CONSTANTINE C. MENGES, PH.D.

Foreword by Bill Gertz

NELSON CURRENT

A Division of Thomas Nelson, Inc.

Published in Nashville, Tennessee, by Nelson Current, a division of a wholly-owned subsidiary (Nelson Communications, Inc.) of Thomas Nelson, Inc.

ISBN 1-5955-5005-4

Printed in the United States of America

The hour was late, the time short when my husband turned to me and said "I want you to make sure that my book is published." He would have been thrilled as I am that his book is now in print. Constantine wrote this book not only to inform and educate the public and our policymakers about China and Russia but to spark a debate about the future possibilities and dangers these two countries present.

This book is dedicated to its author, Constantine Menges, a man of great principle and courage, a man who possessed unusual strategic vision and foresight, who was always able to see the big picture and never failed to connect the dots.

Personally I dedicate this book to Constantine, my life partner, and thank him for our thirty years of marriage, love and friendship during which I cannot remember a boring moment.

—NANCY MENGES

Contents

PART III: CHINA AND RUSSIA

PART IV: WINNING THE PEACE—A COMPREHENSIVE STRATEGY

Foreword

The challenge posed by the People's Republic of China and the Russian Federation represents the most serious long-term threat to American national security, now and for the foreseeable future. As the global war on terrorism remains the immediate and central focus of U.S. policy, looming on the horizon is the growing threat from a rising Beijing. At the same time, China is quickly developing a strategic *entente* with Russia, where the trend is toward dictatorship under Vladimir Putin.

The China-Russia threat became clear in December 2004 when Russian Defense Minister Sergei Ivanov told the Russian president that Russia planned to carry out the first ever joint war games with China's military in 2005. Most significant, Ivanov said that in addition to conventional military forces, Russia would send "strategic bombers" to the exercises. In other words, the two nuclear-armed militaries would practice conducting strategic forces cooperation against a common foe.

"We have agreed with China for the first time in history to hold large-scale exercises on Chinese territory in the second half of next year," Ivanov said, describing the exercises as an "exercise with China in various forms of war exercises." Asked by Putin if strategic nuclear forces would take part, Ivanov said, "It is not ruled out." Several weeks later, Russia confirmed that its strategic nuclear bombers would take part in the maneuvers in China.

Publicly, the war games were supposed to show a joint effort to combat international terrorism. U.S. officials familiar with intelligence reports said the real target of the war games was the United States.

An alarming scenario was played out years earlier in February 2001, when Russian military forces intervened in a mock nuclear conflict between China and the United States over Taiwan. The strategic exercises included Russian preparations to use nuclear weapons on U.S. forces in Asia, according to intelligence reports of the war games. Those games involved practice bombing runs with Russian Tu-22 Backfire bombers that flew close to Japanese airspace. The war games—monitored by U.S. electronic defense intelligence equipment—included military activities in both Europe and Asia and were one of the largest exercises in a decade. During the exercises, Chinese military forces conducted an attack on Taiwan that was followed by U.S. military intervention in the form of ground troops in support of the Taiwanese. China then escalated the conflict by firing tactical nuclear missiles on the U.S. troops in Taiwan, prompting retaliatory U.S. nuclear strikes on Chinese forces. The Russian military then prepared to conduct nuclear attacks on U.S. forces in the region, including attacks on forces in South Korea and Japan. Three Russian strategic nuclear missiles were fired during the exercises, from land-based mobile launchers and from a submarine.

For American intelligence, it was the first time Russian forces had practices fighting U.S. forces in the Pacific region and it highlighted the growing anti-U.S. strategic partnership between Moscow and Beijing.

The unprecedented war games also showed that the rise of China is being assisted militarily by Russia. Moscow's post-communist government remains dominated by veterans of the KGB, the communist secret political police. Under Putin, Russia has moved away from democracy. After the deadly Chechen terrorist attack in Beslan, Russia, that killed more than three hundred people, most of them children, Putin tightened the screws, limiting press freedom and giving himself sweeping powers to appoint governors and to control the Duma.

In Beijing, the communist regime has altered its failed Marxist-Leninist economic system but continues its grip on 1.3 billion people with a Leninist political dictatorship. And when it comes to the United States, Chinese military and Communist party writings make it abundantly clear: the United States is China's "main enemy."

Constantine Menges, whose untimely death in 2004 left a strategic void for the country and the world, understood clearly the danger posed by these two nations. He was an unparalleled strategic thinker who knew clearly that democracy is the last best hope for world peace. Conversely, he knew well that dictatorship and communism are inimical to freedom and prosperity, however they are dressed up.

Several years ago while researching a book on China, I asked Constantine about Beijing's successful strategic disinformation campaign to fool American scholars, journalists, and government officials into believing that China poses no threat to the United States. "You have to understand a fundamental truth," he told me. "China is a threat because it is a nuclear-armed communist dictatorship."

In this book, Menges has produced an important work that captures his views and explains why we need to go on the political offensive against China's communist rulers and bring democracy to China.

More than anything, he understood that promoting freedom and democracy require more than passive resistance. He knew well that passivity toward dictators is a losing strategy.

Menges was a key behind the scenes player in one of the most important actions taken by the United States during the Cold War against the Soviet Union: the liberation of the Caribbean island of Grenada in October 1983. It was the first removal of a communist regime and the restoration of democracy and marked the beginning of the end of Soviet communism. Menges believed that the U.S. action prevented the establishment of a "Soviet Caribbean" that could have led to a new crisis of nuclear weapons in the Western hemisphere.

In addition to his crucial role in rolling back communism in Grenada, Menges, who worked in the Reagan administration from 1981 to 1986, was a key aide to CIA Director William Casey on Latin American affairs.

He was an important contributor to the development of what became known as the Reagan Doctrine of containing and reversing Soviet aggression that was being carried out by armed insurgents and terrorist movements. Menges first drafted elements of the Reagan strategy that were outlined in a 1968 policy paper produced for the RAND Corporation. The paper was presented to the incoming President Reagan as a two-page proposal. Its key elements included:

- Political and communication action to affirm democratic values and to tell the truth about American and other democracies, and to counter hostile propaganda.
- Containment and prevention of communist dictatorships through the timely identification of vulnerable states and the calculated and competent use of U.S. and allied resources to help defeat pro-Soviet groups and prevent them from taking power.
- Restoration of pro-Western forces. The United States must provide help to reasonable and effective indigenous groups in cooperation with friendly governments to bring about pro-Western governments and to replace terrorist-partner and pro-Soviet regimes, like those in Afghanistan, Grenada, Nicaragua, Mozambique and others.

It should be noted that the same strategy drawn up in 1968 could be useful today in waging the war on terrorism, and in dealing with the contemporary problem of Russia and China.

Menges also warned repeatedly about the new threat in Latin America of an axis of evil formed around Cuba's Fidel Castro, Venezuela's Hugo Chavez and Brazil's President Luiz Inácio Lula da Silva.

Throughout his life, Menges was on the cutting edge of promoting democracy and freedom.

In 1979, he proposed waging a pro-active strategy against international terrorism that involved an aggressive approach to liberating terrorist states and discouraging state sponsors of terrorism.

A holder of a doctorate from Columbia University, Menges was more than a federal official. He was a university professor, scholar and author. He was years ahead of his contemporaries in warning of emerging threats and dangers to U.S. national security, ranging from the growth of authoritarian regimes in Spain and Portugal in the late 1960s, to the danger of Islamist extremism in Iran in the late 1970s, to the risk of communist takeover in Nicaragua in the 1970s and the emergence of the threats to Panama under Manuel Noriega in the 1980s.

Menges also had proposed a new strategy of democratization in Saddam Hussein's Iraq after the 1991 Persian Gulf war. His plan called for a program of supporting 1.5 million Iraqi exiles who would set up a coalition government outside the country. The exile government could then be installed once Saddam was ousted. Had his Iraq proposal been accepted, the current effort in Iraq would no doubt have been easier and less costly.

In the 1990s, Menges also called for U.S. policies aimed at preventing the destabilization of the Balkans through preventive political actions.

He also sounded alarm bells in 1998 about the emergence of the pro-communist dictatorship in Venezuela, warning U.S. government officials that Hugo Chavez was an ally of Cuba, China and other anti-U.S. regimes. And he also warned that the radical da Silva regime presents the danger that Brazil will seek nuclear weapons.

In the recent Iraq war, Menges also presented American policymakers with a list of opportunities in the post-Saddam Iraq for democracy and he warned of the danger of "two Irans," as Tehran covertly sought to influence the future of liberated Iraq, a danger that is growing as Tehran is sending both its intelligence operatives and its Islamist paramilitary shock troops to destabilize the new government.

Menges believed that democracy and freedom must go on the offensive in the battle of ideas and that military forces should be used, if necessary, against dictatorships. He was a champion of the concept of "rollback"—reversing dictatorships as the first step toward bringing about a world of peace and freedom.

As he noted months before his death, the battle for freedom does not have to involve troops, bombs and bullets. Countering threats, however, does require political action. Put simply, the correct approach requires first of all insight and understanding of the problems, and then taking action to resolve them.

"The good news," he said at a defense conference in January 2004, "is that this can be stopped through political action alone. It's a political war. It can be stopped through political action. The most important first step is to recognize that it does not require open confrontation; it does not require declaration either.

"It requires, first, a quiet recognition of what's going on. Secondly, it requires honest communication, factual communication country by country to democratic political leaders, government officials, of what's going on, helping them to see the pattern, helping them understand, and then helping them talk about it."

It is on the action side of the China-Russia problem that this book makes a most important contribution. Menges understands that China and Russia represent threats to the United States, by their joint support for the dictatorships in Iran, by arms proliferation to rogue states and unstable regions and by representing an anti-U.S. ideological source.

Menges presents practical solutions for Russia and China. For Moscow, he calls for incentives for democratization and education on why it is in Russia's interest to be wary of communist China.

For Beijing, Menges calls for honest assessments of China by the United States and adopting a pro-active strategy for democratization.

The most important step in this direction is something I have proposed in the past: organizing the so-called overseas Chinese community as a force for democratic reform in China. Menges goes further. He calls for the creation of a democratic Chinese parliament in exile that would provide guidance and inspiration for political reform. Ultimately, the long-term solution to the threat from China is the removal of the communist regime and its replacement with a democratic system.

Constantine Menges will remain a beacon of light because of his reasoned, practical approach to world affairs. Colin Powell, the secretary of state during the first administration of President George W. Bush said that Menges "was a champion of freedom and a passionate defender of his ideas."

"Those who read his prolific work and who knew his life story as a refugee from Nazism understood his steadfast opposition to all totalitarian systems, and appreciated his tireless work on behalf of all its victims," Powell said. "It was true to his nature that after the Berlin Wall fell [in 1989], he seamlessly set out on a new academic mission: to help those former communist countries transform themselves into free market democracies, the only system he knew that maximized human prosperity and happiness."

China: The Gathering Threat presents Menges' solution to the most important strategic threats facing the United States in the years to come.

BILL GERTZ
January 31, 2005

Introduction

"We must bide our time and hide our capabilities."

—DENG XIAOPING, 1994

"War with the United States is inevitable . . . the Chinese armed forces must control the initiative . . . we must make sure that we would win this modern high tech war that the mighty bloc headed by the U.S. hegemonists may launch to interfere in our affairs."

—GENERAL CHI HOATIAN, minister of defense,
People's Republic of China, 1999

"There never was a war [WWII] in all history easier to prevent by timely action . . . but no one would listen . . . we surely must not let that happen again."

—WINSTON CHURCHILL, 1946

A GATHERING DANGER—HIDDEN IN PLAIN VIEW

China and Russia are two globally active major powers that have recently signed treaties of political-military alliance. China remains a Communist dictatorship while post-Soviet Russia is in the process of a fragile, reversible transition to political pluralism and democracy. The United States must be prudent, competent, and realistic in its relations with both countries because, in the case of serious conflict, each has the capability to launch nuclear weapons that in thirty minutes could kill 100 million or more Americans. This book presents the information and perspectives that illuminate little-noticed, gathering but preventable dangers in relations with China and Russia. It also provides suggestions for more thoughtful and balanced policies toward both China and Russia which can maintain peace and increase the prospects for their constructive political evolution toward democracy.

A gathering danger hidden in plain view may seem hypothetical until we know that Communist China has, since 1990, again defined the United States as its "main enemy;" has used espionage to steal the designs of nearly all U.S. nuclear warheads and many other military secrets; has focused its military modernization, doctrine, and increasingly lethal advanced weapons on U.S. forces in the Pacific; and has explicitly threatened to destroy entire American cities if the U.S. were to help the democratic country of Taiwan defend itself against Chinese military assault. China has also involved Russia in backing up that threat through their alliance treaty and numerous joint statements at China-Russia summits followed by large-scale Russian missile and conventional force exercises.

China expects that when it moves to take control of Taiwan the U.S. will not take any military action, even though President George W. Bush said "we will do whatever it takes" to prevent such an event. To reduce the chances that it would be underestimated, China gave the U.S. its war plan against Taiwan, which included nuclear strikes against American targets.

Yet, the main gathering threat derives from China's stealthy strategy of geopolitical and economic dominance. This is a strategy rooted in four thousand years of imperial history and the more recent brutal lessons of Marxist-Leninist power politics.

An increasingly assertive and wealthy Communist regime in China intends to dominate the nine-tenths of Asia Beijing has historically claimed as its sphere of influence, then use that as a springboard to global dominance. This goal puts China on a direct collision course with the United States and its security, political, and economic interests.

China's stealthy pursuit of strategic and economic dominance without open war includes global strategic and economic positioning and its little-noticed but important new alliance with Russia. Additionally, China uses its more than one trillion dollars in cumulative trade surplus gains and an additional $400 billion in Western investment and aid since 1990 to build up its economy and its advanced nuclear, missile, and other weapons systems aimed primarily at the U.S. China officially contends that all U.S. security alliances in Asia constitute an infringement on "Chinese sovereignty" and should be ended. At the same time, China has territorial claims on fourteen of twenty-five nearby countries and asserts that it has full sovereignty over the 450,000 square miles of international waters in the South China Sea, through which half of all world trade passes, including energy supplies vital for Japan and South Korea.

China sells more than 40 percent of its exports to the United States, providing much of the money for its economic growth and military buildup. At the same time, China uses unfair trade practices to take millions of American jobs as it seeks to become the world's factory for high-technology products, software, and services. Therefore, the Chinese Communist regime poses a large but little-recognized threat not only to American security but to the jobs of American workers as well.

The new strategic challenge also includes a politically unsettled and evolving Russian state poised at a political crossroad while still heavily armed with thousands of nuclear weapons on long range missiles. One road leads to increased democracy and peaceful, cooperative, economically productive relations with the West. The other road leads to further political and ideological retrenchment and to the strengthening and broadening of the new Chinese-Russian "strategic partnership." China is seeking to use this alliance to move Russia away from cooperation with the U.S. It also hopes to move Russia away from its fragile, emerging, and reversible democracy so the Chinese people will not have the example of a large, former Communist regime making a successful transition from dictatorship.

China and Russia signed two treaties of alliance in 2001 and have been pursuing a two-level strategy with the United States: normal relations in pursuit of political and economic benefits, while at the same time using discreet means to counter and curtail the United States. In the ongoing major foreign policy challenges the U.S. and the civilized world now face in the war on terrorism—North Korea, Iran, the proliferation of weapons of mass destruction, the stabilization of Iraq and Afghanistan, and the Middle East peace process—China and Russia are partly, secretly on the other side. For example, even after the massive 9/11 terrorist attacks inside the U.S., China and Russia remain the leading suppliers of weapons of mass destruction and ballistic missile components and expertise to the anti-U.S. state sponsors of terrorism with which they have remained political-military allies, including North Korea, Iran, Syria, Libya, and Cuba.

The Chinese Communist regime poses a large but little-recognized threat both to American security as well as to the jobs of American workers. Yet, much as was true of the gathering threat of global Islamic terrorism prior to September 11, 2001, few American political and opinion leaders or citizens are familiar with the facts presented in this book that reveal the emerging threats.

ENDING TERRORISM AND THE SPREAD OF WEAPONS OF MASS DESTRUCTION

Since the horrific attacks of 9/11, the United States has naturally been preoccupied with the dangers—including potentially devastating ones from nuclear, biological, or chemical weapons—that terrorism poses to our well-being and security. Some terrorism has only local or indigenous roots. However, global terrorism is an altogether different phenomenon, both in quality and kind. In large part, global terrorism is the poisonous fruit of a world in which some regimes see the destabilization of peaceful relations among nations as a useful tactic in achieving their power objectives without open war.

Terrorism could be quarantined to more easily manageable hot spots without the military, financial, ideological support, and sanctuary provided by state sponsors such as North Korea, Iran, Libya, and Syria. These and other state sponsors of terrorism would be far less willing and able to continue their hostile actions were they not also receiving political and diplomatic support, as well as components and expertise in developing and deploying weapons of mass destruction and ballistic missiles, from both China and Russia. Therefore, ending global terror will require changes in the current actions of China and Russia—part of the next strategic challenge discussed in this book.

In January 2004, a covert global nuclear proliferation network was revealed to the public. This shadowy network is now commonly called the A. Q. Khan network after the Pakistani scientist who was reportedly at the center of such organizations in nations throughout the world. However, one important part of this network, which is often underreported, was the role both China and North Korea occupied within this proliferation scheme. For example, the plans Libya had received through the A. Q. Khan network and subsequently turned over to the United States were of Chinese origin. This disclosure was widely seen as confirmation of suspected Chinese involvement in the development of Pakistan's nuclear weapons program. Now, whether the secondary transfer of these plans from Pakistan to Libya was with either explicit or tacit agreement by the Chinese is not known from the public record; however, it is illustrative of the danger of past and ongoing Chinese proliferation efforts.

In addition, another of the revolutions to come from the Libyan admissions was the connection to North Korea. According to the International Atomic Energy Agency (IAEA) report North Korea was a key provider of uranium, through the Khan network, to Libya. In a related issue, the United States has tracked by satellite Pakistani cargo planes landing in North Korea to pick up ballistic missile components. It is believed that these planes were also used to deliver gas centrifuges and other necessary equipment for the covert North Korean uranium-enrichment process. Interestingly, these flights would have not only passed through Chinese airspace, but it is also reported that they landed at least once during each leg of their round trip at a PLA (People's Liberation Army) airfield in Western China to refuel. Although not conclusive, this is illustrative of how these types of transnational threats are facilitated and how China has both directly and indirectly over the years contributed to the rapidly expanding threat posed by weapons of mass destruction.

ENDING CHINA'S UNFAIR TAKING OF AMERICAN JOBS AND PRODUCTION

America granted China Most Favored-Nation access to its markets in 1980, and every president since then has said this would lead to greater political freedom for the Chinese people. But, while China's post-Mao economic opening has been accompanied by a welcome decline in the regimentation of daily life for its people, there has been no enlargement of political or religious freedom in China. It remains a Communist dictatorship, where millions are imprisoned in forced-labor camps, and political and religious repression has increased during the years of economic growth funded by China's access to the U.S. market.

A number of American corporations have moved significant amounts of production to China, contending that they were doing this to enter the "vast Chinese market of one billion." Often, their required Chinese partners extract much of the American advanced technology, while the regime and economic factors limit their access to Chinese customers. Therefore, many of these American corporations make large profits not from sales in China, but by using unfree Chinese workers to displace American workers who earn about twenty-six times as much in order to sell their products in the United States.[1]

Economists estimate that every billion dollars in trade surplus that China gains from the U.S. results in the loss of about fifteen thousand American jobs. In 2002, China exported $103 billion more to the U.S. than it imported. This resulted in a loss of 1.5 million American jobs in that year alone. From 1990 to 2003, the current misguided U.S. trade policy with China has resulted in a cumulative trade surplus for China of $732 billion, accounting for a cumulative loss of eight to ten million American jobs. With unemployment in the U.S. at about nine million in 2003, this explains a large part of the current nearly "jobless" economic recovery.

Free trade should be fair and reciprocal. As a Communist dictatorship, China has manipulated trade opportunities in three ways: it has kept its market closed to most American products; it has artificially priced its currency to make its exports 40 percent cheaper; and it has used police power to keep the wages of Chinese workers extremely low. This explains China's massive hard-currency trade surplus earnings with the U.S., the EU, and Japan, which from 1990 to 2004 totaled an astounding $1.5 trillion.

American corporations making profits by using Chinese labor to produce for the U.S. market have set up well-funded lobbying efforts. They endorse the continuation of the current hear-no-evil, see-no-evil, speak-no-truth approach toward China, which rests on the hope, now a convenient myth, that free trade will bring political freedom. The 1989 massacre of peaceful young demonstrators in Tiananmen Square revealed the determination of the Chinese Communist Party to keep total political power, no matter what brutal repression was required. That event sparked congressional proposals by House Democratic Leader Nancy Pelosi, among others, to link economic benefits for China with its actions on human rights. However, that ended in 1994 when President Clinton backed away from the human-rights conditions he had publicly set and returned to the pattern of granting China unconditional, open access to the U.S. market for its exports.

China's unfair trade practices are gradually becoming a visible political issue and will be a major focus of debate in the next several years. A bipartisan group of congressional leaders wrote President Bush in 2003 demanding changes in the U.S.-China trade relationship. This included Democrats, such as Senators Charles Schumer and Joseph Lieberman, and Republicans, such as Senator Elizabeth Dole.

Senator Schumer said, "The fragile coalition for free trade is weakening due to the huge loss of manufacturing jobs in most parts of the country."[2] In 2003, the Bush administration also began to express its concerns about the need for China to take steps to correct the trade imbalance.

Current American trade policy with China has strengthened the Communist regime economically, militarily, and strategically by providing it with vast new resources for power projection, including the purchase of advanced Russian weapons aimed at U.S. forces in the Pacific. It has also facilitated the personal enrichment of the Party elite. Rather then being a source of political freedom, China's access to the U.S. market has given the regime further incentives to keep Chinese workers under dictatorial control, because that increases the profit margin of exports and therefore the money available for the regime's strategic purposes and the personal wealth of its elite members. Therefore, the current U.S. policy is contrary to the economic and national security interests of the American people.

Unless the U.S. establishes a new policy of realistic economic engagement with China along the lines proposed in this book, it risks continuing to provide funding for China's strategy of dominance, the loss of millions more American jobs, and the loss of entire industries, including high technology. This could produce a decline in the standard of living for many Americans. The new trade strategy proposed in the following pages demonstrates how to peacefully link and protect American national security and economic interests.

Preventing a War of Mutual Miscalculation

China's first strategic forays have already begun, with Taiwan as a primary target in the immediate future. This book discusses how missteps by recent U.S. administrations, combined with growing Chinese assertiveness—including explicit threats of nuclear attack against U.S. cities—and the often overlooked contrivance of key businessmen on both sides of the Taiwan Straits who see the possibility of huge financial gains from a Chinese takeover of Taiwan, could all combine to bring us to a flash point.

Present American policies toward China are leading to serious misjudgments on both sides; and in geopolitics, misjudgments between nuclear-armed nations with conflicting interests can be devastating. Our substitution of wishful thinking for realistic policy may lead us simultaneously to underestimate China's military and nuclear capabilities as well as the seriousness of its strategic ambitions. Years of U.S. accommodation and Pollyanna-ish rhetoric may reinforce the views of hard-line Chinese Communist officials that the U.S.—notwithstanding the post–September 11 war on terrorism and the removal of the Saddam Hussein regime in 2003—is indeed only a "paper tiger," when it comes to standing up for its interests against a serious nuclear armed power like China.

To make sure the U.S. leadership takes its threats seriously, China gave the United States a copy of its war plan for the conquest of Taiwan, which included its preparations to use nuclear weapons against U.S. cities if the U.S. tried to defend Taiwan (this is presented in Chapter 8). The Chinese military said it wanted the U.S. to understand that China is "not Iraq or Serbia," nor the Taliban regime in Afghanistan.

In 1962, Khrushchev's misjudgment of American democratic leadership and his belief in Kennedy's weakness in the face of Soviet threats brought the world to the brink of nuclear war during the Cuban Missile Crisis. Bin Laden and his Al Qaeda terrorist network also misinterpreted America's reactive and episodic response to terrorist acts against its citizens during the last twenty-five years, and the timid response by the Clinton administration, as evidence that they could mount a cold-blooded attack on U.S. soil with little fear of an effective reprisal, leading directly to the tragedy of September 11, 2001.

China is estimated to have about twenty intercontinental ballistic missiles capable of reaching U.S. territory and another twelve submarine-based missiles that could hit U.S. cities from international waters. These missiles have very large nuclear warheads (the equivalent of three to five million tons of TNT or, by comparison, 240 to 400 times more powerful than the blast that destroyed Hiroshima), one of which could completely destroy a large city. China is testing and preparing to deploy two new solid-fueled and mobile long-range ballistic missiles, as well as a new submarine-launched ballistic missile, each of which is individually capable of striking multiple targets in the United States.[3] The CIA has estimated that China will quadruple the size of its long-range missile force within the decade.[4]

China also intends to deploy two new ballistic-missile submarines with twenty missiles each by 2008. If its eighty land-based ICBMs and forty submarine-based missiles each had three warheads, that would be a force of about 360 strategic warheads capable of reaching the U.S. The Defense Intelligence Agency estimated that by 2008 China could potentially deploy a thousand nuclear warheads on intercontinental ballistic missiles capable of reaching U.S. territory.[5] History suggests that a nuclear-armed Communist regime in China is likely to be more aggressive and assertive as its armed might grows to match its ever-increasing economic strength.

Currently, China assumes that as long as its deployed intercontinental-range missiles, each armed with a three to five megaton warhead can reach and completely destroy three, five, or ten American cities, the U.S. will be a "paper tiger" when it comes to any U.S. military defense of Taiwan. Therefore, Chinese hardliners believe they must take Taiwan before the U.S. missile-defense system is fully effective against their long-range missile forces, likely in about 2008, but possibly even earlier. These Chinese military and Communist Party officials have said for years that their nuclear attack would probably not be necessary because the U.S. would retreat immediately once China destroyed one or more U.S. aircraft carriers or military bases being used to help defend Taiwan.

These assumptions and purposes may cause China to underestimate U.S. resolve, while misguided U.S. policies contribute to a continuing American underestimation of China's strengths and determination. All this could lead to a shooting war between two nuclear-armed nations, which can be prevented if we recognize the danger and act in time.

China's Strategy: Dominance without Open War

An actual shooting war by miscalculation is one of the possible outcomes of current trends. Another possibility is gradual appeasement and retreat on the part of the West that allows the Chinese to attain their objectives without large-scale conflict. As the ancient but still authoritative Chinese strategist General Sun Tzu famously said, "The supreme excellence is not winning battles . . . but breaking the enemy's resistance without fighting." This is certainly the preferred outcome as far as the Chinese leadership is concerned. Therefore, this book projects an eight-phase strategy by which China might seek domination of Asia, Eurasia, and the world in the next twenty years without fighting a major war.

While projections of Chinese actions in future years are in part speculative, this analysis is thoroughly consistent with China's stated strategic and tactical goals. It also derives from the facts of China's current, virtually unnoticed, global patterns of action, which this book reveals holistically, and through which China hopes to counter and ultimately end the U.S. capacity to restrain its ambitions.

But neither war nor defeat is inevitable. Open, armed conflict with China is a "preventable war," because, as Winston Churchill said about World War II, timely, realistic action is all that is necessary to steer events in more benign directions. There is no doubt in my mind, as I describe in this book, that with a combination of strength, prudence, and foresight—by learning the real lessons of the Cold War and sweeping away the myths that cloud our thinking—the United States can deter open conflict and use its vast economic, political, and diplomatic means to bring about peaceful change. In all this, Russia is a key and all-too-neglected factor.

Russia at a Crossroads

This book provides an in-depth analysis of President Vladimir Putin, including his work for the Soviet foreign intelligence service (KGB) and his actions since assuming the presidency of Russia on January 1, 2000. Putin is an intelligent, disciplined, and systematic leader. He has said Russia should become a "strong state" under a "dictatorship of law" and that it must again play a major role in world affairs. At the same time, Putin expresses support for political democracy and movement toward a market-oriented economy. The reader will learn why Russia now stands precariously at the crossroads of a democratic or autocratic future.

Which road Russia chooses will have historic and long-term consequences for the United States. The path favored by China and hard-line elements in Russia could well plunge the U.S. back into a replay of the darkest days of the Cold War. The U.S. would be confronting two nuclear-armed dictatorships. If Russia takes the road leading West, however, the positive ramifications could be just as great, including real democracy within Russia, improved economic progress, and perhaps even genuine partnership of some degree and kind with the European Union and NATO. Just as important, China would be denied the key ally in its quest for dominance.

An Effective U.S. Strategy

It is time to get serious about strategy toward China and Russia and about geopolitics. The United States must manage the peace in such a way that Russia chooses the Western road and China eventually gives up its ambitions for dominance of Asia and beyond.

The war against terrorism and its state sponsors, and the stabilization of Iraq and Afghanistan are dramatic and important. Yet, if this is the only focus of serious and concerted U.S. international attention, and if the gathering threats posed by China and Russia, as discussed in this book, continue to be ignored, we will miss the closing window of opportunity to bring Russia closer to the West and to deal peacefully with the challenges posed by the rising, globally active, nuclear-armed, and increasingly wealthy Communist regime in China.

This book illustrates the emerging threats by using both recently declassified information and publicly available but little-noticed data to describe: China's international strategies and actions; the recent political evolution of China and Russia; and China's purposes and success in forging the first alliance with Russia in fifty years. The leaders of China and Russia are cited in their own words as they speak among themselves and make frank statements that are often ignored in the Western press.

Having established the geopolitical context, the book concludes with a comprehensive and realistic U.S. strategy to deal prudently and effectively with these emerging threats and encourage peaceful, positive political evolution in both Russia and China. This means that U.S policymakers must deal with China and Russia as they really are, not according to myths or wishful thinking about how they would like those nations to be.

Realistic, sensible, and consistently applied policies can ensure that, when it comes to Taiwan, we never get into a nuclear standoff similar to the Cuban Missile Crisis. An eyes-open policy that understands China's neo-imperial strategy can keep the U.S. and its allies from being maneuvered into a position of increasing weakness—where the only two alternatives are appeasement leading to capitulation or war.

With Russia, the opportunities are as great as the risks. A Russia truly allied with the West, sharing a prudent skepticism of the consequences to itself of Chinese efforts to attain dominance will be central to leading the world to a twenty-first century of peace and global prosperity.

Learning the lessons from the first Cold War with the Soviet Union, the United States can use a combination of strength and foresight to deter open conflict and employ peaceful political and economic means to encourage positive, peaceful change in both Russia and China, resulting in those countries moving toward international cooperation, peace, and democracy.

1 Reform, Repression, and the New China-Russia Alliance

In the late 1980s there was a hopeful sense of positive developments within the two major Communist powers. In the Soviet Union, President Mikhail Gorbachev was attempting to institute limited political reforms and to permit some private economic activities that would not be directly controlled by the state. In China, there had been a shift from the fanatical extremism and brutal repression of the Mao years to pragmatic economic policies intended to gradually open the economic system, but in a manner that would keep the Chinese Communist Party in political control.[1] This economic opening, in turn, led to a marked reduction in the regimentation of daily life in China and to some efforts at political liberalization.

These liberalizing trends produced severe frictions within the ruling Communist parties of each country, however, and on June 4, 1989, dramatic events in both empires, thousands of miles apart, led in two entirely different directions. In Poland, Solidarity, with Gorbachev's approval, competed in a reasonably free and fair election against the Communist Party for control of 35 percent of the seats in the existing parliament and for 100 percent of the seats in a newly established, but entirely symbolic, senate. The result was that Solidarity received overwhelming public support, winning 99 percent of the seats in parliament open for competition. Solidarity's dramatic electoral victory set in motion the events of 1989–90, through which most of the peoples of Central Europe peacefully liberated themselves from Communist one-party dictatorships—a geopolitical sea change symbolized by the opening of the Berlin Wall in November 1989.

Two years after Solidarity's victory, Boris Yeltsin won the first free presidential election in the thousand-year history of Russia and shortly thereafter turned back the August 1991 coup attempt by hard-line Soviet Communists seeking to remove Gorbachev—the leader of the Communist Party and president of the Soviet Union—and reverse the reform course upon which he had consciously set his nation. Ultimately, in December 1991, Gorbachev agreed to the dissolution of the

1

USSR, allowing each of the fifteen constituent Soviet republics to become an independent state, responsible for its own destiny.

In stark contrast, on June 4, 1989, the Chinese Communist leadership decided to stamp out the democratic stirrings in its country, using the full power of the military and secret police to crush peaceful demonstrations by students and young workers in Tiananmen Square and throughout China. This use of brutal military force against unarmed civilians resulted in the deaths of an estimated five to ten thousand persons, with many thousands wounded throughout China. The Tiananmen massacre was accompanied by the arrest and imprisonment in the vast Chinese system of forced-labor camps and prisons of an estimated fifty to sixty thousand.

From the start of the post-Mao era, the Chinese leadership explicitly stated that its plans for economic modernization were to occur under the firm political control of the Communist Party. Contrary to many in the West who saw democratic evolution necessarily following economic liberalization, the Chinese Communist Party worked diligently to ensure that its controlled opening of the economy was not accompanied by the kind of political freedom that might threaten its rule.

In fact, the Chinese leadership viewed the subsequent peaceful removal of Communist dictatorships in Central Europe and the dissolution of the Soviet Union as confirmation that it had made the right choice at Tiananmen. Since then, any and all efforts by the people of China toward political liberalization have been met with swift and brutal repression. Even groups such as Christians, Buddhists, and members of other religions with no political agenda but which seek to exist independently of the Communist regime have been harshly persecuted. In 1999, the Chinese regime began the arrest and brutalization of members of a meditation/exercise association (Falun Gong), and in 2002 further increased the persecution of millions of Christians contending that they were instigated by "hostile Western powers headed by the USA" in order to "perpetuate infiltration."[2]

THE ENSUING YEARS

From the perspective of the Chinese leadership, the decision to crush freedom at Tiananmen has been validated by history. The Communist Party remains in political control and China has made enormous economic and technological progress. China's policy of restricting foreign access to its markets and skill in obtaining access for its exports to the U.S., the European Union, and Japan made it possible for Beijing to gain massive hard-currency trade surpluses totaling more than $1.1 trillion from 1990 to 2002.[3] Those surpluses have financed China's military and technological modernization with its ever-growing military expenditure cumulatively estimated at about one trillion dollars for those same years. China has also obtained foreign direct investments of $340 billion and more than $50 billion in bilateral and multilateral economic aid from Western governments and institutions. In addition, China obtained the return of Hong Kong (1997) and Macao (1999).

There is an enormous irony in the differences in the evolution of Russia and China. The Russian government of Yeltsin attempted both to democratize and to establish a free-market-oriented economy. This led to important positive changes, including a real opening of the political system, freedom of political speech, assembly, and association, opportunities for Russian citizens to choose their political leaders through reasonably open elections, the broadening of civil society, and the avoidance of international conflict. Yet the negative trends of Yeltsin's eight years included a dramatic decline in overall economic production (50 percent), and severe inflation (cumulatively more than 2,400 percent), which virtually eliminated the life savings of most Russians. More than half the Russian population experienced reductions in the standard of living. This was accompanied by a sharp increase in the visibility and extent of the organized crime and corruption that had already been endemic in the Soviet system.

Despite real but fragile democratic changes, Russia's economic problems have led many to characterize it as a failure, a view best illustrated by the words of well-known financier George Soros, who, in 2000, said "Russia is hopeless and there is nothing to be done."[4] That same year, on the other hand, a bipartisan majority of the U.S. Congress came to see China, a repressive Communist dictatorship with a partially open economy, as a country deserving of permanent normal trade relations—meaning full access to the U.S. market for products made by the unfree and coerced. It is noteworthy that the presidential candidates from both major parties in the United States in the year 2000 said that granting China permanent normal trade relations would not only provide economic benefits for both countries, but would lead to further economic liberalization in China, which would in turn lead to political liberalization.

This view—that giving China access to U.S. markets would lead to lessened tensions with that country and ultimately democratic reform—has been a cornerstone of U.S. policy toward that country since President Carter reestablished full diplomatic relations in 1979. It is worth tallying up the exact accomplishments that policy can claim.

The continuing crackdown on religious believers, human rights, and proponents of democracy has already been mentioned. The rule of the Communist Party continues and, in January 2000, then-President Jiang Zemin reiterated that China would remain Communist and that political democracy would never be permitted. He also said: "Western nations led by the United States have intensified their strategic plot to westernize and divide our country, using every conceivable means to attempt to influence us with their political views, ideology, and lifestyles."[5] As to the economic benefits of trade, they have been largely one-sided for China. In addition, China virtually requires U.S. corporations that want to do business there to share their proprietary technology and to use their influence to promote U.S. policies toward China that the regime considers favorable. As a result of the economic benefits it has obtained from the U.S. and other industrial democracies, China has the second largest hard-currency reserves in the world, a resource it uses to buy advanced military weapons and technology and to gain political influence with many governments including that of the United States.[6]

Along with internal repression, during the 1990s China became more aggressive internationally. The Communist regime has accelerated the modernization of its strategic and advanced military forces, continued the sale of weapons of mass destruction and ballistic missiles to anti-U.S. regimes supporting terrorism, and increased its rhetoric against the U.S. China officially declared America its "main enemy" in 1990, with the official press saying that the U.S. is "a dangerous enemy" and a "superpower bully."[7] Deng Xiaoping, China's paramount leader after Mao, propounded the view that China should "hide our capabilities and bide our time."[8] The vice commandant of the Chinese Academy of Military Sciences said in 1996, "[As for the U.S.] it will be absolutely necessary that we quietly nurse our sense of vengeance . . . we must conceal our abilities and bide our time."[9] Most ominously, in December 1999, the Chinese minister of defense, General Chi Haotian, stated his view that "With the United States, war is inevitable."[10] This was the same Chinese general who played a key role in China's invasion of Vietnam in 1979, led the brutal repression in Tiananmen Square in 1989, and who—during an official 1996 visit to Washington to meet with President Clinton in the White House—gave a speech denying that there were any deaths at Tiananmen Square.

The contrast between the disappointment with Russia by many in the Western business and financial world and the enthusiastic support for Communist China led the then-Russian ambassador to the U.S., Yuri Vorontsov, half in jest, to declare that China's success in obtaining economic benefits from the U.S. and the West suggested to many Russians that perhaps Russia might be more successful economically if it returned to Communist rule.[11] Hopefully, Voronstov's jest will not prove to be prophetic.

THE NEW CHINA-RUSSIA STRATEGIC ALIGNMENT

The early failures of Yeltsin's economic program contributed to the political success of the reorganized Russian Communist Party, which won a plurality of seats in the 1993 parliamentary elections and then a near-majority in 1995. The Communists next hoped to win the powerful presidency in the June 1996 election.

The Russian Communists, ultranationalists, and some elements of the military, security services, and state bureaucracy shared the view that the "Chinese model" of a political dictatorship with pragmatic economic policies would be better for Russia. Therefore, in part to broaden his domestic political support before the June 1996 Russian presidential election, Yeltsin visited China in April 1996 where the countries formalized a new "strategic partnership." This was the beginning of the movement of China and Russia from normalization to a new alignment that has evolved and deepened over the years through a number of summit meetings. Of note is that both have agreed in their meetings and said publicly that the United States and its alleged intentions to dominate the world—which Russia called "unipolarism" and China described as "hegemonism"—was the primary international problem each of them faced.[12]

In 1998–99, Russia and China acted in concert to oppose U.S. and Western initiatives intended to persuade Iraq and Serbia to implement existing UN Security Council resolutions. Subsequently, the opposition of Russia and China in the UN Security Council prevented it from authorizing the use of force to compel Serbia to end the killing, persecution, and expulsion of one million ethnic Albanians in Kosovo. This in turn was followed by NATO air attacks in the spring of 1999, without explicit authority from the Security Council. Russia and China condemned those NATO military actions as illegal, took open and covert actions to help the Serbian regime, and objected vigorously to the argument made by President Clinton that massive human-rights abuses of their own citizens by regimes gave the international community, even without UN Security Council approval, the right to intervene on humanitarian grounds. Both Russia and China have concerns about internal separatist movements (Chechnya for Russia and Tibet and Xinjiang in China) and did not want any such precedent established.

At their December 1999 summit meeting, the leaders of Russia and China repeated that they opposed the U.S.-led NATO military campaign that brought an end to the Milosevic regime's persecution of Albanian Muslims, and that all states should "respect each other's sovereignty and not interfere in each other's internal affairs."[13] At that December 1999 summit, the presidents of Russia and China also stated that Taiwan is part of Chinese territory and that "Russia supports Chinese reunification efforts," without limiting this endorsement to peaceful means. Russia also declared that it opposed "the inclusion of China's Taiwan province" in any theater missile defense plan in any form by any country.[14] All of these positions were reiterated in the July 2000 summit held between President Jiang of China and Vladimir Putin, the newly elected and inaugurated president of Russia. Since the early 1990s, Russia has sold China increasing quantities of advanced weapons and has permitted thousands of Russian scientists and engineers to work for China on advanced military development and production. Russia and China have also acted in tandem for years providing components and expertise for weapons of mass destruction to Iran, Saddam Hussein's Iraq, North Korea, and other terrorist-sponsoring regimes.[15]

In the year that followed this first meeting between Jiang and Putin, the governments of China and Russia signed significant documents. In June 2001, they, together with the leaders of what had been known as the Shanghai 5 plus Uzbekistan group, signed a treaty creating the Shanghai Cooperative Organization. In July 2001, Presidents Putin and Jiang signed the "Good-Neighborly Treaty of Friendship and Cooperation" between China and Russia. Although they claimed at the time that there was no military component to this treaty, Article 9 of the treaty reads as follows:

> When a situation arises in which one of the contracting parties deems that peace is being threatened and undermined or its security interests are involved or when it is confronted with the threat of aggression, the contracting parties shall immediately hold contacts and consultations in order to eliminate such threats.[16]

The first alliance between the Soviet Union and Communist China effectively ended in 1959 and the U.S. and its allies have not faced a concerted strategic challenge by the two major powers since. Though Russian conventional military forces at 1.2 million are far weaker than were those of the former USSR, current Russian military doctrine formally declares its large strategic nuclear arsenal may be used first in the event of major conflict. China has the world's largest army (2.3 million), with a growing arsenal of nuclear-armed, intercontinental, medium- and short-range ballistic missiles, and has been modernizing its naval and air forces with Russian and other weapons for the clear purpose of intimidating and countering U.S. air and naval forces in the Pacific.

It is also probable that the U.S. will deploy a theater missile defense in East Asia to protect Japan, South Korea, and the hundred thousand U.S. forces in the region. Given the April 27, 2001, statement by President George W. Bush that the U.S. would do "whatever it takes" to prevent China from using force to take control of Taiwan, it is possible that this deployed system might be used to defend Taiwan if China should decide to use force there. It is possible that Taiwan will obtain the means it needs to construct its own defense against the hundreds of ballistic missiles China has deployed within range of Taiwan. The strong opposition to all of these actions expressed by China and by Russia adds to the potential for serious conflict.

However, it is more likely that Russia and China will continue to align strategically by pursuing a two-level relationship with the United States: normal diplomatic and trade relations to ensure the continued flow of economic benefits, combined with selective opposition to the U.S. and its allies, using mostly methods of indirect conflict.

INDIRECT CONFLICT

During the Cold War there were three potential levels of conflict: strategic nuclear warfare; conventional war—the open use of military forces across international borders; and indirect or secret war—the use of political and covert action to include, in some cases, the arming of indigenous groups or allied states. The U.S. did not use its nuclear weapons again during the time of its monopoly (1945–49), and thereafter, prudence and the strategic nuclear forces of each side deterred their use. After the 1950 North Korean (and then Chinese) invasion of South Korea was repulsed and stalemated by the armed forces of the UN coalition led by the U.S., further open, large-scale conventional conflict was deterred by the rearmament of the U.S. and its allies and by their political cohesion and resolve.

Virtually all of the conflicts of the Cold War era involved mostly indirect conflict. Even the massive Soviet and Chinese military aid to Communist Vietnam was provided discreetly. Soviet success in this domain—bringing twenty pro-Moscow regimes to power on four continents—required a clear sense of strategic purpose, the coordination of a variety of open and secret activities, and the capacity to persuade, coerce, dominate, mislead, or deceive states that might resist.[17]

Generally, expansionist dictatorships are far more effective in this indirect or secret warfare than are political democracies. The dictatorships have the unity of strategic purpose and the capacity to concert all their instruments of statecraft and influence to work toward the desired outcomes. For example, the effectiveness of the Soviet Union against the United States from 1945–1949 demonstrated that a determined Communist regime can use indirect means of conflict to succeed— even against an opponent which is far advanced militarily and economically.

At the end of World War II, the U.S. was a stable, prosperous democracy, with its continental territory untouched by military attack, producing half the world's economic output, with armed forces of 12.5 million and a monopoly on the atomic bomb, which it had twice used to bring about the surrender of a determined opponent. The Soviet Union under Stalin was a repressive dictatorship, with armed forces of 5.5 million, but a homeland where a major part of its industrial and agricultural production had been devastated by four years of invasion and warfare and an estimated 10 to 20 million war-related deaths. Yet from 1945 to 1949, the Soviet Union used the methods of indirect conflict successfully against the ostensibly stronger United States to help bring to power nine new pro-Moscow regimes, controlling 500 million persons in Eastern Europe and China.

China's current use of indirect coercion to secure control of Taiwan, in combination with their threats to use conventional or nuclear force against the U.S., represents a real danger. It should be taken seriously when one considers China's threat to use conventional force against U.S. military assets in the region or attack U.S. cities with strategic nuclear weapons in response to U.S. support for Taiwan. The risk of a preventable conventional, or perhaps even nuclear, war between the United States and China is possible because of a strategic miscalculation at the center of their war plans. This miscalculation is that if People's Liberation Army (PLA) forces successfully sink a U.S. aircraft carrier, under the cover of their nuclear deterrent, then the United States will retreat and end any opposition to Chinese military efforts to take Taiwan.

Until the U.S. has a fully reliable limited missile defense, even the small (but growing) Chinese ICBM force could credibly threaten to destroy twelve to twenty major U.S. cities, possibly killing 60 to 80 million Americans. Many in the Chinese leadership understand that the U.S. has more than six thousand strategic warheads and that a Chinese nuclear attack on the U.S. would result in nuclear retaliation that would be catastrophic for China. Yet, there is a risk of such miscalculation because the Chinese Communist political-military hardliners believe, despite the strong reaction of President George W. Bush in Afghanistan and Iraq, that if they threaten the U.S. with nuclear attack, Washington will either refrain from helping Taiwan defend itself or retreat once China actually sinks a U.S. aircraft carrier or destroys major U.S. bases in Asia.

The more prudent Chinese leadership group would seek to avoid either a conventional or a nuclear military confrontation with the U.S. and would instead use the methods of indirect conflict to attain its objectives. China has a skilled intelligence service and long experience in indirect aggression and international coercion. The intelligence services of Russia also have extensive experience in such activities. The closer their overall collaboration, the more likely that Russian and Chinese diplomatic and intelligence services would jointly pursue some of the most important shared strategic objectives. Both China and Russia are well equipped with the resources needed for indirect conflict: extensive past experience and widespread international agent networks and contacts; organizations with historical memory and skilled, multilayered personnel; the capacity to maintain secrecy; experience in deceiving target governments and their international allies; and, for China, the addition of enormous financial resources which provide a means for gaining both geostrategic and economic advantages that can produce decisive influence with foreign governments.

THE NEW HEGEMON

Ideologically based dictatorships generally have a geopolitical strategy for the future—though not necessarily a timetable. Dictatorships, such as in China, often have a geopolitical strategy that tends toward the domination of other states. For China, this drive toward domination is fueled in part by the doctrine of Marxist-Leninist-Maoist thought, but mostly by the view that domination is the ultimate guarantee of security for the Chinese regime. China's reach for domination also derives from long imperial experience. Until the eighteenth century, China considered Japan, Korea, Vietnam/Indochina, much of Central Asia, and the Russian Far East as its sovereign territory.

The Communist regime believes it will be guaranteed to endure and China will be fully secure only when it is the world's dominant power in the as-yet undefined "new international political and economic order" it has repeatedly declared to be its aim. Also, at home the Communist regime has systematically propounded an intense Chinese nationalism and a belief in the superiority of the Han Chinese people.

How Chinese rulers have viewed their empire in the past has relevance to the present and future. In the traditional view of imperial China "for more than two thousand years the Chinese have considered themselves the geographical-geopolitical center of the world. They spoke of China as the 'Middle Kingdom' or as the Universe under Heaven."[18] In an insightful discussion of the historical evolution of China's political culture, one scholar informs us that beginning 2,800 years ago, "the total control of a state's population and resources was to be concentrated in the hands of the absolute ruler, who would in turn employ it to establish his hegemony, or absolute dominance, over all the states in the known world."[19] He goes on to say that the Chinese imperial rulers viewed "themselves as the highest expression of civilized mankind" and "had their own doctrine of manifest destiny, which is that the Middle Kingdom is destined to recover its traditional place in the world, at its center."[20] Until the rise of Europe with the industrial revolution, the Chinese Empire was, for centuries, the largest, the wealthiest, the most technologically advanced, and the most powerful. Its pattern was to dominate all the states in the then-known world. As a result, "those who refused to kowtow to Beijing were regarded as hostile," and another expert writes that today "China still seems to classify her neighbors into one of two categories: tributary states that acknowledge her hegemony or her enemies."[21]

In the traditional Chinese view, the world needs a hegemon—or dominant state—to prevent disorder. The hegemon is the state that exercises leadership or "predominant influence" over others. The Communist Chinese regime believes China should be that hegemon and that it is threatened by the United States seeking to be the hegemon. After the Communist regime crushed the peaceful human-rights demonstrations in Tiananmen Square in 1989, and the Soviet threat to China ended with the dissolution of the Soviet Union in 1991, the Chinese Communist Party decided it no longer needed the U.S. as a counterbalance to the Soviet Union and soon thereafter formally declared the United States to be, again, its "main enemy."

In 1996 the official publication of the Chinese Communist Party said "the U.S. strategic aim is to seek hegemony in the whole world, and it cannot tolerate the

appearance of any big power on the European and Asian continents that will constitute a threat to its leading position." China's then-leading Communist, Deng
Xiaoping, said that China's geostrategic goals are, "First, to oppose hegemony and
power politics and second, to build up a new international political and economic
order." However, the Chinese have yet to publicly define what this new "international order" is or how it will be achieved, even though they make continued refer-
ences to this as a strategic goal in official documents, including the communiqués
from recent China-Russia summits.

The 1998 Chinese Defense White Paper declared that China should "lead the
world into the twenty-first century"[22] and said that all U.S. security alliances in Asia
were contrary to "stability." Therefore, since 1998 China has opposed the geopolitical and military-security presence of the U.S. in Asia as unacceptable, because it
limits Beijing's capacity to influence or direct states that are American allies or
under its protection. In addition, the Chinese regime has been explicit for decades
that it perceives the very existence of the U.S.—a militarily powerful, prosperous
democracy—a strategic threat, because America provides inspiration for those in
China seeking freedom, human rights, and therefore a democratic alternative to
Communist rule. During the 1950s, the Chinese Communist Party publicly
denounced what it declared to be a U.S. "strategic plot" to encourage "peaceful
evolution" toward democracy in China. Recently, then-President Jiang Zemin again
publicly mentioned and criticized this alleged American plot.

CHINA AND THE WORLD:
THE PURSUIT OF DOMINANCE IN EIGHT PHASES

"To subdue the enemy without fighting is the acme of skill."
—GENERAL SUN TZU

In international relations, policies based on idealistic or wishful thinking create
serious vulnerabilities. By their very nature, such policies are forced to discount or
ignore the stated aims of the other parties involved if these aims in anyway contra-
dict the accepted myths created by the advocates of such idealist policies. Despite
learning a costly lesson of the folly of these types of policies during the Cold War
when we ignored Soviet pronouncements about "exporting revolution" throughout
the world, we ignored the threat represented by the radicalization and anti-
American pronouncements within segments of Islam, which lead to the events
September 11, 2001. We would be just as foolish if we were to make the same
mistakes when it comes to dealing with the Chinese Communist regime in the
twenty-first century and could potentially pay an even greater price.

The Beijing regime, however, is considerably more sophisticated than was the Soviet regime in manipulating foreign states and perceptions about itself. The Chinese have shown themselves more flexible, as well, when it comes to the tactical pursuit of overall strategic objectives, and they hold the decided advantage of possessing a longer time horizon than most U.S. leaders, whose attention span is often measured in a few years, if not months. When Chinese leaders say they seek "a new political and economic international order," they certainly mean what they say, but that does not mean they will necessarily choose outright confrontation. Given China's economic and military situation, its leaders will no doubt seek to use a combination of incentives and coercion, carrots and sticks, to keep their adversary—us—off balance, while they gradually steer events in the direction of their ultimate goals.

This book reveals an open but unnoticed secret: the Communist Chinese strategy of political and economic dominance. China intends to become the dominant global power without a major war. The strategy uses tactics that blend economic ties (including the careful cultivation of U.S., European, Russian, Japanese, and Taiwanese businessmen and entrepreneurs), diplomacy, covert action, military strength, and coercion. Beginning in Asia, the broad outline of the Chinese pursuit of world dominance (which will be discussed in much greater detail in Chapter 18) can be conceptualized as occurring in eight phases, the first two of which are already visible. These phases may overlap, and the dates given are, of course, only approximations, since the timing of each new phase would depend on the strength of the main factions within the Communist regime, Chinese perceptions of the risks in pursuing its international objectives, and the actions or passivity of the U.S. and other major powers. Predatory regimes are by nature opportunistic, so events may unfold with greater or lesser speed, and tactical detours will no doubt occur. Nevertheless, in its broad outlines, the following closely approximates the overall Chinese strategic approach.

PHASE I: Normalization of economic relations with the democracies (1978 and continuing). A period of controlled economic liberalization and normalization with the West to promote the economic, technological, and military modernization of China. The Asian proverb is, "A rich state has a powerful army."

PHASE II: Asian regional persuasion and coercion with global geostrategic and economic positioning (late 1980s and continuing). China strengthens its geopolitical-economic positioning through financial, political, and covert action. It uses the immense wealth generated from trade surpluses, foreign direct investments, and controlled opening of the Chinese market to manipulate the actions of ostensibly independent Chinese business entities within China and Hong Kong, which are either controlled by the regime or subject to its influence. Its policy toward Asian states was summarized by President Jiang Zemin: "Intimidate with force and seduce with money."

Note: in Phases I and II China has, at times, used force and intimidation as well as diplomacy to pursue its territorial claims against eleven Asian states and over the South China Sea and its islands. It has also made systematic use of Chinese spies and companies to extend Chinese influence. Examples are China's success in obtaining control of ports at strategic sea lanes such as those at both ends of the Panama Canal, in the Bahamas, at the Suez Canal, and major positions in Rotterdam, as well as near the Straits of Malacca in Southeast Asia. Since 1992 China has officially asserted its sovereignty over the international waters of the South China Sea, through which 40 percent of the world's shipping moves. China has used force to seize islands claimed by a number of other regional states. Also, China has used political campaign donations to seek influence with U.S. and other foreign political leaders. Beijing grants or withholds contracts, trade, and investment opportunities to selected countries and firms, including in the industrial democracies, as incentives for them to adopt or promote policies desired by China.

PHASE III: China takes Taiwan and is preponderant in Asia (2007–2008?). China takes control of Taiwan, a prosperous democracy of 23 million persons, preferably with the skilled personnel in high technology and the economic-technological resources of the island republic mostly intact. This might be accomplished either by means of political and covert action, with wealthy Taiwan businessmen (as in Hong Kong) working actively with Beijing for "reunification," or by military force and coercion—creating a serious risk of war with the U.S.

Note: The dependence of Taiwanese businessmen on favors from the Chinese regime is already a matter of documented fact. There are more than four thousand Taiwanese businesses that have invested about $70 billion in mainland China, accompanied by three hundred thousand Taiwanese living there.

China touts this success as a geopolitical triumph. It would be perceived as an "Asian Munich" if the U.S. acquiesces to China taking control of Taiwan through coercion. This would undermine the credibility of the U.S. in all of Asia. China would then seek to persuade U.S. Asian allies to reduce current levels of security cooperation with the U.S., by removing some or all of U.S. military facilities from their territories. These conditions also increase their accommodation to China.

PHASE IV: China dominates Asia following the end of the U.S. alliance with Japan (2008–2012). China's control of Taiwan intimidates Asian neighbors and undermines U.S. credibility, while adding $300 billion to Beijing's economic base, as well as an immensely talented labor force with advanced high-technology production facilities and more than $150 billion in hard-currency reserves. Taiwan also provides the advantages of a strategically significant location commanding all the sea and air lanes on which Japan and South Korea depend. China, working covertly with pacifist, anti-U.S. groups in both countries, persuades Japan and South Korea to terminate existing security treaties with the United States. China defines itself as the "guarantor of stability" in Asia and insists that Asian countries no longer permit their territory to be used as bases for any U.S. military forces. The U.S. is no longer an Asian military power.

PHASE V: Neutralization of Western Europe (2010–2014): The economic and technological skills and resources of Taiwan, South Korea, and Japan provide China with valuable advanced military and civilian technology on very favorable terms. China secretly expands its strategic nuclear forces on long-range missiles to one or two thousand warheads, above U.S. and Russian levels after their bilateral reductions. Disputing U.S intelligence reports to the contrary, China denies it is building its own missile-defense system. China uses financial incentives and political/covert action to persuade many states in Europe to end an already tenuous, fractious participation in NATO. China woos European support by shifting a large portion of its economic opportunities from U.S. to European corporations and moving a large part of its massive hard-currency reserves to the euro from the U.S. dollar (thereby weakening the U.S. dollar and strengthening the euro). China secretly uses its significant influence with anti-U.S. oil-producing regimes such as Libya, Iran, Sudan, and Venezuela to urge sharp price increases for NATO members, while offering a discount to neutral countries. Most European powers, seeing the U.S. removal from Asia as a sign of U.S. decline and unreliability, disengage from U.S. commitments. The de facto dissolution of the NATO alliance is visible by 2014.

PHASE VI: China takes the Russian Far East and dominates Russia (2014–2020): With U.S. alliances in Asia and Europe having unraveled, Beijing turns to Russia, its "trusted strategic partner." With the world's largest population and one of its largest economies, China has secretly built offensive nuclear forces far surpassing those remaining in Russia. With the benefit of advanced technology obtained by purchase and espionage from both Russia and the United States, and through the work of its skilled scientists and engineers (along with those in Japan and Taiwan), China reveals to Russia that it has developed, tested, and deployed a missile defense fully effective against the forces of both Russia and the United States.

China "persuades" a demoralized Russia to "return" the Russian Far East, a vast region of great mineral wealth with 1.5 million square kilometers, which the Russian Empire obtained by treaty from the weaker Qing Dynasty in 1860. China offers to "buy" this region for some nominal sum to give Russia a pretext for its submission. China then becomes dominant over Russia and therefore over all the other states on the vast Eurasian continent from the Pacific to the Atlantic.

Note: The Chinese Communist regime has consistently stated that all previous loss of Chinese territory was due to "unequal" treaties imposed by force and is therefore invalid. China's intent to recover its lost territory from Russia when it is stronger was foreshadowed in very heated demands made by Mao to Khrushchev during the alliance of the 1950s. Also, in negotiations to define the Russian/Chinese border in the 1990s, Russia wanted the final agreement to be "in perpetuity," but China insisted that the agreement be reassessed in 2020. Russia accepted that condition.

PHASE VII: Global preponderance for China (2020–2023): By this time, there are pro-China or subservient regimes in key countries of Eurasia, Asia, the Middle East, Africa, and Latin America. The United States is isolated in strategic terms from virtually all major powers, as the Asian alliances and then those in Europe have ended. Former allies in Europe remain neutral, at least publicly, as they pursue individual economic and diplomatic initiatives with China. Asia is wholly subservient. China controls most of the important transit areas for world trade, e.g. the South China and East Asian seas, the Panama Canal, the Suez Canal, and the straits of Malacca.

China, its allies, and client states control much of the world's oil production, including not only the Middle East but also in Russia, the Central Asian oil states, Sudan, Venezuela, and other important producers. China also has a virtual monopoly on advanced computer chips (in 2002 Taiwan produced 85 percent of the world's computer chips) and other high-tech products needed by any industrial economy. This gives China the capacity for "strategic, economic, and technological denial"—the ability to coerce states, including the U.S., by threatening to withhold, slow, or cut off exports of essential products to states not meeting its demands.

PHASE VIII: China is dominant in the world (2025–?): China is far ahead of the U.S. in offensive nuclear-strike capabilities. It has used an amalgamation of technologies to develop means of neutralizing the U.S. missile defense, and it has revealed that it has an effective missile defense. China is now able to require both the U.S. and Russia to reduce significantly their offensive nuclear forces. As a subterfuge, China proposes that all states cut their forces by 80 to 90 percent but implements genuine verification only of the cuts to be made by the U.S., Russia, France, the United Kingdom, Israel, India, and Pakistan—leaving the Chinese offensive nuclear force intact. In the interests of "peace and stability," China prohibits any other country from further developing or deploying missile defenses and requires the U.S. to dismantle its missile-defense system. The penalty for resisting could be the immediate destruction of major economic resources or cities.

With dominance in offensive nuclear forces and an effective monopoly on missile defense, China moves from global preponderance to global dominance.

AN ALTERNATIVE SCENARIO: CHINA AND RUSSIA MOVE TOWARD PEACEFUL DEMOCRATIC EVOLUTION

Fortunately, this possible movement toward global dominance by Communist China can be prevented through a combination of means—none of which need involve military combat. The concluding chapters outline a new comprehensive

U.S. strategy that uses means which are prudent, feasible, and likely to be effective in maintaining peaceful relations with both Russia and China, while providing incentives for both to be cooperative internationally. These new realistic policies would also seek to help the citizens of both Russia and China realize their fundamental aspirations through the attainment of political democracy, which provides the means to protect human rights, including the rights of workers as well as ethnic and religious groups, improve living conditions, and to live in peace at home and abroad.

I. CHINA

2 The First Mao Years, 1949–1965

"Mao was bursting with an impatient desire to rule the world."
                    —KHRUSHCHEV, general secretary of the Communist Party
                                                    of Soviet Union, 1959

"Emperor Qin Shihuang was not that outstanding. He only buried alive 460 Confucian scholars. We buried 460,000 Confucian scholars. . . . We are a hundred times worse than Emperor Qin."
                    —MAO, Tenth Communist Party Congress, 1958

"The peasants recalled how, during the Communist Wind from 1959 to 1960, rice was left to rot in the fields because the peasants were too weak from hunger to harvest it. Many starved to death."
                    —WEI JINGSHENG, Chinese democracy activist and
                                        former prisoner of conscience

China is among the world's oldest continuous civilizations, with a written history that began almost four thousand years ago. The first unified Chinese empire, the Shang dynasty, began in Central China in 1766 B.C. Succeeding dynasties expanded the empire until China reached its greatest extent in the late eighteenth century A.D. under the Qing dynasty, which lasted until 1911.

The political culture of imperial China in the last two thousand years was formulated during what is known as the time of the "warring states." During this time, the emperors were weaker than their nobility who, for about a thousand years (from approximately 1,200 to 200 B.C.) had formed basically independent kingdoms and fought each other for dominance. This millennium of intermittent conflict included the era of "one hundred schools," when political philosophers in the pay of these competing Chinese warlords wrote essays on the proper relationship between man, the state, and society. Confucianism, Taoism, and Sun Tzu's *The Art of War* all derived from this era, though the two doctrines with greatest political influence were Confucianism and Legalism.

Confucianism envisioned a blissful prehistoric time when mythical wise and benevolent emperors ruled properly for the benefit of the whole kingdom. Correct hierarchical relationships among various groups in society were emphasized: emperor and subject; father and son; husband and wife; elder brother and younger brother. The inferior in the relationship always had to obey the superior, but the superior had to show concern for the well-being of the inferior. Traditional notions of ancestor worship and proper ritual were also given emphasis in this philosophy. Thus, the emperor ruled by what came to be known as the mandate of heaven; if the emperor were to lose his mandate by being corrupt, cruel, incompetent, or by improperly performing rituals, then heaven would give him bad fortune and replace him with another. Thus, Confucianism was used to justify both imperial rule and revolts.

In competition with Confucianism was Legalism, a philosophy similar to others taught during this era. Legalism mandated strict adherence to a set of rules instituted by the authorities as the only way for society to function; even if a law were wrong, it still had to be obeyed or society risked falling into disorder. In contrast, traditional Confucianism emphasized relationships over rule by law. At the level of the rulers, the duel between Confucianism and Legalism was won by Legalism, though Confucianism remained part of the official philosophy of imperial China.

Legalism proclaimed, "The ruler occupies the position of power dominating over the people and commands the wealth of the state."[1] In his interesting discussion of the role of legalist political ideas in shaping imperial rule in China during its last two millennia, Stephen Mosher notes that among the means recommended by the legalists to increase the power of the ruler were: "The accumulation of people as an indispensable component of power . . . the suppression of all voluntary associations . . . the establishment of informer networks with a legalist author writing 'the wise ruler forces the whole world to hear and to watch for him . . . no one in the world can hide from him or scheme against him.'"[2]

The forerunner of present-day China is usually taken as the Qin dynasty, established in 221 B.C. The first emperor of the Qin dynasty, Qin Shihuang, unified China and, according to Mosher, is the true inventor of bureaucratic totalitarianism, having established a centralized bureaucratic state which dominated society and used "law as a penal tool of the ruler, mutual surveillance and informer networks, literary persecution, and political practices of coercion and intimidation," along with brutality that included mass executions of enemies and presumed enemies, the burying alive of 463 of the most famous Confucian scholars of the time, and the destruction of virtually all books in the imperial archives except his own memoirs and books on medicine, astronomy, and agronomy.[3] An imperial edict forbade all private schools, all political or philosophical discussion, all work by scholars "who use examples from antiquity to criticize the present, or who praise early dynasties in order to throw doubt on the policies of our own," and condemned "government officials who turn a blind eye to the above mentioned crimes."[4] The Qin emperor also deported some twenty thousand nobles and killed as many as several hundred thousand people during forced labor for massive construction projects.

The French scholar Jean-Louis Margolin informs us, "This emperor was explicitly taken as a model by Mao,"[5] the ruler of Communist China from 1949 until his death in 1976. Speaking to a Communist Party congress in 1958, Mao said "Emperor Qin Shihuang was not that outstanding. He only buried alive 460 Confucian scholars. We buried 460,000 Confucian scholars. . . . We are a hundred times worse than Emperor Qin. To the charge of being like Emperor Qin, of being a dictator, we plead guilty."[6]

For many centuries the Chinese empire was the largest, most wealthy, and most technologically advanced state system on earth. However, with the changes brought by the age of scientific discovery and the industrial revolution in the West, the economic, technological, and military resources of the European states grew.[7] The Chinese empire kept to its traditions and sought to limit its contacts with the European states. In contrast, the nineteenth-century Japanese empire made the decision to learn about and use Western technology and apply it to imperial military purposes, while also seeking to limit the influence of Western cultural and political ideas and practices.

As a result of the growing power of European states, including imperial Russia, the weaker Chinese Qing Empire experienced a series of defeats in the nineteenth century. Britain and the European states obtained extraterritorial privileges in China as a result of two wars: Russia's taking of Chinese territory, which became most of the Russian Far East, was ratified by treaty in 1860; and, in 1895 Japan defeated China, thereby gaining control of Korea and Taiwan.

Imperial rule was undermined by these defeats, as well as by large-scale internal rebellions against the Qing Empire—for instance the White Lotus revolt of the late 1790s, the Taiping rebellion of 1850–1875, and the Boxer Rebellion of 1900. These events, in combination with the attraction and appeal of Western ideas of democratic government among a small but influential group of Western-educated Chinese leaders, resulted in the establishment of the Republic of China in 1911.[8]

The leader of that movement and first president of the Republic, Sun Yat-Sen, had spent some time in the United States and hoped to establish a republic that would be governed democratically. Sun founded the Nationalist Party, but it divided by 1916, and this opened the way for regional political rivals with their own armies to limit the control of the central government. In 1917, the Communist movement seized power in Russia and by 1920 defeated its armed opponents in a civil war. In 1921, inspired and aided by the Russian Communist Party, the Chinese Communist Party (CCP) was founded in Shanghai. It hoped to repeat the success of the Communists in Russia.

The new Soviet government used a double strategy in China, as it did in many other countries. It had diplomatic relations with the nationalist government of China and at the same time, through the Communist International (known as the

Comintern) and through its foreign intelligence services, Moscow supported and encouraged the Chinese Communist movement. In the first years of the Chinese Communist rebellion, Soviet judgment was that the most important tactical step was the defeat of the regional powers, the warlords. To accomplish this, the Soviet Union urged Chinese Communists to join the nationalist government in a tactical alliance.

From 1923 to 1927 the nationalists and the Chinese Communists were in a coalition against the warlords. Following Sun Yat-sen's death in 1925, General Chiang Kai-Shek became the leader of the nationalist regime. Having made progress against the warlords and expecting that the Communists would soon reignite the civil war they had begun in 1921, Chiang Kai-Shek decided to act first. He turned on the Communists, capturing and killing some, although most escaped to southern China. After some years of civil war, imperial Japan invaded and occupied Manchuria in 1931 and in 1934 expanded its invasion and occupation of China. The nationalist regime fought both the Japanese and the Communist armies. Having been driven out of southern China, the Communist armies made the "Long March," a seventy-five-hundred-mile retreat to the western part of China.

In the 1920s, Mao had been one among many leaders in the Communist movement. However, faced with repression by the nationalist government in the cities and the resulting forced movement of the Communists to the countryside, Mao recognized that in a country where the vast majority of the population lived in hundreds of thousands of small villages, a peasant-based Communist movement might be more successful than the urban-based Communism of Russia. In 1927 Mao had observed the success of the Communist-led peasants in Hunan and wrote his *Report on the Peasant Movement in Hunan*. This was the first step in the development of Mao's "people's war," based on a rural, militarized Communism.

This approach worked and gathered enough support in parts of the countryside that on November 7, 1931, the anniversary of the Communist coup in Russia, the Chinese Communists founded the "Chinese Republic of Soviets," and Mao was chosen to preside over the Council of People's Commissars.[9] This established the model that Chinese Communists would pursue into the future: Concentrating the energy of the revolution on the construction of the state, and focusing the efforts of that state—which was to be warlike in nature—on forming an army to crush the enemy, the central government of Nanjing, presided over by Chiang Kai-Shek.[10]

As the Chinese Communist movement grew in the countryside, there was an important dualism in its social base. Most of the local activists came from the more well-to-do elements of the peasants and from families of landowners—they joined the Communist movement because they saw it as a more radical form of Chinese nationalism. However, many of the leaders in the Party center and most of the soldiers in its regular army were recruited mainly from "the lower strata and the marginalized segments of society, including bandits, beggars, mendicant monks, mercenaries, and among the women, prostitutes."[11] Mao said in 1926 that "this second group constituted 'people who can fight with great courage, and led in the right manner, they will become a genuine revolutionary force.'"[12] These social differences would become part of the repeated struggle between the central authorities and provincial authorities in the Communist Party during the decades of Mao's rule.

From 1937 to 1945, the Nationalist government and the Chinese Communists formed an anti-Japanese pact, agreeing to cease their internal war in order to oppose jointly the invading Japanese forces. But in fact, the Nationalist forces did most of the fighting against Japan, while the Communists expanded their areas of control and built up their military forces, preparing safe areas in the west of China for the next stage of the civil war against the Nationalist government.

Following the surrender of Japan in 1945, the Soviet Union continued its dual strategy with China. It formally recognized the Chinese Nationalist government and simultaneously provided significant political and military help covertly to the Chinese Communists. The Soviet Union arranged for the delivery of huge quantities of surrendered Japanese weapons and military equipment to the Communists as they reignited their war against the Nationalist government. Soviet assistance included moving eighty thousand North Korean troops, fully equipped with Soviet weapons and wearing the uniforms of the Chinese Communist People's Liberation Army, into Manchuria to fight against the Nationalist forces.[13]

Because of the importance of the alliance between the U.S. and Nationalist forces during World War II there were many who argued, including U.S. Ambassador to China Patrick J. Hurley, that the U.S. should provide direct support to the Nationalist government in their fight against the Soviet-backed Communist forces. However, in November 1945, the U.S. "adopted a new policy which called for continuing American support of the Nationalist government on the condition that it not employ American arms to conduct a civil war and that it strive to reach a settlement with the Communists." In addition, the United States government repeatedly urged the Nationalists to form a coalition government with the Communists. This left the Nationalists feeling betrayed by the U.S., knowing full well from their experience with Mao and his supporters during the war with Japan, that any coalition government would be taken over by the Communists.

By 1947, the Truman administration decided to contain the Soviet Union in Western Europe and proclaimed what became known as the Truman Doctrine, a policy of helping friendly states resist being taken over by "armed minorities," applying it first to Greece and Turkey. The Truman administration also recognized that in central Europe the Soviet Union was violating the Yalta agreement, which called for free democratic elections as the basis for choosing postwar governments.

Instead, Moscow had established a series of pro-Communist regimes through a process of disguised political coercion. Presumably, the U.S. Department of State understood that the Communist movements in China and the Soviet Union had been close allies since 1921, but nevertheless, it failed to extend the Truman Doctrine to include a coherent strategy to help the Nationalists prevent Communist victory in China.

The Communist movement in China had a systematic propaganda effort to portray itself to the U.S. and the West as a group of "agrarian reformers" who would bring peace and good government to the people of China and free them from what they described as the "brutal and corrupt government of the Nationalist clique." Some Western journalists, experts, and officials came to share that view. This was especially true of some U.S. Foreign Service officers who had direct experience with the many shortcomings and problems of the Nationalist government on the one hand and only a distant knowledge and understanding of the reality of life in rural areas under Communist control. Consequently, the Truman administration did not apply the idea of "containment" to the Communist movement in China, and the Communist armies ultimately defeated most of the Nationalist armies.

The Chinese Communists proclaimed themselves the new government of China on October 1, 1949. Mao, as Chairman of the Chinese Communist Party, said China would reclaim its rightful place in history and in the world:

> The Chinese have always been a great, courageous, and industrious nation; it is only in modern times that they have fallen behind. And that was due entirely to oppression and exploitation by foreign imperialism and domestic reactionary governments . . . ours will no longer be a nation subject to insult and humiliation. We have stood up.[14]

The Nationalist government, most of its military forces, and a large number of civilians afraid of Communist rule fled to the island of Taiwan and established what has come to be known as the Republic of China on Taiwan. They hoped, some time in the not-too-distant future, to be able to return to the mainland after the people there experienced the reality of Communist rule. In 1950, after China attacked the UN forces in Korea, President Truman sent the Seventh Fleet to help Taiwan defend itself. Since then, the Communist regime in China has sought to complete its victory over the Nationalists by taking over Taiwan.

THE MAO YEARS—IN OVERVIEW

As it took power in 1949, the Chinese Communist Party had a membership of about 4.5 million, to rule the estimated 450 million people of China.[15] In considering the future of China, it is important to have an understanding of the major political events and trends during the more than half-century of Communist rule that continues.

Having controlled significant amounts of territory for many years before their national victory, the Chinese Communists had opportunities to reflect on the theory and practice of Marxism-Leninism in the context of their own country's realities and their strategic and tactical purposes. In the remote city of Yenan from 1937 to 1945, Mao wrote his major works on how the Communist Party would rule. To assure that the Party itself would be unified, obedient, and effective, he established the "rectification," or intraparty "struggle" movement. This was a process of intense self-criticism and mutual criticism intended to combat

1. Subjectivism and unorthodox tendencies, 2. Sectarianism within Party ranks, and 3. Formalism in literature. It was . . . aimed at inculcating in the Party members a correct understanding of Marxism, Leninism, the thought of Mao, and the general Party line, in order that they might avoid "leftism" and "rightism."[16]

Mao applied this policy in Yenan, and a Comintern representative commented on the results:

Party discipline is based on stupidly rigid forms of criticism and self-criticism. The cruel method of psychological coercion that Mao calls "moral purification" has created a stifling atmosphere inside the Party in Yenan. A not negligible number of Party activists have committed suicide, have fled, or have become psychotic. The [rectification] method is a response to the principle that "everyone should know the intimate thoughts of everyone else." . . . under the protocol of criticism and self-criticism, the thoughts and aspirations and actions of everyone are in full view.[17]

Also in Yenan, Mao wrote *The New Democracy*, a political blueprint for the future. Mao attempted to follow his blueprint, and this discussion of his rule will begin with the period of consolidating power (the "New Democracy"), followed by the shift to agricultural collectivization and establishment of the five-year plans ("Socialist Transformation"), and then the so-called Great Leap Forward to the communes ("Socialist Construction"). This last factor had disastrous consequences and, after a few years of more pragmatic policy, was followed from 1966 to 1976 by the Cultural Revolution—a movement not originally anticipated in Mao's theoretical writings.

In the first phase of Communist rule, Mao recognized the need to move gradually to consolidate control over existing institutions in society. For that reason, Mao wrote that the initial economic structure should consist of a state economy where the government controlled the major industries, mines, and utilities; an agricultural economy, in which individual farms would develop into collective farms; and a private economy, in which private middle- and small-sized businesses would be allowed to continue. In fact, many of the private firms and factories allowed to remain private in this phase were placed under the de facto control of loyal Communists. For example, the Chinese Communist leader after 1994, Jiang Zemin, was put in charge of two factories in Shanghai during this time.[18]

The political structure in the first phase would be one of "democratic centralism," meaning that the Chinese Communist Party (CCP) would rule but that a few other political parties would be permitted to exist under strict control. Most of these political parties still exist, though they were and always have been captive parties with leadership being used occasionally to add some legitimacy to Communist actions. The historian Immanuel Hsu informs us that these parties "possessed only the right to agree with and cooperate with the CCP and the government."[19] Further, in the New Democracy era there would be a coexistence of the four defined "classes" under the leadership of the Communist Party, which represented the proletariat. Those classes were to be workers, peasants, the small bourgeoisie (middle-income professionals, merchants, etc.), and the national bourgeoisie (owners of large enterprises, assets). These were represented in the flag of the People's Republic by the four small stars surrounding the large star symbolizing the Communist Party leadership as the guiding element of the new state. In cultural terms, Mao's concept was that China would develop a "scientific, anti-feudal mass culture," with the selective acceptance of "useful elements of foreign cultures," and that the state would be "anti-imperialist, able to advocate the dignity and independence of the Chinese nation."[20]

As in the Soviet Union, the overall structure of rule involved the Communist Party as the key institution, which in turn was fully and completely controlled by the Communist Party leadership. Likewise, leadership of both the Party and the government of China were determined by a process that was representative and open in form but, in fact, totally predetermined by the top Party leadership. In form, members of the Chinese Communist Party ostensibly elected delegates who served for five years in the National Party Congress, which convened annually. The Central Committee of the Party was then "elected" for five-year terms and presided over by a Chairman. The Central Committee, in turn, delegated its powers to the Political Bureau or Politburo of the Party, which maintained a Standing Committee of seven, usually the most powerful among the Communist rulers of China. There was also a central secretariat to administer the Party and a Central Control Commission to provide a means for the leadership to assure itself that the Party was carrying out its orders.

Until 1953, the formal government consisted of the Central People's Government Council, which combined executive, legislative, and judicial authority. In 1953 a census was taken, an election law established, and all citizens over the age of eighteen except "landlords and counterrevolutionaries" were permitted to "vote." Starting in 1954, controlled "elections" were held for village, township, and provincial congresses; which in turn selected a legislature, the National People's Congress, nominally the leading institution of the state.

The first National People's Congress adopted a new constitution, recognizing the "alliance of four classes" as well as the four types of ownership: state, cooperative, individual, and capitalist. It also included a bill of rights that applied to all citizens, the exception being that the government maintained the right to "reform traitors and counterrevolutionaries."[21] In the first years of the People's Republic of China, Mao dominated in fact and in form both the Party and government. In the Party, he was Chairman of the Central Committee, of the Politburo, and of the Central Secretariat. In the government, Mao was Chairman of the People's Republic, of the Revolutionary Military Council, and of the National People's Congress.[22] In China, as in the Soviet Union, the process of pseudo-elections for the national government was a means to mobilize the population, to have citizens demonstrate allegiance to the regime, and of appearing modern and contemporary. The existence of a formal government also provided the Communist Party with a means of holding real power while having another set of institutions that could be held responsible for problems or setbacks.

Consolidation of Power, Soviet Alliance, Combat Abroad, 1949–1952

In 1949, as the Nationalist armies were being defeated, the five major Communist armies expanded their areas of control in China. At the start of the new regime these five field armies controlled what came to be called the "Great Areas"; they served as both the initial civil and military administrative apparatus of the new government.[23] After a few years the Great Areas were abolished, but the powerful regional role of the Chinese military in much of the country continued in partnership with the regional Communist Party under the policy guidance of the central Party.

The years of war with Japan and civil war (1931–49) had reduced industrial production in China to about 70 percent of prewar levels and food production to about 60 percent.[24] The new Communist government moved immediately to stabilize the economy and rebuild destroyed infrastructure, such as roads, bridges, and power lines. The regime also sought to reassure those in private commerce and industry that there was a place for them in the new order so that they would continue their productive activities and not flee or defect to Taiwan. At the same time, many Nationalist government officials and former soldiers were offered amnesty as a means of persuading them to remain in China and not go to Taiwan or Hong Kong, where they could add to the potential hostile force China might face in the future.

Establishing an alliance with the Soviet Union, then ruled by Stalin, was a major priority for Mao. In December 1949 Mao traveled to Moscow to visit Stalin and stayed nearly three months, until mid-February 1950. We learn from recently opened Kremlin files that at the first meeting between Stalin and Mao on December 16, 1949, Mao said "China needs breathing space of about three to five years of peace."[25] Mao went on to say that he wanted an alliance with the Soviet Union. Stalin replied that China faced no direct threats at present: "Japan hasn't yet gotten back on its feet. America shouts about war but is afraid of it . . . in Europe they are scared of war. No one wants to fight China."[26]

On February 14, 1950, a formal treaty of alliance was signed between the Soviet Union and China. Stalin agreed to provide a $300 million credit and promised to provide experts to help China with industrialization and military modernization. As a result of that agreement, from 1950 to 1954, the Soviet Union sent China significant numbers of scientists, technicians, and military advisors: from one to twenty-five thousand each to the Chinese air force and navy, five to ten thousand to the Chinese army, and some four hundred thousand technicians to help in industrial enterprises and plants.[27] In 1952, Mao called the alliance with the Soviet Union "lasting, unbreakable, and invincible."[28]

A number of territorial issues were worked out, with the Soviet Union voluntarily abandoning a number of rights and positions in China it had inherited from czarist Russia through nineteenth-century treaties. Stalin also agreed to allow China to reassert control over the area known as East Turkestan to Russia and Xinjiang to China. This largely desert area bordering the Soviet Union had a majority population of about seven million Muslim Uighurs, in a region of 1.6 million square kilometers, or about 20 percent of China's total land. China promised the Muslims that Xinjiang would be a special autonomous region with significant local autonomy.

The same promise was made to Tibet, which had been self-governing for nine centuries, then again in recent decades. In the ninth century, imperial China had agreed that Tibet could govern itself, but the Qing Empire reincorporated Tibet from the eighteenth century to its end in 1911. The Dalai Lama, as the spiritual and secular head of the Tibetan theocracy, resisted the immediate demands from Communist China to accede to its authority. In January 1950, Mao instructed the Chinese army to begin military operations against Tibet in order to coerce it into subordination to Communist rule.[29] This order, by Mao, sent from Moscow indicated Soviet agreement. In 1950, the New Year's message of the Chinese Communist Party proclaimed the "glorious fighting task . . . in 1950 is to liberate Taiwan, Hainan, and Tibet."[30]

A second visible international result of the Soviet-Chinese alliance was the

North Korean surprise attack on South Korea in June 1950. For several years, Kim Il-Sung, the North Korean Communist dictator installed by Stalin, had been asking for Stalin's permission to attack South Korea. With the successful test of a Soviet atomic device in 1949, the consolidation of pro-Soviet regimes in Eastern Europe, and the Communist victory in China, Stalin was prepared to authorize such an attack. This was clearly significant to discussions with Mao, since Stalin gave approval to begin military preparations on February 9, 1950, while Mao was still in Moscow.[31] Stalin was willing to provide Soviet tanks, artillery, rifles, and other military, medical, and fuel supplies, but he also wanted North Korea to pay for this with lead, silver, and gold.[32] After Kim Il Sung made a secret visit to Stalin in April 1950, as the final preparations for the attack moved forward, Stalin wrote Mao that he had agreed "with the Koreans' proposal to move toward unification, but Stalin qualified this by saying that the issue must be settled in the end by the Chinese and Korean comrades jointly."[33] This meant that Stalin and Mao had agreed that, if needed, Chinese troops would fight in Korea.

North Korea launched its surprise attack against South Korea on June 25, 1950. The United Nations Security Council concluded that this was an act of aggression and resolved to take military action to repel it. (The Soviet Union had walked out of the Security Council and therefore could not cast its veto.) On the front lines in Korea the UN coalition was driven out of the South Korean capital, down the peninsula to a small region of the country. Then in mid-September 1950, the United States counter-attacked with a major landing behind the North Korean lines and the tide of battle turned sharply against the invading North Korean army.

At that point Kim Il-Sung asked Stalin for additional help, and Stalin called on Mao, writing, "I understand the Korean comrades are in a desperate situation. At least five or six divisions should be moved up to the 38th parallel. Chinese divisions could figure as volunteers."[34] While Stalin was unwilling to commit ground troops, the Soviet Union established the "64th Fighter Air Corps," consisting of antiaircraft divisions, fighter interception aircraft, and support personnel. These were inserted covertly and over the three years of the Korean War, as Volkogonov reports, "some 15 Soviet air divisions and several antiaircraft divisions gained battle experience" against American aircraft. Soviet records claim that these covert Soviet forces shot down 1,309 U.S. aircraft, about 18 percent of U.S. air losses, while losing only 319 planes.[35]

Then, on October 25, 1950, in a second surprise attack, China sent more than one million of its forces to attack the U.S.-led United Nations forces in Korea. The joint Soviet-Chinese military support for North Korea meant that the Korean War ended in a stalemate. North Korea and South Korea each retained its own government and the same territory it had, and Korea remained divided at the 38th parallel. It is estimated that Communist China sustained nine hundred thousand casualties, including three hundred thousand killed.[36] The total human cost of the Korean War included the death of more than one million South Korean civilians and more than fifty thousand U.S. military personnel.

At almost the same time as China sent its armed forces into Korea, the Chinese regime publicly announced the military occupation of Tibet by more than eighty thousand troops. The Dalai Lama described the outcome: "The Tibetan army, totaling 8,000 officers and soldiers, was poorly trained and equipped. It was no match for the PLA [People's Liberation Army], who quickly encircled the Tibetan army and smashed the entire defense line."[37] Tibet remains under Communist rule.

Since 1950, hundreds of thousands of Tibetans have been killed, thousands of Tibetan religious monasteries and shrines have been destroyed, and China pursues a policy of attempting to repopulate Tibet with Han Chinese to secure and intensify its control.[38] China used its military presence in Tibet as the base for its attack against India in 1962, and in April 2000, the chairman of the House International Affairs Committee, Rep. Benjamin Gilman, warned that Chinese ballistic missiles and fourteen air bases in Tibet threatened India and other states in Asia.[39] Fifty years later, the repression of the Tibetan people by the Chinese regime included "arbitrary arrests, detention without public trial, torture in prison," and "an intensification of controls on Tibetan monasteries and on monks and nuns."[40]

"Land Reform"—Communists Take Control in the Countryside

During decades of warfare in the countryside, the Communists sought to win support by promising peasants that they would have their own land, which would be taken away from the landlords when Communism triumphed. A preview of Communist purposes and methods was visible in one rural region that they governed from 1927 to 1931, the "Jiangxi Soviet." There, in a reign of terror, the Communists killed about 186,000 people who they said opposed their agrarian policies.[41] This was a preview of the brutality that would accompany the nationwide implementation of "land reform" in China, which began with the Agrarian Reform Law of June 1950.

Among China's estimated population of 450 million, about 80 percent, or 320 million people, then lived in the countryside in about one million villages. The Communists understood that most of the rural population was neither for nor against them. Therefore, a very important political goal of the land reform process was to involve the peasants personally in punishing those deemed to be "landlords" or "rich peasants" and taking their property. The Communist reasoning was that this would make the peasants coresponsible with the regime for the executions, starvation, severe beatings, and sentences to forced labor meted out by the Party. Thereby, the peasants would be linked to the regime and would be far less likely to join any future opposition. Later, Mao would also apply this method in the cities and towns, launching mass persecution "campaigns" against designated "enemies" and involving neighbors and coworkers directly in acts of violence and oppression against their fellow citizens.

In the case of "land reform," thousands of teams of Party members went into the countryside, village by village. They first classified the population into five groups: landlords and four categories of peasants ranging from rich to middle to laborers. In many cases, these categories were arbitrary, often the result of quotas set by Party leadership. For example, in a given region 5 percent or 10 percent had to be defined as "landlords" or "rich peasants." The next step was the "bitterness meeting," in which an entire village was assembled and the Communist organizers would begin to shout accusations at the ostensible landlord or rich peasant and urge the peasants to do the same. This process of accusation and vituperation would gain in emotional intensity; often there would be physical violence against the accused, and "the outcome was usually a death sentence for the landowner (accompanied by the confiscation of all goods and possessions) and immediate execution with the active participation of the peasants."[42]

Estimates are that between two to five million persons were executed, another four to six million ostensibly "rich peasants" were sent to forced-labor camps, while an additional eight to twelve million were placed under strict observation by the Communist neighborhood committees.[43] At times, "people were tortured to death in attempts to force them to reveal the whereabouts of alleged treasure. Interrogations were systematically accompanied by torture with red-hot irons. Families were executed and the tombs of their ancestors robbed and destroyed."[44] By the end of 1952, the agrarian changes had been completed, and approximately 110 million acres of land was distributed to about 320 million peasants; or, an average of one-third acre per peasant.[45] In view of the relatively few rich peasants, and the fact that their landholdings were modest—on the order of ten to twenty acres—the net result of this violent redistribution was only a slight improvement in the economic well-being of most peasants.[46]

This bloody process introduced the Chinese people to the power and methods of the new Communist rulers. It also was the beginning of two of the fundamental methods of control established by the regime: the classification of citizens and the mass campaign in which people were directed by the regime to persecute others who had been officially designated as "counterrevolutionaries" or "class enemies."

Two other methods of control established by the regime during these first years were the neighborhood committees, led by loyal Communists, which kept watch on all activities and the division of the population into those who had to remain in the countryside and the relative few who had permission to live in designated towns or cities.[47]

It is worth noting that in a number of other Asian countries, including Japan under U.S. military occupation, South Korea, and Taiwan, the distribution of land had been less equal than in China, yet land reform was carried out peacefully and with compensation for owners. Those land reforms produced the basis for significant improvements in the living conditions of people in the countryside, as well as the savings and capital which made a major contribution to the industrialization and movement toward prosperity of those countries, each of which leapt economically far ahead of China during the Mao years and after.

Agricultural Collectivization, First Five-Year Plan, Differences with the USSR, 1953–1957

Next to assuring its political control in China, the highest priority for the Communist regime was to "build up the industrial base for a strong militarily self-reliant and secure national defense."[48] In imitation of the Soviet Union, the regime launched the first five-year plan in 1953 with a focus on heavy industry, especially those sectors that would support military self-sufficiency. This was to involve about seven hundred major new industrial projects, of which about 160 would be built with Soviet aid.[49] Inexperience caused delays in launching this industrial development plan.

In 1953, confident about its control of the rural areas, viewing its military intervention in Korea as a success in stalemating the U.S. and it allies, and confident that the nationalist regime on Taiwan was incapable of contesting its rule on the mainland, the regime decided to move to Mao's next phase—"socialist transformation"—by collectivizing agriculture. The several hundred million peasants who had just received their "own land" now were forced to give that land to collectives modeled on those in the Soviet Union. By 1957, the collectivization campaign was complete with the establishment of nearly eight hundred thousand collective units, each averaging six to seven hundred persons.[50]

It was also during these years of the first five-year plan for industry that the regime also ended virtually all-private ownership of the means of production and private commerce. Owners were ostensibly "compensated" for some fraction of the value of their property but in fact were forced to surrender ownership to collectively managed organizations under Party and government authority. There was virtually no resistance to this expropriation of private property and business enterprises because, by 1955, years of urban repression had completely intimidated the population of the cities as well as the countryside.

In November 1950, Mao said publicly, "We surely must kill all those reactionary elements who deserve to be killed."[51] By then the Party had built the number of its internal security police to over one million, along with tens of thousands of informers, and expanded the armed militia (under the control of the Party) from nearly six million in 1950 to ten million in 1953. The regime also immediately made use of the neighborhood committees, each with about twenty families, which the

Ming Dynasty (1363–1644) had originally organized. The Communists required these committees to report all movements of strangers into any neighborhood, so they would be known to the police authorities. They also required every person to register with the police and prohibited people from leaving the countryside to live in the cities without special permits.[52]

Party activists conducted nationwide purges in the cities through targeted mass campaigns against "waste, corruption, bureaucracy," starting in July 1950, and in 1951 against "bribery, fraud, tax evasion, and revealing state secrets." These were aimed at elements of the middle class, small business owners, non-Communist former political activists, intellectuals, and even overly independent Communist Party members. Also included as targets were Christians, of whom hundreds of thousands were arrested over the next two decades, and former Nationalist government and military officials, who found that their initial amnesty was no longer honored by the regime.

During the times of urban "red terror" in 1951, official Chinese figures show, for example, that in Shanghai there were three thousand arrests in one night, and thirty-eight thousand arrests in four months, many leading to death sentences and executions. In Beijing, along with thirty thousand interrogations and arrests over nine months, there were 220 death sentences and public executions in a single day; in Guangzhou the official data shows eighty-nine thousand arrests and twenty-three thousand death sentences in ten months.[53] Further, official China data shows that 450,000 small businesses were investigated—one hundred thousand in Shanghai alone—and about three hundred thousand owners and managers received prison sentences.[54]

Mao said that eight hundred thousand "counterrevolutionaries" had been "liquidated" (killed). The very thorough Margolin analysis estimates that more than one million were executed, 2.5 million were imprisoned in "reeducation" camps, and about seven hundred thousand may have committed suicide under the pressure of these urban repression campaigns.[55]

As in the countryside, the Party also sought "that as large a segment of the population as possible took part in the repressions, while being careful to ensure that full control of the proceedings remained with the Party."[56] In practice, this meant that personal associates of the targets of this repression, whether coworkers, colleagues, or neighbors, would be pressured into denouncing publicly the individuals who were subsequently imprisoned or executed.

Intellectuals were required to participate in "submission and rebirth" meetings, in which they had to confess their mistakes and prove they had overcome "liberalism," Westernization, "American cultural imperialism," or face imprisonment and death.[57] Members of the Party were expected to follow the orders of the Politburo without question, to work with inexhaustible energy, to be completely incorruptible, and to be on the lookout for counterrevolutionaries and spies working against the goals of the Communist revolution.

The writing of Jung Chang, the daughter of senior Communist Party provincial officials, provides a great deal of insight into the life experience of Communists in Mao's China. She described the dedication and sacrifices of her parents in helping the Communists win victory in China and their responsibilities as members of the new government. While members of the Communist Party received much better food, living quarters, and medical care than the general population, almost all senior government officials lived in their offices with married Communists usually living in different offices where:

> They were not allowed to cook at home and all ate in canteens [cafeterias]. The canteen was also where everyone got their boiled water, which was fetched in thermos flasks. . . . Saturday was the only day married couples were allowed to spend together. Among the officials the euphemism for making love was "spending a Saturday." Gradually this regimented lifestyle relaxed a bit and married couples were able to spend more time together, but almost all still lived and spent most of their time in office compounds.[58]

All Party and government officials were classified according to seniority in grades one through twenty-six, with one being the highest. All allocations for housing, food, travel, and medical care were dependent on this particular allocation. Jung Chang mentions that in 1990, since her mother was only a grade fifteen (having only been upgraded twice in forty years), she was unable to buy an airplane ticket, a soft seat on a train, or stay in a hotel which had a private bath.[59]

In 1955 Mao initiated a campaign to discover "hidden counterrevolutionaries" within the Party. All eight hundred employees of the office where Ms. Chang's mother worked had to remain on the premises to be interrogated as Party officials assessed their political loyalty. Most were released after some days, but Ms. Chang's mother was held prisoner in her office building for six months of intense "rectification and examination," until finally being cleared of counterrevolutionary activities.[60] This would prove to be a mild preview of what would occur in China during the next decade.

Much in the Communism of Mao was familiar from the experience of the other twentieth-century totalitarian regimes: the dominance of the Party, the brutality of the secret police, forced collectivization, the use of terror and expropriation, mass executions, imprisonment, forced-labor camps, identity papers, and restrictions on free movement within the country. To this Mao added three new features: the political persecution "mass campaign," whereby the Party incited and compelled citizens to turn on those who were targeted for repression; the assignment of class labels to all individuals describing the social origins of the family, which were used in making decisions about individuals' opportunities for work, education, promotion; and the assignment of all individuals in the countryside and towns to work units.

The government-assigned work units "controlled peoples' lives by controlling the assignments of their work and their living quarters."[61] The work unit and the residential permit were needed by all Chinese to "receive housing, medical care, food coupons, and permission to travel."[62] As Professor Andrew Nathan put it, "The work unit locked each individual in place for life with a set of coworkers like scorpions in a jar . . . [and] political campaigns trained people to be vicious."[63] While the class labels would disappear in the post-Mao era, much of the infrastructure for the mass political campaigns, including the neighborhood committees remained despite the post-Mao economic changes.

THE GREAT LEAP FORWARD AND AWAY FROM THE USSR

In January 1956, the new general secretary of the Party, Nikita Khrushchev, gave a speech denouncing the Stalinist "cult of personality" and the crimes Stalin had committed against the Communist Party of the Soviet Union. This surprised and shocked Mao, who became concerned that he too might also be repudiated by fellow Communists were he no longer alive or in power. Khrushchev said the Soviet Party would now rule through collective leadership, rather than one person.

In 1956, Mao still viewed the Soviet Union as the world leader of the Communist movement, and that may have led to his agreeing to a reorganization of the Chinese Communist Party later that year to permit more collective leadership in China. One result of the reorganization was to establish a new six-member Standing Committee of the Politburo, which would be the focus of power in China. Mao was chairman of the Standing Committee, but Liu Shaoqi was the first vice chairman, exercising certain powers for the Chairman. Deng Xiaoping was also a member of the Standing Committee, as the newly appointed general secretary of the Party. Both Liu and Deng wanted to pursue a more pragmatic approach to economic growth in China and sought to maintain a close and cooperative relationship with the Soviet Union as the best source of economic and military assistance.[64] Mao said later that he intended to prepare Liu and Deng as his successors, so that "When I have to see God, the country can avoid great chaos."[65]

Also, in the spirit of collective leadership and greater openness, Mao declared in May 1956, "Let a hundred flowers bloom together, let a hundred schools of thought contend." For nearly a year there was little reaction; the intellectuals in China were afraid. They well knew, as Fairbank wrote,

If you stick your neck out you may lose your head. For a year they said nothing. But then in May 1957 they began to criticize the Chinese Communist Party regime in rapidly escalating terms—its basic premises, working style, common doctrines, and practices suddenly came under severe attack. Within five weeks the Hundred Flowers campaign was closed down.[66]

In addition to the sharp and comprehensive intellectual criticism of the Party, tens of thousands took to the streets to demonstrate against the regime.[67] In Eastern Europe, Khrushchev's "thaw" had encouraged hopes for political liberalization, leading to large-scale demonstrations in Poland and a change in Communist rulers. This was followed by a rebellion in Hungary, which was put down by Soviet military forces. Though the East European Communist regimes remained, the Stalin-era leaders were removed due to public pressures. That may have given hope to those in China, some of whom dared to speak out and demonstrate, in turn leading Mao to end the "Hundred Flowers" opening after just five weeks of criticism.

Mao then launched the "antirightist campaign." All who had criticized the Party and government and hundreds of thousands of others both within the Party and the society were persecuted, with many being sent to forced-labor camps or rural exile. Estimates are that more than one million were subjected to severe punishment as Mao rejected the idea of collective leadership within the Party, extolled the Party center as the "Hall of One Voice," and reemphasized the need for "class struggle."[68] Mao also decided against economic pragmatism and instead pushed for "mass movements, increased speed in collectivization, the Great Leap, and the communes."[69] This division within the Party between economic pragmatists and more hard-line Communist factions continued into the twenty-first century.

The Growing Rift with the USSR and the Taiwan Crisis of 1954–1955

There were a number of dimensions to the gradually widening rift with the USSR after 1956. Sharing a more than four-thousand-mile border, China viewed the treaties signed with czarist Russia as "unequal," and in 1954 Mao began to ask the Soviet government to return territory he viewed as having been stolen by Russian "imperialism." This included Mongolia, which the Soviet Union had converted into an ostensibly independent state in the 1920s, and most of the Russian Far East. Border talks in 1954 and again in 1958 did not result in any progress, and Khrushchev recorded in his memoirs that the Chinese map illustrating the territory of the Soviet Union that Mao wanted returned was "so outrageous that we threw it away in disgust."[70]

There was also growing disagreement on the very important issue of world war. By 1954, the Soviet leadership had decided that in the nuclear age, war with "imperialism" (the United States) was no longer "inevitable." In fact, a series of victories without open warfare was the preferred Soviet method of international conflict. In contrast, Mao proclaimed that China and the Soviet Union together were stronger than the United States and its allies; and that even in the event of nuclear war, the Communist countries would prevail because of their larger populations. In particular, he is reported to have said, "It does not matter if three hundred million Chinese are killed; Chinese mothers will soon make up the difference."

Mao defined the outcome of the Korean War (1950–1953) as a Communist victory, since China had intervened; killed thousands of U.S., South Korean, and UN forces; experienced no open U.S. retaliation against its territory; and kept the North Korean regime in power, despite its having been the clear aggressor. Once the 1954 Geneva Conference ratified the Korean armistice, Mao wanted to move quickly to conquer Taiwan. At the start of the Korean War, President Truman sent the U.S. Seventh Fleet to defend Taiwan from any potential attack by China. Then, on August 14, 1954, China denounced the "American imperialists" for their "occupation of Taiwan," declaring that it must end and that Taiwan must be "liberated."[71] At the same time, China moved military forces with combat experience to bases along the coast opposite Taiwan and began flying its jet fighter aircraft in the Taiwan region.

On August 17, responding to press questions about the threats and military preparations by China, President Eisenhower reaffirmed his order that the U.S. Seventh Fleet would help in the defense of Taiwan and said "any invasion of Formosa [Taiwan] would have to run over the Seventh Fleet."[72] At that time, the United States had a nuclear arsenal far larger than that of the Soviet Union, and it was in this context of confrontation initiated by China that Khrushchev and Mao discussed the issue of nuclear war. Most likely, Mao contended that China had sent a million soldiers to help the Soviet Union and its ally, North Korea, and now it was time for Moscow to back China in its purpose—even if that meant risking nuclear war with the U.S. The post-Stalin Soviet leadership, after five years of experience in testing and developing a nuclear arsenal, had a sense for the enormous destructive power of these weapons and also judged that the U.S. would carry through on its stated commitments. This is when Mao began to consider "Khrushchev a coward because of his unwillingness to risk nuclear war with the U.S."[73]

Without the nuclear military support of the Soviet Union, Mao was deterred from launching a full-scale assault on Taiwan, one hundred miles across the open ocean, but instead attacked a number of nearby islands controlled by the Nationalist regime. The Matsu islands were about ten miles from the Chinese coastline, and the Quemoy (Kinmen) islands were a few miles from the coast. On September 3, 1954, China began an intense artillery attack on Quemoy and the Little Quemoy islands. The Nationalist Air Force immediately retaliated by bombing artillery positions on the mainland.

The U.S. government was divided, with some calling for immediate U.S. bombardment of the Chinese artillery positions, and others arguing that the U.S. should help defend Taiwan but not the offshore islands. The latter was Eisenhower's decision, and it was included in the U.S.-Republic of China [Taiwan] Mutual Defense Treaty of December 2, 1954.[74] As Mosher wrote, China became convinced that Americans would not intervene and then:

> The Chinese Communists assaulted the northernmost island in the Tachen chain . . . on January 20, 1955. The garrison force of 720 soldiers died to the last man. . . . Eisenhower pressured Chiang Kai-Shek to abandon the chain offering the U.S. Seventh Fleet to cover the evacuation of the 20,000 civilians and 11,000 Nationalist soldiers . . . Chiang reluctantly gave way, withdrawing the last of his forces [from the Tachen Islands] on February 6, 1955.[75]

In late January 1955, Eisenhower asked Congress to pass a resolution authorizing him to "assure the security of Formosa [Taiwan], the Peacaores [other Nationalist offshore islands]" and other "closely related localities" which were not identified.[76] By the end of February, the House had passed the Joint Resolution on the Defense of Formosa by 408–3 and the Senate by 85–3. Eisenhower informed China that the U.S. would help the Nationalist government defend the remaining islands.

The result was an end to the Chinese military preparations to overrun the Quemoy and Matsu islands and the announcement by China at the April 1955 Bandung Conference in Indonesia of its "Five Principles of Peaceful Coexistence" and its proposal that China and the U.S. negotiate directly to reduce tensions across the Taiwan straits.[77] The Eisenhower administration agreed to conversations with China, though making clear that this did not imply diplomatic recognition. These discussions were held in Europe over a period of months, while Communist China built up its military forces and air bases opposite Taiwan and the Nationalist regime fortified the offshore islands.

The U.S. requested that China renounce the use of force. This was refused at that time and since. In August 1955, Secretary of State John Foster Dulles said that if mainland China "wants to use force . . . that will almost surely start up a war, the limits of which could not be defined in advance."[78] This warning came from the administration, which proclaimed the doctrine of "Massive Retaliation" for aggression—that it would respond at a "time and place of its choosing" rather than again fighting a limited war such as that in Korea.

This was the context of another important Chinese-Soviet difference—Mao wanted Soviet military supplies and support for his plans to attack the Nationalist-held islands of Quemoy and Matsu, which were close to the Chinese mainland, and ultimately for an attack on Taiwan itself. But instead, the Soviet Union cautioned Mao against taking this risk in light of the nuclear military power of the United States and its mutual defense agreement with Taiwan. For the time, Mao ended further military attacks.

There was also an important Soviet-Chinese difference about economic policy. The Soviet regime tended to side with the Chinese Communist pragmatists, and Mao knew that. He therefore viewed the Soviet connection as not only providing little help in meeting his international goals, but also as potentially dangerous to his control over the Party. In 1957, Mao helped a Soviet Communist faction, later called the "anti-Party group," which tried to unseat Khrushchev. Mao knew firsthand how Communists could conspire against the leadership in both countries.[79] Further, Mao was undoubtedly concerned that Khrushchev had found out about the help Mao had given to his Soviet opponents.

The matter of nuclear weapons also constituted another important difference. Mao had repeatedly requested Soviet aid for China's program to develop its own nuclear weapons. Khrushchev told Mao that China did not need these since the Soviet Union's nuclear forces would protect China from attack. In 1957, an agreement was reached whereby the Soviet Union agreed to give China a nuclear reactor and considerable nuclear expertise. Despite repeated Chinese requests, the Soviet Union did not give China an operational atomic bomb so that China could copy it and thereby develop its own nuclear weapons more quickly. Mao viewed this as a sign of Soviet mistrust and a lack of equality in the relationship.

THE GREAT LEAP FORWARD AND COMMUNISM

These differences led Mao to conclude that China must become more independent of the Soviet Union. This provided Mao with another reason to initiate the Great Leap Forward, a program of crash industrial development intended by Mao to harness China's indigenous human and material resources, and increase its industrial and military capacity quickly, without dependence on the Soviet Union.[80] As announced by the National People's Congress in 1958, the Great Leap Forward called for a three-year program to increase steel and other industrial production by 18 percent. It was a mass campaign, involving everyone in the country: officials, peasants, professors, students, and workers. Estimates are that one million peasants were pulled out of agricultural work to take part in setting up "backyard furnaces" for steel production. By the fall of 1958, there were some six hundred thousand of these furnaces throughout China. They consumed nearly every available piece of metal, including cooking utensils, beds, furniture, iron springs, railings from city streets, as well as enormous quantities of wood including doors, furniture, and mountains of trees.[81]

In August 1958, Mao also decided, and the Party Central Committee officially decreed, that "People's communes" would be created throughout rural China. Mao viewed this as moving ahead of the Soviet Union in "socialist transformation," and he believed China would become the most advanced model for world

Communism.[82] By November 1958, about 98 percent of the rural population had been organized into about twenty-six thousand communes. The average rural commune included five thousand households, or twenty-five thousand people. It took possession of all properties, such as land, houses, livestock, and controlled all administrative and productive activities.[83] Some urban communes were also established in 1958. In these, factory employees lived collectively at the work site.

At the end of July 1958, Khrushchev arrived in China on a visit that the Chinese had asked be kept secret. The first meeting between Mao and Khrushchev lasted for many hours, focused on military issues, and included only one advisor each—Boris Ponomarov on the Soviet side and Deng Xiaoping for China (in addition to translators and note takers).[84] Mao and Khrushchev had a long discussion on "the number of missiles it would take to wipe out this or that country," with Khrushchev saying to Mao, "Right now, with our intercontinental missiles, we have the Americans by the throat."[85]

There was extensive discussion of the idea of building a modern naval fleet. Khrushchev suggested that this could be a joint Soviet-Chinese fleet and that China could make its ports available to the Soviet navy as needed. Mao was opposed to opening Chinese ports to the Soviet navy except during wartime and also opposed the idea of a joint fleet. Later, speaking to a Chinese Communist Party meeting in 1962, Mao told his comrades that "in 1958 Khrushchev wanted to set up a Soviet-Chinese combined fleet in order to seal us off [from attacking the offshore islands held by Taiwan]."[86] Khrushchev also proposed that the USSR establish electronic interception stations on Chinese territory; this was also refused by Mao, who did not want any extraterritorial presence.[87]

Concerning his denunciation of Stalin, Mao told Khrushchev, "The criticism of Stalin's mistakes is correct. We only disagree with the lack of a precise limit to the criticism. We consider that out of Stalin's ten fingers, only three were bad." Khrushchev responded, "I think there were more." Mao replied, "That is not right. The basis of his life was merit."[88]

Clearly, this had not been a successful meeting. Immediately thereafter, Mao decided to show the Soviet Union that China could use its military forces irrespective of whether Moscow provided support. Toward the end of August 1958, China suddenly began a massive artillery attack on Quemoy, with some forty-two thousand artillery rounds landing on the island within the first two hours and jet aircraft strafing the island while Chinese torpedo boats attacked Nationalist ships.[89] Some days later, on August 29, 1958, Radio Beijing announced that an amphibious landing on Quemoy was coming. As described by Mosher:

The 100,000 man Nationalist army on the island was on alert as [Chinese] torpedo boats swarmed about the islands and PLA gunners began concentrating their fire on Quemoy's landing beach and airstrip. The blockade was complete. It was only a matter of time before the garrison force, deprived of reinforcements from Taiwan, would be starved out.[90]

Eisenhower understood that the real Chinese Communist purpose was the conquest of Taiwan and said that this would end "all the Free World positions in the western Pacific."[91] The United States immediately supplied Taiwan with a variety of weapons, including advanced jet aircraft, ground-to-air missiles, and antiaircraft guns. U.S. and Republic of China marines conducted large-scale amphibious landing exercises on Taiwan, and the U.S. Seventh Fleet escorted Nationalist ships that resupplied Quemoy, remaining in international waters but having been given the order to fire upon Communist military forces if they were attacked.

China then proposed a resumption of negotiations with the U.S., which were again held in Warsaw (after a one-year interruption). This represented the classic approach of "fighting and talking," by which the Chinese Communists sought to gain through negotiations what they could not obtain on the battlefield. By the end of November 1958, more than 575,000 rounds of artillery had fallen on Quemoy, causing about three thousand civilian and one thousand military casualties, as well as the destruction of thousands of homes.[92] The Nationalist forces shot down thirty-one Chinese jet fighters, sank sixteen torpedo boats and gunboats, and also destroyed a large number of PLA artillery batteries on the mainland. Sporadic artillery attacks would continue for years afterward, but Communist China did not again attempt to seize the offshore islands from the Nationalists. If Mao launched these attacks in order to show Khrushchev and the Soviet leadership that China could conquer Taiwan without Soviet help and support, he failed. At the same time, Mao's Great Leap Forward and shift to agricultural communes was also failing tragically within China.

The Tragic Human Consequences of Mao's Radical Policies

While the Chinese Communist Party hailed the communes as "the morning sun over the broad horizon of East Asia,"[93] the results for the Chinese people were catastrophic. Party cadres systematically misreported and exaggerated agricultural production by the new communes, causing an enormous famine in the years 1959 through 1961. Since 1988, the Chinese government has officially admitted that there were twenty million deaths, but independent analyses suggest that there were thirty to forty-two million victims.[94] During these years of famine, China continued exporting grain, principally to the USSR, with grain exports rising from 2.7 million tons in 1958 to 4.2 million tons in 1959. The Chinese government hid the famine and refused food aid from the United States.[95]

An eyewitness account captures the tragedy and suffering in the countryside:

> I began to realize that there was nothing at all "natural" about the period known as the "three years of natural disaster," for it was actually caused by misguided policies. The peasants recalled how, during the Communist Wind from 1959 to 1960, rice was left to rot in the fields because the peasants were too weak from hunger to harvest it. Many starved to death watching the ripe rice grains blow in the fields, as not a single person was able to go out to harvest in some fields. . . . I heard stories of how villagers had exchanged babies as food. I felt like I could practically see, hovering up from the weeds in the cracks of those mud walls, the pained expressions of parents chewing the flesh of children they had exchanged with their own babies.[96]

In August 1959, the Chinese Communist Party Central Committee met in Lushan. The economic pragmatists within the Party wanted to change the failing Great Leap and the commune system. There was also discontent within the military, which wanted a closer relationship with the Soviet Union in order to obtain more Soviet help in updating the armed forces, especially in the development of China's own nuclear weapons. The military leaders were also concerned by Mao's intention to use the rural communes to build an armed militia directly responsible to him at the Party center, which could be a counterweight to the People's Liberation Army (PLA). By January 1959, this rural militia already included about 220 million persons, or about a third of China's population.[97]

Just before the August 1959 Party conference, Khrushchev cancelled the 1957 agreement that provided nuclear technology assistance. This was most likely done to increase the pressure from the military on Mao and his Party allies. Marshal Peng Dehuai, minister of defense and prominent military leader, had recently visited Nikita Khrushchev, who had urged Peng to oppose Mao's domestic and international positions. Speaking at the August 1959 meeting of the Central Committee, in his usual blunt style, Marshal Peng attacked the Great Leap Forward as "fanaticism . . . a rush of blood to the brain . . . a high fever of unrealism" and also questioned Mao's views of "People's War."[98] Mao had prepared for this moment and, despite the emerging coalition of military leaders and the economic pragmatists against him led by Liu Shaoqi and Deng Xiaoping, Mao was able to organize a majority of the Central Committee against Marshal Peng and bring about his removal as minister of defense, followed by his imprisonment, torture, and death. Mao's ally General Lin Biao was appointed the new minister of defense in September 1959.

Mao did admit to the Central Committee that "mistakes had been made" and apologized, but also pointed out that in view of the Party's new "collective leadership," the responsibility was also collective. Following that Party meeting, Mao continued the commune system and, through General Lin Biao, increased his role in the military in order to assure that it would support him, even as he moved China away from the Soviet Union.

After Mao won the first round in this questioning of his authority, he was ready for another meeting with Khrushchev to discuss the range of issues dividing Moscow and Beijing. This meeting took place in Beijing on October 2, 1959, with Khrushchev accompanied this time by his foreign minister and several advisors, and Mao "flanked by the entire Chinese leadership."[99] Topics discussed included Taiwan, China's growing conflict with India (Moscow supported the Indian side), relations with the U.S., and American prisoners from the Korean War.

Earlier in 1959, China had sent large numbers of additional troops to Tibet to repress an armed rebellion by Tibetans. With its military control over Tibet assured, China began to make a series of territorial demands on India. Khrushchev "mocked the Chinese version of the conflict with India" and said to Mao, "In our view, five kilometers here or there are not important. I take Lenin as an example. He gave up Kars, Ardahan, and Ararat to Turkey. . . . I think he did the right thing." Khrushchev next criticized China for permitting the Dalai Lama to escape from Tibet, saying, "It would have been better if he had been put in his coffin . . . events in Tibet are your fault." [100]

Mao became extremely angry at these criticisms, and after accusing Khrushchev of "kowtowing to the Americans," Mao said, "You have stuck two labels on us: the conflict with India is our fault, and the Dalai Lama's departure is our mistake. We, however, have stuck one label on you: time servers. Accept it!"

Khrushchev replied in anger, "We don't accept it! We hold a principled Communist position."

At the end of the meeting, the atmosphere was, in Volkogonov's words, "incandescent," and Khrushchev said "You want to subject us to yourselves, but you won't succeed." At that point, Chinese Marshal of the Army Chen Yi reportedly screamed, "I am indignant at your statement that the worsening of relations is our fault," to which Khrushchev replied, "And I am indignant at your statement that we are time servers." The meeting ended with this exchange:

> Khrushchev: I only mentioned some of your blunders. I didn't make fundamental political accusations, whereas you have leveled a precisely fundamental political accusation against us. If you think we're time servers, Comrade Chen Yi, then don't offer me your hand, because I won't shake it.
>
> Chen Yi: Me too. I am telling you your anger doesn't scare me.
>
> Khrushchev: Don't you try spitting on us from your elevation as a marshal. You haven't got the spit. You won't spit on us. It's all very well on one hand, you utter the formula [the socialist camp headed by the Soviet Union] but then you won't let me say a word.[101]

That meeting marked the end of any real Sino-Soviet alliance. On the flight returning to Moscow, Khrushchev reportedly said, "It's hard to make an agreement with an old boot. He can't forgive us for Stalin." This got back to Mao, with "old boot" being translated in Chinese with words that meant "old prostitute," further enraging Mao. Khrushchev later described Mao as "bursting with an impatient desire to rule the world."[102]

Soon after this dramatic meeting, in 1960, the Soviet Union terminated all its assistance to China and withdrew all of its hundreds of thousands of personnel who had been helping build the Chinese military, industry, and agriculture. The next summit between the leaders of the Soviet Union and Communist China would occur forty years later, in 1989, and open the way for a gradual process of reestablishing normal relations. In those four decades, the two major Communist powers cooperated against the U.S. in Vietnam for some years, approached the brink of nuclear war with each other, and each sought relations with the U.S. to counterbalance the other. In the beginning of the twenty-first century, the question for the Russian leadership to consider, and which we will discuss later, is whether nuclear-armed Communist China, with an ever-more developed and advanced economy and modern strategic nuclear forces, is still "bursting with an impatient desire to rule the world," including Russia!

An Attempted Shift toward Economic Pragmatism

Although Liu Shaoqi and Deng Xiaoping attempted to work with the regional Party and government organizations to moderate the disastrous economic and human effects of the commune system, the tragedy and suffering continued from 1959 through 1961. After seeing the mass starvation and economic dislocation for himself, Liu Shaoqi said in 1961, "The problems were not caused by natural calamities, they were man-made." This was understood as stating they were caused by Mao's decisions.[103] After more than 20 million persons had starved to death, in January 1962 the Party Central Committee adopted Liu's proposal for a more pragmatic economic approach to be called "The Three Privates and One Guarantee," in contrast to Mao's "Three Red Banners."[104] This included giving farmers permission to cultivate their own private plots and sell their products at free markets in the countryside, provided they met the "one guarantee" of fulfilling their agricultural production quotas for the state.

In foreign policy, the Central Committee adopted the policy of "Three Reconciliations and One Reduction." This meant China needed to moderate its conflicts with "imperialists, reactionaries, and revisionists," and reduce its support for "national liberation movements" seeking to take power in other countries.[105] Mao was deeply concerned by these Central Committee decisions and "was alarmed by the prospects of the return of capitalism, the rise of a new Mandarin class, and a compromise with Soviet revisionism. If these trends persisted, his life-long work of politicizing the masses would disappear . . . and the country would once again fall into reliance upon the Soviet Union."[106]

To counter this possibility, Mao established the "Socialist Education Movement" in September 1962 to send officials and intellectuals to work in rural areas and factories in order to "learn from the masses." This was not popular within the Party, and Mao found many in the Party apparatus throughout the country resistant to this approach. Therefore, in February 1964, Mao launched the "Learn from the PLA" campaign, which was an effort to use the military and its national, regional, and provincial organizations against the provincial Party organizations.[107]

China Attacks India, 1962

China had cultivated relations with India in the 1950s as part of its overtures to lead the nonaligned movement and maintain good relations with developing countries. In 1955, China proclaimed the "Five Principles of Peaceful Coexistence" as the basis of its foreign policy. One of these principles was that force would never be used to solve disputes of any kind, including territorial disputes. China claimed territory long part of India and opened negotiations to press demands for the "return" of this territory. Beginning in 1958, while those talks proceeded, China built a military road through western Tibet into the area claimed by both sides. The issue became important, as Indian nationalists urged Prime Minister Nehru to be more firm. On October 20, 1962, China attacked India simultaneously on its eastern and western border areas. India lost nearly 3,100 soldiers (1,383 killed, 1,696 missing), and another 4,000 were taken prisoner. No Chinese soldiers were captured. The result was that China seized thousands of square miles of Indian territory.[108]

One strategic purpose of the attack, according to Timperlake and Triplett, may have been to humiliate India and prevent it from having any significant role in Asian or world affairs. The demonstration of India's weakness vis-à-vis China would make it evident which was the major power in Asia. From the point of view of internal Chinese politics, the attack may have been intended to further strengthen Mao's influence with the military; in effect, to repudiate the more conciliatory foreign policy approach the Party Central Committee had decided upon earlier that year. It also weakened the economic pragmatists by putting a major obstacle in the way of improved relations with the Soviet Union, since Khrushchev had told Mao that he disagreed with the Chinese claims and supported India. The 1962 surprise attack on India demonstrated that even with the economic pragmatists in the ascendant, China could be dangerous internationally. This was demonstrated even more clearly in 1979 when the chief economic modernizer, Deng Xiaoping, ordered the Chinese surprise attack on Vietnam.

China's Atomic Bomb and the Threat of Soviet Attacks

During the early 1960s, the policies of the more pragmatic Communists in both China and the Soviet Union disturbed Mao. He did not approve of the Soviet Union having backed down in the 1962 Cuban Missile Crisis, he was opposed to its having signed the nuclear test ban treaty in 1963 without having consulted China, and he criticized the Soviet Union for not supporting China during the war with India.[109]

Mao had first learned about the highly secret U.S. project to develop the atomic bomb (a "super bomb") in 1944 through his intelligence service. In the early 1950s, China persuaded about two hundred Chinese scientists in Western universities to return and help develop its own atomic bomb.[110] Large-scale uranium mining began jointly with Soviet aid in 1950–51, and in the winter of 1951, China built a concealed, closed facility (as its Los Alamos). The Party's Central Military Commission made development of the atom bomb the highest priority in 1958.[111]

In 1964, as China moved closer to obtaining its own nuclear device, the fore-runner to its atomic bomb, there were reports that Khrushchev was considering a preemptive attack on China's nuclear facilities to prevent China from producing its own atomic bomb. Elements of the Soviet Communist Party who disagreed with Khrushchev reportedly warned China, leading Mao to threaten an invasion of Outer Mongolia if attacked. According to historian Immanuel Hsu, the major reason for Khrushchev's removal on October 15, 1964, by a group of Soviet Communist leaders led by Leonid Brezhnev, was to prevent Khrushchev from taking military action to prevent China from testing its nuclear device. The next day, China detonated its first nuclear device, announcing that this dealt a heavy blow to "U.S. imperialism" and "Soviet revisionism," and should encourage "the revolutionary peoples of the world."[112]

3 The Cultural Revolution, 1965–1976

"The Party [must be] shattered in order to be subsequently reconstructed."

—MAO, 1965

"Hanging from their necks were pails filled with rocks. I saw the principal; the pail around his neck was so heavy that the wire had cut deep into his neck and he was staggering. All were barefoot, hitting broken gongs or pots as they walked across the field, crying out, 'I am black gangster so-and-so.' Finally they all knelt down, burned incense, and begged Mao Zedong to 'pardon their crimes.'"

—KEN LING, MIRIAM LONDON, and LEE TA-LING,
Red Guard: From Schoolboy to 'Little General' in Mao's China, 1972

"Red Guards all over China took to the streets, giving full vent to their vandalism, ignorance, and fanaticism. They raided peoples' houses, smashed their antiques, tore up paintings and works of calligraphy. Bonfires were lit to consume books. Very soon, all treasures and private collections were destroyed.

"Many writers and artists committed suicide after being cruelly beaten and humiliated, and forced to witness their work being burned to ashes. . . . Mao hailed the Red Guards' actions as 'very good indeed' and ordered the nation to support them.

"In the city center some theaters and movie cinemas were turned into torture chambers. Victims were dragged in from all over Peking. Pedestrians avoided the spots because the streets around echoed with the screams of victims."

—JUNG CHANG

The policy changes made by the economic pragmatists, led by Liu, now president of China and among the most senior Party officials, began to have visibly positive results after 1962. This was the time when Deng Xiaoping said, "It doesn't matter whether the cat is white or black, as long as it catches mice," his way of countering the emphasis of Mao and his Party faction on how "red" people were rather than on their practical capacities and expertise in different domains of policy and work.

As described by one Chinese citizen, the years right after 1962 were a time when

A stop was put to crazy economic goals, and realistic policies were introduced. Public canteens [cafeterias] were abolished and peasants' income was now related to their work. They were given back household property which had been confiscated by the communes, including farm implements and domestic animals. They were also allowed to till small plots of land privately. . . . In industry and commerce, elements of a market economy were officially sanctioned, and within a couple of years the economy flourished again.[1]

Many of those persecuted were rehabilitated, including "landlords [who] had the label of class enemy removed . . . 'counterrevolutionaries' from 1955, 'rightists' from 1957, and 'rightist opportunists' from 1959 . . . there was greater literary and artistic freedom, and a more relaxed general atmosphere prevailed."[2]

It was within this context that a series of literary articles and new plays appeared that used characters from Chinese history and tradition as an allegorical means of criticizing Mao and his past decisions. The intellectuals writing these works were mostly located in Beijing where the mayor, the eighth-ranking individual in the Party, was closely allied with President Liu. Mao's third wife, Jiang Qing, a former actress, had long been interested in theater, film, the performing arts, and literature, and followed these events closely. She perceived these articles as part of a gathering attack on Mao and told him there needed to be a "cultural revolution" to remove the intellectuals and Party leaders who were responsible.

In 1964, Mao wrote an article that included a list of thirty-nine writers and artists who were to be barred from working in their fields as a result of their criticisms and circulated it to Party officials throughout the country. He demanded that the Party find, expose, and punish similar "reactionary bourgeois authorities"—a new category of enemy.[3] But the regional Party leaders did not respond and "Mao interpreted [this] . . . as an indication that their loyalty to him was weakening and that their hearts were with the policies being pursued by President Liu and Deng. . . . His suspicion was confirmed when "none of the major Communist newspapers would publish the article he had written because they believed he intended "to involve the population in the witchhunt."[4] These were clear signs to Mao that his hold on the Communist Party organization was slipping away. "He saw himself as a Stalin figure about to be denounced . . . while he was still alive."[5]

The economic pragmatists continued to favor closer links with the Soviet Union and reached an agreement whereby the Soviet Union could ship large amounts of its military aid to North Vietnam through China.[6] At the same time, China covertly committed troops and manpower to North Vietnam for the battle against "U.S. imperialism." China sent an estimated total of three hundred thousand military forces, mainly in antiaircraft, engineering, and construction battalions. Then in early 1965, President Liu proposed reviving the Chinese-Soviet alliance so that both powers could provide more military assistance to North Vietnam in its intensifying battle against South Vietnam and the United States.

For Mao, this proposed revival of the alliance with the USSR further raised the risk that the economic pragmatists, led by Liu, would do to him what Khrushchev had done to Stalin. They would supplant and denounce him. This led Mao to decide in early 1965 that "Liu must be disinherited and the Party shattered in order to be subsequently reconstructed."[7]

The source of power that made it possible for Mao to take on the Party organization was the Chinese military, headed by Minister of Defense General Lin Biao. In 1965, Mao was seventy-two years old, suffering from Parkinson's disease, and there were rumors that he had had a stroke the previous year. Having decided to remove the mantle of succession from Liu, it is quite likely that Mao won support from General Lin Biao by promising that he would be the successor once Mao had regained full control over the Party. In the next years of turmoil, General Lin Biao acted as though he expected to succeed Mao.

The opening round in the Cultural Revolution was the November 1965 publication in the military newspaper *Liberation Army Daily* of an article Professor Thornton has called "a declaration of war against the literary world."[8] This article denounced all the intellectuals who had been taking the "capitalist road," a term of political opprobrium used by Mao and his allies during the Cultural Revolution.[9] The coalition Mao assembled for his attack on the Communist Party organization, which was controlled primarily by Liu, had three main elements. First, the Central Cultural Revolution Committee, which consisted of Mao's personal secretary and editor of the newspaper *Red Flag*, Ch'en Po-Ta; Mao's wife, Jiang Qing, as first vice chairperson; and his chief of intelligence, Kang Shang.[10] Second, Zhou Enlai as head of the State Council, the organization responsible for the government institutions, cooperated with Mao. Third, the People's Liberation Army, under the leadership of General Lin Biao, provided both organizational resources and ultimately the armed strength to be used against the Party and the population as needed.

The methods used by the Cultural Revolution group were to magnify the long-established cult of Mao's personality and then mobilize and unleash urban students, ages fourteen to twenty-one, from high schools, technical institutes, and universities. These students were urged to attack the ostensible "capitalist roaders" and "black gangs" (persons who were not "red" in their social origins) within the educational institutions, the local Communist Party branches, and in many government organizations. From the start, however, the military institutions were exempt from attack, as was the military-industrial complex, where work continued on the development of nuclear weapons and ballistic missiles, though this was hampered by the political upheaval.[11] Further, the rural areas were also excluded from the process because they were still recovering from famine and China needed the food being produced there.

The Cultural Revolution can be divided into four broad phases. The first, from November 1965 to the spring of 1966, was the period of verbal attack on intellectuals and ideological propaganda to enhance the cult of Mao. A key part of this first phase was the Mao faction's taking political control of Beijing. This was done when President Liu left China for scheduled state visits abroad on March 26, 1966. On the same day his key ally, the mayor of Beijing, disappeared, never to be seen again.[12] With Liu out of the country, Mao's forces descended upon the Peking Communist Party municipal committee and extracted confessions of "treasonable actions" from those loyal to Liu (the same was done in Shanghai and several other major cities). The military moved in to take control of Beijing and when the city was secure, Mao returned in July 1966. He then appointed General Lin Biao as vice chairman of the Party Central Committee, the second-ranking person in the Communist hierarchy, and demoted President Liu to the eighth position.[13]

The second phase, the mobilization and unleashing of the student Red Guards, began on June 6, 1966. A large-character poster was displayed in the leading university in Beijing and read on the radio. It called for a struggle to "break the evil influence of revisionists and do it resolutely, radically, totally, and completely! Destroy these monsters, these Khrushchev-like reformers!"[14] Thereupon millions of Red Guards throughout China unleashed a campaign of radicalism, violence, persecution, humiliation, torture, and executions, as well as the destruction of priceless cultural artifacts. On August 5, 1966, Mao wrote his first wall poster, "Bomb the (Liu-Deng) Headquarters!"[15]

The third phase began in 1967, when Mao ordered the military to begin reining in the Red Guards, even as their violence continued. Then in 1968, Mao ordered the PLA Main Force Units to use all means to halt the rampaging, out-of-control Red Guards, many of whom had armed themselves with stolen weapons. This led to a violent and brutal process of military repression that involved many armed battles in cities throughout China. It ultimately included the forced deportation of nearly 5.4 million former student radicals to the countryside to live lives of grinding poverty and hard work for many, many years.[16] It was during this third phase that President Liu and his wife were pressured into public self-criticism and then removed from all government and Party positions in November 1968. President Liu and his wife were both sent to prison, tortured, and died there. Deng and hundreds of other senior Party officials, among the economic pragmatists, were sent to hard labor in the countryside.[17] Deng's son was crippled for life as he fell from the third story of a building when he tried to escape the Red Guards.

In April 1969, a National Congress of the Chinese Communist Party elected

Mao chairman of both the Party and the Central Committee and declared General Lin Biao as vice chairman.[18] It appeared that Mao's forces had won and that General Lin Biao was indeed the designated successor.

The fourth, less visible and least well-known phase of the Cultural Revolution, was a process of "continuing investigations," persecution, and prosecutions against "capitalist roaders" that persisted virtually until the death of Mao in September 1976.

Examples of Life During the Cultural Revolution

Initially, most of the Red Guards were the children of the Communist "new class," the sons and daughters of Communist Party and government officials. They had lived comparatively comfortably in the cities and were among the privileged few who could attend academic high schools and study at colleges or universities. Ranging in age from fourteen to twenty-one, they had little, if any, memory of the urban or rural mass persecution campaigns and violent repression that had taken place in the early to mid-1950s. In contrast, most of the adult Party members, who were now the targets and victims of the Red Guards, did remember well the mass campaigns and the violence inflicted by the Party on millions of victims, who were ultimately executed, imprisoned, or sent to work in forced labor.

These adults, many of them Party members who had themselves led and instigated these previous campaigns of oppression, also knew that resistance or defiance was usually fatal. In contrast, however, "self-criticism" and "confession" might somewhat alleviate the consequences of having been designated a target for persecution. The righteousness, fanaticism, and potential brutality of adolescence on the one side was hurled against adults—starting with those in the educational institutions and spreading to Party and provincial organizations—who knew just how terrible the consequences could be if they resisted what they perceived to be the new orders and intentions of the Party.

The first targets of the Red Guards were teachers in their institutions. Throughout urban China, scenes such as the following described by an eyewitness were repeated:

> On the athletic field and farther inside, before a new four-story classroom building, I saw rows of teachers, about forty or fifty in all, with black ink poured over their heads and faces so that they were now in reality a "black gang." Hanging on their necks were placards with signs such as "reactionary academic authority" so and so, "corrupt ringleader" so and so, "class enemy" so and so, "capitalist roader" so and so; all epithets taken from newspapers.
>
> On each placard was a red cross, making the teachers look like condemned prisoners awaiting execution. They all wore dunce caps painted with similar epithets and carried dirty brooms, shoes, and dusters on their backs.

Hanging from their necks were pails filled with rocks. I saw the principal; the pail around his neck was so heavy that the wire had cut deep into his neck and he was staggering. All were barefoot, hitting broken gongs or pots as they walked across the field, crying out, "I am black gangster so-and-so." Finally they all knelt down, burned incense, and begged Mao Zedong to "pardon their crimes."

I was stunned by this scene and I felt myself go pale. A few girls nearly fainted.

Beatings and torture followed. I had never seen such tortures before. Eating nightsoil [human feces] and insects, being subjected to electric shocks, being forced to kneel on broken glass, being hanged "like an airplane," by the arms and legs.

Those who immediately took up the sticks and applied the tortures were the school bullies, who as children of Party cadres and army officers belonged to the five red categories, a group that also included children of workers, poor and lower-middle peasants, and revolutionary martyrs. . . . Coarse and cruel, they were accustomed to throwing around their parents' status and brawling with the other students. They did so poorly in school that they were about to be expelled and presumably resented the teachers because of this.

Greatly emboldened by the instigators, the other students also cried, "Beat them!" and jumped on the other teachers, swinging their fists, kicking. The stragglers were forced to back them up with loud shots and clenched fists.

There was nothing strange in this. Young students were ordinarily peaceful and well-behaved, but once the first step was taken, all were bound to follow. . . .

The heaviest blow to me that day was the killing of my most respected and beloved teacher, Chen Ku-Te.[19]

The Red Guards decided that all "waste of revolutionary energy" should be eliminated, and this meant that people should destroy grass, flowers, their pet cats, and birds. In mid-August 1966, at a mass rally in Tiananmen Square, General Lin Biao, standing next to Mao, called on the Red Guards to smash the "Four Old-Fashioned Things": old ideas, old culture, old customs, and old habits. Jung Chang, an eyewitness, describes what happened next:

Red Guards all over China took to the streets, giving full vent to their vandalism, ignorance, and fanaticism. They raided peoples' houses, smashed their antiques, tore up paintings and works of calligraphy. Bonfires were lit to consume books. Very soon all treasures and private collections were destroyed.

Many writers and artists committed suicide after being cruelly beaten and humiliated, and forced to witness their work being burned to ashes. Museums were raided. Palaces, temples, ancient tombs, statues, pagodas, city walls— anything "old" was pillaged. The few things that survived, such as the Forbidden City, did so only because Premier Zhou Enlai sent the army to protect them, and issued specific orders that they should be protected. . . .

Mao hailed the Red Guards' actions as "very good indeed" and ordered the nation to support them. He ordered the Red Guards to pick on a wider range of victims in order to increase the terror. Prominent writers, artists, scholars, and most other top professionals who had been privileged under the Communist regime were now categorically condemned as "reactionary bourgeois authorities." With the help of some of these peoples' colleagues, the Red Guards began to abuse them.

Then there were the old "class enemies," former landlords and capitalists, people with Kuomintang connections, those condemned in previous political campaigns, like the "rightists" and their children. . . .

A wave of beating and torture swept the country, mainly during house raids.

Almost invariably the families would be ordered to kneel on the floor and kowtow to the Red Guards; they were then beaten with the brass buckles of the guards' leather belts. They were kicked around, and one side of the head was shaved, a humiliating style called the "Yin and Yang head" because it resembled the classic Chinese symbol of dark side (yin) and light side (yang). Most of their possessions were either smashed or taken away.

It was worse in Peking, where the Cultural Revolution authority was on hand to incite the young people. In the city center some theaters and movie cinemas were turned into torture chambers. Victims were dragged in from all over Peking. Pedestrians avoided the spots because the streets around echoed with the screams of victims.[20]

In mid-September 1966, Mao and General Lin Biao presided over another mass rally of the Red Guards in Tiananmen Square. Mao said, "Be violent," and Lin Biao said, "Red Guard fighters: the direction of your battles has always been correct . . . you have done the right thing, and you have done marvelously!"[21]

The Red Guards established their own network of prisons "in every school, government office, and factory . . . in these 'study centers' people were confined, interrogated, and tortured incessantly. One radical militia in Huangzhou . . . had on average 1,000 people in its three 'investigation centers' at any given time."[22] The Cultural Revolution also led to the reimprisonment of many who had previously been released from prison and forced labor, as well as the "systematic arrest of foreigners or Chinese people who had lived abroad."[23]

In parallel with the mass violence conducted by the Red Guards, the Cultural Revolution committee systematically targeted President Liu and his supporters within the Party. Many of the highest-ranking people within the Party had been involved in the long civil war against the Nationalists.

The expanding violence also led to factionalism among Red Guard groups, with some calling themselves the "rebel Red Guards." In late 1967 and early 1968, various Red Guard formations, each claiming to be the authentic followers of Mao, fought armed battles against each other in a number of cities. In 1968, the ever-mounting chaos, economic decline, and the growing military threat from the Soviet Union resulted in Mao ordering the armed forces to act more harshly in ending the activities of the Red Guards and to disband them.

We learn from Margolin that:

Without any doubt, [1968] was the year of the greatest massacres, as worker parties and soldiers took back various campuses and cities [from the Red Guards]. . . . Wuzhou, in Guangxi, was destroyed by heavy artillery and napalm. Guilin was taken on 19th August by 30,000 soldiers and armed peasants after a real military campaign in which political and military teams managed to fan the country dwellers' indifference toward the Cultural Revolution into active hostility. For six days rebels [Red Guards] were executed en masse . . . it was then that the future [post-Mao] chairman of the Communist Party, Hua Guofeng, who was in charge of security for his province, gained the title "the Butcher of Hunan."

The southern part of the country suffered the most: there were perhaps 100,000 deaths in Guangxi, 40,000 in Guangdong, and 30,000 in Yunnan. The Red Guards were extremely cruel, but the worst atrocities were carried out by their executioners, the soldiers and militias carrying out the Party's orders. After the military disbanded the Red Guards, about 5.4 million young people were sentenced to hard labor in the countryside with the expectation that they would remain there for many years. Most stayed for about a decade.[24]

VICTIMS OF THE CULTURAL REVOLUTION

Before Mao died in September 1976, it is estimated that between 12 million and 20 million people, including 5.4 million former Red Guards, had been sent to work at hard labor in the countryside—including one million from Shanghai, about 18 percent of that city's population.[25] Estimates for the numbers of victims killed in this tragic period of China's history vary. A French scholar estimates from one to three million persons.[26] R. J. Rummel, who has done the most thorough analysis of this issue, estimates for the years 1964 through 1975 a total of 7.7 million people were killed by the regime, with another 1.5 million dying in related famine and civil conflict, for a total of 9.2 million.[27] It is estimated that about two million additional persons were confined in forced-labor camps during these years.[28] It is known that about three million members of the Communist Party were punished and imprisoned, and that about 60 percent of the Communist Party members were removed, many of them also being punished with hard labor during this time.[29] In the 1980s, the general secretary of the Chinese Communist Party, Hu Yaobang, publicly stated that one hundred million Chinese had suffered grievously as a result of the Cultural Revolution.[30]

The minister of security, responsible for the secret police, was removed so that Mao's longtime intelligence chief and member of the Cultural Revolutionary Council, Kang Sheng, could take over. A subsequent purge in that organization involved the interrogation and imprisonment of twenty-two thousand employees, many of whom were tortured; there were also more than twelve hundred executions.[31] Among the group that was the initial target of the Red Guards, the intellectuals, it is estimated that 142,000 teachers, 53,000 scientists and technicians, 500 teachers of medicine, and 2,600 artists and writers were persecuted, "and many of them were killed or committed suicide. In Shanghai, where intellectuals were especially numerous, the Chinese government officially estimated in 1978 that 10,000 people had died violent deaths as a result of the Cultural Revolution."[32]

IMPLICATIONS OF THE CULTURAL REVOLUTION FOR CHINA'S FUTURE

Was the Cultural Revolution a nightmare for the people and Communist rulers of China with no relevance for the future of that country? Some might define the Cultural Revolution as an event connected with Mao and his power over one faction of the Communist Party, the military, and urban privileged youth of the time. That was an important part of what happened, but the essence of the Cultural Revolution is that it was a technique used by one group in the Communist Party to remove and punish those whom it opposed. The faction that was removed from power, led at the time by the president of China, Liu Shao-chi, and General Secretary Deng Xiaopeng, was the very group that had helped to rescue China from the nightmare of mass starvation caused by Mao's Great Leap Forward and the communes. There had been four years of relative calm and forward economic movement under the pragmatic policies pursued by Liu and his group within the Party. Those policies had worked well; China was making economic progress and had also succeeded in detonating its first nuclear device.

Nevertheless, Mao and those whom he brought into his coalition were concerned about much more than economic performance. They were concerned with their personal power and used methods of persecution intended to exclude and punish "capitalist roaders" who might ultimately replace them and undo or weaken the essence of the Communist revolution as they saw it. Because of their alliance with military leaders, and their tactical and symbolic moves, the Mao coalition was in fact able to defeat the dominant group of economic pragmatists within the Party center and to do so rather quickly.

There were seven features of the first Mao years. First, the Chinese Communist Party succeeded in establishing a totalitarian regime. Its rule met the characteristics of the classic definition of totalitarianism, including a comprehensive ideology, a single ruling party led by a dictator, secret police or other methods for carrying out political terror, a monopoly of mass communications, a monopoly on political organizations, and dominant control of the economy.[33]

Second, the Communist regime caused immense human suffering to the people of China. During the period of consolidating power from 1949 to 1956, it is estimated that the regime killed from 30 to 60 million persons.[34] This number includes the estimated 20 million people who died among the 50 million who were sentenced as "counterrevolutionaries" to many years of forced labor in prison camps, the Chinese *laogai*.[35] To these victims must be added the 20 to 30 million persons estimated to have starved to death as the result of the decision by Mao to establish agricultural communes and to continue them despite evidence of enormous suffering.[36] Further, according to the general secretary of the Chinese Communist Party in the 1980s, Hu Yaobang, the years of political terror known as the Cultural Revolution swept up and caused enormous suffering to more than 100 million people, including three million members of the Chinese Communist Party.[37] By one carefully researched estimate nearly eight million persons were killed during the Cultural Revolution.[38] Taken together, these estimates indicate that during the Mao years, 1949–1976, the total victims include from 50 to more than 100 million persons killed, and more than 134 million persons were subjected to severe deprivation of human rights and punishment, whether through long confinement in forced-labor camps or by being sent away from their homes and forced to live for years in remote areas in poverty performing hard manual and agricultural labor.

A third characteristic is that factional conflicts within the Communist ruling elite often resulted in sudden, wrenching changes in regime policy, often leading to immense human suffering (e.g., mass starvation resulting from Mao's shift to rural communes). Professor Andrew Nathan described this as "the constant bumbling, desperate insecurity, vicious infighting, and hysterical improvisation that the Chinese Communists disguise behind the bluster of their theory of scientific socialism."[39]

Fourth, on repeated occasions, the military institution and military leaders played a major role in determining the outcome of policy and factional disputes within the Communist Party, and therefore in deciding national policy. Though arguably the military is now more professional, and senior military officers consti-tute a smaller proportion of Politburo members than in past decades, the highly influential role of the Chinese military leadership has continued from the Mao era to the present.

Fifth, the relationship of Communist China with the Soviet Union involved a complex intertwining of Communist Party factional politics in both countries, with groups in both regimes trying to use the relationship for their own purposes. Mao began with a positive view of the Soviet Union as a key ally, but within several years he shifted to seeing the Soviet Union and its allies within the Chinese Communist Party as a threat to his hold on power and the Soviet Union as a potentially grave interna-tional danger to China. In many respects, Mao launched the Cultural Revolution to weaken what he perceived to be the pro-Soviet elements of the Chinese Communist Party. This pattern has important echoes in the newly close relationship between post-Soviet Russia and China which developed in the 1990s. Each seeks certain bene-fits from the other but with the recollection of past suspicions.

Sixth, Communist China initiated major military attacks suddenly and with large forces. This included the military occupation of Tibet in 1950; the interven-tion in the Korean War (1950–53), with nearly one million Chinese troops; the attack on India in 1962; the preemptive invasion of Communist Vietnam in 1979; and a number of smaller military occupations of disputed territories in the 1990s into the present.

Seventh, during the Mao years China was consistently able to deceive and mislead a significant proportion of international observers, both in Western democracies and among developing countries, about the realities of life in China and its internal and international policies. This deception is reflected in China's proclamation since 1955 of the "Five Principles of Peaceful Coexistence" as the basis for its international policies, even while attacking India and providing weapons training and support for insurgencies seeking to overthrow the governments in a number of neighboring countries. The deception was also reflected in the ability of Mao's China to project an apparent sense of purpose, order, and success that led many in the West—not only those sympathetic to Communism—to view China, even at times of its greatest internal upheavals, as a model society and an example to be emulated. This pattern of successful deception has continued.

There is a lesson pertaining to China's future: As long as China is ruled by the Communist Party, there is always the possibility of severe factional conflict, leading to apparently sudden and major changes in the domestic and international policy of the regime. Such events are hard to predict, even for high-level Party officials, as we saw in the fate of President Liu. Since 1978, the economic pragmatists have been in the leading position and have been able to persuade the more hard-line Communist elements that their approach will guarantee China's future as a more economically, technologically and scientifically advanced nation, and that this will lead to ever greater military strength. In turn, the regime's new wealth and military capabilities would permit the hardliners within the Party and the military to accomplish their international objectives, including the taking of Taiwan. The Cultural Revolution warns that hard-line elements of the Communist Party and the military could in the future work together to remove or subordinate the economic pragmatists, leading to a China that is even more repressive at home and far more aggressive internationally.

4 Soviet War Threats and the Opening of Relations with the U.S.

The purges and repression of the Cultural Revolution systematically removed the economic pragmatists from the leadership of the Party and the government; these were also the individuals most in favor of restoring cooperative relations with the Soviet Union. With their removal, "Soviet leaders were no longer able to affect the decision-making process from within, and hence they shifted their tactics to building pressure on the Chinese leadership from without."[1] The Soviet leadership understood that its global position had been set back by the growing distance and estrangement from Communist China. The Soviet leaders also knew that Mao and his faction strongly opposed rapprochement. As they observed the effects of the Cultural Revolution, they concluded that Mao was risking the continuation of Communist rule in China by destroying the Party and becoming ever more fanatical, while also building nuclear weapons and ballistic missiles.

A series of six articles published in an authoritative Soviet magazine in 1968 explicitly attacked Mao and his policies and called for "practical international aid to the forces in China which remain loyal to Marxism-Leninism and resist Maoism."[2] The Soviet Union matched this proposal for an anti-Mao coup with a military buildup along the more than four thousand miles of their border with China. This occupation reached half a million troops by 1968 and included the deployment of Soviet forces in nominally independent Outer Mongolia as well as the movement of Soviet nuclear-armed missiles within range of key Chinese targets.[3]

At the same time, the Soviet Union criticized the events occurring in Czechoslovakia, where a reform Communist leadership was attempting to establish a more open, humane form of rule. In the spring and summer of 1968, the Soviet Union mobilized its troops to intimidate the Czech leadership, and in August 1968 led an invasion by five hundred thousand Warsaw Pact forces to occupy Czechoslovakia, remove the leadership, and replace it with more orthodox, pro-Soviet Communist rulers. This was followed by the "Brezhnev Doctrine," contending that the Soviet Union had the right to intervene in any Communist country to ensure the preservation of a Marxist-Leninist regime. In the view of Mao and his associates, this had ominous implications for China since the Soviet Union defined Maoism as "antithetical to genuine Marxism-Leninism."[4]

Two years of turmoil caused by the Cultural Revolution had weakened China. Mao probably feared the Soviet Union might decide this was the right time to intervene to help the defeated (but not yet all dead) pro-Soviet economic pragmatists and pro-Soviet Party officers remove him from power. Therefore, in the fall and winter of 1968, Mao declared victory in the Cultural Revolution. After completing its repression of the Red Guards, the Chinese Communist political and military rulers immediately began intensive military preparations to deter a Soviet attack and to wage war against the Soviet Union if necessary.

The core of the dispute between the Soviet Union and China was that the rulers in both countries, accustomed to ruthlessness and the use of coercion, were each determined not to be dominated by the other. Starting in the 1950s, the Soviet Union had been concerned about the risks of nuclear war that might arise following China's acquisition of nuclear weapons. As discussed, Khrushchev had told Mao that China did not need the atomic bomb, since it was protected by the Soviet Union. But Mao persisted, stating that China, as a great power, should have its own atomic weapons. The Soviets judged that China, with its huge population also equipped with nuclear weapons, could become an extremely dangerous threat. They also feared that China could begin a war with the U.S. that would spread to the USSR.

The distrust was further magnified as the two powers negotiated about their border.[5] In 1936, Mao told an American journalist, "It is the immediate task of China to regain all our lost territories," including Outer Mongolia, Central Asia, Siberia, Vietnam—all of which Mao believed should again become part of China.[6] The discussions about China's claims on Soviet territory in the 1950s had been intense but inconclusive. As Mao moved away from cooperation with the Soviet Union, his determination to regain China's "lost territories," which included a significant part of the Russian Far East and some five hundred thousand square miles in Soviet central Asia, became stronger.

On March 8, 1963, the Chinese government published a list of "lost territories," which included considerable parts of the Soviet Union. At that time, China also demanded "the Soviets acknowledge, for the record, that the current Sino-Soviet frontier was a product of 'unequal' and therefore 'illegal' treaties. Moscow denied having territorial problems with any neighboring state and refused to admit the illegality of the old treaties with China."[7]

Negotiations regarding the border in 1964 made no progress, and early in 1969 China alleged that the Soviet Union had violated the Chinese border 4,189 times in the preceding four years.[8] It was at this time that China—after ending the most visible tumult of the Cultural Revolution, initiating nationwide preparations for war, and moving military units to the Russian border—decided on an armed attack against Soviet troops. The place was a large island in the Ussuri River, claimed by both sides. The events of March 1–2, 1969, were described as follows:

> Some 300 camouflaged Chinese soldiers reached Chen-Pao [Demansky] Island and dug foxholes in a wooded area in preparation for an ambush. At approximately 11 A.M. the following morning, the Chinese, seemingly unarmed, marched toward the Russians; when they had reached within twenty feet of the enemy, the first row quickly scattered to the side and the second row opened fire . . . other Chinese soldiers rushed out of hiding and overwhelmed the whole Russian unit, taking 19 prisoners and considerable amounts of Soviet equipment. Russian reinforcements finally arrived and drove the Chinese out. Both sides claimed victory while accusing the other of provocation.[9]

On March 14–15, 1969, the Soviet Union retaliated by attacking Chinese forces using tanks, artillery, and large numbers of soldiers, leading to about sixty Russian and eight hundred Chinese casualties. As described by Hsu, "Both sides made feverish propaganda out of the clashes, held exhibitions to illustrate the others' atrocities, and organized vast demonstrations to stir up national sentiments and war scares.[10] Battles were also fought on other border islands in the Amur River and along other parts of the Soviet-Chinese border. At the same time, China sought closer relations with Romania and Yugoslavia (countries which were also concerned about possible Soviet intervention) as a means of facing Moscow with the risk of a two-front war.

It was at this time that the Soviet Union increased preparations for a preemptive nuclear attack on China's nuclear facilities. Moscow's purpose was to assure that China could not further develop nuclear weapons capabilities, which could add to the threat it already posed to the Soviet Union. It is reported that the Soviet Union sent a high-level emissary to the United States, proposing to the recently inaugurated President Nixon (January 1969) that both countries undertake a joint military attack against China. President Nixon, however, gave "a sharply, angrily negative response."[11] In the meantime, both the Soviet Union and China continued preparing for war. China decentralized its economy in preparation for a possible Soviet attack, and Thornton writes that "educational, economic, and political activities all now were linked to the concept of 'peoples war,' the in-depth military defense of China."[12]

It was in this context that the Ninth Congress of the Communist Party, meeting in April 1969, declared the Cultural Revolution to be over and unanimously redesignated Mao chairman of the Party Central Committee. That meeting enlarged the Central Committee to include a substantial proportion of military officers, and the

Ninth Party Congress also officially designated General Lin Biao as Mao's successor.[13] Because the purges had eliminated so many Party leaders, the military was becoming dominant within the Party and potentially the most powerful group.

Yet, Professor Fairbank informs us:

> Though the Cultural Revolution officially ended in April 1969, many forms of its terrorism continued. During 1970–1971, the military security personnel were particularly ruthless . . . innocent people were tortured into confessing . . . and naming others . . . the Cultural Revolution spread its coercion into the countryside, where for example peasants were required to abandon all sideline occupations, such as raising pigs, chickens, and ducks, in order to "cut off the tail of capitalism." For many peasants this meant starvation.[14]

In September 1969, Soviet Premier Alexei Kosygin, while returning from Ho Chi Minh's funeral in North Vietnam, was ordered to fly to Beijing to meet with Chinese Premier Zhou Enlai. After three hours of negotiation, they reached an understanding that an agreement would be signed between the USSR and China on the nonuse of force, the maintenance of the status quo on borders, the prevention of military conflicts, and the separation of forces in disputed regions. The submission of all border disputes to further negotiations was also discussed.[15] A few days after these talks, an article by Victor Louis, seen as an unofficial but authoritative channel to the west for Soviet views, was published in the *London Evening News* entitled "Will Russian Rockets Czech-mate China?" The article made three points which were clear Soviet threats: first, that the Brezhnev Doctrine could be applied to China; second, that Soviet nuclear missiles were aimed and ready to destroy China's nuclear facilities; and third, that the Soviet Union had evidence from within China that anti-Mao forces existed who "could produce a leader who would ask other Socialist [Communist] countries for fraternal help."[16]

The Chinese regime viewed this article as threatening both Soviet nuclear attack and political-military intervention to replace Mao. This intimidated the Mao regime and led to the opening of new negotiations on the border issues. China said that it was beginning these negotiations out of concern that "a handful of war maniacs in Moscow would dare to raid" China's nuclear facilities and that "there is no reason whatsoever for China and the Soviet Union to fight a war over the boundary question."[17] The negotiations were inconclusive, but both sides reduced the public invective they were hurling at each other.

The Soviet Union approached the United States again in 1970 seeking tacit approval for cooperation in military action against China.[18] Both the Soviet Union and China continued a steady buildup of troops aimed at each other. By mid-1973, the Soviet Union had more than a million troops on the border equipped with missiles and nuclear weapons, as well as 150 ships deployed near the Pacific coast of China. It also moved quickly to build antiballistic missile systems around Moscow, as permitted by the 1972 ABM treaty.

China moved one million troops to its borders; built extensive networks of tunnels and shelters in major cities, which were stocked with food, water, and medical supplies; and moved its nuclear installations from Lop Nor to unknown locations in Tibet, while the former sites were made to appear as if they remained genuine atomic weapons facilities. In addition, China deployed its recently developed nuclear-armed ballistic missiles into position to reach the Soviet cities of Vladivostok, Irkutsk, and others in Siberia and Central Asia within range of its 1,200-mile and 2,300-mile missiles. By 1973, China was also beginning to produce missiles with a range of 3,500 miles, which could reach Moscow and Leningrad, and by 1980 they had a 6,000 mile ICBM.[19]

The Death of General Lin Biao

Having used General Lin Biao and the army to defeat the Communist Party factions he opposed, and having designated General Lin as his successor, Mao became concerned in 1970 about the growing political influence of China's military. The military had used its repression of the Red Guards to gain a major role within the Communist Party and all major government institutions, including industry, agriculture, and education.[20] Now, in order to counterbalance General Lin and the military, Mao began to work more closely with Premier Zhou Enlai to rebuild a civilian Communist Party that would be loyal to him and independent of the military. Mao also decided to abolish the State Chairmanship, the formal presidency of the Chinese government, so that General Lin could not succeed to that position. Hsu informs us that "Lin persistently demanded the retention of that position, only to be told by Mao on six occasions that he saw no need for it."[21]

Mao had always said that "the Party should control the gun," and military leaders realized their newly gained political power was being challenged. The issue came to an open confrontation at a meeting of the Party Central Committee held at Lushan in August 1970. There, a new constitution, drafted by the Mao-Zhou group, was challenged by General Lin and several other senior generals, including the chief of the general staff and the commander of the air force. As described by Mao, "At the 1970 Lushan conference, they first conspired covertly, and then launched a surprise attack . . . a certain person [General Lin Biao], anxious to become chief of state, tried to split the Party and was eager to seize power."[22] The "surprise attack" was later described by Zhou Enlai as the first of two unsuccessful attempts to kill Mao. Mao and Zhou used a series of maneuvers to undermine and remove a number of generals supporting General Lin, and also launched a brief public campaign against the "five great generals" who had challenged Mao. In the winter of 1970 and the spring of 1971, no doubt believing he would suffer the fate of former President Liu, General Lin decided to plan a coup against Mao. Documents later issued by the regime describing the plot quote General Lin as saying:

> [Mao] always plays off one faction against another . . . he may talk sweetly today to those whose support he solicits, but tomorrow they may be condemned to death on trumped-up charges. Once he thinks someone is his enemy, he won't stop until the victim is put to death. . . .
>
> If [Mao] falls into our hands, the [other senior leaders] will also be in our hands. They will fall into our trap. We could use a high-level meeting to seize them . . . we could also use extraordinary methods like chemical or bacteriological weapons, bombing, 543 [a presumed secret weapon, nature unspecified], an arranged car accident, assassination, kidnapping, or urban guerrilla units.[23]

Mao also alleged that this coup plan had "the support of Moscow."[24] General Lin Biao and most of the military leadership continued to favor close cooperation with the Soviet Union and opposed the movement they saw in 1971 by Mao and Zhou toward the United States as a means of counterbalancing the Soviet Union. But General Lin and his fellow plotters did not move quickly or effectively enough. The failure of their coup attempt became public when it was reported that on September 13, 1971, an airplane carrying General Lin, his son, and others had taken off for Mongolia in the direction of the Soviet Union and crashed, killing all. General Lin Biao was the second ostensible successor to Mao who was branded a "renegade and traitor" and who died a violent death. At the same time, the generals who were Lin's principal supporters vanished from public life.[25]

NORMALIZATION WITH THE UNITED STATES

The Chinese regime said that General Lin Biao's coup attempt failed due to betrayal by one of the participants.[26] There is also a report that the United States learned of General Lin's secret relations with Moscow and the coup attempt through an Israeli agent in Moscow, and that President Nixon decided to inform Mao when Kissinger first met with Zhou Enlai in July 1971.[27] The official Chinese story of General Lin Biao's death—that he and eight associates were killed in the crash of a small jet aircraft as they were fleeing toward the Soviet Union—emphasized the Soviet connection to the military plot. Speaking to the Tenth Party Congress in August 1973, Zhou Enlai said that General Lin had been a "treasonous super-spy" for the Soviet Union, which was attempting to "reduce China to a colony of Soviet revisionist social imperialism."[28]

The Soviet nuclear threat, the ongoing buildup of Soviet military forces on the border, and Soviet covert efforts to work with the more pro-Soviet elements within the Chinese Party, including the military, all combined to give the Mao regime an important reason to end its years of official hostility toward the United States. Applying the maxim that the enemy of my enemy can be useful, Mao and Zhou clearly saw important strategic advantages in reaching détente with the United States. This could at the least reduce the chances of American acquiescence in a Soviet attack on China and might help counterbalance a range of Soviet pressures.

During his two terms as vice president under Eisenhower (1953–1960), Richard M. Nixon was known as a strong opponent of Communism. During the 1960s, as a private citizen, he traveled extensively in Asia, and in 1967 Nixon published an article in *Foreign Affairs* suggesting a new approach toward Communist China:

> We simply cannot afford to leave China forever outside the family of nations, there to nurture its fantasies, cherish its hates, and threaten its neighbors. There is no place on this small planet for a billion of its potentially most able people to live in angry isolation ... the world cannot be safe until China changes. Thus our aim, to the extent we can influence events, should be to induce change.[29]

After his election as president, but before taking office, Nixon told General Vernon Walters, whom he had known for many years, "Among the various things he hoped to do in office was to manage to open the door to the Chinese Communists ... he felt it was not good for the world to have the most populous nation on earth completely without contact with the most powerful nation on earth."[30]

As president, Nixon received extensive information on the Soviet military buildup around China as well as the battles that broke out between the Soviet Union and China beginning in March 1969. President Nixon rejected Soviet overtures for U.S. acquiescence in a Soviet nuclear strike on China but took the threat so seriously that the United States began to plan for a response in the event Moscow attacked China.[31] From 1965 to 1967, the United States and China met more than 130 times to keep each other informed of their views on major issues. These meetings, held in Switzerland and Poland, maintained a dialogue but did not bring the two countries closer. Communist China under Mao viewed the United States with unmitigated hostility, because of the mutual security agreement the United States had with Taiwan and because of U.S. efforts to help governments threatened by the indirect aggression of Communist China against neighboring countries, including South Vietnam.

The Soviet threats, however, opened an opportunity for possible dialogue; and Nixon, through his assistant for national security, Dr. Henry Kissinger, made a series of secretive overtures through Romania, a Communist country politically distant from Moscow, and Pakistan, a country that viewed China as a possible counterweight to India. In December 1970, these secret overtures led to a response from China that it would be willing to receive a high-level envoy from the United States for the sole purpose of discussing, as Zhou Enlai would put it later, how the United States would withdraw from Taiwan.[32] General Lin Biao and other more pro-Soviet elements of the Party opposed any such discussions. Mao explained his purposes to the Party as being entirely tactical, just as his 1945 negotiations for a "coalition government" with the Chinese Nationalists had been a stratagem to bring victory closer in the civil war. To underline this, Mao's 1945 article on the negotiations with the Nationalists was circulated to Party and military leadership, and Mao made clear that the goal of Communist China remained world revolution.[33]

In July 1971, Dr. Kissinger went to Beijing. The visit was kept secret by mutual agreement so that each country could explore whether a visit by President Nixon would be in their mutual interests. According to the account of a participant and of a declassified secret chronology of U.S.-China relations from 1971 to 1975, Kissinger, in his first meeting with Chinese Premier Zhou Enlai, preemptively gave China what it wanted most by stating that it was the U.S. position that there should be "No two Chinas; no one China, one Taiwan; no independent Taiwan."[34] That led Zhou Enlai to say immediately, "Good. These talks may now proceed."[35] In 1998, this statement of the "Three Nos"—which seems to leave the 22 million people of the democratic, prosperous Taiwan no alternative except unification with mainland China—was stated publicly for the first time by President Clinton during his visit to China.

During Kissinger's first visit, the record shows that he also agreed that Communist China should replace Taiwan in holding the seat of China in the United Nations as a permanent member with a veto on the UN Security Council, and that the U.S. would confer formal diplomatic recognition on the government in Beijing during Nixon's second term in office.[36] During his second visit in October 1971, Kissinger gave China important intelligence information, including photos of Soviet military deployments around China, intercepts, and other useful information . Former National Security Advisor Robert McFarlane, then working for Kissinger, has written that "extremely sensitive exchanges of information had begun by mutual agreement in late 1971," including communications intercepts, high-resolution satellite photos, and other valuable information.[37]

In return for these major U.S. concessions and helpful actions, Kissinger was told by Zhou that the United States should withdraw all its forces from Vietnam. After Kissinger left Beijing, Zhou "made a secret visit to Hanoi, assuring the North Vietnamese of China's continued support, yet also apparently urging some sort of compromise that would end the fighting. The North Vietnamese rebuffed the overture with such vehemence that . . . China turned down later requests by Nixon for further help in ending the war."[38] The end result of Kissinger's missions to Beijing in 1971 was that President Richard Nixon received permission for a visit to China that would take place early the next year.

Nixon in China

As Nixon was en route to China in February 1972, he stopped overnight in Hawaii, where, in his own hand, he summed up his view of the coming discussions with Communist China:

What they want:
1. Build up their world credentials.
2. Taiwan.
3. Get United States out of Asia.

What we want:
1. Indochina (?)
2. Communists—to restrain Chi-Com [Chinese Communist] expansion in Asia.
3. In Future—reduce threat of a confrontation by Chinese Super Power.

What we both want:
1. Reduce danger of confrontation and conflict.
2. A more stable Asia.
3. A restraint on USSR.[39]

President Nixon arrived in China on February 21, 1972. The greeting by Premier Zhou at the airport was described as "not warm, not cold."[40] Some hours after their arrival, President Nixon and Henry Kissinger met with Mao and Zhou in Mao's study for an hour-long unscheduled meeting. That conversation signaled Mao's approval for normalization with the United States, and from that point on, the "somewhat rigid Chinese attitude immediately became warm and enthusiastic."[41] In the course of the next days, the visit combined intense private discussions between Nixon and Zhou, protracted and intensive negotiations on a final communiqué, banquets, and visits to many of the historic and cultural sites in China. These conversations included the geopolitical approach of each and possibilities of coordinating policy toward China's major neighbors, including the Soviet Union, Japan, and India.[42] Because of persistent differences between the two sides regarding Taiwan, the final communiqué was not agreed upon until the last hours of the visit, and was therefore issued in Shanghai, known since as the Shanghai Communiqué.

From the Chinese perspective in 1972, it must have seemed that China had accomplished all its major purposes while giving very little in return to the United States. According to the Shanghai Communiqué, on the issue of Taiwan, the United States

> acknowledges that all Chinese on either side of the Taiwan Strait maintain that there is but one China and that Taiwan is part of China. The United States government does not challenge that position. It reaffirms its interest in a peaceful settlement of the Taiwan question by the Chinese themselves. With this prospect in mind, it affirms the ultimate objective of the withdrawal of all U.S. forces and military installations from Taiwan. In the meanwhile it will progressively reduce its forces and military installations on Taiwan as the tension in the area diminishes.[43]

This public declaration, in combination with the "Three Nos," which Nixon privately reaffirmed during his visit, could well have led the Chinese leadership to believe that it would only be a short time before Taiwan became isolated and was brought under the power of the Beijing government. It is worth noting that China adamantly refused to include any mention of the U.S.-Taiwan Mutual Defense Agreement in the final communiqué.

With respect to Nixon's view of the Chinese intention to "build up their world credentials," the Nixon visit led to major benefits for the Beijing regime. First, it included the private promise that the U.S. would formally recognize China in the future, and the visit itself showed that the U.S. no longer contested the authority of the Beijing regime to rule the mainland. Second, the U.S. had already agreed that China should take Taiwan's seat in the United Nations; this occurred in the fall of 1971. Formally, the U.S. supported a two-China policy within the United Nations, but when this did not occur, Taiwan was effectively removed from its permanent seat on the UN Security Council and from the United Nations. Third, as soon as the United States announced President Nixon's visit, a number of other democratic countries moved to normalize relations with China, including Japan and West Germany among many others, so that within a few years, many governments had transferred their diplomatic recognition from Taiwan to Communist China.

Another Chinese purpose was to use the relationship with the United States as a means of reducing the probability of military attack by the Soviet Union. That purpose was clearly met. The handwritten notes of President Nixon show that in the private conversation with Zhou, he gave China assurances about the Soviet Union, including that the United States would "seek to maintain the balance of power, restrain their expansion (if our interests are involved) . . . not make them agitated at you, make no deals with them we don't offer you, inform you on all deals."[44] These assurances were accompanied by further U.S. promises of intelligence and other useful information about the Soviet Union.

China was concerned about the possibility of Japanese rearmament—especially about Japan obtaining nuclear weapons. Here Nixon's notes show that he explained to Zhou that "our friendship with Japan is within your interests—not against," because by the U.S. providing Japan with a nuclear shield, it helps to "keep Japan from building its own ... [and] to have influence for the U.S."[45] The U.S. also assured China that it would oppose any attempt by Japan to obtain its own nuclear weapons.

Concerning Nixon's prescient view of the longer-range Chinese goal, "the U.S. out of Asia," that was not an operational theme from the Chinese side in the negotiations in 1972, but since the dissolution of the Soviet Union it has become a major goal of Chinese foreign policy.

Looking at U.S. purposes for the 1972 summit, we find that the United States accomplished the broad goal of opening up a new relationship with China, which has continued and which, in the U.S. view, provided an incentive for the Soviet Union to reach arms limitation agreements and to enter into détente with the United States. These were formalized at the U.S.-Soviet negotiations in May 1972. The goal of restraining the USSR and preventing it from attacking Communist China was met. Nixon's goal of a "more stable Asia" was not met because Communist China and the USSR continued helping the Communist movements that took power in South Vietnam, Cambodia, and Laos in 1975. This was then followed by a long Soviet-Chinese proxy conflict in Cambodia, which included a punitive Chinese invasion in 1979 of the border region in Communist Vietnam.

There was no success in obtaining China's help in settling the Vietnam War. Nixon had, in fact, written notes in China on this issue, stating "Taiwan equals Vietnam equals Tradeoff."[46] The Nixon administration secretly requested that China invite Vietnamese leaders to Beijing in 1972 for negotiations on a political settlement, but China would not agree to that action, nor would it agree to play any significant role in attempting to mediate the conflict. China also refused to remove or reduce any of the tens of thousands of Chinese military forces it had secretly deployed to North Vietnam. The Chinese regime did say that Vietnam was "different from Korea," and this was taken as an implicit promise by Zhou that China would not openly send large numbers of combat forces to help the North Vietnamese win their war against South Vietnam and the United States.[47]

At the time, then, it appeared that the U.S. conceded on Taiwan and seemed to have nearly placed it in China's hands without receiving the "tradeoff" of Chinese assistance on Vietnam. Nevertheless, over the years, the Republic of China on Taiwan managed to maintain its existence and in fact has evolved into an economically prosperous and successful political democracy.

With respect to the purpose that Nixon described as restraining "Chi-Com expansion in Asia," this failed, as Communist regimes took power in South Vietnam, Cambodia, and Laos in 1975. However the combination of the internal turmoil in China, its fears of the Soviet Union, the new relationship with the United States, and finally and most importantly, the shift in Chinese internal policy after Mao's death all produced a marked lessening of Chinese armed subversion against a number of neighboring countries such as Malaysia, Thailand, and Indonesia in subsequent years.[48]

Did the 1972 visit result in China becoming aligned with the United States to provide a geopolitical balance against the Soviet Union? The answer is not until after the 1979 Soviet military intervention in Afghanistan and then only in a very narrow but important domain of cooperation. In fact, during the 1970s, the Soviet Union continued its military buildup and helped ten new pro-Soviet regimes take power on three continents all without any Chinese resistance.

This first U.S.-Chinese negotiation set a pattern that would continue over the next decades. In 1972, by any objective measure, the United States was in the far stronger negotiating position. It was China that was menaced directly by the Soviet buildup along its northern border; it was the United States which could and did help counter the effects of that buildup with intelligence information and later with some military assistance. It was Communist China which needed and received assurances that the United States would not agree to participate in or condone a Soviet nuclear attack on China and its nuclear military facilities. Nevertheless, the results of the encounter were that the United States made concessions on the issue of greatest importance to China—Taiwan—and then received virtually nothing on the issue which Nixon had originally defined as of greatest importance to the United States: Chinese help in bringing about a political settlement in Vietnam permitting the removal of U.S. forces without a Communist victory there.

Notably, this 1972 meeting set the stage for the operational style, as James Mann put it, of "high-level negotiations in great secrecy and virtually always on China's territory." As described in a study of Chinese negotiating tactics, "negotiating in the Chinese capital gives the Chinese the opportunity to manage the ambience so as to maximize the sense of gratitude, dependence, awe, and helplessness they evoke in their guests."[49] Mann calls this "an apt description of the psychology of American officials on visits to Beijing."[50] This pattern of one-sided negotiations would be repeated over the years and would have important consequences for the U.S.-China relationship.

THE STRUGGLE FOR SUCCESSION, 1976

Normalization with the U.S. brought China important successes. These included the use of the U.S. to reduce the probability of a Soviet attack on China, the removal of

Taiwan from the United Nations and the recognition that Taiwan was part of China (though only peaceful means could be used), entry into the arena of major powers, and the beginning of financially useful trading relationships. Nevertheless, Jiang Qing and her main associates in the Mao group within the Party, which came to be known as the "Gang of Four," continued to oppose this rapprochement with the U.S. as contrary to fundamental Communist ideology. They also opposed Premier Zhou Enlai and the more pragmatic elements of the Party leadership, especially Deng Xiaoping, whom Zhou had brought back from "reform through labor" exile.

In late 1930, Jiang Qing met Mao while working as a secretary in Yenan. In 1939, Mao divorced his second wife and married Jiang. Even then, the Party leadership viewed her as politically ambitious and extracted a promise from Mao that Jiang Qing would be prohibited from entering politics for twenty years.[51] In the years 1972 through 1976, as Mao's health faded, Jiang Qing and her allies in the Cultural Revolution Group continued the persecution of leaders and elders in the Party, of intellectuals, artists, and regular citizens. Thousands were arrested, tortured, sent to forced-labor camps, and killed with the implicit approval of Mao, in whose name this continued to be done. At the same time, the leaders of the Cultural Revolution Group are described as having "led decadent, privileged, bourgeois private lives." Jiang Qing for example "kept a 'silver' jet for her own use, enjoyed the most expensive of German photographic equipment, wore silk blouses, and received guests in lavish settings."[52]

As we have seen, Mao unleashed Jiang Qing and the Cultural Revolution Group in alliance with the military to assure his dominance of the Communist Party. But after the attempted coup led by General Lin Biao in 1971 and the large presence of senior military officers in the top levels of the Party and government, Mao turned to Premier Zhou Enlai to rebuild the civilian Party as a means of counterbalancing the military.

Born to a gentry family in 1898, Zhou studied in China then went to Japan for further studies, and from 1920 to 1924 he lived in France and Europe as a work-study student. It was in France that he and Deng Xiaoping, a fellow student, joined the Chinese Communist Youth Corps and later the Chinese Communist Party.[53] Zhou had been a firm and steadfast supporter of Mao within the Chinese Communist Party since 1935 and had served as premier of China since its founding in 1949. As the individual responsible for the functioning of the government, Zhou was seen as a person who attempted to moderate the extremes of the policies Mao established for China while always remaining loyal to him.

In 1972, Zhou learned that he had cancer. Concerned about the succession of leadership, Zhou brought about the rehabilitation of Deng Xiaoping and his appointment as vice premier in 1973. This was followed by the Cultural Revolution Group using its control of the Party media to begin an "anti-Lin Biao, anti-Confucius campaign" as a means of harassing and criticizing Zhou by allusion. As Zhou became more ill in 1974, the role and influence of Deng grew, and it became clear that Zhou was preparing him to be the next premier. In January 1975, Zhou appeared before the National People's Congress to give a keynote speech, laying the groundwork for a new national policy that would become known as the "Four Modernizations." This was a clear reflection of Deng's ideas and influence.

A year later, on January 8, 1976, with Zhou near death and Mao gravely ill, the struggle for succession began to gather momentum. One week after Zhou's death, Deng disappeared from view; and on February 6, 1976, the *People's Daily*, controlled by the Cultural Revolution Group, attacked the "unrepentant" members of the Communist Party who wanted to take the "capitalist road."[54] The Cultural Revolution Group had a candidate to become the next premier, but this person was opposed by most of the Party and military leadership. Mao was reluctant to act against the wishes of the military but was persuaded that Deng Xiaoping, the former very close ally of President Liu Shaoqi whom Mao had persecuted and killed, should not become the next premier. Mao then appointed the sixth-ranking Party leader, Hua Guofeng, to succeed Zhou.

Soon after this appointment, in late March and early April 1976, during the days when the Chinese traditionally honor the memory of their ancestors, tens of thousands of people began to visit Tiananmen Square, offering tributes to the late Premier Zhou. On April 5, an estimated hundred thousand people were in Tiananmen with banners praising Zhou and Deng—criticizing Mao by allusion. The demonstrators were dispersed by force and the Mayor of Beijing described the events as part of a "rightist, deviationist struggle," and Deng was blamed. Two days later, the Central Committee, on Mao's recommendation, ordered Deng Xiaoping be dismissed from all Party and government posts. In late April 1976, Mao gave Hua handwritten instructions, including the endorsement "With you in charge I am at ease."[55] On September 9, 1976, Mao died.

Jiang Qing intended to succeed Mao as chairman of the Communist Party and install the Cultural Revolution Group in power. The Gang of Four immediately began working with their allies (Party propaganda and communication organizations, and the People's Militia in cities such as Shanghai, Beijing, Tianjin, and Guangzhou) to bring this about. They had already established a "national general militia headquarters" in Shanghai as a counter to the Party's Central Military Commission responsible for the armed forces in Beijing. The day after Mao's death, six million rounds of ammunition were provided to the militia in Shanghai.[56]

Understanding and fearing the methods used by the Cultural Revolution Group, Deng Xiaoping had fled to Canton and gone into hiding after his dismissal from the Party and government. There he and allied Party and military leaders planned to establish a coalition among several military regions that would be headquartered in Canton. If necessary, they would establish a rival provisional Central Committee of the Party and begin a war against Jiang Qing and the Gang of Four if she became Chairman of the Party. China was on the verge of a potentially major war between competing Communist factions.

The Cultural Revolution Group had made plans to kill key members of the Politburo, including Premier Hua and other senior Party leaders. At the same time, Deng and his allies joined forces with Premier Hua and obtained the cooperation of a number of generals, including the heads of the Peking and Shanghai garrisons and the chief of the elite bodyguard unit for the chairman, a twenty-thousand-strong special unit. On October 5, 1976, at PLA headquarters in Beijing, the Deng-Hua group held a secret meeting and decided on the immediate arrest of Jiang Qing and all members of the Gang of Four and their key allies. The Gang of Four was arrested early on October 6, 1976.

The next day, Premier Hua Guofeng delivered a report on the events to the Politburo and was then designated chairman of both the Party Central Committee and the Central Military Commission. On October 24, Hua, together with top military leaders, appeared at a victory rally in Tiananmen Square, where one million soldiers and civilians praised the defeat of the Gang of Four and hailed Hua as "a worthy helmsman" to succeed Mao. The Gang of Four were expelled from the Communist Party and all official positions, imprisoned, branded as "counter revolutionaries," "conspirators," and even as "representatives of the Kuomintang." They were brought to trial several years later. This intense political and military confrontation and drama ended the Mao years. A new era then began for Communist China.

5 Economic Modernization and China-U.S. Relations, 1979–1986

"The most severe reversal of our socialist cause since the establishment of the People's Republic in 1949 ... leaders are not gods. It is impossible for them to be free of mistakes or shortcomings. They should definitely not be deified."

—MARSHAL YE, October 1, 1979

"The president of the United States wants friendly relations with a strong China. He is determined to join you in overcoming the main obstacles in the way of full normalization of our relations."

—ZBIGNIEW BRZEZINSKI,
assistant to the president for national security, May 1978

"Until Taiwan is returned and there is only one China we will fully respect the realities on Taiwan. We will permit the present system on Taiwan and its way of life to remain unchanged. . . . With this policy, we believe we can achieve peaceful reunification. We Chinese have patience. However, China can not commit herself not to resort to other means."

—DENG XIAOPING, January 1979

"The desperate parents chewing the flesh of children they had exchanged with their own babies ... who had made them do this? ... I could make out the face of the executioner quite clearly ... he was Mao Zedong."

—WEI JINGSHENG, eyewitness, 1957–1959

For the people of China, the Mao years from 1949 to 1976 had been a time of intense personal regimentation, repression, repetitive ideological mobilization campaigns, immense suffering through torture, forced labor, executions, and mass starvation—all with very little economic progress. After Mao, Chinese leaders "openly acknowledged ... that the country remained in a state of dire poverty and widespread scarcity."[1] After a two-year period of transition (1976–1978), Deng Xiaoping and his group of economic pragmatists obtained the support of the Communist Party for their program of "Four Modernizations" in agriculture, industry, technology, and the military.

The Transition to Deng Xiaoping, 1976–78

In October 1976, once the Jiang Qing group had been defeated, the two Party factions that had united against the Gang of Four began to compete. On the one side were those supporting Chairman Hua Guofeng, a former minister of internal security and representative of the Party faction that did not want the radicalism of the Gang of Four but was also uncertain about the economic pragmatists and their program. The second faction, led by Deng, sought to move actively toward the "Four Modernizations."

Once again, the military leadership was decisive in the political outcome. In November 1976, the military mediated between the Party factions resulting in the confirmation of Hua Guofeng as chairman of the Party and of the Central Military Commission. At the same time, Deng Xiaoping was reappointed to his former positions as a member of the Politburo Standing Committee—the inner group controlling the Party—vice chairman of the Central Committee, first deputy premier of the State Council, vice chairman of the Military Commission, and chief of the general staff of the People's Liberation Army.[2] Thus, Deng held senior positions simultaneously in the Party, the military, and the government. These changes were formally announced at the Party Central Committee meetings in July 1977. At that time, the Central Committee also formally condemned the Gang of Four, accusing them of "conspiring to overthrow comrade Zhou Enlai . . . violently attacking and falsely accusing comrade Deng Xiaoping . . . [and being] hostile and extremely opposed to" Mao's choice of Hua, and of "plotting to overthrow the Party Central Committee led by Comrade Hua Guofeng and bring about a counter-revolutionary restoration."[3] The Gang of Four were then expelled from the Party and kept in prison.

Once restored to participation in the Communist leadership structure, Deng moved quickly to bring his former associates back into key positions. Many had also been persecuted and sentenced during the Cultural Revolution to "reform through labor." Most important among these were Hu Yaobang and Chang Ziao, both of whom would serve as Party general secretary and premier of China through most of the 1980s. In August 1977, the Four Modernizations were written into the constitution of the Party, and in March 1978 they were included as part of the state constitution by the National People's Congress.[4] In the spring of 1978, as his influence grew and he moved toward dominance, Deng said that for China it would be "economics in command," rather than Mao's "politics in command." Further, Deng said that to accomplish the Four Modernizations it was now necessary for the Party to use the prescription that it would "seek truth from facts" and that "practice is the sole criterion of truth."[5]

In other words, Deng was returning to the economic pragmatism that he had attempted to introduce in the 1950s and early '60s with President Liu, which had been summarized with the memorable slogan, "It doesn't matter whether a cat is black or white as long as it can catch mice." While Deng emphasized pragmatism in pursuit of the Four Modernizations, he and Hua were in agreement that the "four cardinal principles" of the Party had to be observed at all times: the socialist line, the proletarian dictatorship, the leadership of the Communist Party, and Marxism-Leninism and the thought of Mao.[6] In other words, there would be pragmatism in the pursuit of the modernization of China, but there would be no movement toward political democracy or significant political liberalization.

By 1978, a process began of reopening China to foreign cultural influences, including the performance of music by Beethoven, Mozart, the plays of Shakespeare, and the like. The Cultural Revolution Group had called all music and literature other than that which it approved, examples of "bourgeois decadence." Now there began a new cultural openness and this included the return of the works of major classical Chinese poets whose work had been reviled as products of the feudal past.[7]

In the summer of 1978, the Party began to undo the legacy of Mao Zedong. At the fifty-seventh anniversary of the founding of the Party in July 1978, a speech that Mao made in 1962 admitting some mistakes was circulated so that the criticism of Mao would begin with his self-criticism when he had said: "I myself do not understand many problems in the work of economic construction . . . [or] much about industry and commerce. I understand something about agriculture but only relatively and in a limited way . . . when it comes to productive forces, I know very little."[8]

The next month, the full Congress of the Party declared the Cultural Revolution over, explicitly rejecting Mao's idea that it should be a continuing process. The second anniversary of Mao's death in September 1978 passed with no official commemoration, and soon after the Red Guards were officially dissolved. Mao quotations were removed from newspaper mastheads throughout the country. On the thirtieth anniversary of the founding of Communist China, October 1st 1979, the military signified its agreement with the criticism of Mao's mistakes when Marshal Ye summarized publicly a series of mistakes Mao had made and called the Cultural Revolution "the most severe reversal of our socialist cause since the establishment of the People's Republic in 1949." He went on to say that "leaders are not gods. It is impossible for them to be free of mistakes or shortcomings. They should definitely not be deified."[9]

The rise of Deng as the principal Communist leader was ratified by the December 1978 Party conference, which agreed to accelerate movement toward Deng's policies of the Four Modernizations and the opening of China to economic relations with the major industrial democracies so that China might benefit from exports to those countries and obtain foreign direct investment and assistance from those countries.[10] The decision of the Party conference to move forward with what Deng would call "socialism with Chinese characteristics" represented a rejection not only of Mao's radicalism and ideas of continuous class struggle, but also of "the Stalinist model of state control of the economy, collectivization of agriculture, and emphasis on heavy industry that China had followed since the 1950s. By the late 1970s this model had produced faltering economies, both in China and throughout the rest of the Communist world."[11]

In July 1979, China had a gross national product of approximately $250 billion dollars and Deng said that his goal was to increase that to one trillion dollars by the end of the twentieth century, with a per capita income that would rise to about $800 dollars per person for the projected population of 1.2 billion.[12] As this process began, Deng assured the Party that the open door to foreign capitalism would not erode the Communist regime because the state would continue to own most of the means of production, would maintain the socialist principle of distribution, and would assure that any ventures funded by foreign capital would be at least 50 percent Chinese owned. Deng also made clear that different regions would develop at different rates, and those that became more successful first would constitute examples for the others to imitate.

The international examples of how successful this development could become for China were the East Asian "Tigers": Japan, South Korea, Taiwan, Hong Kong, and Singapore—all of which had used a strategy of export-led economic growth and openness to foreign investment to rapidly increase the size of their economies and improve the living conditions of their populations. A principal market for these exports and source of capital for the East Asian countries had been the United States, and it was in this context that both countries began a new stage in their relationship.

CHINA AND THE UNITED STATES,
MUTUAL DIPLOMATIC RECOGNITION, 1978

The normalization of U.S.-China relations in 1972 had contributed to the fact that there was no Soviet-Chinese war. It also gave the Soviet Union an incentive to improve its relations with the United States. That in turn contributed to the strategic arms limitation agreements of 1972 and to the annual U.S.-Soviet summit meetings from 1972 to 1975. The new U.S. relationship with both the Soviet Union and Communist China was seen as contributing to stability and peace and was undoubtedly part of the reason that the American people decided to reelect President Richard M. Nixon in November 1972.

For the next few years there was little progress in the U.S.-China relationship. On the U.S. side, the administration was distracted by the ever-growing problem of the Watergate scandal, which led to the resignation of President Nixon in August

1974. On the Chinese side, the Cultural Revolution Group had opposed closer relations with the United States, and China insisted that any progress in normalization would require the U.S. to meet three conditions: end diplomatic relations with the Republic of China on Taiwan, abrogate the U.S.-Taiwan defense treaty of 1954, and withdraw all American forces from Taiwan.[13] As long as the war in Vietnam continued, the United States was unwilling to meet these conditions.

By 1978, both the U.S. and China were ready to consider taking further steps in the relationship. Undoubtedly, shared concern about the Soviet Union gave impetus to this, along with the fact that the Deng leadership in China and the Carter administration in the United States no longer faced domestic obstacles to further steps toward normalization. The United States and China were concerned about the Soviet Union because it continued to expand its strategic nuclear forces (though up to the limits permitted by the 1972 agreement), deployed a new category of intermediate range nuclear missiles targeting Europe and Asia, and was increasing the size of its conventional military forces. Further, the Soviet Union's preferred method of expansion, indirect aggression, had been succeeding in country after country on three continents. In 1975, the Communist forces took power in Vietnam, Cambodia, and Laos, as well as in the former Portuguese colonies of Angola, Mozambique, and Guinea-Bisseau. Cuban troops, supplied by Moscow, helped the Communist-led guerillas take over Angola. Two years later, a pro-Soviet regime took power in Ethiopia, and Cuban troops were also sent to support that regime. A pro-Soviet group seized power in South Yemen, and in April 1978 there was a pro-Soviet coup in Afghanistan.[14]

From the U.S. point of view, this pattern of indirect aggression suggested that Brezhnev's intention of having pro-Soviet regimes attain control of Persian Gulf oil and the mineral riches of southern Africa was moving forward. From the Chinese point of view, the strong relationship between the Soviet Union and Vietnam and between the Soviet Union and the new Communist regime in Afghanistan, together with the long-established Soviet relationship with India, suggested a gathering encirclement and growing strategic threat against China. The combination of shared concerns about the Soviet Union's expansionist activities in the world and Deng Xiaoping's intention to obtain significant economic benefits for China from the relationship with the United States and the major democracies made the spring of 1978 a time when China became more interested in moving the China-U.S. relationship forward. The Carter administration also wanted to follow in the Nixon administration's footsteps of attempting to use a closer U.S. relationship with China as a means of persuading the Soviet Union to agree to a major strategic arms limitation agreement and to break the stalemate in the negotiations.[15]

Within the Carter administration, the leading advocate of moving forward in the relationship with Communist China was Dr. Zbigniew Brzezinski, assistant to the president for national security. In May 1978, he led a delegation to meet with the Chinese leadership in Beijing, and announced on his arrival "the president of the United States wants friendly relations with a strong China. He is determined to join you in overcoming the main obstacles in the way of full normalization of our relations." Brzezinski went on to say that the United States shared the intention of China to "resist the actions of any nation which attempts to achieve regional hegemony . . . neither of us dispatches international marauders who masquerade as nonaligned to advance big power ambitions in Africa [Cuban forces]. Neither of us seeks to enforce the political obedience of our neighbors through military force."[16]

According to the very insightful and well-documented study by James Mann reviewing a quarter century of U.S.-China diplomacy, Brzezinski also arrived "laden with gifts." These included briefings on top-secret U.S. assessments of Soviet strategic forces and the balance of power between the Soviet Union and the United States given by Dr. Samuel Huntington.[17] The offer of "exchanges in science and technology, including joint intelligence gathering against the Soviet Union" was presented by NSC official, Benjamin Huberman.[18] Brzezinski informed the Chinese leadership that the United States would sell China technology that it would not sell to the Soviet Union, for example LANDSAT infrared scanning equipment for aerial reconnaissance. Brzezinski also said that the United States would encourage its European allies to sell weapons to China to help with the modernization of Chinese military forces.[19]

Despite these positive initiatives from the United States and China's concerns about Soviet "hegemonism" (meaning the intention to attain international dominance), the Chinese regime refused to commit itself to use only peaceful means in the matter of its claim to rule Taiwan. At the same time, the Carter administration "insisted on the right to sell arms to Taiwan after U.S.-China relations were normalized."[20] Following the successful mediation of the Camp David Peace Accord between Israel and Egypt in October 1978, President Carter made the final decision to pursue the normalization of relations with China. In the course of the negotiations, the U.S. negotiator "had been subjected to a furious lecture from Deng who said that 'China would never agree to these [continuing U.S.] arms sales' to Taiwan."[21]

But, in December 1978, the Party made several decisions: first it ratified Deng as the paramount leader over Hua Guofeng; second, Deng obtained agreement for his new Taiwan policy of "Peaceful Reunification of the Motherland"; third, Deng and the Communist leadership secretly decided to attack Vietnam to punish it for its close relationship with the Soviet Union. Since Vietnam and the USSR had established a security alliance in November 1978, China wanted to establish the relationship with the United States on a more firm basis to reduce the risk of Soviet counteractions after Chinese forces attacked Vietnam. For that reason, Deng requested an invitation to visit the United States, which he received once agreement was reached on the final terms of mutual diplomatic recognition.

China had provided the Vietnamese Communist movement with military, political and economic aid and support since 1950. The battle of Diem Bien Phu in 1954, which turned the tide against France and led to Communist rule over North Vietnam, was in fact fought mostly with Chinese weapons and with significant Chinese military advice and direction.[22] It is estimated that during the Communist war for control of South Vietnam, China provided not only more than three hundred thousand military and technical personnel but also significant military and economic aid, estimated to have totaled between $15 and $20 billion, an enormous amount.[23]

The Chinese regime expected to have a close relationship with Communist Vietnam once it had gained control of the entire country. Instead, Vietnam decided to move closer to the Soviet Union, a major Communist power with which it did not share a border. This angered China, and it is probably why the brutal and fanatical Communist Khmer Rouge regime in Cambodia, a close ally of China, began to launch attacks against Vietnam in 1978. Those attacks, in turn, led the Vietnamese to conclude the military alliance with the Soviet Union before they launched a large-scale military invasion at the end of 1978 to remove the pro-Chinese regime in Cambodia and replace it with a pro-Vietnamese Communist regime.

Deng spoke publicly about the need to "teach the Vietnamese a lesson." And the lesson that China intended to teach Vietnam was that in the Asian region China would be dominant, not the Soviet Union. Hsu also suggests that there was a second and even more ominous lesson that Deng, the leader of the economic modernizers and economic pragmatists, wanted to convey: "To show the world that China did not fear war or the threat of Soviet intervention."[24]

A lesson that the Chinese received from their military attack on Vietnam was that their military forces were not as effective as expected, and this gave a further impulse to the effort to improve Chinese technology and the economy in order to modernize the Chinese military. A relevant lesson for the United States to learn from these events is that even the modernizers and economic pragmatists among the Chinese Communist leadership are ready, willing, and able to launch sudden and massive military attacks if and when they decide it is their interest. The jovial, cordial Deng of the visit to America was also the Communist Party and military commander who risked war with the Soviet Union and caused immense suffering and devastation in northern Vietnam in order to "teach Vietnam a lesson."

Speaking on national television, President Carter announced on December 15, 1978, that the United States and the People's Republic of China would establish full diplomatic relations beginning January 1, 1979. The United States accepted the three Chinese conditions concerning Taiwan, but Carter said that Taiwan "won't be sacrificed"; that the United States would continue to maintain commercial, cultural, and other relations through informal representation; and that the United States would continue to sell weapons to Taiwan adequate to assure its self-defense.[25] President Carter also announced the Deng Xiaoping would visit the United States in early 1979.

In response, the U.S. Congress formulated the Taiwan Relations Act. It specified that the United States would continue to supply to Taiwan "such defense articles and defense services in such quantity as necessary to enable Taiwan to maintain a sufficient defense capability."[26] The Act further said the United States would consider any military action by China including any boycott or embargo of Taiwan to be "a threat to the peace of the Western Pacific and of great concern to the United States."[27] The Taiwan Relations Act passed with an overwhelming veto-proof majority in both the House and Senate and became law after being signed by President Carter. In subsequent years as China has threatened violence against Taiwan and against the United States should it in any way help to defend Taiwan, the Taiwan Relations Act has remained a cornerstone of U.S. policy in the Pacific region.

The Visit of Deng Xiaoping to the U.S.

For Deng, establishing the China-U.S. relationship on more firm ground was not only useful to counterbalance the Soviet Union, it was also entirely consonant with his wish to move forward with the Four Modernizations. Deng wanted an economic opening to the outside world that would provide benefits to China. This was the first-ever visit to the United States by one of the most senior officials of China and was hailed by President Carter as a "time of reunion and new beginnings . . . a day of reconciliation when windows too long closed have been reopened."[28] Both sides treated the visit as the beginning of an important and close relationship. Deng, on several occasions, made indirect attacks on the Soviet Union, saying for example, "The world today is far from tranquil. There are not only threats to peace, but the factors causing war are visibly growing."[29] Deng reminded the American leadership and public that in the joint communiqué establishing diplomatic relations the United States and China had agreed they were "opposed to efforts of any other country or group of countries to establish . . . hegemony."[30] Deng also said publicly on several occasions that Vietnam, which had invaded Cambodia at the end of December, 1978, had become the "Cubans of the orient" and "must be taught some necessary lessons."[31] In addition to Deng's strategic purposes in making the trip, the Chinese leadership also wanted to establish a new image for China with the American public and to open the way to a new relationship with American business, including investment by American companies in production facilities in China.

In addition to Washington DC, Deng also visited Atlanta, Houston, and Seattle, for conversations with civic and business leaders. The secretary of energy in the Carter administration, Dr. James Schlesinger, accompanied Deng to Houston and recalled, "Here we were down in Texas, bitterly anti-Communist Texas, seeing oil and other business executives who regularly proclaimed their belief in free-market principles. And they fell in love with a Marxist dictator."[32]

For the United States, a major priority during the Deng visit was to obtain China's cooperation in replacing intelligence-collection stations against the Soviet Union that had been in Iran but were now no longer available because of the revolution that had just removed the friendly government of the Shah of Iran. During this visit, Deng agreed that the United States could "set up new signals intelligence stations in Western China. . . . These stations were to be installed, equipped, and serviced by the CIA with help from the National Security Agency; Chinese personnel would also help run them and China would share the intelligence gathered at them."[33] Once fully agreed upon in detail, this new cooperative undertaking went far beyond the former occasional intelligence briefings the United States had provided to China and, according to Mann, "formalized their intelligence cooperation . . . under the Carter administration the intelligence Communities and bureaucracies of the two countries began working side by side."[34]

Deng had an important secret that he shared with President Carter, Vice President Mondale, National Security Advisor Brzezinski, and Secretary of State Vance in a meeting held in the Oval Office. He told them China had decided on a punitive attack against Vietnam as a response both to the Vietnamese alliance with the Soviet Union and to Vietnam's invasion of Laos and its removal of the Khmer Rouge regime in Cambodia, which China had supported. Deng also discussed possible Soviet reactions, which might well have included an equivalent Soviet attack against China at some point along the Soviet-Chinese border.

While President Carter's memoirs suggest that he attempted to discourage this attack, Mann informs us that the next day, "Carter handed Deng a note that simply urged restraint in what . . . would be overt military aggression."[35] Former CIA Director Robert Gates wrote in his memoir that merely urging restraint "had to have been the best signal Deng could have hoped for. No mention of disruption of normalization. No mention of a change in economic and military cooperation. No principled objection to the invasion of another state. Just the mildly, albeit firmly expressed, worry that it might create problems. Further, no indication that the secret thus shared would be violated, to warn the intended victim or complicate Chinese plans."[36]

As part of his effort to obtain implicit U.S. support for China's pending military attack on Vietnam, Deng wanted to reassure the U.S. that China would not take military action against Taiwan. Specifically, during his visit, Deng said:

Until Taiwan is returned and there is only one China we will fully respect the realities on Taiwan. We will permit the present system on Taiwan and its way of life
to remain unchanged. We will allow the local government of Taiwan to maintain
people to people relations with other people like Japan and the U.S. With this
policy, we believe we can achieve peaceful reunification. We Chinese have
patience. However, China can not commit herself not to resort to other means.[37]

This statement provided important reassurance to members of the Carter
administration and the Congress who were concerned about possible Chinese military action against Taiwan. At the same time, however, Deng explicitly repeated the
Chinese position that it would not rule out the use of force.

The Deng visit was a political and public relations success for China. Most likely,
Deng intended to create a sense of the warmest and closest possible cordiality and
cooperation so that the Soviet Union would hesitate to take any direct military
action against China once the Chinese regime moved forward with its secret plan to
invade Vietnam.

China Attacks Vietnam, February 17, 1979

Only days after Deng's return from his visit to the United States, Chinese armed
forces attacked Vietnam in twenty-six places, in a coordinated assault using an estimated 360,000 troops, 1,000 tanks, and 1,500 pieces of heavy artillery.[38] The attack
apparently achieved complete tactical surprise, and within a week China had
captured four main provincial capitals in the border region of Vietnam. The Chinese
invasion involved a campaign of deliberate destruction, mostly against the civilian
economy: "Not a single light post was left standing, and even hospitals were blown
up."[39] The best Vietnamese military units were either in occupation duty in
Cambodia, Laos, or South Vietnam, or stationed near the Hanoi area.

Yet second-line Vietnamese forces were able to hold the Chinese military to a
zone within about thirty miles of the border and to inflict very heavy casualties.
Within a month of the attack, China completed the withdrawal of its forces. By that
time it had lost approximately 46,000 killed and wounded soldiers, about 400 tanks
and armored vehicles, and had spent about $1.4 billion.[40] The Soviet Union
provided only modest amounts of military support and supplies to Vietnam; it
made military demonstrations but did not counter-attack China along the Soviet-
Chinese border.

The "Four Modernizations" and the "Newly Outward"

Deng and his associates understood and said publicly in 1979 that the Cultural
Revolution had been "a great catastrophe" and that thirty years of Communism had

left China poor. With the endorsement of the Party leadership, Deng now moved to implement the Four Modernizations program. While there was no master plan, Deng and the Party were explicit that the Four Modernizations would not mean political democracy or threaten the rule of the Party and that opening economically to the outside world would not lead to developments inside China that would threaten the rule of the Party or China's freedom of international action.[41]

The economic failure of the first thirty years of Chinese Communism was most visible and poignant in the countryside where 80 percent of the population still lived. Deng and many of the surviving economic pragmatists had experienced first-hand the misery, unremitting toil, and terrible living conditions of the peasants in the countryside when they were forced to work there during various purges by Mao and his associates. After the period of mass starvation from 1959 to 1962, there had been little improvement in agricultural production and the rural economy was "listless if not lifeless . . . the standard of living on farms had not improved for two decades and a strong incentive to work was nonexistent."[42]

The obstacle to improvement had been the commune system of collective production established by the Mao regime. In December 1978, the Party adopted Deng's proposal that farming should be gradually returned to a situation where each peasant household had control of its own production. This was called the "responsibility system" and provided that each household:

> Received a plot for cultivation and negotiated a contract with the commune production team or economic cooperative. The contract specified quantities of crops to be planted and the output to be handed to the production team or cooperative as payment for the use of the land. This payment also covered such common expenses such as irrigation, health care and welfare. Each household had full control of its labor resources and could either keep or sell on the free market the products that exceeded the contract quota. The farming household accepted and assumed full responsibility for their process of production—from the selection of seeds, choice of fertilizer, labor allocation, work schedule, preparation of soil all the way to the final product.[43]

This new family farming system gradually spread throughout China, and by 1984 nearly all farm households were producing independently. The functions of the commune were gradually supplanted by other arrangements. The effect on agricultural productivity and living conditions was positive, immediate, and dramatic. By 1987, there had been a 50 percent increase in production of major crops, and farmers spent an average of about sixty days a year on crops rather than the 250–300 days a year that had been spent to raise far fewer crops in the time of the communes. By 1999, China had moved to agricultural self-sufficiency.

It now became possible for many of the farmers to become involved in new rural enterprises producing for export and for the emerging market in China. By 1987 there were 85 million "well-trained laborers" in the countryside whose sideline production was actually greater than the entire value of all agricultural production.[44] The combination of vastly increasing agricultural productivity resulting from the personal incentives the farm families had and the new opportunities for participation in rural enterprises meant that, in rural areas during the 1980s: "Cash income quadrupled and the standard of living vastly improved. This newfound prosperity was soon reflected in new brick houses; new televisions and furniture; and new more colorful clothes of the participating households. . . . The farmers lead an ownerlike life."[45]

While land remained publicly owned, in 1987 the Party permitted the "sale of rights to land utilization" by one household to another so that the land could continue to be farmed even if particular circumstances in one family such as sickness or death prevented it from using its parcels of land.[46]

Industrial Modernization

Industrial production in Communist China had been patterned on the Soviet system with an emphasis on heavy industry and complete state planning and management of production. This meant that industrial firms were given quotas of products to produce, that the costs of their inputs were set by a central pricing board as were the sale price of the products produced irrespective of the real cost of production. Workers were essentially given lifetime employment with management having little opportunity to dismiss those who were not working effectively. There was a Chinese expression to describe the system: "Every enterprise eats from the Big Pot of the state and every worker eats from the Big Pot of the enterprise."[47]

Deng and his associates decided to move carefully and gradually in changing industrial production because of the intrinsic complexity and to avoid the risk of inflation which was seen as creating the risk of disaffection and protests in the urban areas. The first phase of industrial modernization was focused on reestablishing incentives for more effective and enthusiastic work. During this period, 1978 to 1984, the method used was to provide a financial incentive for enterprises and workers to produce more effectively. This was done by establishing an "industrial responsibility system," whereby a state enterprise agreed to a "profit and loss contract" with its government supervising organization. The enterprise would provide the state with a share of its "basic profits," but any further profit could be retained by the state enterprise and paid as bonuses to managers and employees or for innovations in production. Further, the government decided there would be more pay for more work and that skilled labor would receive higher compensation. By the end of 1982, all industrial enterprises had become part of this industrial responsibility system.

The results included an upturn in worker enthusiasm, the ability of plant managers to fire and hire employees, set wages, bonuses, and prices within a range of prices preapproved by the state. By January 1985, plant managers themselves were to be appointed for four-year terms, which could be renewed up to three times rather than for life, as had been the situation previously.[48] These changes improved the standard of living and led to a construction boom in the cites, but "there was little evidence of improvement in the efficiency of the enterprises. The performance of Chinese industry had not become more effective as . . . first expected."[49] There was also a sharp reduction in the funds the government received from the enterprises as they and the localities kept more of the money they received for the sale of their products. As a result, in June 1983 the government established an income tax on the profits of the enterprises. By 1984, it is estimated that 30–40 percent of industrial production derived from Central Planning, 40–50 percent resulted from "locally planned or guidance planned output," and 20 percent derived from market demands.[50]

By the fall of 1984, the visible success of the agricultural changes and the major accomplishment of having reached an agreement with the United Kingdom on its transfer of Hong Kong and the associated territories to China, together with the tacit cooperation with the U.S. against the Soviet Union in Afghanistan, all taken together provided the modernizers with the sense that they could move forward with the second phase of reform in the industrial sector. Guided by Deng and his close associate Premier Zhao Ziyang, the Party in October 1984 passed a "resolution on the reform of the economic system," which declared:

> The basic function of socialism is to develop the productive power of the society, ceaselessly to increase its wealth and to meet the increasing material and cultural needs of the people. Socialism wants to end poverty: paupers are not socialism. . . . The difference between a socialist and capitalist economy does not lie in the existence of a commodity economy or the function of the law of value but in the ownership system and the existence or not of an exploiting class, and whether the workers are the masters of the house.[51]

Premier Zhao said that there was too much "averagism" in the industrial sector with people simply taking advantage of the "big pot of the state" and failing to work hard enough. At the same time, Zhao declared that within the Party there still remained a "leftist tendency," opposition to any steps toward a more modern economy. To "overcome averagism," the Party would see that those who worked more received more pay. To increase the dynamism of the industrial sector, the Party decided to reduce government control of large and medium-sized enterprises so that they "could make their own decisions about supplies, sales, capital utilization, hiring and firing, salaries, wages and bonuses and about the prices of the finished products as well."[52] Each enterprise would now become legally responsible for its own profit and loss. At the same time, Zhao and the government supported the continuing expansion of private and collective enterprises that could supplement the state ownership system; the government also agreed that small and medium-sized public enterprises could be leased to private owners to operate on a contractual basis.

These significant changes in the relationship of government and producers in agriculture and industry led to very positive results for China. Between 1978 and 1986, the agriculture and industrial sector both increased output at annual rates of about 10 percent, while national income increased at an average annual rate of about 8.7 percent, among the highest in the world.[53] There was also a large increase in capital construction outside the government budget from about 17 percent of total investment in 1978 to about 57 percent in 1984. This led to a construction boom that was visible in many parts of the country.[54]

"The New Leap Outward"

Deng and the modernizers understood that China could gain three important benefits from the industrial democracies, which they called the capitalist countries: first, direct investments in China to increase and expand the production of products that China wanted; second, hard currency surpluses through the sale of Chinese goods in the markets of the major industrial democracies while China restricted access to its market; third, China could use the hard currency surpluses to buy the economic and military products it wished to have along with managerial and scientific technological skills and resources. In 1979, China established four special economic zones,[55] which were areas along its coast where foreign investors were encouraged to participate and which provided special tax benefits with far less red tape than was involved in investing in other parts of China. Initially, the Chinese regime focused especially on encouraging the very wealthy and successful Chinese business communities in Hong Kong, Thailand, Malaysia, the Philippines, Indonesia, Singapore, and Taiwan to invest in and trade with China.[56]

This developed slowly at first, but by the mid-1980s overseas Chinese communities had invested billions in China, attracted most importantly by the low cost of Chinese labor. At that time, it is estimated that the average Chinese labor cost was only one-eighth of that in Hong Kong and one-fifth of that in Taiwan.[57] By the end of the 1980s, this combination of foreign investment and Chinese low-cost labor made the coastal provinces of China "the most dynamic region not only in the country but in all of Asia."[58]

The success of the four special economic zones led China in 1984 to open fourteen coastal sites and Hainan Island to foreign investment, with preferential terms on taxes and import duties. China also began hosting international conferences where it could advertise new industrial projects that might be aided by foreign technical/managerial advice, capital, and marketing. The regime also gave permission to many local authorities to arrange foreign investment without the prior approval of the central government, and the Chinese government established laws and regulations to clarify the obligations of foreign investors on taxation liability, patent protection, trademarks, and other related matters.[59]

In 1980 President Carter agreed that China could have access for its products to the United States on the same terms as those countries that were most favored under existing trade regulations. This grant of Most Favored Nation Status to China in 1980 was then renewed annually by succeeding U.S. presidents, and China's access to the U.S. market for its export products became a major factor in its export-led economic growth as seen by the enormous trade surpluses which it obtained with the United States and other industrial democracies in the 1990s. During the decade of the 1990s China obtained more than $779 billion in trade surpluses with the industrial democracies of which $426 billion was with the United States alone. And, during the 1990s, cumulative foreign direct investments actually implemented in China were more than $320 billion with a total of $510 billion in total foreign direct investment commitments. The basis for these spectacular economic benefits from abroad were established during the modernization changes of the 1980s.

Mao on Trial and Changes to Prevent a Recurrence

Once the industrial and agricultural changes were launched, the Party under Deng took steps to avoid the possibility of a repetition of the terror and failures of the Mao era. A first step was to bring the Gang of Four and the associates of General Lin Biao to trial. This trial was held from November 1980 to January 1981 and in effect involved the trial of Mao Zedong with his wife, Jiang Qing, serving as the surrogate. The accusations against Jiang Qing and the Gang of Four included: the persecution and harassment of more than 750,000 people, causing the deaths of more than 34,000 individuals; the use of unspeakable tortures and methods of repression, including the revelation that Jiang Qing had a private torture chamber; and, a large number of other acts against the regime, including plotting an armed coup after the death of Mao. The trial was held in secret, but the results were publicly announced. Jiang Qing and one of her associates were sentenced to death, and the rest of those on trial were sentenced to long-term imprisonment.[60] That was followed by the Party moving to pronounce an assessment on Mao and his years of rule. In a 1980 speech, Deng stated: "Even so great a man as Comrade Mao was influenced to a serious degree by certain unsound systems and institutions, which resulted in grave misfortunes for the Party, the state, and himself."[61]

In June 1981 the Party Central Committee issued a statement on the Mao years which included the finding that the Cultural Revolution caused the most devastating setback and heavy losses to the Party, the state, and the people in the history of the People's Republic and that the Cultural Revolution "was initiated and led by Comrade Mao Zedong."[62] The Party Central Committee went on to say that Comrade Mao "confused right and wrong and the people and the enemy . . . herein lies his tragedy."[63] At the same time, the Chinese Communist Party, not wishing to undermine its own legitimacy by following the path Khrushchev had taken in his strong denunciation of Stalin, concluded that Mao's "contributions to the Chinese revolution outweigh his mistakes."[64]

The next step in the effort to create a greater sense of order and predictability in the politics of China was to contend (again) that the leadership of the Party should be collective and that there should be opportunities for different views to be heard and different issues to be discussed. It was for that reason that Deng avoided taking the highest offices; he wanted, in the words of Merle Goldman, "to establish the Party's legitimacy by emphasizing collective rule, regularizing procedures, and reforming political institutions."[65]

Turning from the Party to the government, Deng and his associates decided that government leaders should no longer have lifelong tenure, but be appointed for fixed terms. There was also a decision to attempt a more clear differentiation between the activity of the Communist Party and the government—the Party would provide overall policy guidance, and the government would carry out those policies. This anticipated by some years Gorbachev's efforts to do the same in the Soviet Union. It is worth noting that Prime Minister Zhao attempted to shift some of the Party's power to the government; however, starting in mid-1986 he found strong opposition from hard-line elements of the Party. As we shall see, he was ultimately brought down by the hardliners, removed from office, and placed under house arrest after the Tiananmen demonstrations of 1989.[66]

A new constitution was promulgated in 1982, and article 57 of that constitution again defined the National People's Congress as the "highest organ of the government." Successive heads of the National People's Congress, leading figures in the Communist Party, attempted to give it more of a role in government decision making. A bit of progress was achieved in the 1980s but, for the most part, this was reversed in the 1990s.[67]

Starting in 1980, the Party also attempted to make small changes in the relationship between the people and the local legislative organizations. As with Gorbachev's effort to do the same nearly a decade later, the idea was to provide a means for the citizens to choose among candidates approved by the Communist Party who would compete for their vote in these mostly rubber-stamp local legislatures and organizations as a means of establishing some degree of responsiveness to the citizens and of holding local officials accountable. This was begun in both urban and rural areas in 1980, but it was immediately discontinued in urban areas after it "brought results the Party disliked."[68]

In the 1980s, the movement toward multicandidate elections for village leaders and village assemblies in the countryside, though often rigged, still meant that the local Party and government approved all the competing candidates in advance. Nevertheless, these elections could sometimes make it possible to remove predatory corrupt village leaders and make the local leaders more accountable to their constituents. Evidence suggests that the elected village cadres were relatively successful in securing popular compliance with state policies in return for defending villagers against the illegal, predatory demands of township and county officials.[69] In the 1990s, estimates of the proportion of villages involved in such multicandidate elections ranged from 10 percent given by senior Communist Party officials, to 33 percent estimated by the International Republican Institute, to 80 percent claimed by China's Ministry of Civil Affairs.[70]

The very fact that something as public as multicandidate village elections, suggested as occurring in 10 percent to 80 percent of China's one million villages, cannot be more accurately estimated is a sign of the absence of free expression in China. Further, there is little evidence of this process having yet had any larger effect on the political monopoly of the Party on the issues it chooses to decide. Yet, as we shall discuss in the conclusion, these rural village elections might someday open the way to a process of genuine political competition and elections in the future.

Political and Social Impact of Modernization
In 1978, as the Party leadership made its decision to support the Four Modernizations, a coalition of university students, including now more-moderate former Red Guards as well as workers, began to press for what Wei Jingsheng called the "fifth modernization"—political democracy. Wall posters were put up in Beijing along what became known as the democracy wall. This practice spread to a number of other Chinese cities, including Shanghai, Tianjin, and Nanjing, where thousands of people gathered around wall posters that called on the Communist Party to permit movement toward political democracy.[71]

As with many former Red Guards, Wei was then a young person who had graduated from an elite high school because his parents were senior Party officials. Although his parents had been persecuted in the antirightist campaign (1957–59), Wei describes in his autobiography his fanaticism on behalf of Chairman Mao in the initial year of the Cultural Revolution and then how his views changed when he went out into the countryside and saw the real living conditions of the peasants in

China. In his father's village, Wei heard about the mass famine of the Great Leap Forward and reflected on

> the desperate parents chewing the flesh of children they had exchanged with their own babies . . . who had made them do this? . . . I could make out the face of the executioner quite clearly . . . he was Mao Zedong. It was Mao and his followers who had used their most evil systems and policies to force those parents, starved beyond reason, to give up their own flesh and blood to feed others in exchange for flesh to feed themselves.[72]

Reflecting on his experience in the Red Guards, in the countryside and then in the army, Wei concluded that "Mao Zedong had used class struggle to divide the people and underline interest groups, rendering them incapable of distinguishing their true interests and inciting them to murder one another."[73] Wei and others in the Democracy Wall movement wanted to assure that there would never be another era of terror caused by the Chinese Communist Party and they judged that the best way to do that was for China to establish the institutions of political democracy.

It was also in 1978 that the Congress of the United States enacted legislation which required the Department of State to file annual reports on the human-rights practices of countries receiving direct or indirect U.S. assistance. President Carter had declared that human rights would be an important part of his administration's foreign policy, and he gave a major speech on this theme on December 7, 1978, barely a week before announcing the normalization of U.S. relations with Communist China. We learn from James Mann that the day after this speech by President Carter, a wall poster appeared in Beijing as an open letter to President Carter saying: "The demand for basic human rights is common to all. Your concern for [Soviet human-rights activists] Sakharov, Sharansky, and Ginsburg was very moving . . . we would ask you to pay attention to the state of human rights in China."[74] Mann, having reported on U.S.-China relations for twenty-five years and having lived in China for many of those years, concluded that although Carter was outspokenly sympathetic in the case of dissidents in the Soviet Union, "the president and his aides had no such interest in similarly championing human rights in China."[75]

Human rights in China was not on the agenda in the many discussions Deng held with senior U.S. officials during his visit to the United States at the end of January, 1979. Not long after returning to Beijing, and following the conclusion of China's invasion of Vietnam, Deng ordered the arrest of Wei Jingsheng. Subsequently in October 1979, Wei was sentenced to fifteen years in prison; the only response from the State Department was that the United States was "surprised and disappointed at the severity of the sentence" and, as Mann put it, this left "the impression that it otherwise would have no quarrel with Wei's trial and conviction."[76]

Some years later, illustrating that there had been no consequences for China having imprisoned democratic dissidents, Deng is reported to have said to leaders of the Chinese Communist Party, "Look at Wei Jingsheng . . . we put him behind bars and the democracy movement died . . . we did not release him, but this has not caused any international uproar."[77] This led Mann to conclude that in the "crucial months in which Deng was, in effect, setting the rules for China's political life in the post-Mao era, the Carter administration said and did as little as possible. It kept its distance from Chinese dissidents and avoided condemning Chinese repression, in a way that contrasted markedly with its behavior with the Soviet Union."[78] This is further illustrated by the fact that in 1980 when it was time for the United States to write about China in its first annual report on human rights to the U.S. Congress, Mann reported that then-Assistant Secretary of State for Asia Richard Holbrooke attempted to minimize the prevalent human-rights abuses in China.[79] Wei and many other democracy dissidents were held in prison under conditions of great cruelty and severity. Wei was imprisoned until 1993, and his biographer says that "the severe treatment, beatings, isolation, and other punishments were in Wei's view intended to make him die of 'natural causes.' "[80]

The hardliners in the Party did not want any democracy movement to be established in China. They followed the events in Poland at the time when a group of pro-democratic intellectuals and workers united in the Solidarity movement and challenged the Communist regime. Deng intended the economic and technological modernization of China but opposed movement toward political democracy, which could challenge the rule of the Party. He also derided the separation of powers—executive, legislative, judicial—as constituting "three governments," in his view an impractical arrangement.

In addition to those seeking democracy who were students, former Red Guards, and younger workers, there was another important group of individuals interested in political liberalization: members of the Communist Party who worked with Deng's choice as secretary general of the Party, Hu Yaobang (1980–1987). They wanted to reform the Party so that there could never be a reversion to the terror they had experienced and survived in the Mao years. They began with an effort to rethink and redefine Marxism-Leninism in order to humanize it.[81] Next they sought to argue for reform in governance by concentrating on the need for professionalism in the management of government and on "scientific" methods of decision making. This was consistent with the overall consensus in the Party on the need for administrative effectiveness and predictability in the performance of government as modernization proceeded. This approach was supported by Deng's two main associates in modernization, Secretary General Hu Yaobang and Premier

Zhao Ziyang (Premier 1980–87; secretary general of the Communist Party 1987–89).

Goldman writes that in the early 1980s the modernizing leaders of the Party shared the traditional Chinese intellectual's view that their purpose was to help the existing regime rule more effectively in the interests of the people. However, toward the end of the 1980s, as they reflected on the enormous suffering of the Mao years and saw the continuing efforts by Party hardliners to prevent movement toward political pluralism, and as they "learned more about the workings of Western democracies, they called for a form of checks and balances: a stronger National People's Congress, a more independent judiciary, and freedom of the press. Some even called for civil and individual rights protected by laws and institutions."[82] Year by year in the 1980s, these Party intellectuals, through their "writings, speeches and debates . . . disseminated a variety of democratic ideas that both influenced and reflected the views of important segments of China's urban society, including students, intellectuals, professionals, the new entrepreneurs, and reformist Party cadres."[83]

At the same time, younger individuals explicit about seeking political democracy and pluralism, whom Goldman calls the "democratic activists," followed in the footsteps of Wei Jingsheng, who in 1978 had established the journal *Beijing Spring* to spread the cause of political democracy. After Wei's imprisonment, activists worked in a number of universities to participate in the multicandidate elections that the Communist Party permitted in 1980. As described by Goldman, "These democratic activists used the skills of speech-making, pamphlet writing, and group mobilization that they had acquired in the Cultural Revolution and the democracy wall movement to conduct their election campaigns."[84] The elections at a number of universities and scientific institutes throughout China were welcomed because the Party authorities initially permitted a good deal of open discussion and debate. However, when candidates critical of the Party and supporting political democracy won, the Party decided to discontinue elections to congresses in urban areas and essentially nullified most of those results.

Nevertheless, two of the most important democracy activists, Chen Ziming and Wang Juntou, both of whom shared with Wei the experience of being the sons of members of the Party elite and coming to understand the suffering caused by Communist rule in China, continued their activities for political pluralism throughout the 1980s. Rather than the usual employment available through the Communist Party-State, they found new ways to support themselves. Chen first established correspondence schools that provided administrative training for individuals. He then used the profits from this business to found the Beijing Social and Economic Research Institute (SERI), described as "the first nonofficial social science think-tank in Beijing [they] sought to maintain their autonomy at all costs."[85] Over time, some of the reformers associated with Party Secretary General Hu Yaobang would dare to publish in the journal owned by Chen Ziming and by the late 1980s, some of these Communist intellectuals "asked Chen to help them set up their own publications as they too began to seek more independence from the Party."[86]

Chen and Wang worked toward political democracy in the realm of ideas and the expansion of opportunities for independent intellectual analysis and discussion of the performance of the Chinese state. They stayed away from direct political activism and contact with pro-democratic workers because both were very aware that the Party was extremely fearful of a Solidarity-type coalition between intellectuals and workers.[87] However during the dramatic demonstrations at Tiananmen square in 1989 and subsequent martial law and repression, Chen and Wang made common cause with the students and workers and together suffered the brutal consequences.

U.S.–China Cooperation

There was an unprecedented opening of China to the outside world and especially to the United States. Deng and the Party leadership wanted China to obtain the best of Western advanced technology, management skills, scientific training, investment capital, and trade from the United States and other Western countries. To help bring this about and to help make up for the time lost in the Cultural Revolution, the regime paid for more than eighty thousand Chinese students to visit and study in the United States from 1979–1989.[88] This was one of the most sought-after opportunities among the best Chinese students, and many of the children of the Communist elite, including those of Deng and Jiang Zemin, went to the United States to study. An American journalist living in China observed: The 1980s were the peak period for the Westernization of Chinese society and culture . . . the Communist Party did not yet view American influence and ideals as a threat to its rule over China, in the way that it did after 1989.[89]

As a result, China became open to not only Western scientific, technological, and managerial information and ideas, but also to a great deal of Western music, art, popular entertainment, as well as ideas in many other fields including governance, law, and politics.

The years from 1979 to 1986 saw the closest overall cooperation between China and the United States since both shared a strategic concern about the Soviet Union. These concerns were heightened after the Soviet Union sent 110,000 troops into Afghanistan in December 1979. At the time, President Carter sent the U.S. secretary of defense to China and also authorized the United States to sell nonlethal military equipment to China. This included air defense radar, electronic countermeasure devices, transport helicopters, communications equipment, and perhaps most importantly, the LANDSAT reconnaissance system. While it was ostensibly to be used for civilian purposes related to agriculture and oil exploration, Mann writes that it "amounted to a breakthrough for China's satellite reconnaissance program, giving Chinese military intelligence officials the means to improve greatly the resolution capability of their satellites."[90]

President Carter also authorized the CIA to begin a secret, special relationship with China. We learn from Mann that at the end of December 1980, CIA director Stansfield Turner made the first of these secret visits, which were followed by CIA directors William J. Casey, William Webster, and Robert Gates.[91]

With the inauguration of Ronald Reagan as president in January 1981, the Chinese government understood that it now would be dealing with an individual who had been a lifelong opponent of Communism and who also had been publicly supportive of Taiwan. China moved to obtain a commitment from the new administration that it would cease selling all weapons to Taiwan.

Reagan's first secretary of state, General Alexander Haig, who had worked closely with President Nixon and Dr. Henry Kissinger on the opening to China, argued that the United State should agree to sell China lethal weapons in return for China permitting the United States to continue selling weapons to Taiwan. This led to a sharp dispute over policy within the administration, pitting the State Department against the Defense Department. In the midst of this and other policy disputes, Haig resigned as secretary of state on June 25, 1982. He was succeeded by George Schultz, who appointed a new assistant secretary of state for Asia, Paul Wolfowitz.

As director of policy and planning in the Department of State, Wolfowitz had written a paper in 1982 criticizing the State Department for making "too many concession to China in the Taiwan arms negotiations."[92] Wolfowitz felt that "China needed the United States far more than the United States needed China." In his memoirs, George Schultz described the reason for the new approach he and Wolfowitz brought to the China-U.S. relationship:

> Much of the history of the Sino-American relationship since the normalization of relations in 1978 could be described as a series of Chinese-defined internal "obstacles" such as Taiwan, technology transfers, and trade that the United States had been tasked to overcome to preserve the overall relationship.[93]

The end result was a compromise in which the U.S. and China agreed in a communiqué issued in August 1982 that the United States would gradually reduce the sale of weapons to Taiwan, consistent with providing Taiwan with the means to defend itself. This dispute over policy had pitted Secretary of State Haig against not only President Reagan but also against his skilled assistant for national security,

William P. Clark, and Secretary of Defense Casper Weinberger.

After the U.S.-China communiqué was issued, President Reagan wrote a one-page memorandum in which he made clear that his understanding and purpose in the August 1982 joint communiqué was that the U.S. would restrict arms sales to Taiwan as long as the balance of military power between China and Taiwan were preserved. This Reagan memorandum also said that if China increased its military capabilities, the United States would help Taiwan to acquire the weapons systems needed to match those increased military capabilities.[94] This issue has become even more important as Taiwan requests that the U.S. sell it weapons systems to match the greatly expanded military strength of a wealthier, more highly armed China.

In 1983, Schultz shifted the focus of American policy in Asia toward Japan, a democratic ally, rather than China. In keeping with President Reagan's emphasis on encouraging democracy abroad, Secretary of State Schultz also said, concerning the development of the Asian countries, "We believe that democratic countries are more likely to follow the sensible policies that will best serve the future of the region and the globe."[95] Schultz also spoke directly to the American business interests that were increasingly concerned that U.S.-China policy should support what they defined as being good for U.S. business. During a visit to China in February 1983, a number of American business executives told Schultz that Japan and West Germany issued export licenses much more quickly than the U.S. and helped in other ways to promote business with China. This led Schultz to reply, "Why don't you move to Japan or Western Europe?"[96] In further direct talk, Schultz reportedly told the business leaders that some of them "signed deals [with China], even though they know the technology could not be exported, and then say to the U.S. Government, 'we made the financial commitment, now you've got to approve it' . . . that's your problem when you do that. Don't complain to the government."[97]

Having observed and analyzed U.S.-China relations for twenty-five years, Mann found that the firmness of Reagan, Schultz, and Wolfowitz led to what he called the "golden years" of the U.S.-China relationship when "between 1983 and 1988 the Reagan administration forged a closer, more extensive working relationship with China's Communist regime than the two governments had before or have had since."[98] This included extensive U.S.-Chinese clandestine cooperation in support of the armed resistance against the pro-Soviet regime in Afghanistan and a visit by Secretary of Defense Weinberger to establish a formal Chinese-American military relationship that led to U.S. approval for the export of thirty-two items of military and dual-use technology that the Chinese had been trying to buy since 1981.[99]

President Reagan visited China in 1984 and spoke candidly in several public forums and on television about the fundamental ideas of political reform and political democracy. Unfortunately, these words were not heard beyond those who could speak English and were in the audience when he spoke. Reagan said that Americans "have always drawn tremendous power from two forces: faith and freedom" and that "Abraham Lincoln defined the heart of democracy when he said that 'no man is good enough to govern another man without the other's consent.' "[100]

These comments were censored by the Chinese government and illustrated the fact that China remained a Communist dictatorship. This was also clearly understood by the high level visitors to China who constantly felt that they were under intelligence observation including visual and audio surveillance. For example, Secretary of State Schultz records in his memoirs that during his 1983 trip to China, "I constantly reminded myself to turn my sensitive papers face down because of possible cameras in the ceiling. I was told that even the garden was wired and provided no refuge."[101] Following China's success in negotiating a date for British withdrawal from Hong Kong, Deng attempted to persuade the Reagan administration to make the same arrangements for Taiwan—"one country, two systems." This overture was not taken up and did not succeed.

Problems Associated with Modernization

In addition to the positive economic results stemming from the successful modernization and fast pace of economic growth in the 1980s, there were a number of new problems. Among these was inflation, never before experienced in Communist China, and estimated unofficially at about 15–20 percent annually in the mid-1980s. There was also unemployment resulting from efforts to make industrial and agricultural production more efficient. And there were problems caused by interruptions in social services such as healthcare for the elderly and children, which was no longer provided through the commune or collective enterprises in the emerging mixed economy.[102]

However, the problem that could have the most serious potential political impact was ever-increasing corruption. This resulted directly from the fact that Party and government officials controlled the permits, credit, and other resources needed by enterprises in order to function. There was public anger at the extent of corruption and nepotism involving the families of high-level Party officials who were able to use their political influence to obtain benefits for businesses with which they were involved or to obtain sought-after opportunities such as study in the United States.[103]

A public opinion survey in 1987 found that in twenty Chinese cities, nearly 84 percent of those who answered said they were most disturbed by corruption.[104] Associated with this corruption was the reemergence of criminal groups and secret societies that the Communist regime believed it had eliminated in 1949–50 but had survived underground and overseas and began to reappear. By the end of the 1980s, there were an estimated five hundred criminal gangs identified, increasing to about eleven thousand criminal gangs with a membership of nearly one million by 1995.

Some of these focused on economic activities; others engaged in the usual criminal activities such as drug smuggling, prostitution, gambling, extortion; and some have political aims, including a few committed to the overthrow of the Party.[105]

In the 1980s, China had many of the problems that Russia and other post-Soviet republics would experience in the 1990s as they moved away from the centrally planned economy. The continuing need for approval from the Party and government, even in a more market-oriented economy, was described by one Chinese entrepreneur:

> Everything depends on personal ties *(guanxi)*. If you have good ties with officialdom, everything is easy to deal with. If you do something wrong, your friends in the official bureau will see that the matter is forgotten. But if your ties are bad, then officialdom will make trouble for you even if you have done nothing wrong.[106]

In 1988, a Chinese advisor to the government said succinctly, "Nowadays it is almost impossible to do anything without bribing officials."[107] It is widely believed in China that expanding corruption in official circles is often a harbinger of the end of dynasties. The Communist hardliners decided to counter the changes they viewed as threats to Party rule.

6 Communist Hardliners Crush Political Liberalization, 1986–1989

"There is not rational basis for belief that this kind of dictatorship can overcome the corruption that it has itself bred."
—DR. FANG LIZHI, astrophysicist and pro-democracy activist, 1987

"The truth of course is that the uprising was the greatest show of democratic force in forty years of Communist rule in China."
—LIU BINYAN, former Communist investigative reporter, 1998

"In the whole process of clearing the Square there was no casualty [sic]. No one was shot down or crushed under the wheels of vehicles. The reports that there was a blood-bath and that many people were crushed were incorrect."
—Chinese government spokesman to NBC News, 1989

In 1983, hardliners in the Party obtained approval for a "campaign" against "spiritual pollution," which was the term given to the political and cultural influences from the West, viewed as undermining the authority of the Party. Although this campaign was relatively modest in scale, it led many of those seeking political liberalization to act with caution. However, they did continue, although with greater care, to find formulas for proposing changes that might encourage political liberalization but which could be linked to the modernization goals of the regime—for example, urging the "professionalization" of the government civil service and the use of "scientific methods" in decision making.[1]

The Communist hardliners denounced those proposals and many other popular trends as "raving for anything Western." This included the fact that thousands of Chinese would line up to see a Western art exhibit or Western play, but few visited the Revolutionary Military Museum. As Hsu put it, "Anything foreign was attractive: political thought, social theories, futurology, novels, plays, art, fashion and even such mundane things as Coca-Cola, Maxwell House coffee, and Kentucky Fried Chicken. The most prized wedding gift of the time was a copy of the Encyclopedia Britannica in Chinese."[2]

In 1985, on the fiftieth anniversary of the Japanese invasion of China, students in many cities staged demonstrations. Their purpose was ostensibly to protest the regime's too ingratiating treatment of Japan as it sought Japanese investment and technology. In fact, the demonstrations were a protest against the regime; in particular, against many of the negative trends accompanying the changes of the 1980s including corruption, special privileges for the children of the Party elite, inflation, and other current problems.[3]

These demonstrations alarmed the Communist hardliners. By January 1986, they slowed the pace of economic modernization to consolidate and digest the gains already made.[4] This was a successful attack by the Party hardliners on "the open-door policy as a source of foreign 'spiritual pollution' of Chinese life."[5]

However, 1986 was also the year in which Taiwan made the decision to open its political system and allow the legal establishment of a genuine opposition party; the long-established Marcos dictatorship in the Philippines was overthrown and replaced with a democracy; and, the dictatorship in Haiti was replaced by an elected government. While these events encouraged reformers in China, the Party hardliners decided that they had to act more vigorously to prevent any move toward political pluralism. In September 1986, a resolution at the Party Congress was passed endorsing their policy of opposing "bourgeois liberalization."[6] This victory for the hardliners reflected the fact that Deng had to accommodate to their views.

Deng had chosen his key associates Hu Yaobang and Zhao as head of the Party and of the government with a view toward their succeeding him. He had said that with those two individuals, even if heaven came crashing down, he would have no fear.[7] The Party hardliners, however, felt that both had been too lenient with political protest. Following their success at the September 1986 Party Congress, they began to work with key military leaders to prepare the way for the removal of Hu Yaobang as secretary general of the Communist Party. Their reasons included not only his tolerance of the beginnings of political pluralism, his strong interest in and admiration for democratic Japan's economic development, but also that he had been planning to retire all members of the Central Committee at age sixty and all members of the Politburo at age seventy-two at the next Party Congress.[8] The hardliners in the Party were mostly in the older generation and they wanted to retain their power and privileges. They also felt they had to remain active within the leadership of the Party in order to assure that the process of modernization did not "start a prairie fire."

The first reaction to the Party's pronouncement of its "antibourgeois liberalization" policy and to rumors of the ascendancy of the hardliners within the Party was an upsurge in activism among student supporters of democracy. In December 1986, large demonstrations took place in fifteen major cities in China. More than a hundred thousand students from 150 colleges and universities took to the streets calling explicitly for freedom of speech, assembly, and the press, as well as for genuinely democratic elections. These protests began in early December at the Chinese University of Science and Technology in Anhui Province, where the democratic activist and vice president of the university, Dr. Fang Lizhi, protested the recent "fake" elections to the National People's Congress. The protestors said that these elections had no legitimacy since the Party bosses had picked all of the candidates. Fang Lizhi said that this was the time to launch a struggle for democracy and that democracy could not be given from above but had to be won from below.[9]

That protest evoked sympathy demonstrations at universities throughout China. The most ominous from the viewpoint of the Party were those in Shanghai, where approximately thirty thousand students were joined by an estimated one hundred thousand workers. The Shanghai demonstrators carried placards saying "Long Live Freedom" and "Give Us Democracy." When a committee of the protestors met with Mayor Jiang Zemin, some of them asked who had elected him.[10] The demonstrators made clear that they supported Deng Xiaoping's modernizations, but wanted to add the "fifth modernization," democracy.

In response, hardliners in the Party demanded that Secretary General Hu Yaobang launch a campaign of repression. But, Hu "took the enlightened attitude that youthful idealism should not be blunted but guided to more constructive goals."[11] The vice minister of education pointed out that the demonstrators were fewer than 2 percent of China's two million college students, that they were patriotic but misguided by Western liberalism, and commented that "God allowed young people to make mistakes. When we were younger, we basically did the same thing . . . . Our policy toward them is to educate them and give them proper orientation."[12] Initially, Shanghai Mayor Jiang Zemin said that the student action was "just, legal, and patriotic," that it was permitted under the Chinese constitution, and promised that there would be no retribution.[13] Those December 1986 nationwide demonstrations for political democracy turned out to be the highpoint of political liberalization in the current era of China's history. The hard-line Party leaders, together with key elements of the military, persuaded Deng Xiaoping that the secretary general of the Party had to be removed and that there had to be a campaign to turn back the tide of political liberalization. This opened the way to the second stage in China's contemporary modernization.

As 1987 began, Party Secretary General Hu Yaobang was not seen in public until he appeared at a special session of an enlarged Politburo on January 16, 1987. There he faced criticism from the hardliners, which included, among other points, the accusation that he "advocated an inordinately fast pace of economic reform creating economic imbalances and loss of control of the situation . . . [and that] he showed a tendency toward complete Westernization in his style of work."[14] Hu was then removed as secretary general of the Party but permitted to remain a member of the Politburo and the Central Committee. Deng's other principal associate, Premier

Zhao, then became acting secretary general while remaining in his other positions. This outcome indicated that Deng had kept support for economic modernization in return for agreeing to stronger actions intended to prevent and reverse political and cultural Westernization.

At Politburo direction, the government then established a media and publications office that would lead the way in a stronger "antibourgeois liberalization campaign" decided upon by the Party. It would more closely monitor the news media and the publication of books, newspapers, and magazines.[15] Well-known critics within the Party were expelled, including Fang Lizhi, the investigative journalist Yu, and others. The "antibourgeois liberalization" campaign focused on members of the Party, the government, the military and urban enterprises, but the countryside and independent intellectuals were not to be involved.

There was an explicit decision not to use the harsh and violent methods of persecution and the extreme accusations that had been part of the Cultural Revolution and previous campaigns.[16] For example, not only was Hu Yaobang permitted to remain a member of the Politburo and the Central Committee, but his family and associates were not physically harmed. However, the Party took action against activist college and university students, arresting a number, establishing the requirement for military training and political indoctrination on the campuses, and reinstituting the highly unpopular policy of requiring students to work in factories and farms for a year before being sent to their assigned employment.[17]

Despite the limits on this wave of political repression, it evoked fear, and there was a marked and rapid change in the tone and content of the work produced by China's cultural, literary, and journalistic groups. We are told that "cautious people started to store away their Western clothes in favor of Mao jackets," a sign of concern that there could be a return to Maoist extremism.[18]

The U.S. State Department underestimated the meaning and significance of these events, with a senior official being quoted as saying that the removal of Hu Yaobang was only "a little bump on the road, but perhaps no more than that."[19] After five months of this "antibourgeois liberalization" campaign, acting Secretary General and Prime Minister Zhao confronted the hardliners at an enlarged Politburo meeting on May 13, 1987. He spoke against "excesses of leftism," and thereafter in May and June 1987, Deng on a number of occasions publicly reaffirmed his modernization changes, the open door to foreign economic and technological benefits, but also said there was a need to curb "leftism."[20] This was quickly repeated by a number of major newspapers and journals, as the modernizers planned for the summer conference of the Party leadership to be followed by the autumn Party Congress. Deng was concerned about a repetition of the early 1960s when the pragmatism that he and then President Liu Shaoqi had tried after the failure of the Great Leap Forward had been replaced by the extreme radicalism of the Cultural Revolution.

At discussions among the Party leadership in the summer of 1987, Deng said that he would retire from all positions in the Party except for the chairmanship of the Military Commission. That provided a basis for causing the retirement of more than ninety Party elders who were among the most severe opponents of the market-oriented reforms. The new Central Committee that emerged was considerably younger in average age and about 73 percent of its members were college educated.[21] However, the hardliners kept an important voice in the powerful Standing Committee of the Politburo with the appointment of two younger Communist leaders who shared their views, one of whom was Li Peng, then fifty-nine.

The son of a fallen Communist fighter in the civil war, Li grew up in the home of the late Premier Zhou Enlai. He joined the Party when he was seventeen and studied in the Soviet Union at the end of the Stalin era for six years, from the age of 20 to 26. An engineer and fluent in Russian, Li Peng had risen in the Party, and it was now agreed that he would become the next prime minister of China once the National People's Congress could rubber stamp his appointment early in 1988. Li Peng was trusted by the hardliners, and he would continue to play a major role in the next years.[22]

To increase the prospects for Zhao to succeed him as the paramount leader, Deng had seen to it that Zhao was named vice chairman of the Military Commission in addition to serving as prime minister and secretary general of the Party. In the autumn of 1987, the Thirteenth Party Congress reaffirmed both the Four Modernizations and the Four Cardinal Principles (specifying the continuation of Communist Party rule), the result of a series of negotiated arrangements between the two major competing factions within the Party. It also endorsed the new theoretical formulation given by Zhao of "socialism with Chinese characteristics" and agreed to a series of administrative reforms intended to permit the Party to set policy while the government would actually manage the society. This move toward greater responsibility for the government was also to include the establishment of a government civil service system based on merit.[23]

A new, major step in economic modernization was taken in February 1988 when first Deng and then the Politburo approved the Coastal Development Plan, a new strategy to speed up China's economic growth. The essence of the plan was that China's abundant and very low cost labor would use imported components and raw materials to manufacture finished goods for export to world markets. This would provide China with hard currency such as the U.S. dollar, the yen, and European Union currencies. This hard currency foreign exchange would in turn be used to purchase the high technology and modern industrial equipment that would lead to China itself becoming a major producer and exporter of industrial and high technology. The 1988 Coastal Development Plan assumed three stages: During the first five to seven years, the coastal economy would export mainly textiles, food, small electrical appliances, and light industrial products; in the second stage of about five to seven years, items from the interior of China would also enter international markets and significantly expand China's capacity to earn foreign exchange from labor-intensive products; in the third stage, assumed to occur between 1996 and 2000, China would substantially increase its export of complex technology-intensive products and reduce its export of labor-intensive products, and the resulting higher value-added exports would further accelerate the pace of hard-currency earnings and economic and technological modernization.[24] The original goal was that China would export about $150 billion of goods by the year 2000—in fact China exceeded that goal with total exports over $190 billion by the end of 1999.

By the end of 1987, China already had close to 85 million well-trained and very low-paid workers producing for the export market, and there were tens of millions more who could be available to work producing exports for the major industrial democracies and other countries which could pay with hard currency.[25] In many respects, this plan imitated the economic strategy used by South Korea, Hong Kong, Taiwan, and Singapore during the previous twenty years to dramatically increase the size of their economies and to raise living standards. In fact, China also reached out to the overseas Chinese communities throughout Asia and the world, with a special emphasis on Hong Kong and Taiwan, to encourage the inflow of billions of dollars in investment capital and to encourage overseas Chinese to come into China and establish factories, increasing their profits by using China's low-cost labor to export to the major democracies. China, which could not strike or seek better wages, also encouraged companies from the industrial democracies to establish facilities in China and increase their profits. A political effect was that elements of the business community in many countries, including the United States, became strong advocates for opening the markets of their own countries to exports from China in the name of "free trade" and globalization.

From a Marxist-Leninist point of view, it was perfectly understandable that "greedy foreign capitalists" would want to make money by investing in China and that those that were earning significant profits from their exports from China would then become a strong source of pressure on their governments to continue admitting exports from China irrespective of the political and human-rights situation within China. Further, the immense amounts of hard currency that Chinese exports earned increased the ability of China to purchase some products from the private sector in industrial democracies, including the United States. This became another source of economic interest within the United States and other democracies for maintaining the mostly one-way trading relationship, whereby China since 1990 earned immense surpluses year after year. In approving the Coastal Development Plan in 1988, Deng had said, "It is imperative that you go ahead boldly, speedily, and not miss this key opportunity!"[26]

The foreign-invested enterprises would continue to be at least 50 percent Chinese-owned, whether by individual Chinese with political connections to the Party and government or by state or collective enterprises. By 1989, there were an estimated 225,000 individual Chinese entrepreneurs, including many who became quite wealthy and were millionaires in dollar terms, although their total production amounted to only about 1 percent of China's GNP.[27]

Prelude to Tiananmen

The Solidarity movement in Poland worried China's Communist hardliners because they saw how quickly it grew and seemed to eclipse the Communist Party there. Between 1979 and the suppression of Solidarity in late 1981, millions of members of the Polish Communist Party had ended their affiliation and torn up their Party cards. Chinese leadership had been pleased in December 1981 when, in one night, the Polish government arrested thousands of leaders of the Solidarity movement, apparently causing it to be disbanded. However, by 1989 the Solidarity movement still survived as a clandestine organization and the government of Poland, with the approval of Gorbachev, had begun negotiations with Solidarity for the holding of semi-open elections, which could give Solidarity up to a maximum of 35 percent of the seats in the Polish parliament (which was still, however, mostly powerless under the rule of the Communist Party there). Now, in the spring of 1989, Solidarity was back, recognized as a legitimate negotiating partner and political movement.

At the same time in the Soviet Union, the positive development from the Chinese perspective was that Gorbachev had been reaching out to normalize relations with China and would be making a state visit to Beijing in mid-May 1989. However, Gorbachev's movement in the direction of the reform of Communist rule and his permitting greater openness—including criticism of the Soviet Party, competitive multicandidate elections within the Soviet Communist Party, followed by plans for somewhat more open elections for the parliaments of the Soviet Union and the republics—were undoubtedly matters of deep concern. Chinese leadership understood that Soviet steps toward political liberalization immediately opened the way for similar proposals by reform Communists and others who wanted political liberalization in Eastern European countries. They feared this would provide legitimacy for Chinese Communist political reformers and inspiration for Chinese democratic activists. This was in the same year that marked the seventieth anniversary of the May 4, 1919, democracy protest in China, the two hundredth anniversary of the French revolution against royal tyranny, and the fortieth anniversary of the founding of Communist China. For these reasons, members of the Party were instructed to show extra vigilance in 1989.

In February 1989, the newly inaugurated president of the United States, George H. W. Bush, was flying to Japan to attend the funeral of Emperor Hirohito and suggested that he visit China and South Korea also. In the 1970s Bush had served as one of the first U.S. representatives to China and on this proposed two-day visit he wanted to meet the Chinese leadership and discuss future relations and one new emerging problem. China agreed to the visit.

President Bush decided to host a large banquet to which he would invite the Communist leaders and also Chinese citizens from different walks of life, including several democratic activists, among them the astrophysicist Fang Lizhi. By coincidence, just as Bush was in Beijing, an article by Fang appeared in the *New York Review of Books,* in which he wrote, "Forty years of socialism have left people [in China] despondent . . . there is no rational basis for belief that this kind of dictatorship can overcome the corruption that it has itself bred."[28] Fang had become among the most visible proponents of democracy in China and to the apparent surprise of the U.S. government, the Chinese government began a series of efforts to persuade the U.S. not to invite him to the banquet. This included the statement that neither Premier Li Peng nor another hard-liner, General Kang, then-president of China, would attend the dinner if Fang Lizhi were there. Ultimately, a compromise was worked out in which it was agreed that the Chinese officials would participate at the dinner and that Fang would be seated at a table in a somewhat less visible part of the banquet hall.[29]

However, as Fang was driving to the dinner in the company of a visiting American professor with his invitation from President Bush in hand, Chinese security police intercepted his car and physically prevented him from attending the dinner—in violation of the agreement that had been negotiated. As Mann concluded, "The episode demonstrated, once again, how extraordinarily nervous the Chinese regime had become. The American perception of a strong stable Chinese leadership, steadily reforming the country with strong domestic support, seemed increasingly to be at odds with the day-to-day realities inside China."[30]

The new issue in U.S.-China relations that Bush wanted to discuss was the export of Chinese missiles to the Middle East, specifically to countries such as Iran and Iraq, where China had sold large amounts of conventional weapons when these countries fought a brutal war from 1980 to 1988. The U.S. viewed the sale of medium-range ballistic missiles to Iran and Iraq as risking an expansion of the arms race and war in a region where important U.S. allies were threatened by both of these regimes. China viewed these sales as a means of establishing good relations with these oil producers and earning hard-currency profits. Previous discussions on this issue by both Secretary of Defense Frank Carlucci and CIA Director William Webster had not resulted in explicit Chinese guarantees that such missile sales would stop. President Bush took up the issue directly with Premier Li Peng, but "Li's responses were sufficiently imprecise that American officials spent the rest of the year trying to find out whether or where China would export its M-9 missiles."[31] The February 1989 visit of President Bush crystallized two problematic issues in the U.S.-China relationship that would continue into the new century: human rights and China's export of missiles and components for weapons of mass destruction.

Fang Lizhi had said and written that China needed to move toward political democracy, and this represented the views of an important group of intellectuals and students who were angered by the actions of the security police in preventing Fang from participating in the dinner with President Bush. As a result, they had sought some forum for protest; but they were also afraid, given the influence of the Party hardliners and the most recent "antibourgeoisie liberalization" campaign. Then, on April 15, 1989 the reformist former secretary general of the Communist Party, Hu Yaobang, was reported to have died of a heart attack. As in 1976 at the death of Premier Zhou Enlai, this provided the opportunity for those who wanted to challenge the Party hardliners to come forward and express their hope for political liberalization in the form of eulogies to the late Secretary General Hu. At Beijing University, posters were put up praising Hu and criticizing the hard-line leaders. One said, "A good man has died, but many bad ones are still living," and another said, "A man of sincerity has passed away, but hypocrites are still around."[32]

There were demands that the Party rescind the charges against Hu, but the Party refused to rescind the charges that had led to Hu's dismissal two years earlier. This led to thousands of students marching in the streets and beginning a sit-in at Tiananmen Square, where they shouted, "Long live democracy! Long live freedom! Down with corruption!"[33] Day by day the demonstrations grew, students stopped attending classes in Beijing and week by week there was increasing support from students in the provinces, "as well as from local and provincial workers, intellectuals, journalists, professors, researchers, musicians, actors, ordinary citizens, and even some members of the Party and armed forces."[34] By mid-May 1989, it is estimated that there were about a million peaceful pro-democracy protestors in Tiananmen Square, and there were also large demonstrations in twenty-three other Chinese cities. On May 30, students of the Central Art Institute erected a thirty-foot tall statue of the "Goddess of Democracy," quite similar in appearance to the Statue of Liberty in New York Harbor, placed so that it faced the giant portrait of Mao on the Tiananmen Gate.

COMMUNIST PARTY FACTIONS AND THE
TIANANMAN MASSACRE, JUNE 1989

The hardliners in the Party had continued to oppose significant elements of the Four Modernizations and the economic changes. They had used the student demonstrations in December 1986 as a means to remove Secretary General Hu Yaobang. Now, with the April 1989 demonstrations, the hardliners believed this would provide the opportunity to remove the second of Deng's major allies who had opposed them for years, Secretary General Zhao. The historian Hsu wrote that the Communist hardliners

> saw in student demonstrations a rare opportunity to crush the democracy movement and derail economic reform. . . . [They] masterminded a plot whereby Premier Li Peng was to be absolutely stern and unyielding with regard to student demands, thereby goading students into greater belligerence. Meanwhile Zhao was to be attacked as a secret supporter of the demonstrators—a traitor within the Party. The growing insolence of the students and Zhao's sympathy for them would drive Deng into a rage and cause him to react violently. He could then be persuaded to smash the students and Zhao in one fell swoop, just as he had been persuaded to oust Hu two years earlier.[35]

The Party hardliners took an important step toward their goal on April 24 when they submitted a "war report" to the Central Committee, which was based on secret police compilations of information, including posters, slogans, and secret informants' reports. It concluded that these demonstrations had been planned for two years with the clear purpose of removing the Communist leadership. The next day, Deng declared that the demonstrations were a "conspiracy," and Premier Li Peng refused to meet with student leaders until May 18, when he gave a stern lecture to two of the student leaders Wang Dan and Wu-er Kaixi.

That Gorbachev should be scheduled to visit China while a million demonstrators were in Tiananmen Square was a cause of acute embarrassment to the Party. Speaking for the hardliners, Premier Li Peng told Deng that both Hu and Zhao had been too lax and permissive first during the 1983 "spiritual pollution" campaign and again during the 1987 "bourgeois liberalization" campaign, and that was the reason for the current rebellious actions. He also said that Secretary General Zhao was trying to set up an "alternate headquarters" to the Party, in effect an allegation that he wanted to use the demonstrations to seize power. This convinced Deng, and another potential "successor" fell as Deng branded Secretary General Zhao, his long-time associate, a "traitor."[36]

After Gorbachev concluded his state visit to China, Deng convened a "war council" of the inner circle of the Communist Party leadership. They decided that the demonstrations in Beijing and throughout China amounted to "a war between Communism and democracy," that they could not retreat, that Zhao should be dismissed as secretary general of the Party, that martial law should be declared, and that military and police forces should be used to remove the demonstrators.

On May 19, Deng went to Wuhan to convene a meeting of the Central Military Commission and also to establish an alternate base of operations in the event the situation in Beijing became untenable, and, as Hsu speculates, to prepare for "a secret flight abroad if all else failed."[37] Once again, the Party leadership reached out to the military in order to gain its support at a time of crisis. Part of the military modernization of the 1980s had been to establish an ethic of the military as a professional institution serving China rather than the Party.[38] Now the military once again was clearly to be involved in protecting the Party. The leaders and the armed forces agreed that the military units to be used for the repression in Beijing were to include elements from virtually all of China's major armies, to assure that the entire military establishment would bear equal responsibility for the coming events.[39] This was also the meeting at which the decision was made to appoint the mayor of Shanghai, Jiang Zemin, as the new secretary general of the Party, although this would not be announced publicly until the end of June 1989. Subsequently, Jiang Zemin served simultaneously as the president of China, secretary general of the Communist Party, and chairman of the Central Military Commission until 2003. Then, he kept only the military post until the final months of 2004, when he relinquished his position as chairman of the Central Military Commission.

THE TIANANMEN MASSACRE OF JUNE 3–4, 1989 AND ITS AFTERMATH

As the peaceful demonstrations continued in Beijing, the Chinese government admitted that there were also pro-democracy rallies in 123 other Chinese cities.[40] Further, after the regime declared martial law, pro-democracy leaders among Chinese workers established the Beijing Workers' Autonomous Union and began making speeches at street corners in the capital calling on workers to demonstrate for democracy.[41] Similar labor associations not connected to the Party formed in six places throughout China, and an independent labor newspaper was established in Kunming, a city 1,200 miles from Beijing.[42] When the regime arrested striking workers in Beijing, more than one thousand students appeared at the Public Security Bureau in support of the workers, and they were released.

In April, Secretary General Zhao expressed sympathy with the students, and key members of his staff publicly supported the students' cause.[43] Zhao was placed under house arrest and not seen again for years, and some of his staff were imprisoned. There were also some Communist officials who publicly supported the demands for democracy and a number of journalists for Party publications such as the People's Daily, the Xinhua News Agency, and the English-language China Daily were seen marching in pro-democracy protests carrying the banners of their organizations.[44] Some editors and reporters of Chinese Central Television stated publicly that they had been "propaganda tools for the Communist Party" and expressed their support for the demonstrating students and workers, while three Party-controlled organizations declared that the issues being raised by the demonstrators should be resolved using "democratic and legal means."[45]

These expressions of protest from within the Party gathered momentum with each passing day and went beyond the initial expectations of the hardliners, who became ever more concerned that their fabricated antiregime plot could become reality. The hardliners were also concerned about the loyalty and cohesion of the People's Armed Police, which would normally be responsible for dealing with demonstrations of this type. The students had been peaceful and attempted to develop civil relations with the People's Armed Police. In turn, there were scenes of uniformed police in Beijing "riding around Tiananmen Square saluting the students and giving them the V for victory sign." There were also "Public Security Academy students in the square carrying a banner that proclaimed, 'We have arrived.' "[46] The head of the People's Armed Police was a Politburo member who had spent many years in police and intelligence work, but nevertheless, even he appeared to show sympathy for the striking students by permitting "himself to be photographed smiling as he visited hunger strikers in the hospital."[47] As Deng and the Party leadership decided on repression, they placed the People's Armed Police under the direct control of the PLA. The military, in the words of Timperlake and Triplett, would be the sword that "would protect the Party from democracy."

After declaring martial law on May 20, 1989, the Party ordered to Beijing about three hundred thousand soldiers from ten armies, as well as an armored division, a parachute division, and various special units. Most of this deployment was to prevent deposed Party Secretary General Zhao and those in the military who might support him from resisting the coming repression.[48] This was the third time in eighteen years that the Communist Party faced the prospect of civil conflict in the country between its factions involving the possibility of divisions within the armed forces: 1971, 1976, and 1989.

Many of the local students from Beijing had returned home or to their schools by this time, but thousands more students had come from the provinces. The students were supported by the "local citizenry [who] showed solidarity by offering food, shelter and other necessities."[49] Also, many Beijing residents worked with students to build barricades to block the potential deployment of troops toward Tiananmen Square, the largest public square in the world, encompassing more than one hundred acres. On June 3, 1989, unarmed troops who had come to the Tiananmen Square area were friendly with students, and this reduced their fears of an attack. But then the national television warned all citizens to stay away from Tiananmen Square and student leaders received a warning that the army would attack and thereupon "asked everyone to leave in order to avoid bloodshed, but

40,000 to 50,000 students and 100,000 other citizens vowed to stay and die if necessary in the cause of democracy and freedom. They still believed that the troops
would not fire on their own unarmed people."[50]

On the evening of June 3, 1989, at about 10:00 PM, Premier Li Peng gave the
order for the army to move against the demonstrators in Tiananmen Square and
throughout Beijing. As the army approached, it had to overcome the resistance of
civilians who had erected massive barricades across major streets. At one intersection, an eyewitness reported

> thousands of civilians had turned buses and heavy trucks into a barricade to
> block the PLA's route into central Beijing. Armed only with their defiance, the
> people fended off the army for two hours. But the end was inevitable. . . . PLA
> armor broke through the flaming bus barricade and waves of infantry fired on
> the crowd with their automatic AK-47s. Students from at least four of Beijing's
> universities died with their school banners flying. A dozen fleeing students were
> struck in the back.[51]

The military assault on civilians was witnessed, documented, and written about
by a number of courageous journalists from various Western countries who risked
their lives to record the unfolding massacre. A reporter for the Associated Press, John
Pomfret, reported that at one location on the way to Tiananmen Square, "PLA armor
rolled over Chinese civilians, turning them into human paste."[52] Not long after,
Pomfret saw armored personnel carriers "turn their machine guns on another crowd
of civilians. . . . Bodies littered the streets on both sides of the intersection."[53] The
historian C. Y. Hsu summarized the attack:

> Premier Li ordered the troops to move at top speed to the Square, shoot all
> demonstrators without compunction and clear the Square by dawn. Tanks,
> armored vehicles and soldiers with automatic weapons struck from three direc-
> tions in strict accordance with pre-arranged plans. One column attacked from
> the Revolutionary Military Museum located four miles from the Square, . . .
> shooting and killing everyone in sight. Another column attacked from the
> eastern section of the avenue, and a third descended from the north, all
> converging at the Square. Much of the killing occurred before the troops and
> tanks reached the Square itself. . . . In the early hours of June 4th, 35 heavy tanks
> charged into the main encampment, crushing those students who were still
> inside. At 4:00 AM, the lights in the Square were turned off and loudspeakers in
> the Square again ordered the demonstrators to clear out. . . . Eleven students,
> two from Peking University, nine from Tsinghua University, linked hands in a
> symbolic gesture to protect the goddess of democracy; they were mowed down

together with the statue. By 6:00 AM those who could had already escaped while the dead or maimed were scattered all over the blood-soaked killing field. The soldiers hastily bull-dozed the bodies into large piles for burning on the spot, or packed them in plastic bags for cremation outside the city . . . where no registry was permitted to be divulged.[54]

There was combat not only on the approaches to Tiananmen Square but also in other areas of Beijing. David Aikman of *Time* reported shooting in eight different parts of Beijing, and said: "There were sounds of much heavier fire, probably tank shells or very heavy machine guns."[55]

By dawn, June 4, 1989, the military had taken control of Tiananmen Square. They continued killing unarmed civilians in the area immediately around the Square and throughout Beijing. Thousands of Chinese citizens were enraged by what had happened. A Canadian journalist of Chinese ancestry, who had been very favorable to the cause of Communism in China, witnessed unarmed civilians approaching the Square that morning and soldiers shooting at them, including shooting them in the backs as they ran away. She saw this a number of times: "This scene repeated itself again and again. In all, I recorded eight long murderous volleys. Dozens died before my eyes . . . an hour later, the wounded were still on the ground, bleeding to death."[56] She also witnessed crowds standing on corners screaming, "Kill Li Peng! Kill Li Peng!" in recognition of the fact that it was the hardliners in the Party who had made this decision. After the massacre,

> the capital of China looked like a war zone. Bullet holes pockmarked lamp-posts and subway entrances. Charred buses littered the streets. Torn fences, concrete lane dividers, smashed dumpsters and overturned tractors—futile barricades against the army's onslaught—closed clogged roads all over the city. On the road leading north toward the Great Wall, the carbonized hulks of tanks were still warm to the touch. . . . Tank treads had chewed into the asphalt."[57]

People's Liberation Army troops killed on a random basis for the next five days, including attacks against diplomatic compounds and the homes of foreign diplomats.[58] The regime tried to cut the telephone lines in the hotels where most foreign journalists lived to prevent foreign reporters from informing the world about these events. Estimates of casualties range from about three thousand killed and ten thousand or more wounded to those published in the Communist-owned newspapers in Hong Kong, which were that about five thousand people were killed and about thirty thousand were injured.[59]

The regime acted immediately to conceal the number of casualties. It forbade any hospital from providing any information about those who were killed or wounded. The government lied immediately and said there had been no casualties. On June 16, 1989, the spokesman for the government told NBC News that "In the whole process of clearing the Square there was no casualty [sic]. No one was shot down or crushed under the wheels of vehicles. The reports that there was a blood-bath and that many people were crushed were incorrect."[60]

There is consensus among analysts that the Twenty-seventh army group, which had invaded Vietnam in 1979, was the most brutal and responsible for most of the killing. This army was then under the command of General Chi Haotian, who in the 1990s became China's minister of defense. On an official visit to the United States in 1996, General Chi continued the government's line about the Tiananmen massacre, saying in a speech at the U.S. National Defense University that while there had been some "pushing and shoving" during the Tiananmen events, no one had died in the Square itself.[61]

After crushing the peaceful opposition, cleaning up, burning and hiding the corpses and debris, and lying to its people and the world, the next priority for the Chinese regime was to find, punish, and end the influence of all those who had organized on behalf of political democracy. The Party understood that the former Communist investigative reporter Liu Binyan was correct when he wrote in the fall of 1989: "The truth of course is that the uprising was the greatest show of demo-cratic force in forty years of Communist rule in China."[62] Led by the economic pragmatist Deng; the newly designated secretary general of the Communist Party, Jiang Zemin, who became Deng's successor; the veteran hard-liner, Premier Li Peng, who in 1997 became the head of the National People's Congress; and the principal military leaders who would continue in power through the 1990s into the new century, the regime launched a nationwide campaign of political repression.

Estimates are that about forth thousand people were arrested throughout the country and that hundreds, perhaps thousands, were executed in the weeks after the Tiananmen massacre. Thousands of those arrested were put in prison and in forced labor for years.[63] Many received sentences of thirteen years at hard labor; reportedly "sentences were directly related to the amount of contrition they expressed and the number of colleagues they denounced."[64] The government used the results of modernization, an improved and expanded telephone system, to open up special free telephone lines through which people could denounce individuals they consid-ered opposed to the regime or in support of democracy.

A Western reporter speaking Chinese telephoned and found that the lines were not busy. She subsequently learned that many callers, instead of denouncing their fellow citizens, were reporting "the names of two mass murderers, Deng Xiaoping and Li Peng."[65] This reporter felt that was a turning point; unlike the previous years of repression in China when betrayal was the norm, the citizens of China seemed unwilling to collaborate with the regime. However, the massacre, along with the hunt for dissidents and presumed opponents throughout China, did lead to a new fear of the regime. Mann, who was there, said that Tiananmen "terrorized the Chinese population into submission."[66] Hsu concluded that while most city people did not believe the government lies about the events, there was, nevertheless, a return of fear: "People walked through the street but did not talk; they whispered among themselves and occasionally winked at passing foreigners. Laughter, vivacity, openness disappeared from daily life."[67]

The Communist regime in China had made its decision. The hardliners and economic pragmatists, such as Deng, had joined together with the military and decided that no political liberalization would be tolerated. The Chinese Communist Party decided to continue with modernization but to take all necessary means to assure that there would be no political liberalization and no political democracy.

7 China-U.S. Relations after Tiananmen, 1989–1992

"Foreign hostile forces led the [Tiananmen Square] movement with the intention of exterminating us."
—Confidential Chinese Communist Central Committee Document,
May 1990

"Surplus in trade with the United States 'was the money tree that substantively fueled China's economic development.'"
—IMMANUEL HSU, *The Rise of Modern China*, 1995

"[The visit was] an embarrassing kowtowing to a repressive Communist government."
—SENATOR GEORGE MITCHELL, on the message sent by President George H. W. Bush via special emissaries to China, December 1989

"Conduct necessary business with Beijing authorities in workman-like fashion, not with fawning emissaries."
—WINSTON LORD, former U.S. ambassador to China

"Facing blatant interference by the American hegemonists in our internal affairs and their open support for the debilitating activities of hostile elements inside our country and hostile forces outside the mainland and overseas opposing and subverting our socialist system, we must reinforce the armed forces more intensively."
—GENERAL ZHANG WANNIAN, chief of the general staff, 1994

ON GUARD AGAINST "PEACEFUL EVOLUTION"

Many of the senior Chinese Communist leaders believed that the startling setbacks of 1989–1990 resulted from the strategy of "peaceful evolution," enunciated by U.S. Secretary of State John Foster Dulles in the 1950s. Dulles had said the United States should seek to open up as many contacts as possible with the Communist countries and peoples of Eastern Europe in order to encourage the citizens there to undertake a process of "peaceful evolution" away from Communism and toward political democracy. The Chinese Communist hardliners believed and stated repeatedly that the same strategy was being used by the United States against Communist rule in China. To them, this explained the fact that hundreds of thousands of students and workers joined together to call for political democracy in China in the spring of 1989.

The hardliners said that "foreign hostile forces led the [Tiananmen Square] movement with the intention of exterminating us."[1] After June 1989, they "turned increasingly critical of Deng and his policy of opening which they insisted let in poisonous bourgeois ideas that corrupted the minds of the youths and led to the student demonstrations in 1989."[2]

The unraveling of Communism in Eastern Europe and the dissolution of the Soviet Union meant that the threat posed by the United States as the leading democracy and advocate of "peaceful evolution" was far greater than the Chinese Communist leadership had thought ten years earlier, when the policy of opening to the West had been agreed upon. The Chinese Communist Party decided it would be the "Great Wall of socialism," to counter the American conspiracy represented by "bourgeois liberalism" and "peaceful evolution." The Chinese Communist Party would have to be ever alert and vigilant in order to ensure that it too would not be swept from power as had happened so suddenly and unexpectedly in Eastern Europe and the Soviet Union.

Post-Tiananmen Sanctions by the United States, Japan, and Other Democracies
The Tiananmen massacre changed the U.S.-China relationship on both sides. The Chinese regime became much more suspicious and concerned about the effect of the United States on the people of China. In the United States, there was a sudden awakening to the fact that the regime in China remained a repressive dictatorship, which could be exceptionally brutal. Americans saw television coverage and photographs of the massacre and its aftermath. They also saw repeated television scenes rebroadcast from Chinese television of those the regime was persecuting, "in which defendants with shaved heads, weary voices and bruised bodies were marched before judges, who sentenced them to long prison terms or . . . executions."[3] These images created a new realization among the American leadership and public that China was not just a trading partner.

The day after Tiananmen, June 5, 1989, President Bush returned from a visit to Europe where he had given stirring speeches in Poland and Hungary on behalf of freedom. Bush issued a formal statement deploring the "use of force by the Chinese regime," while Undersecretary of State Robert Kimmitt convened a meeting to examine steps the United States could take to indicate disapproval of the actions taken by China.[4] An interagency group met immediately in subsequent days, resulting in a series of recommendations by U.S. Secretary of State James Baker to President Bush, which were accepted. The actions taken by the United States within days or weeks of the Tiananmen Square massacre included the following:

- Suspension of military-to-military relations between the United States and China, which "uprooted the network of military connections with China that had been nurtured for more than 15 years during the Ford, Carter and Reagan administrations;"[5]
- Establishment of a freeze on further military sales to China—this after a decade in which the United States had sold hundreds of millions of dollars worth of "ammunition factories, torpedoes, radar avionics equipment" to the Chinese military;
- Use of existing American legislation to prevent China from borrowing money in the United States;
- U.S. opposition to further lending by the World Bank to China, which had provided billions of dollars to assist in China's development. This prevented the scheduled lending of approximately $2.3 billion to China in 1989–90. The U.S. also opposed hundreds of millions of dollars in loans from the Asian Development Bank and coordinated its positions with Western Europe and Japan.[6]
- The U.S. persuaded Japan to suspend an estimated $6 billion in loans that it had planned to distribute over the next several years; and
- Secretary of State Baker said that the United States would suspend high-level exchanges with China.[7]

At the time that the Bush administration took these actions, Senate Majority Leader George Mitchell (Democrat from Maine) and Representative Nancy Pelosi (Democrat from California) began calling for a change in U.S. policy toward China that would give China incentives to observe human rights and to stop the selling of weapons of mass destruction. As Mann observed, this marked the beginning of congressional initiatives on matters of U.S. policy toward China after eighteen years in which the executive branch had essentially conducted the relationship with virtually no direct involvement by the Congress. This would lead to proposals by Senator Mitchell and Representative Pelosi, joined by other members of the House and Senate from both parties, to set conditions on the renewal by the United States of Most Favored Nation trade status to China—a decision which the United States made every spring and which had not been an issue of controversy until after the Tiananmen Square massacre.

The term "Most Favored Nation" meant that exports from China would enter the United States on the same terms as those of all friendly countries, in spite of the fact that China was a Communist dictatorship and sharply restricted imports from the United States. To prevent the Soviet Union and other pro-Soviet or Communist regimes from obtaining the benefits of trade with the U.S., American law for decades had prohibited granting those countries Most Favored Nation access. President Carter was the first to recommend a waiver of this prohibition for China. Yet despite Tiananmen and the Mitchell-Pelosi proposals, Congress approved the unconditional renewal every year through 2000, when it granted China "permanent normal trade relations."

Another important change that followed the Tiananmen massacre was the political activism of many among the forty-three thousand Chinese students who were then studying in the United States. These students met together and decided that they would seek to show solidarity with their fellow persecuted students in China who had demonstrated for democracy. They would encourage U.S. and Western economic pressure on China; they endorsed a boycott of the Asian Games, which were to be held in Beijing in 1990; and they also urged changes in U.S. law that would make it possible for Chinese students to stay in the United States if they wished rather than returning to the prospect of imprisonment in China.[8]

At the same time as these post-Tiananmen events were unfolding in the United States, President Bush nevertheless recommended that Congress renew China's Most Favored Nation trade access and sent his national security advisor, General Brent Scowcroft, and Deputy Secretary of State Lawrence Eagleburger on a secret mission to meet with Deng and the Chinese leadership in Beijing. The memo of instructions for the trip indicates that the purposes of the trip included telling the leaders in China that "the president intends to do all that he can to maintain a steady course," that the president "wants to manage short-term events in a way that will best assure a healthy relationship over time," and also to inform them that the president is "not the only factor in the American democratic system. The Congress is a coequal branch of government."[9] It is also possible that a purpose of the trip was to assure the continuity of various secret aspects of the U.S.-Chinese security cooperation against the Soviet Union "particularly to keep in operation the clandestine intelligence facilities in China that monitored Soviet missile and nuclear tests."[10]

Upon returning, Scowcroft and Eagleberger reported that Deng and the Chinese leadership had been "as inscrutable as ever." A long-time observer of the relationship believed that the effect of the secret visit was to tell Deng and the Chinese leadership "not to take so seriously what the administration said and did in public response to the Tiananmen Square crackdown."[11] President Bush also demonstrated his desire for continuity in the U.S.-China relationship by approving the renewal of Most Favored Nation trading status for China during each year of his presidency. This was extremely important to China because, as the historian Hsu so succinctly put it, the dollars that China gained from its surplus in trade with the

United States "was the money tree that substantively fueled China's economic development."[12]

In 1990 there was a sharp cutback in lending to China by the World Bank and its associated institutions and by the Asian Development Bank. In mid-1990, the Group of Seven industrial democracies, while deciding to continue this reduction in multilateral bank assistance for China because of the continuing post-Tiananmen political repression, did support loans for "basic human needs."[13] Not long after, it was also decided that they would make loans to China to promote "economic reform" and "environmental improvement." As a result, the value of these loans to China increased steadily in 1991, and in 1992 the amount was 25 percent greater than it had been the year before the Tiananmen massacre.[14] During the four years 1989–1992, China received a total of $26 billion in subsidized loans from the World Bank and the Asian Development Bank.[15]

In July 1991, President Bush formally announced that he would pursue a policy toward China of "constructive engagement," which would include increased contacts with the Chinese government and people and would avoid the isolation of China.[16] Within a matter of months, the United States, Japan, and Europe ended their objections, and loans from international institutions to China resumed as before. However, various prohibitions on the sale of U.S. military and a number of dual-use (military and civilian) technologies to China continued.

From 1989 to 1993, the Commerce Department in the Bush administration "approved hundreds of licenses worth $75 million for the export of sensitive American technologies . . . involved in the development of weapons of mass destruction and the development of the Chinese military."[17] Yet the total value of the U.S. exports was small in comparison to the billions in exports of sensitive technology during the Clinton years. Perhaps one purpose of the Bush administration in continuing these exports to Chinese military entities was to maintain an atmosphere of cooperation against the Soviet Union, which was still viewed as potentially dangerous by both powers. However, according to the careful research of the Wisconsin Project on Nuclear Arms Control, the pace of exports continued even after the dissolution of the Soviet Union in December 1991.

President Bush continued to seek ways of moving toward the improvement of relations with China. In October 1989, the administration gave permission for Chinese officials and technicians to resume work in the U.S. on a $550 million project to help upgrade the technology of China's fighter aircraft.[18] And in December 1989, a month after the opening of the Berlin Wall, President Bush sent Scowcroft and Eagleberger to Beijing on a second visit that would begin in secret but was intended to become public. On that two-day visit, Scowcroft and Eagleberger were photographed in a cordial toasting at a formal dinner with the Chinese foreign minister, where Scowcroft reportedly said: "We believe it is important that we do not exhaust ourselves in placing the blame for problems that exist. . . . In both our societies there are voices of those who seek to redirect or frustrate our cooperation. . . . We must both take bold measures to redirect these negative forces."[19] China wanted to use this high-level visit to press the case for an end to the economic sanctions and for U.S. permission for Chinese missiles to launch U.S. satellites. This would provide China with significant hard currency earnings and technological benefits.

At the same time, China refused to permit Fang Lizhi, his wife, and son, who had taken refuge in the U.S. Embassy immediately after Tiananmen Square, to leave. The only concession China was willing to make was to repeat a promise it had made over the preceding two years not to sell its medium-range ballistic missiles (M-9) to Middle Eastern countries. This repetition of a promise already made led China expert Harry Harding to comment, "How many times do we get to pay for that concession?"[20]

While President Bush sent his message via special emissaries, Deng stated publicly that the U.S. wanted to resume cooperation with China. Senator Mitchell called the visit "an embarrassing kowtowing to a repressive Communist government," and there was wide opposition to the visit.[21] The recently returned former U.S. ambassador to Beijing, Winston Lord, wrote that the U.S. should "conduct necessary business with Beijing authorities in workman-like fashion, not with fawning emissaries."[22]

CHINA AGAIN DEFINES THE U.S. AS THE MAIN ENEMY

For hardliners in the Party leadership, the 1989 pro-democracy demonstrations in Eastern Europe and China proved that the United States posed a mortal threat to the Communist regime. They said the unraveling of Communism in Eastern Europe and the end of the Warsaw Pact showed that the U.S. strategy of "peaceful evolution" had worked. They believed their campaigns in China against "spiritual pollution" and "bourgeois liberalization" in the 1980s had not been assertive enough. As a result, too many of the leaders among students, intellectuals, and workers were attracted by the U.S. example of an open, prosperous society; by the ideas of political democracy; and by the "decadent" aspects of the more individually oriented lifestyle of the West. The Party hardliners believed that this had produced what amounted to a major rebellion in Tiananmen Square and that they had crushed it just in time. They also believed it could happen again, as was seen by the rise of Solidarity from the repression of 1981 to its success in forming a new government in Poland in August 1989.

Further, the U.S. military intervention in Panama in 1989 and the U.S.-led coalition against Iraq in 1990–91, including the use of advanced military technology to defeat an army of hundreds of thousands with hardly any U.S. casualties, showed the enormous military power of the United States.[23] This American military success, resulting in part from the use of advanced military technology, spurred the Chinese regime and the Chinese military to increase its efforts to build up strategic nuclear forces and to modernize its air and naval forces to counter the U.S. in the Pacific region. As the Soviet threat receded with the dissolution of the Soviet Union and the move to normalize relations that had begun in 1989, China shifted from a focus on preparing for a large land war with the Soviet Union on its long borders to the concept of "warfare under conditions of high technology." Chinese hardliners believed that with the Soviet Union unraveling, the United States would no longer be held in check by the Soviet threat. Therefore, the United States would concentrate its energy in attempting to "contain" China to prevent its emergence as a major world power, and also to bring about a "peaceful evolution" to democracy.

After Tiananmen Square, the hardliners insisted on freezing any further economic modernization as the regime focused on political repression and consolidation. This and the sanctions resulted in a significant economic slowdown in China from 1989 to 1991. From the point of view of the regime, the ability of the United States to withhold technological and economic benefits from China and persuade other countries to do likewise illustrated yet another facet of American power that could be dangerous to China and to its future.

These events and perceptions led to a new strategic consensus in China that combined the intention to continue obtaining economic, technological, and scientific benefits from the United States and other capitalist powers while simultaneously viewing the United States as the main enemy at present and into the future. This strategic judgment became evident both through the statements made by the regime leadership in order to inform the Party throughout China, and in the actions of China in the ensuing years. In 1991, a secret document was drafted by the Party and the foreign ministry warning Chinese officials to be careful in all forms of contact with the United States and alleging that the purpose of the United States was to obtain global hegemony (dominance) by making China weaker.[24]

To back up its new concern, China deployed more of its 7,500-mile-range intercontinental ballistic missiles, which are able to reach major U.S. cities (New York and Washington are about 7,200 miles). While two of these missiles had been deployed as of 1989, with a steady increase during the 1990s, the number was estimated to have reached no fewer than twenty-four by 1998.[25] Previously, the Chinese emphasis had been on deployment of its medium-range ballistic missiles aimed at Soviet targets.

At the same time, during the years of the first Bush administration, China continued selling components and expertise for weapons of mass destruction to states sponsors of terrorism. The administration protested, and China made promises to stop but continued with its proliferation activities.[26] In 1991, demonstrating its mastery of a new and complex military technology, China began deploying a solid-fueled, road-mobile, nuclear-armed, medium-range ballistic missile.[27] This missile (designated the DF-21) represented a technological breakthrough for China, both in the use of solid fuel and in its mobility. This meant that it could be positioned in different parts of China to reach a broad range of targets, including U.S. bases in South Korea, Japan, and Okinawa, as well as the U.S. Pacific fleet in the South China Sea and targets in India and along China's borders with Russia and Southeast Asia. Reports indicate that this new mobile missile could be armed with either three smaller warheads ranging from two to six thousand tons, or a single very large nuclear warhead equivalent to about one million tons of TNT, indicating that it would be targeted against cities or large military bases. By 1998, China had deployed an estimated sixty of these missiles on land and twelve additional missiles of the same type were available for deployment on a Chinese ballistic missile submarine, which had made relatively few voyages.[28]

In 1992, Deng, now advanced in age, used his remaining energy to reinvigorate the Four Modernizations and to obtain agreement among the Party leadership that this policy would be pursued. He opposed defining the United States as the enemy, saying that "China and the United States are different in ideology, but there is no conflict between their fundamental interests."[29] Nevertheless, he did not persuade the Party leadership to move away from the consensus that the U.S. was the main enemy.

Called to the Great Hall of the People in Tiananmen Square in early 1994, Party officials from all twenty-nine provinces and regions were assembled in order to learn that the United States was the main enemy. The chief of the General Staff, General Zhang Wannian, told the assembled Chinese leaders: "Facing blatant inter-ference by the American hegemonists in our internal affairs and their open support for the debilitating activities of hostile elements inside our country and hostile forces outside the mainland and overseas opposing and subverting our socialist system, we must reinforce the armed forces more intensively."[30] In other words, China would accelerate the pace of its military modernization to counter the United States.

A member of the elite Politburo Standing Committee said that "according to the global hegemonist strategy of the United States, its main rival at present is the PRC [People's Republic of China]. Interfering in China, subverting the Chinese govern-ment, and strangling China's development are strategic principles pursued by the United States."[31] Later in 1994, a Chinese submarine and jet fighter aircraft approached an American naval task force led by the aircraft carrier USS Kitty Hawk. The controlled Chinese press then criticized the United States for "harassing" and "unreasonably entangling" the submarine and asked why was the United States

Navy in the Yellow Sea, since this was "right in front of China's gate, a long way from the United States?"[32]

During the presidential campaign of 1992, Governor Bill Clinton of Arkansas, the Democratic candidate for the presidency, was highly critical of the China policy of President Bush. He accused President Bush of "coddling dictators from Beijing to Baghdad." After President Bush again renewed the Most Favored Nation trade status of China in 1992, Governor Clinton made a highly critical speech, stating:

> The people of China are still denied the basic rights of liberty. They are denied the right to choose their own leaders. They are still imprisoned for simply calling for democracy; they continue to suffer torture, and cruel, inhuman and degrading punishment . . . as prisoners, some are forced to produce cheap products for exports abroad . . . we still do not know how many individuals the Chinese government have detained or sentenced for their role in the demonstrations for democracy three years ago, but estimates run into the thousands. And the aging leadership remains defiant and unrepentant in its refusal to allow the Chinese people to exercise their basic rights.
>
> Despite promises from the administration of good behavior from the Chinese on nonproliferation, I am still concerned over possible Chinese sales of sophisticated weapons to regimes such as Syria and Iraq. In addition there are reports that they may be providing dual use technology and training to Syria, Iran, Libya, and Pakistan. And China's explosion last month of its largest nuclear test ever should be another strong warning signal that the Bush administration's policy of "constructive engagement" has been a dismal failure.[33]

As President, from January 1993 to January 2001, Clinton would have the opportunity to establish a more effective policy toward China.

8 U.S.-China Relations, 1993–2000

"No you won't [defend Taiwan]. We've watched you in Somalia, Haiti, and Bosnia, and you don't have the will. . . . In the 1950s, you three times threatened nuclear strikes on China, and you could do that because we couldn't hit you back. Now we can. So, you are not going to threaten us again, because in the end, you care a lot more about Los Angeles than Taipei."
> —LT. GENERAL XIONG, deputy chief of China's General Staff, 1996

"I think there is a genuine movement toward openness and freedom in China."
> —PRESIDENT BILL CLINTON, Shanghai, June 1998

"The Chinese government's human rights record deteriorated sharply."
> —U.S. DEPARTMENT OF STATE, Report on Human Rights for 1998

"In the year 2000, China's human rights record 'worsened,' with 'numerous serious abuses' of religious, political, and press freedoms."
> —U.S. DEPARTMENT OF STATE, Report on Human Rights for 2000

During the eight years of the Clinton presidency, the relationship between China and the U.S. was of enormous importance to both countries and received high-level attention. These were the years in which China's international trade grew enormously and more than 40 percent of its exports went to the United States. These were also the years when both powers began to adapt their international policies to the world after the unraveling of the Soviet Union. For both the United States and China, this meant a sharply diminished sense of risk from the former Soviet Union, and its main successor state, Russia.

As a candidate for the presidency, Clinton expressed three major concerns about China: its human-rights abuses; its selling of expertise and components for weapons of mass destruction to state sponsors of terrorism such as Iran, Syria, and North Korea; and, its strategic nuclear military buildup. Taking office in January 1993, President Clinton was immediately involved in discussions with his own party's leadership in the Congress, led by Senator George Mitchell in the Senate and Representative Nancy Pelosi in the House. They wanted to pass legislation setting conditions for the renewal of China's access to the U.S. market, including specific progress in human rights and an end to the sale of weapons of mass destruction. In the spring of 1993, President Clinton agreed to the unconditional renewal of Most Favored Nation trade with China. President Clinton persuaded the Democrats in Congress that he would seek these objectives through diplomatic means and that rather than legislation, a better approach would be for the administration to explicitly establish the conditions that China would have to meet in order to have its access to the U.S. market granted in the spring of 1994.[1] This was done through an Executive Order issued by President Clinton on May 28, 1993, which specified the following conditions China would have to meet before its complete access to the U.S. market would be renewed:

- that China adhere to terms of the UN Universal Declaration on Human Rights;[2]
- that it release from prison the thousands of individuals imprisoned as a result of peaceful free-speech activities in connection with the 1978 democracy wall movement and the Tiananmen Square events of 1989;
- that China comply with a U.S.-Chinese agreement signed in 1992 that no prison labor would be used for the production of products exported to the United States;
- that the treatment of the millions of prisoners in China's prisons and forced-labor camps would be certified as having improved;
- that Tibet's religious and cultural heritage be protected and safeguarded by the Chinese regime;
- that China permit international radio and television broadcasts to its territory.[3]

Clearly, if adherence to these obligations became a condition for China's access to the United States market, a new political era would have begun there. However, after the Tiananmen massacre, the Chinese regime had made another decision: it decided to strengthen its political dictatorship and to use all means necessary to ensure the Communist regime would stay in power. China did not abide by the conditions set by President Clinton and immediately dismissed them as continuing the U.S. strategy of "peaceful evolution" and interference in its internal affairs.

For the United States or any other nation, there is no obligation to admit the products of any country for sale in its own market. The terms of trade are always subject to mutual agreement and mutual negotiation. President Clinton enunciated conditions in 1993 that were an exercise of U.S. sovereignty in deciding when and how products made in China would be admitted to the United States.

Although China made no improvements in its relevant international or domestic activities, in April 1993 the Clinton administration began lifting a number of post-Tiananmen restrictions on trade with China. For example, the administration permitted the U.S. Export-Import Bank to provide subsidized financing and loans for trade with China, and in the summer and fall of 1993 it waived various trade restrictions. As part of the administration's opening to high-technology trade with China, President Clinton agreed in July 1993 that the China Aerospace Corporation would be permitted to earn tens of millions of dollars by launching satellites made by two U.S. corporations, Motorola and Martin Marietta. Government documents revealed in 1998 that part of the reason underlying the approval was to provide incentives for China to stop selling missile technology.[4] This did not succeed, because only a month later, in August 1993, the Department of State imposed limited economic sanctions on Chinese entities that had sold ballistic missiles to Pakistan. Those sanctions were then lifted in 1994.[5] These missiles and their technology would eventually be filtered out to various nations, including North Korea, Libya, and Iran through the Khan Network. This is, of course, in addition to the Chinese government's own cooperation with those nations in this area and is a perfect example of the effects of secondary proliferation.

In the fall of 1993, Clinton told electronics industry executives that he wanted to "tailor export controls to the realities of a post-Cold War world."[6] The electronics and computer industry wanted to increase exports to China. In December 1993, the administration ordered the loosening of restrictions on computer exports so that more advanced computers with a processing speed of up to 67 million theoretical operations per second (MTOPS) could be exported to China.[7] According to reports in the *New York Times* by Jeff Gerth and Eric Schmitt, President Clinton was directly and personally involved in loosening the U.S. export control system.[8]

CHINA REAFFIRMS THAT THE U.S. IS ITS MAIN ENEMY

Despite Clinton's many actions favoring China, the hardliners only saw the threat of "peaceful evolution." In April, 1993, 116 senior officers of the PLA wrote Deng and Party Secretary General Jiang Zemin, calling for an end to China's policy of "tolerance, forbearance, and compromise toward the United States."[9] This and a similar letter sent in May 1993 by other senior military officers expressed strong anti-U.S. views at the senior levels of the military and, in particular, criticized the government for having failed to act more assertively against the decision by President Bush to sell Taiwan 150 jet fighters at the end of his term in 1992.

The secret police and intelligence organizations of China went along with the military in expressing hostility toward the United States. In October 1993, the minister of state security said that the United States "carries out espionage activities by making use of hostile elements, diplomats, and journalists, and exchanges of academic personnel."[10] The next month, senior officials from the Party, the military, and foreign-policy institutions met for eleven days to discuss China's strategy. Bernstein and Munro, quoting from a Hong Kong publication often used to funnel official Party information to the outside world, report that the meeting concluded that the Communist Party of China regards the United States "as its international arch enemy" and that the final report said that in the next years

> the major target of American hegemonists and power politics is China. . . . Its strategy toward China is through economic activities and trade, to control and sanction China and force China to change the course of its ideology and make it incline toward the West; to take advantage of exchanges and propaganda to infiltrate ideology into China's upper strata; to get financial assistance to hostile forces both inside and outside China's territory and wait for the opportune moment to stir up turbulence; to support and encourage Western groups to impose economic sanctions against China. . . . To fabricate the theory of a China threat to Northern Asian countries . . . and to manipulate Japan and Korea to follow American strategy toward China.[11]

That strategy meeting also concluded that China should seek to reestablish a close relationship with Russia. It is worth recalling that many in Chinese leadership had originally been trained in the Soviet Union, spoke Russian and had worked closely with Moscow from 1949 to 1959. The 1993 strategy meeting also proposed that China seek alliances with important Third World countries.[12] The actions of China in the ensuing years have been consistent with these views.

In January 1994, despite these harsh criticisms by the Chinese Communist Party, the Clinton administration relaxed license requirements for the export of telecommunications equipment. In March 1994, at the initiative of the Clinton administration, the Coordinating Committee for Multilateral Export Controls (COCOM) was disbanded. COCOM had been established by all the industrial democracies to limit the export of militarily useful technology to Communist countries. In the ensuing years, this opened the way for a massive outflow of U.S. high-tech exports to Communist China. The Wisconsin Project on Nuclear Arms Control provided an overview of the nearly $15 billion in permitted U.S. high-tech exports to China by the administration. It found that these legal exports could be used to "design nuclear weapons, process nuclear material, machine nuclear weapon components, improve missile designs, build missile components, and transmit data from missile tests. The equipment, by definition, is of great strategic value."[13] Under American law, the Department of Defense was to review the potential strategic and military implications of such high-technology exports, and the Central Intelligence Agency was to determine whether the nonmilitary end user specified by China really existed and used that equipment. In fact, there is dramatic and moving testimony from career U.S. government officials such as Dr. Peter Leitner and Mr. Michael Maloof of the Department of Defense that political appointees in the Clinton administration frequently recommended approval for high-technology exports despite assessments they would be used for military purposes by China.[14] Further, the Department of Commerce, which viewed American business as its constituency and leaned toward approval of virtually all exports, often made too little time available for the effective review of export license applications.

One of the most dramatic cases occurred in 1994, with the export of a very large, machine-tool factory owned by the McDonnell Douglas Corporation, a major U.S. manufacturer of advanced military aircraft and missiles. The Chinese buyer said that these machine tools would only be used for civilian products. But it was later determined that the address to which the strategically valuable machine tools were delivered was a vacant lot near Beijing and that some of these machine tools were "diverted to a facility involved in the production of military aircraft and antiship cruise missiles."[15] This was a case where the Navy, Air Force, and the Defense Intelligence Agency had all objected to the export, but it was approved by the Clinton administration.

While the Clinton administration was attempting to show goodwill to China in 1993–1994 by loosening export restrictions and other actions, the Beijing regime, for its part, began deployment of ballistic missiles opposite Taiwan.[16] Government documents also reveal that the United States had information that China continued its sale of weapons of mass destruction in 1994, including the sale of ballistic missiles to Pakistan. This raised the risk of war between Pakistan and India.[17]

In 1994, China sharply devalued its currency. This made its exports much less expensive and much more competitive in comparison to those of South Korea, Thailand, Indonesia, and other Asian producers. This resulted in a sharp increase in China's export earnings and in its trade surplus with the U.S., because China continued to maintain tight restrictions on access to its market. The devaluation in China reduced the export earnings of neighboring Asian countries friendly to the United States that competed in many of the same product areas in the markets of the industrial democracies. As their hard-currency export earnings declined in 1995 and 1996, China's devaluation set the stage for the very difficult and economically damaging Asian financial crisis of 1997–1999, which required about $100 billion in emergency loans from the U.S.-supported International Monetary Fund.

Clinton's Retreat, 1994

By May 1994, China had met none of the conditions for the renewal of Most Favored Nation trading status specified by President Clinton the year before. Yet many of the American corporations that were exporting to the U.S. from China or wanted to begin doing business with China argued that there was a greater likelihood of improvements in the regime's internal and international behavior if the United States increased its economic relationship with China. They wanted the removal of all conditions on the renewal of Most Favored Nation trade status for China, and this is exactly what President Clinton announced on May 26, 1994. He would renew Most Favored Nation status for China without imposing any conditions. Clinton explained his reversal:

> Will we do more to advance the cause of human rights if China's isolated or if it is engaged in a growing web of political and economic cooperation and contact? I am persuaded that the best path for advancing freedom in China is for the United States to intensify and broaden its engagement with that nation. I believe . . . that there are far more likely to be human-rights advances when it is not under the cloud of annual renewal of MFN.[18]

Since then, this same rationale has been repeated, even though the complete change in Clinton's policy had no positive impact on the actions of the Communist regime. China continued to define the United States as its "main enemy" and continued its proliferation of weapons of mass destruction and military buildup. In addition, China also continued its aggressive and coercive actions in some of its many territorial disputes, and the annual U.S. Department of State reports on human rights showed that political and religious repression became worse.

China had been testing new nuclear weapons since 1992. By 1995, there was an understanding within the United States government that these tests were of powerful, smaller nuclear warheads, indicating significant advances in Chinese capabilities.[19] In July 1995, an individual from China provided the U.S. government with Chinese documents labeled "secret," which confirmed suspicions that Chinese spies had obtained the designs of five of the smallest, most powerful, and most advanced U.S. nuclear warheads. Within a matter of several months, the CIA reached the judgment that this information had been provided at the direction of the Chinese government.[20] During this time, China continued to deploy more intercontinental ballistic missiles that could reach the United States.

The 1995–1996 Taiwan Missile Crisis

During the 1990s, the most visible and dramatic focus of China's international aggression and coercion was the Republic of China on Taiwan. This country had evolved over the years from an authoritarian, very poor country to a pluralist political democracy with a very good standard of living, far above that of mainland China, and with one of the most equitable distributions of income in the world.

The last step in a nearly ten-year process of political liberalization was a free and open presidential election to be held in March 1996.

The Chinese regime had two concerns if Taiwan successfully conducted its first free presidential election and completed its transition to democracy. First, a democratic Taiwan, far more prosperous than China, would be a beacon of freedom for the mainland. Second, this could increase prospects that Taiwan might declare itself an independent state rather than submit to Chinese control.

In early 1995, President Jiang Zemin made a speech that has become known as the "eight point proposal," in which he said that China's policy of "one country, two systems" would guarantee that the people of Taiwan could continue to maintain their "way of life" after "returning to the mainland." The speech also continued the formulation China had used since the establishment of the Communist regime in 1949—that Taiwan is an intrinsic part of China and that no other state should interfere in the matter of "reunification."

Yet Communist China has no more "right" to control Taiwan than North Korea does to control democratic South Korea or the former East Germany had to control West Germany. Taiwan has all the attributes of statehood, including a functioning government, a defined territory and population, the ability to enter into international agreements, and a long history of international diplomatic recognition. Taiwan, with a population approaching 23 million, is larger than two-thirds of UN member states.

On the Taiwan issue, the pattern of the Communist regime is to assert its "right" to what it has taken to calling "China's Taiwan" and then to attempt to coerce the Taiwanese and all other governments into acceding to China's demands. While the U.S. "acknowledged" that "it is China's view" that Taiwan is part of China and has said since 1971 that there should someday be reunification, all U.S. presidents, including President Clinton, repeated that China and Taiwan have to come to a mutual agreement and that the U.S. opposes the use of force by China to take control of Taiwan. This bipartisan consensus was given additional emphasis as U.S. policy by the Taiwan Relations Act of 1979, which was renewed in 1999.

In the summer of 1995, China took a new step in international coercion. To intimidate the people and leaders of Taiwan, China decided in the period July 21–26, 1995, to fire six of its short-range ballistic missiles into an area about forty miles from the capital of Taiwan. The advance notice of these "missile tests" closed the air and sea communication lanes around the island and caused fear in Taiwan.

The response of the Clinton administration to China's unprecedented coercive firing of ballistic missiles was ambiguous. Therefore, China moved forward with further plans to coerce Taiwan, seeking to prevent the March 1996 election. China built up its military forces opposite Taiwan, including its short-range ballistic missile forces. A former Clinton administration official met with Lt. General Xiong

Guangkai and said that China risked a reaction from the United States if it were to attack Taiwan. The General, deputy chief of China's General Staff, responded: "No you won't. We've watched you in Somalia, Haiti, and Bosnia, and you don't have the will. . . . In the 1950s, you three times threatened nuclear strikes on China, and you could do that because we couldn't hit you back. Now we can. So, you are not going to threaten us again, because in the end, you care a lot more about Los Angeles than Taipei."[21]

The effects of China's intimidation against Taiwan were felt immediately on Taiwan. The stock market in Taiwan went down sharply—by about 33 percent—after the military exercises and missile firings began. At the same time, airlines serving Taiwan had to change the routes of scheduled flights and "Taiwan's fishermen kept their boats in port" for some weeks.[22] When asked in public whether the United States would come to the aid of Taiwan if China attacked, the Department of State was ambiguous in its response, notwithstanding the fact the Taiwan Relations Act is explicit in requiring the United States to assist Taiwan if it were to come under attack or blockade from mainland China. However, we now know that President Clinton acted to appease China by sending a secret letter to President Jiang of China in August 1995, inviting him for a state visit to the United States and assuring China that the U.S. would also resist any effort Taiwan might make to become independent.[23]

Clinton's retreat on his proposal for conditions on Chinese trade access and the secret letter received by the Chinese Communist leadership during their annual policy retreat and vacation at a seaside resort in August 1995, seem to have convinced them that the United States would offer no real resistance if China stepped up efforts to coerce Taiwan into accepting its conditions for what China called "reunification." China continued deploying short-range ballistic missiles opposite Taiwan, which could be armed with conventional, nuclear, electromagnetic warheads or neutron warheads—these kill people but leave property intact. China had stolen the design for the neutron warhead from the United States and successfully tested it in December 1984. China announced this publicly in 1995 as part of the intimidation of the leadership and people of Taiwan. (This was an example of China secretly deploying new weapons, which it later publicly disclosed.)[24]

In November 1995, China established a "war headquarters," transforming the "Nanjing Military Region" into the "Nanjing Theater," where the vice chairman of the Central Military Commission, General Zhang Wannian, established the Military Command Headquarters Targeting Taiwan (MCHQTT).[25] President Clinton seemed to ignore these facts, because late in 1995 he instructed his secretary of commerce to take more action to "streamline and liberalize," that is, reduce controls on U.S. high technology exports to China.[26]

However, the Chinese threats may have played a role in the decision of the United States to send the aircraft carrier *Nimitz* through the Taiwan Straits in December 1995. This was an unusual route, ostensibly due to "bad weather."[27] Most likely it was an attempt to send a message to the Chinese Communist leadership rather different than the one contained in Clinton's secret August 1995 letter. Neither Clinton's overtures to Jiang, nor commercial benefits, nor the aircraft carrier deployment had any effect on Chinese actions. China continued deploying ballistic missiles near Taiwan, scheduled large-scale military maneuvers for February–March 1996, and continued threats against Taiwan as the March 1996 presidential election approached.[28]

CORPORATE INTERESTS AND NATIONAL SECURITY

During this time, President Clinton continued his policies to help U.S. corporations expand their business with China. In a trip to China with the U.S. secretary of commerce in 1994, Bernard Schwartz , the head of the Loral Corporation, obtained permission from the Chinese government for satellite transmission rights for a mobile telephone network that could be "worth billions" to his company.[29] Following that trip, the White House deputy chief of staff wrote a memo to President Clinton urging that he invite Schwartz and other potential political campaign donors to coffee at the White House, to "impress on him the need to raise three million dollars in the next two weeks" for Democratic Party candidates in the November 1994 congressional elections.[30]

In January 1995, Bernard Schwartz wrote President Clinton asking that he shift authority to approve satellite exports to China from the State Department to the Commerce Department, where he undoubtedly expected approvals to be given more readily. The reason U.S. corporations wanted to launch their satellites in China is that the costs were considerably less and, therefore, potential profits would be much greater.

In April 1995, the secretary of state established an interagency committee to examine the issue, and in October 1995, the departments of State, Defense, and the CIA all recommended against any change.[31] But on February 6, 1996, in the midst of the potential confrontation with China over its coercion of Taiwan, President Clinton overrode his administration's unanimous recommendation and signed waivers permitting the launch in China of four satellites owned by Loral and Hughes,[32] despite new information that China continued to transfer missiles to Pakistan and nuclear technology to Iran.[33]

Also in January 1996, the Clinton administration further reduced restrictions on the export of high-performance computers to China. Within two years, more than six hundred high-performance computers had been sold to China, many of which increased China's ability to develop advanced nuclear weapons, missiles, and high-technology weapons.

There were three important benefits to China from these Clinton decisions. First, the rocket used by China to launch satellites was in essence the same as its long-range intercontinental ballistic missile. Therefore, the more often these were launched, the more practice China had in the launch of long-range ICBMs, which led to improved reliability.[34] Second, China gained hundreds of millions of dollars in hard-currency earnings from the fees for these launches. This money would be used by China to purchase other high technology that could help its strategic and advanced weapons military buildup. Third, China gained friendly relations with important U.S. corporations, which it knew would lobby in the United States for further administration actions permitting China to buy military-related high technology.

Clinton's decisions did nothing to reduce China's declared opposition to the U.S. or persuade it to stop coercing Taiwan. During the first week of March 1996, China held military maneuvers opposite Taiwan, involving an estimated 150,000 troops. Given months of threats, it was possible that China might go beyond these large-scale maneuvers and seize control of a number of islands under Taiwan's jurisdiction but close to the Chinese mainland. China also announced that it would again launch its ballistic missiles within forty miles of Taiwan's northern and southern cities. This again led to the closing of air and sea lanes around Taiwan and caused fear. "Taiwan's stock market fell again, and people on the island lined up at banks to change their money into dollars. Taiwan's foreign exchange reserves began dropping at the rate of 300 to 500 million U.S. dollars a day."[35]

During the week of March 3, 1996, as China increased its coercion of Taiwan, President Clinton publicly announced that he decided to reverse the decision of his secretary of state and the interagency committee and shift authority to review the export and launch of U.S. satellites from the State Department to the Department of Commerce. While Clinton was considering this reversal, Loral's Bernard Schwartz donated $150,000 to the Democratic Party. After Clinton's shift of approval authority to the Department of Commerce, which directly benefited Schwartz, he donated $300,000 between April and December 1996, for a cumulative total of $600,000 before the November 1996 presidential election.[36] When the possible connection between the fact that Bernard Schwartz was the largest single contributor of soft money to the Democratic Party in the 1996 presidential election cycle and the decisions favoring Loral that President Clinton had personally made came under investigation, President Clinton said that "campaign contributions never solely influenced my decisions on these kinds of issues."[37]

On Friday, March 8, 1996, China fired three ballistic missiles north and south of Taiwan near two major ports and cities, and one directly over the capital, Taipei.

After the first three missiles were fired, Secretary of Defense Perry, together with National Security Advisor Anthony Lake and Secretary of State Christopher, met with a senior Chinese national security official who was then visiting Washington, General Liu Huaqiu. Perry told him that there would be "grave consequences" if any Chinese missiles were to hit Taiwan. This was "universally understood as a code for a military response" by the U.S.[38] Perry said that as a former U.S. Army artilleryman, he understood that the "routine tests" were in fact being used to "bracket" Taiwan for actual attacks and considered this extremely reckless.[39]

On Saturday, March 9, Secretary of Defense Perry convened a group of officials to review the escalating crisis. This was the second time China had used the firing of its ballistic missiles coercively. In the effort to prevent the people of Taiwan from freely electing their president, there was a risk that China might take further direct military action in the time remaining before the election.

To prevent a miscalculation or further use of force by China, the United States immediately sent two aircraft carrier battle groups to the Taiwan area. As Secretary of Defense Perry said later, "We did not want this to escalate. We considered sending one carrier, but decided that wasn't strong enough."[40] To make the purpose of this largest naval deployment to Asia since the Vietnam War crystal clear to the Communist leadership, Perry said publicly at the time: "Beijing should know, and this U.S. fleet will remind them, that while they are a great military power, the strongest, the premier military power in the Pacific is the United States."[41] A senior Chinese military leader responded with fury that if any U.S. aircraft carrier were to enter the Taiwan straits, it would never emerge.[42] On March 13, before the aircraft carriers arrived, China fired another ballistic missile near Taiwan. Once the two aircraft carrier battle groups arrived, they remained near Taiwan. They did not enter the Taiwan straits but their presence ended the escalating Chinese military threats.

Within days, the sense of crisis passed, and the people of Taiwan elected a new president in free, fair, and open democratic elections, thereby completing their peaceful transition to political democracy. This was a beacon of peaceful democratic change for the people of mainland China.

Then in April 1996, it was revealed that the United States had evidence that China continued to sell nuclear-weapons-related technology to Pakistan. In a departure from its usual denials, China admitted these sales. According to U.S. law, this should have triggered specific economic sanctions, but none were applied.[43] That same month, the presidents of China and Russia met in Beijing and declared that they were going to establish a "trustworthy strategic partnership." This was the beginning of their emerging alignment against the United States. It was also in April 1996 that the U.S. and Japan signed a joint declaration on security, intended to strengthen their existing security alliance.

Also during that time, the deputy national security advisor to President Clinton, Samuel Berger, was informed by a courageous intelligence professional, Notra Trulock, that the administration was doing too little to investigate recently confirmed Chinese nuclear espionage, nor was it acting to prevent the further theft of nuclear weapons secrets by China.[44] By then, the U.S. government knew that China had stolen the designs for the most advanced U.S. thermonuclear warheads, including the very small, powerful W-88 warhead, which the United States used in some of its missiles with multiple thermonuclear warheads. The administration now also knew that China had not only stolen the designs for these weapons, but it had tested nuclear devices that had characteristics resembling the most advanced new small warheads developed by the United States after years of effort and billions of dollars in expenditures.[45] Remarkably, Berger testified to the U.S. Congress three years later that he had not mentioned this important information to President Clinton until July 1997, some fifteen months later. President Clinton, for his part, waited another seven months to issue a directive requiring more strict security procedures at the nuclear weapons laboratories of the United States.[46]

However, China illegally obtained U.S. military technology not only by spying but also from U.S. corporations. In February 1996, a Chinese Long March rocket failed and destroyed a satellite that was to have been launched for the Loral Corporation. This led to a process of consultation whereby Loral and the Hughes Corporation illegally "identified for the PRC the true cause for the failure as a particular element of the Long March guidance unit and provided the PRC with technical assistance which might be useful not only for the PRC's commercial and military space launch programs, but for ballistic missiles as well. In so doing, Loral-Hughes deliberately acted without the legally required license and violated U.S. laws."[47] These illegal actions followed previous episodes in 1993 and 1995 when U.S. corporations provided illegal technical information for improvements that helped China deploy multiple warheads on each missile.[48]

CHINA AND THE 1996 PRESIDENTIAL ELECTION

Shortly before the 1996 presidential election, allegations surfaced that China had given illegal campaign donations to the Democratic Party through intermediaries. In the case of Mr. Johnny Chung, a business and political consultant, the Democratic National Committee decided to return $366,000 because it could not verify the sources of his donations. There were reports that these came from various Chinese government officials or entities. Not long after that money was returned, Mr. Bernard Schwartz of the Loral Corporation decided to donate $366,000 to the Democratic National Committee.[49]

As the 1996 presidential election approached, there was overwhelming evidence that a number of Chinese government-related sources used intermediaries to make various illegal donations to the Democratic party or to the Clinton reelection effort.[50] One dramatic example was testimony by one intermediary that the chief of Chinese military intelligence, General Ji Shengde, gave $300,000 in cash to be denoted to the Clinton reelection campaign, saying "We like your president."[51] Very active in this process of providing money for Clinton reelection was Lt. Col. Liu Chaoying, whose father, General Liu Huaqing was a member of the Chinese Politburo Standing Committee (the inner circle of rule) and vice chairman of the Central Military Commission. This was the same general Deng had brought out of retirement in 1989 to improve military support for Jiang as he moved toward the succession. General Liu also had responsibility for missile sales abroad. It is documented that his daughter was involved in providing at least $80,000 in illegal cash contributions to the Democratic Party and, in fact, was photographed with President Clinton at a Hollywood fundraiser in July 1996. Throughout this time, the "automatic" U.S. economic sanctions on U.S. firms doing business with the 250 involved Chinese organizations were not implemented.

The Clinton administration knew that these continuing Chinese sales included eight publicly reported shipments of weapons of mass destruction components to Iran and Pakistan.[52] The United States had also discovered that China and Pakistan were colluding together to evade detection.[53]

On November 5, 1996, the day of President Clinton's reelection, the Department of Commerce published—two hundred days after the event—the regulations implementing Clinton's March 1996 decision to shift approval for satellite launches to the Department of Commerce. On November 24, 1996, Presidents Clinton and Jiang met at the APEC summit meeting in Manila and agreed that they would exchange state visits in the next two years. China declared that it "does not, did not, and will not transfer any nuclear weapons related technology or missiles to any country," but a few days later China announced that it was going to continue its "nuclear cooperation" with Pakistan.[54] The Chinese disavowal of its proliferation was false, while the statement of "nuclear cooperation" with Pakistan was true and two years later resulted in Pakistan having nuclear weapons. The successful completion of these weapons and the expertise in the illicit transfer of technology would provide key lessons and contacts for the Khan network.

In early 1997, the Department of State issued its annual *Report on Human Rights* for 1996. This said that China remained a repressive Communist dictatorship and that human-rights abuses had become more severe as China used intimidation, exile, prison terms, or other forms of detention to repress all independent groups. President Clinton admitted that his policy of "constructive engagement" had not brought about progress on human rights.[55] China responded to the human-rights report by saying that it contained "malicious attacks and lies about China's human-rights condition."[56]

In February 1997, the *Washington Post* reported that a Justice Department investigation revealed that there had been unlawful efforts by the Chinese government to send contributions through foreign sources to the Democratic National Committee prior to the 1996 presidential election. President Clinton said that the allegations should be "thoroughly investigated," and China said these were a "fabrication."[57] Congress thereupon decided to expand its investigations into improper political fundraising to include allegations that the Chinese government had attempted to provide funds improperly for the Clinton reelection campaign.[58]

Soon after, the Chinese foreign minister and minister of defense visited the United States. China's foreign minister denied any Chinese involvement in the U.S. political campaign.[59] In May 1997, as in every year during his two terms in office, President Clinton recommended to Congress that Most Favored Nation trade status for China be extended for another year.

In July 1997, Hong Kong peacefully reverted to the control of China. The terms of the agreement negotiated with the United Kingdom in 1984 were that the political and economic institutions of Hong Kong would essentially remain unchanged for fifty years after reunification. China summarized this commitment to Hong Kong as "one country, two systems" and had made the same proposal to Taiwan, promising that the institutions within Taiwan would remain unchanged. The United States and the United Kingdom both said they would observe closely whether China carried out its treaty commitments in Hong Kong. But, even before taking full control, China violated its promise to leave the institutions of Hong Kong unchanged by establishing a new legislative assembly and a new executive that would be controlled by its handpicked allies, mostly wealthy businessmen with major investments in China. In this way, China assured its control over the political governance of Hong Kong. There was no U.S., British, or other international protest. These unilateral Chinese actions have stood, although China has permitted Hong Kong to continue functioning economically much as it had before.

THE U.S.-CHINA SUMMITS OF 1997 AND 1998

The visit of President Jiang Zemin to the United States in October 1997 was the first time a Chinese leader had visited since 1985. In welcoming President Jiang, President Clinton said:

> The emergence of a China that is stable, open, and nonaggressive, that embraces free markets, political pluralism and the rule of law, that works with us to build a secure international order—that kind of China, rather than a China turned inward and confrontational, is deeply in the interests of the American people . . . we have the opportunity to build a new century as China takes its rightful place as a strong and stable partner in the community of nations, working with the

United States to enhance peace and prosperity, freedom and security for both our people and for all the people of the world. We have to take that chance.[60]

Later, referring to conversations in which both leaders had expressed their differing views on human rights and other issues, President Clinton said:

We also have fundamental differences, especially concerning human rights and religious freedom. I am convinced the best way to address them is directly and personally, as we have done yesterday and today, as we will continue to do until this issue is no longer before us, when there is full room for debate, dissent, and freedom to worship as part of the fabric of a truly free Chinese society. . . . In the information age, the true wealth of nations lies in the people's ability to create, to communicate, to innovate. Fully developing these resources requires people who feel free to speak, to publish, to associate, to worship without fear of reprisal. It is China's extraordinary human resources that will lift it to its rightful destiny of leadership and widely held prosperity in the 21st century . . . On this issue [human rights] we believe the policy of the [Chinese] government is on the wrong side of history. There is after all, now, a Universal Declaration of Human Rights.[61]

President Jiang expressed his different views in direct language. After the summit in Washington, DC, President Jiang traveled to a number of cities across the United States, meeting with business and civic leaders having an interest in relations with China. In December 1997, China issued regulations establishing government censorship of the Internet to make unlawful "harmful information" or anything on the Internet that would "defame government agencies."[62] Thereby, China again showed that it could take modern technology and control it in a way that would secure the priorities of the regime.

During 1997, China continued selling components for weapons of mass destruction and advanced weapons to Iran and other terrorist-sponsoring states. In June 1997, Secretary of Defense Cohen told China that its continued sales of anti-ship cruise missiles to Iran could have negative effects for China as well as the United States by halting oil shipments from the Middle East in the event of a war there.[63] Yet, the administration continued to overlook Chinese sales of weapons of mass destruction to state sponsors of terrorism and pressured government employees who sought to analyze these issues objectively. One career Defense Department official who was pressured to conclude that China was not continuing its nuclear proliferation activities said that the administration wanted to approve the sale of nuclear power equipment following the October 1997 summit and under U.S. law could only do so if President Clinton certified that China had stopped its proliferation activities.[64]

In April 1998, Secretary of State Albright was still referring to the mythical "strategic partnership" between China and the United States proclaimed by the Clinton administration. Yet by May 1998, public revelations of China's continuing weapons of mass destruction sales activities included the following:

- the judgment by the Defense Department that the thirty-four ballistic missiles China provided Pakistan in 1992 were now operational and could be armed with nuclear warheads;
- the fact that in 1996 China had provided [Pakistan] a complete production factory for the M-11 ballistic missile;
- China was discussing the sale of telemetry equipment for missile tests and sending missile technicians to Libya to assist with that country's missile program.[65]

These and many similar revelations led Secretary of State Albright to inform Congress that President Clinton would raise U.S. concerns about these Chinese activities at the forthcoming summit meeting with President Jiang.

The Clinton-Jiang Summit, June 1998

It was in this setting that from June 24 to July 3, 1998, President Clinton visited China, traveling to a number of regions and scenic places in the country and holding several discussions with President Jiang. However, there was no major breakthrough on U.S. concerns about China's sales of weapons of mass destruction or their human-rights violations; the summit events consisted mainly of ceremonial occasions. Speaking in Shanghai, President Clinton said: "I think there is a genuine movement toward openness and freedom in China, which obviously as an American and an American president I hope will continue and increase and which I believe is right—morally right—and I also think that it is good for China."[66]

The day before, Clinton had given President Jiang something that had been requested of American presidents by China since 1972—a public statement of the "Three Nos" on Taiwan, which had been secretly promised by Dr. Kissinger and President Nixon at the opening of relations with China. At a radio discussion in Shanghai, President Clinton explicitly stated that the United States did not support independence for Taiwan, nor a "two China policy," nor did it believe that Taiwan should be a member of any international organization that required statehood. This public statement represented a major success for President Jiang, both internationally and in the context of the Chinese Communist leadership. It is not evident what, if anything, the United States received from China.

As he was departing China, President Clinton made a series of statements in Hong Kong that were surprising to many, saying:

I believe there can be, and I believe there will be [democracy in China] ... clearly China is changing, but there remain powerful forces resisting change, as evidenced by continuing governmental restrictions on free speech, assembly, and freedom of worship ... what I would like to see is the present government, headed by this president and this premier, who are clearly committed to reform, ride the wave of change and bring China fully into the twenty-first century and basically dismantle the resistance to it.[67]

Clinton went on to say that President Jiang had the imagination necessary to transform China from a single-party Communist state to a pluralist democracy and "there is a very good chance that China has the right leadership at the right time."[68]

These statements seemed all the more out of touch with reality because of Jiang's frequent, public declarations to the Chinese leadership and people that China must maintain Communist one-party rule at all costs and that the current regime would never permit pluralist democracy. Clinton also totally ignored the facts presented by the Department of State annual reports on human rights, which documented the intense, brutal, and increasing political repression in China during these years.

For example, on June 25, 1998, just as Clinton began his visit, courageous individuals had established the China Democracy Party and publicly began efforts to expand membership and obtain legal status for it to exist and to compete with the Chinese Communist Party. During Clinton's visit, many of these individuals seeking to exercise their rights of free speech were arrested, sometimes almost within sight of the visiting American delegation. One American commentator wrote:

Clinton's summit visit to China was in fact a trip dedicated to changing American perspectives and politics ... to get the American public at large to accept the ... uncritical view of China firmly entrenched in the ranks of American business leaders and academic specialists ... [the administration] agenda is to change the way the U.S. thinks about a Chinese leadership that still refuses to change the way it thinks about the United States and democracy.[69]

It had been customary for American presidents and senior officials who visited China to stop in Japan either before or after the visits and discuss U.S. policy with the leadership of America's closest Asian ally. This time, the Chinese government publicly said that it did not want President Clinton to visit Japan during his trip to China. Also, the Chinese government insisted publicly for weeks before the visit that President Clinton had to be received officially in Tiananmen Square, the very place where the tragic massacre had taken place in 1989. President Clinton gave in to those Chinese conditions before his trip, and publicly stated the "Three Nos" on

Taiwan. Once again, the U.S. gave China what it wanted and received nothing, except the "opportunity" to continue adding to China's annual trade surplus earnings. These gains have gone toward the modernization of the Chinese military, which in turn embolden the Chinese leadership.

China's War Plan Delivered to the U.S., 1999

Each August, the leadership of the Chinese Communist Party gathers in the seaside resort of Beidaihe to plan for the future and to relax. One of the perennial issues discussed is Taiwan. In 1999, the Party had two concerns. First, President Lee Teng-hui of Taiwan had said on July 10, 1999, that further discussions on relations between Taiwan and China should occur on a "special state to state" basis.[70] That had elicited immediate and vehement protest from the Chinese government because it seemed to suggest that Taiwan was trying to define a "two China" situation, which Beijing rejected. Another concern was that Taiwan would hold a second round of democratic presidential elections on March 18, 2000, and the candidate of the Democratic Progressive Party, Chen Shui-bian, who had long favored an independent Taiwan, seemed to have a chance of winning.

For many years, China had said that it would use force immediately should Taiwan declared independence. To back up these threats, China accelerated the build up of missile and military forces so they could be used for an attack or for a blockade if Taiwan elected a new president who would dare to declare Taiwan an independent state, not subject to "reunification."

In August 1999, the Central Military Commission of the Party produced an analysis of the Taiwan situation for both the military and civilian leadership of China. It discussed how China could wage war to take control of Taiwan and specifically described the means, including nuclear threats and attacks, China would use against the United States should it intervene to protect Taiwan. This document offers insight into the thinking of the senior Chinese military leadership. It is confident and assertive, arguing that China would defeat the United States in any conflict that might occur about Taiwan. This document declares:

> Based on strategic considerations, the CMC [Central Military Commission] has decided to disclose . . . some information on strategic weaponry so that the U.S. will exercise some caution in decision making and be aware that it would have to pay a price if it decided to intervene in a military conflict. The purpose is to prevent the U.S. from becoming deeply involved, even if a war becomes unavoidable, so that the losses on both sides of the Taiwan straits will be minimized throughout the war. The main point is deterrence, which is the test for a peaceful solution.[71]

This explains why in 1995 China provided the United States with the information that it had obtained the designs for a number of its most advanced thermonuclear weapons.

This CMC analysis is, in effect, a war plan. It begins by stating that the delay in "unification" has damaged China's "interests and dignity" and "has long since become a trump card for the anti-China forces and deteriorated into a malignant tumor that hinders the development of our motherland. Playing the Taiwan card and using it to contain China is a manifestation of the old Cold War thinking . . . and an important means of opposing China by a handful of politicians in the U.S. Congress who cling desperately to the old Cold War thinking."[72] The document continues: "Lee Teng-hui's comment on 'state to state discussions' [involves his putting] his foot across our bottom line, actually providing us with solid ground to achieve unification by military power."[73] The military analysis makes clear that the "obstacles to the resolution of the Taiwan issue" have been erected by the United States, while "Japan has a complicated attitude toward our handling of the Taiwan issue."[74]

The Chinese military analysis is explicit in stating that "bias and prejudice" on the part of Western governments, specifically the United States, have led to a misunderstanding of "the ability of our armed forces to fight a modern war."[75] The "warfare model" that China will use is one of "instant, large scale, and fully extended operations," which means that there will be a "first fatal strike against Taiwan," destroying its ability to "organize effective resistance."[76] China would then take total control of Taiwan "before the U.S. intervention" and then "concentrate our forces to fight the U.S. Based on this scenario it is impossible for the U.S. to force us to fight on two fronts to protect Taiwan."[77]

This explained the buildup of ballistic missiles across from Taiwan, which can be equipped with any one of four types of warheads: high explosive, neutron (which kill people but do not destroy property), nuclear, or electromagnetic/radio frequency warheads (which destroy or disrupt anything electronic, including communications, computers, and power lines and grids). China has tested these four types of warheads and has supplies of all four types but would be least likely to use nuclear warheads because of radioactive fallout and levels of blast damage. Also, most Chinese nuclear warheads are very large and China wants to take control of Taiwan with its high-technology production facilities, scientists, engineers, and skilled labor mostly intact.

The Chinese military analysis proclaims the "certainty of winning the war should it break out"[78] and points out that all operations would be carried out from its own territory, which has strategic depth, and that China "would completely destroy the attacking enemy [United States] forces from the sea and their auxiliary bases."[79] This would refer to U.S. air/naval forces and the bases from which they come in Japan,

Okinawa, South Korea, and elsewhere in the region. These bases are within range of China's medium-range ballistic missiles, which could be equipped with nuclear or high-explosive warheads. The Chinese military also write that they are "willing to sustain major losses," but "if the United States loses thousands of men under our powerful strikes, the antiwar sentiment within their country would force the U.S. government to take the same path as it did in Vietnam."[80] This Chinese military view is reinforced by its perception that China defeated the United States in Korea, where the conflict ended at the status quo, and also that China helped North Vietnam defeat the United States. Turning to the issue of nuclear weapons, the military analysis states:

> Unlike Iraq and Yugoslavia, China is not only a big country, but also possesses a nuclear arsenal that has long since been incorporated into the state warfare system and played a real role in our national defense. During the last crisis across the Taiwan straits, the U.S. tried to blackmail us with their aircraft carriers, but when their spy satellites confirmed that our four submarines which used to be stationed at Lushun harbor had disappeared, those politicians addicted to the Taiwan card could not imagine how worried their commanders were.
>
> In comparison with the U.S. nuclear arsenal, our disadvantage is mainly numeric, while in real war, the qualitative gap will be reflected only as different requirements of strategic theory. In terms of deterrence, there is really no difference in practical value. So far we have built up the capability for our second and third nuclear strikes and are fairly confident in fighting a nuclear war. [This means China's long-range weapons can kill twenty million or more Americans if necessary, provided the U.S. has no missile defense.] The Communist Party of China has decided to pass through formal channels this message to the top leaders of the U.S. This is one of the concrete measures we will take to prevent the escalation of war. . . .
>
> We are fully prepared for prolonged warfare. Judging each by his domestic situation, the U.S. will not be able to keep up for long. Historically, China has experienced prolonged warfare against foreign invasion and the People's Liberation Army has the ability to safeguard the peaceful production facilities of the peoples of all nationalities of China during the war. We do not want to fight a prolonged war but this is because our country's basic principle is preserving peace . . . not because we are afraid. Prolonged warfare will work to our advantage and enable us to defeat the enemy, which will be one of our options to win the war in extreme circumstances.
>
> China has certain abilities of launching strategic counterattack and the capacity of launching a long distance strike. It is not a wise move to be at war

with a country such as China . . . the U.S. military will even be forced to [make] a complete withdrawal from the East Asia region as they were forced to withdraw from Southern Vietnam.[81]

The Central Military Commission (CMC) document concluded by demonstrating a systematic approach to geostrategy. First, it mentioned that President Jiang Zemin would meet with the leaders of Russia, Kyrgyzstan, Kazakhstan, and Tajikistan in Bishkek in late September 1999. The agreements reached there to "expand cooperation in the fields of security" would "not only eliminate security concerns in the rear . . . but also serve to ensure our exchanges with the outside world by land routes during the war . . . in case we are forced to fight a full-scale war against the U.S."[82] This has been the reason for Chinese efforts to increase strategic cooperation with Russia leading to the formal alliance signed in 2001.

The CMC also noted that President Jiang Zemin would meet President Clinton at the APEC summit in New Zealand in September1999 and would inform the United States of China's views on the Taiwan issue. Presumably this meant providing President Clinton with a copy of this war plan and summarizing the threat in a clear statement made face to face.

Yet, there was no visible response from the Clinton administration to either the China-Russia meeting or to the explicit nuclear war threats made by the CMC. Rather, on November 6, 1999, the United States and China announced that they had reached agreement on terms for China's accession to the World Trade Organization.[83] On December 20, 1999, Macau returned to Chinese sovereignty under the terms of a previously negotiated agreement with Portugal. And in December 1999, the Chinese minister of defense was quoted as saying, "war is inevitable" with the United States, suggesting that the agreement on the trade issue, of enormous economic and military advantage to China, had little effect on the strategic thinking of the military or the regime.

CHINA'S SECOND THREAT OF NUCLEAR ATTACK ON THE U.S.

The new century and the new millennium began with China continuing to increase its ballistic missile and military forces opposite Taiwan and with the announced arrival of a new Russian-built guided missile destroyer, which included advanced antiship missiles capable of being armed with nuclear warheads. On February 1, 2000, the House of Representatives passed the Taiwan Security Enhancement Act by a vote of 341–70. This mandated the administration provide additional defensive weapons systems for Taiwan in view of the continuing buildup of Chinese military forces and the threats being made by China. China strongly protested the Act as interference in its internal affairs. On February 18, 2000, a U.S. delegation led by

Deputy Secretary of State Strobe Talbott met Chinese officials in Beijing. Talbot reportedly said, "President Clinton is determined to further promote U.S.-China relations along the lines of a constructive strategic partnership in the remaining months of his tenure" and that the administration "opposed the proposed Taiwan Security Enhancement Act and would prevent it from becoming law."[84]

Virtually at the same time as the high-level U.S. delegation was in Beijing, Jiang Zemin, speaking as secretary general of the Communist Party, told the Party leadership to "get ready to liberate Taiwan." This was the first time in more than twenty years that the term "liberate" had been used for Taiwan, and it was reported that Jiang also instructed the Party to be prepared in all areas required to support warfare.[85] At the same time, the Central Military Commission of the Communist Party established a new operational headquarters in Fujian province, immediately opposite Taiwan. On February 11, 2000, this headquarters reportedly conducted for the first time a "routine military exercise," using submarines to block the Taiwan strait. It also assumed command of submarines and the missiles in the region. The combination of submarines, Chinese-manufactured destroyers with antiship missiles, and the Russian-built *Sovremmenny* missile-armed destroyer would, according to mainland sources speaking through the Hong Kong press, "form a powerful fleet, responsible for the strategic blockade of the Taiwan straits and for dealing with U.S. aircraft carriers."[86] These Chinese military preparations were communicated through Chinese-language Hong Kong newspapers to the leadership and citizens of Taiwan. China's intended purpose was again to intimidate the voters of Taiwan so that they would not choose the candidate of the pro-independence party, whom polls showed leading in the final weeks.

On February 21, 2000, the Chinese government issued a White Paper which said that China would use force against Taiwan not only if it declared independence or were occupied by a foreign power, but also if Taiwan "indefinitely postponed negotiations on reunification."[87] This was a new threat that had not been mentioned to U.S. Deputy Secretary of State Talbot. A few days later, *Liberation Army Daily*, the main official newspaper of the Chinese military, repeated the military threats against Taiwan and went on to directly threaten the United States with a nuclear attack. The Chinese military newspaper said that if the United States were to defend Taiwan, China could use its "long range" missiles to inflict "serious damage" on the United States—an obvious reference to the 7,500-mile-range ICBMs that carry large thermonuclear warheads capable of destroying an entire city.[88] At the same time, it was reported that the Chinese military had received $7 billion in extra funds in 1999 so that it could either buy or produce additional advanced "killer weapons systems," presumably including nuclear weapons.[89]

President Clinton responded to these serious threats by saying, "We'll continue to reject the use of force and we'll continue to make clear that the issues between

Beijing and Taiwan must be resolved peacefully and with the consent of the people of Taiwan."[90] The head of the Taiwan Navy, Admiral Lee Jye, said, "China has so many missiles that antimissile defense and air defense is our highest priority . . . in the end, Communist China wants to be a superpower. We [on Taiwan] just want to exist."[91] A senior Department of Defense official stated that any use of force by China would "cause incalculable damage to China." A leading Taiwan newspaper said about this pattern of threat that China "thinks Taiwan will surrender to its power. It does not understand such threats will be counterproductive . . . the Chinese Communist war of words is the same mistake it made in 1996 when it intended to intimidate Taiwan voters with missiles."[92]

As the March 2000 Taiwan presidential election approached, the United States deployed a carrier battle group in the vicinity of Japan, able to reach Taiwan quickly. It was said privately that this was to deter China "from conducting threatening wargames," as occurred in 1996.[93] On February 29, 2000, Admiral Dennis Blair, Commander of U.S. forces in the Pacific, made a visit to Beijing. The official Chinese news agency reported that Admiral Blair was "warned" that the Clinton administration should stop Congress from passing the Taiwan Security Enhancement Act and that China "resolutely opposed" any linkage between an end to China's threats against Taiwan and U.S. support for China's entry into the World Trade Organization or for the grant of Permanent Normal Trade Relations to China.[94] In addition, as an indication of China's sense of military confidence and its feeling of control over the South China Sea, the Chinese military leaders are reported to have told Admiral Blair, "to his face," that should U.S. aircraft carriers again sail close to the Taiwan straits as they had in 1996, the People's Liberation Army would take decisive acts—meaning attack them. In this report through a Hong Kong newspaper, an authoritative Chinese source was quoted as saying that this direct confrontation shows that the Chinese military is "psychologically ready to fight a battle against the United States at any cost."[95] It should be noted that the U.S. carrier battle group that was positioned near Japan did not in fact go near the Taiwan straits as the presidential election took place in Taiwan.

On March 18, 2000, the people of Taiwan chose their new president in free and fair elections. Despite the threats from China, the winner of the election was Chen Shui-bian, a member of the opposition movement which had long competed with the Nationalist Party. Immediately upon winning the election and again in his inaugural address on May 20, 2000, President Chen Shui-bian stated that Taiwan would not declare independence and would not hold a referendum on independence. He also said "both sides possess enough wisdom and creativity to jointly deal with the question of a future one China."

The official mainland China news agency called the inaugural speech "evasive and unclear" and criticized President Chen for a "lack of sincerity."[96] Unlike the situation in 1996, the military threats from mainland China did not subside after the election. Instead, during April and May 2000, in the very weeks that President Clinton was urging the United States Congress to grant China permanent access for its exports to the U.S. market, the Communist regime continued a large number of threatening military maneuvers in the vicinity of Taiwan.

For example, from April 19 to 23, 2000, along the south and east China coast, more than one thousand jet fighters and three regiments of missile forces, with more than eighty ballistic missiles were involved in maneuvers that the Chinese military called "one attack and two prevents." These simulated a military attack on Taiwan and then missile strikes against the military forces of the United States and Japan to prevent their aiding Taiwan.[97] Leaked reports indicated that Chinese generals were urging the political leadership to agree to an attack against Taiwan, presenting the Politburo with petitions, some of which were ostensibly written in blood by soldiers willing to "sacrifice their lives for the cause of liberating Taiwan." The same reports indicated that many factories were increasing the production of weapons and military supplies and that in visits to the coastal Taiwan region of China opposite Taiwan, the most senior general, Zhang Wannian and Chi Haotian, minister of defense, were emphasizing the military use of civilian facilities.[98]

As the Clinton administration urged the U.S. House of Representatives to approve Permanent Normal Trade Relations with China, there were reports of additional missile units being transferred to areas near Taiwan to participate in a possible military attack against the island democracy.[99] At about the same time, Chinese naval ships surrounded the main islands of Japan, just outside the twelve-mile limit. They were believed to be gathering military intelligence on U.S. and Japanese bases, including the exact coordinates for missile targeting. Japan formally protested these activities.[100]

None of these events had any impact on the view of the Clinton administration that Permanent Normal Trade Relations for China should be approved. On May 24, 2000, the House of Representatives gave its approval by a vote of 237 to 197.[101] In July 2000, Secretary of Defense William Cohen visited China for discussions, just as it was reported that Russia had finished a second *Sovremmenny*-class destroyer with advanced antiship missiles that had been bought by Beijing.[102]

After Permanent Normal Trade Relations—Clinton Says No to Missile Defense

Reports from the August 2000 annual vacation and policy gathering of the Communist Party leadership indicated that a focal point of discussions was President Jiang's view that China must intensify its efforts to develop what he called "killer weapons." Presumably, by these he meant nuclear and other mass-destruction weapons that China could use to deter the United States and any other country which might seek to oppose its international activities.[103] Additional funds would be made available in the military budget for this category of weapons.

In September 2000, there were reports of sharp increases in the persecution of Christian religious groups other than those under the control of the Chinese government. The regime had enacted a law against "evil cults" in the summer of 1999 to use in its repression of the Falun Gong exercise-meditation movement. In the summer of 2000, it began applying this to the underground Chinese Catholic Church—for example, in one province twenty-four individuals were arrested including a priest who was severely beaten.[104] A total of fourteen Christian groups were branded "evil cults" and the Hong Kong Information Center for Human Rights and Democracy reported that on August 23, 2000, that 130 members of one Protestant evangelical group were arrested in one Chinese province.[105] It is estimated that there are millions of Christians in underground churches, called "house churches." They wish to practice their religion peacefully. The Chinese constitution permits freedom for five religions: Buddhism, Taoism, Islam, Protestantism, and Catholicism, but these must be practiced within organizations controlled by the government. This round of religious persecution and repression illustrated the Party's continued determination not to permit the people of China to participate in any institutions outside its control.

For nearly two years, China had waged an intense diplomatic campaign against the U.S. deploying a limited national missile defense or an Asian regional missile defense. On September 1, 2000—the sixty-first anniversary of the day that Nazi Germany began World War II, President Clinton announced:

> I have decided not to authorize deployment of a national missile defense at this time ... we should ... not move forward until we have absolute confidence that the system will work and until we have made every reasonable diplomatic effort to minimize the cost of deployment and maximize the benefit ... the best judgment of the experts who have studied this question is that if we were to commit today to construct the system, it would most likely be operational by 2006 or 2007. If the next president decides to move forward next year, the system still could be ready in the same time frame. ...
>
> We need to move forward with realism, with steadiness and with prudence, not dismissing the threat we face or assuming we can meet it while ignoring our overall strategic environment, including the interests and concerns of our allies, friends and other nations.[106]

This decision was unwise, given China's explicit threats of nuclear attack delivered repeatedly since 1996 and given the known fact that Chinese-backed Stalinist North Korea was developing intercontinental ballistic missiles and, as is now known, was cheating on their promise to halt work on nuclear weapons.

President Putin of Russia commented that Clinton's decision was "well thought out and responsible . . . [and that it would] lead to strengthening strategic stability in the whole world and will raise the United States' authority in the eyes of the international community, especially on the eve of the millennium summit."[107] The Embassy of China in the United States, through its spokesman said "this is certainly a good sign of caution" by the United States.[108] China probably believed its threats had intimidated Clinton and the U.S.

While Vice President Gore supported the decision, the Republican candidate for the presidency, Governor George W. Bush, was critical. He said that the postponement "underscores the fact that for seven years, the Clinton-Gore administration has failed to strengthen America's defenses. I welcome the opportunity to act where they have failed to lead by developing and deploying effective missile defenses to protect all fifty states and our friends and allies."[109]

To mark the new millennium, the United Nations invited the heads of state of all member nations to convene in New York in early September 2000. More than 150 heads of state accepted, and this offered opportunities for many informal summit meetings. Presidents Jiang Zemin of China and Putin of Russia undoubtedly were pleased that their joint effort against the limited U.S. national missile defense program had succeeded to date.

President Clinton and President Jiang had not met for a year, and they decided to meet in New York on September 8, 2000, for a discussion of trade and nonproliferation issues. This was an attempt to obtain yet another promise that China would end its missile exports to Pakistan. National Security Advisor Samuel Berger said, "We have to get this resolved and we are seeking further commitments on restraint."[110] In that conversation, the United States would also urge "flexibility, restraint and dialogue" in China's dealings with Taiwan. Jiang met with Clinton and made no comment or commitment on the nonproliferation issues. Instead, China had what it wanted: Permanent Normal Trade Relations (PNTR), with Clinton's full support.

President Jiang used the UN millennium summit to gather more international support to persuade the United States not only to postpone but also to cancel all forms of missile defense.[111] At the meetings, President Clinton tried to persuade Jiang that neither the limited national missile defense nor the Asian regional missile defense were directed against China.[112] That was not the Chinese view.

China continued to sell weapons of mass destruction expertise and components to Iran, North Korea, Libya, and Pakistan, as reported by the CIA on January 10, 2001. Nevertheless, the Clinton White House in its last days, announced that it would significantly relax controls on the export of U.S. high-performance computers to China, the sixth time controls were loosened.[113]

By the end of the Clinton presidency, it could be said that China had achieved virtually all of its major objectives with the United States. China continued to have open access to the U.S. market for the largest portion of its exports, thereby earning huge hard-currency surpluses that could be used for economic and military modernization. Despite China's military actions and threats, President Clinton consistently supported the annual unconditional renewal of Most Favored Nation status and thereby waged a vigorous and successful political campaign to obtain congressional approval for China's unconditional and permanent access to U.S. markets. The United States also agreed to the one-sided favorable terms for China's admission to the World Trade Organization. On human rights, China continued its political and religious repression and continued to insist any discussion of human rights in China was intervention in its internal affairs.

China signed or even ratified various international human-rights commitments during the Clinton years and was at times willing to engage in a dialogue with the United States on human-rights issues. However, none of these had any effect on its actual practices—aside from encouraging the occasional release of a few particularly well-known individuals who were being held in forced-labor camps for expressing their hopes for democracy and human rights. On proliferation of weapons of mass destruction, China made many promises but continued doing most of what it had been doing and wanted to do throughout the Clinton years. The decision of President Clinton to postpone national missile defense could well have been perceived by China as yet another major success against the United States and against the Clinton administration.

Perhaps the best summation of China and the United States in the Clinton years might be the observation of an American political leader: "The administration's policies have led the Chinese leaders to believe they are free to take whatever actions they please without a meaningful reaction from the United States."[114] Clinton said this in 1992 while criticizing the China policy of President George H. W. Bush.

9 A New Congressional Approach to China

"America's China policy should aim to bring freedom, human rights, and the rule of law, religious and political freedom, free trade and free markets."

—House Republican Policy Committee,
U.S.-China Relations: A Policy for Freedom, 1997

"China poses a threat to the U.S. as a significant proliferator of ballistic missiles, weapons of mass destruction, and enabling technologies."

—Rumsfeld Commission Report, 1998

"China has been a long time major proliferator of weapons of mass destruction materials and technologies . . . moreover the Chinese leaders have a very poor record of living up to their commitments to the U.S. and in the name of national sovereignty they resisted U.S. efforts to put in place any methods to verify their compliance with bilateral or international agreements."

— DR. GORDON OEHLER,
former director of the CIA Nonproliferation Center, 1998

The November 1994 congressional elections resulted in a Republican majority in the House of Representatives and Republican control of Congress for the first time in forty-four years. The dramatic events and revelations in U.S. relations with China in 1995 and 1996, especially the Chinese firing of ballistic missiles near Taiwan and the need to deploy U.S. carrier battle groups to deter further coercion of Taiwan in March 1996, led the Republican leadership in the House of Representatives to become increasingly concerned with the single-minded commercial focus of the Clinton administration's China policy.

Representative Christopher Cox, the Chairman of the Republican House Policy Committee, with the full support of the House leadership, took the unusual step of introducing a resolution summarizing a number of serious concerns about current U.S. policy toward China. The resolution urged the various committees of the Congress, within their jurisdiction, to enact legislation that would establish the basis for a comprehensive and constructive U.S. policy toward China. This resolution passed in the House by an overwhelming bipartisan vote of 411 to 7 on June 7, 1996. The result a year later was a series of eleven bills in the House of Representatives and one combined bill in the Senate, introduced under the leadership of Senator Connie Mack (Republican from Florida), Chairman of the Senate Republican Conference, and Senator Tim Hutchinson (Republican from Arkansas), which together defined a "policy for freedom" toward China.[1] The purpose of these legislative initiatives in the words of the House report which brought all of the legislation together was that:

> America's China policy should aim to bring freedom, human rights, and the rule of law, religious and political freedom, free trade and free markets. For our longstanding relationship with China can only reach its full potential when its people enjoy the freedoms we cherish—freedoms which increasingly flourish along China's own borders. And America's China policy should aim to promote peace and security for China and all of its neighbors—the essential precondition for further economic, political, and social progress in all of the region. . . . The Chinese people have repeatedly shown their strong support for these common goals. It is time for the United States to enshrine them in law.[2]

The proposals for legislation were grouped in three broad areas. Under promoting human rights, the proposals sought to assure the funding necessary to enforce the ban on importation of products made by slave labor—to prevent China from using the millions of people in forced-labor camps to produce products for sale in the United States. There were legislative initiatives calling for prohibitions on travel to the United States of individuals in China involved in religious persecution or forced abortion, and there was a proposal to increase by a factor of six the number of U.S. Foreign Service personnel at the Beijing U.S. embassy involved in monitoring human rights. The reports criticized the overwhelming focus of the U.S. embassy in China on commercial and trade issues.[3]

To promote freedom and free trade, the House Republican Policy Committee suggested expanding the broadcast time and reach of Radio Free Asia, ending subsidized below-market-interest loans from multilateral development organizations to China and preventing Chinese Communist military-controlled corporations from operating in the United States. The proposed legislation would also authorize the president to "monitor, restrict, seize the assets of, and ban" Chinese military-owned companies in the United States because of their involvement in the use of slave labor, spying, and the transfer of weapons of mass destruction.[4]

In the third area, ensuring U.S. security, the Republican congressional initiative called on the Clinton administration to enforce the Iran/Iraq Nonproliferation Act of 1992, under which the president is required to impose economic sanctions on entities in any country that transfer "destabilizing numbers and types" of advanced conventional weapons or any weapons of mass destruction to Iran and Iraq. The House Policy Committee report pointed out that from 1994 to 1997, "Communist China has transferred at least sixty C-802 antiship cruise missiles to Iran, but the Clinton administration refuses to apply the Act's sanctions."[5] Some of these same "antiship" cruise missiles were fired by Saddam Hussein at Kuwait City during operation Iraqi Freedom.

Another proposal, in view of the coercive missile firings by China in 1995 and 1996 that came "within 40 miles of Taiwan's largest population center . . . blockaded both ends of the Taiwan strait as well as Taiwan's commercial airspace," recommended that the administration "help Taiwan develop and deploy an effective theater missile defense system."[6] Another of the House Republican Policy Committee proposals was a requirement that the administration issue classified reports to Congress and public reports to the American people concerning "Communist Chinese espionage within the United States, including industrial spying and commercial theft, propaganda and intelligence efforts and attempts to manipulate American elections."

By November 1997, virtually all of the initiatives proposed by the House Republicans had passed the House with large bipartisan majorities. Some also passed in the Senate and were enacted into law, but most of these legislative proposals were not passed by the Senate before the end of the congressional session. Therefore, consideration would have had to begin anew when the next Congress convened in January 1998. Although the entire set of proposals was not enacted into law, a number did become law. These included the Freedom from Religious Persecution Act, which was enacted in 1998 and which applied worldwide but had its origin in concerns about the persecution of religious believers in China.[7]

Congress also enacted a number of reporting requirements that were intended to assure that the executive branch provided timely information to Congress and the public on issues that were of concern to the majority in Congress. These included reports to Congress on:

- Chinese espionage activities in the United States;
- Chinese advanced technology to modernize its military;
- the military balance between China and Taiwan; and
- the activities by China, Russia, and other states to transfer weapons of mass destruction and or components to hostile countries.

In addition, in 1998 Congress enacted legislation to overturn President Clinton's decision to have the Department of Commerce review the export of U.S. satellites to China; the legislation returned that authority to the Department of State so that security issues would be part of the consideration. Further, within the terms of the Defense Authorization Act, Congress required that the administration establish a China Analysis Center at the National Defense University that would provide objective analysis of the strategic, military capabilities and intentions of Communist China, with a focus on the extent to which these posed a threat to U.S. forces and allies. These actions were in addition to congressional investigations into illegal donations to American election campaigns including from the Chinese government, as well as to the bipartisan Cox Committee on national security concerns. Despite these efforts by the Republican majority in the U.S. Congress to introduce an emphasis on freedom and realism into U.S. policy toward China, President Clinton and his administration essentially ignored these aspects and continually worked to grant China more economic benefits.

CONGRESSIONAL INVESTIGATIONS

Continuing its rapid growth, China's trade surplus with the United States reached $48 billion in 1997. At the same time, the United States was selling China hundreds of high-performance computers, directly useful in its military industries, and billions of dollars in other high technology with direct military applications. The most specific outcome of the October 1997 summit meeting was a U.S.-China agreement on nuclear energy cooperation, which set the stage for President Clinton's certification in January 1998 that China had provided "clear and unequivocal assurances" that it was not helping any state to acquire nuclear weapons.[8] But in fact, CIA reports required by Congress show that the administration knew China was continuing to deliver nuclear weapons components to Iran, among other countries.[9]

In February 1998, Clinton gave permission for the Loral Corporation to provide the kind of advanced assistance to the Chinese rocket program it had already done illegally in 1996. This undermined the ongoing federal investigation of Loral's actions. Not long after, Loral chief Bernard Schwartz sent the Democratic National Committee an additional $55,000 contribution.[10] And not long after that, China announced it would launch five Loral satellites. This was worth many millions of dollars in fees for China and potential profits in the hundreds of millions of dollars to Loral through the year 2002.[11]

These events and many revelations and allegations in the media all contributed to decisions by the U.S. Congress to investigate several aspects of the relationship between China and the Clinton administration. On March 5, 1998, the House of Representatives opened hearings on the issue of China's attempts to influence U.S. elections, specifically the 1996 presidential election.[12] Then, in June 1998, the House established the bipartisan Select Committee on U.S. National Security Concerns with the People's Republic of China, under the chairmanship of

Representative Christopher Cox. It would focus on China's theft and acquisition of nuclear secrets and other advanced military technology.[13]

In the first few months of 1998, press reports indicated that China had added six additional long-range ICBMs to its arsenal, and the CIA reportedly estimated that thirteen were targeted at U.S. cities.[14] In March 1998, the United States discovered China's intention to secretly sell large amounts of uranium-enrichment material useful in producing nuclear weapons to Iran. This was in direct violation of promises made by Jiang at the October 1997 summit with Clinton.[15]

The consequences of the continuing sale by China of components, technology, and assistance in the production of nuclear weapons were dramatically demonstrated in May 1998 when India detonated three nuclear devices, the prelude to a nuclear weapons capability. India stated it needed nuclear weapons and missiles because of concerns about China and Pakistan. Within a matter of days, Pakistan also conducted nuclear tests, a large step toward having nuclear weapons. These two countries had fought three wars in the past and remained in a state of high military tension because of a territorial dispute in the Kashmir region. For India and Pakistan to have a combination of nuclear weapons and ballistic missiles posed the danger of a regional nuclear conflict that could cost the lives of tens of millions of people. It also posed the risk of a wider nuclear war, should China decide to support Pakistan openly in a confrontation with India.

China had rejected a U.S. offer to increase commercial and scientific space cooperation in return for China's promise to end missile exports to Iran, Syria, and other countries not members of the Missile Technology Control Regime.[16] During congressional hearings on administration policy toward China, the former director of the nonproliferation center at the CIA, Dr. Gordon Oehler, told the Senate: "China has been a longtime major proliferator of weapons of mass destruction materials and technologies . . . moreover the Chinese leaders have a very poor record of living up to their commitments to the U.S. and in the name of national sovereignty they resisted U.S. efforts to put in place any methods to verify their compliance with bilateral or international agreements."[17] Following that testimony, Senator Jesse Helms, chairman of the Senate Foreign Relations Committee, said, "The administration has sought to shield China and U.S. satellite vendors from the effects of U.S. sanctions"[18] that should have been imposed because of China's continuing WMD sales.

The Rumsfeld Commission

Only weeks after Clinton's return from his June 1998 summit in China, the Commission to Assess the Ballistic Missile Threat to the United States, chaired by former Secretary of Defense Donald H. Rumsfeld (who would again serve as secretary of defense beginning in January 2001), reported its findings to the United

States Congress. The commission was established by Congress in 1997[19] and was composed of independent citizen experts who had received the support of the secretary of defense, the director of Central Intelligence, and other government agencies, which provided full access to relevant classified information. Part of the reason that Congress sought to establish the commission was a concern that the intelligence estimates of the CIA understated the imminence of the ballistic missile threat from countries such as China, North Korea, Iran, and Iraq.

Regarding China, the commission concluded that it was modernizing its long-range missiles and nuclear weapons in "ways that will make it a more threatening power in the event of a crisis."[20] The commission also concluded that China "poses a threat to the U.S. as a significant proliferator of ballistic missiles, weapons of mass destruction, and enabling technologies."[21]

Concerning North Korea's intercontinental ballistic missile, the Taepo-dong II, the commission said "a test flight could be conducted within six months of the decision to do so."[22] This contrasted with the view of the CIA that it would be a matter of several years before that North Korean ICBM could be flight tested. The commission also concluded that a "light payload version of North Korea's new long-range ballistic missile, the Taepo-dong II, could reach as far as 6,000 miles, putting at risk U.S. territory in an arc extending west from Phoenix, Arizona to Madison, Wisconsin."[23] The commission judged that North Korea had developed and deployed a ballistic missile with a range of approximately eight hundred miles that could "threaten Japan, South Korea and U.S. bases in the vicinity of North Korea."[24] This missile, the No-dong, was, in the view of the commission, "operationally deployed long before the U.S. government recognized the fact. There is ample evidence that the North Korean government has created a sizable missile infrastructure and therefore it is highly likely that considerable numbers of No-dongs had been produced."[25]

Since the United States intelligence organizations had such difficulty in assessing the North Korean medium-range ballistic missile program, the commission stated that "the U.S. may have little warning prior to the development of the Taepo-dong II. North Korea also has an active program for the development of nuclear weapons, and in the view of the Commission, possesses biological weapons production and dispensing technology, including the capability to deploy chemical and biological weapons on their missiles."[26] Therefore, "North Korea, also poses a major threat to American interests and thus to the United States itself . . . it is a major proliferator of the ballistic missiles it possesses [as well as of] missile, technology, technicians, transporter-erector-launchers (TELs), and underground facility expertise—to other countries of missile proliferation concern: Iran, Pakistan, and others."[27]

The concerns raised by the commission report on the capacity of North Korea to develop an ICBM quickly and secretly were validated almost immediately. In August 1998, to the apparent surprise of the U.S. and Japanese governments, North Korea fired a six-thousand-mile-range Taepo-dong II ballistic missile over the territory of Japan. North Korea said that this actually had been an effort to launch a satellite into orbit. The North Korean launch raised deep concerns in Japan about its vulnerability to attack by the belligerent and repressive Communist regime in North Korea. This North Korean missile launch led to serious consideration and work on the establishment of a regional missile defense among Japan, South Korea, and the U.S., and increased pressure on the Clinton administration to move toward a national missile defense. This was not the sequel to the U.S.-China tourism summit of 1998 that had been expected by the Clinton administration.

Since 1994, China had ostensibly been working with the United States, South Korea, and Japan to find ways to reduce the likelihood that North Korea would produce nuclear weapons. The findings of the commission pointed to Chinese aid for the North Korean ballistic missile program and also to North Korea's actions as a secret intermediary for the transfer of Chinese weapons of mass destruction that it sought to conceal or deny. In 1999, the Chinese minister of defense, General Chi Haotian, said that China and North Korea were as close as "lips and teeth."

Report of the Bipartisan Committee on China

On January 3, 1999, the House of Representatives Select Committee on National Security and Military/Commercial Concerns with the People's Republic of China submitted its top-secret report to the House and to the president. After many months of negotiations with the administration, a declassified version of the report was released to the public in May 1999. As a result, we know that the investigative work of the committee documented the Chinese theft of secrets about advanced U.S. nuclear weapons, and missile and space technology. This practice intensified during the years of the Clinton administration but had been going on since the 1970s.[28] The dramatic findings about China's successful theft of nuclear and military secrets led a bipartisan group of American leaders to express concerns about the implications for U.S. national security. The Clinton administration requested that the CIA undertake its own assessment of the facts and their implications and provide a report to Congress. In April 1999, the CIA reportedly informed the Congress that "as a result of espionage, China had obtained significant classified nuclear weapons information" from the United States.[29]

At the same time, in early 1999, there were reports that China was further increasing its ballistic missile buildup opposite Taiwan, begun in 1994, and also that China was building military facilities on some of the Spratly Islands in the South China Sea.[30] A further issue involving U.S. relations with China was the increasing revelation and discussion of the evidence uncovered by the Senate Committee chaired by Senator Fred Thompson (R-Tennessee) and the House Committee chaired by Rep. Dan Burton, both of which investigated illegal Chinese donations to the Democratic National Committee and the 1996 Clinton presidential campaign. These donations were provided directly by Chinese government sources and by other individuals who allegedly worked on behalf of China.[31]

These disturbing revelations also came at the time when President Clinton faced a Senate trial on impeachment, voted by the House of Representatives in December 1998. China-related national security issues added to the sense of crisis surrounding the Clinton presidency. On February 12, 1999, the Senate vote did not reach the required two-thirds that would have removed President Clinton from office. This dramatic Clinton political crisis, which had gone on for more than a year, was over just as the Serbian dictator Milosevic began the brutal murder and expulsion of Muslims in the Kosovo region.

The NATO air campaign against the Milosevic regime in Serbia began in late March 1999 and was vigorously opposed by both China and Russia. Nevertheless, in early April 1999, Prime Minister Zhu Rongji became the first prime minister of China to visit the U.S. since 1984. Arriving in the midst of widespread public and congressional attention to Chinese military espionage and illegal Chinese funding of the Democratic National Committee, Zhu said with emphasis, "It is not the policy of China to steal so-called 'military secrets' from the United States."[32] He denied any illegal funding of U.S. political candidates by China but said that he would urge his government to make an investigation of this issue. Prime Minister Zhu went on to explain that China believed it had the right to use force against Taiwan and remarked that "Abraham Lincoln, in order to maintain the unity of the United States and to oppose the independence of the southern part, had resorted to the use of force and had fought a war for maintaining the unity of the United States."[33] This visit demonstrated clearly that economic pragmatists and those seeking an expansion of the role of private economic organizations in China, such as Prime Minister Zhu, nevertheless fully supported both military action against Taiwan and Chinese military spying.

Soon after Zhu's return from his American visit, a peaceful and sudden sit-in demonstration was staged in Beijing by more than ten thousand members of an exercise-meditation group called the Falun Gong. This was done near the Zhongnanhai, the living quarters and offices of top government and Party officials, and it took the regime by surprise.[34] Within a matter of weeks, China outlawed the movement and began nationwide repression that involved the arrest of thousands accused of being Falun Gong members.[35] Since membership in the Falun Gong movement was estimated in the millions, including members of the Communist Party and government officials, the Party instituted a series of required indoctrination meetings for all Party members at which the Falun Gong was criticized and condemned. All Party members had to renounce any participation and denounce those they knew who were involved. The persecution of the Falun Gong began to take on some of the characteristics of the vicious campaigns in the Mao era, illustrating once again how quickly the Party could revert to its violent ways.

The Clinton administration issued pro forma protests. These were ignored by China, as it ignored or countered all concerns expressed by the United States about human rights. The Department of State Human Rights Report for 1998, said, "The Chinese government's human-rights record deteriorated sharply" pointing specifically to the repression of the China Democracy Party and all those associated with it.[36] Typical of Clinton administration comments on human rights were those of Secretary of State Albright, who in a 1999 visit to China said that while the Clinton administration is "very disturbed" by what is going on (meaning political repression), it must be understood that the United States nevertheless has "a multifaceted relationship with the Chinese . . . it is very important for countries such as China which has great responsibilities and is a hugely important country to be able to really benefit by the free participation of all of its people."[37]

During the NATO air campaign to prevent mass deportations and killing in Kosovo, China sided with Russia in the UN Security Council in opposing these U.S./NATO actions, arguing that they were counter to international law because they had not been approved by the Security Council. As will be discussed later in greater detail, this was an extremely dangerous time during which some elements within Russia clearly were considering moving toward a large-scale covert or perhaps even open military assistance effort for the Milosevic regime. Fortunately, President Yeltsin decided not to give military support to Milosevic.

However, before that happened, on May 7, 1999, U.S. aircraft accidentally bombed the Chinese embassy in Belgrade, Yugoslavia, killing three and wounding a number of other persons. This led to the Chinese regime inciting mob attacks against U.S. and NATO embassies and facilities in Beijing and throughout China. It also led to strong condemnations by China, the termination of China-U.S. military-to-military relations, and China's decision to end "cooperation" on human-rights and nonproliferation issues.[38] Following those dramatic events, President Clinton apologized to China on several occasions for the accidental bombing, ordered an investigation, and agreed to pay a mutually negotiated indemnity to the families of the Chinese victims.

A few weeks later, on May 25, 1999, the unclassified version of the bipartisan House Select Committee report on Chinese spying was released to the public. The report captured nationwide attention as it became clear that China had stolen the designs and secrets of seven advanced U.S. nuclear warheads. China had also engaged in a large number of other illegal activities through which it had successfully obtained technology useful to its military systems. The committee judged these systems enabled China to "design, develop, and test strategic nuclear weapons sooner than would have otherwise been possible."[39] The following is a brief summary of the Select Committee's findings.

The Select Committee found that Communist China had "stolen design information on the United States' most advanced thermonuclear weapons . . . that the PRC's next generation of thermonuclear weapons currently under development will exploit U.S. thermonuclear weapon information . . . PRC penetration of our nuclear weapons laboratories continues and almost certainly continues today."[40] This stolen information included the design information for the neutron bomb, which only Communist China has deployed; and design information on six other U.S. nuclear warheads, five in the current U.S. nuclear arsenal, including the very small, light and destructive W-88 warhead used on U.S. Trident submarine-launched ballistic missiles.[41] The United States learned about the theft of this warhead in 1995. The committee also concluded that stolen U.S. secrets "gave the PRC design information on a par with our own . . . the PRC has leaped, in a handful of years from 1950s-era nuclear capabilities to the more modern thermonuclear weapon designs. These modern thermonuclear weapons took the United States decades of effort, hundreds of millions of dollars and numerous nuclear tests to achieve."[42]

In May 2001, it was reported that China was preparing to conduct "covert nuclear testing" using "special containment equipment from Russia" to test its version of the stolen W-88 thermonuclear warhead.[43] This test would help China move toward multiple warheads on its missiles and also violated its declared 1996 nuclear test moratorium.

MISSILE AND SPACE TECHNOLOGY: The select committee determined that "Communist China has stolen U.S. missile technology and exploited it for the PRC's own ballistic missiles . . . [and] has proliferated such military technology to a number of other countries, including regimes hostile to the Untied States."[44] To illustrate the negative effects of such successful spying, the committee also noted that "currently deployed PRC ICBMs targeted against the United States are based in significant part on U.S. technologies illegally obtained in the 1950s."[45]

ANTISUBMARINE WARFARE: The Cox Select Committee found that during the late 1990s, "U.S. research and development on electromagnetic weapons technology had been illegally obtained by the PRC as a result of successful espionage. Such technology, once developed, can be used for space based weapons to attack satellites and missiles [and] to threaten U.S. submarines."[46] China's successful launch of an astronaut into orbit around the earth in October 2003 provides evidence that it could soon have the means to use such new weapons from space.

It is worth recalling that the United States learned about China's theft of U.S. nuclear weapons secrets in 1995 and that Samuel Berger, then deputy assistant to the president for national security affairs was briefed specifically on this matter by Mr. Notra Trulock of the Department of Energy in the spring of 1996. Nevertheless, despite four years of notice to the Clinton administration, the bipartisan select committee concluded that as of January 1999: "Despite repeated PRC thefts of the most sophisticated U.S. nuclear weapons technology, security at our national nuclear weapons laboratories does not meet even minimal security standards."[47] President Clinton indicated variously that he had been briefed on the latest nuclear espionage problems that became known in 1995 either in mid-1997 or early 1998.[48] A Presidential Decision Directive was issued in July 1998 to improve security at the nuclear weapons laboratories—therefore the finding nearly a year later that the security situation still did not meet "even minimal standards" was cause for continuing concern.

The bipartisan report said in January 1999 that four years after learning that the Chinese had stolen the designs of at least five advanced nuclear warheads (1995 to 1999), the Clinton administration had launched a serious investigation into only one case and had not yet investigated the others. Further, the report concluded that successful Communist Chinese espionage in obtaining "nuclear test codes, computer models, and data from the United States . . . could further accelerate its nuclear development . . . in conjunction with high performance computers already acquired by the PRC, the PRC could diminish its needs for further nuclear testing to evaluate weapons and propose design changes."[49]

The House Select Committee also reported that "Loral and Hughes provided valuable additional information that exposed the PRC to Western diagnostic processes that could lead to improvements in the reliability of all PRC ballistic missiles."[50] Further, these two U.S. corporations had undertaken these illegal actions because they expected future sales of satellites to China or to those serving the market in China, and they hoped to reduce the cost of their future satellite launches in China.[51] A Department of Defense damage assessment concluded that as a result of the activities of these two corporations, "U.S. national security has been harmed."[52] In 1997, the Department of Justice decided to investigate these illegal actions and to bring the activities of the Loral Corporation to a grand jury. In 2002, Loral paid a fine for having illegally transferred missile technology to China and in 2003 declared bankruptcy.[53]

For its part, China contended that the Cox Report was false and a series of lies.

In a July 1999 refutation, China said that since it already had developed the atomic bomb and the hydrogen bomb, "it is quite logical and natural for it to master the neutron bomb technology through [our] own efforts."[54]

The White House issued a formal statement in contrast to the administration's passivity on these issues, which said:

> The administration is deeply concerned about the threat that China and other countries are seeking to acquire sensitive nuclear information from the U.S. national laboratories . . . the administration agrees with the Select Committee on the need to ensure that the launch of U.S. manufactured civilian satellites by China or any other foreign country does not inadvertently transfer military technology.
>
> The administration agrees with the Select Committee that the end of the Cold War and the dissolution of COCOM in 1994 have complicated efforts to control transfers of militarily important, dual use goods and technology. . . .
>
> The administration is well aware that China, like other countries, seeks to obtain sensitive military technology for military purposes . . . as recommended by the Select Committee, the FBI and CIA plan to complete their annual comprehensive threat assessment of PRC espionage by the end of May, 1999 and the Inspector Generals of State, Defense, Commerce, Energy, Treasury, and CIA expect to complete their review of export controls by June 1999.[55]

Republican political leaders were extremely critical. Senator John McCain (R-Arizona) said the administration was responsible for "a complete failure to effectively bring these security breaches to a halt . . . questions will be asked: why, in the face of overwhelming evidence that these operations were taking place, didn't the Justice Department and this administration do more to stop it."[56] Then Governor George W. Bush of Texas said, "Presented with detailed information about China's espionage, this administration apparently did not take it seriously, did not react properly, and it is still trying to minimize the scope of the damage done."[57]

In the midst of the controversy that followed publication of the complete House Select Committee Report, President Clinton said,

> We have to do more to prevent China from stealing U.S. nuclear secrets, but at the same time I strongly believe that the new engagement with China has produced enormous benefits for our national security . . . for example, we have persuaded China to end nuclear cooperation with Iran and with Pakistan's unsafeguarded nuclear program. China is working with us to help eliminate North Korea's nuclear program and reduce its missile threat.[58]

In that spirit of continuing "engagement," on June 3, 1999, the day before the tenth anniversary of the massacre in Tiananmen Square, Clinton recommended that Congress approve the renewal with China of Most Favored Nation status, now called Normal Trade Relations (NTR). In July 1999, President Clinton further loosened restrictions on the sale of high-performance computers to China.[59] That same month, China successfully tested its new solid-fuel, road-mobile, long-range ICBM, capable of reaching the West coast of the United States.

II. RUSSIA

10 The Soviet Era in Overview

"With our intercontinental missiles we have the Americans by the throat."
—KHRUSHCHEV, speaking to Mao, July 1958

Modern history has been decisively affected by Russia and the United States—two powers occupying vast and generously endowed continents. Many in the West have been drawn to Russia, intrigued by its rich historical and cultural legacy and attracted by its vast expanses, forests, steppes, and natural resource potential. There has also been concern to learn more about the formerly Communist-ruled Soviet Union in order to prevent its expansion, as well as to reduce the risks of conflict by building bridges of mutual interest and understanding.

The year 1992 marked the beginning of a hopeful yet fragile and potentially reversible process of transition in post-Soviet Russia. The reformist leadership of Russia sought to make three types of systemic changes simultaneously: from Soviet Communism to political democracy; from a centralized command economy to mixed free market institutions; and from colonial empire to a new relationship with the fourteen former subject republics that declared themselves independent and sovereign states in December 1991.

This transition effort held both promise and uncertainty. The U.S. and the major democracies committed significant human and financial resources to help the pro-reform leadership succeed in a process of change that will take many years. This process could fail through the reimposition of another authoritarian regime, which might again become a serious international threat. Much that has occurred since the hopeful beginning in 1992 suggests reasons for deep concern about the future political system in Russia.

There were two other times of hopeful opportunity: from 1906 to 1917 when the Russian monarchy made political and economic reforms, opening the way toward the establishment of a British-type constitutional monarchy; and, after the end of the monarchy in 1917, when a provisional government based on an elected parliament was established. The first effort ended as a result of the crisis brought on by the costs of World War I, which led to the abdication of the Russian monarchy, and the second was ended by a Communist coup against the reformist government. Today, the specter of an authoritarian regime again looms over Russia. To understand the present and future of Russia it is important to have a sense for its modern history—especially the more than seven decades of Communist rule.

LENIN LEADS THE COMMUNISTS TO POWER

The democratic experiment in post-Czarist Russia was short-lived. On November 7, 1917, a small band of Communists led by Leon Trotsky and Vladimir Lenin seized control of Petrograd (St. Petersburg), the Russian capital. Taking advantage of the power vacuum in the Russian capital, Lenin's Bolshevik Party rapidly established control over the city's communication and transportation networks, and effectively cut Petrograd off from the rest of the country. More importantly, the now-deposed provisional government, under the leadership of Aleksander Kerensky, lost all contact with the front, thereby denying the government any military support.

The German government had provided secret help to Lenin and his Communist movement. It hoped that this would foment political unrest that would lead to Russia's withdrawal from the war where, as an ally of France and Great Britain, Russia opposed Germany and Austria-Hungary. According to newly available evidence uncovered by the Soviet/Russian military and political historian, General Dmitri Volkogonov, who obtained access to long-secret Communist Party records, Germany covertly spent large sums to help Lenin with "the printing and distribution of newspapers and leaflets, the purchase of arms, and salaries for a large number of 'professional revolutionaries.'"[2] Germany also helped Lenin return to Russia from his exile in Switzerland.

After the Bolshevik coup the German government spent millions more to support Lenin's fragile new regime. One German goal was achieved as Lenin signed the Treaty of Brest-Litovsk in March 1918, ending Russian participation in World War I on terms favorable to Germany. This included ceding one million square kilometers of Russian territory and paying Germany 245 tons of gold.[3]

In 1921, Lenin agreed to provide secret military help for Germany, in violation of the disarmament required after Germany's 1918 defeat and codified in the Versailles Treaty. Volkogonov notes that it was this "secret game with Berlin that would ultimately lead to the [Hitler-Stalin] Pact in 1939, with its secret protocols and 'friendship' with Nazi Germany."[4] The Hitler-Stalin Pact, in turn, set the stage for Germany to begin World War II in 1939 by attacking Poland jointly with the Soviet Union and agreeing to the Soviet occupation and forced annexation of the three Baltic countries—Lithuania, Latvia, and Estonia. The Hitler-Stalin alliance ended when Germany invaded the Soviet Union in June 1941.

In the immediate aftermath of the 1917 coup, the Bolsheviks' hold on political power was exceedingly tenuous. Although a broad range of political parties had evolved since 1906, the Communist regime pronounced all but two illegal. Not surprisingly, these political movements decried the Communist coup as illegal. Lenin then used cunning political tactics and brutality to subdue his opponents.

In December 1917, to counter and break all resistance to his regime, Lenin established the *Cheka,* the Soviet Union's first secret police. Under its first chief, Feliks Dzerzhinskii, the *Cheka* played a key role in the institutionalization of the one-party state. All whom the Communist Party defined as enemies became victims of the *Cheka's* Red Terror.[5]

Political opposition to the Communists soon evolved into military opposition, with royalist and pro-democratic elements joining in a White Army, battling the newly formed Red Army across the territory of the former Russian empire from 1917 to 1920. While the Russian Communist regime secretly aided Communist movements in Europe, hoping to spark successful revolutions in the aftermath of the political and economic problems caused by World War I, the United Kingdom, France, and the United States provided military aid, including some troops, to help the White forces.

The Russian Civil War resulted in the devastation of the economy and claimed hundreds of thousands of lives. The Bolsheviks pursued a policy called "war Communism," designed to eradicate much of the existing political, social, and economic system. But it also destroyed incentives to work and save, fueled hyperinflation, and reduced the domestic flow of food and products to a trickle.[6] Lenin said: "We decided that the peasants would supply sufficient grain through requisitioning, we would distribute it to the factories and enterprises, and thus we would have Communist production and distribution." And in order to take this grain without payment, Lenin said in 1920, "We did not hesitate to shoot thousands of people."[7]

Lenin's Communist regime established the new pattern of modern totalitarian dictatorship when it authorized its secret police to use "extra-judicial executions" and to establish "exile and concentration camps" in the name of "revolutionary legality."[8] Four years of civil war and war Communism destroyed much of the modernized sector of the Russian economy and, in essence, wiped out most of the economic gains of the preceding twenty years.

By the middle of 1921, the Red Army had reduced the armed opposition to a variety of ill-clad, scattered groups. With peasants seeking to keep their grain and the urban population desperate for food, and with every financial and monetary tool in disarray, the Communists sought a means to rebuild the Soviet economy. They decided on a "breathing spell" to be called the New Economic Policy (NEP), a series of measures designed to encourage market practices and incentives at all but the "commanding heights" of the economy.

Advanced by Nikoli Bukharin, one of the founding Bolsheviks, and legitimized by Lenin's writings, the NEP sought, ultimately unsuccessfully, to blend

Communism[9] with some aspect of a market economy. This has similarities to the views of Russia's main Communist Party in the 1990s and to that of the Chinese Communist regime since 1978. Yet Lenin was explicit that the NEP was temporary and tactical. He said, "We are doing it [NEP] in order to retreat and then take a run and leap forward more strongly." In 1922 Lenin wrote, "It would be the biggest mistake to think that the NEP put an end to terror. We shall return to terror and to economic terror."[10]

During the Lenin era (1917–1924), the institutions and practices of Soviet Communism became firmly established: dictatorship over society by the Communist Party, controlled by the Central Committee, which was, in fact, subservient to a very small group within it called the Politburo (which from Stalin on would be dominated by one person, the general secretary of the Party); and, the use of terror and coercion to maintain power and to achieve Party objectives at home and abroad, with the secret police as the main instrument. The Communist Party also established the *nomenklatura* (list of names) system, whereby it decided which persons (virtually always Party members) would hold all important jobs "from the economic ministries and *Gosplan* [State Planning Agency] to the diplomatic service, the Supreme Court, the army and the security organs."[11] The Communist Party was the instrument of rule while all formal institutions of governance were simply given orders to obey.

The extent to which the Communist regime increased the coercive activity of the state can be seen by comparison with the evolving monarchy of the last Czarist era. Since the late nineteenth century, the monarchy had executed an average of seventeen individuals each year for all causes. Once Lenin established the Communist secret police in December 1917, executions began at a rapid pace and in only two years, by 1920, an estimated fifty thousand had been killed for political reasons alone.[12] In addition, hundreds of thousands were imprisoned in work and concentration camps, where most died.

At the time of the Bolshevik Revolution, the Russian empire consisted of three broad groups: Europeanized upper-, middle-, and working-class persons, mostly in the cities and the Russian Far East; a large, mostly illiterate peasant population; and the traditional Muslim societies of Central Asia. By the time Lenin died in 1924, the differences among these groups had been increased by the devastation in all sectors of the economy, the direct result of the combination of civil war, economic mismanagement under war Communism, and the repression of Lenin's Red Terror. The Lenin regime's effort to make some use of market forces had a positive economic impact but did not overcome the social devastation. By 1928, a growing disparity between the prices of industrial and agricultural goods fueled a widening dispute within the ruling Communist Party leadership, bringing an end to the NEP.

THE STALIN ERA: 1929–53

Just prior to his death, Lenin wrote members of the Politburo concerning a number of policy issues. In the letters that would become his "Testament," Lenin remarked that the Party's General Secretary Josef Stalin was "too rude," and that the position of general secretary should be abolished altogether.[13] Indeed, Stalin was often regarded by his Bolshevik contemporaries as uncivilized and unnecessarily brutal, particularly when dealing with issues of ethnicity.

By 1929, however, Stalin had become dominant by either outmaneuvering or discrediting his Politburo rivals. To increase Soviet military power and to assert more central control over the Soviet economy and society, Stalin adopted a course of crash industrialization and forced agricultural collectivization—the first Five Year Plan. This meant that individual farmers were required at gunpoint to turn over most of their crops to the regime, which sold grain on the international market for hard currency, which was then used to build industrial and military production factories.

This led to mass starvation in the countryside, especially in the Ukraine, where, during the 1930s, an estimated six million persons died of starvation caused by Stalin's policies. Those who resisted or were perceived by the regime as opponents were executed or imprisoned in a vast archipelago of labor and concentration camps. According to formerly secret information from Soviet sources, as described by Volkogonov, the first five years of agricultural collectivization "cost 9.5 million lives. More than a third of these had been shot or tortured, perished on long death marches into exile, or died in the frozen wastes of Siberia and the far north. The rest had died of famine."[14]

In 1932, Stalin decided to strengthen and rename the secret police as the State Security Police (*Natsionalnii Komitet Vneshnom Delo,* NKVD, the precursor of the KGB). Its repression went beyond the brutal practices of its predecessor, Lenin's *Cheka.* Further, the system of centralized economic planning concentrated both economic and political power in Moscow. Limited political pluralism, which had enjoyed a brief if ill-fated resurgence during the time of the NEP (1922–28), was crushed by Stalin. The institutions of the Soviet Party regime fused with Communist ideology, elements of Stalin's personality, and the modern communications media to establish the world's first totalitarian state.[15]

In 1933, Stalin began the Great Purge, a "war against the nation" that would ultimately claim from nineteen to thirty-three million lives.[16] Volkogonov concludes from Soviet sources that "between 1929 and 1953 the state created by Lenin and set in motion by Stalin deprived 22 million citizens of their lives."[17]

Stalin intended to have absolute control over all Soviet institutions, using as pretext a theory that "class struggle" would intensify as society approached the realization of Communism. The purges and the terror reflected Stalin's view that Soviet society "harbored countless members of the old middle classes, former officers, unreconstructed members of the pre–1917 political parties, covert saboteurs and spies."[18] While the 1930s were the most repressive, Volkogonov, who lived through this era, observes that "the entire period of Stalin's rule was a bloody one. The population, silent except when told to shout the slogan of the day, was made to expose and 'uproot' a seemingly endless succession of hostile groups."[19] This also frequently occurred during the years of Mao's rule in Communist China (1949–1976). This pattern prompted numerous observers to conclude that both Stalin and Mao were paranoid and unstable.

The victims of Stalin's bloody repression included not only the general population but also the ranks of Soviet bureaucracy, the military leadership, the intelligentsia, leaders and members of the Communist Party, and many foreign Communist leaders living in Moscow. Perhaps the most glaring example of the irrationality behind Stalin's terror was his purge of the military leadership from 1937 to 1939, resulting in the arrest of forty-five thousand officers, the execution of fifteen thousand, and the imprisonment of the remaining thirty thousand.[20] Among the eighty-five most senior generals, sixty-eight were shot. These actions effectively decapitated the Red Army, leaving it vulnerable to the visible and increasing threat posed by the Hitler regime in Germany and the aggressive military regime in Japan.

The Hitler-Stalin Pact, a mutual accord on nonaggression, economic cooperation, and territorial aggrandizement, evidently lulled Stalin into a false sense of security.[21] Upon Germany's "blitzkrieg" invasion in June 1941, Stalin was overcome by incomprehension and disbelief. Evidence suggests that he directly ordered advance Russian units not to resist the invading Germans.[22] Only after four days of silence did Stalin recover his composure enough to deliver a radio address to the nation, notably addressing the stunned populace as his "brothers and sisters," rather than with the Communist salutation, "comrades." Facing the need to drive back the Nazi invasion, Stalin emphasized nationalism and sought to blend the theory and institutions of Leninism with the religious symbols of Russian czarism.[23] There are echoes of this nationalist-Communism in the political ideas of the post-Soviet Russian Communist Party in the 1990s.

The German invasion and subsequent four years of warfare killed an estimated ten million Soviet citizens and destroyed almost all the cities and industrial facilities of the eastern Soviet Union. After the alliance between the U.S., the United Kingdom, and the Soviet Union defeated Nazi Germany in 1945, Stalin tightened repression inside the USSR. He also took immediate steps to use all means short of open military attack to help pro-Soviet Communist parties take power in Eastern Europe, China, and North Korea, where they succeeded. He also tried but failed in Greece, France, Italy, and the Philippines.[24] This marked the end of the wartime alliance with the West and the beginning of the Cold War.

Post-war Soviet reconstruction was done in significant measure through the use of Soviet citizens in forced-labor camps. In his five-year economic plans, Stalin emphasized massive factories geared to producing machine tools, steel and military hardware, with consumer goods and light industry lagging far behind. In 1949, the Soviet Union ended the U.S. nuclear monopoly by successfully testing an atomic device; and in Asia, Communist forces took power in China. This was followed by an alliance between the USSR and the People's Republic of China, personally agreed to by Stalin and Mao Zedong. In Europe, Stalin's Berlin Blockade (1948–49) failed to prevent the establishment of West Germany and the NATO alliance (1949).

In 1950, Stalin secretly approved and provided covert military assistance for the North Korean Communist regime's invasion of South Korea. By prearrangement with Moscow, this was cast as a defensive action against what North Korean radio described on June 25, 1950, as "troops of the puppet government of South Korea launch[ing] a sudden attack on North Korean territory."[25] Newly available Soviet sources show that Stalin personally ordered Soviet military advisors to "join front army group headquarters in civilian clothes as Pravada correspondents," and urged China to intervene with its "volunteers" in October 1950. Stalin also ordered a large covert Soviet air force contingent to counter U.S. aircraft (Soviet records claim they destroyed 1,309 U.S. aircraft while losing 319 Soviet planes).[26]

As the U.S.-led United Nations coalition turned the tide of battle and its forces moved toward North Korea, Stalin wrote Mao about the possibility of a Third World War: "The USA might become involved in a big war; China will be drawn in and with it the USSR, which is tied by a pact of mutual assistance with China. Should we be afraid of this? I don't think so because together we are stronger than the USA and England."[27] The immediate response from Mao was: "I am very glad that in your reply you speak of the joint struggle of China and the USSR against the Americans. Without question, if we are to fight, we should fight now."[28] The Soviet and Chinese Communist leaders' sense of confidence and readiness to wage a world war against the United States illustrates the risks that might arise from the current emerging strategic alignment between China and Russia.

There is considerable evidence that by 1952 Stalin was planning another major purge, this time with a focus on prominent Jewish individuals. Following the trials and executions of those involved in the Jewish Antifascist Committee, established by the regime in 1942 to rally support for the Soviet Union, and the allegations made against Jewish Kremlin physicians (the "Doctor's Plot"), "many Jews were arrested and shot or exiled to the Gulag for periods of fifteen to twenty-five years."[29]

At the time of Stalin's death in March 1953, there were more than five million persons in Soviet concentration/labor camps or in forced exile, and the secret police had an informer network numbering eleven million persons—nearly one-tenth of the population.[30] With some important modifications, this totalitarian institution would survive until 1991.

INSTITUTIONAL COMMUNISM: 1953–1985

Stalin's death, in 1953, left political power in the hands of the "collective leadership" of the Communist Party's Politburo. The secret police (the NKVD, later the KGB) was Stalin's instrument for arresting, executing, and imprisoning whomever he defined as a threat. The then-chief of the secret police, Lavrentri Beria, was perceived by many members of the Politburo as the person who might try to take power and then purge the other leaders. As related by Volkogonov, Nikita Khrushchev took the lead in organizing a majority of the Politburo against Beria, then getting support from key military leaders to bring about his arrest, trial, and execution.[31]

After an interim of collective leadership by Khrushchev and two other members of the Politburo, Khrushchev emerged as the dominant ruler of the Communist Party and therefore of the Soviet Union. At the twentieth Party Congress in 1956, Khrushchev, despite opposition from many of the Politburo members, delivered a secret report, "The Personality Cult and Its Consequences." Khrushchev revealed and condemned Stalin's "mass terror against the Party cadres."[32] As later recounted by Khrushchev:

> It was so quiet in the huge hall you could hear a fly buzzing. You must try to imagine how shocked people were by the revelations of the atrocities to which Party members had been subjected. This was the first time that most of them had heard of the tragedy which our Party had undergone—a tragedy stemming from the sickness in Stalin's character which Lenin had warned us against in his Testament and which Stalin himself had confirmed in his confession to Mikoyan and me—"I trust none, not even myself."[33]

This "secret speech," repudiating the terror of the Stalin years against the Party leadership, had the effect of making the Soviet regime safe for its Communist rulers. From that time there would be no further campaigns of repression and terror directed against Communist Party leaders and members. It also ushered in a period of gradual and partial liberalization, which included rehabilitating many of Stalin's Communist victims. In 1956 there were more than five million persons in Soviet forced-labor camps and exile, and over the next years significant numbers of those were released and permitted to return to their homes.[34] Khrushchev's "thaw" also led to substantial reductions in the number of citizens who would be arrested, executed, or sent to forced-labor camps—though these actions continued.

In foreign policy, however, Khrushchev became ever more assertive as Soviet breakthroughs in nuclear and missile technology led him to believe that the USSR could counter the strategic nuclear military power of the U.S. and NATO. Meeting with Mao in July 1958, Khrushchev told him: "With our intercontinental missiles we have the Americans by the throat."[35] Examples of Khrushchev's aggressiveness include his six-month ultimatum on Berlin given in late 1958, his decision to provide all forms of assistance to pro-Soviet movements seeking to take power in all regions of the world (1961), and the 1962 decision to deploy eighty nuclear-armed Soviet missiles and fifty thousand overt military personnel to Cuba.[36]

The Soviet missile deployment in Cuba would have changed the strategic military balance significantly. To prevent this, in October 1962 the U.S. demanded the immediate and permanent withdrawal of missiles, nuclear warheads, and Soviet troops. After tense weeks, Khrushchev agreed in return for a U.S. pledge not to invade Cuba and to remove its missiles from Turkey. While both sides claimed success in this tense crisis, it was a visible Soviet defeat. This, along with serious tensions with China and the fact that some in the Communist Party leadership remained angry over the damage to its prestige resulting from de-Stalinization, led a faction in the Politburo to plot Khrushchev's removal from power. In 1964, with support from both the KGB and the military leadership, Aleksei Kosygin and Leonid Brezhnev secretly organized a majority of the Politburo and compelled Khrushchev to resign. While Krushchev was permitted to live in retirement, instead of being purged as he would have been in the Stalin era, the institutions of Communist rule continued to function for nearly three more decades.

THE COMMUNIST PARTY-KGB REGIME

Within the Soviet Union, the era of General Secretary Leonid Brezhnev (1964–82) was a time of stability and, in the view of many, of stagnation. Brezhnev himself was described by a Russian member of the Communist elite as "a man of one dimension, with the psychology of a middle-ranking Party functionary, vain, wary and conventional. He was afraid of sharp turns, terrified of reform, but was capable of twisting the Party line in whatever direction the hierarchy desired."[37] Contrary to the apparently impulsive changes in policy that were undertaken by Khrushchev, the Brezhnev years were marked by the steady functioning of the Communist Party institutions. For major national decisions, the Central Committee of the Party would "prepare the appropriate documentation, draft a resolution, and submit analytical arguments, texts of speeches to be made, and guidance. Party functionaries played an enormous role, as the preparation of decisions invariably took place in departments of the Central Committee."[38]

This is illustrated by a 1980 report to the Politburo summarizing its work of the previous year: they had met 47 times; examined 450 issues; passed more than 4,000 decrees, including 46 on ideology, 159 on industry, transportation and capital construction, 330 on personnel, 227 on defense and 1,845 on foreign trade and foreign policy.[39] This report also discussed the 51 sessions of the Central Committee Secretariat, which had issued 1,327 regulations. The minutes of this Politburo meeting indicate that then-KGB Chief Andropov said: "Like the Politburo, the Secretariat also conducted its business in complete unanimity."[40]

This "unanimity" during the Brezhnev years included decisions to undertake a massive buildup in Soviet strategic nuclear and conventional military capabilities; to invade Czechoslovakia in 1968 in order to remove its reformist Communist government; followed by enunciation of the "Brezhnev Doctrine," which stated that the Soviet Union would use all necessary means to assure that no existing Communist regime would be replaced. The Politburo also sharply increased Soviet support for Communist guerrilla and terrorist organizations, leading to the establishment in the 1970s of ten new pro-Soviet regimes from Afghanistan to South Yemen.[41] In 1978, the bloody repression of the Afghan people by their new Communist rulers led to a growing armed resistance. In December 1979, the Politburo decided to intervene openly with armed force, leading to nine years of combat. This resulted in hundreds of thousands of civilian deaths, many thousands of Soviet dead and wounded, and drove nearly five million Afghan civilians (one-third of the population) from their homes to refuge in Pakistan.

In 1980, the Soviet Politburo took steps to prepare for military intervention in Poland to suppress the emerging Solidarity workers movement. The Politburo agreed to support the Polish Communist regime, taking this action on its own in December 1981. As Volkogonov concludes from the evidence in formerly top-secret Soviet documents, Brezhnev "did not initiate these actions but carried out the will of the hawks in the Politburo and the almighty KGB."[42] This era of rule by the Communist Party leadership and staff with strong support from the KGB, the military and the military-industrial complex demonstrated that the system itself, even without dynamic leadership, could challenge the West strongly and that greater Soviet military power and economic/technological progress leading to perceived strategic parity with the U.S. made the regime more not less aggressive.

At the same time, despite the efforts of the Brezhnev regime to emphasize Communist orthodoxy and conformity, ever-growing numbers of Soviet citizens sought greater personal, religious, and intellectual freedoms. This movement was given momentum by mounting concerns about the extremely hazardous environmental pollution in much of the Soviet Union,[43] by opposition to Soviet casualties in Afghanistan, and by the protests of leaders such as Andrei Sakharov (a physicist who participated in designing the first Soviet hydrogen bomb) against "the ruinous super-militarization of the country [which prevents] reforms in the consumer economy and social sphere."[44]

The KGB kept all such dissenters under surveillance and used a wide array of pressures, threats, and punitive means—including incarceration in forced-labor camps and psychiatric hospitals—to limit and suppress them.[45] As head of the KGB since 1967, Yuri Andropov decided on a strategy of selective, preventive, and less-visible repression because he believed it would be more effective than the mass physical terror of the Stalin years and it would do less damage to the international opportunities of the Soviet Union. Nevertheless, through the 1980s the KGB retained a "web of informers, 'observers' and secret agents . . . [involving] literally millions of . . . workers, farmers, soldiers, intellectuals, priests, cultural figures and clerks."[46]

During the Brezhnev era,

> Public apathy grew. Corruption flourished at every level, the higher the worse. Brezhnev's entourage consisted of a court with numerous favorites, intrigues and machinations, to which he, being a mild soul, tended to turn a blind eye. . . . Because the central structures were in a state of decay, something like a feudal system came into being in the local Party committees in the republics. . . . The First Secretary or Regional Party Secretary acquired virtually unlimited power in his own bailiwick and this corrupted him.[47]

These conditions set the stage for the pervasive collaboration between some senior Communist Party officials, government enterprise managers, and criminal groups, which would become a growing and major issue in the 1990s.

After years of visibly declining health and capabilities, Brezhnev died in 1982 and was succeeded by Yuri Andropov (1982–84), who both was chairman of the KGB and had strong support from the military. During his fifteen years as KGB head, Andropov had made it a "state within the state," increased its relative power within the ruling group, and assured that a special KGB unit monitored all members of the Politburo—including their office and personal communications—so that "everything about the lives of the Politburo members was known to the KGB."[48] This era of KGB preeminence may well have left an important mark on Yevgeny Primakov, who worked with the Andropov KGB for many years and who, during the Yeltsin years, served as head of the Russian foreign intelligence service, as foreign minister, and then as prime minister. It also had a major impact on Vladimir Putin, who was a KGB officer from 1975 to 1991, became prime minister in 1999, and was elected president in 2000.

As the new general secretary of the Communist Party, Andropov attempted to spur the economy by seeking ways to "strengthen production and labor discipline" and by reaffirming Marxist-Leninist ideology.[49] In foreign affairs, he continued Soviet support for guerrilla and terrorist organizations, and "approved the continuing supply of billions of dollars worth of aid to Syria, Iraq, Libya, South Yemen, the PLO, Cuba and North Korea," which involved the delivery of thousands of tanks, fighter aircraft, and artillery systems so that these regimes would cooperate against the U.S. and its allies in various regions of the world.[50] The Andropov regime made a major but unsuccessful effort to use a mixture of nuclear deployment and coercive threats, covert action, and propaganda to block the deployment by NATO of medium-range nuclear-armed missiles in Western Europe in 1983. These were put in place to counter the earlier Soviet deployment of similar weapons. This indirect conflict continued, even though newly available information indicates that Andropov believed that the administration of President Ronald Reagan might be giving serious consideration to a preemptive first strategic nuclear attack to defeat the USSR.[51]

Taking power at age sixty-eight, Andropov had serious health problems (including kidney failure that required dialysis) and spent nearly half of his fifteen months as general secretary in the hospital. Following his death in February 1984, Konstantin Chernenko (1984–85), Brezhnev's close confidante on the Politburo, was designated the next general secretary. Already seriously ill with emphysema at age seventy-two, Chernenko was an interim choice who undertook no innovations in policy. Chernenko was the "precursor of change" and the unintended "symbol of stagnation," because "even closet Stalinists, orthodox Leninists and adherents of class dogma saw at last that the system had come to the end of its trajectory. It had shown itself incapable even of choosing an acceptable leader."[52] After thirteen months, Chernenko died of his illness in March 1985, and the Politburo immediately chose its youngest member, Mikhail Gorbachev, as the seventh general secretary of the Communist Party Central Committee.

11 Gorbachev and the End of the USSR, 1985–1991

"For a long time I really did think that the CPSU [Communist Part of the Soviet Union] could be reformed. But the August [1991] coup destroyed those hopes."
—MICHAEL GORBACHEV, *The August Coup*, 1991

The deaths of three General Secretaries in three years and their visible infirmities and limitations over a longer time personified the stagnant institutions of Communist rule. This—together with the continuing gap between the Communist Party's claims about its accomplishments and the dreary realities of daily life in the Soviet Union, marked by endemic shortages of food and consumer goods along with endless waiting in lines—prepared the way for efforts to improve the system and its results.

Gorbachev grew up in the Caucasus region in a peasant family. He joined the Communist Party at the age of eighteen, studied agricultural economics at Moscow University, and then rose in the ranks of the regional Party until he was promoted in 1979 to the Soviet-level Central Committee with responsibilities for agriculture. As a result of his cordial personal style, energy, and economic training, Gorbachev was then appointed to the Politburo. As the youngest member of the mostly aged Politburo, and with a lifetime of proven loyalty to and work for the Party, Gorbachev was the consensus selection as the seventh general secretary of the Party. The Politburo members expected Gorbachev to be a vigorous and articulate representative of their collective Party leadership.

Until virtually the end of his rule, Gorbachev described himself as a Leninist committed to the reform of the Party, which he believed should determine the direction of the Soviet Union. At the March 1985 Politburo meeting, after he had been selected as the new general secretary, Gorbachev said: "We must not change our policy. It is a true, correct and genuinely Leninist policy. We have to raise the tempo, move forward, expose shortcomings and overcome them, and see our bright future clearly."[1]

Throughout his nearly seven years in office (1985–1991), Gorbachev understood that the economy was in steady decline and was failing to produce sufficient food and consumer goods. Gradually, he brought a new team of experts and advisors to his personal staff, to the top ranks of the Party Central Committee, and he also changed the membership of the Politburo as the Brezhnev-era members were encouraged to retire with generous pensions and honorific appointments.

The attempt to reverse steadily worsening trends in virtually every sector of the economy initially focused on traditional efforts to reinvigorate the Soviet system by combating and weeding out corruption and enforcing greater discipline. This failed to produce the desired results, as did Gorbachev's anti-alcohol campaign, the only notable effects of which were a significant decrease in the state's tax revenues and a huge shortage of sugar in stores, the result of home distillation.[2]

During his first two years, Gorbachev also took a conventional Soviet approach to foreign policy. In July 1985, the Politburo concurred with Gorbachev's proposal that Eduard Shevardnadze, a Communist official from Georgia with no foreign experience, become foreign minister. After Gorbachev's first meeting with President Reagan in November 1985, he described the encounter in an "orientation report," sent to allied Communist leaders such as Castro and Kim Il-Sung of North Korea, as "a real skirmish; we had no intention of letting Reagan get away with just a photo session, which he loves so much."[3] After the 1986 summit with Reagan in Iceland, where Gorbachev failed to persuade the U.S. president to agree to end efforts to develop defenses against strategic missiles, Gorbachev told the Politburo: "We are dealing with people who have no conscience, no morality. . . . In Reagan at Reykjavik we were fighting not only with the class enemy but with one who is extremely primitive."[4]

Gorbachev continued Soviet military operations in Afghanistan for another four years despite his personal misgivings because, in Volkogonov's words, he was "unwilling to oppose the hardliners, the Defense Minister and the KGB."[5] In fact, from 1985 to 1987 there was a marked increase in Soviet military, economic, and political support to pro-Soviet regimes in Afghanistan, Cambodia, Angola, and Nicaragua, which faced armed anti-Communist resistance movements supported by the U.S. or its regional allies.[6]

TOWARD REFORM COMMUNISM

There were several reasons why Gorbachev decided to try new approaches in both foreign and domestic policy in 1987. These included: the lack of domestic improvements after two years; the failure of Soviet-aided regimes to suppress the armed resistance movements, especially in Afghanistan, where Soviet soldiers were being killed and wounded; the NATO deployment since 1983 of nuclear-armed intermediate-range ballistic missiles, countering Moscow's initial deployments; and, the

1986 Chernobyl nuclear accident in Ukraine, which provided a warning about the lethal dangers of nuclear conflict.

The Chernobyl disaster contaminated tens of thousands of Soviet citizens with radiation; it also spread radiation through the air and through particles on crops and other food sources. The Soviet regime lied to its own citizens, minimized the devastation, and lied to neighboring countries in Europe. Soviet neighbors could, however, make their own assessments of some types of radiation dangers faced by their citizens.

In July 1986, a few months after Chernobyl, Gorbachev announced: "Global nuclear war can no longer be the continuation of rational politics, as it would bring the end of all life and therefore of all politics."[7] The glowing radioactive crater at Chernobyl helped produce Gorbachev's "new thinking," which he expressed in his 1987 book *Perestroika and New Thinking for our Country and the Whole World* as a Soviet intention to have "moral and ethical norms as the basis of international politics."[8]

That was followed by the December 1987 U.S.-Soviet summit in Washington DC, where, as had originally been proposed by Reagan in 1981, both sides agreed to dismantle, redeploy, or destroy all the intermediate-range nuclear missiles that had threatened both Western Europe and the Western USSR, including Moscow. This, in turn, opened the way to a series of agreements beginning in 1988 that would bring about the withdrawal of Soviet military forces from Afghanistan in early 1989, as well as 70,000 Cuban troops from Angola, Ethiopia, and Mozambique; and, in time, of about 140,000 Vietnamese forces from Cambodia.

Gorbachev's prescription for the reform of Soviet Communism focused on glasnost (openness) and perestroika (restructuring). As described by a participant in the Soviet leadership, the effect of *glasnost*—"openness, publicity or just telling the truth . . . was to widen the avenues of public access to information of all kinds. The process was begun by Gorbachev, but continued to evolve without regard to his decisions. The system based on the class lie was destroyed from within by glasnost."[9]

The objectives of these policies were to foster more openness and reduce corruption and unnecessary regimentation, hoping thereby to encourage improved economic efficiency, higher rates of growth, and enhanced administrative effectiveness of the existing political system. While seeking to reform Communism, Gorbachev was explicit that he was not talking about "bourgeois liberalization" that would end the rule of the Communist Party.[10]

Gorbachev's efforts to change Soviet foreign and domestic policies received strong support from one sector of the Communist Party leadership and organizations, but evoked strong opposition from hardliners who feared that it might endanger the Communist monopoly of power at home and Soviet interests abroad. As a result, throughout Gorbachev's efforts to reform Communism, just as Yeltsin experienced when he attempted post-Communist democratization and movement toward a market economy, there was a nearly continuous conflict with Communist hardliners who wanted to stop and reverse first Gorbachev's and then Yeltsin's changes. This reflected the fact that hard-line Communists who did not want to risk losing power had more than seventy years to build their organizational networks.

The policy of openness required a combination of leadership and decisions by the Party and KGB to widen the domain of permitted speech by reducing repression and supervision in daily life. However, the institutional reform of the Communist governing system was a more formidable task. Since Stalin, the Soviet political system had had a dual structure, in which the Party and government bureaucracies functioned side-by-side at the three levels of rule: federal (pertaining to the entire USSR and directed from Moscow); republic (for the fifteen constituent republics of the USSR, ostensibly independent entities that had "voluntarily" joined the USSR); and local (cities, towns, ethnic "autonomous areas"). Before his death, Lenin had emphasized the importance of the government structures and warned against the use of the Party to administer day-to-day government affairs.[11]

When Lenin died in 1924, the government institutions administered the Soviet Union, while the Party provided ideological guidance and made all major policy decisions. Under Stalin, and thereafter, the Party's Politburo and Central Committee became the institutions of de facto governance. The formal governmental institutions, including both executive-branch ministries and the legislatures (councils or "soviets"), remained in place, enacting orders received from the Party as administrative decisions or laws.

By the time Gorbachev set out to change and partially open the system, the Party had been directly running the Soviet Union for over fifty years. Linden summarized Gorbachev's evolving approach to the reform of that system as beginning with efforts to "alter the regime's mindset," then moving to "changing the method of rule" by the Communist Party (1987–88), followed by the effort to "leap to a new base of power" in 1989.[12]

"Changing the Method of Rule"

Having taken the first step with *glasnost* and *perestroika*, Gorbachev took the second in January 1987 when he told the senior Communist officials at a plenum of the Central Committee that "henceforth the Party's leaders were to be chosen by secret ballot and no longer by designation from above. He met a wall of opposition . . . from leading members of the nomenklatura who saw it not only as an attack on their status but as a danger to the Party regime itself."[13] Gorbachev's "new economic mechanism" reforms, approved by the Party in 1987 and implemented starting in 1988, began to disrupt the economy and lead to increases in the budget deficits.[14] The combination of threats posed to the dominance of the Party and the apparent ineffectiveness of Gorbachev's economic reforms led Communist hardliners to try to recapture the Party from Gorbachev. They did this by working from within and by opposing his specific proposals for the internal democratic reform of the Party made in June 1988 at an extraordinary Party conference. There, for the first time in Soviet history, "the country at large witnessed on television what heretofore had been closed Party proceedings [and saw] an unprecedented open and freewheeling debate over fundamental issues."[15] Gorbachev chaired the meeting, but since the hardliners had the votes to defeat his proposals, "Without forewarning, Gorbachev closed the conference with a dramatic call for elections to new parliamentary institutions which he would head as president."[16] In Linden's words, "This action struck at the heart of the [Communist Party's doctrine] and counterposed a new principle of legitimacy, the electoral, against the ideological."[17]

While there is much evidence that Gorbachev was determined to keep ultimate power in the Politburo and Party, he sought both to increase his authority vs. the Communist Party hardliners and to improve administrative performance by reinvigorating the long-subordinate institutions of the Soviet state. Gorbachev could also view himself as true to Lenin's prescriptions in his proposals to bring government institutions into the policy process by restructuring the legislative system and through the establishment of the office of USSR president.

Gorbachev's 1988 proposals called for changing the legislatures at both the federal and republic levels by reducing their size and entrusting them with actual legislative work. The new USSR Supreme Soviet would serve as the standing parliament, its membership drawn from the 2,225-person Congress of People's Deputies to be chosen in nationwide elections to be held in 1989.

Turning Points in 1989–1990 in the USSR and Eastern Europe

In the March 1989 elections for the USSR Congress of Peoples Deputies, the Communists were still the only legal political party. Further, 85 percent of the seats in this legislature were reserved for the Communist Party and its affiliated organizations, such as the *Komsomol* (Young Communist League), Communist trade unions, the Leninist Youth League, and so forth.[18] However, the fact that different Communist factions, including reform Communists, could compete for votes to become the nominee for Party-controlled seats was a major change. Further, 15 percent of the seats were open to individual candidates who could campaign expressing some opposition to the Communist Party because *glasnost* had created an entirely new atmosphere of more open political discussion and debate.

The result was that, while 87 percent of those in the new Congress were members of the Communist Party, a higher proportion than in 1985,[19] many reform-minded individuals were elected and hundreds of long-established Party officials were defeated. This election was a major turning point because it was, in part, "a referendum on the Party and marked the beginning of the end of totalitarianism in the USSR."[20] In May–June 1989, this newly elected Congress convened and

> the entire Soviet Union came to a halt. Everyone was watching [on television] the Communist Party's legacy being publicly demolished from the highest rostrum of the nation [as] one Peoples deputy after another exposed the horrible state of affairs in the country. The principal point of criticism was the miserable and humiliating living conditions of workers and peasants ... and the appalling corruption among the nomenklatura. Yeltsin pointed out that this flagrantly unfair system was upheld by a monstrous apparatus of repression, the KGB had such enormous power that it could shape society. The deputies demanded a drastic overhaul of this "state within the state" placing it under the control of the Supreme Soviet and curbing the power of the Party ... expressed in Andrei Sakharov's proposal to eliminate article six from the Soviet Union's constitution, which asserted the Communist Party's sole prerogative to rule.[21]

The economy continued to decline, with visible shortages of food and necessities. This led to proposals for more comprehensive, wide-reaching economic changes. By the end of 1989, the Supreme Soviet adopted a plan (offered by Prime Minister Ryzhkov) for a "regulated market economy."[22] It is quite possible that the experts who helped formulate their new approach had analyzed the gradual economic opening in China (beginning in 1978), implemented by a Communist Party that kept power.

"A New Base of Power"

The federal level all-Union Congress of People's Deputies elected in 1989 (with 2,250 members) met in the spring and fall of each year and designated 750 of its members to serve as the Supreme Soviet, responsible for day-to-day governance. The Supreme Soviet, in turn, elected Gorbachev as its chairman—even while he remained general secretary of the CPSU.

In March 1990, the Congress abolished Article 6 of the Soviet constitution, which began: "The leading and guiding force of Soviet society, the nucleus of its political system, its state and public organizations is the Communist Party of the Soviet Union." Eliminating Article 6 ended the guarantee of the Party's leading role in society and opened the way for democratic movements and parties to organize. We learn from secret Politburo records that after this occurred, Gorbachev "did all he could to maintain the influence of the Party in society "which included open and secret measures to transfer state properties to the Party" and to hide "large sums in

Russia and abroad" as the "Party was quietly preparing to live in the new 'demo-cratic society.'"[23] It is reported that Yevgeny Primakov, who played a major role in the 1990s, assisted Gorbachev and the Party leadership in this still-mysterious hiding of Party financial resources in Russia and abroad. Volgogonov notes that the successor Communist Party in Russia clearly benefited from these funds in the 1990s, as evidenced by the fact that "in 1995 when the democratic parties and groups within Russia had only a handful of publications . . . the Communist organ-izations owned more than a hundred central and provincial newspapers."[24]

After the Soviet Congress easily passed the law abolishing Article 6, there subse-quently emerged a widespread belief that Gorbachev was moving away from the Party and that he would eventually leave it. This impression was reinforced by the declining frequency with which numerous time-honored Party organizations met. Although reports in *Pravda* seemed to indicate that the Politburo still served as the Soviet Union's most important policy-making body, its activity sharply declined. For example, between 1981 and 1986, the Politburo met 238 times and made more than 200,000 decisions. Between 1986 and 1990, however, it met 187 times and made just over 11,000 decisions.[25] This suggests a redistribution of policy initiative among a number of government and Party institutions, some old and some new. The Communist Party, however, remained the preeminent institution and main-tained the option of exerting its will indirectly, through the legislature; or directly, through the traditional Party hierarchy.

Eastern Europe

Gorbachev and his team undoubtedly saw the results of the 1989 election, and much that followed, as part of the renewal of the Party after the stagnant Brezhnev era and movement toward the more dynamic "Communism with a human face" that he sought. Certainly Gorbachev welcomed the support he received from the reform Communists and emerging democratic groups within the Soviet Union. Gorbachev was also seen as a symbol of reform by many within the Eastern European Communist-ruled countries and became a popular celebrity there and in the democracies where he was often cheered and warmly welcomed during frequent summit meetings.

Soon after the March 1989 Soviet election, the regime in Communist Poland opened serious negotiations with the revived Solidarity labor movement (which had been repressed in 1981 but gradually rebuilt its organization), hoping to gain its cooperation to stabilize the Polish economy. The Polish Communists, after consulting Gorbachev, offered Solidarity the chance to compete in the first reason-ably open elections under Communist rule for 35 percent of the seats in the existing lower house of the parliament (65 percent would be reserved for Communists and their allies) and for 100 percent of the seats in a new Senate. The Senate would have only nominal powers. The intention from the Communist side was to assure the continuation of Communist rule but provide the Solidarity-led opposition with an institutional means of political participation and opposition other than repeated strikes and labor slow-downs, which were harming the economy.

The date of the Polish election, June 4, 1989, marked a major turning point in the history of Communism. In Communist China, that was the date the regime began its violent repression against young, peaceful demonstrators for human rights and democracy in Tiananmen Square, killing thousands and arresting tens of thousands throughout China. In contrast, though the Polish Communist rulers were surprised by the extent to which the people repudiated them in the election, they kept to the spirit of Gorbachev's reforms by permitting the political process to continue. The pro-democracy movement, Solidarity, won all but one of the 100 Senate seats and all of the 35 percent of the seats in the lower house for which it could compete. Solidarity then surprised the Communist regime by forming a coalition with several small, non-Communist parties that had been forced into an alliance with the Communists in the Polish parliament (as a sign of the ostensible freedom of the previous controlled elections). As a result, in August 1989 Solidarity was able to obtain a majority of votes in the parliament for its proposed prime minister and then form the first democratically led government in Eastern Europe since the late 1940s.

The ruling Polish Communist president, General Jaruzelski, acceded to this undoubtedly after consulting Gorbachev again, but pointedly reminded the Polish people that the Communists still controlled the "organs of security," meaning the secret police and the military, as well as the government bureaucracy. Nevertheless, this was a stunning political breakthrough in a Communist state allied to the Soviet Union. To many in Eastern Europe, it now seemed possible that the Gorbachev regime would indeed permit a degree of political openness that most believed had been ruled out by the past Soviet military interventions in East Germany (1953), Hungary (1956), and Czechoslovakia (1968).

The summer and autumn of 1989 marked the time when the pro-Gorbachev, younger, reform Communists in Eastern Europe sought to use their own *glasnost* and *perestroika* to take over from the now-elderly Brezhnev generation of Communists who still ruled. At the same time, the citizens in one Eastern European country after another began to lose their fear of the Communist regimes, as it seemed they would not be backed by Soviet military force (an impression heightened by Gorbachev's changes and by the withdrawal of Soviet forces from Afghanistan after ten years of casualties). This was dramatically visible in the flight of hundreds of thousands of mainly young East Germans to West Germany through Hungary's newly opened border with neutral, democratic Austria.

That exodus from East Germany helped spark the events which led to the unraveling of Eastern Europe's Communist regimes in a rapid and dramatic process summarized by one democracy activist as "Poland ten years, Hungary ten months, East Germany ten weeks and Czechoslovakia ten days."[26] There were joyful and exuberant celebrations as hundreds of thousands of East Germans visited West Berlin following the opening of the Berlin Wall on November 9, 1989. That event symbolized a new era for the people of Eastern Europe. It was followed in the next months by genuinely free national elections in Hungary, Czechoslovakia, and East Germany, which led to democratic governments replacing the Communist regimes.

Then, after months of complex negotiations between the U.S., the United Kingdom, France, the Soviet Union, West Germany, and East Germany to overcome Soviet objections, Gorbachev agreed in July 1990 that Germany could be reunified while remaining a member of NATO (with certain continuing and additional limitations on German armaments in the future). German reunification took place in October 1990, followed in November 1990 by the signing of the Conventional Forces Europe treaty, which set far lower limits on permitted NATO and Soviet forces deployed in Europe. All of these momentous events in 1989 and 1990 in Eastern Europe had important effects inside the former Soviet Union—encouraging those seeking political liberalization and causing the hard-line Communists to become ever more wary of and opposed to Gorbachev's reforms. The end of Communist rule in much of Eastern Europe illustrated the dangers to Soviet and to Chinese Communism, about which hardliners in both countries had warned.

The Republics vs. the USSR

Throughout the spring of 1990, it became increasingly apparent that the Soviet Party organization was resisting democratization more sharply and more successfully, spurred on by the fact that the free elections in many Eastern European countries were removing Communists from power.[27] Even as *glasnost* continually evolved toward the more free exchange of ideas, existing communication media favored the Communist Party. Yet at the same time, Gorbachev appeared unable to achieve his goals in the newly restructured system, and the new office of president did not give Gorbachev the means to overcome the strong opposition by the Party's hardliners.

It was in this context that Gorbachev faced the new challenge of national assertiveness by the fifteen constituent republics of the Soviet Union. This began in the three Baltic states—Estonia, Lithuania, and Latvia—with revelations permitted by the greater openness of the media. In 1988, an Estonian newspaper published the secret protocols of the 1939 Hitler-Stalin Pact, which included agreement that the USSR would annex the three sovereign Baltic states. This was followed in November 1988 by the Estonian Supreme Soviet declaring Estonia to be sovereign, with the right to veto Soviet laws.[28] Then, in the March 1989 national elections for the USSR

Congress of Peoples Deputies, proindependence "popular fronts" won 31 of 41 Lithuanian seats, 25 of 29 in Latvia, and 15 of 21 in Estonia.

The dramatic success of Solidarity in the elections in neighboring Poland (June 1989), the first-ever official Soviet admission in July 1989 that the Hitler-Stalin Pact had included the coordinated Nazi-Soviet occupation of Poland and "granted" the Baltics to the Soviet Union, and the fiftieth anniversary of the beginning of World War II (September 1, 1989), all combined to bring hundreds of thousands of Baltic citizens to commemoration and proindependence ceremonies in August 1989. Then in the fall of 1989 and the spring of 1990, as Communist rule unraveled in one Eastern European country after another with no military intervention by the USSR, there was a gradually expanding process of republic-level assertions of independence within the Soviet Union. By August 1990, all fifteen republics had declared themselves sovereign. Many republic-level Communist Party leaders wanted more autonomy from the central control of the Soviet Party, and they used this revived nationalism as a means of keeping themselves in power.

In 1990, Yeltsin saw the assertion of the authority of the Russian Federation in broader terms—he believed the formal authority of the newly elected Russian Congress of Peoples Deputies and its appointed Russian Supreme Soviet could be used to accelerate the pace of political and economic reform. Elections for the new Russian Congress of Peoples Deputies in early 1990 had not been multiparty elections and Communists won 90 percent of the seats, but about 35 percent of the deputies supported reform, as did a majority of those elected to local government in many of Russia's major cities. The Russian Congress then chose the Russian Supreme Soviet, which in May 1990 elected Yeltsin as chairman of the Presidium— in effect, president of Russia.[29] Under Yeltsin's leadership, in June 1990, the Russian Congress proclaimed Russia a sovereign state and declared that its laws would have primacy over those of the USSR on Russian territory.[30]

This was followed in July 1990 by a Soviet Communist Party Congress that marked the high point of Gorbachev's influence: he was reelected as head of the Party, the Politburo was enlarged to include representatives from all fifteen republics, and various hard-line opponents of Gorbachev were forced to resign. At the same time, Yeltsin publicly resigned his membership in the Party and declared that his goal was a Russia that would be fully democratic with a free market economy.[31] That was followed by the parliament of the Russian Republic ending Party control of the media and taking actions to reduce the influence of the KGB.[32] In essence, Yeltsin was using the full constitutional powers of the republic-level governing institutions to attempt the dismantling of the Communist Party regime.

During 1990, the shortages of consumer goods in the stores continued, and a group of Soviet economists produced a plan for a five-hundred-day transition from central planning to an economy based on private ownership and markets.

Gorbachev and Yeltsin jointly endorsed a plan close to this approach in September 1990, and the parliament of the Russian Republic then voted to implement this plan in Russia, whether or not the USSR legislature agreed.

Return of the Hard-liners

The hard-line Communists saw these actions as a major internal challenge to the authority of the Soviet regime at the same time that Gorbachev's permission for German reunification in NATO and the end of the Soviet-led military alliance with Eastern Europe (the Warsaw Pact) created a potential external danger. As a result, in the fall of 1990 Gorbachev faced growing pressure from Communist hardliners in the Party, the KGB, and the military. Those pressures included reports of military deployments near Moscow and rumors of a coup. Gorbachev was clearly intimidated or persuaded, and he took a number of actions demanded by the Party, KGB, and military hardliners. First, in October 1990, Gorbachev rescinded his agreement with Yeltsin and endorsed a far less comprehensive economic reform plan, which did not permit any private ownership of the means of production.[33] The USSR Supreme Soviet rapidly approved this. The fact that the USSR and Russian legislatures had enacted two different economic plans for Russia undoubtedly contributed to the continuing decline of the economy.

Next, the USSR Supreme Soviet declared on October 24, 1990, that the assertions by the republics that their laws took precedence over those of the USSR were invalid. The Russian and Ukrainian parliaments immediately voted again to declare that their laws had primacy.[34] Clearly, this difference between the Soviet Union and its two largest republics could lead to serious conflict. Gorbachev met with military leaders and assured them he would preserve the unity of the USSR. Gorbachev ordered the military to take steps to guarantee that the republics would not obtain access to Soviet nuclear weapons on their territory and to use force if attacked or harassed by individuals in the Republics.

In December 1990, Gorbachev replaced the reform oriented minister of the interior with a hard-liner. Subsequently, the KGB chief, Vladimir Kryuchkov, appeared on Soviet television to say the KGB would use "'all the means at its disposal' [against] the 'anti-Communist forces' that are working against central power in the USSR."[35] Gorbachev followed with warnings to the Soviet Congress about the "dark forces of nationalism" and the statement that twelve to eighteen months of "executive rule" would be needed to keep the USSR from falling apart. A few days later, Gorbachev's close confidante and partner in international "new thinking," Eduard Shevardnadze, resigned as foreign minister, warning that "a dictatorship is approaching."[36] Immediately thereafter, to illustrate the new ascendancy of the hardliners, the KGB chief told the Soviet Congress that bloodshed might be necessary to restore order and alleged that the CIA and other Western intelligence services had been fomenting dissent in the USSR. Gorbachev then ordered the parliament of Moldova to rescind various nationalist laws and it complied. This was a sign of the fear caused by the reassertion of KGB-backed centralism in Moscow.

In early 1991, there were a series of paramilitary assaults against the proindependence leaders in the three Baltic states. These were most likely covertly organized by the KGB. Gorbachev accused the Lithuanian parliament of "implementing a policy aimed at restoring a bourgeois system" (meaning democracy) and demanded that it "restore constitutional order" (meaning subordinate itself to the central government).[37] Gorbachev appointed as premier an individual strongly opposed to comprehensive economic reform, ordered the confiscation of all currency in fifty- and one-hundred-ruble notes (ostensibly to stop corruption, but this step undermined the beginning of expanded retail marketing), and authorized the KGB to search domestic and foreign businesses if it suspected economic crimes. At the end of January 1991, the Ministries of Defense and Interior announced joint patrols in many Russian cities to preserve order, an indirect move toward martial law intended as a warning that the military would be used if needed.

Yeltsin organized demonstrations and protests against these reassertions of the Party-dictatorship and denounced Gorbachev for his complicity and acquiescence. In March 1991, Gorbachev mobilized fifty thousand paramilitary police in Moscow to halt a Yeltsin pro-democracy demonstration but decided not to risk the confrontation.[38] Instead, Gorbachev persuaded Yeltsin to join him and leaders of the other republics in formulating a new political arrangement with the republics to be called the Union of Sovereign States. Gorbachev and Yeltsin met and reached agreement in May 1991, with the understanding that the final treaty establishing the new union would be signed in August 1991.[39]

Gorbachev's attempts to revitalize the Soviet system using a hybrid approach of Party and governmental institutions, both of which he headed, had failed to produce the hoped-for economic results, but it did lead to the coalescence of powerful hard-line anti-Gorbachev Communists. Similarly, Yeltsin, Russian democrats, and other members of the intelligentsia had criticized Gorbachev for failing to move toward full democratization. Gorbachev, trying to placate both, was too authoritarian for those seeking democracy and far too experimental, hesitant, and open for the Communist hardliners. They decided on the August 1991 coup attempt.

THE UNRAVELING OF THE SOVIET UNION

In June 1991, a reasonably open and competitive election was held for the newly established presidency of Russia. Boris Yeltsin soundly defeated the Communist candidate, former USSR Premier Nikolai Rhyzhkov, as well as the ultranationalist Vladimir Zhirinovsky, to become Russia's first democratically elected leader in its thousand-year history. This gave Yeltsin the unique and powerful legitimacy of a genuine popular mandate, unmatched by any other leader in the USSR, including Gorbachev. Following his formal inauguration as president of the Russian Federation in July 1991, Yeltsin continued his campaign to use the authority of the Russian Republic to challenge and reduce the Communist Party's political influence. At his urging, the Russian parliament made it illegal for the Communist Party of the Soviet Union to continue its cells within the KGB, the armed forces, police and state enterprises located in Russia (which included Moscow).[40]

On August 19, 1991, Gorbachev's vice president, Gennadi Yannaev, and his hastily assembled "State Emergency Committee," including the hard-line ministers of interior and defense and the chief of the KGB, announced that they were now in charge since Gorbachev had resigned for "reasons of health." Meanwhile, their forces held Gorbachev prisoner at his vacation residence in the Crimea. Yeltsin immediately led a series of popular demonstrations in opposition to the coup and used his authority as president of Russia to issue orders to the military, KGB, and other government organizations in Russia that contravened those of the Emergency Committee.

This led to divisions within the military and KGB units that the Emergency Committee had deployed. Various armed units did not obey orders to arrest Yeltsin and take control of the Russian parliament building Yeltsin used as his countercoup headquarters. The coup plotters had planned poorly and were overconfident in their ability to intimidate the people and leaders of Russia. Facing internal splits and popular resistance, the coup collapsed within three days. As Gorbachev wrote after the coup was defeated:

> The whole of society had changed, including the army. Officers and privates refused to go against their own people. . . . The forces of law and order and even the special commando troops behaved similarly. That was where the plotters went wrong: they did not realize the society was now not at all what it had been a few years back. . . . It had breathed the air of freedom and no one could now take that away from it.[41]

Yeltsin personally flew to Gorbachev's summer residence and accompanied him and his family back to Moscow, where Gorbachev initially spoke about the need and opportunity to reform the Communist Party. But after some weeks of assessment and reflection, Gorbachev wrote that while "the army turned out to be with the people . . . it turned out to be possible to bring out on to the streets a huge number of troops, tanks and other armored equipment without any agreement on the part of the country's supreme legislative body.... The Supreme Soviet of the USSR failed to exercise its constitutional powers" because it failed to oppose the coup.[42] Gorbachev went on to write that "for a long time I really did think the CPSU [Communist Party of the Soviet Union] could be reformed. But the August coup destroyed those hopes.... Many Party committees decided to help the plotters."[43]

At the same time, in the fall of 1991, Yeltsin quickly moved to consolidate the gains of Russia's independence and exercise the fullest possible authority of the Russian presidency. Yeltsin acted immediately to "suspend" the Communist Party in Russia, physically expelled the Central Committee and Politburo from its elegant Moscow headquarters, and prohibited the continued functioning of Communist Party networks within the military and government organizations. Yeltsin also sought to insure that the Communist Party of the Soviet Union, in power since 1917, would be held directly responsible for the illegal coup attempt. Rather than oppose Yeltsin on this, Gorbachev resigned as general secretary of the Party (the first person ever to do so) and proposed that the Central Committee dissolve itself.

Yeltsin immediately appointed individuals he considered to be proreform and loyal to positions of authority throughout Russia, thereby hoping to establish a counterweight to the existing institutions that continued in place. In October 1991, Yeltsin accepted the advice and plan of Yegor Gaidar and his group of reform-oriented economists and agreed that Russia would carry out large-scale economic changes that came to be known as "shock therapy" once they were begun in January 1992. The purpose was both to stimulate economic growth and to begin dismantling the Party-controlled economic institutions, thereby reducing the risks of a Communist restoration.

One of the greatest ironies of the attempted coup was that by moving against Gorbachev and his changes, the hard-line Communists hastened the collapse of the Soviet Union. Yeltsin joined with other presidents of the Soviet republics to press for the replacement of the existing union with a far looser association. On December 8, 1991, Russia, Ukraine, and Belarus declared their full independence, and on December 25, 1991, Gorbachev resigned as president of the USSR.[44] The formal dissolution of the Soviet Union followed, and most of fifteen republics agreed to establish a voluntary Commonwealth of Independent States. With those events, Russia became fully independent, and the post-Soviet era began.[45]

The defeat of the August coup made clear that some elements of civil society, social organizations independent of the state, had returned to the USSR. The seven tumultuous Gorbachev years (1985–1991) had partially removed from Russia the dark veil of secrecy that had enshrouded society since 1929. Not so clear was how Russia and the other post-Soviet republics would evolve as independent states.

12 The Yeltsin Era, 1992–2000

> "The Communist Party [was] one of the main problems ... since the beginning
> ... ever since 1991 the Communists were obsessed with getting rid of Yeltsin ...
> a reform government could not work together with a Communist parliament."
> —BORIS YELTSIN, *Midnight Diaries,* 2000

Born in 1931, Yeltsin lived in Sverdlovsk (now Yekaterinburg), an industrial city in the Urals. He received a degree in civil engineering in 1955 and married Nainia Girina in 1956. Their first child, Ydena, was born in 1957; their second daughter, Tatyana, in 1960. Yeltsin joined the Communist Party in 1961 and rose in the ranks as he worked on construction and industrial development until 1976. Yeltsin then became first secretary of the Sverdlovsk Regional Party Committee until 1985, when he was called to Moscow to serve as first secretary of the Moscow City Party Committee, and in 1986 Yeltsin became a candidate member of the Politburo. From there, Yeltsin moved toward reform Communism and then to public criticism of Gorbachev in late 1987 for not seeking more liberal political and economic reforms. This led to Yeltsin's being publicly criticized, his removal as first secretary, and his first hospitalization for heart problems.

At the end of 1991, as Yeltsin looked forward to his role as president of a newly independent Russia and to the challenge of bringing about political democracy and a market-oriented economic system, he must have considered what lessons the Gorbachev years might hold for him about efforts to liberalize the Russian political system. These years showed, first, that there was an important group among the public that strongly supported democratic and market reform and which could be mobilized when challenges called for it, as Yeltsin himself had done on several occasions.

Second, it was evident that hard-line Communists in Moscow, throughout Russia, and in the institutions of the state would continue to oppose moves toward democracy and free markets in the future, as they had in the recent past. Looking back from the year 2000, Yeltsin wrote that "ever since 1991, or even 1990, the Communists had been obsessed with one idea: getting rid of Yeltsin."[1]

Third, there would be a constant danger to his government from a military coup if Communist hardliners should be able to win over significant elements of the "power ministries," which controlled armed force. Yeltsin knew how close the coup of August 1991 had come to succeeding, and he believed that another coup attempt might be made.[2] This was a reason to monitor and keep close relations with the Ministries of Defense and Internal Affairs and the intelligence agencies. He also knew that elements of the Communist Party and the military had cooperated in removing Khrushchev (1964), and in the leadership transition after Stalin's death (1953–54).

Fourth, in the context of the economic problems facing Russia in the autumn of 1991—inflation over 138 percent, an 18-percent decline in GNP, the possibility of severe food shortages in the cities—Yeltsin concluded that limited economic reforms of the type Gorbachev had tried simply did not work in either economic or political terms.[3] Gorbachev's economic changes had failed to improve the economy and failed to create new institutions and interests that could challenge the dominance of the Communist Party.

A fifth lesson from the Gorbachev years derived from the fact that Russia is a republic, with over one hundred ethnic groups, a number of ethnically based autonomous territories, and many regional authorities. Having just witnessed and led a political process whereby republic level nationalism had precipitated the dissolution of the Soviet Union, Yeltsin understood the potential threat of the fragmentation of Russia if ethnic assertiveness led to demands for secession, as the Chechen region had begun voicing in 1991. These five "lessons" would affect Yeltsin's actions during his years as president of Russia.

Two Fateful Decisions

The new parliament of the Russian republic had been chosen in the spring of 1990, in a Communist-dominated election with some competition within the Party between pro- and anti-Gorbachev reform candidates. The Russian parliament had supported Yeltsin as he challenged Gorbachev and the Soviet Party state. After his success in opposing and stopping the August 1991 coup against Gorbachev, support for Yeltsin increased within the Russian parliament.

Yeltsin's first fateful decision as president of an independent Russia was to leave the existing Russian parliament in place. He focused instead on changing the command economic system rather than taking steps to create a political opening to a fully democratic political system. This could have been done by following the examples set in Eastern Europe: the Communist era parliaments were disbanded by the transitional governments, genuinely democratic parties were given a chance to organize, and new elections were then held to establish a new democratic basis of governance. This resulted in the establishment of pro-democratic political parties with grass-roots citizen support and also led to shared executive-legislative consultation and decision making about the major economic and other reforms to be undertaken.

Yeltsin worked with a team of energetic young Russian economists who persuaded him that their plan for comprehensive economic reform would work within a year or two and could produce visible improvements in living conditions.[4] Yeltsin believed that this would provide political support for democratization, and he also assumed that making rapid and comprehensive economic changes would remove much of the institutional power of the Communist Party. Yeltsin's purposes were political as much as economic. The Russian parliament, enthusiastic about the independence of Russia, provided Yeltsin with authority to rule by decree for one year until December 1992, so that he could implement his economic reform plans.

Its principle architect, Yegor Gaidar, Russian minister of economics and finance and deputy prime Minister, described the key elements of this economic reform plan in January 1992. His "clear strategy" included:

> First, the freeing of markets—for goods, services and for foreign exchange. On January 2 [1992] most consumer prices were freed . . . after 75 years of price control this was a big step. . . . Freeing markets is the first element in the reform. . . . [Next] the task of stabilization is the most difficult and involves three steps. First the budget must be balanced . . . freeing prices means that most subsidies would be removed . . . drastic cuts will also be made in defense procurement. . . . [It is also necessary] to impose effective limits on lending to enterprises. Here the government is engaged in urgent discussions with the Central Bank since effective limits are essential to the success of the program. . . . The final need is to stabilize the ruble.[5]

This economic reform proposal was greeted with praise by a number of prominent Western economists. Two American specialists in Soviet economic affairs wrote early in 1992, "Yeltsin has proposed what may be the most promising program for a successful transformation to a market economy yet offered in the Soviet Union. It is comprehensive in nature, avoiding a piecemeal approach, and it is aimed at the most critical areas, such as monetary stability, budgetary control, and privatization."[6] These experts did, however, add this cautionary note: "In spite of the program's many virtues, formidable obstacles to its success remain. . . . This could cause public disillusionment and a reversal of some aspects of the plan."[7] To provide assistance, the West moved by April 1992 to admit Russia to the International Monetary Fund and the World Bank, and the seven leading industrial democracies (G7) committed a total of $18 billion to Russia—$8 billion for balance of payments support, $6 billion for a stabilization fund, and $4 billion for International Monetary Fund "standby" borrowing rights.[8] This was in addition to various bilateral assistance funding provided by the U.S. (more than $300 million in humanitarian food supplies), Germany, and others.

Yeltsin's reformist intention became focused on his economic program, which became the test of the entire reform movement. A Russian political scientist offered an interesting analysis of the thinking of Russia's democratic reformers of that time. He contended that they saw the state

> as the main obstacle to an ideal democracy and the maximum weakening of the state was believed to be the most important condition for its creation . . . [Russian] Democratic activists view democracy not as a system of compromises among various groups and interests or as a separation of powers but as the unlimited power of "democrats" replacing the unlimited power of the Communists.[9]

Yeltsin decided not to take the risks of dealing with hard-line Communist opponents in the parliament or society during a lengthy consultative political process to define a new economic reform agenda, because he had observed the negative consequences for Gorbachev. There was also a sense of deep concern about how the Russian people would cope with scarcities of essentials such as food and fuel during the "terrible winter of 1991–92," when the Soviet-era institutions were hardly functioning and new post-Soviet governments had not yet fully emerged. Gaidar describes the perceived threat of massive food shortages and economic collapse in a December 1991 Moscow scene when he saw, "Grim food lines. . . . Pristinely empty stores. Women rushing about in search of some food, any food for sale. . . . Expectations of disaster were in the air."[10]

Yeltsin formulated and implemented major economic changes by presidential decree, but he did not remove the Communist-dominated parliament that had been elected in the Soviet era. Then, by omitting the process of broad political consultation and debate, which parliamentary elections and a new democratically elected Russian parliament might have provided as it participated in shape a reform program, Yeltsin missed an opportunity to empower democratic political parties. Therefore, in the public mind, Yeltsin became solely responsible for the economic changes and their consequences. These in turn became the focus of a political division between Yeltsin and his allies on one side and Communists and ultranationalists in the Russian parliament and the bureaucracy on the other, which continued through the entire period of the Yeltsin presidency.

The Realities of the Soviet-era Economy

The challenges facing Yeltsin derived from realities of the Soviet-era economy which had a four-tiered system for providing goods and services to its citizens: the regular system of state-managed stores and facilities; the legal private markets where foods and other goods were normally available at higher prices; the closed state-run retail stores where abundant goods were available but only for high-ranking members of the Communist elite or when purchased with Western currencies such as dollars or Deutschmarks; and, the black market (also known as the *na levo* market, literally "on the left"), where goods and services were sold without legal sanction.[11] Perhaps the most widely known example of the legal private markets for the general public were the peasant and farmers' markets that sold agricultural commodities legally at whatever price the market would bear. Food from the state and collective farms was generally of low quality and often in short supply, but on private plots accounting for only about 2 percent of the Soviet Union's arable land, about 40 percent of the country's meat, vegetables, and fruits were produced and sold through the legal private market.

Although private initiative ultimately kept some food on most Soviet tables, the huge gap between the supply and demand of consumer durables remained largely immune to entrepreneurial endeavors. From this arose the intricate system of hard-currency stores throughout the Soviet Union. Since only a small minority of Soviet citizens had legal access to hard currency, high-quality consumer goods remained out of reach for the vast majority. Only Party members and foreign tourists could enter the special shops and purchase Japanese televisions, German refrigerators, American jeans, and other sought-after goods. The *nomenklatura* used its special retail stores and other distribution systems to ensure that its members lived well and were not burdened by the shortcomings of the regular state distribution system. Average Soviet citizens were, by contrast, forced to contend with whatever the system could produce. *Pravda,* the newspaper of the Party, reported in 1987 that nearly 40 percent of all apartment fires in Moscow had been caused by faulty Soviet-made television sets, a fact that served to underscore the vast gap between average Soviet citizens and the Party leaders.

There is some degree of corruption in every governmental system, but the potential for corruption grows in dictatorships where the regime lacks legitimacy and moral authority, and where there are no independent means of holding corrupt officials to account. It is also true that a political economy of chronic shortage and rationing will inevitably lead to extralegal means of acquiring desired, scarce resources such as food, housing, raw materials, medical care and supplies, personal services, and the like. During Brezhnev's rule (1964–82), corruption became wide-spread. To understand this aspect of the Soviet economic culture, it is well to recall what one well-informed Soviet exile wrote at the end of the Brezhnev era in 1982:

> Massive and ubiquitous corruption at the district level of the Party-state apparatus has forged such close ties between it and the criminal world that . . . a

system of organized crime has come into existence in the Soviet Union, a system that has permeated the political power centers of the districts as well as the administrative apparat, the legal system, and key economic positions. Although not conceived as such by its creators, this Soviet variety of organized crime naturally is derived from and has become an organic part of the dictatorship of the apparat of the Soviet Union. Organized crime in the Soviet Union bears the stamp of the Soviet political system.[12]

Ten years later, at the close of the Soviet era, a book written by a Russian concluded that:

It was as if the entire Soviet Union were ruled by a gigantic mob family known as the CPSU [Communist Party of the Soviet Union]. Between an agricultural government minister's order for, say, the production of ten tons of meat and Ivan Ivanov's purchase of a kilo of veal for a family dinner, there were countless opportunities for mischief. No one could afford to avoid at least a certain degree of complicity. It was impossible to be honest.[13]

In fact, much of the behavior that could officially be called "corruption" was, in a command-economy dictatorship like the former Soviet Union, the simple imperative of making the system work to meet what they perceived as their vital needs. Far from having any sense of committing immoral or dishonest acts, a majority of participants in the myriad "informal" arrangements, including the barter and sale of state supplies and services, school admissions, jobs, medical care and the like, viewed themselves as simply doing what they had to do because of the shortcomings of the system. Not only individuals but organizations outside the privileged circle of the *nomenklatura* or the KGB military complex also had to make "special arrangements" to meet their needs. Out of this developed what came to be known as the "shadow economy."

For example, workers in a washing-machine factory would steal the appropriate tools and spare parts from the factory during the day and at night moonlight as private washing-machine repairmen, charging whatever price the market would bear. In a system notoriously weak in the area of service delivery, these "entrepreneurs" could often earn many times their monthly salaries in just a week's worth of work. When cash payment was unavailable, many would barter their services for goods and services they needed. Thus, the washing machine repairmen might earn "free" medical care from the local doctor or have their unreliable cars repaired by a grateful auto mechanic.

Various reports issued during the Gorbachev period suggest that the shadow economy at one time accounted for between 30 and 40 percent of all business done in the service sector.[14] One Soviet reform economist cited an official government estimate that in the late 1980s about 20 million people provided services through the "underground business" of the shadow economy.[15] In major cities, these private businessmen "accounted for roughly half of all shoe repairs, nearly half of all apartment repairs, 40 percent of repairs on private automobiles, 40 percent of tailoring, 33 percent of repairs to household appliances," and millions of illegal abortions— all responsible for an estimated 10 percent of the Soviet GNP.[16]

In 1987, as part of his economic reforms, Gorbachev decided to legalize much of the shadow economy by permitting the formation of private enterprises to be officially designated as "cooperatives." These organizations, according to the Law on Cooperatives enacted in May 1988, were permitted to operate in virtually all economic activities with no limit placed on the number of members or on their assets. Gorbachev recalled, "Lenin had equated the growth of cooperatives with the growth of Socialism," as he found the new movement opposed vehemently by hard-line Communists contending that cooperatives were a "malignant tumor" and legalized "the plunder of the working class."[17]

All these activities—the individual "adaptations" to the endemic scarcities, the shadow economy, and the burgeoning cooperative and private farm sectors—testify to the entrepreneurial interests, motivations, and skills of significant parts of the population. Yet despite some constructive legacies of the Russian shadow economy, the omnipresent Soviet-era Russian "mafias" presented a greater challenge to those wishing to encourage free markets in Russia. It has been said that the entire Soviet Communist Party structure resembled most closely that of a typical mafia "family." But, as Hedrick Smith noted, when most Soviet citizens uttered the term "mafia," few meant organized crime in the Western sense, merely its dark connotation: "In Soviet parlance, the mafia is a stratum of society that includes powerful Party and government officials, economic managers, and criminal elements, an amorphous, privileged layer held in popular contempt for its corrupt lifestyle and evil tentacles that reach into all walks of life."[18]

There was the absence of the institutions and practices needed for the fair, legal functioning of a market economy, such as the enforcement of contracts through an independent judicial system, and an established, reliable means to ensure and protect the rights of private property. Clearly, the Russian economic reformers intended that these institutions would be developed in parallel with the process of reform and privatization. Perhaps this might have happened in a harmonious way had there not been such strong, continuing hard-line Communist opposition from the very start of the reform process.

There was also an important structural impediment to making state and privatized enterprises more cost-effective. In the former Soviet Union, employment in state enterprises was not only the source of a salary, but was also directly linked to employees' access to many other essential goods and services in the society—food, housing, medical care, child care, vacations, and the like. This fact raised the political and social costs of reducing employment in any of the inefficient state enterprises, whether government-owned or under the auspices of new private ownership. Losing employment meant a potential catastrophe in the lives of millions of families. In the absence of social insurance and support institutions, which Russia could not quickly fund or develop during the initial period of the reform process, it was not politically prudent for a government that sought to be democratic and avoid coercion to cause large-scale unemployment.

Results of the Economic Reform Program

The results of Yeltsin's "shock therapy" were quickly felt. On the positive side, by the end of January 1992 most price controls had been lifted (excepted were utilities, communication, rail transport, natural gas, and some basic consumer items), imports were liberalized, government expenditures were reduced, and "goods were finally beginning to appear in stores."[19]

Within a matter of weeks, inflation began to rise sharply and there was an immediate fall in industrial production, agricultural production, investment, and in wages.[20] As a result of the negative effects, the opposition within the Russian parliament to Yeltsin's economic program brought together an ever-stronger coalition of hard-line Communists and others. They began demanding changes in Yeltsin's reform program. By April 1992, Yeltsin was forced by this opposition in parliament to remove Gaidar as minister of finance, but he remained as deputy prime minister.

Gaidar himself reflected the immediate pressures that the negative economic results brought when he noted that the industrial managers starved of credits and with debts to each other and to their workers would be given large-scale new credits "to ease their problems."[21] Gaidar went on to say in April 1992 that he was being criticized by the Communists and by Russian ultranationalists "who will say that I am selling the country to the IMF and the Western powers. We will be criticized by the agrarian deputies because we don't care about agriculture and we will be criticized by the enterprise managers because they face serious problems of industrial restructuring."[22] In that statement, Gaidar summed up the opponents of the reform program who would continue to oppose it throughout the 1990s: Communists, ultranationalists, state industrial mangers, collective farm mangers—essentially the political-managerial elite of the Communist era, whom Yeltsin would describe in his memoirs as "the Soviet directors corps."[23]

These opponents combined to bring about changes in Yeltsin's policy, including the large-scale printing of money, since the parliament and not the president controlled the Russian Central Bank.[24] The resulting inflation reached roughly

2,600 percent by the end of 1992, essentially wiping out the life savings of virtually all of the Russian population. This had extremely negative political effects.

Maintaining employment in Russia became a major purpose of the credits provided to the industrial and agricultural state enterprises by the Russian Central Bank, which responded to the Communist-controlled parliament. These credits both maintained employment and preserved many of the state enterprises, albeit at far lower rates of productivity. These credits also helped produce the enormous inflation, which accumulated to more than 4,000 percent in Yeltsin's first five years. In effect, there was a sharp decline in real wages and a total elimination of personal savings as a result of the economic changes, but employment and the access to some social services continued for the most part through the entire Yeltsin era. At the same time, a large shadow economy and illegal mafia-type relationships continued and expanded at all levels of the post-Soviet economic systems in Russia and most of the other republics. This would have enormous consequences for the actual evolution of the intended economic reforms.

THE POLITICAL STRUGGLE: 1992–1993

The political results of Yeltsin's fateful decisions on economic policy were exactly opposite of those intended: a sharp increase in opposition from Communists and little, if any, support from the public, because "shock therapy" produced economic hardships. Before 1992, the Russian parliament, even though 90 percent Communist, had been divided approximately one-third in strong support of Yeltsin's democratic and economic reform efforts, one-third potentially willing to support him in the hope that things would work out, and one-third strongly opposed.[25] Within a matter of several months, in early 1992, the Russian parliament had shifted strongly against Yeltsin's economic reform program and, as Gorbachev had done, Yeltsin moved to compromise.

The first step taken in April 1992 was to remove Gaidar as minister of finance. The second was the appointment of two individuals from the Communist managerial elite who were to bring a more "practical" approach to the issues of privatization and economic reform. This was done in the summer of 1992 but did not reduce the opposition in the parliament, which in the fall rescinded its grant of authority to rule by decree. Next, the hard-line Communists attempted to obtain a two-thirds vote to amend the Russian constitution to reduce the powers of the Russian president to that of a nominal head of state, transferring all real decision-making powers to an executive committee of the parliament. Described by Communist hardliners as an effort to put Yeltsin in the same position as the "Queen of England," this failed by only a few votes in November 1992.

This opposition coincided with a very important decision reached by the new

Constitutional Court, which the Russian parliament established in late 1991 in an effort to begin the creation of an independent judiciary. The Constitutional Court had taken on the case brought by Yeltsin against the Soviet Communist Party (the CPSU) for its responsibility in the August 1991 coup attempt. This included the trial of a number of the coup plotters who had remained in prison since that time. In November 1992, the Constitutional Court ruled that "Yeltsin has indeed acted properly in disbanding the national governing bodies of the CPSU for their role in conspiring against the state. The justices, however, also found that the millions of rank and file Communists had not engaged in a conspiracy and therefore, had a right to reconstitute the Party."[26] This decision was followed by the reestablishment of several different Russian Communist parties, with the most important being the Communist Party of the Russian Federation (CPRF), which would become the focus of strong opposition to Yeltsin in society and in parliament.

Describing the time when the parliament had removed his power to rule by decree, Yeltsin recalled: "No Gaidar law could pass . . . not a single reform that would be painful for the population got through without encountering fierce political hindrances. Instead of common efforts and patience, we encountered stark dissatisfaction and vehement resistance. . . . A reform government could not work together with a Communist parliament. So I was forced to say good-bye to the Gaidar government."[27] Yeltsin then appointed as prime minister a member of the Communist managerial leadership, Victor Chernomyrdin, the director of Gazprom, the large natural gas monopoly from the Soviet era. In Yeltsin's words, "A completely different era began, a slow, careful and rather contradictory era of economic reform. . . . The banking and loan systems started to function, privatization began, a market of goods and services emerged and the first class of Russian entrepreneurs appeared. This was a real revolution for our country, where people had spent decades fearing the bosses and were completely devoid of initiative and competition."[28]

As Yeltsin made additional compromises with the hard-line opposition, he found himself losing support from some elements of the democratic reform movement who had supported him for years (much as he had moved away from Gorbachev). At the same time, in 1993, the hard-line Communist opposition grew stronger and more demanding. Yeltsin considered dissolving the parliament in the spring of 1993 but decided not to do so when he found no support for this step within Russia or within the major democracies. Instead, Yeltsin decided to call a referendum so that the Russian people could vote on the reforms. This referendum, held in April 1993, provided the Communist Party and the ultranationalist party of Zhirinovsky with an opportunity to mobilize supporters and organize for this vote. Although there was no major pro-democratic or pro-Yeltsin party at the time, Yeltsin won the vote, with 59 percent supporting reform versus 39 percent opposing. With that popular endorsement, Yeltsin hoped to move toward compromise with the parliament on a new constitution but found instead adamant and implacable opposition. Yeltsin's own vice president in effect joined the opposition by agreeing with the Communist view that the economic changes were "genocide against the Russian people."

In August 1993, as a prelude to reversing the economic reforms, a Communist-led coalition in the Russian parliament again tried to gather the 67 percent of the vote needed to amend the Russian constitution and reduce Yeltsin's authority to that of a figurehead. Yeltsin countered in September 1993 by dissolving the Russian legislature. He then called for national elections for a new legislature to be held in December 1993. This was to be coupled with a referendum on Yeltsin's draft of a new constitution, which provided for a strong presidency and a weaker legislature.

Yeltsin had come to this decision after concluding that it was impossible to reach an effective compromise with the current parliament elected in the Soviet era, which remained strongly opposed to his government no matter his compromises on the economic reforms. He and his advisors took as their precedent the decision of President Charles de Gaulle to unilaterally dissolve the Fourth Republic in France (in 1958) and establish a new, strong presidential constitution by means of a referendum and new elections. Yeltsin would say later that he had to act against the letter of the constitution in order to preserve the opportunity for the rule of law and democracy.

A core group of hard-line Communists and ultranationalist deputies of the parliament refused to obey the order to dissolve the parliament, and instead armed and barricaded themselves inside the Russian parliament building. This group was led by General Alexander Rutskoi, Yeltsin's vice president and the speaker of the Russian Supreme Soviet. Rutskoi and his group declared themselves to be the legal government of Russia and announced that Yeltsin's actions were unconstitutional and illegal. They chose their own defense minister and ordered army units to support them.[29] At the same time, a number of activists from various Communist movements organized armed groups that moved to attack and occupy Russian telecommunications facilities in Moscow.

Yeltsin met this challenge with forceful action. He ordered troops from the Ministry of the Interior (MVD) to intercept these rebel armed units in Moscow and to forcibly remove the rebelling armed deputies and their supporters from the Russian parliament. The regular armed forces of the Ministry of Defense hesitated, but after receiving a written order from President Yeltsin, they committed military forces to support him.[30] This dramatic armed confrontation demonstrated for the second time in as many years that the armed forces hold the balance of decision when politics moves toward violent confrontation.

The U.S. and all the democracies supported President Yeltsin in his actions.

Perhaps that is why there has been relatively little comment about one very important aspect of the crisis. During the tense two weeks of confrontation and for some weeks thereafter in the fall of 1993, Yeltsin ruled under a state of emergency. It proved relatively easy for even the reformist government of Yeltsin to curtail or roll back significant elements of the freedom of press, assembly, and association during and immediately after the crisis. With the stroke of a pen and the perception of the predominance of military and police forces behind President Yeltsin, there was a marked change in the Russian print and electronic media toward support of the regime or withholding of criticism. There was a suspension of civil liberties, not only for those arrested with weapons, but also for thousands of members of ethnic groups believed to be associated with organized criminal activities. Those arrested were held in prisons and improvised detention facilities, then deported by the thousands to their home regions, where some continued to be imprisoned. Several pro-Communist newspapers were closed or had their editorial management changed.

These steps against "disorder" and armed opposition were widely perceived as justifiable both inside and outside Russia. Nevertheless, the actions of October 1993, following the defeat of the armed opposition to Yeltsin, illustrated the fragile, reversible nature of the transformations in the political institutions of Russia. Recall that years of market-oriented changes and some liberalization instituted by Lenin during the New Economic Policy phase of his rule were quickly ended beginning in 1929, as Stalin consolidated his power.

Largely missing from the struggle in September–October 1993 was the mass of Russian citizens. They did not answer the call of those opposed to reform to come by the tens of thousands and protect the legislators opposed to Yeltsin. Neither did they demonstrate in large numbers for President Yeltsin. They did not visibly support or oppose Yeltsin's suspension of civil liberties. They were on the sidelines of their own history—perhaps too disappointed by the results of Yeltsin's economic policies to give him enthusiastic and sustained visible support as in August 1991, but also not ready to support a return to the Communist regime.

Yet, the crisis did mark another defeat for the Communist-led forces and especially for their attempted use of violence. They had failed in August 1991, they had failed in November–December 1992 using legislative means, failed in the April 1993 referendum, and failed again with violence in September–October 1993. However, the Communist groups once again showed political determination and resilience as they immediately organized to compete in the December 1993 national election for the Russian parliament, which would complete the two years remaining in the term of the previous parliament (1990–1995).

The largest Communist Party, led by Gennadi Zuyganov, used its more than five hundred thousand members to organize its election campaign activities throughout Russia. The ultranationalists led by Vladimir Zhirinovsky had already participated in two Russian national political campaigns, June 1991 and April 1993. They immediately set about using and expanding their regional and national networks. Both the Communists and the ultranationalists quickly gathered the one hundred thousand signatures necessary to get on the ballot and both ran campaigns focusing on the negative economic and social results of Yeltsin's program of "shock therapy."

Following Yeltsin's success in withstanding the September–October 1993 armed revolt, most observers in the major democracies underestimated the resilience of the antireform groups and the possibility that the Communists and ultranationalists might, in fact, perform very well in the December 1993 vote for the new national legislature.[31] During the brief campaign, the antireform movements called on their existing national organizations, criticized shortcomings of the present, and promised a better future. In contrast, the proreform political parties supporting the Yeltsin program had the double burden of being newly established and of having to defend the Yeltsin economic record and its consequences. In addition, since nearly all public opinion polls showed the pro-Yeltsin parties far in the lead, with about 70 percent of the vote, there was an element of overconfidence.[32]

After the December 12, 1993, balloting, the Yeltsin government announced that a majority of the population had endorsed the new constitution. This significantly increased the powers of the president of Russia. The new constitution established the Federal Assembly as a new bicameral legislature: the upper house would be the Federation Council, composed of two representatives from each of the eighty-nine regions and territories within Russia; a lower house, or State *Duma*, would consist of 450 members, half elected by proportional representation through party lists and half chosen on the basis of single-mandate candidacies. The constitution also granted president Yeltsin important new powers and established what some have called "super presidentialism."[33] The Russian president could veto legislation and only be overridden by a two-thirds majority of both the upper and lower houses. Under some conditions, he could dissolve the lower house of parliament and call for new elections. For example, this could be done if the State *Duma* failed three times to endorse his proposed prime minister.

The Russian president would be the head of state, the commander in chief of the armed forces, and had the authority to nominate and dismiss all government ministers. The head of the Central Bank would now report to the president rather than to the parliament, as had been the case before. This was a very important change and undoubtedly contributed to the fact that inflation, which had totaled 3,800 percent in 1992–23, was sharply reduced in subsequent years as the Yeltsin government obtained control of the money supply.[34]

While Yeltsin obtained the new constitution he wanted, the result of the December 1993 parliamentary election was a major setback for Yeltsin and the reform movement. The three main parties supporting political democracy and economic reform received 44 percent of the votes and won 26 percent of the seats of the State *Duma;* the Communist and ultranationalists, strongly opposed to Yeltsin and the reform program, received 43 percent of the popular vote and 31 percent of the seats in the *Duma;* and the market authoritarian parties, which favored some degree of economic reform but were indifferent to democratic reforms, won about 9 percent of the popular vote and 16 percent of the seats in the *Duma.*

The main party supporting the Yeltsin program headed by Yegor Gaidar, widely seen as the architect of economic reforms, received about 15 percent of the popular vote. It was burdened by its direct association with the negative economic results of the first two years. All three proreform parties were far less organized and had far fewer resources than did the Communist Party of the Russian Federation (CPRF) and Zhirinovsky's ultranationalist party.

Given the short time available for the campaign, mid-October to mid-December 1993, there was an even greater premium on grass-roots organization. It was the Communist Party which had twenty thousand local branches and a membership in excess of a half million, which could and did campaign throughout Russia. The Communist Party and its country cousin, the Agrarian Party, led by Communist collective farm mangers, together obtained 21 percent of the vote. The ultranationalist party of Zhirinovsky received 23 percent of the vote—a clear protest against the direction of Russian policy.

While Yeltsin had hoped that a freely elected Russian legislature would produce a majority in support of his program and government, in fact, the ironic result was that his coalition was diminished by doing less well than expected, and the antireform Communists and ultranationalists were strengthened. This election result would define the political struggle in the years ahead.

THE THREE PILLARS OF THE EMERGING "PARTY OF POWER"

In the context of hard-line Communist opposition and severe economic difficulties that seemed to grow worse following the 1992 "shock therapy," Yeltsin understood the potential fragility and reversibility of his effort to establish democratic and market-oriented reforms. With Chernomyrdin as prime minister (1993–98), Yeltsin had an individual who, in his words, "sat through the compromise between the market and the Soviet directors' corps" and who could bring some of the state industry managers into a more cooperative relationship with his government.[35] Yeltsin's gradually growing coalition included many of his original supporters, those he appointed to government or state sector managerial positions, those state sector managers working with Yeltsin/Chernomyrdin, and later a number of major private-sector business tycoons. Collectively, these would come to be called the "party of power."

The December 1993 elections gave Yeltsin the presidential constitution he sought and he used it and three evolving main sources of support to govern through a series of crises to the end of his time in the presidency, despite the continuing opposition of the well-organized Communists. These three pillars of the Yeltsin coalition were the "power ministries"; the United States and the major democracies; and a number of the newly wealthy Russian businessmen.

The "Power Ministries"

From the early twentieth century, when the Russian monarchy established constitutional governance in "royal ministries," the Ministry of Internal Affairs, Ministry of Defense, the secret police, and intelligence service "were empowered to report directly to the Czar" rather than the prime minister who dealt with economic, financial, and social issues.[36] This continued into the Soviet era, when they reported to the general secretary of the CPSU. Yeltsin, from the start, viewed these as "presidential ministries," which would report to him personally. By his account, at most times of major political crisis or decision he would consult with the power ministries—for example when he considered whether to postpone the presidential election scheduled for June 1996.[37]

The armed revolt and conflict of September–October 1993 had demonstrated again to Yeltsin the importance of the power ministries in determining the future of Russia. As 1994 opened, he used his presidential authority to issue a decree subordinating all "organs of force" strictly to himself, establishing them as a Security Council. This included the Ministry of Defense, the Ministry of Internal Affairs (MVD), the Foreign Intelligence Service (SVR), the Federal Security Service (FSB), and the government information and communications agency responsible for all electronic eavesdropping and intercept operations.

Yeltsin had always understood the importance of these organizations and maintained good relations with them. He did this by taking their views into account on issues of direct interest to them and by promising them salary increases, bonuses, and better budgets—promises which he often did not, in fact, implement. Yeltsin also balanced the various institutions against each other. By 1994, the regular military armed forces had approximately 1.4 million men, while the "multiple militaries" had a nearly equivalent number. These included the armed forces of the MVD, the Border Guards, the Presidential Guards, the federal security service, and others. In fact, Yeltsin generally provided better weapons and resources to the multiple militaries in contrast to the conventional armed forces. [38]

Soon after the military backed him during the October 1993 crisis, Yeltsin agreed with the military on a new defense doctrine for Russia, which was more assertive than the views of Foreign Minister Andrei Kozgrev. However, Yeltsin never provided the military with the funds necessary to implement that blueprint.[39] Yeltsin also deferred to the views of the military on issues of the "near abroad," as the former Soviet republics were called, agreeing to maintain Russian troops in a number of the former republics. Yeltsin deferred to the military on issues related to the conversion to civilian production of the military-industrial complex, which the military resisted; and on a number of other national security issues, such as the military's strong opposition to returning the Russian-claimed Kurile Islands to Japan. Perhaps most importantly, Yeltsin acquiesced to the military's insistence that it remain essentially self-managing with little real oversight by the legislature.

Yeltsin's own actions and the 1996 defense law gave the parliament only two powers relevant to military matters—the power to pass the defense budget and to write laws regulating military organization.[40] But the military was not exempt from the pervasive problem of unpaid wages and benefits that became endemic in these years of economic difficulty, as the Russian government tried to meet targets for reducing its budget deficits by withholding wages of government employees, including the military, as well as payments to pensioners and others.

As Yeltsin moved to solidify his support from the military and the other "power ministries" in 1994, he made two decisions about the Chechen separatist movement. First, the government would provide covert support to pro-Moscow Chechens to help them remove the separatist regime. When that failed, in late 1994 the "Security Council passed a decision to launch a military operation" to defeat the Muslim separatist movement.[41] This decision was made with strong support from the minister of defense, General Pavel Grachev, who "believed firmly in a lightening strike military operation."[42] This decision reflected Yeltsin's deferring to the military and his preoccupation with the risk of Russian fragmentation through cascading separatism.

As it turned out, the Russian armed forces were unprepared for this combat that led to an estimated one hundred thousand persons killed on both sides, including many thousands of totally unexpected Russian military casualties. The commanding officer who overcame the defenses of the Chechen capital, General Lev Rokhlin, refused the medals offered by Yeltsin and subsequently became one of Yeltsin's strongest opponents in the parliament and among military officers.[43] More than five hundred officers resigned from the Russian military rather than participate in the Chechen war.[44] Nevertheless, Yeltsin maintained the support of the power ministries throughout his presidency. His expanding relations with China after 1996 were part of this pattern.

The United States and the Major Democracies

There was an immense initial feeling of hopefulness for a future of good relations among the leaders of the major democracies as the Yeltsin-led reformers emerged to govern a newly independent Russia. The United States immediately offered and sent by air large quantities of food and other humanitarian assistance, and in January 1992 the Bush administration convened a large conference of all major democracies and the emerging democracies of Eastern Europe to discuss how best to organize large-scale assistance in support of the Yeltsin government.

Yeltsin and Gaidar visited the United States in late January 1992. There were extensive discussions on how help might be provided; some held in the relaxed setting of Camp David, where Bush and Yeltsin spoke at length. This began a process whereby the United States, Germany, other major democracies and the Western financed IMF and World Bank provided Russia with more than $120 billion in bilateral and multilateral assistance and credits from 1992 to 1999.[45] As noted, the first large-scale commitment was $18 billion in April 1992, the same month in which Bush sent the U.S Congress his proposal for a multiyear program of bilateral U.S. aid for Russia and the other post-Soviet Republics .

Yeltsin and Bush met three times in the course of one year and made progress on a number of major issues. This included reaching agreement on the advisability of having a missile defense to cope with accidental/unauthorized launches or third-country attacks.[46] Yeltsin was immediately invited to join the Group of Seven industrial democracies (which became the G8), Russia was quickly brought into the IMF and World Bank, and there were many reciprocal summit meetings and state visits with all the leaders of the major democracies.

These symbolic and practical actions were intended to help Yeltsin meet the immense political and economic challenges of the post-Communist transition, and he believed these were helpful. For example, in 1996 as Yeltsin faced an uphill battle for reelection with only 3 percent approval in the polls, he described the G8 summit on nuclear security held in Moscow in early 1996 as "an invaluable show of moral support" which "alone was of tremendous political significance."[47]

From early 1992, this international democratic support evoked recurrent criticism from the Communists that Yeltsin was selling Russia to the west. Yeltsin tried to counter the criticism by adding Communist China as a "Strategic Partner" in the spring of 1996. As it would turn out, after the 1999 NATO-Russia crisis and the ever closer Russia-China alignment, the international democratic "pillar" seemed to become less important internally as Vladimir Putin moved toward the presidency.

Financial-Industrial Groups (the "Tycoons")

The first war in Chechnya ended in 1996 when General Alexander Lebed, at Yeltsin's direction, negotiated a truce. That war had a very disillusioning effect on the political coalition supporting Yeltsin. As with Gorbachev, Yeltsin found himself in 1994 and 1995 criticized from both sides of the political spectrum—by his former democratic allies for the Chechen war and by the Communists and ultranationalists for the consequences of his economic policies.

The continuing economic problems in 1995 led the Communist and ultrana-tionalist opposition to believe they could win an even larger proportion of the seats in the parliament in elections scheduled for December 1995. The Communists hoped the 1995 election would be the prelude to their winning the scheduled June 1996 presidential election. They believed that if they could build on public dissatis-faction with the economic results of the Yeltsin years they could win the presidency. If so, they would, in essence, have the power to implement their agenda of restoring much of the Communist system.

An important aspect of Yeltsin's economic reforms was privatization—the selling to private owners of production and commercial assets owned by federal, regional, or local governments. Privatization was intended to bring the efficiency of private ownership to the productive process, with the hope that this would lead to all the benefits of entrepreneurship—greater investment, better management, more efficient use of labor, lower prices, and the production of goods that people wanted to buy. It was also hoped that privatization would have two important political effects: undercutting the political power of the Communist managerial elite and dispersing political influence and interests among private owners, who would themselves become an important social group in support of democracy and further economic reform. By 1995, about 70 percent of Russian industrial production was counted as having been privatized.[48]

A large proportion of the new owners were, in fact, former Communist managers. They had been given shares in the state enterprises and had also bought up shares that had been given to workers. In effect, in many of the now-privatized enterprises the management continued as before. There were strong institutional inhibitions on reducing employment and the government continued to provide credits and funds to pay part of the wages in order to avoid unemployment. In retrospect, this would be viewed as having contributed to a continuing budget deficit and as essentially the continuation of much of the former Communist economic policy.[49] Many in this Communist managerial elite, now the "owners" of nominally privatized enterprises, in essence continued their previous practices and also supported the Communist criticism of the reform program because of the difficulties they encountered.

There were essentially two economies in Russia, one focused on the Russian internal market, which was burdened by the overall economic problems; the other was the sector connected to export markets, where Russian products could be sold for hard currency. These included precious metals, oil, natural gas, and similar products. This lucrative market came to be dominated by a comparatively small group of politically well-connected financial-industrial groups presided over by newly wealthy individuals. Most trace the origin of the financial barons to 1987, when the Russian financial system was liberalized and a number of individuals, mostly members of the Young Communist leadership who wanted to become businessmen, started up their own banks. They learned the art of finance and of international financial operations and, as described by one observer, "They made fortunes because the government was weak and ripe for the picking."[50]

In the post-1992 Russian economy, these individuals gained large sums of money by selling commodities for hard currency and then speculating against the exchange rate, at times using money borrowed from the government for their financial operations. The Russian government generally deposited its funds with "authorized" banks, including those owned by individuals who would later become the leaders of the main financial-industrial groups. The government not only decided in which banks it would deposit its money, but also which individuals would be permitted to receive which opportunities derived from the economic changes.

Among the competing business interests in Russia, by 1995 six industrial-financial groups emerged as the wealthiest. Each of these six major groups usually each included a bank with financial holdings, export-oriented industries, and some media properties. The financial-industrial oligarchs or barons, as they were variously called, also worked cooperatively together. In fact, in a rare moment of candor, one of them said publicly, "When we see a critical situation in the government, we draw lots in order to pick out a person from our milieu for work in power."[51]

These financial-industrial barons understood that their wealth, influence, and future prospects depended upon a Yeltsin government continuing in power and on the Communists not returning to power. Communists were incessantly critical of these "tycoons." They were viewed as exploiting the resources and people of Russia and as "criminals" whom the Communists repeatedly said they would "bring to justice" when they took power again.

In 1995, the Russian government approved a "loans for shares" project: bankers lent money to the cash-poor government and in return received shares in Russia's most lucrative enterprises.[52] As described by David Hoffman, "If the government failed to pay back the loans, the bankers could sell off the companies and they did—to themselves; many of the auctions were rigged from the inside."[53] Through that process, the six major financial-industrial groups gained control of many of Russia's most lucrative producers of metal and oil in 1995. In turn, they used a part of their profits in 1995–1996 to obtain control over most Russian television and major print. These financial-industrial-media groups became the third major pillar of institutional support for Yeltsin and his government. They used their financial and media assets to help Yeltsin win the 1996 presidential elections, to help the "party of power" in the December 1999 parliamentary elections, and to help Yeltsin's preferred successor, Vladimir Putin, win the March 2000 presidential election.

The Elections of 1995 and 1996—the Communists
Seek Restoration

As the parliamentary elections of December 1995 approached, Yeltsin had lost the support of many of the democratic reformers who had been with him over the years. They were disappointed by the negative results of his economic program, and were deeply opposed to the war in Chechnya. They were also concerned about the evolution toward both *"nomenklatura* capitalism" and the financial-industrial group dominance that suggested large-scale corrupt relationships between the government and private interests. There was also deep disappointment with the growth of organized crime, which expanded as the power of the state weakened and as the new economic arrangements offered many more opportunities for corrupt and coercive dealings with both government and private sector interests.[54]

A new political party was established to carry the banner of the government in the 1995 election. This party, Our Home is Russia (NDR), was headed by Prime Minister Chernomyrdin and was strongly supported by the financial-industrial-media groups. The economist Gregori Yavlinsky continued his pro-democratic reform party, *Yabloko,* and campaigned actively, as did several other smaller pro-reform parties. Led by Genadi Zyuganov, the main Communist Party and its allied parties were active and optimistic. They felt they had a message that would resonate with the people of Russia: the Yeltsin government had failed in its economic program, had failed to maintain orderly life in Russia by permitting extensive corruption and the expansion of crime, and had failed to assure Russia's independence from Western pressure, especially from the Western financial institutions (IMF, World Bank), which provided funds linked to economic conditions that harmed Russia. The ultranationalist party, led by Zhirinovsky, emphasized Yeltsin's failure to maintain the "greatness" of Russia.

The national election for the State *Duma* was held as scheduled on December 17, 1995. About 65 percent of Russia's 108 million registered voters participated. International observers pronounced the elections reasonably free and fair, although some believed the election campaign had not been fair because the pro-Yeltsin party had far greater access to the radio and television, which was mostly controlled by the financial barons or the government.

In broad terms, the result represented a continuation of the December 1993 election. The main parties supporting Yeltsin received about 10 percent of the vote. This was seen as a setback for Yeltsin and a bad portent for his run for the presidency in 1996. But all the parties supporting democratic and economic reform together received about 30 percent of the vote, an increase from the 24 percent they had received in 1993. The Communist-allied parties also increased their vote from about 28 percent of the total to 35 percent. Zhirinovsky's ultranationalist party fell sharply from about 23 percent of the vote to about 11 percent. Both Yeltsin and the Communists took these results as a sign that they could well win the Russian presidency in June 1996.

The newly elected State *Duma* convened in January 1996 and chose as its chairman Genady Scleznev, a member of the Communist Party. Among the twenty-eight committees, Communists and their allies headed thirteen. As a result of the Communist dominance of the *Duma,* they replaced "the permanent staffs of committees [they] dominated . . . and the parliamentary facilities served as the CPRF's [Communists'] campaign headquarters."[55] The Communist Party intended by its "discipline and cohesion" in the parliament to demonstrate that it was prepared to govern seriously if it won the presidency in 1996.

Half of the *Duma's* 450 seats were decided on the basis of party list votes and half were single-mandate seats, for which individuals campaigned. In order to qualify to receive seats from the party list, political parties had to obtain more than 5 percent of the total vote. This provision in the constitution was intended to prevent the parliament from being divided into a number of very small parties. In December 1995, only four parties received more than 5 percent of the vote—the Communists (CPRF), the pro-Yeltsin Our Home is Russia, *Yabloko,* and Zhirinovsky's party. According to their share of the total vote, each of these parties received a proportionate number of the party-list seats, which led to a situation where the proportion of total *Duma* seats was larger for these four parties than their proportion of the popular vote. As the *Duma* considered legislation, the Communist Party organized a group of its allied parties together into a coalition that generally produced about 213 votes on most issues. The coalition of pro-Yeltsin parties usually had about 152 votes, and Zhirinovsky's party often voted with the pro-Yeltsin coalition, adding its 50 votes.[56]

Until July 1996, the question dominating Russian politics was: would the Communists win the presidency? This certainly seemed a possibility. The economic situation continued to be difficult, although there was a significant reduction in inflation during 1996 and the fall in GDP was "only" 5 percent. To help Yeltsin, the U.S. led the way in providing $10 billion in IMF financing and additional bilateral economic assistance. Yet, Yeltsin was at a very low point in popularity, with some polls showing him having support in the single digits. The Communist Party made every effort to present itself as reasonable, constructive, and determined to improve the well being of the Russian people.[57]

With the situation in early 1996 appearing hopeless, at the urging of General Korzhakov, chief of his bodyguard for many years, and others of the "Soviet mentality," Yeltsin gave the order to prepare decrees banning the Communist Party, dissolving the parliament, and postponing the presidential elections.[58] But first Yeltsin met to discuss this with the "power ministers," who advised him that they were not certain they could contain public protests by the Communists. At the same time, Yeltsin's daughter Tanya, who had been working in the election campaign with Anatoly Chubais, an economic reformer, persuaded Yeltsin that it would be unconstitutional and a grave mistake to postpone the elections. That led to Yeltsin's decision to move away from those with a "Soviet mentality" and work instead with a modern-style campaign team, whom he described as "young people with clear heads and straightforward language, unburdened by the heavy weight of the [Soviet] past."[59]

While the Communists had their nationwide organization, the leading financial-industrial-media barons gave Yeltsin their full support during the campaign. According to one informed observer, they contributed millions of dollars, providing Yeltsin with "virtually unlimited resources."[60] Most importantly, they used their ownership of radio and television to provide favorable media coverage for Yeltsin throughout the election campaign, while virtually ignoring other competing candidates and providing only nominal overage of the Communist candidate.

The media campaign on behalf of Yeltsin not only showed him at his energetic best as a campaigner, highlighting the positive aspects of the changes that had occurred since 1992, but also used archival film footage and documentary material to vividly remind the Russian people about the immense suffering caused by the Communists during the years of Stalinist rule. There were many dramatic televised episodes of never-before-seen film of Stalin-era concentration camps—including concentration camps for children, who were shown in fear as they suddenly found themselves in prisons. The television documentaries also showed many other aspects of the brutality and terror of the Communist years.[61] The message was clear and simple: a vote for Yeltsin is a vote for a new Russia, while a vote for the Communist Party is a vote for a return to dictatorship and state terror.

The candidacy of democratic reformer Gregori Yavlinsky was handicapped by the fact that in the two previous national elections his party had received only about 7 percent of the vote. This reduced the prospect that he could become the reform alternative to Yeltsin. Yavlinsky's party and the other small pro-democratic reform parties had far fewer resources and a very small membership base in comparison to either the Communist Party or Yeltsin's "party of power," which was fully backed by the financial-industrial-media elites.

The first round in June 1996 gave Yeltsin and Zyuganov the most votes, but neither received more than 50 percent, so a second round was needed. Before the second round, Yeltsin replaced a number of those in the power ministries, including Minister of Defense Grachev (seen as responsible for the Chechnya war), Presidential Security Chief Alexander Korzakov (by then known to have urged postponing the election), and the director of the Federal Security Service, Mikail

Barsukov. Yeltsin's purpose was to encourage his disaffected democratic supporters to vote for him in the second round rather than abstaining. Moreover, the dismissed officials had been seen by the financial barons as allies of the military-industrial complex and opposed to them. As McFaul described it, "Their departure from the Kremlin and the government created a new balance of power within the state more favorable to the new economic elite."[62] Yeltsin also sought to appeal to the 15 percent who had voted for General Lebed by appointing him head of the newly reconstituted Security Council, as well as special envoy to end the war in Chechnya. Yeltsin's strategy paid off as he was reelected with 54 percent of the vote compared to 40 percent for Zyuganov.

The Russian presidential election in June and July 1996 was the second time that the people of Russia had the opportunity to choose their president in a reasonably open and competitive national election. The results suggest three conclusions about the political evolution of Russia. First, despite all of the political and economic problems surrounding the Yeltsin government, a majority of the Russian people preferred to continue in Yeltsin's direction rather than risk a return to Communist rule. In fact, it is worth noting that in the three Russian national votes, June 1991, April 1993 referendum, and the presidential election of 1996, Yeltsin received between 54 and 59 percent of the vote, while his Communist opposition received between 36 and 40percent.[63] This showed that while a large proportion of Russians were willing to vote for the Communist Party, a still larger proportion provided support for Yeltsin and his program, even in the face of many disappointments. At the same time, the large vote for Communist candidates certainly gave the Communist Party hope that it might prevail in future elections. Second, all contending political groups were willing to use political means alone to compete for power. There were virtually no instances of violence or direct hostile action during the generally peaceful election process. Third, the 1996 Russian presidential election further illustrated and reinforced the shift to open, competitive elections as the basis of legitimacy in governance.

Dangerous Challenges to Yeltsin

Yeltsin campaigned very vigorously for reelection. He knew that there was every possibility that the Communist Party could win and undo the changes he had made. Yeltsin traveled the country and gave speeches in all regions across eleven time zones of the vast nation. He had appeared with rock bands for youth groups, danced vigorously on stage, and shown enormous energy for a person who had had recent serious illnesses. All this took its toll, and between the first and second rounds of the presidential election, Yeltsin again became very ill, though this fact was hidden from the electorate. After the election, Yeltsin needed a major heart operation, which many thought he might not survive, and an extended period of convalescence which lasted months.

In this context, Anatoli Chubais, the person who had organized his reelection campaign, was appointed chief of staff, an appointment with even greater importance because of Yeltsin's illness. Chubais had a good relationship with a number of the financial-industrial barons, and two of those individuals wanted to enter the government directly. Berezovsky, one of the barons, became vice chairman of the important Security Council. Chernomyrdin remained as prime minister. Within the Yeltsin administration, there was continuing competition for influence between the camp of Chernomyrdin, more oriented toward the state enterprise mangers, and that of Chubais, more oriented toward the financial-industrial-media barons.

General Lebed, as the newly appointed head of the Security Council, undertook direct and high-profile negotiating missions with the Chechen leadership. By the end of August 1996, he had concluded a truce that was widely welcomed within Russia. Fresh from that success, Lebed began organizing his staff to take more forceful action against organized crime, including a plan for a combined military and internal police unit that would "fight the criminals with their own methods." From his sickbed, Yeltsin became concerned as Lebed seemed to be reaching for more and more control over the "power ministries." As described by Yeltsin, "Even after Lebed had brought the Defense Ministry under his control, he didn't stop. He began an attack on the Ministry of the Interior and went after Minister Kulikov."[64] Yeltsin decided Lebed had to be removed, but carefully, as he considered the "worst case scenario of a military coup with absolute seriousness: paratroopers landing in Moscow, the buildings of the power ministries being seized ... the paratroopers ... idolized Lebed."[65] As General Lebed's popularity continued to increase, Yeltsin, having made careful preparations, dismissed him in a dramatic televised address in October 1996. General Lebed had served an important purpose, but he now seemed potentially dangerous.

In the United States, as part of his presidential election campaign, Clinton stated in October 1996 that he believed NATO should be enlarged to include Poland, Hungary, and the Czech Republic. In December 1996, NATO moved ahead with plans to begin the enlargement in 1997, with the final acceptance of the new members to occur on the fiftieth anniversary of NATO in 1999. This led Russian Foreign Minister Primakov and Prime Minister Chernomyrdin to make a number of strong statements opposing NATO enlargement. In February 1997, Prime Minister Chernomyrdin visited the U.S. and said that NATO enlargement could well result in a revival of Russian military production and an expansion of Russian military forces.[66]

In the former Soviet Republic of Belarus, Alexander Lukashenko, a hard-line Communist, had taken power and was proposing a treaty of unity with Russia. Both

Chernomyrdin and Primakov agreed to the text of a treaty of unification, which included provisions that "would have enabled a coalition between the Belorussian president . . . and the anti-Yeltsin opposition in Russia to [in effect] legally remove Yeltsin from power by permitting the Communist dominated parliaments in both countries to jointly choose a new president for the unified federation."[67] This draft treaty permitting a stealth coup to remove Yeltsin had been approved by every part of the Russian government, as well as by Prime Minister Chernomyrdin and Foreign Minister Primakov.

It was only because the independent press raised the issue of this potentially anti-Yeltsin part of the treaty that Anatoli Chubais, chief of staff, looked into the matter and persuaded Yeltsin not to sign the treaty as written, thereby avoiding a potentially serious mistake.[68] Once alerted, Yeltsin learned that the foreign minister of Belarus was "an active member of the Russian Communist Party" and that those behind this move were not only the Communists in both countries but also those "who dream of restoring the Soviet Union at all costs."[69] This episode undoubtedly further persuaded Yeltsin that he needed more allies at the top of his government and that he needed to find new leadership for the future.

In March and April 1997, Yeltsin made major changes to his government. He appointed Chubais deputy prime minister and finance minister, with overall responsibility for economic management; and brought in Boris Nemstov, who had been a reformer as the governor of Nizhny Novgorod. Nemstov became deputy prime minister for social affairs, housing, and reforming of monopolies. These changes reduced the influence of Prime Minister Chernomyrdin, as both new deputy prime ministers sought to reduce corruption by removing corrupt officials and reducing the power of Russia's natural resource monopolies—not excluding Gazprom, with its close ties to Prime Minister Chernomyrdin. They also attempted to reduce the special government benefits for the financial-industrial allies of the Yeltsin administration. Yeltsin held a meeting with the main financial barons in September 1997, whom he now viewed as "illegitimate centers of power in quiet bankers' offices. [Who] tried to run government offices. . . . It was necessary to set some clear boundaries."[70]

That was followed in 1997 by a "war of the bankers," in which two of the financial-industrial leaders accused Chubais of favoring a third in the allocation of a 25 percent share of a telecommunications company. Further, the barons opposed Chubais using the media they owned to contend that a publishing firm connected to the winning baron had given a four-person group headed by Chubais $490,000 each for publishing a book on privatization in Russia. The press accused the Chubais team of accepting an indirect bribe. Yeltsin fired Chubais and his team and recounted in his memoir that "the book scandal was the banana peel on which the whole team of young reformers slipped."[71] The end result of these disputes was that

Communist criticism increased, public perceptions of official corruption were reinforced, and in November 1997, Yeltsin dismissed one of the financial-industrial barons, Boris Beresovsky, as deputy secretary of the Security Council. All of this again increased the influence of Prime Minister Chernomyrdin, which lessened the impetuous for further reform just as the Asian financial crisis began to reduce the willingness of foreign investors to provide funds for Russia.

Meanwhile, there had been improvement in the Russian economy. Real wages increased by 5 percent in 1996 and again in 1997, inflation was down to an annual rate of 11 percent, and the first small increase in GNP was recorded since 1989.[72] As Yeltsin returned to the Kremlin in March 1998, after another long illness, he decided to remove prime minister Chernomyrdin and make a new start by appointing the minister of energy, thirty-five-year-old economist Sergi Keriyenko, as his new prime minister. While Yeltsin felt that Chernomyrdin's five years were marked by some steps forward, mostly he saw: "Huge defeats. We didn't manage to overcome the monopolization in the economy, the fall in production, and the decrepit system of mutual payments that fostered corruption and theft. We didn't manage to invest major funds in industry. . . . We didn't manage to improve People's lives."[73]

Thinking of the presidential succession in 2000, Yeltsin wanted a person of the new generation, "free from group interests and political ties . . . a technocrat. . . . a manager, an economist . . . a clean person."[74]

This nomination led to very strong opposition from the Communists in the *Duma,* which voted twice to reject Yeltsin's appointment of Keriyenko as prime minister. The month-long political standoff was a time of tension, but it was dealt with entirely within the constitutional political framework. According to the Russian constitution, if the *Duma* rejects the president's appointment for prime minister three times, the *Duma* is dissolved and new national elections for the lower house of parliament are held. Yeltsin held firm to the appointment of Keriyenko, and on the third vote, the *Duma* acceded, since even the Communist opponents of Yeltsin did not want to risk losing their seats in a new election. A week after his confirmation, Keriyenko proposed and Yeltsin appointed a strongly reform-oriented cabinet.

THE RUSSIAN FINANCIAL-POLITICAL CRISIS OF 1998: THE RISE OF PRIMAKOV

Commenting on Chernomyrdin's five years as prime minister (1992–1998), one informed observer summed up having "gone along with Russia's stutter-step journey toward capitalist democracy. But he had also presided over the insider deals and half-measures that led to its economic quagmire. . . . As the former head of Gazprom, Russia's huge natural gas monopoly, he was an unofficial member of the oligarchy.

He also enjoyed close ties with the Communist leadership in the parliament."[75] According to a Russian economist, the Chernomyrdin government showed "weakness and inconsistency in strengthening budget revenues and implementing structural adjustments; that is why the budget debt crisis in Russia was inevitable."[76]

In plain language, the Chernomyrdin government had been unwilling to tax the state enterprises or the wealthy financial-industrial barons, who by 1997 and 1998 were estimated to control nearly half of Russia's economy. The new Kiriyenko government intended to adopt a more assertive national-interest-oriented approach to the economy. It intended to increase tax revenue from the financial-industrial barons and others and reduce government expenditures, while at the same time obtain additional assistance from Western financial sources—most importantly the IMF, to help Russia over its serious problem of international and domestic debt.

In addition to long overdue hard-currency debt payments, the Keriyenko government faced a number of additional and immediate problems. In the first quarter of 1998, Asian businessmen withdrew nearly $2 billion from Russia in reaction to the Asian financial crisis. There was also a substantial drop in oil prices, which reduced hard-currency earnings for one of Russia's main exports. The Communist led *Duma* "cut by ⅔ the revenues that could be obtained as a result of the anticrisis program" and tried to block the reforms of the Kiriyenko government at every step.[77]

In July 1998, the Keriyenko government received commitments of external financial support amounting to $22.6 billion from the IMF ($15.1 billion directly from the Fund, $6 billion from the World Bank, and $1.5 billion from Japan). This was an important vote of confidence and an opportunity, but it came too late. Confidence in the Russian economy had been undermined by the political struggle with the Communists in the *Duma,* by the financial barons who did not want to pay taxes, and by the "contagion" effects of the Asian financial crisis.

On August 17, 1998, the Kiriyenko government and the Russian Central Bank announced a ninety-day moratorium on repayments of some foreign debt and a restructuring of ruble-denominated debt. This led to a dramatic loss of confidence in the ruble, which in a matter of days fell by nearly 50 percent against the dollar and other hard currencies. That, in turn, caused foreign portfolio investors to begin withdrawing funds from Russia and ended the inflow of foreign investment to Russia. These events produced an atmosphere of acute political and economic crisis. Living costs immediately increased for most Russians, since imports of food and other items were now 50 percent more expensive in rubles and the purchasing power of newly accumulated savings was cut in half.

The immediate reason for the financial crisis of August 1998 was that the Russian government continued to spend too much in relation to the resources it received through taxation.[78] At the same time, there was a pattern of "irresponsible monetary and exchange rate policy" from July 1995 through the beginning of the crisis in May 1998, when the foreign-exchange assets of the Russian government rose by only 8 percent while its liabilities in rubles increased by 137 percent. This gap made "the subsequent devaluation inevitable."[79]

In broadest terms, this financial crisis revealed the political-economic conse-quences of the absence of a broad-based democratic political movement, with substantial support in Russian society. Instead, on one side, the Communist oppo-sition opposed virtually everything the Yeltsin government did, and on the other, the Yeltsin government was politically dependent on and catered to the financial-industrial barons who essentially used the state for their own enrichment.[80] Yeltsin himself went from describing the constructive role of the Russian business tycoons, his "partners in government" in 1995–96[81] to strong criticism of their conduct in 1997–98, when he said they were seeking to establish "new illegitimate centers of power," a perspective Putin had already come to share.[82]

But it was Keriyenko and the reformers who were in office at the time that the financial crash occurred, again hurting the cause of market-oriented economic reform in the public mind and serving as a basis for renewed Communist attacks on Yeltsin. His response to the crisis was to remove the Keriyenko government and reappoint Chernomyrdin as prime minister. As Yeltsin put it, "Five months ago, no one expected the world financial crisis to hit Russia so hard. Today, we need those who are commonly referred to as heavyweights."[83]

But the Communists, knowing that the financial crisis was a strong setback for Yeltsin, were not ready to endorse his nominee as prime minister and steadfastly refused to do so. They voted twice against the nomination of Chernomyrdin. On September 10, 1998, Yeltsin nominated Primakov as prime minister, and the parlia-ment gave its approval the next day.

SEVEN DAYS IN MAY 1999

In late 1998, the Communist-led *Duma* decided to investigate articles of impeach-ment against President Yeltsin. Charges against Yeltsin included that he was respon-sible for the "illegal dissolution" of the Soviet Union; "genocide" against the Russian people as a result of the negative consequences of his economic policies; and waging an "illegal war" in Chechnya. With the beginning of debate and the vote on the impeachment articles scheduled for May 13, 1999, President Yeltsin took a major step the day before this procedure was to begin in parliament. He dismissed Prime Minister Primakov and announced that the newly appointed vice prime minister, Sergei Stepashin, would become acting prime minister.

This shocked many of the political leaders in Russia and caused immediate protests by the Communist leaders of the *Duma*. Yeltsin had acted at virtually the last moment. The Russian constitution provides that once the lower house of parliament has passed any article of impeachment against the president, until the impeachment issues are fully resolved the president cannot dissolve the *Duma*. Yeltsin understood that most of the Communists would strongly object to his removal of Primakov, and assuming that he survived the impeachment process, which Yeltsin expected to do, his main bargaining power with the *Duma* to bring about the confirmation of his designated successor to Primakov would lie in his capacity to threaten the dissolution of the parliament, forcing its members to compete for new elections before those scheduled in December 1999.

The impeachment debate was dramatic. The Communist leader Zyuganov called Yeltsin "absolute evil" and said in his closing remarks that Yeltsin was responsible for losing the Russian empire:

> a thousand year old power; a power that Hitler failed to conquer, but which through the efforts of Yeltsin and his team was torn to pieces .... Our country took almost five centuries to gain access to the seas, the Baltic Sea and the Black Sea, and today we have been thrown back from theses seas and we have sustained colossal economic and moral losses. We are all humiliated because the old people and the children, the women and the workers have been robbed. The strategic reserves of this country amounted to more than $200 billion. Everything has been wasted—sold and drunk away. We have lost almost all property which was accumulated not during the 70 years of Soviet power, but during all of the history of Russia.[84]

The ultranationalist Zhironovsky blamed not just the Yeltsin government, but what he called a two-hundred-year process of Western hostility to Russia:

> It cannot be said that the country was ruined in 1991. That decision was made in 1717 in Paris; two hundred eighty years ago, the West made a decision to destroy the Russian empire. Do you think Napoleon invaded Russia just for kicks? That Hitler attacked Russia just like that? That Yugoslavia is being bombed just like that? The target is one—the Russian empire, the Soviet Union; never mind that we are now a democratic country. They are moving closer and closer to Russian borders.[85]

Yeltsin was defended by the leader of the Our Home is Russia party in the *Duma*, Vladimir Ryzhkov, who pointed out that the *Duma* had approved the military action in Chechnya in 1994. However, Ryzhkov also criticized Yeltsin, saying: "In 1991, when he had the support of 97 percent of the population, he did not use the historic opportunity to create a truly democratic and stable state with a genuinely responsible parliament."[86]

None of the five articles of impeachment received the required two-thirds vote (300 out of the 442 active *Duma* members). The Yavlinsky democratic group voted for the charge that Yeltsin had begun the war in Chechnya illegally, which received the most votes: 283 for, 43 opposed. The votes on the other charges were as follows: genocide against the Russian people—283 for, 88 against; destroying the Russian army—240 for, 77 against; dismantling the Soviet Union illegally—239 for, 78 against; and staging a coup against the parliament in 1993—263 for, 60 against.[87] The charges summarized the Communist and ultranationalist grievances against President Yeltsin and represented deeply felt, serious allegations about the actions of the Yeltsin government.

It is notable that nearly ninety members of the *Duma* did not vote and some members of the *Duma* checked into Moscow clinics with various illnesses in order not to have to vote. Some suggested that this indicated that there was bribery or coercion at work.[88] The vote was seen by many in Russia as a victory for Yeltsin against the Communist Party and its allies. It was of some interest that the ultranationalist party of Zhironovsky, which often agreed with the Communists on issues of Russian foreign policy, opposed the impeachment process. Zhironovsky stated after Yeltsin won the vote that this was an opportunity to "crush the leftists," and he predicted that Yeltsin would move to ban the Russian Communist Party.[89]

With the impeachment vote having fallen short on May 15, 1999, Yeltsin's next challenge was to persuade the *Duma* to confirm Sergi Stepashin as the new prime minister of Russia. Born in 1952, Stepashin had received a law degree and then a graduate degree from the Soviet Interior Ministry's Senior Political School, at which he subsequently became a lecturer. He spent most of his time in the Soviet internal security organizations, but in August 1991, following the hard-line Communist coup attempt, Stepashin resigned from the Communist Party, and from that point forward became a strong and consistent supporter of President Yeltsin.

A member of parliament, he was viewed as a "centrist lawmaker" and served as the deputy internal security minister for Russia in 1992–1993, where he remained loyal to Yeltsin during the September–October 1993 armed confrontation following the dissolution of the parliament. Yeltsin then named Stepashin as first deputy director of the Federal Counterintelligence Service (FSK), the successor to the counterespionage functions of the Soviet KGB. In 1994, Stepashin became head of the FSK, and he kept that position when the organization was reorganized to form the Federal Security Service (FSB).[90]

On May 19, 1999, one week after having been nominated by President Yeltsin, the *Duma* confirmed Stepashin as the prime minister of Russia by a vote of 301 to 55. Publicly, Yeltsin said that he had removed Primakov because he had failed to act vigorously enough on economic issues, and Stepashin had told the *Duma* that he would be more active and move beyond the approach taken by Primakov: "A simple continuity of the course of political and economic stabilization is no longer enough. Changes have ripened in the very tactics of pursuing this course, there is no more place for half-hearted measures and compromise."[91] Stepashin's confirmation was viewed as a major victory for Yeltsin and his allies and another major political setback for the Communists and their allies. The Communist leader, Zyuganov, said after Stepashin's confirmation: "One government crisis is over, but another is just starting . . . . [Stepashin] has no clear program or team yet. I am certain that the crisis will only get worse."[92]

There were three related dimensions in Yeltsin's concern about Primakov's growing power: his institutional alliances in the power ministries and military-production complex and with the Communists; foreign policy; and the threat posed to some of Yeltsin's key backers, such as the financial barons and even his own family members.

In foreign policy, Primakov led a delegation to meet with Milosevic on March 30, 1999, which included his foreign minister, defense minister, the head of external intelligence, and the head of military intelligence—a group clearly intended to provide assistance and probably covertly support the Milosevic regime. In contrast, Yeltsin made his annual state of the nation speech and spoke with moderation about the Kosovo crisis:

> Russia's citizens are of course concerned about Yugoslavia, but even more concerned about Russia. . . . Our weight in the world depends upon how we solve our problems at home. . . . At the turn of the century, Russia must keep abreast of the leading world powers and build relations with them on a basis of self-respect and partnership. If we miss our chance again . . . the gates to the future will be slammed shut forever.[93]

As the Primakov government leadership issued increasingly hostile statements against NATO and the U.S., Yeltsin clearly became concerned that this and various covert activities could bring Russia into unintended or intended conflict with the U.S. and NATO. As a result, Yeltsin attempted to step back from the path being taken by Primakov by appointing former prime minister Chernomyrdin as his special negotiator.

The West welcomed Chernomyrdin's appointment and worked with him immediately to make Russia a constructive part of an effort to find a politically negotiated settlement. It was only in that context that Primakov and his foreign and defense ministers changed course and tone, as illustrated by the statement of Foreign Minister Ivanov on April 21: "There is violence in Kosovo in all directions, and as a result, everyone suffers, Albanians and Serbs."[94] This was the first time that the Primakov group had acknowledged, albeit indirectly, that there was suffering on the part of Albanians in Kosovo. Ivanov went on to say, "despite NATO's aggressive actions, we cannot break with Western countries, we cannot find ourselves in isolation. Russia continues to be a world power."[95] That change seemed to come after Primakov and his allies understood by Yeltsin's words and actions that Yeltsin was moving away from support for Primakov. Also, while billions in IMF Western financing were promised, they were not being provided as long as Russia seemed to be moving toward covert or open military aid to Milosevic.

After the Stepashin government was confirmed by the *Duma* and Yeltsin had prevailed, one of Yeltsin's top aides was quoted as describing former Prime Minister Primakov as "strategically dangerous . . . a man who demonstrated some characteristics of Stalin."[96] Speaking in the U.S. after Yeltsin's removal of Primakov, Anatoli Chubais, former deputy prime minister of Russia and confidante of Yeltsin, said that Yeltsin removed Primakov to prevent increasing Communist influence in the *Duma* and the upper house of parliament. In fact, Chubais said that the firing of Primakov was a "rational and timely decision," because it is linked to Yeltsin's most fundamental political goal, to build a new Russia where "the Communists will never be able to come to power."[97]

The result of the dramatic events of May 12–19, 1999 was that Yeltsin removed a key competitor for power by undercutting the gathering institutional momentum of Primakov and his Communist allies. Yeltsin also halted and reversed the Communist-ultrantionalist momentum toward potentially dangerous confrontation with NATO about Kosovo. Instead Russia moved toward pressure on Milosevic to withdraw his forces. This set the stage for the restoration of normal relations with the major democracies and for the allocation of international financial assistance. Yeltsin had returned to his three pillars of political support but also permitted the expansion of significant strategic and military cooperation with China.

THE YELTSIN ERA IN PERSPECTIVE

Since 1987, the Russian people were participants in and witnesses to a dramatic political struggle. Gorbachev tried to reform Communism and opened the way to an important degree of political liberalization that was met by sharp resistance from hard-line Communists seeking to keep the Soviet Party regime solidly in power. Their coup attempt in August 1991 failed, and Yeltsin led those seeking democratic reform and the independence of the constituent republics of the Soviet Union, bringing about the dissolution of the USSR in December 1991.

Given Yeltsin's stated commitment to political democracy and a market-oriented economy and his strong opposition to the Communist dictatorship, the hope in

1992 was that as the first popularly elected president of a newly independent Russia, Yeltsin could lead his country to the establishment of democratic institutions and economic changes that would bring economic growth, with better living conditions for all. At the same time, the fear was that the Communists would reorganize, establish a coalition with elements of the KGB and military and stage a successful coup to restore a Communist dictatorship. By the end of 1999, as Yeltsin resigned his office, neither the bright hopes nor the darkest fears at the beginning of 1992 had been met by the course of subsequent events. Instead, there were both negative and positive trends that left the direction of Russia's political future uncertain.

Negative Aspects

The first, and perhaps the most important, negative aspect is the continuing institutional weakness of the genuinely pro-democratic political parties and related civic associations, such as independent labor unions.

A second major negative aspect of the Yeltsin era was the continuation and expansion of the pattern of regime-criminal collusion from the Soviet era. In the words of David Satter, who has written perhaps the most powerful critique of what has evolved: "The society which exists in Russia today is run by and for criminals. The Russian government operates like a business in which every license, contract, or permission must be paid for; businesses adopt the methods of gangsters, criminals pretend to respectability and ordinary persons live in fear, convinced that they cannot count on the slightest protection of the law."[98]

The Russian Ministry of the Interior officially estimated that 40 percent of the Russian economy and nearly half of the banking sector was controlled by organized crime.[99] This has obviously contributed to the delegitimization of the idea of democracy and market-oriented reform in Russia and to the disappointment of the Russian people in Yeltsin, from whom they had expected so much more.

The combination of well-intentioned errors in public policy and the expansion of corruption and collusion with organized crime and semicriminal business elements in the economic realm have also contributed to the third major negative aspect of the Yeltsin era, the continued poor economic performance of Russia.

There had been some but too little progress toward an effectively functioning and independent judicial system in Russia. In the Communist era, the entire judicial system was simply an instrument to formalize the decisions of the Party and regime against individuals in the society.

There have been a number of changes in the legal system, including the phased introduction of a jury system beginning in 1993 and revisions to the criminal code in 1994, so that many of the normal practices of private business in a mixed economy were no longer defined as illegal. These revisions also provided guarantees for the protection of all forms of property. In 1995, the Russian parliament passed legislation intending to improve the independence and professional qualifications of judges, followed in 1996 by further legislation to assure the courts had adequate financial support, which had been a problem.[100] However, the Federal Security Service, the successor to the KGB for internal matters, still "enjoys extra-judicial powers, including the right to search premises without a court order."[101] And Freedom House notes that "pre-trial detention centers are generally deplorable and prisoners presumed innocent often languish for months in filthy, overcrowded cells before coming to trial."[102] These limitations on the fair functioning of the judiciary are compounding the pattern of corruption and organized criminal activity that has become endemic in Russia.

After decades in which only the Communist viewpoint was heard in the Russian mass media, during the Yeltsin years there was a flourishing of print and electronic media. By 1997, there were more than 150 independent television and radio companies operating in Russia. Russian citizens also had access to foreign cable and satellite radio and television broadcasts. The end of state control of the media meant the end of government subsidies. However, it also opened the way to a new development that raises new questions about the independence of much of the major electronic media. According to a Freedom House analysis,

> Russia's powerful financial syndicates, some with close ties to the government, have acquired control over or fund major media assets, raising the issue of press independence. . . . Berezovsky's LogoVaz owns shares in Russian state television (ORT) and TV6 and has a controlling stake in the newspaper *Nezavisimaya Gazeta* through the Obediodinionny bank. Gusensky's Media-Most controls 70 percent of NTV, an influential television station that broadcasts nationwide, and also owns *Segodnya,* and other leading newspapers. Onexinbank, along with Lukoil, has stakes in several papers, including *Ivestia.* SBS-ABRO is part of a consortium that owns 38 percent of ORT televisions and several newspapers and periodicals.[103]

The major financial-industrial-media barons close to Yeltsin clearly understood that their ownership of both electronic and print media could give them added political influence. They demonstrated this in the 1996 election, when they reduced coverage of the Communist challenger to Yeltsin, and again in the December 1999 parliamentary elections. At the same time, the Communist Party of Russia had received control of more than one hundred regional newspapers that had belonged to the former Communist Party of the Soviet Union. It uses these newspapers to promote its views. It could be argued that the role of both financial institutions and political parties in controlling elements of the media is simply part of political pluralism. Yet the dominance of the financial barons in national television limited the ability of competing political parties to reach the voters. This would become a major issue in the Putin years.

Another negative trend involving the independence of the media concerns the fact that while official censorship ended, the 1990s law on mass media limited the freedom of journalists to criticize public figures. That law and the law on the Protection of the Honor, Dignity and Business Reputation of Citizens (1991), in the view of human-rights monitoring organizations, has been and could be used to limit journalists' independence in criticizing and commenting on the public activities of public officials. There also is a very important provision of the law on mass media that permits "the compulsory suspension of the activity or the closing down of a medium of mass information . . . on the basis of the law and in accordance with a ruling of a court of law."[104] This suggests that individual courts in different regions of Russia could act against the independence of the media; also that there is a risk to the independence of the regional media because of the lack of independence of the courts in many of the regions of Russia where lower court officials are both appointed and paid by regional and local governments. These factors and existing limits on the pluralism and independence of the media in Russia suggested that even the limited levels of media independence at the end of the Yeltsin years were fragile.

A last negative trend is the change in the attitude of the Russian public toward political democracy and the process of political and economic change. The Yeltsin era of transition began with a population overwhelmingly opposed to the rule of the Communist Party and, for the most part, endorsing the idea of democracy and market-oriented economic reforms.[105] By 1995, opinion polls found that 60 percent of the Russian population "opposed the practice of democracy" and 81 percent believed that "elected officials do not care what the people think." That trend has continued.

Positive Aspects

Despite the negative aspects of the Yeltsin era, there are a number of important positive trends that give hope that Russia may evolve peacefully in a positive direction in the future. The first is the establishment and maintenance of the rights of political speech, assembly, and association, which has been a fact of life in Russia throughout the Yeltsin years. This has been complemented by a new freedom of worship and religion that began in the Gorbachev years, which has continued and expanded.

Another major positive trend during the Yeltsin era has been the institutionalization of a constitutional political system, in which the citizens of Russia, through reasonably open and competitive elections, make the major changes in the leadership of the executive and legislative branches of government.

A third positive aspect of the Yeltsin era has been the absence of extensive political persecution and repression.

A fourth and very important positive trend has been the maintenance of formally peaceful relations with the former Soviet republics. There was, however, some degree of Russian covert involvement in a number of the former Soviet republics, which seemed to be part of Yeltsin's placating of the military and security forces by allowing them to have their way on issues involving the "near abroad."

This balance of positive and negative aspects of the Yeltsin era suggests that at the end of 1999, Russia was a country of both political opportunity and fragility. The opportunity lay in building on the positive developments so that the struggle for political authority and political direction of Russia would remain within the bounds of constitutional means respected by all major political competitors. The fragility of Russian political institutions derived from the self-seeking financial-industrial barons, the political goals of the Communists, and the absence of broadly based democratic political parties and movements.

There are four possible futures for Russia: a continuation of the current situation of partial democracy and endemic corruption; an increasingly authoritarian regime under the Putin-led party of power; a full Communist restoration; or evolution toward a more open democratic system where the government is more effective and reduces significantly the power of the financial barons and organized crime. It is unfortunate for Russia and for the West that the alternative of a reformist democracy that would build on the positive aspects of the Yeltsin years and move beyond the negative ones seems least likely.

13 The New Century with President Putin

"Putin . . . combined both an enormous dedication to democracy and market reforms and an unwavering patriotism."
— BORIS YELTSIN, *Midnight Diaries,* 2000

"The government is not sure that democracy is essential . . . this is a very serious mistake and very dangerous."
— YEGAR GAIDAR, speaking of the Putin government, February 2001

"Putin has decided to follow the Korean model of development—but he is not sure if this will be that of North Korea [Stalinism] or of South Korea [democracy]."
— A Russian joke in the year 2000

PUTIN—THE PATH TO THE KREMLIN

It was a surprise to Russia and the world when, on August 9, 1999, President Yeltsin appeared on television and announced that he was appointing Vladimir Putin as prime minister and that he believed that Putin would be a good choice for president in the year 2000. After one year as head of the Federal Security Service (FSB), Putin was still unknown to the public and there was immense interest in knowing more about him.

Putin was born in October 1952 and lived with his parents in a crowded communal apartment in Leningrad. His father had served in the Russian military and was wounded in World War II. After the war, he worked as a skilled laborer in a factory that made railroad cars.[1] Putin's mother was described by a friend of the family as "a very nice person—kind, selfless, the soul of goodness. . . . She worked hard her whole life. She was a janitor, took deliveries in a bakery at night, washed test tubes in a laboratory."[2] The same friend describes Putin's father as "much liked and appreciated as a ready and willing worker."[3] Both parents suffered immensely during the Second World War, as had so many Soviet citizens. They clearly loved their son deeply and this closeness was mutual.

Until his sixth year in school, Putin describes himself as more interested in playing than his studies and not a member of the Young Pioneers because "I was a hooligan. . . . I really was a bad boy."[4] His parents and teachers were concerned and worked together to try to motivate young Vladimir. He changed when he became involved in a martial arts program, becoming proficient in judo, which he described as "not just a sport . . . it's a philosophy. It is respect for your elders and for your opponent. It's not for weaklings. Everything in judo has an instructive aspect."[5] At about that time in his life, young Vladimir saw the Soviet movie *The Sword and the Shield,* which celebrated the exploits of the KGB in defending the Soviet Union. He then began reading books and seeing other movies about spying and became ever more fascinated because he was impressed that through espionage "one man's effort could achieve what whole armies could not. One spy could decide the fate of thousands of people. At least that was the way I understood it."[6]

As a teenager, Putin approached the KGB and tried to join, but he was told that he had to finish his studies, preferably law, or join the military, and that if they were interested they would contact him in the future. Putin completed his high school studies and then went on to Leningrad University Law School, while continuing to compete in judo competitions where he became prominent and successful.

Putin was eighteen when he began the university, and he graduated at the age of twenty-three in 1975. He clearly enjoyed his time at the university, combining study, social life, and judo. In his third year, Putin's mother won a car through the state lottery, and his parents decided to give him the car. Putin recalled, "I lived the good life in that car. I used to drive everywhere, even to my [judo] matches."[7]

At the end of his university studies, he was contacted by an individual in the KGB and invited to apply. Asked whether at the time he had thought about the past terror against the Soviet people that had been inflicted by the KGB, Putin replied, "To be honest, I did not think about it at all. Not one bit . . . my notion of the KGB came from romantic spy stories. I was a pure and utterly successful product of Soviet patriotic education."[8] Perhaps part of the reason for the success of this "Soviet patriotic education" is that no one in Putin's immediate family had suffered directly during the Stalin years of pervasive state terror. Also, in his formative years, as Putin put it, "We lived under the conditions of a totalitarian state. Everything was concealed. . . . How serious was it? My friends and I did not think about that."[9]

Putin served in the KGB from 1975 to 1991, from age twenty-three until he was thirty-nine. Initially, he was trained in counterintelligence and then, being viewed among the most intelligent and capable new officers, was moved into the elite intelligence service and sent to Moscow for a year of special training. After that, Putin returned to Leningrad where he worked for nearly five years before going back to Moscow for training in foreign intelligence activities. In discussing methods used against democratic dissidents by the KGB, Putin said that during his time, "The way they did things was covert. It was considered indecent to be too obvious."[10]

In 1983, Putin married Lyudmila Putina, an attractive airline stewardess and student whom he had been courting for three years. Their first daughter was born in 1985, and soon after a second daughter was born. Putin and his new bride lived with his parents for several years in a small apartment. By all accounts, the Putins are happily married and remain a close couple and very devoted parents.

As the Gorbachev era was beginning in the Soviet Union in 1985, Putin and his family were assigned by the KGB to live in Dresden, East Germany. There Putin said his work was:

> political intelligence—obtaining information about political figures and the plans of the potential opponent . . . we were interested in any information about the "main opponent" . . . and the main opponent was considered NATO . . . [this involved] the usual intelligence activities: recruiting sources of information, obtaining information, analyzing it and sending it to Moscow. I looked for information about political parties, the tendencies inside these parties, their leaders. I examined today's leaders and the possible leaders of tomorrow and the promotion of people to certain posts in the parties, and in the government.[11]

Once Putin became a celebrity, a large number of reports surfaced about his alleged activities for the KGB in East Germany. These suggest that he had a major role in the efforts to steal advanced technology from the West, to plant East German scientists and engineers under false West German identities in "deep cover" assignments in Western companies, so they could provide technological and scientific information of interest to the Soviet Union. It was also rumored that Putin had an important role in guiding the younger generation of East German Communist leaders, who tended to emulate Gorbachev's changes, and that he was involved in work with Soviet military intelligence on a special project intended to uncover evidence of a possible surprise attack by NATO on the Soviet Union.[12]

We may never really know what is true or not true about Putin's work for the KGB in East Germany. We do know that he and his wife enjoyed living there, that Putin found the work stimulating, and that he and his wife both learned to speak German fluently. Also, as Putin described it, "We had come from a Russia where there were lines and shortages and in the GDR [East Germany] there was always plenty of everything. I gained about twenty-five pounds and weighed about one hundred and sixty-five."[13] Putin went on to admit that his weight gain was due to the fact that he did not exercise as he usually did and that he enjoyed the German beer.

In 1989, as the dramatic political changes swept over the Communist countries of Eastern Europe, Putin and the KGB in East Germany were burning papers day and night and removing their most valuable items to the Soviet Union. When angry crowds began breaking into the East German secret police offices and threatening the KGB offices, calls to Moscow were met with silence. After the Berlin wall fell,

Putin said he came to view that as "inevitable," but "regretted that the Soviet Union had lost its position in Europe, although intellectually I understood that a position built on a wall and dividers can not last ... we would have avoided a lot of problems if the Soviets had not made such a hasty exit from Eastern Europe."[14] One of Putin's closest friends described him as "confused and upset" about the end of the Soviet intelligence network in Germany and quoted Putin as saying, "I know that I can be wrong, but how can the most highly qualified professionals be mistaken?"[15] Putin also told this friend that he was going to leave the KGB.

On returning to the Soviet Union, Putin rejected offers to work in the KGB headquarters in Moscow, instead becoming a member of the "active reserve" and returning to Leningrad State University Law School to write a doctoral dissertation. There, through friends, he became assistant to the president of the university with responsibilities for international liaison. He described himself as being "under-cover" at the university.[16] The chairman of the Leningrad City Council, Anotoly Sobchak, who had taught Putin economic law during his time as a student in the 1970s, asked him to join his team as an assistant in order to help with a series of political and administrative tasks. Putin says that he told Sobchak that he was in the active reserves of the KGB and had been with the KGB since 1975. Putin went to inform his superiors in the KGB of this invitation and that he would then have to resign his post at the university. As Putin tells it, he said he would resign from the KGB if necessary in order to begin the work with Sobchak. His superiors gave him permission to work for Sobchak and the City Council, and Putin goes on to say that they never "once tried to use me for any operations. I think they understood it would have been pointless. Moreover at that moment, everything including the law enforcement agencies were falling apart."[17]

In June 1991, as Yeltsin was elected president of the Russian Federation, Sobchak was elected mayor of St. Petersburg. Sobchak then appointed Putin as chairman of the city government's Committee on International Relations. Putin was responsible for attempting to encourage foreign investment and a foreign banking and commercial presence in St. Petersburg. He did this by building on his German language and associations to bring in German companies and banks, among others. In 1992, Putin was being called the "deputy mayor" because Sobchak was often away from the city and involved in other national political issues. Putin was given the formal title of first deputy mayor in March 1994. In addition to inter-national relations and international business promotion responsibilities, Putin also oversaw the "power ministries" in St. Petersburg and handled relations with the media and interest groups.

The hard-line Communist coup of August 19, 1991, against Gorbachev was a turning point for many individuals in the Soviet Union. Putin was on vacation but returned to Leningrad and recalls that he and Mayor Sobchak opposed the

Communist coup and organized against it. We "practically moved into the City Council ... we drove to the Kiron factory and to other plants to speak to the workers ... we even passed out pistols, although I left my service revolver in the safe. People everywhere supported us. It was clear that if someone tried to disrupt the situation there would be a huge number of casualties."[18] Putin had taken a clear stand with Yeltsin and the reformers by working with Sobchak and sending a second letter of resignation to the KGB. He indicates that his first resignation had not been accepted, but on August 20, 1991, he insisted that he was leaving the KGB and did so. In fact, Putin recalls that Sobchak personally called Vladimir Kryuchkov, then head of the KGB, about Putin's second resignation letter and was told the next day that Putin's resignation had been accepted. Typical of his judgment of people according to how they dealt with him personally, Putin said: "Kryuchkov was a true believer in Communism, who decided with the coup plotters. But he was also a very decent man. To this day I have the greatest respect for him."[19]

During the Communist-armed uprising against Yeltsin in September–October 1993, a similar confrontation occurred in St. Petersburg. Putin again was with Sobchak against the armed Communists and he recalls that the then-head of the Federal Security Service (FSB), Victor Cherkesov—who had been one of the most active among those who persecuted democratic dissidents in the 1980s—supported Sobchak and Yeltsin and "introduced a number of measures advocating the arrests of extremists who were plotting provocations, planning to blow things up, or trying to destabilize the situation."[20] Some years later, President Putin named the same Victor Cherkesov to a key appointment as the presidential representative for the entire St. Petersburg region of Russia.

In 1996, after a political campaign involving what Putin believed were false allegations of corruption, Sobchak was defeated for the post of mayor. Putin, along with others of Sobchak's team, left government employment and for some months Putin explored various employment possibilities, including private law practice or joining the Yeltsin administration in Moscow. Through connections with St. Petersburg officials in the Yeltsin presidential administration, Putin was offered a job to work in the office of the president in charge of the legal division and of Russian property in foreign countries.[21] In this role, Putin was deputy to Mr. Pavel Borodin, who served during the Yeltsin years as the manager of all Kremlin property and who would subsequently be accused of having participated in the diversion of money to the Yeltsin family through schemes involving contracts with Swiss companies.[22]

After only seven months in that position, Yeltsin promoted Putin to deputy head of the presidential administration and head of the main oversight department (equivalent to inspector general) that was responsible for assuring that decrees issued by Yeltsin were carried out. In early 1998, Putin was promoted again to first deputy chief of staff to the president, with responsibility for the eighty-nine regions of Russia. It was reported in the *Moscow Times* and other Russian papers that Putin would, in KGB fashion, collect "special information" on the regional leaders (meaning examples of improper official, financial or personal conduct) in order to have a basis for persuading or pressuring them to carry out Yeltsin's policies. It may well be that this is when Putin reached the conclusion that the Russian presidency must have stronger control over the regional leaders—something he implemented after becoming president. This was the time when Putin began to bring people he knew well from his time in St. Petersburg and the KGB into the presidential administration. For example, a close associate from their KGB days, Nikolai Patrushev, was brought into the presidential administration in May 1998 and was appointed head of the Federal Security Service by President Putin in 2000.

In July 1998, Yeltsin appointed Putin director of the Federal Security Service. According to informed observers, Putin immediately began to move his allies into key positions within that organization, and according to one source, "resumed the KGB's domestic espionage activities."[23] Putin said that he did not welcome this appointment. As he put it,

> A military style of organization is after all a very difficult kind of service . . . it puts you in a constant state of tension. All the papers are secret. This isn't allowed, that isn't allowed. . . . And you couldn't even go out to a restaurant. They thought only prostitutes and black marketeers went to restaurants. What would a decent officer of the security agencies be doing in such company and then if you were an intelligence officer you were always the object of a potential vetting. They are always checking up on you.[24]

A sign of Yeltsin's confidence in Putin and also a result of Yeltsin's concerns about Primakov is that in March 1999 Putin was appointed secretary of the Security Council. In that role, he would coordinate the activities of the power ministries, including the Federal Security Service, Defense, Foreign Intelligence, and Ministry of Interior, while remaining head of the FSB. Putin had these responsibilities during the tense months of the Kosovo conflict (March–June 1999) and at the time of increasing tensions before armed Chechan fighters staged an incursion into the neighboring region of Dagestan in August 1999.

When Yeltsin named Putin prime minister on August 9, 1999, most believed that Putin would be just another short-term prime minister. The Communist leader in the *Duma*, Gennady Seleznoyv, said, "Why did they do that to you? They've buried you."[25] Putin said in an interview that his immediate reaction to the appointment was that he had a "historical mission" to use the authority as prime minister to end the danger posed by the Chechan separatist movement. Putin said that when the armed Chechans attacked the neighboring region of Dagestan some days after his appointment, he felt that

> if we don't put an immediate end to this, Russia will cease to exist. It was a question of preventing the collapse of the country. I realized that I could only do this at the cost of my political career. It was a minimal cost, and I was prepared to pay . . . so when Yeltsin declared me his successor everyone thought that it was the beginning of the end for me, I felt completely calm. . . . I calculated that I had several months to consolidate the armed forces, the interior ministry and the FSB, and to rally public support. Would there be enough time? That is all I worried about.[26]

Days after becoming prime minister, as Putin prepared for this battle, his father died. A friend said that in the last weeks of his father's life, Putin had flown every weekend to spend at least half a day with his father and was with him at the end.[27]

Putin as Prime Minister

As the new prime minister, Putin faced an immediate challenge. About twelve hundred Chechans and radical Islamic guerillas attacked the neighboring Russian Republic of Dagestan and occupied about a dozen villages.[28] Putin immediately deployed Russian troops and forced the guerillas back into Chechnya. In September, two thousand Chechan guerillas again occupied villages in Dagestan. In the same time period, bombs exploded in four apartment buildings in Moscow and several other Russian cities, killing more than three hundred persons and creating a widespread sense of insecurity among the Russian population. The Russian government immediately rounded up about ten thousand ethnic Caucasians in Moscow and deported them to their regions. Yeltsin said on September 13, 1999, "Terrorism has declared war on . . . Russia."[29]

Putin took command and described meeting with the heads of all the power ministries once, sometimes twice, daily: "The first thing I had to do was overcome the disarray among the ministries. The army did not understand what the interior ministry was doing and the FSB was criticizing everyone and not taking responsibility for anything. We had to become one team, one single organism. Only then would we be successful."[30] Starting in early September 1999, Russia began air strikes inside Chechnya and also began the massive use of ground-based missiles. On September 27, 1999, Putin explained this use of overwhelming military force by saying that Russia was "now the victim of aggression by international terrorism. In no way is this a civil war."[31] The Chechan guerillas were, in Putin's words, "bandits" who "rustled livestock, kidnapped people into slavery [and] engaged in violence and murder . . . [they have decided to] annex Russian territory from the Black Sea

to the Caspian . . . we will use all modern forces and means to destroy the terrorists."[32] From September 1999 through December 1999, Russian combat forces were
estimated at one hundred thousand military troops and forty thousand armed
police. This compared with the estimated forty thousand Russian military and
police forces that were involved in the 1994–1996 conflict with the separatist
Chechans. About five hundred thousand people lived in Chechnya before the
beginning of the 1999 war, and within months this had been reduced to about two
hundred thousand, with thousands killed and the displaced population fleeing to
neighboring republics.

While the United States and European governments explicitly acknowledged
the right of Russia to end armed separatism, these governments called on Russia to
conduct its military operations in accordance with international human-rights
provisions and the Geneva Convention on the law of war, which safeguarded
unarmed civilians. The international media reported numerous human-rights
abuses by Russian forces, and some months later, the UN High Commissioner for
Human Rights issued a report confirming the validity of the charges of the disproportionate use of force by Russia, resulting in heavy loss of civilian life, and
concluded that there were "mass killings, summary executions, rape, torture, and
pillage" by Russian military and police forces.[33]

In November 1999, the parliamentary assembly of the Council of Europe, the
organization comprising all the democratic states of Europe, urged Russia to cease
the human-rights violations, and in April 2000 it suspended Russia's right to vote in
the parliament by assembly and recommended a suspension of membership
because Russia continued to violate human rights in Chechnya.[34] The Organization
for the Islamic Conference (OIC), representing the world's Islamic states, sent a
delegation to Moscow in December 1999 to condemn the Russian campaign
against primarily Muslim Chechans as "disproportionate" and said this was
increasing tensions between Russia and the Islamic world. In January 2000, the
foreign minister of Iran said that the human suffering in Chechnya was "unacceptable" to the Muslim world and urged a cease-fire.[35] In contrast, China expressed
unqualified support for Russia.

In the fall of 1999, the Russian government did permit various international
assistance organizations to provide humanitarian assistance to the tens of thousands of displaced Chechan refugees. Aside from that, there was little evidence that
the international criticisms and concerns had any effect on Russian military and
police operations. The Putin government did attempt to restrict both international
and Russian media access to Chechnya. The Russian government did not want any
reporting of actual or alleged human-rights violations by its forces, and it did not
want any questioning of the low casualty figures for Russian forces that it provided
to the Russian public. Putin was perceived as a resolute, effective, and strong prime

minister who was saving Russia from the risk of widespread terrorism by Islamic radicals, and his popularity increased during the fall of 1999 as the Russian parliamentary election approached.

Both Yeltsin and Putin understood clearly that the December 1999 parliamentary election would be a prelude to the scheduled 2000 presidential election. If the new party supporting Moscow Mayor Luzhkov and former Prime Minister Primakov, Fatherland-All Russia, did very well, this would give Primakov political momentum toward the presidency. Yeltsin also understood that the previous political parties associated with his regime had failed to gather significant political support and that a new party would need to be established by Putin. The new party was called Unity. As public support for Putin rose dramatically during the fall of 1999, more and more political leaders and groups decided to join the new, broad Unity coalition.

For the parliamentary election campaign, the economic reformers associated with Anatoly Chubais formed a party called the Union of Right Wing Forces. The democratic reform economist Gregori Yevlensky continued with his *Yabloko* Party, hoping to increase its share of the vote. The main Communist Party used its nationwide organization expecting to maintain or expand its control in the parliament as a prelude to the presidential race. The ultranationalist party led by Zhirinovsky was also competing.

As the parliamentary election approached, the momentum grew in favor of the newly established Unity Party, which was also supported by most of the business and media tycoons who had sided with Yeltsin in the past. The Unity "party of power" was also helped by the fact that higher world oil prices and other factors had led to positive economic growth in Russia for the first time in years (GDP increased by 3.2 percent in 1999) and by an inflation rate that was considerably lower than the 1998 crisis year (36 percent compared with 84 percent).

In November 1999, Primakov publicly opposed "large-scale" ground operations in Chechnya, and Yavlinski proposed an immediate halt to military operations and the opening of negotiations with the head of the Chechan government. Criticism of those views came from many directions and reduced support for their parties. At the same time, Putin's popularity and, therefore, that of Unity continued to increase, partly as a result of what appeared to be low Russian casualties during the military operations in Chechnya.

The Russian people voted for a *Duma* on December 19, 1999, with the following results: the Communist Party received 24 percent of the vote and 111 of 450 Duma seats; Unity received 23 percent of the vote and 76 seats; Fatherland-All Russia (Primakov) received 13 percent of the vote and 62 seats; the Union of Right Forces received 9 percent of the vote and 29 seats; the ultranationalist group of Zhirinovsky received 6 percent of the vote and 20 seats; and, the democratic reform party *Yabloko* received 6 percent of the vote and 22 seats.[36] The results were viewed as a major success for Putin and for Yeltsin. The Communists and allied parties did not have enough seats to nearly dominate the parliament as they had done from 1995 to 1999, and Unity had enough seats to make coalitions with what were presumed to be reasonably sympathetic deputies from the Union of Right Forces and among many in Fatherland-All Russia, so that Putin could have a working majority. Undoubtedly, it was Putin's apparent success, both in the Chechnya military operations and the political contest for the Duma, that led Yeltsin to his final decision that Putin could and should succeed him. There remained only the question of timing. Yeltsin decided that with his surprise resignation on December 31, 1999.

Putin as Acting President

Under the constitution, Russia began the new century with Prime Minister Putin automatically becoming acting president, with the requirement that a presidential election be held within three months. These were scheduled for March 26, 2000. Putin began his acting presidency with a dramatic New Year's Eve visit, accompanied by his wife, to front-line Russian troops in Chechnya. Describing his fundamental political perspectives, Putin said there was a need to restore "moral values," that Russia needed an "effective state" that would meet its responsibilities to citizens and fulfill its promises. He said that Russia should follow "the path of democracy."[37] At the same time, Putin also made clear that he considered it a vital Russian national interest to prevent fragmentation through separatist movements such as that in Chechnya and said bluntly, "We will destroy those who take up arms against the state."[38] Putin's record in the federal government during the Yeltsin years showed that he combined a directness of purpose with the use of political and other methods that would often be discreet, secretive, and at times deceptive—much as he had described the methods of the KGB in the 1970s and 1980s.

Among his first actions as president, Putin kept his promise to Yeltsin and issued a pardon for Yeltsin and his entire family against prosecution or investigation for any and all alleged wrongdoing. Putin then requested that Yeltsin's daughter relinquish her Kremlin position and offices and also dismissed Mr. Pavel Borodin, who had managed the Kremlin properties.[39] Next, Putin moved to strengthen his relations with the power ministries. He placed many of his former associates from the KGB and his various Yeltsin-era jobs in key positions. These were people he felt he could trust. Within two weeks, Putin's government issued a new *National Security Concept*, which replaced the 1997 version. This accepted the view predominant among the military leadership that Russia was threatened by NATO enlargement, by disintegration through armed separatism, and by the lack of control over former Soviet Republics. It also lowered the threshold for Russia's use of nuclear weapons—they could be used first if deemed necessary for defense, whether or not an opponent had used such weapons. A Russian commentator, himself a former KGB officer, called this a "weak imitation of a new Cold War . . . this is a political step by Putin aimed at winning the military's support . . . it is still very dangerous because it gives the military a legal basis to act more aggressively, and it will feed into anti-Western sentiments among the public."[40]

Significant elements of the Russian military were concerned that in order to win the presidential election Putin might do what they perceived Yeltsin had done in 1996—negotiate an unacceptable truce with the Chechan separatists. A leading Russian general commanding forces in Chechnya said that he would resign if ordered to halt fighting and warned that such an order could result in a "civil war." That general also openly opposed acting president Putin's call for a cease-fire in Chechnya on the Orthodox Christmas, January 6, 2000.[41]

Putin sought to ensure the military's support by promising a 50 percent increase in the military budget and by reestablishing compulsory military training for all Russian schoolboys. This had been eliminated in 1992, but Putin reinstituted the training to build public support for the Russian army and to increase the willingness of young men to serve in the Russian army. This program included forty hours of intensive military instruction every summer for all boys aged fifteen and sixteen.[42]

On January 17, 2000, Putin and the Communists in the *Duma* reached an unexpected political arrangement behind closed doors. Most likely, Putin emphasized to the Communists that he was determined to strengthen and restore the power of the Russian state, that he would work against corruption and disorder in Russia, and that he would restore Russia's influence and greatness in the world. The following day, Putin's Unity Party voted with the Communists and their other allies so that the Communist Gernady Seleznyov again became chairman of the *Duma*, and the Communists received the chairmanships of nine of the twelve *Duma* committees. Seleznyov was elected by a vote of 282 to 2, as the economic reformers in the Union of Right Forces and others walked out in protest against Putin's deal. The democratic leader, Gregori Yavlinski, head of the *Yabloko* Party told the *Los Angeles Times* that Putin's surprising arrangement showed that Unity and the Communist parties are "one and the same and that we must fight this."[43] This surprising tactical move not only gave Putin an overwhelming majority for most of his legislative proposals over the next months, but also out flanked Primakov, who shortly thereafter decided not to contest the presidency of Russia in the coming election. Putin was left facing Zuganov, the Communist Party leader, as the most serious competing candidate.

With the major democracies, Yeltsin's second pillar of support, Putin emphasized his strong commitment to democracy and market-oriented reforms and his wish for good relations. His economic team was oriented toward moving forward on market-oriented reforms. During Putin's first month as acting president, U.S. Secretary of State Albright called him a "prime reformer," one of Russia's "leading

reformers" and commended his "can do . . . [and] problem solving approach."[44] In
early February 2000, Albright had a long meeting with Putin in Moscow and made
no progress on any of the main issues discussed: Chechnya, arms control, or nuclear
and missile technology proliferation to Iran. Nevertheless, she repeated her compli-
mentary words about Putin, and the U.S. agreed to provide additional food aid to
Russia. Soon thereafter, major U.S. and other Western creditors gave Russia an estimated $32 billion in debt relief by agreeing to write-off 37 percent of Russia's multi-
billion dollar Soviet-era commercial debt and convert the remainder into
thirty-year Euro bonds with lower interest rates.[45] This was an enormously important benefit provided to Acting President Putin, because at the end of 1999, Russia
had been scheduled to repay $17 billion in loans to foreign creditors, an amount
that exceeded Russia's total expected annual tax revenue.

The financial-media tycoons supported Putin's reelection. For them, he was
preferable to the Communists or Primakov. However, Putin did not need the financial-media tycoons in the way that Yeltsin had needed them in 1996. Rather, Putin
adopted a strategy of being above politics: he did not debate any of his opponents
on telelvision; he did not offer a formal political platform other than an open letter
to Russian voters that was highly general; he did not use free television time that was
available to all candidates.[46] In the words of one well-informed analyst, the combination of government-controlled electronic media and that controlled by financial-
media tycoons resulted in broadcast news coverage of the acting president "so
extensive and fawning that some called it 'all Putin, all the time.'"

The great majority of print and broadcast media have also cast the war in
Chechnya in the most favorable light for Putin, heralding military victories, mini-
mizing or ignoring military and civilian casualties, and denouncing opponents of
the war as traitors.[47]

On March 26, 2000, Putin was elected to the powerful presidency of the Russian
Republic with about 53 percent of the vote, while the Communist Party leader
received slightly less than 30 percent of the vote.

President Putin: Words, Actions, and Their Implications

Putin's declared objectives for Russia included strengthening the Russian federal
government, reviving the economy, obtaining economic benefits for Russia through
participation in the world economy, reversing the decline in Russia's military strength,
and asserting a major role for Russia in the world. In addition to these objectives, the
question facing the Russian people and the world is whether Putin will govern using
means which maintain human rights and movement toward democracy or whether
there will be a step-by-step reestablishment of an authoritarian regime.

Concerns about the possibility of an emerging dictatorship in Russia were heightened in May 2000 by the publication in Russia of parts of a planning document prepared by some of the many KGB people who worked with Putin in the presidency. According to the published excerpts, this document said that President Putin needed a staff able to "forecast and create the 'requisite' political situations in Russia [and] also to really control political and social processes in the Russian Federation and also countries in the near abroad."[48] The document went on to say that Putin's staff would become "an organ exerting powerful influence . . . [on] political parties and movements, their leaders, regional leaders and legislatures, candidates for any significant political post, including journalists and the activities of electoral committees and their staffers."[49] The work would be done in typical KGB fashion, through what the document called a "double line" in organizing its work—"open" and "clandestine."[50] Putin would be helped through this open and clandestine work while opposition elements would be discredited with "special information." The document went on to give examples of how to discredit political parties and undermine independent journalists. The Russian newspaper that published this concluded that if this is "not yet totalitarianism, then at any rate it is tightly administered democracy."[51] Much of what has occurred during the Putin presidency can be understood in the light of the approach outlined in this document, allegedly prepared by key members of Putin's presidential staff on the eve of his inauguration as the elected president of Russia.

Putin was inaugurated as president on May 6, 2000. He kept virtually all of his government intact, submitting the name of Prime Minister Kysyonov, an economic reformer, to the parliament for its approval (which was soon provided). He also retained the minister of defense and minister of foreign affairs who had worked closely with Primakov. Putin kept his close associate Patrushev in charge of the Federal Security Service (FSB) and maintained the practice of close presidential control and coordination of the power ministries, while the prime minister mainly focused on the economy and social issues.

In July 2000, as required by the Russian constitution, President Putin delivered a state of the nation address to both houses of the Russian parliament. This provided a guide to his public views on the current state of Russia and how his government would seek to improve matters. The tone of the talk was very candid in accessing the current problems facing Russia and provides a basis for comparing Putin's stated purposes and his actions during the first years of his presidency.

A Strong Central Government

Putin emphasized the importance of strengthening the central government of Russia saying: "Only a strong—effective, in case someone does not like the word strong—democratic state is able to protect, civil, political and economic freedoms and to create the conditions for a good life for the people and the prospering of our native land."[52] It was the weakness of the Russian state in recent years that, in Putin's words, "facilitated the dictatorship of the shadow economy and gray schemes, the raging corruption and massive outflow of capital. The state has contributed to this because the rules were vague and restrictions were not well defined or justified."[53] He also said that "an ineffectual state is the main cause of the lengthy and profound economic crisis. I am totally convinced of that."[54]

Putin's first act as president was to establish seven large regions for Russia, in which federal agencies would function under the control of his personal representatives. These regions coincided in their geography with the seven military districts of Russia and also had their headquarters in the same cities as these military districts. The Russian presidency announced that the purpose of this new approach was to "make the work of federal bodies of state power more effective and improve the control over compliance with their decisions."[55] Next, Putin introduced legislation to change the way in which the upper house of the federal parliament was selected. The Federation Council had consisted of the elected governor and head of the regional legislature from each of Russia's eighty-nine regions. Their membership in the Federation Council gave them parliamentary immunity from criminal prosecution, and they, not the Russian president, decided whether the federal prosecutor could be removed. In Yeltsin's view, these regional political leaders had used that power to encourage the federal prosecutor to investigate him as president in 1999, and he viewed this as part of "the political warfare against him" and an unexpected consequence of a "mistake in the Russian constitution."[56]

Putin moved to change that by introducing two bills that would have the members of the Federation Council appointed by the regional legislature. The Federation Council vetoed both of these proposals, but Putin used his overwhelming majority in the State *Duma* to enact these changes for the Federation Council taking office in February 2001. These changes gave Putin new authority over all levels of government in Russia and opened the way for federal law to be implemented equally in all regions. Putin said this was essential to economic reform because of the need to have, as he called it, "a single economic space" with uniform laws throughout the country, instead of what he had described as a Russia having evolved in the regions as "separate islands of authority."[57]

Economic Revival

Putin described the Russian economy as very weak and fragile, in spite of the positive growth in 1999 and 2000. The essence of the problems, he said, is that

> The state interferes excessively in spheres where it should be absent and is absent where its presence is needed . . . the main obstacles to economic growth are high taxes, the arbitrary actions of functionaries and the rampage of criminals. . . . A

state that is subject to corruption and with imprecise delineation of competencies will not deliver entrepreneurs from the arbitrary actions of functionaries and the influence of crime.[58]

Putin said that he was for the protection of ownership rights, equal conditions for all in business, liberty of businesses from "administrative dictatorship," an easing of the tax burden, and a simplification of the customs and tariff system among other needed changes.[59]

Working with a large coalition in the parliament, Putin was able to obtain a number of the economic changes he had proposed. These included a uniform lower tax rate of 13 percent, which was to end confusion and opportunities for corruption through tax evasion; it was also intended to stimulate the private sector. Further, federal control was strengthened over regional governments' resources and budgets, and the *Duma* enacted lower tariffs and customs duties. A major step not taken in Putin's first years was the enactment of the right of private property in agricultural land—this continued to be strongly opposed by the Communist Party and its Agrarian Party allies in the State *Duma*.

Overall, there were positive economic results in Putin's first year with the GDP growing by an estimated 6 percent in the year 2000, industrial production by 9 percent, and inflation declining from 37 percent in 1999 to about 20 percent in the year 2000. Average wages also increased to $89 per month, compared to $66 per month in the autumn of 1999. Nevertheless, severe economic problems continued as about 36 percent of Russians were thought to be living below the subsistence level (defined at $35 per month). Unemployment was officially at about 10 percent and, according to U.S. government analysis, "Corruption continued to be a negative factor in the development of the economy and commercial relations."[60]

Political Democracy, The Media

Putin has frequently emphasized his commitment to political democracy and the observance of human rights. He did this in his first state of the nation address, emphasizing that the "effective state" would establish and protect freedoms. In the first internet interview with a Russian president, Putin said in March 2001: "As long as I remain head of state, we will adhere precisely to democratic principles . . . this country simply has no alternative but democratic development and a market economy."[61] Three years later he told the Russian parliament in his overall address: "Russia must become and will become a country with a flourishing civil society and stable democracy."[62] Yet a large number of actions by the Putin government have led many in Russia and abroad to question this commitment. Yeltsin's first prime minister, Yegor Gaidar, said that many in the Putin government seem to approve "the Chinese model," meaning market-oriented reforms and international economic benefits from the democracies combined with dictatorship. Gaidar went on to say the Putin government "is not sure that democracy is essential . . . this is a very serious mistake and very dangerous."[63] The Department of State Human Rights Report said that there were "serious problems" with the overall human-rights situation in Russia, especially with respect to events in Chechnya where "Russian security forces demonstrated little respect for human rights, and there were credible reports of serious violations."[64] The United States government report went on to say that the Putin government had been "mostly silent about violations of human rights and democratic practices" and that in Putin's first year, "the government's record on media freedom worsened."[65]

As Putin took office, the Russian government owned about 150 of the 550 television stations and about 20 percent of the registered newspapers and periodicals. There were three national television stations, the government-owned Russian Television and Radio (RTR), and the government had a majority stake in Russian Public Television (ORT), in which the financial-media tycoon Boris Berezovsky also had ownership. The Russian government also controlled or owned the major radio stations and news agencies (ITAR-TASS and RIA-Novosti).[66] Outside Moscow, at the regional and local levels, government entities operated and controlled a much larger percentage of the media, so that "in many media markets, citizens received information mainly from unchallenged government sources."[67] A further indication of the media's dependence on the Russian government is that about 90 percent of the print media rely on government entities for paper, printing, and distribution, and many television stations depend on government organizations for access to the airwaves and office space.[68]

A Russian nongovernmental organization, the Glasnost Defense Foundation, monitors the condition of the media in Russia and the other post-Soviet Republics. It reports that one government means of pressuring the media was to bring lawsuits against journalists and their organizations. In 1999, about three hundred such lawsuits were filed against journalists, and "judges rarely found for the journalists; in the majority of [those] cases, the government succeeded in either intimidating or punishing the journalist."[69] A new Information Security Doctrine promulgated by the Putin administration in September 2000 is also of concern. While the doctrine expressed the government's intention to uphold freedom of the press, there were contrary provisions, such as the provision for an "increase in propaganda activity to counter the negative effects of the dissemination of misinformation about the internal policies of the Russian state." There was also the intent to clarify "the status of foreign journalists and media . . . to place them on an equal footing with the domestic media."[70]

The three national television networks have immense political importance in shaping public opinion in Russia. Before Putin, the government controlled one television network; the financial-media tycoon Berezovsky controlled another (ORT); and the financial media tycoon Gusinsky controlled the third (NTV), along with a radio station in Moscow, an important news daily *Segodnya,* and a weekly news-magazine, *Itogi.* In his July 2000 state of the nation address, Putin was explicit in his criticism of business tycoons saying: "There are those who turn the lack of an effective state to their own advantage.... this vacuum of authority has led to state functions being appropriated by private corporations and clans. They have surrounded themselves with their own shadowy groups, lobbying groups and dubious security services using illegal means to obtain information."[71] While contending that there had to be a genuinely independent media, Putin also explicitly criticized the "weighty financial groups" who use the media as "a convenient instrument in the inter-clan struggle ... censorship can come not only from the state and interference can be not only administrative."[72]

Putin said further that the financial baron-controlled media had become "mass misinformation outlets and . . . a means of struggle against the state; therefore, we are obliged to guarantee real freedom to journalists . . . and to create legal and economic conditions in the country for a civilized information business."[73] Yeltsin wrote that in a September 1997 Kremlin meeting he had told the financial barons that they could not "go on getting discounts from the state treasury."[74] In March 2000, the state energy company Gazprom began demanding that Vladimir Gusensky's company Media-Most repay a $211 million loan at once. Only days after Putin's election as president, an armed and masked group of individuals believed to be from the tax police raided the offices of Media-Most and took documents and technical equipment. In June 2000, Gusensky was arrested and charged with tax evasion.

Progovernment media said the raid on Media-Most and Gusinsky's arrest were part of everyone being "equal before the law," and Putin claimed to have no specific knowledge of the event. Yet many in Russia and abroad agreed with the Russian Union of Journalists, which said the raid on Media-Most headquarters was "an unconstitutional act aimed at intimidating the independent media."[75] Criticism from within Russia and abroad (which overshadowed Putin's high-level international meetings) was followed by Gusinsky's release after three days in prison. Soon after, armed government personnel again raided Media-Most and Gusinsky's private residence and took an inventory of the property. This was purportedly in connection with a criminal investigation into the 1995 privatization of a television production company in St.Petersburg. Thereafter, on July 27, 2000, Gusinsky left Russia to join his family at their home in Spain.

On September 19, 2000, a Russian official, Media-Most, and Gazprom announced that Gusinsky had agreed to sell Media-Most to Gazprom for $300 million in cash and $473 million in debt. This agreement included the Russian government dropping criminal charges against Gusinsky. From Spain, Gusinsky denounced the agreement as "null and void" saying it had been signed "at gunpoint" with the threat of imprisonment. Gazprom then made the allegation that Media-Most hid assets in foreign companies, and the deputy prosecutor general said that if the allegations seemed substantiated, he would launch another criminal probe of Media-Most.[76] After prosecutors conducted additional searches of Media-Most and banks holding its accounts in February 2001, the deputy prosecutor general said on national television that this was not about politics: "I investigate criminal cases, there are no political cases in Russia. That is the law."[77] In April 2001, Gazprom took control of NTV, the daily newspaper *Segodnya* and the weekly newsmagazine *Itogi,* despite days of protesting by many journalists and by thousands of Russian citizens. New managers fired most of the journalists, and many others resigned in protest. The Gusinsky media holdings were in new hands, and this was presented as a matter of business—foreclosure due to nonpayment of the debt owed. Gusinsky said the Putin government had indirectly prevented Ted Turner of Cable News Network from providing the funds to pay the Gazprom loans. He argued that all of these events showed that in Putin's Russia, press freedom, private property, and basic human rights "are no longer respected."[78] The Russian Union of Journalists declared that "attacks on freedom of expression are not only becoming more determined but they are trying to . . . label the press as the enemy."[79]

A series of pressures on the national television network that had been controlled by Boris Berezovsky, another financial-media tycoon, led a Western group with extensive experience in Russian media issues to conclude in September 2000: "The Kremlin is trying to assert control over Russia's main television networks—RTR, ORT, NTV—and formulate the ideology of a new state with their support. . . . It is sending a powerful signal that only media supporting 'state interests' will be tolerated and supported."[80] After Berezovsky lost control of the ORT television station, he wrote a dramatic article in the American press contending that after the Communists had been defeated in the 1996 presidential campaign, they and the remnants of the KGB "started a concerted smear campaign against our new Russian capitalist class."[81] Having failed to impeach Yeltsin in 1999, Berezovsky said under President Putin:

> The KGB has gained prominence in the Kremlin while the influence of big business has been reduced to zero. The results are . . . the democratic system of checks and balances has been dismantled. . . . Private owners of independent media are blackmailed by a government that is unhappy with news coverage. And fear of the authorities is creeping back into the hearts and minds of millions of Russians.[82]

At the start of his presidency, Putin said, "Without a really free press, Russian democracy simply will not survive."[83] Were these pressures on the media tycoons simply part of an effort to reduce corruption and end the tycoons use of the media for their political and economic purposes? Or was this also an example of what had deeply disturbed Yeltsin about Primakov—the wish to control the media and the use of what Yeltsin called "economic repression . . . economic regulations used to intimidate and control people"?[84] A clear indication that Putin was determined to control both the tycoons and the national media is the statement made in February 2001 by a former news anchorman for the ORT television network. He said that Putin's chief of staff met every Wednesday with the heads of the TV networks, except for Gusinsky's still-independent NTV, and gave "strict and clear instructions as to how they are to work, and how to interpret each particular news event in their news programs."[85] This new (and old) conformity led to a Russian joke—the offer to trade two televisions for one short-wave radio (to listen to Western news broadcasts). But the Gusinsky-owned media continued to operate independently and in February 2001, Gusinsky was quoted as saying: "Every day Putin sees [on NTV] how people are freezing in the [Russian] Far East . . . how people are dying in Chechnya. . . . And every day, everyone sees that he lied."[86]

In addition to these legal-financial-administrative pressures on journalists, under Putin there has been a continuation of the years-long pattern described by the U.S. government as the "threat of physical violence, beatings and murder" of journalists, especially those pursuing investigative stories on "corruption and organized crime."[87] In Putin's first year (as in 1999), numbers of journalists were killed and dozens of journalists were severely beaten with the police virtually never finding the perpetrators.[88] This included the beating murder in Moscow of Iskander Khatloni, a jounalist with the U.S.-funded Radio Free Europe/Radio Liberty.

In July 2000, the Russian tax police moved not only against the financial-media tycoons but also against a number of other very wealthy businessmen. This included allegations that the head of a major privatized oil company (LUKoil) had falsified exports and obtained fraudulent tax refunds; demands that Norilsk Nickel, owned by another major tycoon, Vladimir Potanin, reimburse the government $140 million as the fair value of his purchase in 1997; and allegations that a car manufacturer (AvtoVAZ) owed the government $600 million in taxes.[89] The business leaders declared their innocence and said the confusion in current Russian laws permitted "law enforcement bodies to persecute virtually any successfully operating corporation."[90] In response, Putin said that those who have "fished in muddy waters" and "who have already caught a lot of fish would like to keep the system as it is," which is not acceptable. However, Putin's staff said there would be amnesty for past violations and on July 28, 2000, Putin met with a large group of business leaders (Gusinky, Berezovsky, and Roman Abramovitch were not invited). During this meeting, Putin said there would be no overturning past privatizations, that there should be a statute of limitations for past violations of law, and that there should be regular consultations with business.[91] These actions made clear that Putin would not depend on the political and economic support of the tycoons and would require them to comply with the law, but without the threat of having their property nationalized—unless they became too much of a threat.

Political Parties and Independent Labor Unions

In his first address on the state of Russia, Putin also spoke about the vital role of political parties in a democracy: "They provide a constant link between the people and the authorities. . . . Russia needs parties that enjoy mass-scale support and stable authority. Russia does not need another bureaucrats' party that sucks up to the authorities."[92] Yet, the Federal Security Service (FSB) headed by Putin's close friend attempted to coerce two *Yabloko* student activists into spying on their party—threatening them with dismissal from the university and immediate conscription into Russian units in Chechnya if they refused.[93] In December 2000, Putin proposed a draft law that was presented as intended to strengthen political parties, but would also have given the central government and the prosecutors "broad powers to regulate, investigate and even close down parties."[94]

Putin was eloquent in arguing the need for truly independent trade unions, which "protect the rights of hired labor in both the state and the private sectors" and are not just bureaucracies acting as middlemen in "distributing social benefits." This was the role unions played in the Communist era and continued to play now with 90 percent of those in labor unions still in the Communist-era organizations.[95] A free media, genuinely competitive political parties, and independent labor unions—these are the basic institutions of political democracy. While Putin claims to support these, the evidence to date indicates that his government is, in fact, pursuing a KGB-like "double line" as described in the leaked planning document of the presidential office. Putin endorses democracy and democratic institutions in principle, while using hidden, disguised, often covert or indirect actions to gain significant control over political life in Russia without appearing to be doing so. Putin, when exposed, offers implausible denials for these actions.

The Law Enforcement System and Espionage

In Russia, as in much of continental, democratic Europe, a government allegation that an individual may have committed a crime often leads to immediate arrest and imprisonment pending a trial. In principle, when any person is in the custody of the government, it has the obligation to assure treatment that respects human rights and individual dignity. During the Soviet dictatorship, as in China at present, persons imprisoned by the state were subject to severe physical and mental abuse including torture.

Unfortunately, this has remained the situation in Russia during the entire post-Soviet era. After Putin's first year as president, the U.S. Department of State found that:

> Although the government generally respected the human rights of its citizens . . . serious problems remain, including . . . the condition of pre-trial detention and torture of prisoners . . . Beatings by security officials throughout the country resulted in numerous deaths and injuries . . . law enforcement personnel regularly use torture to coerce confessions from suspects . . . the government does not hold most of the torturers accountable for their actions. . . . Police also beat, harassed and extorted money from persons. . . . Prison conditions [are] frequently life-threatening.[96]

Russian human-rights groups charge that about eleven thousand persons die in prisons each year due to overcrowding, disease, and lack of medical care.[97]

In an April 2001 annual address to the Russian legislature, Putin criticized the "groundless violence and arbitrariness in the institution of criminal proceedings" and the fact that there were "over a million people in prisons or remand centers."[98] Every society, even long-established democracies such as the United States, has to maintain vigilance to prevent the abuse of persons by police and prison officials. Yet the repressive practices from the Communist dictatorship continues in Russia even though laws prohibit this mistreatment, even though Putin emphasized he intended that all follow the "dictatorship of law," and despite Putin's new authority over regional officials provided by his large coalition in the State *Duma*.

Further, as with virtually all the documented examples of atrocities by Russian forces in Chechnya, government officials from Putin down remained "mostly silent about violations of human rights."[99] In contrast, Lev Ponomarev, a courageous human-rights activist since the Soviet era held a demonstration in Moscow on February 22, 2001 marking the fifty-seventh anniversary of Stalin's mass deportation of the Chechen people, protesting the human-rights violations of the Russian forces in Chechnya, stating that these "threaten democracy in our country."[100]

Yeltsin continued this, but the Putin government issued new guidelines for the Federal Security Service (FSB) that revives the Soviet-era practice of "investigating anonymous allegations of crimes" by Russian citizens.[101] A member of the Union of Right Forces, Sergei Yushenkov, called this "a retreat to Soviet times when the state prosecuted those people whom the state did not like with the help of anonymous letters." In the year 2000, the Federal Security Service is said to have received sixty-five thousand "anonymous signals."[102]

Further, in February 2001, Putin withdrew support from his own proposed legislation that would have conformed the criminal code from the Communist era with the democratic constitution by curbing "the ability of security agencies to conduct searches and make arrests without court warrants."[103] This limitation was strongly opposed by the chief prosecutor and minister of Internal Affairs. After Putin withdrew the legislation, a member of parliament from the liberal Union of Right Forces concluded that this demonstrated "his dependency on the law enforcement institutions."[104]

In this domain also, Putin has taken actions moving Russia toward authoritarianism. Among the important positive changes during the last Gorbachev years was that the domestic security organizations (KGB, MVD) were prohibited by the legislature from soliciting anonymous denunciations against citizens for alleged wrongdoing. Another example would be the fact that the Federal Security Service said that in the year 2000 it was monitoring 350 Russian citizens allegedly working for foreign intelligence agencies—a sharp increase.[105] This has been accompanied by a number of espionage arrests and trials of "distinguished mainstream academics, researchers, journalist and diplomats . . . the charges against them are transparently trumped up."[106] Examples include a Russian diplomat arrested, publicly characterized by Putin as one whose case was "proven beyond any doubt," then months later tried and convicted for having given a South Korean diplomat a "secret document" that was the text of a public speech he made. The Russian Supreme Court overturned the conviction, a judge withdrew from the second trial, and the FSB initiated a third prosecution, threatening also to bring charges against the Russian diplomat's daughter, a student in South Korea.

Other recent espionage cases involved writers using only public information who concluded the Russian military had caused radioactive contamination of national and international waters adjacent to Vladivostok. The human-rights activist Sergei Grigoryants said if these individuals are guilty of compromising "state secrets," then the same could apply to any writer "who criticizes the government or who has contact with foreigners."[107] The editors of the *Washington Post* concluded in February 2001 that these spy trials suggest that the Putin government is "inclining toward rule by means of secret police, rather than by parliament, elections or law."[108] Having distanced himself from the business-media tycoons, Putin's main pillar of domestic support is in the power ministries, among which the internal security organizations are very important.

Patriotic Education and Soviet Symbols
In every country there is a strong interest in young persons and adults having a sense of pride in and loyalty to their homeland. This is often called civic patriotism and is distinct from an aggressive, domineering ultranationalism sometimes misla-

beled as patriotism. Putin clearly feels a strong personal sense of civic patriotism. He has said candidly, "I am a successful product of a Soviet patriotic education," and he believes that the political and economic changes of the last years have undermined public morality, civic patriotism, support for Russia by young people, and the willingness of young men to serve in the military.

During his time as prime minister and his first year as president, Putin took many actions to revive symbols of the Soviet past that he associates with civic patriotism rather than the terrors of Communist repression. On the date of the founding of the first Communist secret police organization (which conducted the Red Terror under Lenin, as it did again in the Stalin era), Putin dedicated a plaque honoring Yuri Andropov, a former chief of the KGB. He invited two of the major plotters in the hard-line Communist coup attempt of August 1991, who were former KGB chairmen during Putin's term of service, Vladimir Kryuchkov and Marshall Dimitry Yazov, to participate in major national ceremonies.[109] Putin revived compulsory military training for high-school aged males and restored the Soviet-era national anthem for Russia (with different words). This produced the first public criticism from Yeltsin who said, "I am categorically against the restoration of the Soviet anthem."[110] Putin's political party, Unity, created a youth branch that "some [in Russia] compare to the Komsomol [youth] league of the Communist era."[111]

In early 2001, the Unity Party drafted a bill on national security calling for restrictions on some constitutional rights, giving greater emphasis to "military power" in foreign policy, and the establishment of a system of "education for the formation of law-obedient citizens."[112] In March 2001 the Russian government announced its plan for the "Patriotic Upbringing of Citizens of the Russian Federation" to be jointly carried out by the Ministries of Education, Culture, and Defense in order "to promote public stability, restoration of the national economy and strengthening of the country's defense potential . . . to ensure the consolidation of society [and] the unity and friendship of the peoples of the Russian Federation."[113] In addition to activities in the schools, the new program may produce computer games for teenagers emphasizing the exploits of Russian heroes; a new state lottery to be called "Patriot of Russia;" awards for writers and film-makers who produce patriotic works; a Slavic youth festival near the borders of Russia, Belarus, Ukraine; and the naming of schools and businesses "after Soviet heroes."[114]

Time will tell how this will evolve. The question is whether Putin's government will distinguish between patriotism and public morality that is consistent with the democratic aspirations he expresses for Russia—for example, the view that criticism of government is an inherent right and part of constructive debate about policy, rather than an act of disloyalty. Or whether patriotism will be defined to mean only loyalty and obedience to the state irrespective of its actions and political purposes. A program of patriotic education for citizenship in a Russia moving toward democracy would emphasize the rights of citizens, the need for both citizens and the government to act within the law, the noble history of dissent by those seeking to help free their fellow citizens from the Communist dictatorship, and the immediate welcome and massive economic/humanitarian support that post-Soviet Russia received from the major democracies. There is no evidence yet of this approach. Rather, the new initiative seems aimed more toward a revival of the "successful Soviet patriotic education" that Putin believes worked well in his youth.

In foreign policy, Putin has continued much of the approach taken by Primakov during the last four Yeltsin years. This has meant a dual policy toward the major democracies of actively seeking continued and increased economic support and opportunities, while working more closely with China and with a number of regimes hostile to the U.S. (North Korea, Cuba, Iran, Saddam Hussein's Iraq) to counterbalance the alleged American impulse toward "unipolarism" or dominance. Further aspects of Putin's very active foreign policy will be discussed at greater length as we examine Russian-U.S. relations in the post-Soviet era and in the analysis of the new China-Russia strategic alignment.

It is still possible that Russia under Putin will evolve in a positive way internally, leading to greater cooperation with the democracies. This would mean that the visible authoritarian tendencies of Putin's government were in fact checked and that the "strong state" being established was used against corruption, organized crime, and the unlawful actions of regional authorities, rather than to give Putin ever-greater political power and inhibit any effective political opposition.

However, it is equally possible that the negative aspects of the Putin government—the effort to control and shape expression by the major media; the use of masked, armed tax police in raids on political opponents for alleged economic wrongdoing; the return to the systematic use of anonymous informants; and the spurious prosecution of alleged spies—will worsen.

Domestically, Putin continued his recentralization of authority and power within Russia throughout his first term as president. This included the continued crackdown on independent media as well as using the power of the state to isolate and then neutralize the power of the oligarchs. This was illustrated most dramatically by the arrest of Yukos's founder Mikhail Khodorkovsky for tax evasion and fraud. With the future of Yukos in doubt, as it faces an auction of its assets to pay a reported $20 billion tax bill, this would represent an end to the large private domestic Russian companies. These companies, of course, represent the only private centers of power that could have potentially challenged Kremlin rule. However, one aspect of the Yukos drama that was missed in the numerous financial headlines was Yukos's involvement in the pipeline debate between China, Russia, and Japan.

Although little noticed in the West outside of the energy sector, there was a major diplomatic battle waged between the Chinese, Russian, and Japanese over whether a proposed pipeline would go directly to China or to the coast of Russia, from which point it could service Japan and potentially other markets. In the weeks before the actual clamp down on Yukos, there were several indications that the Kremlin was going to go with the Japanese-financed option when the leadership of Yukos announced that they would build a private pipeline to China. This could represent increased weariness on the part of the Kremlin, however, at the same time the Kremlin does not seem to be letting up on its moves toward greater centralized control.

Another recent example of Putin's use of security concerns in order to increase the control of Moscow over the nation can be seen in the events following the tragic terrorist attacks in Beslan, Russia. Under the guise of reforming the system to fight corruption and to better position the state to pursue terrorists, Putin announced that he was going to reform the system by which the regional leaders were selected. Rather then elections, future leaders will be appointed by the Kremlin.

If Putin continues to pursue increased centralization, as well as the strong and growing alignment with Communist China, this will lead to Russian policies that increase the challenges to the United States and its allies, reduce cooperation with the democracies, and sharply increase the risks of a new dictatorship and future conflict. The following brief review of Russian-U.S. relations since 1992 will provide perspective on Putin's future foreign policy.

14 U.S.-Russia Relations Since 1992

"Russia will strive toward the stable development of relations with the United States, with a view toward strategic partnership and, in the future, toward alliance."

—Yeltsin's Foreign Policy Concept
of the Russian Federation, January 25, 1993

"The Russian government has managed in the last three or four years to restore a Soviet world outlook, where on the one side there is Moscow, and on the other, all democratic countries."

—ANDREI KOZYREV, *Russian Reform Monitor*, April 14, 1999

THREE PHASES IN RUSSIAN FOREIGN POLICY

Cooperation and Integration, January 1992–October 1993

In 1992, President Yeltsin and his foreign minister, Andrei Kozyrev, expressed their clear intention to establish a new, peaceful, and cooperative relationship with the major democracies, which would include the integration of Russia into the political and economic institutions of the free world. Yeltsin had supported Gorbachev's "new thinking" as an effort to shape Soviet foreign policy in a more cooperative direction and expressed his intention to go beyond that to develop a "partnership" with the major democracies. Kozyrev had written one of the first articles in the time of *glasnost* strongly criticizing many aspects of Soviet foreign policy as having been detrimental to the interests of the Soviet Union and the well-being of its people.

President George H. W. Bush welcomed the independence of Russia and the other former Soviet republics and stated clearly that the U.S. wanted to be helpful in supporting President Yeltsin in his objective of moving toward political democracy and a free-market economy. In January 1992, Secretary of State James Baker convened a conference in Washington of all leaders from the major democracies, the recent post-Communist states in Eastern Europe, and multilateral institutions such as the World Bank and IMF to consider how best to coordinate a new program of assistance for Russia and the other post-Soviet republics.[1] President Bush had already asked Congress in January 1992 to provide $645 million in immediate humanitarian and economic assistance to the post-Soviet republics, and then he submitted to the Congress in April 1992 a larger multiyear program of assistance to be called the Freedom Support Act.[2] With the encouragement of the Bush administration, the World Bank and the IMF admitted Russia to full membership in record time, by April 1992. Immediately, the World Bank and the IMF agreed to provide $16 billion in financial stabilization assistance for Russia's program of economic reform, while President Bush proposed to the Congress that the U.S. establish a large program of bilateral assistance. It is noteworthy that as early as April 1992, while the U.S. and the major democracies were working to provide immediate assistance to Russia, the Communists in Russia were already denouncing this assistance and Yeltsin for accepting any such assistance as "selling Russia to the imperialists."[3]

Russia and the U.S. also moved immediately to discuss the opportunities to enhance their mutual security in tangible ways. At the end of January 1992, Russia and the U.S. participated in a conference of all fifteen members of the UN Security Council to discuss the structure of the international community after the Cold War. Thereafter, Presidents Bush and Yeltsin met together at the U.S. presidential retreat at Camp David for intensive discussions of arms control opportunities and proposals.[4] That was followed by a visit to Moscow by Secretary of State James Baker, where the U.S. agreed to provide $400 million to assist Russia in the dismantling and safe disposal of its nuclear weapons and to fund a scientific research center with locations throughout Russia that would provide alternative scientific employment for scientists and engineers who had worked on the development of nuclear and strategic weapons. These funds had been made available by the U.S. Congress as a result of an initiative taken by Senators Nunn and Lugar in the fall of 1991 and provided a major opportunity for the U.S. to assist Russia in meeting its objectives of reducing the size of its strategic nuclear forces.[5]

In the first months of 1992, the U.S. and Russia also conducted intense negotiations on reductions in their strategic nuclear arsenals. As a result, in June 1992, at a summit meeting held in Washington D.C., Presidents Bush and Yeltsin announced that they had agreed to reduce American and Russian nuclear arsenals from the approximately 9,000 strategic warheads that each then had to about 3,500 warheads in two phases by no later than 2003. This agreement would require Russia to essentially eliminate most of its land-based missiles, which had multiple warheads, and substitute a new single-warhead missile, so that the agreed limits on warheads could be more accurately counted and verified. At the same time, the U.S. would reduce the number of its submarine-launched warheads by more than 50 percent (from 3,840 to 1,750).[6] Presidents Bush and Yeltsin also discussed the U.S. opening its market to Russian exports by granting Most Favored Nation trading status and a series of other bilateral agreements, including cooperation in space exploration.

President Yeltsin called the agreement to reduce strategic arms concrete evidence of "the partnership and friendship" between Russia and the U.S., and he went on to say "We know one thing . . . we shall not fight against each other."[7]

In January 1993, Presidents Bush and Yeltsin met in Moscow to formally sign the Strategic Arms Reduction Treaty II (START II). At that third meeting of the two presidents, President Yeltsin said, "We have every right to say that relations between our two countries have undergone a genuine revolution." President Bush said, "We seek no special advantage from Russia's transformation. Yes, deep arms reductions, broader and deeper economic ties, expanded trade with Russia are all in the interest of my country. But they are equally in the interest of the Russian people."[8]

While the START II agreement symbolized the new relationship between Russia and the U.S., its ultimate fate illustrated the problems that later emerged. The U.S. Senate ratified the START II agreement in 1995, but the Russian parliament did not ratify the treaty during the entire period of Yeltsin's presidency. In fact, the issue of ratification of START II has constantly been used by the Communists in the parliament as a means both of opposing aspects of Russian foreign policy and of registering their opposition to actions of the United States. Ratification finally occurred in the spring of 2000 only as a result of President Putin's de facto coalition with the Communists in the Russian parliament.

The U.S. and Russia also shared an interest in persuading the post-Soviet republics—Kazakhstan, Belarus, and Ukraine—to give up the more than 2,200 strategic nuclear warheads that remained deployed on their territories from the Soviet era. Both Russia and the U.S. judged that the risks from these nuclear weapons would be fewer if the newly independent former Soviet republics did not keep them. Initially, the U.S. suggested that these strategic weapons be put under international control but then acceded to the view of the Russian government, particularly the Ministry of Defense, that Russia should take possession of the warheads and provide for their dismantlement.[9] In the end, both governments were able to persuade Belarus, Kazakhstan, and Ukraine to transfer all of their strategic warheads to Russian control. The U.S. agreed to provide funding from the Nunn-Lugar Cooperative Threat Reduction program for transporting and dismantling those nuclear warheads. The U.S. also provided significant funds to purchase uranium from those warheads as well as for other major items of Russian technology related to space exploration.

During this cooperative time, President Yeltsin had a very positive attitude toward the NATO alliance. While on a visit to Poland, he told the Polish leadership that Russia would have no objection to Poland joining NATO and later suggested that Russia should also become a member of NATO. Some U.S. analysts felt that the U.S. missed a major opportunity by not having immediately taken up President Yeltsin's suggestion and moved toward incorporating Russia into NATO.[10] But neither the U.S. nor the other NATO members were ready to deal with this informal proposal. Nevertheless, these initial expressions about NATO reflected Yeltsin's view that since 1949 NATO had demonstrated that it was a defensive alliance and posed no offensive threat to Russia. This also mirrored the views of those in the democratic community within Russia who saw the U.S. and NATO as positive and benign and not as a potential threat to Russia.

Only weeks after taking office in January 1993, President Clinton met with President Yeltsin in Vancouver, British Columbia for a wide-ranging discussion of U.S.-Russian relations and international politics. Congress had enacted the Bush proposal for a multiyear assistance program for Russia and the other post-Soviet republics in October 1992, and President Clinton went to the summit with the ability to commit hundreds of millions of dollars annually in bilateral assistance. It is noteworthy that President Yeltsin candidly stated before this 1993 summit that while he needed a great deal of assistance, he would not ask for too much because the Communist opposition in Russia would use it against him and say that he is making Russia beholden to the West. As a result, Yeltsin asked for more emphasis on economic cooperation rather than direct assistance and requested that the assistance focus on aid to the private sector.[11] President Clinton was supportive and announced a large number of U.S. assistance initiatives for Russia. A meeting of the Group of Seven industrial democracies on April 16, 1993, shortly followed the U.S.-Russia summit.[12] At that G7 summit, an aid package totaling more than $28 billion was approved for Russia and, in addition, $15 billion of Russia's foreign debt inherited from the Soviet Union was restructured to reduce Russia's annual payments.[13] This U.S. and Western political and financial support for President Yeltsin came at a time when he was facing ever more strident Communist opposition to his programs in Russia and a national referendum in Russia to decide whether or not the Russian people supported his economic changes.

Another example of Western support for Yeltsin came during the September–October 1993 armed confrontation between Yeltsin and Communist members of the *Duma*. In September 1993, Yeltsin acted in an extraconstitutional way to dissolve the Communist-dominated parliament elected in the Soviet era, which had obstructed and opposed his reform efforts. It was important to President Yeltsin that the Western democracies understood his actions as a means to reform the political system in a constitutional and democratic direction. The withdrawal of Western support at that time or sharp criticism could well have turned the balance internally against Yeltsin. In fact, the U.S. and the major democracies all supported President Yeltsin through the crisis, and, at its conclusion, a senior U.S. government official said that the task of the Russian government is "not only a restoration of order, but a reaffirmation of the Russian government's commitment to get on with the process of democratization."[14] In addition, Yeltsin also needed the support or acquiescence of the power ministries, including the Russian military. This would become a major factor in changes in Russian foreign policy that followed soon after the September–October 1993 crisis.

Limited Cooperation and Increased Russian Assertiveness, November 1993— December 1995

Russia was invaded by Napoleon early in the nineteenth century, then again by Nazi Germany in 1941. In the absence of natural defenses to the west, the south, and the east, Russia has always been concerned with maintaining secure borders and having, if possible, aligned friendly states on its borders. For those in the Russian military and foreign intelligence services who focus on issues of national security, there was undoubtedly a sense of shock at the rapid pace of events since 1989. It could be said that in the space of two years, Russia had lost two sets of buffer states—the Communist regimes in Eastern Europe and the constituent republics of the Soviet Union.

However, an even greater perceived threat to Russian national security was the prospect of the disintegration of Russia itself. The Russian Federation is a multi-ethnic state, where a large number of ethnic groups live in their own regions, some having had the formal legal status of being "autonomous" during the Communist era. Muslims account for approximately 15 to 20 percent of the Russian population and are among those with the greatest sense of identity. Many of the Muslim and other non-Russian peoples living inside Russia had suffered severe repression during the Communist era, and they were inspired by the political liberalization that began during the Gorbachev years to become more assertive of their ethnic and national identity, just as their neighbors were doing in the fourteen newly inde-pendent post-Soviet republics. The theoretical possibility of the disintegration of Russia replicating the disintegration of the Soviet Union became concrete in November 1991 when the newly self-designated government of Chechnya declared its secession from Russia, saying that it had become an independent state.

Yeltsin well understood that if one part of Russia were permitted to secede it could lead a number of other regions to attempt the same, and this could quickly threaten the continued existence of the Russian state. Yeltsin did not take immediate or precipitous action against the secessionist Chechen regime because he knew this could trigger a war against a group known from history as fierce fighters against the Russian empire. Instead, Yeltsin sought to work out a political accommodation, while at the same time establishing the Security Council (1992), which brought together the "power ministries"—defense, interior, internal security, and the foreign intelligence service.[15] This Security Council did not include the foreign ministry under Kozyrev and was intended to coordinate Russian security policy to preserve the state and defend it from outside intervention using both open and covert means.

As political negotiations and a series of ever more intrusive and violent Russian covert/paramilitary actions failed to end the secessionist movement in Chechnya, the threat it posed to Russian unity during 1992–1994 seemed to grow greater. Ultimately, this led Yeltsin to authorize a full-scale military assault against the Chechen regime in December 1994. The perceived risk posed by the Chechen secession was also a factor in shifting Russia's relations with post-Soviet republics in toward increasing efforts by Russia to dominate their foreign relations.

Initially, Yeltsin took the lead in proposing the establishment of the Commonwealth of Independent States (CIS), a voluntary association to maintain cooperative relations and assure mutual collective security, including joint peace-keeping endeavors on the territory of the former Soviet Union. In the December 1991 Declaration of Alma-Ata, Russia and other post-Soviet member states pledged:

> to build democratic, law-governed states, the relations between which will develop upon the basis of mutual recognition and respect for self-determination, principles of equality and noninterference in internal affairs, the rejection of the use of force, the threat of force and economic or any other methods of pressure, the peaceful settlement of disputes, respect for human rights and freedoms, including the rights of national minorities.[16]

As liberalization had reduced the power of the Gorbachev regime over the former Soviet republics and made national assertiveness more possible, this led to positive trends in a number of the republics, but also to a series of interethnic conflicts that grew in intensity with time. These included conflicts between Azerbaijan and Armenia, and within Georgia, Moldova, and Tajikistan. The Russian government was concerned by these conflicts, first because they could endanger some of the 25 million Russian-speaking citizens living in the "near abroad" of the post-Soviet republics; and secondly because they might lead to the involvement of other countries that might support different factions, such as Iran, Islamic fundamentalist regimes, or Turkey, a member of NATO. There was also a concern that the conflicts could escalate and involve the use of some of the thousands of tactical nuclear, chemical, and biological weapons that still remained on the territories of the former Soviet republics.[17] A fourth concern was that these conflicts could stimulate ethnic national groups within Russia to arm themselves and press their demands for secession, as had been done in Chechnya.

These concerns and constant pressure and criticisms from the Communist and ultranationalist opposition about Yeltsin's alleged failure to defend Russian citizens in the "near abroad" led to a series of military interventions by Russian forces in 1992 and 1993. Many of these were called peacekeeping, with the ostensible multi-lateral agreement of the CIS. But in fact, Russia was the only power supplying forces and essentially determining these activities. To deal with international concerns about Russian interventions, Russia evolved the practice of calling on the international Organization for Security and Cooperation in Europe (OSCE) to have formal international oversight, while only Russia had operational responsibilities in the actual deployment of armed units for peacekeeping or peace making.[18]

The OSCE consists of fifty-four countries, including all members of NATO, the countries of Eastern Europe, and the post-Soviet republics. It acts only on the basis of consensus reached by all member governments; therefore, each, in effect, has a veto. The OSCE established a number of mediation and peacekeeping missions to help settle and prevent conflicts in some of the post-Soviet republics, but Russia assertively saw to it that only its military forces would be involved if any were to be used. At the same time, Russia also sought to involve the UN to obtain "its legal and financial backing for Russian peacekeeping efforts in the ex-USSR, [but] not its interference in its internal affairs."[19]

Undoubtedly, Yeltsin's close work with the heads of the power ministries in the Security Council throughout 1992 and 1993 reinforced his relationship with this important pillar of his regime. The grave internal political-institutional crisis of September–October 1993, during which Yeltsin relied upon the power ministries to overcome armed resistance by Communist groups, increased their mutual concerns about the continued stability and territorial integrity of the Russian state. This might in part explain why, in the aftermath of the surrender of those armed Communists in October 1993, the Russian government arrested, detained, and then deported from Moscow tens of thousands of members of non-Russian ethnic groups, including Chechens, who had been living in Moscow without official permission.

In November 1993 the Russian government issued a document defining its security strategy for the future. The chief threat to Russia was identified as "armed conflicts engendered by aggressive nationalists and religious intolerance," meaning the threat of disintegration within Russia.[20] Concerning conflicts and peacekeeping in the states of the former Soviet Union, the national security strategy enumerated Russia's rights as follows:

1. Russia as a successor to the former Soviet Union has a special role to play in the region;
2. The territory of the former Soviet Union is a geostrategic space in which Russia has special interests;
3. Russia has a special responsibility to the security and well being of Russian citizens, ethnic Russians and Russian speaking communities, throughout the CIS;
4. Russia is a great power with regional and global responsibilities.[21]

A decade later, President Putin would reaffirm this: "We see the CIS area as the sphere of our strategic interests."[22]

The conventional forces of the Russian military had been in decline for several years, as a result of budget cuts, draft avoidance, low troop morale, and officers leaving to pursue other opportunities. In addition, it was estimated that "some 70 percent of the most up to date military technology and weapons of the former Soviet Union [had been] left outside Russian borders."[23] However, Russia retained a formidable nuclear arsenal, and the new security doctrine stated that Russia could use nuclear weapons first if necessary against any attack—conventional or nuclear—on its "key communications, command, electric, and nuclear and other strategic sites by a power owning nuclear weapons or allied to nuclear weapon states."[24] This was a revision from the 1990 security doctrine of the Soviet Union that it would not be the first to use nuclear weapons. According to Stephen Blank, this change to a doctrine of both first and if necessary preemptive use of nuclear weapons was intended "not only to deter potential nuclear armed opponents of Russia but also to establish Russian 'military superiority' over all other CIS states.... And remind [the] CIS states of Russia's military potential and the shadow its military power could cast over the CIS."[25]

The December 1993 national elections gave Yeltsin a new constitution with a strong presidency, but also saw the Communists and ultranationalist parties dominate the new Russian parliament. The new security doctrine and increased political momentum that the Communists and ultranationalists gained as a result of their electoral successes set the stage for the shift of Russian foreign policy that became more visible in the following two years.

In the "near abroad," Russia became more interventionist and assertive. It made clear that none of the former Soviet republics would be permitted to consider joining NATO or become allied with any other major power. The Russian military and security services became more active in a number of the conflicts within the republics, and in May 1994, Yeltsin issued a decree stating that twenty-nine new Russian military bases would be established in countries that had been part of the former Soviet Union.[26] At the same time, the Russian defense minister gave an ultimatum to Armenia and Azerbaijan to settle their conflict and accept a large Russian peacekeeping and monitoring presence in the region.

The sale of weapons and nuclear reactor components to Iran also began in 1994. At that time, the Russian intelligence service, led by Yevgeni Primakov, argued that "Russia must sell arms to prevent Iranian support for Islam in the southern CIS and Russia. It is best to influence Iranian policy by these sales to eliminate the threat."[27] Primakov continued that Russian and Iranian nuclear cooperation was allowed under the nonproliferation treaty, which permits "equitable, non-discriminatory cooperation in the field of peaceful atomic power."[28] At the time, Foreign Minister

Kozyrev, while confirming the sale of weapons and nuclear components to Iran, said that this had been on condition that Iran renounced the possession of nuclear weapons and its support for the expansion of Islamic fundamentalism into Central Asia.[29]

The combination of Russian assertiveness and unilateralism toward the former Soviet republics, the Communist and ultranationalist's political resurgence as seen in the December 1993 elections, and the continuing difficulties and lack of success in the economic reform process created increasing concerns and anxiety about Russia among the Eastern European countries. They hoped for the protection that membership in NATO could provide and pressed for the opportunity to join NATO. In early 1994, the U.S. proposed the Partnership for Peace (PfP) program, seeking to find a means for taking steps to increase the sense of security in East Europe without threatening Russia. This would be an association with NATO open to all the states of Eastern Europe and all the former Soviet republics, including Russia. The conditions for participating in the PfP were that states were moving to resolve their interstate and internal conflicts through peaceful means and were committed to making progress toward political democracy.[30] There was an immediate movement by the states of Eastern Europe to join the PfP and many of the post-Soviet republics sought to participate as well. Russia initially refused to participate, and the Communists and ultranationalists criticized Yeltsin for permitting this "indirect encirclement" of Russia to occur.

The events of 1995 almost mirror the ongoing struggle within the Russian government between the cooperative and the assertive approaches to Russian foreign policy. Kozyrev, as foreign minister, and Primakov, as head of the foreign intelligence service, were waging a battle for these two approaches and each had some success in persuading Yeltsin at various points in time. On the cooperative side, at the May 1995 Clinton-Yeltsin summit, Russia agreed to join the PfP and also said it would not sell Iran specific nuclear components that might help it develop nuclear weapons. Russia also signed the update of the 1969 nonproliferation treaty and gave notice to North Korea that it was ending its long-established treaty of mutual defense, which would therefore expire in one year.[31] Russia agreed to contribute peacekeeping forces under the terms of the Dayton Accords, which were intended to settle the conflict in the Bosnia-Herzegovina region of the former Yugoslavia. Russia also decided to begin a dialogue on security issues with NATO. This invitation was extended following the June 1995 NATO foreign ministers conference as a way of opening a new forum for discussion between Russia and NATO, hoping to reduce Russia's concerns about NATO enlargement.

At the same time, reflecting Russian assertiveness, a number of agreements were imposed upon some of the post-Soviet republics. These involved permission for the stationing of Russian troops on their territory, and the reestablishment of close relationships between their internal security and intelligence organizations and those of Russia. The drive for Russian dominance over the post-Soviet republics was focused on the Central Asian states. In September 1995, Yeltsin issued a decree that "sought to reintegrate Central Asia with Russia in economics and military affairs along lines that serve Russian interests and clearly undermine those states' real sovereignty."[32]

Also, a major opening to Communist China occurred at the 1995 Russia-China summit that would be a prelude to ever-closer political and military collaboration. This reflected the preferences of those who believed that Russia's main international threat came from the West and not from China in the East. At the same time, as part of a return to Soviet international strategies of the type that Primakov had pursued and advocated in the past, Russia became more supportive of Iraq and Iran, and this would increase year by year.

The December 1995 parliamentary election in Russia saw a significant increase in the number of votes for the Communists and in their representation, a decline in the ultranationalist vote, and the vote for Yeltsin's "party of power" and the democratic parties remaining about the same. As a result, Communists and ultranationalists essentially controlled the parliament and exuded optimism as they looked toward the June 1996 election for the powerful presidency. This political fact led Yeltsin to remove Kozyrev and appoint Primakov as foreign minister in January 1996, hoping a more assertive foreign policy might draw votes from the Communists and ultranationalists.

Dual Foreign Policy: "Cold Peace," Increasing Opposition to the U.S. and NATO, January 1996–Present

During the first four years of the Yeltsin era, the Communists and ultranationalist political leaders had incessantly propounded the view that the U.S. and the other major Western democracies were deliberately attempting to exert dominance in the world, to weaken Russia, and that Russia's serious political and economic problems were in large part the result of purposeful, negative Western actions through the World Bank and the IMF, among others. The Communist leader, Zyuganov, had a theory about the purpose of the U.S., which he expressed in 1994 as "nothing less than an attempt to consolidate on the planetary scale the leading role of the oceanic powers—the USA and its satellites—by way of the forcible imposition on the entire world community of the liberal market values of mercantile, oceanic civilization."[33]

While Primakov may not have accepted this echo of early twentieth-century geopolitical theory that there is an inevitable competition between the "Eurasian heartland" and the "oceanic powers" of the world, he continually stated that Russia had to find a counterweight to the power of the U.S. and the NATO alliance. This was in marked contrast to the foreign policy views expressed both by Yeltsin and by

Foreign Minister Kozyrev from January 1992 to January 1996, that Russia should endeavor to cooperate with Western powers and become integrated in a cooperative political and economic relationship with the major democracies.

Primakov essentially favored a three-level international strategy. First, all major security policy issues should be dealt with by the UN or the OSCE, where Russia had a veto and could in the end define or limit the activities of the organization. Second, Primakov understood that Russia urgently needed continuing financial assistance from Western multilateral organizations, such as the IMF and the World Bank, as well as from Western governments and investors. Therefore, he adopted a cooperative style in negotiations on differences with the U.S. and NATO. This was intended to encourage the continuing flow of public and private aid and investment resources into Russia to help in its economic recovery. Third, Primakov articulated a geopolitical doctrine of "multipolarism," in contradistinction to "unipolarism," which was the alleged intention of the U.S. and its allies to dominate the world. To counterbalance the global political influence of the U.S., Primakov believed that Russia should build a closer relationship with Communist China and support China in Asia.

The Primakov approach to China is illustrated by the results of the April 1996 Russia-China summit in Beijing, which marked the shift from the normalization of relations to a strategic alignment opposed to the United States. There, Presidents Yeltsin and Jiang Zemin signed a treaty that included Kazakhstan, Kyrgyzstan, and Tajikistan in delineating borders and began a series of confidence-building measures.[34] Russia promised to increase exports of high-technology weapons systems and components to China, and Yeltsin joined with Jiang in issuing a communiqué that attacked "hegemony," meaning "U.S. policy in Asia and NATO."[35] As described by two informed observers, Russia "aligned itself with Beijing's policies . . . whereas China only pledged cash for Russian arms and opportunities for Russian investors."[36]

This 1996 summit meeting with Communist China began an important deepening of Russian commitment to provide weapons technology and other military related supplies to China and produced the beginning of expanded Russian-Chinese geopolitical cooperation against the United States. It occurred one month after a summit between Presidents Clinton and Yeltsin in Moscow that included expressions of resolve to cooperate together on the Middle East peace process and explicit pledges by President Clinton to be helpful to President Yeltsin in his uphill battle for reelection. In fact, thanks to the publication of the memorandum from that meeting, we learn that President Clinton told President Yeltsin that in the time leading up to the June 1996 Russian elections, "Everything that the U.S. did would have a positive impact and nothing would have a negative impact."[37] Looking to his own presidential reelection campaign in the fall of 1996, President Clinton also suggested to President Yeltsin that nothing Russia did should have a negative impact on U.S.-Russian relations.

President Clinton met with President Yeltsin shortly after the U.S. succeeded, in early 1996, in encouraging the IMF to provide a special credit of $10 billion to Russia. This had a very positive impact on Yeltsin's reelection prospects because the IMF funds helped the Russian government meet its promises to pay the back wages of government employees, the military, and pension recipients, and to undertake other projects in Russia. Clearly, this was timely support for President Yeltsin.

Russia has always viewed the Middle East as a region of immense geopolitical importance. Middle Eastern countries that border the former Soviet republics could have a direct effect on the security situation in those republics and, therefore, on the security situation in Russia. This has been particularly so since the rise of Islamic fundamentalism and Russia is acutely aware of its potential appeal for the 90 million Muslims in the former Soviet republics. Also, the Middle East had been seen as important because of its immense energy supplies and the potential geopolitical influence and economic benefits to having those energy supplies in the hands of regimes friendly to Russia. Primakov, Yeltsin's new foreign minister, spent more than two decades in the Soviet era working closely with the regimes in the Middle East that the Soviet Union aided and supported in political and military terms because of their hostility to the U.S. and the West—specifically Iraq, Iran, Libya, and Syria.

The leaders of Russia and the U.S. decided that one of the highest shared priorities was to prevent the spread of weapons of mass destruction, including nuclear, chemical, and biological weapons and the means to deliver them at long range, such as cruise and ballistic missiles. In November 1994, President Clinton issued an executive order stating that "the proliferation of nuclear, biological and chemical weapons ('weapons of mass destruction') and the means of delivering such weapons constitute an unusual and extraordinary threat to national security, foreign policy, and economy of the U.S."[38] President Clinton then said that the U.S. would enter into international negotiations, and impose controls and sanctions against foreign organizations, persons, and countries in order to end the proliferation of weapons of mass destruction and the means of their delivery. In 1995, Russia signed the missile technology control regime, which obligated those signing it to prevent the export from their territory of components for ballistic missiles or dual-use technologies that could help countries make ballistic missiles.

The government of Iraq, after its invasion of Kuwait in 1990 and its defeat by a UN-sanctioned military coalition led by the U.S., was required by the UN Security Council to completely dismantle all its weapons of mass destruction and the means for their delivery. A UN inspection organization was established to see that this was, in fact, done. In spite of the fact that it was a member of the UN Security Council and a participant in these decisions, Russia, nonetheless, took a variety of actions both to impede the inspection process and to covertly provide Iraq with a variety of prohibited weapons and missile-related technology.[39]

The U.S. Congress passed the Missile Technology Control Act in 1996. The act required the Director of Central Intelligence to provide an unclassified report to Congress every six months, beginning in 1997, on which countries were providing weapons of mass destruction and which countries were obtaining them. These reports all show that China was the country most involved in proliferating components and expertise for weapons of mass destruction and that Russia was also heavily involved in those years in proliferating to Iraq, Iran, and Libya, among others.[40]

With respect to Iran, Russia did acknowledge that it had agreed to build a nuclear reactor in Iran under an $800 million contract. But Primakov insisted that this was entirely in keeping with its obligations under the nonproliferation treaties, since there would be no assistance for Iran's acknowledged intention to acquire nuclear weapons and missiles. Nevertheless, the periodic public CIA reports, the annual public testimony of the CIA director, and the revelations of internal U.S. government documents published by Bill Gertz, make clear that the U.S. government had information that after 1996, Russia was providing important assistance to Iran in developing its ballistic missiles and other weapons systems.[41] In 1997, in response to questions about Russian assistance to Iran, Primakov said, "Not a single such project by our government channels has been undertaken by Russia with Iran."[42]

In June 1997, as Presidents Clinton and Yeltsin met after the G7 summit in Denver, Colorado, President Yeltsin promised that Russia would stop its missile technology transfers to Iran.[43] This did not happen, and in 1998, Clinton's National Security Advisor, Samuel Berger, had extended conversations in Moscow with the Yeltsin government seeking to persuade Russia to end this proliferation. According to one account of Berger's meetings, he tried to persuade Russia that Clinton did not want to invoke the terms of the Iran-Libya Sanctions Act passed by Congress in 1996 and preferred instead that Russia halt the proliferation assistance to Iran. The Berger delegation included no officials from the CIA or the Department of Defense and in the end, Berger is quoted as stating, "Our own assessment is that assistance to Iran was still flowing."[44]

Not long after these conversations, Iran successfully tested a medium-range ballistic missile that could reach much of Europe and the Middle East, including U.S. forces stationed in the area. After that, the Communist-led majority in the Russian *Duma* passed a resolution calling for increased Russian military cooperation with Iran. It is important to note that at the same time, in the spring and summer of 1998, the U.S. supported a program of nearly $22 billion in IMF and Japanese assistance to Russia to help the Yeltsin administration overcome a serious crisis in the Russian economy.

This dual Russian foreign policy was supported by a number of different elements in Russia. First, it met the purposes of Primakov's definition of "multipolarism" by ostensibly counterbalancing the U.S. Second, it was supported by significant elements of the military-industrial complex, which wanted to obtain the hard currency paid by Iran, Iraq, China, and other regimes from the sale of conventional weapons, weapons of mass destruction, and missile systems. Third, it appealed politically to those who would support the Communist and ultranationalist views that Russia should do whatever the U.S. did not want it to do, to assert its independence, and build up a coalition of states that Russia could use to counterbalance the U.S. and its allies.

While Iran may accommodate these Russian purposes during the time it needs to acquire ballistic missiles and nuclear weapons, it is quite possible, even probable, that the religious and ideological regime could well undertake a foreign policy opposed to Russia's national interests once it had what it believed was a proportionate nuclear deterrent against Russia. If the current Islamic fundamentalist regime in Iran continues in power for some years, it is also possible that Russia would have succeeded only in creating a significant political danger through its arming of Iran and potentially a military danger in the future. An Islamic fundamentalist Iran armed with ballistic missiles and biological, chemical, or nuclear warheads could well become much more assertive in spreading its Islamic doctrines in Central Asia. In the Russian view, this would pose a threat that these states could turn in a direction hostile to Russia and that Muslim groups inside Russia might be assisted by Iran directly or covertly, thereby becoming more assertive and risking the disintegration of the Russian state. This is just what Putin has identified as Russia's great security risk.

Yet to counterbalance the U.S. in the Middle East, Primakov decided to work with Iran and Iraq. One dramatic and early example of this cooperation was a joint statement issued by Primakov and the Iranian foreign minister in early 1996, stating that any foreign military presence in the Persian Gulf was "totally unacceptable." Military presence was defined not only as the regular U.S. naval presence but also the military forces of the U.S. and Western powers that sought to enforce the UN Security Council resolutions against the Iraqi regime.[45]

On another front, the tragic wars in the former Yugoslavia that began in 1991 and continued through several phases, Primakov moved Russian foreign policy toward support of the Communist-ultranationalist Milosevic regime. He did this while, at the same time, partially cooperating with the Western powers in enforcing the Dayton Accords of 1995 and the UN Security Council resolutions in Bosnia.

This was illustrated when, in 1999, the CIA reportedly concluded that despite ostensible Russian cooperation with the West to contain the Serbian regime, the Russians were, in fact, engaged in intelligence collection activities and cooperation with the Milosevic regime. These actions by Primakov "reduced the effectiveness of the international effort and increased the risks to other observers while advancing Moscow's interests."[46] Specific examples included Russian activities as members of an observer mission carried out by the International Conference on the Former Yugoslavia, Serbia, and Montenegro in the years 1994 to 1996, supported by international funds.

Among actions taken by Russian members of that ostensibly peace-keeping international group, which included many former KGB and military intelligence officers among the Russian staff, were the following: efforts to recruit the president of Montenegro as a Russian agent; undermining the group's operations by its Russian chief of staff; the selling of data from a UN election monitoring system to the Serbs; and frequent visits by a Russian UN observer who, according to the CIA report, had many meetings with "high ranking Serbs . . . he was an unreconstructed, pedantic Communist . . . he decried unacceptable U.S. hegemony in the world and longed for the return of the USSR and a strong Russian leader."[47] These covert Russian activities took place in Primakov's last years as head of the Russian foreign intelligence service and during his first year as foreign minister.

In 1997, Primakov led the way in opposing the enlargement of NATO. However, when Russian objections and threats to undertake rearmament failed to dissuade NATO, Primakov negotiated over a period of months to establish a Joint NATO-Russia Council for consultation on security issues, which was ceremoniously adopted at a meeting of NATO heads of state with President Yeltsin in May 1997. This Joint Council gave Russia a "voice but not a veto" in NATO decisions on security matters and, in the same way, gave NATO a "voice but not a veto" over Russian decisions on security issues. It was viewed, at the signing by president Yeltsin, as "a great day" for peace in Europe, although Yeltsin repeated his objection to NATO enlargement.[48]

In 1998, Saddam Hussein shifted from obstructing UN weapons inspections to ending all cooperation, which led to the UN inspectors leaving Iraq. As a result, the U.S. threatened air attacks on military facilities to pressure Saddam Hussein to implement the UN Security Council resolutions on the destruction of weapons of mass destruction and access for international inspectors. Primakov once again attempted to prevent the use of force against Iraq (as he had in 1990–1991), while ostensibly seeking to abide by Russia's international obligations. In December 1998, U.S. and United Kingdom forces launched air attacks on Iraq as a result of its continuing refusal to comply with the UN Security Council resolutions on weapons inspection. China and Russia strenuously objected, and Russia temporarily withdrew its ambassador from Washington. Shortly after, Primakov visited India and publicly stated that it would be desirable for Russia, India, and China to form an alliance to counterbalance the United States.[49] The following day, Russian Communist Party leader Zyuganov publicly supported that proposal.[50]

The 1999 Kosovo Crisis and Its Political Effects

For the former Yugoslavia, the Kosovo crisis began in 1989 when the Yugoslav Communist dictator, Slobodan Milosevic, decided unilaterally to end the status of Kosovo as an autonomous province. As part of his effort to incite and inflame extremist Serbian nationalism as a means of keeping his Serbian-based Communist Party in power, Milosevic began to persecute the 90 percent ethnic Albanian population of Kosovo. The Albanian Kosovars resisted through peaceful means for a number of years, and efforts were made by moderate elements in the Kosovo Serbian and Albanian communities to bring about a fairer and less repressive Serbian administration of the province. The majority of the mostly Muslim Albanian Kosovars became affiliated with a nonviolent civil resistance that established parallel institutions such as schools and other civic organizations to meet their needs.

In early 1998, as Milosevic increased repression, small groups of armed Kosovars began to attack Serbian forces in the province. Milosevic sent more Serbian units to Kosovo and sharpened the repression. The U.S. and other NATO countries denounced the violence. In February 1998, Secretary of State Madeline Albright said that the U.S. and its allies would not permit the Milosevic dictatorship to again drive hundreds of thousands of people from their homes and persecute them on the basis of their ethnicity.

The U.S., several European nations, and Russia established a "contact group" that attempted to negotiate with the Milosevic regime on Kosovo all through 1998. By late summer, as the diplomatic process continued, Serbian forces had driven nearly three hundred thousand men, women, and children from their homes; they were hiding inside Kosovo or had fled into neighboring countries. As the situation worsened, the U.S. and NATO threatened to launch air strikes against Serbian forces if they were not withdrawn from Kosovo. Milosevic refused, contending the Serbian forces were a response to the armed attacks of the Kosovo Liberation Army (KLA), which Serbia denounced as terrorists. During these negotiations, Russia contended that only the UN Security Council could authorize military attacks against Serbia, and both Russia and China said they would veto any such action. Russia did not publicly condemn the persecution of civilians in Kosovo, nor did it condemn the KLA. In the UN, Russia and China also took the Serbian position in support of Milosevic against the NATO military threats.

In October 1998, a special envoy representing the U.S. and NATO reached an agreement with Milosevic that permitted unarmed international observers to enter Kosovo to monitor the human rights situation as Serbia withdrew most of its units from Kosovo, thereby ending the repression of Kosovo Albanians. Those negotiations took place in the context of repeated threats of air strikes by the NATO countries if the ethnic persecution in Kosovo continued. Prime Minister Primakov appointed his trusted deputy, Igor Ivanov, as foreign minister. During the critical October 1998 meetings between the U.S. special envoy and Milosevic, the Russian ministers of foreign affairs and defense also visited the Yugoslav capital. According to the Yugoslav press, they expressed the political support of Russia for the Milosevic regime and promised that if NATO attacked, Russia would break the UN embargo on the export of weapons to Yugoslavia and supply the Yugoslav army with advanced missile and anti-aircraft systems.[51] A German magazine published what it said was German intelligence information indicating that in the event of a NATO attack on Serbian forces, Russia had promised to provide Yugoslavia not only with advanced defensive weapons, but also with military aircraft and pilots.[52]

An accord on Kosovo was announced on October 13, 1998: Serbia would end its persecution of the Albanian Kosovars and withdraw its armed units, and NATO would rescind the threat of air strikes. On October 25, 1998, the UN Security Council adopted resolution 1203, which urged Yugoslavia to comply immediately and unconditionally with the agreement signed by Milosevic and U.S. special envoy Richard Holbrooke. Russia and China abstained. This resolution was intended to reinforce the accord negotiated by the Contact Group in early October.

In the fall of 1998, policy toward Iraq and Serbia were two simultaneous points of major difference between the U.S. and Russia. With respect to the former Yugoslavia, and the Kosovo crisis in particular, Russia did not want the U.S. or NATO to threaten force against the Milosevic regime and insisted that any use of force could occur only if the UN Security Council authorized it. By that means, Russia and China intended to have a veto over the ultimate question of the use of force. At the same time, as we have seen, Primakov followed a policy of participating in negotiations and conflict resolution efforts with the West on the one hand while supporting the regimes of Milosevic and Saddam Hussein on the other. Primakov, through his ministers of defense and foreign affairs, promised Milosevic both political support and potential military and covert support in the event of a conflict. It is likely that this Russian support emboldened both Milosevic and Saddam Hussein.

The crisis in U.S.-Russian relations in the fall of 1998 occurred just after the September 1998 summit between presidents Yeltsin and Clinton in Moscow, where President Clinton had said that Russia and the U.S. "have a partnership . . . even though we do not agree on every issue."[53] At that summit, both presidents were in a situation of great domestic political difficulty. Yeltsin was in the midst of a confrontation with the Russian parliament on the selection of a new prime minister, following the August financial crisis. President Clinton had just admitted publicly that he had lied since January 1998 about a personal scandal and was facing impeachment proceedings by the U.S. Congress. He was accused of lying under oath, which is a felony. That summit meeting established an agreement on a joint center for Russia and the U.S. to share early warning information and for working groups on improved export controls to prevent the proliferation of weapons of mass destruction.

It was in this context that in the fall 1998 Russia conducted its strategic military exercises, launching ICBMs and air-launched cruise missiles against simulated U.S. and NATO targets, as would be done in a war. Perhaps the intended message was that Russia remained a powerful country in terms of its strategic nuclear weapons and that this power needed to be respected by the U.S. and the other NATO countries by not acting unilaterally against the wishes of the Russian state.

For some weeks, the October 1998 agreement seemed to work. On November 17, the UN Security Council adopted resolution 1207 (with China abstaining and Russia voting in favor), which required Yugoslavia and leaders of the Albanian community in Kosovo to cooperate with the international tribunal investigating war crimes committed in the former Yugoslavia. However, in subsequent weeks, a series of incidents led to the resumption of fighting by both sides. On January 16, 1999, when the bodies of forty-five Albanian civilians were discovered in a Kosovo village, U.S. diplomat William Walker, the head of the Kosovo Verification Mission, said that Serbian security forces had committed the murders. Two days later, this led to a UN Security Council resolution condemning those murders and a decision by the Yugoslav regime not to allow the chief prosecutor of the International War Crimes Tribunal for the former Yugoslavia to enter the country to investigate the killings.

In February and March 1999, an extended series of negotiations between the Serbian regime, representatives of the Kosovo Albanians, and the international community were held in Rambouillet, France. These concluded in March with the Kosovo Albanians signing a new agreement and the Serbian government refusing to sign. The Rambouillet Agreement provided for implementation, in essence, of the October 1998 commitments. The Serbian government justified its opposition by stating that it would not permit an international military presence in Kosovo. Instead, the Serbian regime began adding to its military and paramilitary forces in Kosovo. By early March 1999, there were reports that Serbians were using artillery and tanks.

As the winter snows thawed, the Serbian forces began systematic attacks against towns in Kosovo, both to remove the forces of the Kosovo Liberation Army (KLA) and to expel tens of thousands of men, women, and children from their homes. On March 24, 1999, NATO threats having failed to persuade Milosevic to halt these attacks, NATO began a campaign of air attacks against military targets in Yugoslavia. President Clinton described the purposes of the NATO air attacks as follows:

> We act to protect thousands of innocent people in Kosovo from a mounting military offensive. We act to prevent a wider war, to diffuse a powder keg in the heart of Europe that has exploded twice before in this century with catastrophic results. We act to stand united with our allies for peace. . . . As the Kosovars were saying yes to peace [in the Rambouillet peace agreement], Serbia stationed

40,000 troops in and around Kosovo in preparation for a major offensive in clear violation of the commitments they had made. Now they have started moving from village to village, shelling civilians and torching their houses. We have seen innocent people taken from their homes, forced to kneel in the dirt and sprayed with bullets. Kosovo men dragged from their families, father and sons together, lined up and shot in cold blood. This is not war in the traditional sense. It is an attack by tanks and artillery on a largely defenseless people whose leaders already have agreed to peace. Ending this tragedy is a moral imperative. It is also important to America's national interests.[54]

From the NATO point of view, its air and cruise missile attacks against Serbian forces were justified to prevent an escalating pattern of crimes against humanity by the Milosevic regime and were consistent with the purpose of the existing UN Security Council resolutions on the Yugoslav issue. From the Russian and Chinese point of view, the NATO military attacks were an act of aggression against a sovereign state and were not permitted under international law because the UN Security Council had not specifically authorized the use of force.

While there was general support for the NATO air campaign within the member states of NATO, there was sharp opposition across the political spectrum in Russia. The Communist opposition in the Russian *Duma* moved immediately to make the case to the Russian public that the NATO attacks demonstrated exactly what it had been warning about since 1992—that the U.S. and NATO were a danger to Russia and would use military force coercively to obtain dominance in international politics. As the NATO air strikes began, Primakov was on his way to the U.S. to meet with the U.S. leadership and the IMF in order to negotiate a new $4.5 billion IMF loan to Russia. In mid-flight, he decided to return to Moscow. Primakov strongly condemned the NATO air attacks and with China went to the UN Security Council in an attempt to obtain a resolution condemning the NATO bombing. His efforts were unsuccessful.

There were essentially three broad phases in the strong Russian reaction against the NATO air strikes, the first of which was a Communist-led demand for forceful condemnations and counteractions. Some Russian Communist leaders suggested that Russian nuclear missiles be targeted on all NATO countries; that Russia send full military assistance to the Milosevic regime, including Russian "volunteer" ground forces; and that Russia take unspecified military counteractions. Also, President Yeltsin warned that this conflict could lead to "a Europe wide or even a third world war."[55] Yeltsin's immediate reaction also was, "In Russia, there is deep shock at the military actions of NATO against the sovereign Yugoslavia, which is nothing other than naked aggression."[56]

During this first phase, Primakov acted to forge an even closer coalition with

China opposing the NATO actions, while acting covertly to send military assistance to the Milosevic regime. Shortly after the start of the NATO air war, Primakov visited Milosevic on an ostensible mediation mission. However, he went accompanied by the Russian foreign minister, defense minister, the head of military intelligence, and the head of foreign intelligence. The composition of this delegation suggested a program of covert assistance. The covert military aid came to light when the Azerbaijani government impounded a large Russian cargo plane, which landed in Azerbaijan on a refueling stop. It was discovered that the cargo plane carried six Russian jet fighters, other military equipment, and thirty pilots and technicians. Various false statements were made about the destination of the plane, and most observers concluded that it was an example of a Russian covert action that had been discovered.[57] Subsequent press reports would confirm the presence of Russian officers and soldiers with Serbian fighting forces.

The NATO air strikes did not prevent the Milosevic regime's military and para-military forces on the ground in Kosovo from systematically attacking and burning hundreds of towns and villages. This led, in a matter of weeks, to the expulsion of an estimated eight hundred thousand ethnic Albanians from Kosovo. Most fled to neighboring countries. At the same time, there were estimates of approximately three to four hundred thousand ethnic Albanians hiding in the hillsides and forests of Kosovo, fleeing persecution that included the systematic murder of thousands of men who were separated from their families and taken away. NATO released aerial photographs of fresh mass graves, suggesting large-scale executions. Estimates of those killed by the Serbian forces in March, April, and May ranged in the thousands.[58]

That all of these victims of the Serbian regime were Muslim Albanians and Kosovars had a political effect inside Russia, where about 20 percent of the population is Muslim and where the government hardly commented on or criticized the brutal actions of the Milosevic regime. The Russian Muslims wanted Russia to condemn Milosevic as well as NATO, and this view was also held by many of the 90 million Muslims living in the former Soviet republics in Central Asia that border Russia. The Central Asian countries rebuffed Primakov when he sought to have them condemn the NATO air strikes. That response may have reminded the Russian government that its support for Milosevic could lead to problems at home and in the "near abroad."

The second stage of the official Russian reaction to the NATO air campaign was more measured. There were probably four reasons for this. First, President Clinton spoke with President Yeltsin and invited Russia to act as mediator in attempting to bring about a political settlement. This reaffirmed Russia's status as a major power. Second, Yeltsin understood that the Communist and ultranationalist proposals for military support to Milosevic could, in fact, lead to a much wider war, and this was contrary to Russian interests. Third, there were risks of problems within Russia and from Central Asian Muslims from continuing what seemed to be Russian endorsement of massive repression against the Muslim Kosovars. Fourth, Russia had an urgent need for funding from the IMF, if it were to avoid another major financial crisis. Until Russia moved toward a more constructive mediation role, no progress was made in its request for IMF funding, suggesting that behind-the-scenes pressures from the U.S. might well be having a role in that matter.

A major step in Russia's new approach was Yeltsin's appointment of former Prime Minister Chernomyrdin as his special negotiator for Kosovo. This occurred at the same time that Yeltsin gave his first public indication that Prime Minster Primakov did not have his full support by stating publicly, Primakov "is useful to us for now—later we shall see." Yeltsin's decision to move away from Primakov's diplomatic and covert strategy by appointing Chernomyrdin, who undertook a strictly diplomatic approach to mediation, began to produce results. On April 25, 1999, Yeltsin telephoned President Clinton, and it was reported that they had a useful discussion on Kosovo. Four days later, the IMF approved the $4.6 billion loan to the Russian Central Bank, and on the following day, April 30, President Yeltsin named the head of the Ministry of the Interior, Stepashin, as deputy prime minister. That set the stage for Yeltsin to remove Primakov as prime minister. In contrast to most Russian political leaders, who condemned the NATO air attacks on Yugoslavia and were silent about the ethnic deportations and murders, Yeltsin's first foreign minister, Andrei Kozyrev, spoke and wrote candidly. In early April 1999 he said:

> The Russian government has managed in the last three or four years to restore a Soviet world outlook, where on the one side there is Moscow, and on the other, all democratic countries. . . . This obviously is a happy hour for our corrupt bureaucracy. . . . We are recreating an international situation in which nobody asks anymore if there is corruption or not [in Russia], if the economy is managed in a qualified way or not. . . . Now the talk is already about building a big prowar camp against imperialism. . . . This situation did not start today. AntiNATO hysterics have been inflated in the last three years. . . . We dropped the postulate of partnership. . . . and we adopted the postulate of a so-called multipolar world. This means basically [creating] an antiimperialism front.[59]

Former foreign minister Kozyrev further discussed his criticism of the change in Russian foreign policy under Primakov as prime minister and foreign minister in an essay:

> Instead of defending the true interests of Russia through partnership in the economic sense with the leading democratic powers—who were, by the way,

our allies in the Second World War—we have taken a course which all but resembles one of defending the interests of bloody dictators like Milosevic in Serbia and Saddam Hussein in Iraq. . . . Russia alone . . . and Milosevic . . . both head toward political and economic isolation. [Primakov's] turning back of the plane on his flight to Washington is the price we pay for pursuing the blind alley policy we are following today. We ourselves are erasing the possibility of receiving credits.

In this way, once again, we show that our bureaucracy thinks least of all of the interests of our people. . . . We have disinformed our population about the situation in Kosovo with the result that at present, European states and other foreign countries are beginning to get the impression that . . . we overlook ethnic cleansing in Kosovo, just as we did in Bosnia, just as we ignored the fact that it was the leadership in Belgrade that unleashed conflict on the territory of the former Yugoslavia. This impression casts a long, very grim shadow. It is in the interest of Russia [not to be] the only state marching in step with Milosevic.[60]

These words courageously stated by Kozyrev in public at a time when most political leaders were unwilling to criticize Primakov's policies, much less speak out about the full dimensions of the Kosovo conflict, were also undoubtedly stated in private to Yeltsin by those who shared Kozyrev's viewpoint. These would include important individuals both in the political leadership and among the financial-industrial barons who recognized that their interests, as well as Russia's, lay in avoiding a major war and in a continued economic partnership with the West. They also knew that additional Western financial support was critical to maintaining the Russian economy.

After the 1999 Kosovo Air Campaign Against Serbia

The mediation efforts had begun with Milosevic insisting that any international forces in Kosovo must be under the direct authority of the UN and could not include any from NATO countries. Russia initially supported that position, but after some weeks of discussions and NATO's insistence that an international force must have "NATO at its core," the combination of NATO air strikes and Russia through Chernomyrdin persuaded Milosevic to accept the following: all Serbian police, military, and paramilitary forces would withdraw from Kosovo; the international force would be comprised primarily of NATO troops, with some participation from Russia and other countries, and NATO would have primary functional direction of the force; an international force to protect the Kosovars and its civilian counterparts would be under the overall authority of the UN Security Council; and Russian forces would not directly report to NATO but would have the same command arrangements as in Bosnia, where Russian commanders in the field reported to appropriate military officers from the various NATO countries who, in turn, reported to the UN.[61]

Once this agreement was accepted on June 12, 1999, NATO ceased its air strikes. With the Kosovo issue decided, the G8 summit meeting in Cologne, Germany, provided an opportunity, as Prime Minister Blair put it, "to put our differences behind us and map out a set of common interests for the future."[62] The leaders of the other seven industrial democracies told Russian Prime Minister Sergei Stepashin that they would now urge the IMF to release the promised $4.5 billion and that they would also help Russia restructure $69 billion of its $159 billion debt from the Soviet era. This restructuring was very important because it would reduce immediately billions of dollars in annual debt repayments that Russia would otherwise have to make. The IMF credit, when finally approved, would also open the way to other financial assistance for Russia from the World Bank, which planned to lend $3 billion, and from other sources of public and private investment. Further, they would "expand funding to assist Russia in dismantling obsolete nuclear warheads, safely disposing of plutonium stocks and finding long term employment for scientists who might otherwise be tempted to sell their nuclear expertise to foreign tyrants."[63]

The following day, President Yeltsin arrived to participate in the G8 summit meeting and said, "We need to make up after our fight. That is the main thing." He also suggested reviving the regular meetings between Vice President Gore and the Russian prime minister and agreed (as he had in 1992) to consider U.S. proposals for changing the 1972 ABM treaty to permit a ballistic missile defense system against threats from accidental or rogue state attacks. This important statement came in return for U.S. agreement to consider deeper cuts in both nuclear arsenals.[69] But the Communist speaker of the Russian *Duma* said once again that it was unlikely that the *Duma* would ratify the 1993 START II agreement and that despite the results of the G8 summit, his view was that bilateral relations with the U.S. were still on hold. Any ratification of START II would require the U.S. to continue adherence to the 1972 ABM treaty with no changes.[64]

The day after this summit meeting, June 21, 1999, Russia began its "West 1999 Maneuvers," a six-day exercise involving its entire range of weapons, including strategic nuclear weapons, designed to simulate a hypothetical NATO attack. That exercise led to "the first airborne face-offs between American and Russian pilots in a decade."[65] The head of the Russian air force said that the flights of Russian bombers near Iceland and Norway, both NATO members, had been planned in advance, "Nothing more, and nothing less."[66] A senior U.S. official commented that the maneuvers Russia "reminded us that they are a force to be reckoned with."[67]

Following the maneuvers, Yeltsin reportedly urged Russian generals to cooperate with NATO in Kosovo, saying, "The problem of our relations with NATO and the USA is very subtle, delicate and difficult . . . everyone of you must pursue the same line—the President's line. We shall certainly not quarrel with NATO outright, but nor do we intend to flirt with it."[68] In late July, Russia returned to meetings of the permanent Joint Council between Russia and NATO.[69] This step was followed by the visit of Russian Prime Minister Sergei Stepashin to Washington, DC for conversations with American business leaders to promote increased U.S. investment in Russia and for a meeting with Vice President Gore and President Clinton. Stepashin indicated that Russian priorities were to obtain greater economic aid, U.S. investment and to resolve various trade issues.[70] U.S. priorities were focused on security issues and Russian cooperation in the former Yugoslavia.[71]

The post-Kosovo Russian foreign policy with the U.S. suggested an end to confrontation and a return to dualism and limited cooperation. On the positive side, the U.S. and Russian foreign affairs ministers signed an agreement establishing a new telephone "hotline" to improve communication between the two capitals. At virtually the same time, it was revealed that Russian intelligence and espionage operations in the U.S. had increased to their Cold War levels and that the U.S. government had formally asked Russia to reduce these activities.[72] A U.S. official was quoted as saying that the Russian intelligence services were "operating in full swing without missing a beat. . . . In some cases they had the same KGB personnel here now who were working against us in the Soviet period."[73]

PUTIN's FOREIGN POLICY

The foreign policy approach of President Putin has continued that of Primakov—a style of normalcy and cooperation with the major democracies in order to obtain economic benefits for Russia, together with a wide range of actions to counterbalance the U.S. and divide it from its allies in Europe and Asia on key issues. In his first years as president, Putin has shown a strong sense for international maneuver, and he has been active in building or deepening international relationships that he believes will be useful for Russia, such as those with China and Iran. As prime minister and president, Putin initially continued in their offices two key individuals who worked closely with Primakov: Minister of Foreign Affairs Igor Ivanov and Minister of Defense Igor Sergeyev. However, Putin worked most closely with Sergei Ivanov, a contemporary from St. Petersberg who had also been in the foreign intelligence directorate of the KGB and whom he appointed secretary of the Security Council. Toward the end of March 2001, Putin named Ivanov as minister of defense.

Preserving Russia, the Near Abroad
The renewal of the Chechnya war in 1999, just as Putin became prime minister, meant that the threat of the fragmentation of the Russian Federation through a series of armed separatist movements returned as the highest national security

concern. Therefore, the first priority for Russian foreign policy under Putin was to prevent any other states from providing military or political support to the Chechens or any to other separatists within Russia. This in turn reinforced the effort begun by Russia in 1994 to prevent hostile actions by groups operating from the former Soviet republics, the "near abroad," which involved the placement of military bases and reestablishment of operational links to the intelligence and internal security agencies of most of the former Soviet republics.

A leaked plan, prepared for Putin in May 2000, called for open and covert actions to restore Russian dominance over the former Soviet republics. This was to be done step-by-step, mostly in a "discreet" manner, not being "too obvious," much as Putin had described Soviet-era KGB operations to affect internal political groups. The Communists within the former republics were the most eager for the de facto restoration of the Soviet Union (or as much of it as possible). This could be seen in the Central Asian republic of Tajikistan, where the Communists took power in 1992 and invited a large Russian military presence; in Belarus, where the Communists returned in 1997 to be followed by the "reunion" with Russia; and in 2001 in Moldova, where the Communists' winning control of the parliament was followed by their proposal to join the Russia-Belarus union. The Communists in Russia have long favored this reestablishment of a de facto Soviet Union. As former republics ask to rejoin Russia, there is little apparent debate about this by other parties in Russia; nor would there be a basis for the international community, the UN, or the OSCE to object. These are, after all, the apparently voluntary decisions of sovereign states, which some might compare to the voluntary political-economic steps taken by members of the European Union.

Even in Ukraine, long viewed by some as highly unlikely to return to Russia, the main Ukrainian Communist leaders urge the restoration of the Soviet Union. President Kuchma, a former Communist leader, ran his 1999 presidential campaign on the basis that he could best "consolidate" relations with Russia.[74] Among the invisible and indirect means of influence Putin has used in relations with Ukraine (and other former republics) is dependence on Moscow for energy supplies and for financial support or credits. There are reports that Putin spoke with the former president of Ukraine frequently. In February 2001, it was reported that Ukraine had agreed to the reintegration of the Russian and Ukrainian energy supply systems, that Ukraine would cooperate with Russia in missile building and in aerospace production (many of the Soviet Union's most important facilities were in Ukraine), and that a new bridge would be jointly built to connect the sunny, warm Crimea with Russia.[75]

The Republic of Georgia, bordering Turkey and Chechnya, has been a focus of Russian pressure for some years. In 1999, former President Shevardnadze refused to give permission for Russian military forces to attack Chechen guerillas from

Georgia. Putin has used Georgia's debts to Russia and its dependence on Russia for energy and employment to gain more control over Georgian policy. The head of the majority party in the Georgia parliament said: "There is no acceptance [in Russia] that Georgia can be a country or that any of the former Soviet republics except the Baltics can go their own way."[76]

This movement toward a restoration of a Russian-led union of former Soviet republics, especially the mainly Muslim republics to the south and west, could be seen by Putin and by many in Russia as among the actions necessary to prevent further Chechnyas from erupting in the future. The concern over the "Islamic Question" in Russia could explain the curious attendance by Putin at the Organization of Islamic Conference (OIC) summit in Kuala Lumpur in October 2003, after which he expressed an interest in Russia joining the OIC as a member state. However, on a geostrategic level, it is a means to prevent and preempt any other major or regional powers—whether members of NATO such as Turkey or "strategic partners" such as China—from displacing Russian influence and interests in the contiguous regions.

This is increasingly a concern for Russia as it walks the tightrope between its own interests, working with China for both economic and geostrategic considerations, and its justifiable concerns over Chinese intentions—not only in the Central Asian states that make up the Shanghai Cooperative Organization, but also in the Russian Far East, which is increasingly drifting more toward the geographically closer Beijing and away from the distant influence of Moscow. The former head of the SVR, now First Deputy Foreign Minister Vyacheslav Trubnikov, has expressed this concern publicly when in respose to a question in an interview with a Russian newspaper in May 2004 about the U.S. presence in Central Asia said:

American presence has greatly increased in the post-Soviet space. This is not only Transcaucasia, but also Central Asia. Much will depend on how we build our relations with the CIS countries. Should we enter into a confrontation, or, on the contrary, raise our hands up or generally ignore the U.S. presence? I don't think we can be happy with the presence of extra-regional powers whether it is the U.S., China or some other country. After all, it is a sphere of our vital interests. It is our priority and the presence of extra-regional powers there cannot be good news for us. There is a limit to everything. There are agreements with us regarding the goals of their presence there.[77]

Interestingly, this interview was removed from almost every place it was available within the Russian government within days of being published, except for the Russian embassy in Canada's website.

This statement has not been the only potential sign of friction between China and Russia. For example, recent actions taken by the Russian government—such as the pipeline debate in which Moscow sided with Japan over China; or the ongoing strengthening of the bilateral economic, political, and military relations between Russia and the individual members outside of the framework of the SCO—could indicate growing weariness on the part of Moscow about the intentions of Beijing. The distancing between these two states could provide some unique opportunities if they were seized upon. An example of the potential this might offer was seen in the report in the summer of 2004 that President Putin would be willing to sell eight Kilo submarines, the same number and class Russia is selling to China, to the U.S.— with the understanding that they would be resold to Taiwan.[78]

The Stated Purposes of Putin's Foreign Policy

On July 10, 2000, Russia publicized a statement of foreign policy doctrine signed by President Putin. It continued using the Primakov and Chinese terminology by stating that Russia seeks a "multipolar" world rather than the "unipolar structure of the world with the economic and power domination of the United States."[79] At the same time, reflecting the Russian need for economic support from and relations with the democracies, the doctrine stated that the essence of Russia's approach would be "pragmatism" and that the core purpose of Russian foreign policy is to "effectively help solve domestic tasks," especially by providing "favorable conditions for Russia's economic growth."[80]

In January 2001, after months of international activism, Putin said that Russia had neither a Western nor an oriental "direction" in foreign policy and that "because of its geopolitical allocation, Russia has its national interests everywhere."[81] In that same talk to Russian diplomats, Putin said the main objectives of Russian diplomacy were to integrate Russia into the world economy, to protect Russian business interests abroad, and to improve Russia's international image. In keeping with those objectives, Putin has adopted an active policy of seeking to assure the continuation of economic support from the major democracies and has sought to establish special relationships with Germany, France, and the European Union. In June 2000, Putin and German Chancellor Schroeder agreed on a new "strategic partnership."

In March 2001, Putin became the first Russian leader invited to participate in a summit meeting with the fifteen leaders of the member states in the European Union. He was welcomed with the words: "We want to engage and not exclude Russia from the process of European integration."[82] The meeting ended with agreements on new cooperation in the export of Russian oil and gas to meet the growing energy needs of Europe and on maintaining stability in the Balkans. At the same time, Chancellor Schroeder urged Putin to make further progress on economic reforms and on ending endemic corruption so that Western entrepreneurs could have the confidence needed to invest in Russia.

From his first visit to Europe as president in June 2000, Putin had urged the European members of NATO to oppose U.S. plans for missile defense and proposed instead a vaguely defined joint Russian-European missile defense.[83] In February 2001, Putin presented NATO Secretary General George Robertson with a proposal that NATO and Russia build a joint defense system against third-country missile attacks, reportedly listing as possible threats Iran, Libya, and North Korea—all countries to which Russia sells weapons. In the view of a senior European defense official, this meant that Putin had rejected the view of many in the Russian military leadership that NATO was Russia's greatest threat and had, instead, accepted the view of Russian "intelligence and security services [that] the threat from Muslim extremists" is the most important.[84] Following his meeting with Putin, NATO Secretary General Robertson said on the record: "Putin is moving along precisely the same tracks that we are."[85]

It remains to be seen whether this judgment is correct or whether this is what Putin wants the Europeans to believe as part of a political strategy to divide them from the United States on as many major international issues as possible (such as missile defense and further NATO enlargement). A good example of increased activism in this direction is the report that Putin requested the very large sum of $50 million from the Russian parliament to pay for an international media campaign against NATO enlargement.[86] This proactive Russian approach to the democracies—seeking economic benefits from all, while simultaneously trying to divide the U.S. from Europe—shows that Putin has learned much from past Soviet and KGB strategies and tactics.

Relations with the United States

With his emphasis on the need to strengthen the Russian economy and the resulting importance of good economic relations with the United States, Putin has continued in Primakov's style of seeking constructive relations. At the same time, Putin has been explicit about Russian opposition to further NATO enlargement, to the inclusion of the Baltics in such an enlargement, and to missile defense plans as announced by the United States in 1999 and again proposed by President George W. Bush in May 2001.[87] Putin's minister of defense, Sergei Ivanov, said in February 2001 that if the United States moved away from the 1972 ABM treaty, it would "crush the very foundations of international strategic security and force the expansion of the arms race into space."[88] Yet the proposal for cooperation on missile defense that Putin presented to the secretary general of NATO in February 2001, and a promise by Bush to Putin that the U.S. could not unilaterally change the strategic balance, illustrate that there may be an opening for compromise on this issue.[89]

At Putin's initiative, the Russian military leadership was tasked with restructuring the Russian military in order to make it more cost-effective. Presiding over this effort was Putin's close associate Igor Ivanov, and the result was a months-long debate between two perspectives within the Russian military. The chief of the general staff, General Anatoly Kvashnin, contended that the Strategic Rocket Forces should reduce the number of land-based nuclear warheads from 3,500 to 1,500 and merge the heretofore-separate Strategic Rocket Forces into the Air Force. The defense minister, a former commander of the Strategic Rocket Forces, contended this would be a grave mistake and denounced the proposed changes as "a psychotic plan" that would "undermine Russia's status as a leading world power."[90] For months, there was an impasse on this issue, but in March 2001 Putin decided that he would adopt the proposed plan for reducing the strategic missile forces and that Russia would reduce its conventional forces from about 1.2 million to about 850,000 in the next several years.[91] In making this decision, Putin removed the minister of defense and appointed Sergei Ivanov, a civilian, in his place, saying this change "is a step toward the demilitarization of Russia's public life" and that "it is high time to get to the practical implementation of our plans" for changes in the Russian military.[92]

This military restructuring is to be accompanied by a sizable increase in the defense budget (estimated for 2001 at $8 billion of Russia's $40 billion national budget[93]). The new defense minister said that the additional budget will provide increased salaries for personnel and will also lead to a "more professional, mobile, and more combat ready" military. The proposed reductions in the total size of Russia's forces should be reassuring to Europe, and the proposed reductions in strategic nuclear forces will undoubtedly be a major factor as Russia seeks to persuade the United States to pursue its approach to missile defense.

Shortly after the Bush administration took office, Russia conducted a days-long strategic war exercise involving simulated conflict with the United States and other NATO members, and the actual launching of land-based and sea-based ballistic missiles and strategic bombers.[94] A former Director of Central Intelligence for President Clinton, James Woolsey, said that he viewed this large-scale strategic combat exercise as "Russia deciding to deal with the West after the fashion of the Soviet Union in the 1980s . . . to prevent an American strategic overture, in this case missile defense." For their part, the Russian military gave advance notice of the exercises and said that these were aimed at "checking notification systems, combat and mobilization readiness."[95]

This exercise coincided with two unexpected events. It was revealed that the United States had information that Russia had moved nuclear warheads into the Kaliningrad region, a Russian enclave of nine hundred thousand contiguous to Poland and the Baltics. Putin personally denied the allegation when it was published, but subsequent information published at the time of the Russian strategic exercise indicated that there was conclusive proof that Russia had transferred these weapons contrary to its previous promises and declarations.[96] Poland,

Lithuania, Latvia, and Estonia requested inspections of the Kaliningrad area, but Russia refused. It is worth noting that in addition to its strategic nuclear warheads Russia has an estimated four to fifteen thousand tactical nuclear weapons, including short-range missile warheads, nuclear armed torpedoes, and nuclear bombs—none of which is included in existing U.S.-Russian arms control agreements.[97] The transfer of these nuclear weapons could be interpreted as a means of threatening the Baltic countries and NATO in order to prevent any future affiliation.

The second unexpected event was the revelation that a senior official of the U.S. Federal Bureau of Investigation, Robert Hanssen, had been spying for Russia since 1985. The U.S. government's public statement on the matter disclosed that Hanssen's responsibilities were for counterintelligence against Soviet and then Russian espionage and suggested that a large amount of highly sensitive information had been compromised. Before the Hanssen arrest, a Russian weekly magazine reported that Putin had increased political and military intelligence gathering in the United States and put Sergei Ivanov in charge of those efforts.[98] This was in addition to the large increase in Russian espionage activities that had occurred under Primakov and about which the United States had protested in 1999. The Hanssen spy scandal was followed in March 2001 by the U.S. government expelling about fifty members of the Russian embassy and Russia expelling an equal number of U.S. embassy employees from Moscow.

Russia and Regimes Hostile to the United States

During his first months as president, Putin moved to reestablish or deepen relations between Russia and a number of regimes hostile to the United States or its allies. This included the reopening of relations with North Korea that Yeltsin had ended in the early 1990s; a personal visit by Putin to Castro in Cuba, broadening the relationship after years of distance; diplomatic support for Iraq; and overtures to Libya and Syria. All of these were among the most important pro-Soviet regimes, and Putin seemed to be moving toward a restoration of cooperation and weapons sales that had a long history as part of Soviet strategy.

In March 2001, Presidents Putin and Mohammad Khatami of Iran announced a cooperation agreement in Moscow providing for the open sale of Russian weapons to Iran (contracts were expected to total more than $300 million annually—$2 billion over five years); increased Russian work on helping Iran build a nuclear reactor, a project begun in 1994, for which Iran would pay Russia an estimated $1 billion; and joint opposition to a U.S.-supported oil pipeline from Central Asia that would move oil from Central Asia to the West on a route bypassing Russia—thereby depriving it of revenues and a means of influencing or controlling the governments of Central Asia.[99]

Putin said, "Iran has the right to arm and defend itself," in reversing the policy

Yeltsin had adopted of limiting announced arms sales to Iran in deference to U.S. concerns about the impact on peace in the Middle East.[100] The public testimony of the Director of Central Intelligence in February 2001 identified Russia as selling ballistic missile technology to Iran in recent years. In 1999, the U.S. had placed economic sanctions on seven Russian companies and three institutes that were judged to be providing Iran with help in the development of nuclear weapons.[101]

Since 1979, Iran has been a militant Islamic state and has protested the brutality of Russian forces against Muslims in Chechnya, calling those Russian actions "unacceptable." Since Putin and his closest advisers consider the greatest threat to Russia to come from Islamic extremists, it seems self-defeating and dangerous to be providing weapons and technology for nuclear weapons and ballistic missiles to Iran. This would also apply to China, which is persecuting the Muslim Uygur people in its Western region that borders Central Asia. After the Russia-Iran agreement was announced, a liberal newspaper in Russia expressed concern that "the patron of international terrorism [Iran] has been promised increased sales of arms and broader cooperation in the nuclear energy field;" and *Izvestia,* a major Russian paper, said Putin should not be surprised if in a few years "a group of Islamic terrorists or separatists armed with military hardware which Moscow had just sent to Tehran" arrive in Russia or at its borders.[102] In the opinion of some well-informed Russian analysts, Putin shared the concern that Russian help for Iran on nuclear power could lead to assistance for Iran's nuclear weapons program. For that reason, he removed the minister of atomic energy, Yevgeny Adamov, who was viewed as "excessively active in reaching nuclear deals with Iran."[103]

Putin's activities with these regimes closely parallel those of China. Both Russia and China have increased their level of political and military support to a number of regimes hostile to the United States, while moving to cooperate more closely on a number of shared strategic objectives. Putin has also deepened the China-Russia strategic alignment, as will be discussed subsequently at greater length.

In addition, one must consider what President Putin said at a press conference while visiting President Bush at Camp David in September 2003. In response to a question about the nature of U.S.-Russian relations, President Putin said,

> I have never said this in public, I'm going to do it today. When counterterrorist operation began in Afghanistan, we were approached by people, through several channels, we were approached by people who intended to fight against Americans in Afghanistan. And if by that time President Bush and I had not formed appropriate relationship, as we have, so no one knows what turn would the developments in Afghanistan had taken. You know what was Russia's position, and it helped, to a great extent, to achieve further results that we have achieved in Afghanistan, and was for a very good purpose.[104]

President Putin has never answered publicly who those people that approached him were or what groups or countries they represented.

U.S. RUSSIAN RELATIONS IN PERSPECTIVE

The Russian Perspective

For the Yeltsin and Putin "party of power" regime in Russia, the positive aspects of the relationship include the fact that the U.S. government and the major democracies consistently provided political, symbolic, and immense financial support for his stated objectives of moving toward political democracy and market-oriented reforms. This support was continuing and especially visible at key times of crisis for Yeltsin, including in 1993 when he dissolved the Russian parliament, in 1996 when he faced an uphill struggle for reelection as president, and in 1998 as Russia faced a severe economic crisis. Support continues also for Putin in the ongoing economic assistance.

Another very important positive aspect of the relationship was U.S. political and financial assistance in persuading Ukraine, Kazakhstan, and Belarus to give their strategic nuclear weapons to Russia and declare themselves to be nonnuclear powers. This removed an enormous domain of potential threat to Russia. Another positive aspect of the relationship was the strong affirmation by the U.S. and the major democracies of the quest for partnership with Russia and of its global importance through the welcome Russia received to the G7 summit meetings and its full membership in that group, along with the immediate inclusion of Russia in all the major international financial organizations. The frequent summit meetings held with President Yeltsin and then Putin by the leaders of the U.S., Germany, France, and the United Kingdom demonstrated this resolve.

At the same time, Yeltsin and the Russian leadership benefited from the tacit acceptance by the Clinton administration of many Russian unilateral actions, including: Russia's influence over the post-Soviet republics' foreign policy activities; Russia's strategic nuclear modernization activities, which cost billions in resources while Russia continued to receive significant financing from the West; Russia's proliferation of weapons of mass destruction to Iran, Iraq, and other potentially hostile powers; and Russia's use of force to end separatism in Chechnya in 1994–1996 and since 1999. Whatever the occasionally disapproving words of the Clinton administration on these issues, it never actually linked any significant reductions in U.S. economic or other benefits to Russia ending those activities.

From the point of view of the Yeltsin and Putin party of power, the negative aspects of U.S. foreign policy would include the unilateral use of force by the U.S. against Milosevic in the fall of 1995, against Iraq in December 1998, the U.S.-led

NATO air campaign against Serbia in the spring of 1999, and the U.S.-British removal of the Saddam Hussein regime in 2003. Those actions were taken without authorization by the UN Security Council and, therefore, from Russia's point of view, were both illegitimate and prevented Russia from having a veto over the use of force, even though Russia had agreed to the various UN Security Council resolutions that laid the substantive basis for the actions taken.

A second negative aspect would undoubtedly be the repeated requests from the U.S. that Russia cease its proliferation of weapons of mass destruction, as Russia had promised to do on numerous occasions at summit meetings and through its participation in the nonproliferation treaty and the missile technology control regimes. Even if ineffectual, those pressures, demands, requests, and revelations of Russian action through the U.S. media would be viewed as negative.

The Communists in Russia would add to these negative aspects of U.S. foreign policy that the U.S. and its allies had acted purposefully to force "the wrong economic model on Russia," using the IMF and World Bank grants and loans to undermine Russian sovereignty and rob Russia of its resources. From their point of view, the purpose was to weaken Russia and, as the Communists repeated since 1992, make it no more than a source of raw materials for capitalist countries. The allegations are untrue but believed by many in Russia after years of deprivations and economic problems.

The U.S. Perspective

From the U.S. perspective, there were a number of positive consequences of Russian foreign policy in the Yeltsin era. First was the end of the open and covert Soviet-era support for anti-Western insurgencies and terrorist organizations on a worldwide scale. This had already decreased after 1989, with Gorbachev's "new thinking," but it was in the Yeltsin era that there was a marked and noticeable end to these activities. This included, from 1992 to 1994, a sharp reduction in Russian support for state sponsors of terrorism such as Iran, Saddam Hussein's Iraq, Libya, Cuba, and North Korea, though this was reversed as the Primakov view became more dominant.

Another positive aspect was the compromise on NATO enlargement. An agreement by the Yeltsin government to participate in the NATO-Russia Joint Council provided a forum for a dialogue that could be constructive in the future, even though it failed to prevent the serious differences on the Kosovo issue in the spring of 1999. It could also be said that the twelve U.S.-Russia summit meetings from 1992 to 1999 established a process of dialogue that offered the opportunity for both nuclear superpowers to discuss major differences.

A third positive aspect was the agreement in January 1993 on the START II treaty for mutual reductions in strategic nuclear weapons. It was an expression of the Yeltsin administration's intentions, even if the Russian parliament refused to ratify it. It could also be counted as positive that Russia significantly reduced its military budget for conventional military capabilities, while also permitting its strategic forces to decline from roughly 9,000 warheads in 1992 to about 6,200 by the year 2000. The U.S. also significantly reduced its military forces by more than 45 percent and removed all of its deployed nuclear weapons from Europe. Both Russia and the U.S. indicated their mutual peaceful intentions through symbolic actions, such as the 1994 detargeting agreement (which, however, either side could reverse in a matter of minutes).

Much of the reduction in Russian strategic nuclear forces was the result of attrition and reduced budgets caused by Russia's economic difficulties. Those changes in Russian conventional and strategic nuclear military strength also led to one of the most important negative aspects from the point of view of the United States. This was the change in 1993 to a Russian doctrine of the first use of strategic and tactical nuclear weapons in order to make up for its perceived conventional military deficiencies. In the July 1999 Russian strategic military exercise against a hypothetical NATO attack, this new doctrine was employed. The Russian minister of defense explained:

> The exercise tested one of the provisions of Russia's military doctrines concerning the possible use of nuclear weapons when all other measures are exhausted. . . . We did pursue such an option. All measures were exhausted. Our defenses proved to be ineffective. An enemy continued to push into Russia and that is when the decision to use nuclear weapons was made.[105]

This strategic military exercise in June 1999 occurred in the context of Yeltsin's 1998 decision to continue significant economic investments in modernizing Russian strategic nuclear weapons. According to Andrei Kokoshin, secretary of the Security Council, Russia would continue to maintain strong nuclear forces, including land-, sea-, and aircraft-based systems until 2010 and beyond.[106] While the U.S. is not developing any new ICBMs, the Russian modernization includes the development of new types of ICBMs and the development of a new ballistic-missile submarine, on which construction began in 1996. The newest Russian ICBM, the Topol-M, which is road mobile, was described by the commander of the Russian strategic rocket forces, General Vladimir Yakovlev, as "second to none and by some parameters exceed[ing] all existing weapons of this kind."[107] He indicated that it was Russia's intention to deploy ten silo-based and mobile Topol-M systems (announced as having one warhead each) annually until 2001 and then thirty-one systems annually from that point on. He estimated the cost of deploying these 450 new strategic missiles by 2005 as $42 billion.[108]

This strategic nuclear modernization was matched by Russia continuing the

Soviet-era program of building large underground bunker complexes, described as necessary to assure continuity and protection of the leadership in the event of nuclear war. Based on a variety of contemporary U.S. government reports, Bill Gertz summarized the enormous scope of the secret underground rail lines to leadership quarters in the Moscow region, as well as two additional complexes. One, called Kosvinsky Mountain, is a "nuclear survivable strategic command post." The other is called Yamantau Mountain.[109] According to a U.S. government report, "the command post at Kosvinsky appears to provide the Russians with the means to retaliate against a nuclear attack; the rationale for the Yamantau complex is unclear."[110]

The Yamantau Mountain underground complex is described as being as large as the area inside the Washington DC beltway, costing billions of dollars, being built by thirty thousand workers living in two closed cities.[111] Gertz informs us that after an article about the mysterious Yamantau complex appeared in the U.S. press, the "Strategic Rocket Forces issued a statement suggesting nuclear missiles may be secretly deployed at the site as part of . . . a nuclear command program designed to fire nuclear missiles automatically in the aftermath of a first strike on Russia."[112] Former CIA analyst Peter Prye concludes that these extensive facilities are "a manifestation of Russia's continued war fighting attitudes. They believe in the idea that you can survive and prevail in a nuclear conflict. These kinds of facilities are designed to survive for weeks and months."[113] Gertz notes that in distinction to this Russian activity, virtually all U.S. facilities for leadership protection against nuclear attack had been closed, including facilities in West Virginia and Virginia.[114]

The serious issue posed by Russia's strategic nuclear modernization and evident preparations for wartime leadership survival and command are accompanied by a great deal of information that suggests the command and control system for Russian nuclear weapons is unreliable. This was first reported publicly by then Russian Minister of Defense Igor Rodinov, who in 1997 warned President Yeltsin in a letter and then publicly stated that "the components of Russian command centers have already been asked to operate twice or thrice, as long as their useful life. Today no one is able to guarantee the reliability of our command and control systems. . . . Russia may soon approach a threshold beyond which rockets and nuclear systems become unmanageable."[115] A Russian former career officer in the Strategic Rocket Forces who had helped test the system in the 1970s supported this by writing that even during the 1980s, "the equipment ceased functioning properly . . . certain parts of it spontaneously went into combat mode."[116] This significant risk is increased further when considered with a U.S. government report that concluded, "An array of evidence indicates that political authorities could not prevent the General Staff from launching nuclear weapons on its own initiative."[117] That 1996 report referred to a total of almost 22,000 nuclear warheads that were potentially beyond the control of Russian political authorities, including, at that time, 7,500 deployed strategic warheads, 4,400 battlefield nuclear warheads, and 10,000 in storage.[118]

Taken together, all of these aspects pertaining to Russian strategic nuclear weapons—the "first use" doctrine, the strategic modernization, difficulties with and uncertainties both technical and political about the command and control system, together with the continuing preparations of large-scale leadership protection facilities—suggest that, looking into the future, the risks from Russian nuclear weapons remain extremely serious.

A second major negative aspect in U.S.-Russian relations from the U.S. perspective is the movement by Russia from an emphasis on international cooperation with the major democracies to the geopolitical view of "multipolarism" vs. "unipolarism" as the basis for establishing an international coalition to counter the alleged attempt by the U.S. to exert global dominance. This led directly to Russia's resumption of supportive relations with China and with a number of currently anti-Western states formerly allied with the Soviet Union, including Iran, Iraq, Libya, North Korea, and Cuba. It also justified and rationalized the sales of Russian components and technology for weapons of mass destruction and missile and aircraft delivery systems to a number of these countries and to China.

Third, Russia has continued the Soviet practice of violating major arms-control agreements. In the Russian case, this has included agreements on the elimination of chemical and biological weapons, the 1989 agreement on Conventional Forces in Europe, and aspects of the nonproliferation treaty and the missile technology control regime. A fourth negative aspect is the lack of acknowledgement by the Russian government of the more than $120 billion in grants and credits provided by the industrial democracies and the major Western-funded international financial institutions. This has been matched by a failure of the Russian government to cooperate effectively to provide for transparency in the use of those funds and to work with Western governments to prevent the corrupt diversion of assistance monies.

The fifth and most serious negative aspect is the expanding Russian strategic alliance with China. What began as a movement toward the normalization of relations with Communist China has become an axis between Russia and China with ever more strategic aspects ostensibly directed against "unipolarism," but, in fact, directed against the U.S. and in explicit support of many Chinese foreign policy purposes. The new China-Russia geopolitical relationship, in fact, poses risks to international security and U.S. foreign-policy interests in the future. For that reason, we now turn to the contemporary political evolution and strategic objectives of Communist China.

III. CHINA & RUSSIA

15 China's International Actions

"The mind of the enemies and his leaders is a target of far more importance than the bodies of his troops."
> —Mao Zedong, during the civil war for control of China

"Intimidate with force, seduce with money."
> —President Jiang Zemin, 1998

"Chinese authorities have also claimed authority over the South China Sea. The resulting uncertainty over Chinese intentions of using force . . . creates concern throughout the entire Asia Pacific region."
> —Admiral Dennis C. Blair,
> commander of U.S. forces in the Pacific, March 2000

Building military bases on foreign territory, or on territory that is disputed under international law is a clear act of aggression."
> —James Webb, former secretary of the navy, 1999

In 1998, China issued its first White Paper on National Defense that declared, "Hegemonism and power politics [by the U.S.] remain the main threats to world peace and stability." It went on to state that the U.S.-Japan security treaty was an infringement upon and interference in China's "internal affairs."[1] This official document also said that all U.S. security alliances in the Asian region had to end because they threatened China.

This White Paper publicly expressed the views that the Chinese Communist elite had reached in 1990 and that have since formed the basis for China's strategic activities. China's view of its right to dominate Asia, including Japan, is evident in its calling a mutually agreed upon defensive security treaty between two sovereign states an infringement on China's "internal affairs." This neoimperial definition of what constitutes interference in China's internal affairs is something that may be seen more frequently in the coming years.

During the August 1998 vacation and policy sessions at the Chinese resort of

Beidaihe, the Politburo decided on a strategy toward Taiwan that President Jiang summarized as having two parts: "intimidate with force" and "seduce with money."[2] In November 1998, the intimidation component was demonstrated by the Chinese military conducting war exercises with simulated missile firings against not only Taiwan, but also against U.S. forces and bases in Japan and Okinawa.[3] One senior Clinton administration official was quoted as saying that Chinese missiles "had never been pointed our way before"—presumably, he meant in military exercises. This was part of the pattern of Chinese preparations for military threats and possible war with the U.S. and its allies if they opposed China's purposes. China also has territorial claims and disputes in the South China Sea—with Japan and India, among others.

In the 1998 National Defense White Paper, China explicitly declared its opposition to the bilateral security alliances that the United States has with Asian states, calling them "factors of instability both globally and regionally."[4] In reply, the senior official in the Department of State responsible for East Asian and Pacific Affairs testified to the U.S. Congress that the U.S. Security Alliances "with Australia, Japan, the Philippines, the Republic of Korea, and Thailand remain the bedrock of our regional security policy."[5] Then two years later, China's 2000 National Defense White Paper clearly warned the United States that it will seek to remove the U.S. military presence from Asia and end all American security alliances in the region. The Chinese White Paper said the fact that "the United States is further strengthening its military presence and bilateral military alliance in the region" is a "new negative development . . . China's fundamental interests lie in . . . the establishment and maintenance of a new regional security order."[6]

INTERNATIONAL AGGRESSION/COERCION IN TERRITORIAL DISPUTES

The South China Sea
The Communist Party's Central Military Commission stated in its August 1999 war plan given to the U.S. that Taiwan was China's "last territorial demand." That is not true. China has claimed that all of the South China Sea, an international ocean of 450,000 square miles, is its sovereign territory, and it also claims that all of the islands surrounding this sea are its sovereign territory.[7]

There are two main island groups in the South China Sea. The Paracel Islands are in the northern part, about two hundred miles from the coast of Vietnam, and they are claimed by Vietnam as well as by China. The Spratly Islands are spread throughout the southern part of the South China Sea and include about one hundred small islets, sand bars, reefs, and rocks, comprising a total area of less than 3 square miles in a vast ocean.[8] While China claims all the Spratly Islands, they are also claimed by Vietnam, which currently occupies twenty-seven of the one hundred; the Philippines, which occupies eight; Malaysia, which occupies three; Taiwan occupies one; and China currently occupies seven.[9] To date, there has been no definitive international arbitration of these competing claims.

In February 1992, the rubber-stamp National People's Congress of China adopted a law claiming Chinese sovereignty over all the Spratly Islands and authorizing its navy to use force in "evicting trespassers."[10] This alarmed the other claimant countries. Acting through the Association of Southeast Asian Nations (ASEAN), they proposed multilateral negotiations on this issue, but China has shown no willingness to enter into any serious negotiation or discussion of its claims of jurisdiction over all of the islands.

China has a history of using force to assert its claims of either sovereignty or influence. In 1974, Chinese military forces evicted South Vietnam from some of the Paracel Islands. In early 1979, China decided to punish Communist Vietnam for its alliance with the Soviet Union by invading its northern region for some weeks. In 1988, China again attacked Communist Vietnamese forces and drove them from Fiery Cross Reef in the Spratly Islands. In that military action, China sank three Vietnamese ships with an estimated seventy Vietnamese killed or missing.[11]

In February 1995, the Philippines revealed that one of the Spratly Islands, Mischief Reef, which was 150 miles from the island of Pelawan and nearly 1,000 miles from Mainland China, had been occupied by China. In May 1995, the Clinton administration privately told the Philippines not to invoke the mutual defense treaty. Instead, the U.S. urged diplomacy and officially stated that it has

> an abiding interest in the maintenance of peace and stability in the South China Sea. The United States calls upon claimants to intensify efforts to address issues related to competing claims, taking into account the interest of all parties and which contribute to peace and prosperity in the region. The United States is willing to assist in any way the claimants deem helpful. The United States reaffirms its welcome of the 1992 ASEAN declaration on the South China Sea.[12]

This formal pronouncement by the Department of State was ignored by China. In turn, the United States mostly ignored China's further aggressive actions. Yet, the May 1995 U.S. statement provides a preview of possible conflict with China in addition to that which might occur over the issue of Taiwan. The United States totally rejected the Chinese claim of sovereignty over the South China Sea by stating further:

> Maintaining freedom of navigation is a fundamental interest of the United States. Unhindered navigation by all ships and aircraft in the South China Sea is essential for the peace and prosperity of the entire Asia-Pacific region, including

the United States. . . . The United States would . . . view with serious concern any maritime claim or restriction on activity in the South China Sea that was not consistent with international law.[13]

In November 1996, it was reported that China was dredging the entrance to Mischief Reef so that it could accommodate larger Chinese ships.[14] Initially China said that it had put "fisherman's huts" on Mischief Reef in order to provide tempo-rary shelter for its fisherman who might need it. As Winncek points out, this action is in keeping with China's three-phase process of building on the reefs it occupies. First, there are "sheds" made of bamboo; second, there are "octagonal pavilions" built of iron sheeting; and third, there is permanent construction in the form of "three-story white buildings and concrete platforms which China refers to as 'fortresses in the sea.' "[15]

When China first occupied Mischief Reef, there were subsequent negotiations with the Philippines. Both agreed that neither would place any new construction on any of the Spratly Islands they respectively claimed.[16] However, in October–November 1998, China moved to the "fortress in the sea" phase on Mischief Reef, with significant new construction. Congressman Dana Rohrabacher and Al Santoli flew over Mischief Reef in 1998 and photographed this. They saw three Chinese naval vessels anchored near the "fortress in the sea" structures.[17]

One of the Paracel Islands, Woody Island, is almost two square kilometers in size. By January 1999, the U.S. government confirmed that China had built a runway about 7,300 feet long that could accommodate all of China's fighters, bombers, refueling aircraft, and command and control planes—including their most advanced jet fighters, the Su-27, which China had received from Russia.[18] In 1996, a U.S. Defense Department report said that China had converted twenty of its B-6 bombers into long-range refueling tankers and also equipped about twenty-four jet fighters with aerial refueling pods for extended-range missions, concluding that "steady progress in air refueling will give China a power projection ability over the South China sea by the turn of the century."[19] U.S. military intelligence officials were quoted as saying that the building of military facilities on Woody Island and claims on the Spratly Islands were "part of China's 'outward expansion' to move forward on its 'island chain strategy' in which China would control all the territory in an arc stretching from Japan to Indonesia."[20]

Woody Island not only has a Chinese long-range air strip, but also port facilities, docks, power plants, fuel oil tanks, ammunition storage bunkers, and gun emplace-ments.[21] By early 1999, the upgrading of Chinese structures on the Philippine-claimed Mischief Reef had led to a "helopad, radar, gun emplacements, and a four story structure."[22]

An expert on the Chinese military, Richard Fisher summed up China's strategic purposes: "As we look into the next decade, airborne warning and control jets could operate out of Woody island, directing both offensive and defensive operations aimed at controlling access to the South China Sea."[23]

Former Secretary of the Navy James Webb, in examining China's new military installations in the South China Sea, put it clearly: "Building military bases on foreign territory, or on territory that is disputed under international law, is a clear act of aggression. That these islands were uninhabited until the appearance of the Chinese military does not lessen the importance of this historic principle."[24] The Philippines was alarmed by these Chinese actions and in early 1999 proposed an international forum under U.S. auspices to discuss all of these disputes. The response from the Chinese foreign ministry was unyielding: "China's sovereignty over the Nansha [Spratly] Islands is indisputable. External interference in this matter is unacceptable."[25]

Testifying to the U.S. Congress in March 2000, the commander in chief of U.S. Forces in the Pacific, Admiral Dennis C. Blair, said that in addition to their Taiwan claims, "Chinese authorities have also claimed sovereignty over the South China Sea. The resulting uncertainty over Chinese intentions in using force to resolve territorial claims creates concerns throughout the Asia Pacific region."[26]

The effect of continuing acquiescence in these Chinese claims and actions could be to cede China de facto control over the islands in the South China Sea. China could then use the full sovereign rights under international law over waters extending to twelve miles from land boundaries and the economic exclusion zone of two hundred miles from the land border recognized under the 1982 United Nations Law of the Sea to essentially establish large domains of sovereign control that would, in effect, give it operational or economic control over much of the South China Sea.

China has acted and spoken in a tone of belligerent entitlement in pressing its claims in the South China Sea and to the Paracel and Spratly Islands. China has used force and has made clear that it is willing to use more force in the future if other claimant countries fail to acquiesce in China's purposes. Control of the South China Sea would both symbolize and facilitate China's dominance of Asia, since U.S. ships and aircraft, as well as those of Japan, South Korea, and other countries, would have to have Chinese permission to transit the South China Sea, a major supply route. It is estimated that 50 percent of world commerce and more than 41,000 ships annually transit the South China Sea (in comparison with about 4,000 ships transiting through the Panama Canal each year). If China controlled the South China Sea, it could decide which country's ships could transit and which could not, and thereby have a means to exert political influence on countries in the region that depend on supplies moving through the South China Sea for their energy and commercial deliveries. Oil and other supplies could sail around the South China Sea, but this would increase costs markedly.

China has an enormous need for energy resources, and some estimate that there could be significant oil beneath the waters of the South China Sea. By claiming all of the Spratly and Paracel Islands, China would have an exclusive claim on the seas within twelve miles of each, and the UN Convention on the International Law of the Sea would support its claims to exclusive economic rights within two hundred miles of those islands. By asserting and ultimately obtaining sovereign control of all the Spratly and Paracel islands, China would, in effect, gain control of any energy supplies that might be found under the South China Sea.

A new geopolitical doctrine of the "first island chain of defense" was advanced as a strategic concept by General Liu Huaqing, a close associate of Deng Xiaoping, vice chairman of the Central Military Commission and member of the Politburo elite until his retirement in 1997. The first island chain of defense doctrine holds that to be secure China needs to control the entire region off its shores in a line from Japan to Taiwan and the Philippines.[27]

The Chinese Communist leadership knows that should China attempt to enforce its claim to sovereignty over the South China Sea by regulating or limiting, for example, U.S. Naval transit, or by seeking to limit the flow of 75 percent of Japan's oil through the South China Sea in order to extract political concessions from Japan, this could lead to conflict with the United States. Perhaps that is why, in December 1999, the Chinese minister of defense said that "war is inevitable" with the United States. He may have had an understanding of where China's policy is moving in the future.

China's Territorial Disputes with Japan, India

China and Japan have a difficult history because of past Japanese aggression against China. In 1895, Imperial Japan defeated Imperial China in war and the Qing dynasty ceded to Japan the island of Taiwan and its surrounding islands. In 1931, militarist Japan invaded first Manchuria and then China in 1937, remaining as occupier through 1945. Japanese military forces committed terrible atrocities against the people of China, and the current regime in China remains deeply suspicious of Japan despite its more than half-century of democracy and peaceful international relations.

Democratic Japan has tried to develop a cooperative relationship with China.[28] It recognized the Communist government immediately after the United States normalized relations in 1972. Japan has been the largest single source of economic assistance to China, providing a combination of grant aid and low-interest loans for a variety of Chinese development projects that are estimated to have totaled approximately $23 billion from 1979 to 1996.[29]

As in its relations with the United States, China has had two purposes with Japan. First, to obtain "the capital and technology required to modernize China's economy and defense capabilities;"[30] and second, to persuade Japan not to oppose

China internationally. Until the 1990s, China seemed to agree with President Nixon that the U.S.-Japan security relationship had a stabilizing effect in Asia and was in the interest of China as well as in the interest of the United States because it provided assurance that Japan would not develop its own nuclear or advanced military capabilities and that Japan would be peaceful and cooperative.

The Chinese view of this relationship changed following its redefinition of the U.S. as its "main enemy" in 1990. Then, after the United States and Japan decided to explore the feasibility of regional missile defenses, China said these would be "clearly aimed at China" and therefore would be part of a "China containment policy."[31] Following the March 1996 Taiwan missile crisis, the United States and Japan held a summit and agreed to increase their cooperation for mutual security. The Chinese media contended that this was a "dangerous signal" and that now Japan and the United States would try to "work hand in hand to dominate the Asia Pacific region."[32] Japan, for its part, felt threatened by China's extensive program of nuclear weapons testing from 1992 to 1996 and by its expanding strategic and tactical nuclear military buildup. Chinese military threats in 1996 and in 1999–2001 against Taiwan and against U.S. forces and bases in Asia should there be any effort to help Taiwan affected Japan directly, because at least ten major U.S. air and naval bases are located on Japanese territory. Therefore, Japan recognized that China's threats of attack against U.S. forces involved a threat of attack by China's missiles with either nuclear or high-explosive warheads on Japanese territory. Japan is also very concerned about and feels threatened by China's actions to establish control over the entire South China Sea.

China has two ongoing territorial disputes with Japan. The first dispute involves small islands and reefs called the Senkaku Islands by Japan and the Diaoyutai Islands by China. These cover an area of about three square miles and are located about 120 nautical miles northeast of Taiwan, 200 nautical miles east of China's mainland, and about 200 nautical miles west of Japan's province of Okinawa. These islands passed to Japanese control as a result of the 1895 Treaty of Shimonoseki, by which China ceded Taiwan and the surrounding islands, including the Senkakus, to Japan. As with other nineteenth-century treaties signed by a defeated Qing dynasty, Communist China declares that the 1895 treaty was not valid and, therefore, Japan has "stolen" those islands from China.

After World War II, Japan and the United States signed a peace treaty in 1951 whereby Japan ended its claim to Taiwan and many other islands but kept control of the Senkaku and others, all of which were under U.S. occupation at the time. The Communist Chinese government lodged a protest against the U.S.-Japanese peace treaty and, to the present, China continues to call it "illegal," because China was not party to it. In 1951, China protested against Japan's retention of the Senkaku Islands; since 1958, China has demanded the return of those islands from Japan.

As the United States returned Okinawa to Japanese control in 1971, it also returned the Senkaku Islands. According to the Chinese government, Japan has improperly included these islands in the air defense perimeter of its Self Defense Forces.[33] On December 30, 1971, China declared that the Senkaku/Diaoyutai islands are "attached" to Taiwan and, like Taiwan, "have always been an inalienable part of Chinese territory since ancient times." After normalization of relations in 1972, both China and Japan agreed to "shelve" the issue for future discussions. But in the year 2000, China said "the Japanese side has broken its promises repeatedly and has provoked incidents one after another in recent years in an attempt to seize the islands."[34]

A second and related dispute concerns the rights China and Japan have over the potentially oil-rich continental shelf beneath the East China Sea. Under the United Nations Convention on the Law of the Sea, China has economic rights under the East China Sea as an extension of its continental shelf, and Japan has rights to the same area as an extension of the continental shelf from Okinawa.[35] Japan has indicated to China that it would like to negotiate for the sharing of rights to oil drilling under the East China Sea, but China has not been willing to do this.

As in other disputes, China is following its pattern of first making economic incursions in the disputed territory and then adding a military presence. In 1995, China began sending oil-drilling ships in the neighborhood of the Senkaku/Diaoyutai Islands. Before an August 2000 Japanese-China summit meeting, Japanese sources revealed an increasing pattern of Chinese penetration of waters within the Japanese economic exclusion zone. This began in 1999, when Chinese "research ships" were inside Japan's two-hundred-mile economic exclusion zone on thirty occasions without required permission. Through August 2000, this occurred seventeen additional times. The Japanese speculated that the Chinese ships were mapping the sea bottom, which has military value as well as potential oil-drilling operations.[36] In addition to those incursions, in May 2000 Japan observed Chinese naval vessels, not research ships, surrounding Japan's main island just outside Japan's twelve-mile territorial limit. According to the Japanese Foreign Ministry, they were "apparently gathering intelligence."[37] This occurred again in July 2000. The intelligence could well be the exact locations of U.S. and Japanese air and naval facilities in Japan—measured with the precision needed to aim ballistic missiles.

Japan sent a formal protest to China about these disturbing naval activities. In the days before the August 2000 China-Japan summit meeting, the Japanese governing party said it would not provide another $161 million in planned loans to China because of these intrusive naval actions. The Chinese response was to criticize Japan for hesitating to allocate the funds, calling the linkage of the two matters "irrelevant."[38] Some members of the Japanese legislature, concerned about China's military buildup, also called for China to publish its full military budget and the facts about its military forces as a prerequisite for obtaining any further low-interest loans from Japan.[39] Japanese political leaders also called for the use of Japanese naval forces to protect its territorial waters.[40]

At the summit meeting, Foreign Minister Kono of Japan raised these issues and said that in Japan "feelings of distrust" toward China are rising.[41] The meeting ended with an agreement that both Japan and China would notify each other of the movement of ships into disputed zones and that they would begin negotiations about disputes on maritime borders. Japan called this a "step forward." It reflected the Chinese view that, for the moment, any large-scale rift with Japan should be avoided. Nevertheless, the pattern of Chinese actions toward Japan in these disputed areas shows the willingness of China to attempt to dominate and impose its view of its territorial claims on even such an economically important, potentially powerful country as Japan.

In the 1950s, China made a series of territorial claims on India in the region of the two countries' borders. China proclaimed, then and since, that it believes in the Five Principles of Peaceful Coexistence—one of which is that all territorial disputes must be settled peacefully. In 1962, without warning, China attacked India and seized many thousands of square miles of territory, which it continues to hold. Currently, India states that China occupies sixteen thousand square miles of Indian territory in Kashmir and that it claims additional Indian territory in the eastern state of Arunachal-Pradesh.

In 1998, Minister of Defense George Fernandes gave a very candid assessment of India's view of China. He said that China is the biggest threat to India, even greater than Pakistan, revealing that Beijing had deployed nuclear-capable missiles in Tibet and that "China has its nuclear weapons stockpiled in Tibet, right along India's borders."[42] Fernandes said further that China had expanded its military airfields in Tibet, that China was heavily involved in constructing harbors on Burmese islands where Chinese naval ships could be based, and that "[China's] senior officials have stated that the Indian Ocean is not India's Ocean. There is no doubt in my mind that China's quickly expanding navy, which will be the biggest in this part of the world, will be getting into the Indian Ocean fairly soon." Fernandes also pointed to the fact that China was involved in training the Burmese Army and had established "a massive electronic surveillance" organization on Burma's Coco Islands very near India. The Indian defense minister said that though "these are Burmese territory, China has taken them over. Although there is a massive electronic surveillance establishment, . . . there are moves to convert that into a major naval base which would be a direct threat to us."[43]

Because of the continuing sense of threat from China—heightened by Chinese deployment of aircraft, nuclear weapons, missiles targeting India and Chinese naval activities in neighboring Burma—Fernandes said in 1998 that India had "come to a point where we believe we need to make a review" of defense policy in order to decide whether to build nuclear weapons.[44] The combination of China's past and recent actions toward India and China's providing Pakistan with nuclear and missile technology created a sense of threat within the leadership of India, which was a major reason for India's developing nuclear weapons.

PROLIFERATION OF WEAPONS OF MASS DESTRUCTION

For decades, there has been a shared consensus among the democracies that the spread of nuclear weapons to more countries, especially dictatorships, could sharply increase the risk of nuclear war. In 1980, Iraq invaded Iran and began an eight-year conflict that caused millions of dead and wounded on both sides. In that war, both sides attacked with short-range ballistic missiles and sought to develop nuclear, chemical, and biological weapons for use against the other.

China sold weapons to both Iran and Iraq during and after the war. These military sales by China provided hard-currency earnings for the Chinese military-industrial complex and a means of developing close relations with two oil-rich dictatorships that could meet China's oil needs in the present and future. Both Iran and Iraq wanted to develop ever more destructive weapons to use to deter each other or to use against each other if another war should occur. They were also both hostile to the United States and its allies in the region, especially Israel.

In 1990, Iraq invaded Kuwait. The United States led a broad coalition in 1990–91 to enforce UN Security Council resolutions requiring Iraq to withdraw from Kuwait. This meant that the United States and several of its NATO allies faced the possibility of dealing with an opponent that might use chemical or biological weapons, as well as ballistic missiles.

In 1997, the Office of Naval Intelligence stated: "Discoveries after the Gulf War clearly indicate that Iraq maintained an aggressive WMD [weapons of mass destruction] procurement program. A similar program exists today in Iran, with a steady flow of materials and technologies from China to Iran. This exchange is one of the most active WMD programs in the third world."[45] In succeeding years, public congressional testimony of the director of Central Intelligence and the director of the Defense Intelligence Agency indicated that China and Russia continued to actively provide weapons-of-mass-destruction technology, expertise, and components to a number of hostile and potentially dangerous countries; including Iran, Iraq, and North Korea.[46]

Although Saddam Hussein's regime in Iraq did fire a number of ballistic missiles in 1991, it was deterred by threats of massive retaliation from using chemical or biological warheads. But the fact that four hundred thousand U.S. and allied troops had faced that threat for many months added impetus to the expressed policy of the first Bush administration, that preventing the spread of these weapons of mass destruction and the means to deliver them was one of the highest priority concerns of U.S. foreign policy. As a candidate for the presidency, Clinton gave this special emphasis.

As China shifted in 1990 to the view that the United States was its "main enemy," it viewed the sale of components for weapons of mass destruction and the sale of technical assistance in building these to Iran, Iraq, North Korea, Syria, Libya, and other states hostile to the United States, as not only financially profitable but also a way to strengthen the enemies of its "main enemy." During the 1990s, a great deal of government information became public in the United States; first about Chinese, then later Chinese and Russian activities in transferring weapons of mass destruction to the main state sponsors of terrorism.[47]

Yet, year after year the Clinton administration seemed to ignore and overlook these facts. Therefore, the Republican majority in Congress added to the intelligence authorization act of Fiscal Year 1997 the requirement that the director of Central Intelligence submit a report twice each year on "the acquisition of technology relating to weapons of mass destruction" received by specific countries viewed as hostile or as states supporting terrorism. These reports were also to describe the activities of key countries supplying these weapons and were to be submitted to Congress in both a classified and unclassified form, the former presumably more complete and detailed. As a result of these unclassified reports, and of the report by the House Select Committee on U.S. National Security and Military/Commercial concerns with the People's Republic of China, a great deal of information has become available about China's proliferation activities, which continue to the present.[48]

We learn from the public CIA proliferation reports that China, together with Russia, has been the leading source of nuclear, chemical, and missile technologies for North Korea, Libya, and Iran, and that China increased its supply of missiles and equipment to Pakistan.[49] China provided significant components for its ballistic missile program to North Korea, which the CIA informs us "produces and is capable of using a wide variety of chemical and possibly biological agents, as well as their delivery means."[50] This activity by the North Koreans is in addition to the known and potential assistance both of these nations provided to the Khan network.

The pattern of relations between China and North Korea suggests that China is using North Korea as a partner in the sale and distribution of missiles and missile components as one way of coping with, evading, and avoiding U.S. concerns and possible sanctions. It is also important to note that North Korean sales of its No-Dong medium-range ballistic missiles have been, in the view of the director of Central Intelligence, responsible for "the complete altering of strategic balances in the Middle East and Asia."[51] Those ballistic missiles, of course, could also be used against the armed forces of the United States in the Middle East and Asia.

During the 1990s and since, China has provided Iran with ballistic missile components as well as air-, land-, and ship-based cruise missiles. By 2001, the director of the CIA testified that these, along with Iran's submarines, mines, and missile patrol boats, can attack ships including U.S. naval forces in the Middle East "and stem the flow of oil from the [Persian Gulf] for brief periods."[52] China also sent Iran key ingredients for the development of nuclear weapons, ingredients for poison gas production, rocket propellants, and a "research" nuclear reactor. The CIA noted that in 1999 Iran "continued to seek production technology, training, expertise, and chemicals that could be used as precursor agents in its chemical warfare program from entities in Russia and China."[53]

In early 2001, the newly inaugurated Bush administration publicly accused Chinese organizations of breaking UN Security Council prohibitions by providing advanced fiber optics support for the military command and control systems of Iraq.[54] During the 1990s, China reportedly provided ingredients that Iraq used for nerve gases, missiles, and nuclear weapons; and China also sold Iraq chemicals that are used to produce missile fuel.[55] There has been no United Nations inspection of Iraq since the autumn of 1998, when Saddam Hussein refused to cooperate any longer with the inspection system set up under the terms of the UN Security Council Resolutions. As permanent members of the Security Council, China and Russia colluded to undo the inspection regime and to delay its resumption until November 2002.

From 1990 to 1997, China provided extensive support for Pakistan's development of nuclear and other weapons of mass destruction, as well as for its ballistic missile program. One of Pakistan's missiles is an extended range copy of a Chinese missile. Chinese firms provided technical specifications and assistance for the missile's development.[56] In addition, China has also facilitated flights of cargo planes between Pakistan and North Korea that involved the proliferation of both uranium-enrichment technology and ballistic missiles.

In 1998, Pakistan detonated nuclear weapons, and the CIA concluded that "Chinese entities had provided increased assistance to Pakistan's ballistic missile program. North Korea continued to give Pakistan assistance as well. Such assistance is critical for Islamabad's efforts to develop ballistic missiles."[57] China promised in May 1996 to stop providing assistance to nuclear facilities in Pakistan that were not part of the International Atomic Energy Agency system (to assure they were only used for peaceful purposes). But the CIA reported it could not "rule out ongoing contacts." This suggests that the U.S. government had information that China's assistance to Pakistan's nuclear weapons program continues.

Obviously, the combination of China's moving its own aircraft, nuclear weapons, and missiles within striking range of India; providing Pakistan with assistance in developing ballistic missiles; and shipping complete short-range ballistic missiles to Pakistan strongly increased the risk of a potential conflict between India and Pakistan, which could potentially become nuclear. The House Select Committee chaired by Representative Cox included much of this information when it discussed the proliferation activities of China and added this important point: "The select Committee is aware of information of further PRC proliferation of missile and space technology that the Clinton administration has determined cannot be publicly disclosed without affecting national security."[58]

Quite clearly, the large amount of information publicly available on what China has been doing in its secret proliferation activities is only part of the whole story. Limiting ourselves to what is known, China's activities in spreading weapons of mass destruction and components to hostile, dangerous regimes have certainly contributed enormously to the risk of regional nuclear wars. In addition, we note that the director of Central Intelligence stated in February 2000 that North Korea "could test an ICBM capable of delivering a light payload to the United States in the next few years."[59] In February 2001, the CIA said that the existing, already-tested North Korean space launch vehicle could be converted to an intercontinental ballistic missile (ICBM) "capable of delivering a small biological or chemical weapon to the United States."[60] Admiral Thomas R. Wilson, director of the Defense Intelligence Agency, testified that North Korea, Iran, and Iraq could potentially develop or acquire ICBMs, which "could fundamentally alter the strategic threat."[61] This is an example of how Chinese proliferation activities directly threaten not only U.S. forces in Asia and the Middle East, but also U.S. cities and citizens.[62]

PROMISE AND FORGET: CHINESE REACTIONS TO U.S. PROLIFERATION CONCERNS

Beginning with the Reagan administration, expressing its opposition in 1987 to China's transfer of ballistic missiles to Iran, the United States government at the very highest levels has repeatedly stated its concerns about China's proliferation actions. In response, China has made blanket denials that it is involved in proliferation activities and has officially and explicitly denied specific U.S. government allegations. Another response by China has been to make a series of commitments at summits or other high-level meetings with the United States and/or to sign agreements that ostensibly preclude China from proliferation in the future. Examples of this response include, but are not limited to the following:

1. 1991: China agreed to adhere to the 1987 Missile Technology Control Regime Guidelines. This is not a formal international treaty and it has no intrinsic legal authority, but participation indicates acceptance of its voluntary guidelines.[63]

2. 1992: China promised again to abide by the Missile Technology Control Regime and reaffirmed this in 1994.
3. China acceded to the Nuclear Nonproliferation Treaty in 1992 and the Chemical Weapons convention in 1993—both prohibit providing assistance for the development of nuclear or chemical weapons.
4. May 1996: China promised to make nuclear transfers only to facilities that were safeguarded as being for peaceful activities.
5. July 1996: China announced a moratorium on nuclear testing and signed the comprehensive test ban treaty in 1996.
6. October 1997: China joined the Zanger Committee, a group of governments established to limit exports of militarily useful advanced technology.
7. June 1998: the Chinese government announced that it issued new regulations to control the export of dual use nuclear related items.[64]

Although China may have kept one or two of its many pledges and formal commitments, in fact, the phrase that best characterizes its policy is "promise and forget." Interestingly, the Clinton administration, which sought to ignore much of the evidence that its own intelligence services produced on Chinese proliferation activities, frequently used many of the formal commitments and international agreements signed by China to indicate that the promise on paper showed that "progress was being made." A good example is a 1997 briefing paper on China by the Department of State, which cites China's promises and declarations and concludes that China has "taken substantial steps to strengthen its nonproliferation policy."[65] But further in the same document, we learn that the "substantial steps" had little impact, because the Department of State "remained concerned about possible PRC cooperation with Pakistan and Iran and are pressing Beijing to expand on its 1994 commitment not to export ground to ground missiles."[66]

Speaking before the June 1998 U.S.-China summit, then Senator Ashcroft recalled that in January 1998 President Clinton had certified that China had made "clear and unequivocal commitments not to proliferate military technology."[67] Following that certification, the Senator said, the United States "sent its best nuclear reactor technology to Communist China—the country which the Central Intelligence Agency identified as the 'most significant supplier of weapons of mass destruction, related goods, and technology to foreign countries.'"[68] The Senator went on to say, only two months after this presidential certification, the *Washington Post* reported that China "was caught trying to ship Iran hundreds of tons of hydrogen fluoride, a material used in enriching uranium to weapons grade. This material reportedly was destined for . . . one of Iran's principle research sites to manufacture the explosive core of an atomic device [a major step toward an atomic bomb]. The administration reportedly discovered this effort by China even before the President certified China's nonproliferation commitments to Congress."[69]

A third Chinese reaction to U.S. concerns has been to work more diligently to hide its transfer of weapons of mass destruction. This is documented clearly in a government report published by Bill Gertz that provides details of how China and Pakistan discussed ways to evade detection by the United States intelligence services.[70] In fact, Defense Department officials who participated in discussions with China on proliferation issues have said that the Chinese use these discussions "to consistently deny that Chinese firms are involved in the transfer of weapons technology to states seeking nuclear weapons and missile delivery systems . . . and then make requests for additional information to find out about U.S. intelligence capabilities and how to avoid detection of further covert sales."[71]

Another method of evasion has been China's work with North Korea and, most likely, the Khan network in Pakistan. China provides them with advanced nuclear weapon and missile technology and North Korea or the Khan network then becomes the ostensible source of that technology to other states. There were revelations that, contrary to its promises, China had provided North Korea and Pakistan with extensive missile-related technology.[72] A further example of cooperation is the fact that China permitted Iran to use its airspace to transport ballistic missiles provided by North Korea, as well as reports of Chinese and North Korean technicians working together to help Iran produce its own missiles.[73] A sign of how self-destructive the profit motive can be is that some of the technology China provided North Korea for its missiles comes from Japanese high-tech companies that pass their products and technology though Chinese partners.[74]

A fifth Chinese reaction has been to repeatedly use the amount and type of its proliferation activities to bargain with or threaten the United States. For example, China says that it will reduce its WMD sales if the Untied States ceases the sale of weapons of any kind to Taiwan. The State Department says that "China consistently tries to link proliferation initiatives, particularly on missiles and missile components . . . to our own arms sales to Taiwan, a link which we reject." A variant of this use of its proliferation occurred before the June 1998 U.S.-China summit, when the *South China Morning Post* reported that "China was willing to trade Pakistan and Iran for Taiwan," meaning that it would stop its sales of weapons of mass destruction to those countries if the United States would stop selling weapons to Taiwan.[75] Year after year, China threatens to expand its proliferation of weapons of mass destruction and missiles to hostile and dangerous countries if the United States transfers certain kinds of technology to Taiwan or if the United States moves forward with either an Asian regional missile defense or a national missile defense. This threat, typical of the coercive style of diplomacy adopted by assertive dictatorships, has been reported in the U.S. and international media, but has not met with any effective response.[76]

China has not yet demanded payment to stop its proliferation activities. North Korea has done this since 1998, when it admitted for the first time it was selling missiles abroad. North Korea said it would stop doing this if it the United States would pay compensation, starting at one billion dollars annually for its "lost revenues."[77]

The scale of Chinese proliferation activities can be judged by the fact that in its 1998 White Paper on National Defense, China reported that from 1993 to 1997 it had exported 168 ballistic missiles and launchers. Western analysts believe the actual number is several times higher, which could mean China had exported about 500 missiles and launchers in those years.[78]

China continues these dangerous activities, in part, because there have been almost no consequences. U.S. laws require that the president of the United States apply economic sanctions against the organizations in China transferring weapons of mass destruction. These sanctions would prohibit firms in the United States selling dual-use technology or making contracts with them. The Clinton administration invoked sanctions once in 1993, then lifted them in 1994 based on promises. An exception to the lack of response was the decision in 1997 to impose sanctions on several Chinese organizations. These remained through the year 2000 because of those organizations' direct involvement in the transfer of chemical weapons to Iran.[79]

Meetings between Presidents Clinton and Jiang in June 1998 and in September 2000 perhaps best illustrate the lack of effectiveness of the Clinton administration in dealing with this aspect of China's international actions. Before the June 1998 summit meeting, U.S. intelligence agencies detected a Chinese ship bringing weapons materials to Pakistan's major nuclear weapons laboratory. This was just after the dramatic May 1998 nuclear tests by India and Pakistan.[80] On the way to the June 1998 summit with China, Secretary of State Albright said that President Clinton would raise proliferation issues with China: "We have repeatedly made clear to China our concerns about Chinese exports of missile related equipment and technology to Tehran [Iran] and we will continue to do so . . . the president is going to raise all of these issues when he is in Beijing."[81] Nothing changed.

More than two years later, in the summer of 2000, President Clinton sent a special delegation to China to persuade Beijing to end its supply of missile technology to Pakistan. There were no visible results. At the August 2000 policy meeting of the Chinese leadership, the decision was made to move more rapidly to develop high-tech "killer weapons." In order to finance these more expensive weapons, the Chinese government would adopt a "military-finance-military" policy, meaning that arms exports would be used to pay for this advanced military technology.[82] This would be implemented by increasing its already high level of sales of weapons of mass destruction in the future.

In September 2000, Clinton and Jiang met in New York, and the main topic for Clinton was Chinese proliferation. As they met, it was reported that Iran would soon flight test one of its medium-range ballistic missiles that could reach U.S. allies Israel, Turkey, Saudi Arabia, the Persian Gulf States, as well as Russia and Uzbekistan.[83] At their meeting, President Jiang listened politely to President Clinton's concerns about China's continuing proliferation, made no reply, and then moved on to another subject. Later, an aide to President Clinton was quoted as saying, "This is going to take a while."[84] That certainly remains true.

VIOLATION OF INTERNATIONAL ARMS CONTROL TREATIES AND AGREEMENTS

The available evidence indicates that China has violated virtually all of the arms-control agreements it has signed.

In January 1993, the U.S. Arms Control and Disarmament Agency reported that China continued to have an offensive biological-warfare program and for years had violated its commitments under the Biological Weapons Convention (BWC), which it signed in 1989.[85] The same U.S. government agency reported that China had an offensive biological-warfare program before and after it became party to the biological weapons convention and that China's "declarations have not resolved U.S. concerns, that China probably maintains its offensive program. The United States, therefore, believes that . . . it is highly probable that it remains noncompliant with these obligations."[86] The Department of Defense concurred with this view and added that "China has a wide means of delivery available, including ballistic missiles, cruise missiles, and aircraft and is continuing to develop systems with upgraded capabilities."[87] Secretary of State Albright also testified that the United States knows that China has exported biological weapons to Iran.[88]

China signed the nuclear nonproliferation treaty in 1992. The first article of that agreement requires that "each nuclear weapons state Party to the Treaty undertakes . . . not in any way to assist, encourage, or induce any nonnuclear weapons state to manufacture or otherwise acquire nuclear weapons or other nuclear devices, or control over such weapons or explosive devices."[89] In 1995, the U.S. Arms Control and Disarmament Agency said that China was continuing to aid Pakistan's nuclear weapons program, and in 1996, a senior State Department official testified in Congress that China was in violation of its obligations under the Nuclear Nonproliferation Treaty.[90] This has continued.

China signed the Chemical Weapons Convention in 1993 and ratified it in 1997. The Chemical Weapons Convention prohibits signatory states from transferring "chemical weapons to anyone . . . directly or indirectly."[91] One of China's methods of making political use of signing various agreements, whether in the area of weapons limitations or human rights, is to claim credit for signing the agreement and then delay the ratification of the agreement by the rubber-stamp National People's Congress for some years. In political democracies where the legislative branch may have views different from the executive branch, a delay in ratification might well be part of the normal political process and part of the reality of pluralist political negotiation. In China, however, this gap in time between signature and ratification merely reflects the tactical intentions of the regime, because the National People's Congress acts at the direction of the Chinese Communist Party.

Not long after signing the Chemical Weapons Convention, China sent Iran a nearly complete poison gas factory—perhaps China believed that it could do this as long as it had not yet ratified the treaty. But in fact, Article 18 of the Vienna Convention on the Law of Treaties holds that when any country signs a treaty it has an "obligation not to defeat the object and purpose of a treaty prior to its entry into force."[92] As Timperlake and Triplett write, sending a poison gas factory to Iran would "clearly defeat the purpose of the Chemical Weapons Convention."[93]

China says that it maintains an "antichemical warfare corps" that seeks to develop protective measures in the event of a chemical attack. It also indicates that it has on its territory "large quantities of chemical weapons abandoned by Japanese aggressor troops" at the end of World War II.[94] However, the Department of Defense concluded that despite China's claims not to produce or possess chemical weapons, it does in fact have:

> an advanced chemical warfare program, including research and development, production, and weaponized capabilities . . . in the near future China is likely to acquire the necessary expertise in delivery capability to integrate chemical weapons successfully into all military operations. China's current inventory of chemical weapons includes the full range of traditional agents, and China is conducting research on more advanced agents. It has a wide variety of delivery systems for delivery of chemical agents.[95]

On two occasions, in February 1992 and October 1994, China gave written promises to the United States that it would not export ballistic missiles having a range greater than 150 miles (300 kilometers) or a throw weight/payload greater than 1,100 pounds (500 kilograms).[96] In fact, the M-11 missiles that China subsequently sold to Pakistan violated those commitments. As Timperlake and Triplett put it, China's "written promises . . . to [the United States] . . . created valid bilateral agreements under international law," and therefore China was again in violation of valid international agreements on weapons limitations.

16 "A Rich Country and a Strong Army": Military Modernization and Buildup

"Credible intimidation . . . victory through inferiority over superiority."
"Active defense—gaining the initiative by striking first."
"Winning victory with one strike."
—Key elements of China's new military doctrine from 1990s to present

"The first rule of unrestricted warfare is there are no rules with nothing forbidden."

—COLONEL QIAO LIANG and WANG XIANGSHUI,
Beijing, 1999

The Chinese Communist Party took power on the battlefield. Mao said, "Political power grows out of the barrel of the gun," and the Party has always been serious about issues of war and military strength. China fought against the United States in Korea and, by preventing the defeat of North Korea, believes that it won that war. In the 1950s, when Mao attacked the offshore islands controlled by the Nationalist government, it was the United States Navy and, according to Chinese military officials, U.S. nuclear threats that stood in the way of Chinese military success and conquest.

Despite the serious economic crisis and mass starvation caused by its actions at the time, the Chinese Communist Party decided to give the development of nuclear weapons and missiles the highest priority.[1] The result was that China developed an atomic weapon by 1964 and tested its first ballistic missile in 1965. During the 1960s, China began work on three ballistic missiles. Two medium-range ballistic missiles were focused on the Soviet Union and the long-range ICBM was targeted against the United States.[2]

Throughout the intense turmoil of the Cultural Revolution (1966–1976), work on nuclear weapons and missiles continued. During this time, the Chinese regime knew that the Soviet Union was considering a nuclear attack to prevent China from further developing these weapons. China prepared for war against the Soviet Union by moving large ground forces to the border regions, establishing nationwide secure command facilities with food and weapons storage for the Party and military leadership, and by moving the nuclear-armed missiles it already possessed into position to destroy Soviet cities within reach. Given the Soviet invasion of Czechoslovakia in 1968, China perceived the threat of Soviet attack as a deadly, serious issue and prepared to fight both a conventional and nuclear war against the Soviet Union.

After Deng Xiaoping persuaded the post-Mao Communist Party to agree to major economic changes in 1978, the "Four Modernizations" specifically included the modernization of China's military forces. The Chinese military had not performed as well as had been expected when China invaded Vietnam in 1979, and despite normalization with the United States, China continued to be concerned about the potential danger posed by both the Soviet Union and the United States. As a result, in the 1980s China developed six new types of ballistic missiles. Some of these were able to survive attack by either the Soviet Union or the United States because they would be solid-fueled and mobile, rather than being launched from fixed silos or deep-tunnel areas that might become known and therefore targeted in advance. As these missiles were moving from design to early development in the 1980s, China also used espionage and its own skilled personnel to begin developing the smaller, lighter nuclear warheads that these missiles would deliver to their targets. During the 1990s, China tested the newly manufactured nuclear warheads and moved the new ballistic missiles from development to testing and into the production phase.

There is an Asian proverb: "A rich country has a strong army." As the Chinese regime became immensely wealthier, it had more economic resources and a growing technological base to expand its weapons modernization. At the same time, the lightning speed of Operation Iraqi Freedom and the defeat of Iraq's large ground forces with almost no casualties, the normalization of relations with the Soviet Union, and the definition of the United States as the main enemy, led to a rethinking of Chinese military strategy and a new, more intense focus on obtaining more modern weapons.

The Communist regime has the purpose of making China a "strong, unified, modern, and wealthy nation," which will be "the preeminent power among the regional states of Asia."[3] With the Soviet threat in the west and north gone, in the 1990s, in the view of the U.S. Department of Defense, China decided to focus on its "sovereign interests to include Taiwan, the South China Sea, and elsewhere on its periphery," and the purpose for modernizing its military forces was to obtain control of Taiwan and to "defend its claims in the East and South China Seas."[4] Additionally, Beijing believes the United States to be a "significant long-term challenge"[5] to the Chinese realization of "a favorable 'strategic configuration of power.'"[6]

This view of China's current strategic objectives is sobering for the United States because since opening relations with Beijing in 1971 the United States has said that the issue of relations between China and Taiwan must be resolved without coercion. The United States has also taken a clear position that both the South China Sea and the East China Sea are international waters, not the sovereign territory of China or any other state. This divergence in viewpoint would suggest the possibility of conflict between the United States and China in the coming years. That the Chinese regime perceives this prospect of war with the United States can be seen in the fact that, according to the Department of Defense, "a cross-strait conflict between China and Taiwan involving the United States has emerged as the dominant scenario involving PLA [People's Liberation Army] force planning, military training, and war preparation."[7]

In the years when normalization with the United States was useful to China as a counter to the Soviet threat, Mao had said that the issue of Taiwan could "wait 50 or 100 years." But since the 1990s, a wealthier Chinese regime with ever more modern, high-tech weapons has placed increasing pressure on Taiwan to submit to its control under the rubric of "one country, two systems." At the same time, China declared a new geopolitical imperative as a means of defending China and establishing its preeminence in East Asia. China contends it must control "the first island chain" off its coast —a region including the East and South China Seas, bounded by the Japanese Islands, Taiwan, the Philippines, and Borneo.[8]

ESPIONAGE AND COVERT ACTION

In the three millennia of Chinese statecraft, spying and shaping the opponent's perception in useful ways have always played a major role. More than two thousand years ago, General Sun Tzu codified the important role of espionage and influence operations in his writings and summed up the benefits for the state when he said, "To win the war without a battle is the highest success." To this important imperial tradition must also be added the experience of Communist political movements and Communist dictatorships. In the years of fighting for power, the Communist movements of the Soviet Union and of China emphasized using spies to obtain information about the actions governments might take against them and to prevent the penetration of their movements by those governments. Once in power, Communists placed the highest priority on spying to obtain information about activities that might be taken by internal opponents of the regime and also by foreign powers. For Communist rulers, spying internally and internationally and seeking to shape perceptions at home and abroad is an intrinsic part of governance.

In its long years of warfare with the Nationalist government of China, the Chinese Communist Party used extensive spy networks and political influence operations. In the final phase of the war to control China from 1945 to 1949, the Chinese Communist Party worked with the Soviet Union and its networks in the United States in a successful effort to limit the amount of military aid the United States might give the Chinese Nationalist government. There were also unsuccessful efforts to sabotage aid shipments from the west coast of the United States to China at that time.[9] A major purpose of Chinese Communist intelligence was to recruit agents in the United States from the American Chinese community and to gather information about possible U.S. support for the Nationalist government. Recall that Mao Zedong received information from his U.S. spy networks in the late 1940s about the U.S. development of the atomic bomb in Los Alamos—at the same time Stalin was receiving information from the Soviet spy network. The difference was that Mao learned about the program in broad terms whereas Stalin got the actual plans for building an atomic device.[10]

Upon taking power in 1949, the Chinese Communists, together with the Soviet Union, defined the United States as the main enemy. Both Communist powers undertook aggressive espionage operations against the United States. Yet, in the 1950s, the Federal Bureau of Investigation prosecuted few spy cases involving Chinese Communist agents.[11]

A former senior U.S. counterintelligence official indicates that during the 1950s and 1960s there was a significant effort by the Chinese intelligence service to coerce Chinese Americans who had family members living in China to be cooperative.[12] These included efforts to obtain personal information on Chinese Americans from their financial records in order to find those who would be might be vulnerable to financial inducements. After the normalization of U.S.-Chinese relations in the 1970s, it became possible for the Chinese intelligence organizations to operate under diplomatic cover in the United States. According to one analysis, China's intelligence agents have carried out secret espionage activities with the assistance of extensive, well-organized, nationally active networks. Very often, these networks are "family based," with the senior operative being the "wife" who is supported by a "sister" or "mother," while the "husband" is actually the most junior participant.[13]

Perhaps one of the best-known recruits for China during the 1950s was Qian Xuesen. Qian left China in 1935, at the age of twenty-four, because of the Japanese occupation. Subsequently, he received a master's degree from MIT and a Ph.D. from the California Institute of Technology, where he worked in the rocket research group of the jet propulsion laboratory. Based on that work, Dr. Qian was invited to join the U.S. Army Air Force long-range missile program and commissioned a colonel. He worked on the development of the Titan, one of America's first ICBMs, until there were allegations that he was spying for Communist China. As a result of negotiations with China, he and four other members of the Titan design team returned to China. Once there, Dr. Qian became "the leading figure in the PRC's ballistic missile effort . . . Qian and his associates were able to apply the knowledge gained from U.S. ballistic missile programs to the PRC's ballistic missile program."[14]

In 1985, as a result of a high-level defection from China's Ministry of State Security (MSS), responsible for foreign intelligence, a well-known case of long-term Chinese penetration was discovered.[15] Mr. Larry Wu-Tai Chin had worked for the U.S. intelligence community for thirty-seven years, until his retirement in 1981. Among the many valuable documents he was believed to have obtained from the Central Intelligence Agency was the very highly classified overview of President Nixon's purposes in seeking to open relations with China prepared before his first visit. Mr. Chin was convicted of espionage and was awaiting sentencing at an Alexandria, Virginia prison when he was found in his cell, dead by suffocation— suicide was ruled.[16]

In 1981, a Taiwan-born scientist working at the Lawrence Livermore National Laboratory resigned during the course of an FBI investigation into whether he had passed secrets to China about the neutron bomb.[17] This weapon uses lethal radiation to kill humans but does not damage physical structures. It was intended for use against Soviet forces that might be attacking in Europe with large formations of tanks and armored personnel carriers. The United States did not actually develop the neutron design into a weapon, but in July 1999 China announced that it had success-fully developed the neutron bomb and that it was in its inventory of weapons.[18] In the early 1990s, the FBI began an investigation of Chinese espionage at the Los Alamos National Laboratory. In 1997, this resulted in a confession by Taiwan-born scientist Dr. Peter Lee that he had provided secret information to China.[19]

The Los Alamos Nuclear Weapons Secrets

Perhaps the most dramatic case of apparent Chinese espionage during the 1990s involved Dr. Wen-Ho Lee, an employee of the Los Alamos nuclear weapons labora-tory from 1980 to 1999. Suspicions were first raised about Dr. Lee in 1982 when the FBI intercepted a telephone call he made to a scientist at the Livermore laboratory who was known to have been conducting espionage. Reportedly, Dr. Lee had told that individual that he would try to find out how his identity had been uncovered.[20] When asked about this by the FBI, Dr. Lee first denied knowing the other scientist whom he had called but admitted the telephone call when confronted with irrefutable evidence. Nevertheless, the 1982 investigation of Dr. Wen-Ho Lee did not proceed further.

Dr. Lee visited China in 1982, 1986, and 1988. In the view of federal investiga-tors, it was during those years that nuclear weapons information may have been passed to Chinese officials. As a condition of his employment, Dr. Lee was required to report all contacts with Chinese government officials or scientists involved in nuclear weapons development. He had not reported any contact with an individual known as the "father of the Chinese atomic bomb," the vice president of the Chinese organization in charge of developing nuclear weapons. But when this Chinese scientist visited the Los Alamos National Laboratory in 1994 and met with a group of Chinese-American scientists, he embraced Dr. Wen-Ho Lee and told the other scientists that Dr. Lee had made important contributions to the nuclear weapons program of China.[21] This encounter raised obvious questions. In 1995, when the United States received a packet of Chinese documents indicating that China had obtained the design for a number of the most advanced U.S. nuclear weapons, a new investigation began that led, once again, to Dr. Lee.

On September 26, 2000, Attorney General Janet Reno and FBI Director Louis Freeh testified together before the Senate in the case of Dr. Wen-Ho Lee. This followed Dr. Lee's plea bargain with the government, in which he admitted to the "mishandling" of classified national security information and promised the government that he would fully disclose what he had done with the highly classified nuclear weapons information copied from the secure computers at Los Alamos into his personal computer. Dr. Lee made no admission that he had provided any information to China or any other foreign power.

The attorney general and FBI director testified that they judged it more important to obtain Dr. Lee's cooperation in recovering the information he had removed, along with the computer tapes and discs, than it was to prosecute further in the context of a court proceeding where they were concerned that the government might have to reveal secrets in order to make the case for espionage.[22] Their joint finding was that between 1993 and 1998, Dr. Lee had removed the equivalent of "400,000 pages . . . stacked up that's a thirteen story building . . . from the most secure computers of the Los Alamos nuclear weapons laboratory, to his own personal computer." And while doing this he had, according to the attorney general,

> moved files in such a way as to defeat security measures he knew were in place. He went further. He copied the information from the unsecure computer onto ten portable tapes. The FBI recovered three however seven are still missing. What is more, he made copies of the portable tapes, and those copies are also missing. When Dr. Lee found out he was being investigated, he took steps to cover up his actions. After his access was revoked to the part of the lab where the computer was located, he tried over and over again to get in, including at 3:30 am on one Christmas Eve.[23]

The FBI director summarized the information that Dr. Lee removed from the Los Alamos secure computers and copied onto his personal computer as:

> the complete nuclear weapons design capability at Los Alamos at that time . . .
> 50 years of weapons development at the expense of hundreds of billions of

dollars . . . [this data], in the wrong hands, [could] change the global strategic balance. They enable the possessor to design the only objects that could result in the military defeat of America's conventional forces. The only threat, for example, to our carrier battle groups. They represent the greatest possible risk to the United States.[24]

These disturbing revelations, from the highest levels of the Clinton administration, came a year and a half after the public release of the information in the House Select Committee Report on Chinese spying.

A U.S. government report written in late 1998 provided an overview of the efforts of a number of countries, including Russia, India, China, and North Korea, to obtain information about U.S. nuclear weapons. In writing about China, the report said that China had

successfully employed a combination of open source collection, all forms of cyber-collection, elicitation, and espionage needed to aid their weapons program . . . China has specifically targeted DOE [the Department of Energy and the nuclear weapons laboratories], responsible for the collection of technical intelligence related to the design of nuclear weapons, and seeks information related to stockpile stewardship and reliability. This effort has been very successful and Beijing's exploitation of U.S. laboratories has substantially aided its nuclear weapons program.[25]

COVERT ACTION

When governments use covert action to advance their interests, they seek to obtain results without their involvement being known or visible. This usually involves the use of intermediaries to carry out specific activities. These intermediaries might be "witting" or "unwitting": witting means they understand that they are acting as agents or conduits for a particular government; "unwitting" that they do not know that another government is secretly directing their actions.

In the 1990s, China decided to undertake a new effort to influence the actions and decisions of the United States government. It went beyond the normal conduct of diplomacy and espionage, including secret agents of influence, and beyond the means of hiring lobbyists and public affairs companies to influence U.S. policy in a direction favorable to China. The Chinese leadership had always believed that, as Mao said, "The mind of the enemy and his leaders is a target of far more importance than the bodies of his troops."

In October 1996, allegations first surfaced in the press of the United States that various Asian organizations were making illegal cash donations to the reelection campaign of President Clinton and Vice President Gore. Under American law, only U.S. citizens or persons and organizations in the territory of the United States may make contributions legally. While these allegations did not change the result of the 1996 presidential election, they did lead to a Senate investigation chaired by Senator Fred Thompson beginning in June 1997 and later to an investigation in the House of Representatives chaired by Representative Daniel Burton.

In February 1997, the *Washington Post* reported that the FBI had definitive information that the Chinese embassy was involved in political influence operations with a focus on the Democratic Party.[26] The method was to transfer money from entities with connections to the Chinese government, through intermediaries who were U.S. citizens, to the Democratic National Committee and other organizations connected with the 1996 Clinton-Gore reelection campaign. After Senator Thompson held hearings on this topic, he concluded, "Chinese government officials crafted a plan to increase Chinese influence over the United States' political process."[27] Bill Gertz concludes from his overview of the available information that roughly $3 million was provided by China through various intermediaries during the 1996 election campaign. Senator Thompson said one of the funding go-betweens could be viewed as an agent of Communist China because "We had information, both public and classified, that showed she was doing work for the PRC surreptitiously."[28]

The public record of those investigations and the results of a great deal of effective investigative journalism by Bill Gertz, Kenneth Timmerman, Jeff Gerth, James Reisen, and others led, in turn, to a number of insightful articles and books that examine these issues in depth.[29] With the record, public and classified, of the congressional investigations available to it, as well as the in-depth investigative reports in the press and the cited books, the bipartisan House Select Committee concluded that China "adopted policies in recent years aimed at increasing its influence within the United States in order to increase access to U.S. military as well as commercial technology . . . agents tied to the PRC's military industries provided illegal contributions and may have used these contributions to gain access to U.S. military and commercial technology."[30]

A large number of the persons named in the press and congressional reports were subsequently convicted in U.S. Courts for various illegal actions in connection with large campaign contributions made to the Democratic Party. Many others refused to testify, even under grants of immunity, and took refuge in foreign countries, especially China. Several brief examples will illustrate this covert Chinese campaign to gain influence with the Clinton administration.

In the summer of 1996, the head of intelligence for the Chinese military, General Ji Xingde, gave $300,000 in cash to Mr. Johnny Chung, a fundraiser for the Democratic Party. According to Mr. Chung's testimony, General Ji said that this money was to be contributed to the Democratic Party because, "We like your president." This was not very good tradecraft, because it involved the Chinese government so directly and visibly. In December of 1999 it was reported General Ji was demoted and assigned to a military research institute.[31] The relationship between the Riady family business complex of Indonesia, Mr. John Huang, China, and the Clinton administration is another example that was extensively discussed and documented in the congressional investigations of the late 1990s.

During the serious crisis with China in the Taiwan Straits (March 1996), Mr. Charlie Trie, a Chinese intermediary who had for many years operated a restaurant in Little Rock, Arkansas and knew Clinton, sent him a letter through his White House contact for pro-Clinton fundraising. The letter contained a serious warning: "It is highly possible for China to launch real war, based on its past behavior in the Sino-Vietnam war, [and the] war with Russia."[32]

In 1998, an internal Department of Justice investigation of the campaign financing allegations by Charles Labella cited Mr. Trie as "acting as a conduit for PRC [People's Republic of China] money into the Presidential campaign."[33] That report also said that in the matter of financing the 1996 Clinton-Gore campaign, "Abuse was rampant and indeed the norm . . . the campaign was so corrupted by bloated fundraising and questionable 'contributions' that the system became a caricature of itself. . . . The timing of the 'Trie donations' is at least as curious as the timing of contributions of Bernard Schwartz and the waiver sought by Loral in connection to the satellite project in China."[34] The Senate Select Committee on Intelligence reported in May 1999, after its investigation, that China's "covert effort to influence the U.S. political process does represent a threat to U.S. national security.[35] Three years after beginning his investigation, Senator Thompson said it was his belief that the Chinese Communist political influence effort "continues today."[36]

DIVERSION AND EXTRACTION OF MILITARILY USEFUL U.S. TECHNOLOGY

A major purpose of Chinese spying and covert action in the United States has been to ensure the continued flow of advanced military technology to assist the modernization of China's military forces. In 1999, the House Select Committee concluded: "The PRC has vigorously pursued in the past decade the acquisition of foreign military technologies. These efforts represent the official policy of China and the Chinese Communist Party leadership . . . the PRC uses a variety of techniques including espionage, controlled commercial entities, and a network of individuals that engage in contact with scientists, businesspeople and academics."[37] The Select Committee went on to say that China's "pervasive efforts pose a significant threat to U.S. export controls and counterintelligence efforts."[38] Three of these approaches will be discussed briefly.

It is estimated that China has established hundreds, and perhaps several thousand, front companies in the United States to obtain advanced U.S. military technology. In the words of Representative Curt Weldon, a member of the House Select Committee, the Chinese military set the priorities for technology to be obtained and these front companies in the United States bought and sent it back "to those entities that wanted to improve their missile capabilities, their nuclear programs, their computing capabilities, the design of their fighter aircraft, whatever the need might be."[39] A very skilled investigative journalist, Kenneth Timmerman, looking into this issue found that there were hundreds of Chinese front companies in California, many in a small area not far from Los Angeles. In one building alone, he found 150 Chinese trading companies, many of them having a listing in the building but neither telephone numbers nor offices, normal aspects of doing business. Some major Chinese companies operated under their own names; others established corporations in the United States under other names. For example, Timmerman found that the China National Electronics Import-Export Corporation—which manufactures radar, communications gear, and cryptography systems for the Chinese military and for export to countries like Iran and Iraq—was incorporated in California under the name Catronics.[40]

While many of these Chinese companies were established to secretly ship militarily useful products back to China, other Chinese military-linked companies produced products for sale in the United States to increase hard-currency earnings. An AFL-CIO project led by Mr. Jeffery Fiedler reported on the many military-related companies now doing business in the United States. One example is Xinxing, which in China operates more than three thousand factories for the military and is a major exporter to the United States of "consumer goods, building materials, and frozen fish . . . well over one million pounds of fish fillet . . . as well as a million pounds of men's pants."[41] Timmerman reports that since 1993, the Chinese military has established about three thousand commercial entities in the United States and that through 1999 China had raised about $10 billion in the U.S. financial markets.[42]

Another approach used by China to obtain advanced militarily useful technology is to require U.S. companies seeking to do business in China to share their advanced technology with Chinese scientific, research, or production entities. This was documented in a report by the U.S. Commerce Department that found: "Most U.S. and other foreign investors in China seem willing to pay the price of technology transfers—even state of the art technologies—in order to 'establish a beachhead' in China with the expectation that the country's enormous market potential will be realized."[43] This comprehensive study notes that as a result of technological advances, China is becoming increasingly competitive in high-technology sectors such as aerospace and electronics and concludes that "continued pressures on foreign high technology firms to transfer advanced commercial technologies, if successful, could indirectly benefit China's effort to modernize its military."[44] Related to this is the fact that in the 1990s more than one hundred thousand Chinese students and scholars have studied in America (fifty-three thousand in the year 2000 alone), the overwhelming majority of which have been in the fields of science and technology. Most of these individuals and many thousand Chinese who work in American high-technology companies return to China. They are a valuable, highly trained resource, which can be used by the Chinese government to improve its high-technology science, military research, and production sectors.

A third approach is the enticement of technology from U.S. companies that intend to do more business with China in the future. Perhaps the best-known examples of this have occurred in China's space and satellite launch program. The first reported launching of a satellite by China was in 1970. By 1997, China had launched about forty domestic satellites—seventeen retrievable reconnaissance satellites, three meteorological satellites, eight communications satellites for broadcasting, and twelve possible military satellites.[45] In 1988, the Reagan administration permitted China to launch U.S. origin satellites because of a lack of U.S. satellite launch capability, due to recent problems with the U.S. space shuttle and other possible launch vehicles. An agreement was signed with China to protect U.S. technology from "possible misuse or diversion," and U.S. satellite exporters understood that they had to abide by the terms of U.S. export policies.[46]

In 1992, 1995, and 1996, three Chinese rockets failed catastrophically in efforts to launch satellites for U.S. companies. The Chinese satellite-launch vehicle is identical to the Chinese long-range ICBM in essentially all characteristics, except that in one case the payload is satellites and in the other it is nuclear warheads.[47] In 1994, the Lockheed Martin Corporation provided China with a detailed technical assessment of the problems with its space-launch rocket, without first clearing this with the appropriate U.S. government authorities. In April 2000, the U.S. government charged Lockheed Martin with thirty violations of the Arms Export and Control Act; Lockheed Martin paid civil penalties of $13 million in June of that year.[48] As already discussed, the Loral Corporation and the Hughes Corporation provided considerable technical assistance to improve Chinese rockets in 1995 and 1996 and, in the words of the U.S. government, "Any assistance to China that enhances its abilities in space launch has the potential to be applied to missile development."[49] An expert on these issues who served in the Department of Defense wrote, "All of our satellite transfers have helped China improve its military rocketry." In particular, the writer pointed to the fact that the help given by U.S. corporations to China in developing multisatellite dispensers for its space-launch rockets would help China significantly in developing the ability to put multiple nuclear weapons on its ICBMs.[50]

The results of all these systematic Chinese efforts to improve its advanced military weapon systems could be seen in its military forces at the beginning of the twenty-first century.

Asymmetric Warfare: "Gaining the Initiative by Striking First"

The combination of China's strategic objectives and its assessment of the implications of advanced technologies for warfare have resulted in a number of fundamental shifts in military approach. In broadest terms, China ended its emphasis on "protracted, large-scale land warfare" and began to focus on "regional conflicts along China's periphery ... officially called 'people's war under modern conditions' but also described as 'local warfare under high technology conditions.' "[51] This new Chinese approach assumes the need for "rapid response to an array of contingencies along China's land and sea borders, particularly in a strategic envelope which composes the East and South China Seas."[52]

One of the corollaries of the new Chinese military doctrine, which evolved during the 1990s, is the idea of asymmetric warfare. This means that China is focusing on military programs that give "China the most effective means for exploiting critical vulnerabilities in adversarial defenses. This approach could give Beijing the 'credible intimidation' needed to accomplish political and military goals without having to rely on overwhelming force on force superiority, a concept known as 'victory through inferiority over superiority.' "[53]

Another major aspect of China's new military strategy is given the name "active defense," but what it means, as the Chinese describe it, is "gaining the initiative by striking first."[54] As China has considered the possibility of conflict with the United States or Japan, the assumption is that it has a window of opportunity for a first strike against the most critical targets of the opponent—military and civilian command and control system, communications and computer systems, and advance forward bases within reach of China's missiles and assembled forces. Chinese strategists refer to this as "winning victory with one strike" and believe it can be achieved by attacking the "core" of the enemy's defense.[55]

The U.S. Department of Defense finds, in fact, that the actions China is taking in deploying weapons and developing new weapons are intended to accomplish exactly this kind of attack. As we shall see, China's large investment in ballistic missiles and other long-distance means of attack, such as cruise missiles, is an example. China is also very active in developing "electromagnetic warfare" and has reportedly developed electromagnetic weapons capable of destroying many types of high-tech warfare capabilities.

China has also decided to reduce its large ground forces by more than one million. As seen by the United States, "China in essence has defined its military force to include three components: a small number of high technology forces for flexible use in regional contingencies; a larger number of forces equipped with low to medium technology weapons for internal security and a modest nuclear force to maintain a viable deterrent against the other nuclear powers."[56] In addition, China has engaged in a comprehensive modernization strategy under the operational framework of fighting and winning a regional war under "high-tech" conditions. This includes the nearly continuous emphasis on the operational concept of using waves of attacks from multiple sources to defeat and, if possible, sink a U.S. aircraft carrier; thus, the acquisition of air, land, sea, and subsurface platforms. Although there are indications that some within China are rethinking the reduction of traditional ground forces following operation Iraqi Freedom, there are no signs of a reduced interest in finding an "assassin's mace" that can be used to counter U.S. Pacific regional assets such as the Seventh Fleet and its carriers.

China has organized its military forces into five branches: the Second Artillery for ballistic missiles, the Navy, Air Force, Army, and the new information warfare organization.

SECOND ARTILLERY/BALLISTIC MISSILES

The main Chinese organization for attack by ballistic missiles is the Second Artillery, with about ninety thousand personnel deployed in six to seven major launch areas. It has its own communications regiment as well as four research institutes, two command and training academies, and perhaps an early-warning unit.[57] While the Second Artillery is located in different regions of China, it is not subordinated to regional military commanders.[58] Originally, the ballistic missiles of the Second Artillery were armed with nuclear weapons, but after the 1991 Gulf War, China decided to add conventional, chemical, and electronic warheads as it saw the Second Artillery as a means of conducting "long-range precision strikes."[59] Stokes indicates that the total number of China's nuclear warheads is unknown, but an informed estimate as of 1999 put the estimated number of both tactical and strategic at 450 to 1,200.[60]

Intercontinental Ballistic Missiles

By the year 2004, China had deployed a publicly estimated number of more than eight hundred ballistic missiles—the majority of them short- or medium-range. In the absence of missile defenses, China's weapons, armed with nuclear, conventional, chemical, biological, or electromagnetic warheads can serve its declared purposes of having the ability to strike Taiwan, Japan, or the United States first, with surprise at critical vulnerabilities.

During the Korean War (1950–1953), China fought America under the potential threat of a U.S. nuclear counterstrike. Since then, China has worked to build its own nuclear missile force. A CIA assessment published in 1999 sums up the goal: "Chinese strategic nuclear doctrine calls for survivable nuclear missile force that can hold a sizable proportion of the U.S. population at risk."[61] An important step toward that goal was China's long-range intercontinental ballistic missile with a range of 7,500 miles (DF-5). This missile's range makes it capable of hitting all of the United States, except for Southern Florida. It reportedly has a very large single nuclear warhead in the five megaton range—about 192 times more powerful then the bomb dropped on Hiroshima—easily enough to destroy a large city completely and kill most of the inhabitants.

Due to China again defining the U.S. as its "main enemy" in 1990, the regime increased the number of these ICBMs from two to an estimated twenty-four during the 1990s. The CIA reportedly concluded that thirteen of these ICBMs were targeted against U.S. cities—if fired these could cause the loss of eighty million or more U.S. lives.[62]

In the 1980s, China began developing three new missiles that could strike directly at the United States and would be less vulnerable than its existing ICBM. One of these, the mobile solid-fuel, five-thousand-mile-range DF-31 was flight tested in 1999.[63] By the end of 2004, eight were deployed. This missile was probably originally designed for use against the Soviet Union, but it can reach Alaska, Hawaii, and the Western states of the United States. The DF-31 can be armed with either 250-kiloton or 650-kiloton single nuclear warheads, or three 90-kiloton multiple independently targeted reentry vehicles (MIRVs). There are also reports that a series of launch sites for the mobile DF-31, connected by highways, is under construction in southern China. The second successful flight test of the DF-31 in August 1999 also included its launching decoy warheads to confuse potential missile defenses.[64]

China has also been working on a new seventy-five-hundred-mile solid-fuel and mobile missile (the DF-41), which could reach virtually all cities in the United States. Third, a new submarine-launched version of the DF-31, which will be designated the JL-2 (Ju Lang/Great-Wave) is being developed and will be available some time in the next few years.[65] China has experienced challenges with its earlier attempts to deploy the indigenously developed Xia class ballistic missile submarine (SSBN), which is capable of carrying approximately twelve JL-1 sea-launched ballistic missiles (SLBM). The next generation Type 094, together with the JL-2 SLBM, will likely avoid many of the problems confronted by the Xia because of the coordinated effort between the shipyards and missile-development teams, as well as the hull design having been proven by the Type 093 attack submarine program.[66]

Because of the immense secrecy surrounding all Chinese military activities, especially those concerned with advanced nuclear weapons and missiles, it is difficult to say whether current estimates of numbers are reasonable. It would be prudent to treat these as minimum estimates. Any estimate of Chinese ICBMS should also take into account the number of Chinese space-launch vehicles potentially available to carry weapons. Since these are virtually identical to the DF-5 ICBM, these space-launch vehicles could also deliver nuclear warheads against cities in the United States.

In 1997, the Department of Defense estimated that by 2008, China could have 1,000 ICBMs.[67] If China continued its progress in the area of multiple warheads, this could mean that China could have two, three, or more warheads on those 1,000 ICBMs and would pose a far more formidable and deadly threat than it does today.[68] Concerning the uncertainty of the estimates of China's nuclear weapons, it is worth noting that an ostensibly internal document of the Chinese defense ministry published in Hong Kong in 1996 showed that China had at that time not 300 nuclear warheads, as estimated in the West, but about 2,350 warheads; of which 550 were tactical and 1,800 were strategic. The document goes on to say that annual production of nuclear warheads was about 110 in the 1980s and 140 in the 1990s.[69] Much of the progress China made with its nuclear weapons and missiles in the 1990s derived from technology stolen from or provided by the United States.[70] If this level of production continued from 1996 to 2004, it is possible that China already has 3,470 nuclear warheads.

Medium/Intermediate Range Ballistic Missiles

After the successful test of its first liquid-fueled missile in 1965, China immediately moved to develop other missiles. The DF-3, with a range of 1,900 miles and a nuclear warhead, was liquid-fueled and silo-based and could reach targets in the Soviet Union, Korea, Japan, and the Philippines. Starting in 1971, about one hundred of these were deployed. Some believe that these are no longer in service.[71] This might be the case, but such weapon systems can be deployed again and it would be prudent to assume that this capability remains available to China.

Begun in 1965 and first deployed in 1980, the liquid-fueled DF-4, with a range of 3,400 miles, can reach targets in Russia, Japan, India, South Korea, Guam, and the U.S. base at Diego Garcia. Estimates are that there are twenty to fifty of these in service. Also begun in 1965, the DF-21 was the first solid-fueled missile China sought to develop. It was produced in a version for deployment on a ballistic missile submarine in 1983 under the designation JL-1, but the submarine has been plagued by trouble and rarely leaves port. Nevertheless, there are twelve of these missiles called, in their sea-based version, the JL-1, with a large nuclear warhead estimated as the equivalent of one million tons of TNT. If fired from the submarine, those missiles could reach any place within a 1,200-mile range from where the submarine was able to maneuver. The land version of this missile was first deployed in 1987, with possible targets in the Soviet Union, Japan, South Korea, Okinawa, Southeast

Asia, and the South or East China Sea regions if it were deployed at the borders. It is estimated that about fifty of these missiles are deployed.

An improved version of the DF-21 missile has a longer range of 1,900 miles, a smaller nuclear warhead (in the range of 250 kilotons), and is probably significantly more accurate. The numbers deployed are unknown, and the targets it could reach include all of those previously mentioned for the DF-21 plus U.S. bases in Japan.[72]

Short Range Ballistic Missiles

Starting in 1984, China began the development of short-range missiles with a clear intention that these would be targeted on Taiwan, and possibly U.S. or other naval forces that might be operating in areas near its borders. The DF-11 has a range of 170 miles and was first deployed in 1992. At this time, estimated deployment is about 200. This mobile, solid-fueled missile can use nuclear, chemical, biological, or electromagnetic warheads. The second short-range ballistic missile is the DF-15 with a range of 370 miles, first deployed in 1991. By 2003, the Department of Defense estimated that there are 450 short-range ballistic missiles aimed at Taiwan.[73] Although this represented an increase of one hundred missiles over the pervious year's estimate in the annual report to Congress, the Department of Defense only revised the figures on the estimated production/deployment from fifty to seventy-five missiles per year.[74] Reports indicate that the PLA has a goal of more than 650 deployed short-range ballistic missiles by 2004–2005, in areas within range of Taiwan.[75]

These hundreds of ballistic missiles opposite Taiwan most likely "target air defense installations, airfields, naval bases, C4I [Command, Control, Communications, Computers, and Intelligence] and logistics facilities."[76] It is believed that most are armed with high-explosive conventional munitions or chemical or electromagnetic warheads, to disable and destroy the military command and support infrastructure of Taiwan without the use of nuclear weapons. The Chinese believe these short-range missiles could also be effective in attacking U.S. aircraft carriers and other naval forces if they were operating in the area of the Taiwan Straits to help defend Taiwan.

Air Forces

According to publicly available figures, the Air Force and the Naval Air Force have combined personnel of over 426,000, with over 1,360 tactical fighters, 228 bombers, more then 776 close air support fighter aircraft, and 453 transport aircraft. However, some experts estimated that by 2005 there would be about 2,300 tactical fighter aircraft, about 500 ground attack aircraft, and 400 bombers.[77] The Department of Defense judges, "there is no comprehensive, integrated air defense network . . . and aerial refueling and airborne early warning programs remain behind schedule."[78] China's jet fighters arc being upgraded by the addition of about 80 Russian Su-27 all-weather advanced aircraft, with the expectation that by 2006 there will be about 400 Su-27 fighters and around 100 Su-30 fighter-bombers available to China.[79] From the point of view of possible conflict with the United States, it is significant that some of the naval air force planes are capable of carrying three advanced air-to-surface cruise missiles, which could be highly effective against U.S. naval ships.[80]

In comparing the balance across the Taiwan Straits, the Department of Defense notes that although Taiwan has only 400 jet fighters, about 300 of these are the most modern type. However, it says that by 2006, if current trends continue, the balance would shift in China's favor because China would have about 500 modern and aerial-refueled-capable fighter and fighter-bomber aircraft, as well as active radar air-to-air missile and airborne early warning aircraft, which would be a large-force multiplier.[81] In one view, China already has air-to-air missiles on the Russian Su-27, superior to those Taiwan has—perhaps shifting the balance of airpower earlier.[82]

A shift in the balance in favor of Mainland China could significantly increase the chances for war across the Taiwan Straits. However, the balance can be maintained. Taiwan already has a strong air force, with a very effective pilot training program, and enough aircraft in strategic positions to defend the island. Thus, if Taiwan keeps up with Communist China in terms of both defensive and counterattack weapons, the balance of airpower can be maintained. This has been the professed goal of U.S. policy in delivering the latest air-to-air weapons to Taiwan.

NAVAL FORCES

The Chinese navy includes about 260,000 personnel, approximately 63 destroyers and frigates, about 62 diesel submarines, five nuclear attack submarines, one ballistic missile submarine, and over 337 amphibious landing ships of various sizes. In addition, the naval air arm has roughly 500 aircraft. During the 1990s, the navy modernized its forces and eliminated significant numbers of older ships, replacing these with fewer, more modern ships. The number of submarines has declined by about 50 percent; however, there are indications that the Chinese view the use of submarine warfare as the key to victory in any effort to blockade Taiwan or a direct confrontation with the U.S. Navy. Chinese strategists view submarines armed with a combination of Russian-produced antiship cruise missiles and advanced wake-homing torpedoes, in combination with other assets, as the key to sinking a U.S. aircraft carrier.[83]

The Department of Defense concludes that in the year 2000 the Chinese navy "continues to lag behind other regional navies, in most technological areas, especially air defense, C4I [command, control, computer, communications, intelligence] and surveillance."[84] China is judged to have "an overwhelming advantage in submarines over Taiwan," both in numbers and in quality because of new submarines purchased from Russia.[85] As a result of technological and training improvements in the year 2000, the submarine fleet of China is a "force capable of controlling sea lanes and mining approaches around Taiwan, as well as a growing threat to submarines in the East China Sea."[86] The surface ships of the Chinese navy all carry antiship cruise missiles, ranging from first-generation to advanced. The first two of four Russian-built destroyers of the *Sovremmeny* class were delivered in the year 2000 and are equipped with an advanced antiship cruise missile, which is viewed as posing a direct threat to all ships of the U.S. Navy. This is the SS-N-22 "Sunburn" antiship cruise missile, which skims on the surface of the ocean at a speed over two times the speed of sound and can be armed with nuclear and conventional explosives. It cannot be defended against at present. There are also reports that air-launched versions of these antiship missiles have or will be sold in connection with the purchase by the Chinese of the Su-30 ground attack fighters.

A further advance in Chinese naval capabilities occurred in 2002, with the launching of the lead hull in their indigenously developed Type 093 attack submarine, which is expected to carry antiship cruise missiles, and wake-homing and wire-guided torpedoes.[87] In addition to these domestically produced nuclear submarines, the navy has also taken delivery of two Russian export Kilo and two improved Kilo-class Russian-built diesel electric submarines.[88] Although this diesel-powered submarine has a short range, the Kilo class are considered among the quietest submarines in the world and as such pose a particularly dangerous threat to U.S. forces.[89] There has also been growing interest by the Chinese in purchasing Oscar-class cruise-missile-carrying submarines, armed with up to twenty-four cruise missiles each, to be used in swarm attacks against enemy ships. This strategy might also involve the use of the older Chinese diesel submarines as either decoys or a screen force to protect the advanced equipment.[90]

GROUND FORCES

Chinese ground forces number approximately 1.6 million and are reinforced by a reserve estimated at about 1.5 million, as well as by the People's Armed Police, which functions as an internal security force.[91] During the 1990s, China reduced its regular ground forces by about five hundred thousand. Since 1991, special emphasis has been given to establishing Special Operations Forces (SOFs) as about 20 percent of the ground forces. Each of China's twenty-four group armies includes a special operations battalion. The purpose of these troops would be sabotage and ambush operations behind enemy lines to include: "conducting reconnaissance, surveillance, locating or destroying C4I assets, transport nodes, and logistics depots, capturing or destroying airfields and ports, and destroying air defense facilities in the event of a military attack on Taiwan."[92] There are reports of a full-sized replica of one of Taiwan's major airfields having been constructed inside China so that Special Operations Forces can practice assaults to seize control of the airport.

The Chinese press describes the men of the Special Operations Forces in almost superhuman terms, capable of excellent camouflage and concealment, qualified in combat swimming and parachuting, much like the Special Operations forces of the Western world. State television regularly runs footage of these soldiers performing incredible feats normally seen in martial arts movies, such as breaking bricks with their heads or withstanding being run over by a jeep. Since China has a talent pool of over one-quarter of the world's population, it is quite likely that China will field many such commandos. Although there are continuing cuts in the legacy forces, there are indications that following the U.S. operations in Afghanistan and Iraq, the Chinese military leadership is reevaluating the structure of their ground forces.

Information Operations/Warfare

The military forces of Taiwan, the United States, Japan, and other advanced industrial powers are heavily dependent on highly complex electronic systems; including communications, radar, and electronic control devices of many kinds. The traditional Chinese approach to warfare from the time of Sun Tzu has emphasized the importance of "collecting, controlling, and manipulating information," and this, in combination with the contemporary idea of asymmetric warfare against more powerful, technologically advanced opponents, makes information warfare a natural focus of Chinese interest and development.[93] According to Stokes, the first book in this field was *Information Warfare,* written by a Chinese officer in 1985. Since then, but especially in the 1990s, information warfare and operations have been of major interest to the Chinese military and a major focus and priority for development. A forum of Chinese military experts in 1995 concluded that the development of information warfare weapons, which could "throw the financial systems and army command systems of the hegemonist into chaos" should be a major priority for the Chinese military.[94] The definition of information warfare is:

> All types of warfighting activities which affect the exploitation, alteration, and paralysis of the enemy's information and information systems, as well as those activities involved in protecting one's own information systems from exploitation, alteration, and paralysis by the enemy.[95]

Reflecting the high priority being given to this aspect of warfare, China established this as a separate branch of the military in the year 2000.

Already in 1991, the Chinese government made the development of its indigenous microelectronics and telecommunications sector its top priority. There was
recognition that dual-use microelectronics and telecommunications equipment
would assist both in economic and military modernization.[96] During the 1990s,
these sectors were the fastest-growing segment of China's economy, increasing at an
annual rate of about 30 percent.[97] According to Stokes, foreign companies "have
been key to China's initial successes in telecommunications technology. Leading
companies include Alcatel, Ericsson, Siemens, Nokia, Northern Telecom, AT&T,
Sprint, Motorola . . . [as well as] Hughes . . . Lockheed Martin, and Loral."[98]

While China's command, control, communications, computer, and intelligence
systems before 1991 were "disjointed and devoid of interconnectivity," by 1996 this
had changed dramatically, and China had "constructed ten of the largest networks in
the world . . . this rapid modernization is expected to continue and progress toward
informationalization [sic] has prompted some to assert that China has the potential
to become the world's most advanced telecommunications infrastructure."[99] In the
1990s, the capacity of the military communications network increased by a factor of
ten (that is by 1,000 percent). There was a significant investment in the security of
the military communications network, with four redundant networks being established by the end of the 1990s.[100] All this is designed to maintain the ability of China's
military and Party systems to function even under conditions of war. The Defense
Department concluded, "China's military national level command and control
communications are carried over multiple transmission systems . . . in order to create
a military communications system which is survivable, secure, flexible, mobile and
less vulnerable to exploitation, destruction or electronic attack."[101]

Looking at the offensive side, China is working diligently on computer attack
systems. The Department of Defense concluded that China in 2000 already had the
ability to "penetrate poorly protected U.S. computer systems and could potentially
use CNA [Computer Network Attack] against specific U.S. civilian and military
infrastructures and information networks. This antiaccess strategy is centered on
targeting operational centers of gravity, C4I centers [Command, Control,
Communications, Computers, and Intelligence] air bases, and aircraft carrier battle
groups located on the periphery of China.[102]

In March 2000, Admiral Dennis Blair, commander in chief of the U.S. Forces in
the Pacific Command, testified in Congress that the United States had a severe
vulnerability in the domain of its information systems. Admiral Blair summarized
this deficiency in the most technologically advanced military forces by saying, "Our
top warfighting deficiency is . . . inadequate theater C4 [Command, Control,
Communications, Computers]. Basic classified network access capacity [is] well
short of major theater war requirements."[103] He also pointed out that the Pacific
Command relies "heavily on strategic satellite communication."[104] A preview of

information attacks occurred during the times of tension over Taiwan in the 1990s when there were reports of hundreds of cases of computer attacks from Mainland China against Taiwan and from Taiwan against Mainland China. And in May 2001, the FBI reported that Chinese hackers "unlawfully defaced a number of U.S. Web Sites, replacing existing content with pro-Chinese or anti-U.S. rhetoric."[105]

Through a combination of reverse engineering, espionage, and purchases from Western companies, China is seeking to develop the most advanced technology to "improve its intercept, direction finding, and jamming capabilities."[106] In addition, China is developing an unmanned aerial vehicle that can be used for the "collection of electronic intelligence, reconnaissance, surveillance, and also as a platform for radio and radar jamming of opposing forces."[107] China also has the ability to interfere with satellite communications by using electronic facilities on its territory. Given China's allocation of $200 billion for the further development of dual-use telecommunications and their continued access to the most advanced Western and Russian technology, it is highly likely that the already well-developed capabilities of China in this domain will increase significantly year by year.[108]

China has also purchased foreign technologies and is developing its own in order to interfere with or destroy satellites. All modern military forces rely heavily on satellites for communication and for the positioning and guidance of many precision weapons. China is working on a variety of means to attack satellites from the ground, including high-energy lasers, which it has, and it also "may be developing jammers which could be used against global positioning system (GPS) receivers."[109] These kinds of capabilities could interfere with an opponent's weapons systems in a number of potentially decisive ways. At present, China can track most U.S. satellites for targeting purposes. It could destroy them by firing a ballistic missile or space-launch vehicles armed with a high explosive, electromagnetic, or nuclear weapons.[110]

Mutual Misjudgments: "Winning Victory with One Strike"

In November and December 1998, China conducted military maneuvers that simulated missile attacks on Taiwan and nuclear missile attacks on U.S. military forces in the Asia region. The simulated nuclear attacks against U.S. forces included those in South Korea, on Okinawa, and mainland Japan.[111] An experienced observer of Asia wrote that further Chinese military maneuvers in July and August 2000 demonstrated:

significant new firepower, coordination, and command and control capabilities ... the PLA's modernization and joint warfighting capabilities are developing at a rate far more rapid than the Pentagon's previous predictions. The Nanjing region exercises have showcased the PLA's new high tech capabilities, based on

U.S. military tactics and information technology and weapon systems purchased or stolen from the U.S., Russia, and Israel. The PLA's growing ballistic and cruise missile inventory; recently acquired Russian fighter aircraft and supersonic antiship missiles and information and electronic warfare pose an immediate, potent threat to Taiwan's military . . . the PLA boasts of "asymmetrical" 21st century weapon systems such as antisatellite and electromagnetic pulse weapon systems.[112]

These combined force military exercises were repeated in October 2000 and often since using coordinated attacks by the army, navy, air force, and ballistic missile services. These were the largest operations the PLA has ever undertaken, overshadowing the large-scale 1962 exercises held by Mao Zedong, which occurred the same year as the invasion of India. Jiang seemed to be putting himself in Mao's shoes by presiding over those exercises from the same compound in the Beijing suburbs from which Mao had commanded the 1962 exercises; Jiang also wore a Mao suit. Perhaps he intended to convey a Mao-like determination to take Taiwan.

These military exercises represented the enactment of the war plan that China delivered to the United States in August 1999. This included explicit threats of Chinese attack against U.S. forces if they should help Taiwan defend itself. There were also threats of a potential Chinese nuclear attack on the United States as a means of preventing the U.S. from using nuclear coercion to stop a Chinese attack on Taiwan or to prevent the United States from a major counterattack against Chinese bases on the mainland.

The issue is not whether China has attained Western levels of capability, but whether it has developed the military forces it feels will both guarantee success in its immediate offensive operations and either counter or deter the United States and its allies. We learn from Stokes that by the end of the 1990s, some Chinese military analysts believed they could establish air superiority over Taiwan "in 45 minutes or less."[113] A military conflict becomes more likely the more confident China is of rapid military success against Taiwan and the more confident China is that it could destroy U.S. Pacific forces and bases or deter the U.S. from coming to the assistance of Taiwan.

The scenario of a Chinese attack on Taiwan, as given in its 1999 war plan, was to begin with simultaneous attacks using missiles and information warfare against Taiwan's Command, Control Communications, Computers, and Intelligence, top leadership, naval and air bases—using four hundred or more ballistic missiles. This would be accompanied by warnings to the United States and other powers not to interfere and accompanied by threats to attack U.S. Asian-based forces if military aid was provided to Taiwan.

Dr. Michael Pillsbury has published two important collections of contemporary Chinese writing on military strategy and tactics. The recurrent theme is that the

United States does not have the will to sustain casualties or take the risks that China has made clear would be involved if the United States were to provide military aid to Taiwan.[114] Pillsbury informs us that Chinese military analysts have concluded that the United States has failed to exploit the new technology in warfare effectively. Chinese military analysts and officers continually cite the following problems in U.S. strategic planning: interservice rivalry, shortages in defense budgets, problems with technology, "laxity in sharing its military technology abroad," and ostensibly vulnerable U.S. information networks.[115]

Looking at U.S. military capabilities, Pillsbury notes that Chinese analysts continually argue that U.S. success in the 1991 Iraq war was due to mistakes of the Iraqi government. These included its failure to make surprise attacks on U.S. bases and its permitting the United States time to build up its logistics, as well as having failed to use harassing "special measures" such as commando attacks and other means against U.S. forces and their command and control structures.[116] Chinese analysts also point to a large number of shortcomings in deployed U.S. military forces including, in the Asian context, lack of means to transport forces to Asia, the inability of U.S. munitions to damage deep underground bunkers (of which China has many), and various weak areas that can be used to disable major U.S. weapons systems. For example, the Chinese military has analyzed the vulnerabilities of aircraft carriers in great detail.[117]

The Chinese regime and military leadership believe that the United States was defeated in Korea and in Vietnam. The regime believes that the United States is unwilling to accept any significant number of casualties in order to defend its interests in Asia, and, as the Department of Defense report concludes, in the event of U.S. involvement in a conflict involving China, the regime "would employ all means necessary in the hope of inflicting high casualties and weakening the intervening party's [the United States] resolve."[118]

In 1999, two Chinese military officers published a book entitled *Unrestricted Warfare*.[119] This book examines the strategy of asymmetric warfare based on striking at the weak points of an opponent and indicates, in the words of one of the authors, "The first rule of unrestricted warfare is that there are no rules, with nothing forbidden." This Chinese analysis of contemporary warfare proposes that China strike inside the territory of the United States using many means simultaneously in order to inflict serious harm on the population—many of their proposed actions involve the use of information warfare. The authors say that unrestricted warfare is the corollary of economic globalization and that "on this battlefield . . . the weapons are more advanced and the means more sophisticated . . . [but] it is just as brutal."[120]

In 1995, the U.S. Defense Science Board Task Force on Information Warfare reported to the president: "Because of its ever increasing dependence on information and information technology, the United States is one of the most vulnerable nations to information warfare attacks."[121] In an incisive and sobering analysis of how this might be used by China against the United States, Timperlake and Triplett point to the fact that computer control systems have become nearly ubiquitous in all major sectors of the American economy. As a result, they suggest that information war operations could inflict many types of very serious damage on the United States, including: disrupting the supply of power from major utilities; causing major fires and explosions in refineries, sewer systems, and natural gas pipelines; totally disrupting financial markets and transactions, including transferring funds out of bank accounts on a large scale; changing computer controls resulting in processed food provided for industry, restaurants, and hotels becoming toxic; and changing the potency of prescription drugs during manufacture "so that thousands of people could be poisoned."[122] Civilian deaths and injuries from such nearly invisible attacks, if mounted on a large scale, could easily reach many millions of persons. China is giving serious attention to this form of attack and to defending itself against such risks.

Chinese military analysts see the United States as weak. They believe that their threats to inflict massive casualties, strike at U.S. advance forces and bases in Asia, use information warfare attack, and strike first in a nuclear attack on U.S. cities would cause the United States to avoid or halt any military resistance to China's coercive actions in Taiwan (and probably the South China Sea thereafter).

At the same time, most U.S. military analysts view China as weak in terms of its operational forces. This can be seen in the Defense Department report that stated that while China's military communications were "survivable, secure, flexible, mobile, and less vulnerable to electronic exploitation and attack," that China never-theless does not have a command infrastructure "capable of controlling or directing military forces in a sophisticated, Western-style joint operating environment. . . . China still lags far behind Western standards for controlling joint operations."[123] The Defense Departments concluded that China "lacked the technology and logistical support to project and sustain conventional forces much beyond its borders."[124] In May 2003, the Council on Foreign Relations published a report concluding that the military in China was many years behind that of the United States.

In the view of skilled U.S. military analysts, the repeated underestimation of China's military capabilities in recent years reflects a normal tendency to "mirror image" the potential opponent.[125] As stated by Pillsbury, "American specialists who forecast future Chinese military backwardness [due to weapons systems limitations] are mirror imaged in Beijing by specialists who believe in the weaknesses of the United States military [due to a lack of political will]."[126] This mutual misperception and mutual underestimation significantly increases the risk of conflict given China's strategic purposes and Communist regime. As long as the United States continues to underestimate the threat from China, it will fail to take the corrective actions that could clearly and visibly increase the risks to China of beginning a conflict.

There is also a disturbing sense of time urgency in the August 1999 war plan of the Central Military Commission discussed earlier. There, the Chinese military leadership said, "Taking into account [the] possible intervention by the U.S. and based on the development strategy of our country, it is better to fight now than in the future—the earlier the better."[127] It is worth recalling that in 1941, another Asian country with a highly educated political and military leadership reached the judgment that if it attacked first, suddenly, and decisively, and sank the American fleet in the Pacific, the United States would no longer challenge its aggression across the wide Pacific Ocean. Japan was wrong at Pearl Harbor and the Chinese regime would be wrong if it believed that sinking U.S. naval ships and perhaps attacking U.S. forces and bases in the region would lead the United States to withdraw from Asia. Unfortunately, the historical analogy of Pearl Harbor appears to be lost on the Chinese, even after the terrible events of September 11th and the corresponding U.S. response. This type of blindness to the realities of U.S. cultural and political will could have devastating consequences for all parties involved.

Since 1990, as the economic relationship with the United States provided China with enormous benefits worth hundreds of billions of dollars, these parallel negative actions were underway: defining the United States as the main enemy, international aggression and threats, transferring weapons of mass destruction to state sponsors of terror hostile to the United States, and large-scale spying to obtain nuclear and weapon secrets from the United States. Now, China's efforts are focused on the extraction of militarily useful technology from the United States and U.S. corporations in China and a buildup of strategic nuclear missile forces targeted on Taiwan, U.S. forces in the Pacific Region, and the U.S. homeland. Perhaps the most important new aspect of Chinese policy, however, has been the establishment of a strategic alignment with Russia, which year by year has become more significant. We shall now explore the Russia-Chinese relationship and its implications for the future.

17 The New Russia/China Alignment

"The stronger China becomes the more peace and stability in the region will benefit."

—PRIMAKOV, Russian foreign minister, 1996

"China is Russia's Strategic partner and . . . number one foreign policy priority."

—PRESIDENT VLADIMIR PUTIN, July 18, 2000

China used the normalization of relations with the United States beginning in 1971 as a means of counterbalancing the Soviet Union, as the United States sought to use China for the same purpose. During the years of mutual hostility, the Chinese Communist regime described the Soviet Union in all international forums as a hegemonic power that wanted to rule the world and as the greatest danger to peace on earth. In Afghanistan, the United States and China were tacit allies in supporting the armed resistance against the Soviet-established Communist government in a conflict extending from 1978 through 1989.

In 1984, the post-Mao leadership in China and the post-Brezhnev leadership in the Soviet Union began discussions on the opening of relations. There had always been significant elements in the Communist parties of both countries that believed closer relations would better serve their political and national interests. In particular, the economic pragmatists surrounding Deng Xiaoping, including virtually the entire leadership of China during the 1990s, had long been involved in relations with the Soviet Union. Many spoke Russian, and they and China experts within the Soviet Union wanted to see the relationship reestablished. As a result, a joint commission to explore and facilitate economic trade and technological cooperation was established as a first step on the road toward normalization.

With Gorbachev's ascent to power in the Soviet Union in 1985, the military and KGB leadership first intensified Soviet efforts to defeat the armed resistance movements that were opposing newly established pro-Soviet regimes in Afghanistan, Africa, Central America, and Southeast Asia. As those efforts failed, and as Gorbachev sought to open the Soviet system, he and newly established pro-Soviet regimes agreed in negotiations on a number of withdrawals of Soviet Allied military forces, totaling about 320,000 troops.[1] From the viewpoint of Communist China, the withdrawal of Soviet troops from Afghanistan, Vietnamese troops from Cambodia, and Cuban troops from Africa opened the way for normalization with the Soviet Union.

The official visit of Gorbachev to Beijing in May 1989 marked the restoration of normal relations. This also included the reestablishment of relations between the two Communist parties and the beginning of limited Russian weapons sales to China. In the spring of 1990, Premier Li Peng, a hard-liner very interested in reestablishing relations with the Soviet Union, and Admiral Liu Huaqing, vice chairman of the Central Military Commission, visited Moscow to begin consultations on Russian military sales. Russia was willing to sell China weapons for hard currency but was careful not to provide weapons that might significantly enhance China's military capabilities against the Soviet Union.[2]

In 1991, Jiang Zemin, then general secretary of the Chinese Communist Party and chairman of the Central Military Commission, visited Moscow to negotiate an agreement demarcating a large part of the border about which there had been serious disputes. The Chinese leadership welcomed Gorbachev's efforts to normalize relations but was very concerned that his internal changes could lead to an unraveling of the regime in the Soviet Union, as had occurred in Eastern Europe in 1989 and 1990. They were very critical of Gorbachev for that reason, and in August 1991, China publicly supported the coup attempt against Gorbachev by Soviet hardliners.

The Chinese Communists did not want to see political liberalization in the Soviet Union. In their view, that could be very dangerous for their own continued rule. Second, they also felt a liberalizing Soviet regime would move closer to the West, especially the United States.

Russia and China: From Normalization to "Strategic Partnership"

In the first year of the Yeltsin administration, the primary purpose of the relationship with China was to ease tensions along the border and thereby reduce the sense of military threat and the possibility of conflict. This was a purpose shared by China, which welcomed Gorbachev's 1988 decision to end the Soviet military presence in Mongolia by 1992. China also said it would reduce conventional forces by half a million troops. Following eight rounds of negotiations on troop reductions along the border, Russia and China reached an agreement in 1992 that would reduce their troops and offensive weapons in a sixty-mile zone on either side of their border.[3] The first Russia-China summit in the post-Soviet era took place in

December 1992 when Yeltsin visited Beijing. There, Russia and China signed an agreement on "mutual relations," which included their joint renunciation of the use of force against each other and their promise not to enter into "military alliances directed against the other."[4]

A second reason for the Russia-China relationship was that Russia had a large number of advanced military weapons and military production capabilities that were not being utilized, and China wanted to build up its military forces. China also had ever-increasing hard-currency amounts from its trade surpluses. These weapon sales to China became more important economically and politically because Yeltsin's economic changes had led to enormous inflation and sharp reductions in production beginning in 1992. This, in turn, provided a basis for the strong Communist Party of the Russian Federation and the ultranationalist movement to oppose Yeltsin. To counterbalance the political pressures from the Communists, Yeltsin relied increasingly on the military and on compromise with the state industrial sector, especially the military production industries. These employed a significant proportion of Russian scientists and engineers and dominated the local economies in a number of regions of Russia. Therefore, arms sales to China not only provided income for Russia and employment for the military production sector, but also were a means for Yeltsin to strengthen his support among the military and its industrial allies, one of what we have called his three "pillars of power."

The December 1992 Russia-China summit led to agreements on the sale of a number of Russian weapons systems to China, including jet fighter aircraft.[5] In June 1993, Admiral Liu Huaqing, vice chairman of the Central Military Commission, led a high-ranking military delegation to Russia. As the Russian economic crisis deepened, and as Yeltsin faced implacable Communist opposition in the parliament, the political and economic benefits for the Yeltsin administration of military sales to China increased. In the first few years, 1992 to 1995, official estimates are that roughly $500 million in armaments were sold to China annually, though experts estimate that weapon sales totaled $1.3 billion.[6] In September and October 1993, Yeltsin dissolved the Communist-dominated Parliament and faced an armed insurrection by Communists and their sympathizers. He was able to contain and end this only with the support of the Russian military. That increased his political dependence on this pillar of his power. The December 1993 parliamentary election resulted in a large proportion of votes for the Communist Party and the ultranationalists, giving them a near majority of Parliament. This again made it important for Yeltsin to have the support of the Russian military and the military production organizations.

The 1994 Russia-China summit was held in Moscow, with newly installed President Jiang visiting Yeltsin. They agreed on a "constructive partnership" that included commitments that neither would use nuclear weapons first against the other and that there would be no targeting of the other with strategic nuclear weapons. Further, they agreed on virtually all border demarcation issues.[7] Then, beginning in the spring of 1994, a series of regular working meetings were established between the premiers of Russia and China, who would meet approximately twice annually from then on, and also between the leadership of the parliaments of China and Russia. These exchanges, while focused on domestic matters such as increasing trade, regulating customs duties, and trade, also provided a means for the Chinese Communist Party to broaden its relationship with key individuals inside the Yeltsin government. At the same time, the relationship between the Chinese Parliament, a rubber stamp of the Communist Party, and the Russian parliament, where the Russian Communists had a plurality, established another link between the Communists of Russia and China that would become stronger year by year. In many respects, the institutional form of the relationship between Russia and China began to replicate that which had existed during the Sino-Soviet alliance from 1949 to 1960.

In May 1995, President Jiang again visited Moscow. The occasion was the fiftieth-anniversary celebration of the victory in World War II, and he was one among many foreign dignitaries present. However, Presidents Yeltsin and Jiang had a private informal summit meeting. At its conclusion, President Jiang said that the two countries had agreed to establish "a constructive Sino-Russian partnership."[8] At this time, in Yeltsin's fourth year as president of Russia, the strong Russian Communist opposition and the ultranationalists continued their criticism of his government for being too close to the United States and too subservient to the West. Russian Communists and ultranationalists continually pointed to Communist China as an example of economic success and reform from which the Yeltsin government should learn as the Russian economy continued to perform poorly. For Yeltsin, the relationship with China was a way of countering these allegations and criticisms of Russian subservience to the West.

In the December 1995 parliamentary elections, the Russian Communist Party increased its plurality with a few allies and essentially controlled the *Duma* (the lower house). The Russian Communist Party fully expected to move from that electoral success to winning the powerful presidency of the Russian Federation in the presidential elections scheduled for June 1996. Yeltsin was at a very low point in the opinion polls, and his political movement was greatly concerned that the Communists would succeed in winning the Russian presidency. Part of the strategy used by Yeltsin to increase support for his government was to appoint the head of foreign intelligence, Yevgenny Primakov, as foreign minister. Having worked against the West for years in the Middle East as a Soviet Party official, Primakov favored taking a far more assertive position against the United States and the West on a number of issues. This included greater international political cooperation with

China. This was formalized when Yeltsin visited Beijing in April 1996. He and president Jiang jointly declared that they were now establishing a "strategic partnership of mutual coordination." The joint Yeltsin-Jiang statement also criticized "hegemonism, power politics, and repeated imposition of pressures on other countries ... [and] new manifestations of bloc politics."[9] These critical statements were directed against the United States. It was the first time that Yeltsin and the Russian government used the same language of criticism that China had been using for some years. This marked the beginning of the change from Russian-Chinese normalization to their alignment against the United States. The April 1996 summit also included a near doubling of Russian military sales to China. Some months later, Foreign Minister Primakov said that "the stronger China becomes, the more peace and stability in the region will benefit."[10]

In March 1996, Presidents Yeltsin and Clinton held a cordial summit meeting in Moscow. The United States had played a major role in obtaining a special IMF loan package of nearly $10 billion for Russia, which could contribute both to improving the Russian economy and to Yeltsin's reelection prospects. Yeltsin believed that the declaration of a "strategic partnership with China" also contributed to his prospects in the coming presidential election and helped to counter criticisms from the Communists and ultranationalists. The additional military sales to China helped the Russian economy and increased Yeltsin's support in the Russian military and the military production complex. This involved no problems with the United States, since the Clinton administration was talking about a "strategic partnership" with China at the same time, an example of how a self-deceptive slogan can have negative effects.

At the conclusion of the April 1996 summit in Beijing, Presidents Yeltsin and Jiang traveled to Shanghai where they met with the presidents of Kazakhstan, the Kyrgyz Republic, and Tajikistan. China was interested in having these former Soviet republics accept the Russia-China demarcation of the border as mutually agreed, in order to end disputes from the Soviet era. China was also interested in a broadened economic relationship with the Central Asian republics, some of which had significant supplies of energy, which China might want to obtain in the future. China wanted to involve Russia as a partner in these discussions, perhaps so that there would be no suspicions on the Russian side of Chinese purposes in seeking to establish closer relationships with the Central Asian countries. This meeting led to an agreement on "confidence building in the military field and in the border areas in the People's Republic of China" and began a process of regular meetings among the "Shanghai Five" that would continue into the future.

Following Yeltsin's successful reelection in June 1996, he was frequently absent for many months as a result of severe health problems. In that context, Foreign Minister Primakov used the opportunity to exert ever-greater influence on Russian foreign policy. Primakov agreed with elements of the military as well as the Communists and ultranationalists that the enlargement of NATO being discussed by the United States and its NATO allies potentially posed a threat to Russia and represented an effort to weaken Russia in the world. For Primakov, a closer relationship with China, which constantly criticized American "hegemonism," was a useful means of seeking to counterbalance the U.S. and the possibility of NATO enlargement. In October 1996, President Clinton announced his decision that the United States would support the admission of three Eastern European countries— Poland, Hungary, and the Czech Republic—to NATO, and that this would likely occur on the fiftieth anniversary of NATO's founding, in April 1999. The Russian government immediately expressed its strong objections.

A telling episode in the development of the Russia-China relationship occurred in the winter of 1996–1997. During a monthly news conference, Minister of Defense Igor Rodionov indicated that Communist China should be considered one of the countries potentially threatening Russia and the other members of the Confederation of Independent States. The Russian Foreign Ministry immediately publicly reprimanded the Russian Defense Minister for this statement, as did a spokesman for President Yeltsin; subsequently, in January 1997, the Russian defense minister "sent an official message to the Russian Armed Forces praising Sino-Soviet relations and disavowing his earlier statement."[11]

The following month, the Russian prime minister visited the United States seeking to persuade the administration not to go forward with NATO enlargement. In the course of his discussion of possible Russian responses, he indicated that Russia might significantly increase its military forces. Those talks were unsuccessful, and in April 1997, President Jiang visited President Yeltsin in Moscow for their fourth formal summit meeting. They issued a joint declaration that included their intention "to promote a multipolarization of the world and the establishment of a new international order . . . no country should seek hegemony, practice power politics while monopolizing international affairs."[12]

This marked a further important change in tone for Russia, which now seemed to fully endorse the Chinese view of international politics and joined China in criticizing the United States for an alleged intent to dominate the world. Russian military sales to China increased further, and there are reports that at this 1997 summit Yeltsin agreed to sell China two to four Russian *Sovremmeny*-class destroyers, each of which would be equipped with twenty-four nuclear-capable supersonic antiship missiles, a weapons system specifically designed to attack U.S. aircraft carriers and their accompanying Aegis equipped naval escorts.[13] Despite the fact that Russian economic policy in 1997 and 1998 was in the hands of individuals viewed as pro-Western and market-oriented reformers, and that Russia and the United States had agreed in May 1997 on a consultative mechanism for Russia in matters of NATO policy —a "voice but not a veto"—the movement toward the Chinese view of the world by Russia was pronounced and significant but ignored by the United States.[14]

A second meeting of the "Shanghai Five" followed the April 1997 Russia-China summit. These countries agreed on "mutual reductions of military forces in the border areas," a further step toward confidence building and political cooperation.[15]

The fifth formal Russia-China summit took place in Beijing in November 1997. Yeltsin and Jiang declared that the 1991 agreement on their eastern border demarcation had been implemented fully and that they would complete work on the Western border in the near future. Their joint statement focused on new domains of bilateral cooperation, to include large-scale supplies of Russian natural gas, oil, and nuclear energy to China. It was also agreed that Russia would help China by providing "state of the art high technology for production and basic research" in a number of areas, including military technology.[16] The agreements on Russian energy exports involved plans for a Russian pipeline from Eastern Siberia to China and permission for China to exploit a gas field in Russia. This would help China meet its energy needs and provide an additional source of hard-currency earnings for Russia.

By May 1998, the international political alignment of Russia and China became visible in one crisis point after another. Russia and China supported the Iraqi regime in resisting the requirements for effective UN inspection of its dismantling of weapons of mass destruction. Russia and China jointly supported the Communist dictatorship of Milosevic in the former Yugoslavia as it sought to help its allies evade the provisions of the Dayton Accords and various UN Security Council resolutions. Russia and China both transferred weapons of mass destruction and other weapons systems to Iraq, Iran, and other countries hostile to the United States, while the United States sought to restrict this process. In many respects, Foreign Minister Primakov was reviving patterns of Soviet activity in the Middle East in support of Iraq, Iran, Syria, and Libya that he had helped establish during the 1980s.[17] For Russia and China, the sales of weapons to these countries provided a useful means for increasing their hard currency earnings—both had sold weapons to Iran and Iraq during the 1980–88 war. Strengthening these regimes hostile to the United States was again viewed as being in Russia's interest as part of the strategy to counterbalance the United States. These actions were a key of the new Russia-China alignment.

As this was occurring, the United States continued to provide bilateral economic assistance to Russia. In the summer of 1998, as it approached a severe financial crisis, the United States helped Russia obtain an emergency financial assistance package from the IMF and Japan totaling nearly $18 billion. Despite this, in August of 1998, the Russian currency was sharply devalued and Russia experienced severe economic contraction as foreign investment declined sharply. The savings of many Russian citizens once again became worthless, as had occurred in the sharp inflation of 1992–1995. The Russian economic crisis resulted in strong criticisms of the Yeltsin administration from both the Communists and ultranationalists. They contended that the pro-Western reformers had failed and that this new sharp economic setback for Russia was the result of deliberate efforts by the West, and especially the United States, to weaken Russia.

The Russian economic crisis brought the removal of the pro-Western reformers and led to Primakov becoming prime minister in September 1998. Reflecting Primakov's growing power, the sixth Yeltsin-Jiang summit held in Moscow in November 1998 included Primakov in a number of discussions. These two presidents took positions on a large number of international issues ranging from the Balkans to South Asia, where Pakistan and India had both tested nuclear weapons in May 1998. They declared that their strategic partnership was "neither an alliance nor directed at a third country." At the same time, they raised a new issue in opposition to the United States by expressing their view of the "great importance of maintaining and ... restricting the antimissile defense system."[18] Russian suspicions were expressed by the minister of defense, who said in June 2000:

> The true reasons for deploying the U.S. national missile defense do not lie in imaginary threats from certain pariah countries. Apparently some people in the United States are in the grip of a temptation to acquire strategic dominance by means of increasing the technological gulf between them and the rest of the world in creating exceptional conditions of invulnerability that is implementing the forgotten doctrine of fortress America.[19]

THE RUSSIA-CHINA ALIGNMENT INTENSIFIES, 1999

In the fall of 1998, the Saddam Hussein regime ended its reluctant, partial compliance with UN Security Council resolutions requiring inspections and monitoring to assure that Iraq was not producing weapons of mass destruction or the means to deliver them. The United States sought to apply pressure on Saddam Hussein, while Russia and China opposed this in the UN Security Council and sought to have the sanctions on Iraq lifted. In December 1998, the United States and the United Kingdom launched a series of air strikes against military targets to pressure Iraq into compliance. China and Russia adamantly opposed these military strikes.

In the former Yugoslavia, beginning in February 1998, Milosevic had begun to move military and paramilitary forces into Kosovo. The United States sought action by the UN Security Council to prevent Milosevic from undertaking yet another campaign of military assault, forced deportation, and "ethnic cleansing" of the type which since 1990 had resulted in the loss of hundreds of thousands of lives and the displacement of millions of people in the former Yugoslavia. Again, Russia and

China jointly opposed the United States in the UN Security Council. As tens of thousands of Milosevic's military and paramilitary forces moved into Kosovo and forced hundreds of thousands of Albanians to flee, the United States and the NATO decided to use force to prevent the future loss of life and forced deportations. NATO air strikes began in late March 1999 and continued for several months.

President Clinton cited as the basis for this action, which was not authorized by the UN Security Council, the prevention of crimes against humanity (forcible deportation and mass murder of civilians). He said the NATO countries believed humanitarian concerns could override national sovereignty and permit intervention within countries to act, even with UN Security Council authorization. Russia and China strongly disagreed with this, and both were concerned that this type of U.S./NATO military intervention on behalf of the Muslim Kosovars could set a precedent. Russia was concerned about Chechnya, where it had fought a war against Muslim separatists from 1994 to 1996 and where it faced the possibility of a revival of that war or other separatist movements. China was concerned about the precedent set for intervention if it decided to use force against Taiwan, which it defined as an internal issue, or against Tibetans, Muslims, or other minority groups within China.

Within Russia, the Communist opposition stridently demanded that Yeltsin send Russian air and combat forces to help Milosevic against NATO. Clearly such actions could have risked expanding the crisis, perhaps bringing both powers to the brink of a nuclear war. Fortunately, as previously discussed, Yeltsin made the decision not to escalate Russian involvement and helped to bring about the withdrawal of Serbian forces from Kosovo. In moving toward negotiation rather than confrontation, Yeltsin removed Prime Minister Primakov and appointed former Prime Minister Chernomyrdin as a special envoy for Russia.

The accidental bombing of the Chinese Embassy in Belgrade, Yugoslavia, by the United States on May 7, 1999, produced a furious reaction by China. The Chinese government orchestrated mobs that attacked the U.S. Embassy and other facilities in China. This was followed by the beginning of another aspect of the Russia-Chinese alignment—the stage of crisis consultation—and expanded Russian weapons sales to China. Special Envoy Chernomyrdin visited China on May 10–11, 1999 to discuss the "NATO bombing of the Chinese Embassy . . . and the question of Kosovo."[20] While we do not know exactly what was discussed, it is reasonable to surmise, given subsequent actions, that Chernomyrdin informed the Chinese that Russia would move toward a negotiated outcome in the former Yugoslavia but that Russia would be willing to sell China a large number of advanced weapons systems that it had been holding back until that time. Russian Foreign Minister Ivanov visited China for further consultations on June 1–3, 1999.

Then, from June 7 –15, 1999, General Zhang Wannian, vice chairman of the Central Military Commission, went to Russia with a delegation of senior Chinese military officials for talks on expanding military and technological cooperation. Subsequently, General Zhang was permitted to visit a number of secret Russian military facilities, including air force/air defense command facilities and a strategic rocket-forces base, where he was shown a Topal SS-25 intercontinental ballistic missile and told how it could overcome the missile defenses of a "potential foe."[21] This new phase in Russian-Chinese strategic consultation and Russian military sales occurred at the same time that Yeltsin met in Europe as a member of the industrial democracies Group of Eight, where he received commitments for further economic assistance from the West.

The leaders of Russia, China, Kazakhstan, Kyrgyzstan, and Tajikistan held another meeting toward the end of August 1999. As he arrived for that meeting, Yeltsin bluntly told the press that he was "in fighting form, ready for battle, especially with Westerners . . . the current summit is taking place in conditions of an aggravated international situation. Some nations are trying to build a world that would be convenient only for them ignoring that the world is multipolar."[22] Yeltsin and Jiang used the "Shanghai Five" meeting as an occasion to meet alone for further discussion. The final statement issued by the five countries essentially repeated the major themes of Chinese foreign policy during the 1990s, indicating that not only Russia but also the three Central Asian countries were now in agreement with Chinese views on these issues. It is important to note that the three Central Asian republics involved in these meetings had all essentially followed the "Chinese model" in maintaining politically authoritarian regimes while seeking to open their economies somewhat and obtain Western investment and economic aid. The Central Asian presidents were all former Communist rulers who had renamed their parties as nationalist and essentially prevented any genuine political competition. In the case of Tajikistan, there had been a restoration to power of the former Communist Party of the Soviet era.

In their joint statement, all five countries said they "are faithful to the principle of respecting human rights stipulated in the UN charter and other international documents pointing out that in implementing the principle, the sovereign countries characteristics must be taken into consideration. Human rights must not be used as a pretext for interfering in other countries internal affairs."[23] This formulation was intended to make clear their joint opposition to the principle enunciated by the United States, that in cases of extreme abuses of human rights, intervention for humanitarian reasons could be done. The formulation in this statement is typical of the Chinese view that it can endorse the "principle of respect for human rights" but reject any evaluation of their behavior by third parties, since every country must determine for itself how its "characteristics" have to be "taken into account."

The August 1999 joint statement also endorsed "multipolarism" and condemned "nationalist splitism and religious extremism."[24] This particular condemnation was aimed at any Muslim or other separatist groups that might challenge the authority of any of these regimes. Russia was at that time moving toward the second Chechen war, and China continued to be concerned about Taiwan, Tibet, and the Muslim Uygurs in Xinjiang. As a sign that relations among the five countries were moving from what had begun as confidence-building measures along the borders and military reductions to broader strategic cooperation, the joint statement also agreed that there would be regular meetings among the foreign ministers and defense ministers of the five countries.[25] China was beginning to move the Shanghai Five into a group of countries endorsing its main foreign policy purposes and perspectives.

Following that summit, there were reports of expanded Russian military sales to China. These included $1 billion for the sale by Russia of two nuclear-powered attack submarines (*Akula* class) and $2 billion for advanced fighter aircraft (Su-30 MKK).[26] One report by two experts who have studied Russian military sales to China in great depth, contends that in the fall of 1999 Russia also agreed that it would transfer to China two of its ballistic-missile submarines (*Typhoon* class), each of which carried twenty submarine-launched ballistic missiles armed with ten nuclear warheads.[27] The report's authors do not say this has occurred, but such a transfer of military capability from Russia to China, whether by sale or lease, would be dramatic in its impact on Chinese military capabilities.

Allowing for the time required for Chinese crews to be trained in all facets of submarine and missile operations, this type of Russian military sale to China could have, in effect, provided China with four hundred nuclear warheads by 2002, which could reach any point in the United States when launched from those ballistic-missile submarines. The same authors also report that at the August 1999 summit, Russia agreed to provide air-defense weapons to China (A-300 antimissile and anti-aircraft) and discussed the establishment of a joint air defense system with China.[28] Russian Foreign Minister Ivanov echoed his mentor Primakov's 1996 statement by commenting at the end of the 1999 summit, "The closer relations are between Russia and China, the more stable the world."[29]

In August and September 1999, a series of events including bombs placed in several civilian apartment buildings, led the Yeltsin government to use large-scale military force in an effort to totally suppress the armed separatists in Chechnya. To lead this effort, Yeltsin choose a former KGB official, Vladimir V. Putin, as prime minister. Russian military attacks in Chechnya used overwhelming force, irrespective of consequences for the civilian population in Chechnya. At the same time, the Russian military promulgated a new military doctrine, which said that Russia would resort to the use of its nuclear weapons "to repel armed aggression." This is in contrast to the earlier doctrine that said nuclear weapons would only be used if the existence of Russia were at risk.[30]

Simultaneously, from October to December 1999, Russia launched seven strategic nuclear missiles in tests to demonstrate that its formidable nuclear arsenal still was functioning and effective.[31] The tests included nuclear missiles launched from a Delta submarine on October 1 and 2, 1999; an SS-18 ICBM launched on October 20, 1999; the November 3, 1999 testing of short-range antimissile systems in Kazakhstan; two additional nuclear missiles fired from submarines on November 17, 1999; and the firing of a Topol-M ICBM on December 14, 1999, with Prime Minster Putin, Minister of Defense Igor Sergeiev, and the commander of the Strategic Rocket Forces at the launch site, "to emphasize the importance of the event to the rest of the world."[32] The Russian regime clearly was intent on demonstrating to the United States and NATO countries that there should be no interference in its internal affairs, irrespective of their views about Russian military actions in Chechnya. Putin said after the launch that Russia would use "all diplomatic and military-political leverage" to deal with Western criticisms of Chechnya.

The United States and the Western powers did not question the right of Russia to end an armed rebellion on its territory. However, after the president of France and the German Chancellor criticized the brutality of the methods used in Chechnya, Yeltsin canceled a scheduled December 1999 meeting with them.[33] On December 6, 1999, President Clinton also publicly criticized the Russian military operation for causing unnecessary civilian casualties. This was followed the next day by the Chinese Foreign Ministry announcing its full support for the Russian military campaign as an effort to prevent national disintegration.

On December 9, 1999, Yeltsin arrived in Beijing for his seventh (and last) formal summit meeting with President Jiang. He spoke to the media quite deliberately and loudly:

> President Clinton permitted himself to put pressure on Russia. It seems he has for a minute forgotten that Russia has a full arsenal of nuclear weapons....It has never been and never will be the case that he will dictate to the whole world how to live....A multipolar world—that is the basis for everything. We will dictate to the world. Not him, not him alone."[34]

Russian Foreign Minister Igor Ivanov followed that dramatic statement with the announcement that "President Jiang said he completely understood and fully supported Russia's actions in combating terrorism and extremism from Chechnya."[35] A Foreign Ministry spokesman for the Chinese added that China has "taken note of the fact that in the Chechnya action, the Russian side has tried to avoid civilian losses as much as it can."[36] The next day, in an article published in a Russian military newspaper, Russian Defense Minister Igor Sergeiev said that Russia would use nuclear weapons to protect its interests. This was reported in one Russian newspaper under the headline, "The Iron Curtain Falls Again."[37]

In Washington, DC, President Clinton's response to Yeltsin's remarks was that "we can't get too serious about that."[38] This apparently reflected the view that both Yeltsin's threatening comments and the recent decision by Russia to reunify with Belarus, which was ruled by a restored Communist regime, were all part of the actions Yeltsin was taking to demonstrate Russian strength and nationalism in order to compete more effectively with the Communists and ultranationalists in the coming parliamentary elections. In Beijing, Yeltsin and Jiang issued another joint statement listing many domains of cooperation and their "determination to take coordinated actions and oppose any threat to global stability." They also agreed to expedite bilateral cooperation in a number of areas, such as advanced technology, communications, engineering, and electronics, all of which could help China's military modernization and buildup.[39]

The Communists retained their plurality and near dominance of the lower house of parliament in the December 1999 election. Once again, they hoped to win the Russian presidential election the next year. Apparently to prevent this, on the last day of the century and millennium, Yeltsin resigned as president of Russia and, as specified by the Constitution, Putin became acting president. Putin then won the presidential election in March 2000 and was inaugurated as president of Russia in May 2000.

As acting president and then as elected president, Putin initially kept the minister of defense and foreign minister who had worked so closely with Primakov in previous years. Putin also continued the dual strategy that Russia had adopted since 1996, continuing to preserve normal relations with the United States and the Western countries in order to maintain a flow of international economic assistance and investment on one hand, while at the same time moving closer to China in strategic and military cooperation. This Russian policy was explicitly reflected in the formal statement of Russian foreign policy doctrine signed by President Putin on July 10, 2000. This document stated that the essence of Russia's foreign policy would be "pragmatism," and that the fundamental purpose of Russian foreign policy would be to "effectively help solve domestic tasks" by promoting economic growth.[40]

China had successfully pursued this double approach in foreign policy. It sought permanent normal trade relations with the United States and welcomed the support of the Clinton administration in persuading the U.S. House and Senate to approve this in May and September 2000. At the same time, the Chinese leadership sought to expand its strategic, political and military cooperation with Russia and continually spoke out against its view of the alleged U.S. intention to dominate international politics. The Russian foreign policy doctrine of July 2000 also used virtually the language used by China when it stated that Russia sought a "multipolar" world rather than "the unipolar structure of the world with the economic and power domination of the United States."[41]

THE NORTH KOREAN STRATAGEM

During the early months of the Putin era, international events involving North Korea illustrated how Russia and China work together to advance their shared strategic purposes. One of the threats cited by the Clinton administration, giving rise to the need for a limited national missile defense and an Asian missile defense, has been concern about North Korea's development of nuclear weapons and long-range missiles. The following events seem to be the result of Russian and Chinese decisions to provide incentives for the North Korea Communist regime to reduce its appearance of danger and aggressiveness, as a means of undercutting the U.S. contention that emerging North Korean missile capability necessitates a national and Asian missile defense system.

China and North Korea, two Asian Communist regimes that fought the United States in Korea (1950–1953), have had military-strategic relations for decades. As already discussed, China's transfer of components for North Korea's missile program and both countries' ties to the Khan network suggest that North Korea is a partner in China's proliferation of weapons of mass destruction to other regimes hostile to the United States.

However, since 1978, the closed North Korean dictatorship had not followed China's example of opening its economy, instead keeping its Stalin-era command economy. In 1999, China invited a high-level North Korean delegation to view the positive results China had obtained through its economic strategy. China's president told the North Koreans that economic development "is an absolute necessity" and that economic resources were essential for a country to be internationally powerful.[42] China then began providing additional economic and technical aid to its North Korean ally.

In 1992, Yeltsin ended the security relationship that the Soviet Union had with North Korea. With the ascent of Putin to the presidency, Russian Foreign Minister Igor Ivanov visited Pyongyang in February 2000 and concluded a friendship agreement in which both sides pledged not to take "any action or step . . . against the sovereignty, independence or territorial integrity" of the other.[43] Since Russia had relations with democratic South Korea, this was interpreted as a Russian guarantee to North Korea that it would not participate in any effort to encourage or bring about a German-type reunification in democracy.[44]

In May 2000, the North Korean "Great Leader" Kim Jong-Il made a secret visit to China for three days, during which both sides reached "important consensus" on many issues of mutual concern.[45] Most likely, this was the occasion for China to promise that both Russia and China would guarantee the continued rule of the Communist regime and would provide economic and military assistance to make the North Korean military even more powerful—provided that North Korea participated in a "peace process" designed to remove the appearance of its posing a nuclear or missile threat against the United States and its Asian allies, especially Japan and South Korea.

In early June 2000, presidents Clinton and Putin met in Moscow. Putin, in Clinton's words, agreed "there is an emerging ballistic missile threat that must be addressed" but disagreed with the U.S. intention to deploy even a limited national missile defense.[46] Putin then immediately left for Western Europe, where he opposed the U.S. approach to missile defense and suggested that Russia work with Europe and NATO to create a joint missile defense system for Europe.[47] On June 14, 2000, German Chancellor Schroeder met with Putin and said that Germany was establishing a new "strategic partnership" with Russia. At the same time, Putin said that he was visiting Germany, in part, because of "the special place Germany, its people and its culture have in my heart." There he continued his efforts to have NATO allies oppose the U.S. national missile defense plan.[48] Putin also sought the rescheduling of payments due on the Russian debt, 60 percent of which it owed to Germany.[49]

These Russian overtures in Europe coincided with North Korea's invitation to the democratically elected president of South Korea to visit for a summit meeting, ostensibly intended to begin a process of reconciliation. After years of North Korean isolation, vituperation, probing actions, and threats in the context of its forward deployment for sudden attack, the summit meeting was held in North Korea on June 14, 2000. It was not only cordial, but also led to agreements on first steps toward reconciliation, including limited visits among divided families and further discussions.[50] This summit meeting led many in South Korea and among the democracies to hope that a new era might be at hand.

Before the North-South Korea summit meeting, Putin announced that he would visit North Korea in July 2000. This would be the first such visit by a Soviet or Russian head of state. Following the North-South summit, the United States announced that it would drop economic sanctions against North Korea, and on June 22, 2000, North Korea promised to "stop flight testing its long-range missile."[51] A few days later, North Korea was admitted as a member of the Asian Regional Forum, where regional governments sought to promote cooperation and defuse conflict.

There are a number of indications that North Korea's actions are a stratagem intended to use the prospect of "peace and reconciliation" as a means to its former purposes. When its new approach to South Korea and apparent forbearance on missile testing did not quickly result in a U.S. decision to cancel both missile defenses, a senior North Korean official said on July 12, 2000, "The United States has no right to make such unjust claims for the freezing of our missile capabilities," since the U.S. has deployed "thousands of missiles" that threaten North Korea.[52] When Putin visited North Korea on July 19, 2000 (the day after his summit with

Jiang in Beijing), he received a promise that North Korea would not test any more long-range missiles if another country would provide assistance in launching its satellites.

However, some weeks later North Korean sources were reported as saying this offer was, in fact, a "joke." In negotiations with the U.S. a few days before Putin's visit, the North Korean regime had repeated officially its offer to stop exporting missile technology only if it would be paid $1 billion annually, "for our economic and political losses in case of suspension." The American negotiator said the North Koreans should not be paid for ending proliferation activities that "they should not be conducting in the first place."[53]

A few months after the June 2000 Korean summit, the defense ministers of North and South Korea met, the second-ranking North Korean official visited the United States, and President Clinton agreed to visit North Korea. Yet an analysis by the Department of Defense reportedly found that though North and South Korea had held discussions about family visits (under highly controlled conditions in the North), about "confidence building measures," and about opening one highway and one railroad connection, there was in North Korea "no evidence of economic reform, of reform minded leaders, of a reduction in the military or a lessening of anti-U.S. rhetoric."[54] Also indicative that the North Korean regime remained much the same was its response to inquiries from Japan about the fate of Japanese citizens, including adolescent girls, whom North Korean defectors said were kidnapped by the regime to be used to train North Korean infiltrators and spies in the Japanese language. (It is estimated that ten persons have been kidnapped from Japan and four hundred from South Korea).[55] The North Korean response in October 2000 was, "Japanese politicians . . . [should] feel ashamed of their crime-woven past and present and should stop talking about 'suspected kidnappings,' a by-product of their anti-Korean policies."[56] Over the next months, North Korea remained threatening in its military deployment and mostly hostile in its statements toward the U.S. and neighboring countries, except China and Russia.

Today the Communist regime in North Korea continues in power and remains a close ally of China. As the Chinese have said, North Korea and China are "as close as lips and teeth." North Korea maintains a million-strong army, which is deployed for a sudden invasion of democratic South Korea. North Korea's "missile, chemical, and germ warfare programs threaten Japan, India, and American friends and allies in the Middle East." North Korea is also developing long-range ballistic missiles that could reach U.S. territory and, in 2003, admitted to developing nuclear weapons.

Initially within the framework of the six-party talks was the potential that the Chinese and Russians would work honestly toward a reasonable solution to the issue of the North Korean nuclear weapons program. Unfortunately, as the talks continued, there were increasing indications that not only were the Russians following the lead of the Chinese, but also that the Chinese were not truly interested in the denuclearization of the Korean peninsula if it maintained the status quo within the U.S.-Asia-Pacific security relationship. If the Chinese and, to a lesser extent, the Russians truly wanted to see the end of the North Korean program, they could use their influence to encourage the North Koreans to accept a fair offer on behalf of the U.S., South Korean, and Japanese delegations. Instead, it appears that the Chinese are using the negotiations as part of an overall strategy to accomplish their stated goal of eventually ending all U.S. strategic alliances within the region, rather than to further the global interests of the threat of a nuclear North Korea.

PUTIN AT THE RUSSIA-CHINA SUMMITS

In early July 2000, China, Russia, and three Central Asian states held another summit meeting of the "Shanghai Five plus Uzbekistan" in Dushanbe, the capital of Tajikistan. There they issued a joint declaration pledging further political cooperation and condemning "international terrorism," meaning the various Muslim armed groups opposing their regimes. The participants also discussed expanding this Eurasian coalition to include Uzbekistan (which also attended the meeting), Iran (where Jiang visited at the end of June 2000), and possibly India.[57] While the Russian minister of defense accompanied Putin, Jiang brought only economic planners and foreign ministry personnel—indicating that, for China, this group was not yet a focus for military planning or cooperation.

On July 18, 2000, Presidents Putin and Jiang held their first formal summit meeting in Beijing, the eighth Russia-China summit since 1992. Before that meeting, Putin had told the Chinese press that "China is Russia's strategic partner and . . . number one foreign policy priority" and that he frequently speaks with Jiang on the telephone (Jiang speaks Russian as a result of his studies in the Soviet Union).[58] Presidents Jiang and Putin jointly stated that Russia and China had agreed to "push toward a global, multipolar process and establish a new political and economic order."[59] This was the first time that Russia had associated itself with this often repeated and somewhat ambiguous Chinese purpose of bringing about "a new political and economic order." Clearly, Putin was ready to move the Russia-China alignment to what Jiang called a "new stage" of even closer strategic cooperation.

This was reflected in the two joint statements issued, as well as by the fact that the Russian delegation included the Russian minister of defense and senior officials involved in arms exports and advanced weapons production. The "Antimissile Joint Statement" said that the purpose of U.S. missile defenses "is to seek unilateral military and security advantages" and that "implementing the plan will have the most grave adverse consequences not only for the security of Russia, China . . . but also for the security of the United States and global strategic stability."[60]

The joint "Beijing Declaration" repeated and gave emphasis to the points made at the December 1999 Russia-China summit and also added important commitments, such as that both countries "support all of each other's efforts to safeguard national unity," not just peaceful efforts; and, concerning Taiwan, both agreed that "no outside force should be allowed to interfere in resolving the Taiwan issue."[61] They also said that "military-related technology cooperation . . . represents a major orientation for expanding and deepening the Sino-Russian strategic cooperation partnership."[62]

According to a report published in Hong Kong, China's Foreign Minister Qian Qichen, in briefing senior Chinese officials on the Russia-China summit, said that "Putin pledged to unreservedly support China on the Taiwan issue and that if foreign forces became involved, Russia would make a military response and in addition increase its supplies of weapons to China."[63] This ostensibly occurred during a secret two-hour discussion at the summit. This report may or may not be true. It does illustrate the dangerous trajectory of the new Russia-China alignment, which would become more explicit a year later. If true, this would constitute a large and potentially very dangerous military commitment by Russia—it also might be that the Chinese government was exaggerating the extent of Russian assurances.

From Beijing, on July 19, 2000, Putin went to meet the North Korean ruler, Kim Jong-il, whom he subsequently described publicly as a "comfortable and pleasant interlocutor . . . a modern man, a person who evaluates many situations in the world objectively [and] is well-informed."[64] From there, Putin went to Japan for a meeting of the Group of Eight, where he described North Korea's offer to him that it would give up developing its ICBMs in return for help in launching its satellites. At that meeting, Putin continued his efforts to persuade all the major U.S. allies that the U.S. should not build an antimissile system against countries such as North Korea.[65] Putin also met privately with President Clinton on the issue.[66] During the G8 summit, Putin heard the German and French leaders repeat their agreement with him.[67]

On September 1, 2000, Clinton announced that he would postpone a decision leaving the question of missile defense to the next administration. The Russian and Chinese leaders must have felt a sense of satisfaction at their success but it left the question—why their adamant opposition to missile defense? For China, the answer is that even the limited missile defense proposed by the U.S. could sharply reduce the ability of China to threaten tens of millions of U.S. citizens with nuclear death. Therefore, since China has an agenda of expansion including Taiwan, it wants to be sure that the U.S. cannot use its nuclear forces to coerce it to halt its aggression and that China can use the threat of nuclear attack against U.S. cities to prevent the U.S. from helping Taiwan or any other country with which China may have a confrontation.

For Russia, the limited missile defense proposed by the Clinton administration would not interfere much with its ability to use nuclear weapons against the U.S., since it has a force of about 1,000 strategic missiles with 4,500 nuclear warheads.[68] But the Russian military leadership probably believes that once the U.S. has a limited system, it could quickly expand it to a more complete system. Putin's first priority is Russian economic recovery and he does not want even a limited U.S. missile defense system to require Russia to invest large resources either to counter it with additional or more effective offensive systems or by speeding up the long-established Soviet/Russian effort to obtain its own missile defense. Most likely, both China and Russia each hope they will be the first to develop and deploy an effective system while the U.S. remains undefended.

While in Beijing, President Putin also met with Li Peng, then the chairman of the Chinese National People's Congress, who, in that role, continued making visits to Russia. Putin also met with Premier Zhu Rongji. In addition, the ministers of defense of Russia and China met jointly "to strengthen military cooperation"; the Russian delegation to Beijing included a large number of key individuals from the Russian military production complex. As the Speaker's Advisory Group on Russia concluded, "The collective presence of such powerful figures was eloquent testimony to the pervasive military orientation of the Sino-Russian partnership."[69]

CONSEQUENCES AND IMPLICATIONS

A number of consequences and implications derive from this evolution in Russia-China relations from hostility to normalization to ever-closer strategic alignment, not the least of which is the creation of the "Good-Neighborly Treaty of Friendship and Cooperation" and the Shanghai Cooperative Organization. Within the Central Asian region, the Shanghai Cooperative Organization or (SCO) has the potential to provide a vehicle for the Chinese to gain a significant position of influence in this strategically vital region. Originally founded for the purpose of confidence building on border issues between China, Russia, Kazakhstan, Kyrgyzstan, and Tajikistan, the organization was known as the Shanghai Five. In 2000, Uzbekistan was invited to attend the annual heads-of-state meeting and when the formal treaty was signed in June 2001, Uzbekistan joined the newly formed Shanghai Cooperative Organization. Following the September 11th attacks on the United States, the SCO sought in the intervening months between the signing of the treaty and signing of the SCO charter to redefine their mission under the context of the U.S.-led global war on terror. Rather than focusing on relations between the various states, they defined their mission under the rubric of fighting what they call the "three evils" of terrorism, extremism, and separatism. There are also efforts directed toward the coordination and, to a lesser extent, integration of the various nations within a security, legal, transportation, and economic framework. This is facilitated by monthly meetings of senior governmental leaders of the member nations as well as yearly summits of the chief executives.

A more recent example of the international consequences of this potential alignment of Russia and China was evident in the UN Security Council debates in the months leading up the U.S. liberation of Iraq. Although many may dismiss this as a coming together for basic mutual economic self-interests, or perhaps even connected to the issues surrounding the fraud in the UN oil-for-food program, that does not answer the questions of the aid that was provided by both Russia and China in and up to, possibly even during, the U.S.-led invasion. In addition, when viewed outside of the isolation of this one issue, there is great cause for concern.

1. China-Russia Agreement on Major International Issues

A very important first consequence is that both Russia and China now have defined most major issues of international politics in the same way, using the same terms, and share the intention to oppose and contain the United States. This was said directly in the *Foreign Policy Concept of the Russian Federation*, signed by President Putin in July 2000:

> The concurrence of the fundamental approaches of Russia and the PRC on the key issues of world politics is one of the basic mainstays of regional and global stability. Russia seeks to develop mutually advantageous cooperation with China in all areas.[70]

While the United States views the NATO alliance in Europe and its alliance relationships in Asia as strictly defensive in character and contributing to peace and stability, Russia and China, especially after NATO's Kosovo intervention in 1999, share the view that both U.S.-led alliance systems are threatening and dangerous. In the 1998 and 2000 White Papers on national defense, China explicitly denounced U.S. alliances, called "military blocs," as contributing to "instability." In 1999, the Russian Foreign Ministry said that "NATO does not help increase stability in the European region and only leads to the creation of new dividing lines."[71] The shared agreement between Russia and China has gone from their initial stated opposition to "hegemonism" and "unipolarism," which meant the assertive actions of the United States, to the shared view that a "new international political and economic order" must be established. This implies current and future plans to coordinate their international activities in opposition to the United States and its allies as necessary. This makes it likely that the level and depth of their coordination may grow year by year and become an ever-greater issue.

Another fundamental element of shared perspective between the two powers is that there may be no intervention within any state except by a resolution of the UN

Security Council, where both Russia and China have a veto. Their immediate concerns are with the separatist movements within their own borders. Some within both Russia and China continually accuse the United States and some of its allies of providing secret help to those separatist groups. Fueled by hard-line elements in both countries, those suspicions may well grow over time. That would provide another important domain of unity between Russia and China in opposition to the United States.

The U.S. proposals for a limited national missile defense and for both Asian and European regional missile defenses have mostly been met by a China-Russia campaign of threats, denunciations, and opposition. This is another example of their growing and effective strategic cooperation. In October 1999, Russia and China cosponsored a United Nations General Assembly resolution opposing any change in the 1972 ABM treaty. The vote on this resolution was preceded by Russian threats that if the United States modified the ABM Treaty, Russia would terminate all nuclear-arms agreements and add new multiwarhead ICBMs to its arsenal.[72] During this time, Russia also conducted seven tests of its nuclear-armed ICBMs in November 1999. Yeltsin said that changing the ABM Treaty would have "extremely dangerous consequences."[73]

One of the most explicit Russian statements in opposition to the U.S. missile defense proposals was made by the minister of defense, who said in June 2000:

> The true reasons for deploying the U.S. national missile defense do not lie in imaginary threats from certain pariah countries. Apparently some people in the United States are in the grip of a temptation to acquire strategic dominance by means of increasing the technological gulf between them and the rest of the world in creating exceptional conditions of invulnerability, that is implementing the forgotten doctrine of fortress America. . . . Furthermore, in my opinion, some people in the United States are under the illusion that by deploying an NMD system capable of intercepting a few hundred strategic missile warheads and reducing the number of warheads and delivery vehicles, as a result of the accords under Start III and subsequent treaties, it is possible to acquire the potential to destroy Russia strategic nuclear potential as a result of a preemptive strike and the interception of those Russian missiles and warheads that will remain for a retaliatory strike. . . . We regard the deployment of NMD as only the first step toward the future emergence of a multifunctional global system for combating all types of . . . targets. This comprehensive defense system will be directed first and foremost against the deterrent potential of the Russian Federation and of the People's Republic of China. Russian defense ministry experts are in no doubt about this."[74]

This was not a Communist or an ultranationalist, but the minister of defense who said that his organization has "no doubt" that the real U.S. purpose for having missile defense and nuclear arms reduction is to have the potential to launch a first strike that would disarm Russia. This recalls the views of General Secretary and KGB Chairman Andropov in the early 1980s, when he believed President Reagan intended to launch a surprise nuclear attack.[75]

The Chinese government also made a number of threats indicating that if the U.S. deployed missile defense it would no longer abide by any limits on proliferation of weapons of mass destruction and would build up its nuclear forces more rapidly. Those threats have continued beyond those issued by the first Putin-Jiang summit of "most grave, adverse consequences" for going beyond the ABM treaty. Examples of the effectiveness of the joint Russia-China campaign against U.S. missile defense plans include the North Korea stratagem discussed earlier, the fact that a number of European allies (no doubt persuaded in quiet briefings by Russia) have opposed U.S. plans, and, in the end, the September 1, 2000 decision of President Clinton to leave the issue for the next administration.

However, in a meeting held in August 2000 after months of debate among Russian national security officials, Putin reportedly decided both to reduce Russian troop strength by about 30 percent, in order to field smaller but more modern forces; and to reduce sharply Russia's offensive strategic arsenal to about 1,500 warheads, fewer than half the number permitted under the current START II arms reduction agreement with the United States.[76] This decision followed the accidental sinking of a Russian nuclear attack submarine in August 1999, and Putin said the military reductions would be done because "one has to live within one's income. . . . [Russia had] . . . wasted money . . . in seeking to support a military force of the same level that the Soviet Union had."[77]

2. Transfer of Weapons of Mass Destruction
It is a fact of international politics that virtually all Soviet-linked anti-U.S. dictatorships of the Cold War era outside Europe survived during the 1990s. These include Iran, Iraq, Libya, Syria, North Korea, and Cuba—all of which have been judged by the United States government to be states that support international terrorism. The Middle Eastern anti-U.S. regimes—Iran, Iraq, Libya, and Syria—continue to seek to build weapons of mass destruction for possible use against the United States as well as against U.S. allies such as Israel and the Persian Gulf oil states. These are the states that during the 1990s were supported by Russia and China politically and with weapons transfers at ever-increasing tempo. In congressionally mandated public reports, the director of Central Intelligence has indicated that Russia and China are the countries that provide the largest number of conventional weapons and the most weapons of mass destruction to these and other hostile regimes.

The Soviet purpose in working for thirty years with these regimes in the Middle East was essentially to use them and their hostility against Israel and its ally the United States as a means of helping radical pro-Soviet groups gain control of the Middle East oil wealth. This included attempts to overthrow the moderate Persian Gulf oil regimes—Saudi Arabia, Kuwait, and the United Arab Emirates. The Soviet view was that with radical pro-Soviet regimes in charge of those oil resources and Europe and Japan dependent on these for about 70 percent of their energy supplies, it would be possible to neutralize Europe and Japan by placing political conditions such as leaving NATO and other U.S. security alliances on further supplies of Middle Eastern oil. In the 1990s, Russia and China sold weapons to the anti-U.S. regimes in the Middle East to earn hard currency, to support their own military producers, and also to establish closer relations and build up these regimes as another means of counterbalancing the United States.

In addition to China's transfer of weapons of mass destruction to these countries, starting in 1994 Russia began to sell large numbers of weapons to Iran along with nuclear-weapons-related equipment, which a 1999 U.S. government analysis concluded, "if not terminated, can only lead to Iran's acquisition of a nuclear weapons capability."[78] The weapons Russia supplied to Iran during the 1990s included three submarines, a large number of antiship mines, and a variety of long-range guided torpedoes for the submarines, as well as tanks and armored personnel carriers.[79] Reports revealed that in 1995, Vice President Gore entered into a secret agreement with Prime Minister Chernomyrdin of Russia that the United States would not implement sanctions required by the Gore-McCain Nonproliferation Act of 1992 if Russia promised to stop selling these conventional weapons to Iran by December 31, 1999. This surprising revelation led Senate Majority Leader Trent Lott and Senator Jesse Helms to write President Clinton on October 13, 2000 saying, "Please assure us . . the Vice President did not in effect sign a pledge with Victor Chernomyrdin in 1995 that committed your administration to break U.S. law by dodging sanctions requirements."[80] In fact, Russia did not stop selling such weapons. Despite U.S. diplomatic protests, Russian weapons transfers continued and increased into the year 2001.

Since U.S. and British forces have sought to enforce UN Security Council sanctions against Iraq and maintain stability through a military presence in the Middle East, quite clearly these Russian weapons systems increase Iran's capabilities to attack U.S. forces in the region. While Russia and China have added to the military capabilities of regimes opposing the United States, it may well be that in the future the missiles—as well as the nuclear, chemical, or biological weapons that Russia, China, and North Korea have provided to these Middle Eastern radical dictatorships—may, in fact, be directed against either Russia or China or both. It is Russia and China, not the United States, that have repressed or persecuted Muslim minorities in their territories.

3. Russian Sale of Advanced Weapons to China

A third major consequence of the Russia-China alignment has been the sale of increasing quantities of ever more advanced weapons and weapons technology by Russia to China. Beginning with carefully limited sales at a level of somewhere between $400 million and $2 billion in the first year of the Yeltsin government, the value and scope of military sales increased steadily as the relationship became closer. Open sources and experts led to an estimate that the cumulative value of Russian sales to China from 1992 to 1999 ranges between $9.5 and $22.5 billion. Many of these sales were announced, but many were also conducted in secret. The reason for the wide range in estimates, according to Nemets and Scherer, is that the openly available figures used in most compilations of data on this topic do not include: exports to China secretly approved by the Russian government, mostly ICBM-related technology and the items related to strategic nuclear weapons; black market exports to Russia, where China buys directly from Russian research centers, defense plants, and military units; equipment and technology for Chinese nuclear-related production facilities located in China and supported by Russia; and materials and services provided to the Chinese space program, which have clear military applications.[81]

Most, if not all, of Russia's major weapons systems were designed to counter those of the United States in the Cold War years. The massive transfer of weapons and advanced technology from Russia to China that gained momentum during the 1990s and continues, in combination with China's extensive national program to develop the most advanced weapons systems and its successful espionage, could well mean that China's future military systems might combine the most advanced aspects of science and technology from both the United States and Russia.

One of China's highest priorities is developing its own national missile defense system and to be the first power that deploys such a system. The extensive Russian cooperation with China in helping China develop its missile and air defenses and other domains of high technology may well make a large contribution to this Chinese purpose. From 1992 through 1999, Russia sold China eight systems of its long-range missile and air-defense missiles (S-300). Each has twelve or more mobile launchers, and each of these is capable of firing four air-defense missiles with a range of ninety miles and capable of reaching an altitude of nearly ninety thousand feet. According to Nemets, these missiles can "destroy the most advanced aircraft, cruise missiles, and tactical missiles."[82] In addition, China also bought fifty-five medium-range air-defense systems (Tor-M1). Each has four mobile missile launchers. In addition, Russia is aiding China in producing another 160 units of the Tor-M1 system. Taken together, the Russian air-defense systems give China the capability of launching 1,264 long- and medium-range air-defense missiles simultaneously. The S-300 system was originally developed to defend Russia from the American Pershing Theater ballistic missile. Thus, Nemets concludes that, in effect,

China is building not only a powerful air-defense system, but "a TMD [theater missile defense] network covering the coastal regions of China . . . an essential part of preparations for conflict around Taiwan."[83]

There are also estimates that at least two thousand Russian scientists and technicians are "employed by Chinese research institutes working on laser technology; the miniaturization of nuclear weapons; cruise missiles; space-based weaponry; and nuclear submarines."[84] Most directly threatening to the United States are the Chinese nuclear-armed ICBMs. We have discussed China's significant investment in developing two land-mobile ICBMs that could reach the United States (the DF-31 and the DF-41). As chairman of the House Armed Services Committee, Representative Floyd Spence concluded in May 2000 that these new Chinese ICBMs "may be armed with multiple independently targetable warheads (MIRVs) based on technology provided by Russia and illicitly acquired from the United States."[85] It was also reported that, in 1995, Russia violated its commitments under the missile technology control regime by selling rocket engines to China.[86] The Defense Intelligence Agency estimated in 1997 that China could produce one hundred ballistic missiles annually, which means that by 2008, China could have one thousand ballistic missiles. If these were armed with multiple warheads, it would give China a nuclear power roughly equivalent to those of the United States and Russia.[87]

In addition, Russia could quickly and substantially increase China's nuclear ICBM potential by transferring one or more *Typhoon*-class ballistic missile submarines, each of which carries twenty missiles armed with ten nuclear warheads, or 200 per submarine. It has been reported that since 1995, Russia has been considering selling China its largest ballistic missile, the SS-18, a number of which Russia agreed to leave in storage. Each of these could reach the continental United States to deliver ten to twenty nuclear warheads.[88] Russia also agreed to permit China to use its satellite-based global positioning system *(Glonass)* to improve the accuracy of China's missiles. Further, for China's known existing ICBMs to attack the United States, they require permission to fly over Russian air space. This apparently is assumed by China to have been granted or to be irrelevant.

China is concerned about the demonstrated U.S. air attack capabilities, and it has bought significant numbers of Russia's advanced jet fighter aircraft. In 1992, it reportedly contracted for advanced jet fighters (SU-27s), while in 1994, China contracted for an advanced long-range attack version of the SU-30. China has also received the license to produce hundreds of advanced Russian aircraft in Chinese factories including, for example, the MIG-31 long-range fighter interceptor.[89] In addition, Russia has sold to China what some U.S. analysts call the best air-to-air missiles in the world, the R-77 Bympel. This is a beyond-visual-range air-to-air missile, which can strike from a distance of fifty-five miles and is viewed as effective against U.S. fighter aircraft (such as the F-16, the F-15, and even the newest F-18 E/F and F-22).[90]

The warships Russia has sold China are those which would be most effective against U.S. naval forces in the Pacific. This includes the sale of four of Russia's advanced *Sovremeny*-class destroyers, each of which can carry eight antiship missiles (SS-N-22), which skim just above the water's surface at over twice the speed of sound and can carry a conventional explosive or a 200-kiloton nuclear warhead. These were specifically designed by Russia to destroy U.S. aircraft carriers and their escort ships. Representative Dana Rhorbacher, a member of the House International Relations Committee who monitors these events closely, said, "The SS-N-22 is the most dangerous antiship missile in the Russian and now the Chinese fleet. Our Navy admittedly has scant ability to defend against this 200-kiloton nuclear-capable weapon."[91]

Russia delivered two of these destroyers to China in 2000; they were to be manned by what is called a mixed Russian and Chinese crew. Since it requires intensive training to use the complex modern weapons systems of the *Sovremeny*-class destroyer, it is possible that one further Russian contribution to China's military power might be that Russian crews essentially man some of these advanced ships and weapons under the Chinese flag. This would be a contemporary variant on the covert Russian deployment of its air force to North Korea, which shot down large numbers of American aircraft. American defense analysts say that this destroyer and weapons systems provides China with a "quantum leap" in naval capabilities and that the "U.S. Navy has nothing that can stop it."[92]

Beginning in 1995, Russia sold China four attack submarines (*Kilo* class), which the director of Naval Intelligence, testifying in 1999, called "among the quietest diesel submarines in the world."[93] These could be used to enforce a blockade on Taiwan or the South China Sea or to attack U.S. aircraft carriers and other ships China viewed as "trespassing" in its territorial water or helping Taiwan. Some reports indicate that China has promised in the range of three to ten more of these attack submarines in the years 2000 to 2003.[94] China also wants to obtain the licensing rights from Russia to build these submarines, and the Department of Defense has concluded that China's own submarine production is using advanced technology from both Russia and the West.[95] This is another example of China's fusion of military technology from Russia and the West where the results may be a superior weapons system.

Russia also is reported to have sold China a new weapon it has developed to protect its ballistic missile submarines.[96] This has direct relevance to China as it deploys its existing ballistic missile submarine and a more advanced submarine is being developed. It is also reported that China has purchased a small Russian aircraft carrier, the *Kiev*, which is being updated with advanced Russian weapons systems. In addition, Russia is providing assistance to China in the building of its own aircraft carrier. Estimates are that each of these would carry about thirty-six Chinese-produced versions of the Russian SU-27 jet fighters.[97] This extensive delivery of naval weapons to China is complemented by the fact that in October 1999 Russia and China held joint naval exercises for the first time since normalization.[98]

In the summer of 2000, President Jiang told the Communist leadership that China would invest more heavily in developing what he called "killer" special high-technology weapons. Year by year, after the declaration of the strategic partnership, Russia began to provide China with some of its most advanced military technology and production capabilities. This continued and expanded until, in January 2000, the Chinese and Russian ministers of defense agreed on a "15-year military cooperation plan." Information published in a Hong Kong newspaper, often used by China to informally provide intimidating information, said this included the following:

- Russia will continue to supply advanced high-technology equipment including aircraft, naval vessels, and guided missile systems;
- Russia and China will jointly manufacture military equipment with Russia supplying the technology and materials and China providing payments to a military research and development fund;
- China and Russia will complete by 2003 the first anticruise missile system to intercept, for example, the U.S. tomahawk cruise missile. It will be jointly manufactured by both countries;
- Joint military exercises will increase as will the number of exchange participants;
- twenty to fifty delegations will visit each other annually to review military exercises, and eight hundred Chinese military personnel will study in Russia annually.[99]

Further, that same report indicated that China would have its stealth high-speed guided missile gunboats, intended to attack U.S. and other naval vessels, ready by 2005; that it would also have a new generation of fighter aircraft; and that it is conducting final checks on new laser and velocity-beam weapons, which China would begin to produce in 2002.[100] If these projected weapons developments materialize, this would reflect the cooperation Russia has provided in laser and high-technology weapons; China's own advancing skills in high-tech weapons and production; and the results of Western sales, technology transfers, and successful Chinese and Russian espionage.

These extensive Russian military sales and transfers of advanced weapons-related technology not only strengthen the military capabilities of China, but they help Russia to modernize its military. The billions in hard currency that China pays for these weapons makes more resources available for Russia to continue the development of its most advanced weapons systems. The Soviet Union had a highly developed military-industrial complex that employed about 60 percent of its skilled scientists and engineers. While some portion of that complex has ended its work and some of the scientists and engineers have moved into civilian production, the alternative opportunities have been fewer than hoped for due to Russia's economic problems. The Russian military leadership wanted to continue developing Russia's most advanced weapons systems, especially its nuclear missiles and related capabilities. Money received from its large sales to China, along with money received from Russia's transfer of weapons to Iran, Iraq, and other anti-U.S. states, has paid for the continuation of significant amounts of Russian military development.

4. Strengthening Authoritarian Forces Within Russia

The Russia-China alignment is also having the effect on Russia's internal political development of supporting those forces tending toward authoritarianism, including those seeking to restore Communism and weakening those seeking more political democracy and a market-oriented economy in cooperation with the West. From the start of the post-Soviet years, the Communist Party of the Russia Federation continually pointed to the "Chinese model" as that which Russia should follow—specifically meaning rule by the Communist Party with some economic changes in order to encourage economic growth.

In 1995, the ultranationalist politician Vladimir Zhironovsky visited China and urged closer Russian-Chinese ties as a way of asserting Russian national interests against those of the United States and the West.[101] In 1997, Lukashenko, who restored a Communist dictatorship in Belarus, which was united with Russia in 1999, also strongly urged closer Russia-Chinese international political alignment.[102] What the Communists and ultranationalists of Russia understand is that the closer Russia works with China internationally, the more it will oppose the United States and the West. The resulting disputes will open a political distance, which will grow larger over time. In the view of the Russian Communists, this will increase the opportunity for restoration of Communist rule there. At the same time, while the Chinese government develops relations with the Putin government, especially with the military, the Chinese Communist Party has revived its direct relationship with the Communist Party in Russia and supplements this through the new ties between the Chinese and Russian parliaments. These multiple relationships, all coordinated from the Chinese side through the Communist Party, provide many opportunities to cultivate allies in Russia, and perhaps to carefully and subtly encourage a Communist restoration in Russia.

From the Chinese point of view, this would reinforce its own rule because it could tell the people of China that Russia had failed economically as it sought to move away from the former Communist system and only began to recover its economic vitality as it restored authoritarian and, ultimately, Communist rule. Conversely, for the Chinese Communist Party, the economic and international success of a pro-democratic Russian political leadership would offer the wrong example to the Chinese people—the ability of even long-established Communist regimes to make a transition to political democracy with economic growth.

The ever-expanding and mutually profitable relationships between the Chinese and Russian military and the military production complexes in both countries reinforce suspicion of the United States/NATO and a return to authoritarianism as being in Russia's national interest.

ALIGNMENT OR ALLIANCE: THE RUSSIA-CHINA TREATY OF 2001

Both Russia and China state that their "strategic partnership" is not "directed against any third party." China says that it does not enter into any alliances and, as we have discussed, takes a position against military alliances. The U.S. Ambassador to China, Admiral Joseph Prueher, former commander in chief of U.S. forces in the Pacific, said at the end of February 2000 that the ties between Russia and China were "a relationship of convenience . . . the Russians want cash, the Chinese want military equipment."[103] Yet the evidence and pattern of Russian-Chinese international political cooperation suggests it is much more than simply an arms transfer relationship—even though 90 percent of Chinese military imports for the year 2000 were from Russia.[104]

The visit of President Putin to India in October 2000 was the first visit there by a Russian head of state since 1993. Building on the long Soviet-Indian military relationship, Putin signed weapons contracts that included India's purchase of 310 of the most advanced Russian battle tanks, licenses for India to produce 140 advanced Russian jet fighters (SU-30 MKI), and a contract through which Russia would give India its aircraft carrier, the *Admiral Gorshkov*. In return, India would spend about $2 billion in Russia to refurbish and equip it, which would include a fleet of Russian MIG-29K fighter aircraft.[105]

Russia also agreed to establish a relationship with India for "peaceful uses for atomic energy" at the same Indian facility where advanced nuclear research and nuclear weapons are developed. This was done in spite of the fact that India has not yet agreed to international inspection of its nuclear facilities.[106] The Russian-Indian memorandum on nuclear cooperation was kept secret. China has decades-long and continuing border disputes with India and views this democracy with a billion citizens as a major competitor in Asia. Russian overtures to India suggest that Putin considers it in Russia's interest to revive the former relationship, perhaps, in part, as a counterbalance to China.

While the newly intensified Russian-Indian relationship may be unwelcome to China, it nevertheless remains that Russia and China have moved toward greatly expanded international military and political cooperation. The reports from August 1999 of their preliminary agreement on a joint air-defense system suggest a high level of planned future military cooperation.[107] We cannot confirm the reports of Russian agreement on transferring two Typhoon ballistic missile submarines with four hundred strategic nuclear warheads to China—perhaps with a substantially Russian crew under Chinese command—but if that were to occur, it would also suggest a high degree of planned future military cooperation. The most disturbing reports, which also cannot be confirmed, are those that Putin promised in July 2000 that the Russian navy would participate in seeking to block U.S. naval forces in the event of Chinese coercion of Taiwan. If true, this would constitute a de facto secret military alliance.

It has been reported that Putin and the head of the National People's Congress, Li Peng, one of the most pro-Russian Chinese leaders, agreed in September 2000 that when President Jiang visited Moscow in the summer of 2001, Russia and China would sign a formal treaty of "friendship and cooperation."[108] Subsequently, Russian and Chinese sources indicated that the treaty would include a full range of political, economic, and military cooperation, as well as the possibility that China might provide Russia with $10 to $15 billion in economic assistance.[109]

A senior Russian official directly involved in negotiating the thirty-year cooperation treaty said that it will include "the main trends of our cooperation, the basic principles by which we will be guided . . . the border . . . each other's support as regards sovereignty and combating terrorism."[110] Leaked reports from the Chinese government are more explicit in emphasizing that the shared defense of "sovereignty" means opposition to "international hegemonism, power-politics, and military blocs, military invasion and blackmail against sovereign states."[111] The Chinese view of the coming treaty also emphasizes that when one of the parties to the treaty "experiences military aggression," the other signatory state should, at its request, provide "political, economic, and military support and launch joint attacks against the invading forces."[112]

While these comments from the Chinese side do not represent acknowledged official positions, they do reflect a consistent expressed intention by China to involve Russia as a military ally if for any reason the United States should either threaten China (which in China's view would be a violation of sovereignty "or blackmail") or become involved in military hostilities with China for any reason. It remains to be seen whether the Russian or the Chinese version of the new treaty of cooperation is presented publicly or becomes the basis for their actual joint future strategic and military planning. While China may at the present time feel it has much to gain by using the nuclear military potential of Russia to counter that of the United States, it is not clear that this involvement by Russia on behalf of China's claim to Taiwan, the South China Sea, or other territory, is in Russia's national interest. That may explain the noticeable difference in the way Russian officials and Chinese sources discuss the Russia-China cooperation treaty.

After the Stalin-Mao treaty was signed in 1950, North Korea was given approval by Stalin to attack South Korea, with the understanding that Chinese military forces would help if needed. Jiang's decision in August 2000 to allocate $8.5 billion annually for four years to accelerate the purchase and production of the most high-tech Russian weapons and the coordination of this special program by his likely successor, Vice President Hu Juntao, is part of China's preparations to have the means to take control of Taiwan and deter any U.S. military help for Taiwan.[113] China seeks to draw Russia in to back its military threats against the U.S. and will seek to use the new treaty relationship for that purpose.

Looking to the future, the Russia-China alignment poses a great military and political challenge to the United States and its allies. In military terms, the premise of U.S. policy during the Clinton years was that the United States would not face a peer military competitor in Asia for two decades (until 2020). But as described by the chairmen of several international security committees of the House of Representatives, the evidence from the Russia-China military relationship suggests that the "combination of Russian and PRC technology and resources would truly produce a peer competitor for the United States more quickly than is otherwise commonly supposed."[114] In terms of international political strategy, the Russia-China alignment permits both powers to jointly work against the United States and its allies on all the issues that they deem significant. As each helps the other accomplish its national political objectives against the United States and its allies, both become more effective, and the United States faces a challenge in the present and future that it has not faced since the Soviet-Chinese alliance in the 1950s. For China, the alignment with Russia sets the stage for its approach to dominance in Asia and to geopolitical global dominance, which we shall now discuss.

18 China: Stealthy Strategy toward Global Dominance

"To subdue the enemy without fighting is the acme of skill."
— SUN TZU, *The Art of War*

"We shall hide our capabilities and bide our time"
— DENG XIAOPING, 1994

"Facing hegemonism, China should . . . develop an elite and effective military intimidation force and fully and cunningly organize and apply all kinds of non-military intimidation factors . . . political, foreign relations, economic, market, financial, media, and other kinds of non-military threats and methods."
— MAJOR GENERAL XU HEZHEN, *Zhongguo Junshi Kexue*, October 2000

Beginning in the 1950s, the Communist government of China said that its goal in international politics is to promote peaceful relations with other states. Therefore, its international conduct would always be governed by the "five principles of peaceful coexistence," which China defined as:

1. Mutual respect for the other's territory and sovereignty;
2. mutual nonaggression;
3. mutual noninterference in each other's domestic affairs;
4. equality of relationship for mutual benefits; and
5. peaceful coexistence.[1]

Yet, during the 1950s, China committed many acts of aggression including: sending a million troops to battle the United Nations forces in Korea; threatening invasion and attacking island territories controlled by Taiwan; and supporting armed Communist insurgent movements seeking to overthrow regional governments. Nevertheless, these five principles of peaceful coexistence served to persuade many Asian states to remain neutral. As the historian Hsu put it, "Peking succeeded to a large extent in preventing these states from aligning with the West,"[2] even India after China's surprise attack in 1962.

In the post-Mao years, with China's economic opening to the industrial democracies and other countries, there have been major changes in the methods of

Chinese action in the world. While China continues to say that it seeks to promote peace and the five principles of peaceful coexistence, it has now added the major purpose of promoting its own economic development. During the 1990s, China increasingly repeated, as stated in its October 2000 *Report on National Defense,* that it seeks " a new international political, economic, and security order, responsive to the needs of our times."[3] While the content and structure of this "new international order" has not been made clear, obstacles to its realization that China often mentions are the alleged intention of the United States to dominate the world by what it calls "unipolarism" or "hegemonism." Also preventing the Chinese "new world order" are the alliances maintained by the United States in Asia, Europe, and the world, all of which are condemned as contrary to peace and relics of "the Cold War mentality." China also opposes the plans of the United States for national missile defense and for Asian missile defense involving Japan, South Korea, and potentially other countries.

There is an important contrast in the international actions of the three major powers in Asia: Japan, India, and China. Japan, with the world's second-largest economy and a highly developed technological infrastructure, has maintained a relatively small self-defense force; has been cooperative internationally, providing especially large amounts of aid and development loans for China; and has not moved toward acquiring its own nuclear weapons. Japan, as a democracy after World War II, has never used direct or indirect aggression or coercion internationally, as has China.

China has spoken about building peaceful relations but, in fact, has been aggressive. China has territorial disputes with eleven of twenty-five bordering and neighboring states;[4] has transferred enormous quantities of technology for weapons of mass destruction to potentially aggressive dictatorships; has conducted large-scale espionage and covert action operations against the United States and undoubtedly many other countries; and has engaged in an intense, rapid effort to build up its advanced military force, including ballistic missiles, nuclear weapons, aircraft, and other power-projection forces. It is the pattern of actions by Communist China and China's own official pronouncements that indicate its purpose to seek dominance—first in Asia, then more widely in the world.

REASONS FOR CHINA'S PURSUIT OF DOMINANCE
IN ASIA AND THE WORLD

The history of the twentieth century demonstrates that it is the inclination of political democracies to seek international security through conflict resolution, conflict prevention, and defensive alliances. In contrast, ideological or expansionist dictatorships, such as the regime in China, seek international security through the domination and the neutralization of potentially threatening governments. As the twenty-first century began, the government of China defined the world situation as follows:

> In today's world, factors that may cause instability and uncertainty have markedly increased. The world is far from peaceful. There is a serious disequilibrium in the relative strength of certain countries. No fundamental change has been made in the old, familiar and irrational international political and economic order. Hegemonism and power politics [the actions of the United States] still exist and are pursuing and developing further in the international political, economic, and security spheres. Certain big powers [the United States] are pursuing neointerventionism, neogunboat policy, and neo-economic colonialism, which are seriously damaging the sovereignty, independence, and developmental interests of many countries and threatening world peace and security.[5]

This negative assessment echoes accusations also made publicly by then-President Jiang Zemin of China. These are the public declarations of the private conclusions reached by the Chinese Communist rulers in 1990, following their repression in Tiananmen Square. To protect itself from the actions of the United States, defined as hostile "neointerventionism," "neogunboat diplomacy," and "neoeconomic colonialism," China must become dominant for a number of reasons.

1. Preserve the Power of the Communist Party of China

The first reason China seeks international dominance is to preserve the power of the Communist Party and its unquestioned rule. Party leadership has been concerned since the 1950s about what it perceives to be an American plot of promoting "peaceful evolution" from Communist dictatorship to democracy. It believes that the United States and the democracies caused the end of Communist rule in Eastern Europe and the unraveling of the Soviet Union. Speaking publicly in June 2000, President Jiang reflected these concerns when he said, "Our struggle to fight against Western hostile forces infiltrating and seeking to overthrow [the Party] is a long and a complicated struggle that at times will be very intense."[6] A few months later, the Chinese leadership witnessed the people of Serbia removing the long-established Communist dictatorship of that country (1945–2000) through an essentially peaceful popular uprising, which some believed was secretly encouraged and aided by the United States and other democracies.

The democratic, prosperous, and powerful United States of America is seen as an intrinsic threat to the continued existence of the Communist regime. It provides an appealing political and economic example for the people of China and is a potential barrier to China's aggressive purposes.

Immediately across a one-hundred-mile strait, the people of Mainland China can see the reality of a democratic, much more prosperous, and peaceful China. They know that this is the result of Taiwan's own "peaceful evolution," which occurred without the enormous suffering, persecution, and bloodshed that was imposed by the Communists on the mainland. This Chinese democracy, as well as prosperous democratic Japan and other Asian democracies, show clearly that the peoples of Asia can also establish successful democratic self-government. A major reason that the Chinese Communist regime wants to take control over Taiwan is to end the idea that there can be another democratic alternative for the people of China. Taiwan is also an important prize because of its highly skilled scientists, engineers, and workers, together with its high-technology industries and GDP of $286 billion, as well as its $175 billion in hard-currency reserves—all of which would make an immediate contribution to the overall military, technological, and economic potential of China.

To take control over Taiwan, China must prevent any other country from interfering with its purposes. This involves a form of dominance. In a recent *National Defense Report*, the Chinese regime criticizes the U.S. and Japan for having "failed to explicitly undertake to exclude Taiwan from the scope of the 'areas surrounding Japan' referred to in the Japanese security bill that could involve military intervention. These actions have . . . seriously undermined China's sovereignty and security and imperiled the peace and security of the Asia-Pacific region."[7] These strong words along with the many Chinese threats made against the U.S. in the event it acts to help Taiwan defend itself are in themselves an exercise in dominance and deterrence.

2. Counter the Military Power of the United States and Its Allies
China's second concern is the military power of the United States, which is perceived as limiting its ability to take control of Taiwan and attain its territorial aims in Asia. It is this military power that permits the U.S., virtually alone in the world, to announce the sale of a large number of defensive weapons to Taiwan on April 23, 2001, followed the next day by the statement of President George W. Bush that if China attacked Taiwan, the U.S. would do "whatever it took to help Taiwan defend itself."[8] This military power was demonstrated in the 1991 Gulf War, in the 2001 removal of the Taliban, and in the 2003 overturning of Saddam Hussein's regime in Iraq. It is inherent in the U.S. arsenal of six thousand strategic nuclear weapons and in its system of alliances.

In 1999, China and Russia were deeply disturbed by the military action of the U.S.-led NATO alliance against the Communist-nationalist dictatorship in Serbia. They viewed that as a potential precedent for U.S. intervention in their countries, as they use military repression against separatism and ethnic autonomy. Yet, the Chinese military says and believes that its explicit threat of nuclear attack on U.S.

cities (February 2000) will deter the United States from intervening if China uses force to take over Taiwan or accomplish other purposes to exercise its "sovereignty," as China might define it; for example, by closing or restricting access to the South China Sea or its airspace in the future.

In contrast to this professed confidence in the ability of the Chinese military to deter the United States or defeat its Asian-based air and naval forces, Chinese military writings indicate a deep concern about the potential military capacity of Japan. Chinese military analysts believe that Japan could produce and deploy one to two thousand nuclear warheads in a matter of months and that Japan could quickly develop other formidable military forces that could be a threat to China.[9] There is a vivid memory in China of the enormous brutality of Imperial Japan during its years of military attack and occupation in China from 1931 to 1945 and a sense that an aggressive ultranationalist Japan could emerge at any time in the future. At one point, the Chinese leadership believed that the U.S. alliance with Japan was a stabilizing influence and contributed to the security of China by preventing unilateral Japanese nuclear rearmament. However, the present Chinese regime has international objectives in mind that it knows could lead to potential conflict with the United States and with Japan, making the U.S.-Japanese alliance dangerous to China. As a result, the neutralization of Japan is one of the major objectives China will seek to achieve in the coming years.

3. Ensure Access to Economic Resources

A third reason for China to seek dominance is to ensure its continued economic modernization and growth. Chinese strategists have defined "comprehensive national power" to include the political will and leadership of a country; its economic, scientific, and technological resources and development; and its military capabilities.[10] China's involvement with the world economy since 1978, its rapid economic growth, and enormous success in developing advanced civilian and military technology all have made clear to the Communist leadership that access to the economic, technological, and mineral resources of the world are essential to its future success.

Oil imports are an example of China's inevitably growing dependence on resources from abroad. In the year 2000, China used about four million barrels of oil a day and produced about three million barrels a day.[11] A comprehensive analysis by Robert A. Manning has shown that China's energy production may increase slightly in the next years, but also that its oil and other energy import requirements will rise steadily as China's economy continues to expand and become more developed, and as more motor vehicles are used. The economy of China has grown by more than 7 percent annually for many years. Assuming that in the next years China's economy grew at a rate of about 5.5 percent, China is estimated to need to import about four million barrels of oil a day by 2010 and six million barrels by 2020. If China's annual economic growth were in the range of 8 percent from 2000 to 2020, this could mean that China would need to import roughly eight million barrels a day by 2020. One informed projection is that global demand for oil could grow by thirty-five million barrels per day by 2010, with total production substantially less. This indicates that major oil importers such as the U.S., Europe, and Japan will be in even greater competition with China than was experienced throughout the summer and early fall of 2004, if world oil supplies do not meet increasing global demand.[12] China also needs to continue importing significant amounts of advanced technology, including advanced military technology, in order to meet its current objectives. Obtaining these imports means that China must have both the money to pay for them and must have access to them.

China has witnessed economic sanctions imposed under U.S. leadership on Serbia, Iraq, Iran, North Korea, Cuba, and other countries. China also experienced the negative effects of the temporary reduction in economic assistance and benefits imposed by the United States, Japan, and other countries after the Tiananmen massacre. For the Chinese regime, the best way to avoid the potential of future economic denial is to undertake an extensive program combining geopolitical influence building and geoeconomic positioning, as it has been doing. Also, China intends to gain positions of dominance and political influence such that no major power would consider denying it the resources it considers vital for the function of its economy and society. This, obviously, is linked to China's plans for a "new international political and economic order," which it expects to define.

4. The Fusion of China's Imperial and Communist Traditions

A fourth impulse toward dominance is the visible fusion in the Communist regime of its Marxist-Leninist-Maoist ideology and the historical traditions of imperial China. As discussed in the introduction, the imperative of ideological dictatorships, especially those with a worldview that is assumed to apply to all peoples on the planet, is to spread their ideology because it is declared best for humanity and because it further legitimates their own dictatorship at home. Currently, this is less important to the contemporary Chinese Communist leadership than the centuries-long tradition of China as the center of a world in which all other states either pay tribute and accept the dominance of the Chinese regime or are viewed as hostile.

As discussed so eloquently by Mosher, the Chinese emperor would exercise power over all the subjects of China while China would, in turn, exercise power over all the known states on earth. This traditional Chinese conception of global dominance is less totalistic than the view of some other recent expansionist dictatorships, which intended either to invade, occupy, and directly administer many foreign countries (Nazi Germany) or have this done by its indigenous, ideological allies (the

Soviet Union). China's pursuit of first Asian, then Eurasian, and finally global dominance to be discussed here is more in keeping with the ancient Chinese tradition. China does not seek to occupy and administer all the countries of the world, but rather to assure that no important country acts contrary to its purposes and that the resources China wants and demands from other states will be provided on its terms.

METHODS: THE STRATEGY OF GLOBAL POLITICAL-ECONOMIC DOMINATION

The foundation for China's pursuit of international dominance will be the continued increase in the political, economic, and military resources available to the regime. The basic method of action will be to use political, economic, and secret means to advance Chinese purposes, keeping military threats and military forces available to be used as needed. This very much follows the decades-long Soviet model of often-successful indirect war against a stronger United States and other democracies, with one important difference—the Soviet leadership proclaimed it sought to bring Communism to the world. The Chinese Communist leadership proclaims its peaceful intentions and in the post-Mao period has avoided any discussion of a global mission of bringing Communism to the world. However, China has proclaimed ever more clearly since the mid-1990s that it seeks a "new international political and economic order." This most likely is a world system where nominally independent states continue to be administered by their national governments, which, in turn, take no major international actions without permission from a dominant China.

It is worth recalling what Khrushchev said in 1957 and 1958 describing Soviet methods of international action:

> We do not need wars of conquest, or interference in the affairs of other states and peoples, or Cold War, hatred and distrust . . . we shall not foist our socialist system on other countries by force of arms. We are against interference of other countries in the defense of other countries. But we are attacking capitalism from the flanks, from economic positions, from the positions of the advantages of our system . . . we shall never take up arms to force the ideas of Communism on anybody . . . we shall defeat the capitalist world by using this powerful ideological weapon rather than the hydrogen bomb. We produced the hydrogen bomb with the sole object of cooling the ambitions of some excessively zealous politicians and generals in the capitalist countries. After all, living among wolves, we must have the means to let them know how dangerous it is to let them show their fangs.[13]

By all objective measures, the Soviet Union was much weaker than the United States and its allies from 1945–1949 and for many years thereafter. Yet, by using the methods of political and indirect warfare, the Soviet Union was able to help pro-Soviet groups take power in twenty-two countries after World War II, without a large-scale direct military confrontation with the United States. The success of Soviet political warfare methods was especially vivid in the time from 1945 to 1949, when the United States was a prosperous democracy with a homeland untouched by World War II, armed forces in 1945 of twelve million (unilaterally reduced to 1.2 million by 1946), and a nuclear monopoly. In contrast, Stalin's Soviet Union had been invaded, fought over, largely destroyed in its industrial regions, and more than ten million killed. Yet, using indirect means, deception, and propaganda it was Stalin who, in only four years, succeeded in helping bring ten pro-Soviet regimes to power, including that in China.

While the Chinese method of indirect political warfare shares much with Soviet Communist methods—such as the use of diplomacy, deceptive propaganda, sympathetic groups in other countries, espionage, agent networks, and secret coercion—it differs in two basic ways. First, China professes that it seeks "a new international political and economic order" that would be for the benefit of all reasonable countries. This is cast to be especially appealing to developing countries, which are a majority in the United Nations and the World Trade Organization, among other global forums. Secondly, China has accomplished the feat of linking Communist rule with many of the economic institutions of the industrial democracies, thereby obtaining enormous benefits for its own development. This linkage has also created inside the democratic countries vested interests by large and powerful business organizations in the continuation of good relations with China and in interpreting Chinese purposes and actions internationally as benign. This has already had a profound effect on the policies of the United States and other major democracies toward China and, in the view of the Chinese Communist regime, will continue to help China accomplish its purposes in the years ahead.

This connection between the Chinese Communist regime and private business abroad is consistent with Marxism-Leninism-Maoism, which assumes that all private businessmen are self-interested and self-seeking and that they do not consider or care about the broader national or geopolitical consequences of their actions. It is also consistent with democratic political theory and practice, which holds that it is proper for private interest groups to seek government policies that help their immediate interests. In this tradition, it is up to government officials, not businessmen, to decide what is in the broader national interest of the United States and the other democratic countries.

The words of Sun Tzu best express the long Chinese tradition of using political war methods: "To subdue the enemy without fighting is the acme of skill." This was given a contemporary rendition by President Jiang Zemin, who said China will "intimidate with force and seduce with money." A Chinese military expression of this approach is the following statement by General Xu Hezhen, one among many examples of Chinese strategic writing on the means of political warfare:

> Facing hegemonism, China should . . . develop an elite and effective military intimidation force and fully and cunningly organize and apply all kinds of non-military intimidation factors . . . political, foreign relations, economic, market, financial, media, and other kinds of non-military threats and methods . . . a nation applies overall political, economic, scientific, military, diplomatic, ideological, cultural or other forces.[14]

The political action approach to the pursuit of dominance is evident in the pattern of China's contemporary diplomacy with a large number of states around the world. China always declares that "peace is the best policy," and repeats its commitment to the five principles of peaceful coexistence and, in recent years, to the sanctity of the United Nations charter and the role of the United Nations Security Council. China also emphasizes historical and cultural affinities and connections with a particular country that Chinese leaders are visiting. Other authoritarian regimes comprise more than 110 of the world's 192 governments. China deals with regimes as they are, no matter how brutally repressive. It always emphasizes that, in its view, "human rights," which it "endorses," are to be conditioned by the historical and cultural experiences of each particular country and that no country (especially the United States) should make suggestions to other sovereign states about those issues.

The Chinese leadership also consistently offers significant economic inducements in its dealings with foreign countries where it seeks influence. These include, as useful, offers of Chinese economic assistance, Chinese investment in the country, new business arrangements, the building of Chinese factories in developing countries, and the purchase by China of products for hard currency from the countries it is courting. Many of these economic relationships are structured to include elements of the politically and economically influential national elites in profit-making arrangements. This is part of President Jiang's approach of "seduce with money" and is used both with dictatorships and democracies. When foreign governments are helpful, the Chinese regime is also quite willing to reward them with additional contracts and economic benefits or threaten to withhold them if particular governments act in ways that China considers unhelpful.

Another characteristic is that in foreign countries of interest, China often attempts to establish "people-to-people relationships" among professional groups, the media, and others with their professional equivalents in China. This is especially prevalent in many of the developing and neighboring countries where China seeks to establish a broader network of relationships in the society, often providing funds for extensive visits and exchanges. These relationships provide a useful way to recruit and organize a pro-China lobby within the countries.

Where China has territorial disputes with a country and it is in the phase of seeking to develop more friendly relations, it virtually always proposes that the two countries "shelve their differences" until some undetermined future date and focus instead on cooperative economic relationships for mutual benefit. It is noteworthy that China proposes not compromise on these differences, but only to postpone their discussion to a time when China will be even stronger politically, economically, and militarily than at present. China has done this with Russia, India, and Japan, as well as with many smaller states.

There is also a consistent, strong, but often subtle effort by China to oppose the idea that China might be a threat to any country now or in the future. This campaign against what China calls the "China threat theory" includes very close monitoring in important countries of those who believe otherwise. China makes an effort to find ways to isolate, defame, and discredit these people within their own countries so that the very idea that China might be a present or future threat is something that is rarely, if ever, discussed in influential circles within the major democracies or in many developing countries.

The Chinese regime, as in the case of all Communist regimes, has in-depth experience in the instrumental use of political, economic, symbolic, and coercive means to accomplish its objectives in its own country, as well as internationally. The Chinese Communists have a long tradition of "United Front work," where the Communist Party reaches out to non-Party business people, intellectuals, religious leaders, overseas Chinese, and people of influence in order to persuade them to work with the Party in accomplishing its objectives. The United Front has been called the "magic weapon" of the Chinese Communist Party. The techniques of persuading, coopting, manipulating, and deceiving non-Communists whose support is needed for particular purposes, having been used effectively to win the Chinese Civil War and maintain the dictatorship since 1949, are also relevant in persuading and manipulating foreign groups and states to adopt policies useful for China.

EIGHT STAGES TOWARD GLOBAL DOMINATION

From the point of view of the Communist regime, it must either dominate the world or be dominated by the United States and its allies. The regime judges that as China becomes ever more economically and technologically advanced and better armed year by year, it is inevitable that the United States will take actions that China defines as intending to "prevent the rise of China." For the regime, the question is whether this will happen sooner or later. This may be one of the reasons why the Chinese minister of defense said, at the end of 1999, that "War with the United States is inevitable," and the reason why a similar statement was repeated more recently by another senior Chinese military official.[15] From the point of view of hard-line Communists, who are intrinsically suspicious of the United States and its allies, especially Japan, the onset of efforts to restrict China's continued economic and technological advance is highly probable for two reasons: first, to avoid the potential of being faced with China having nuclear arsenals equal to the United States; second, because China, with its low-wage workers who are not free to organize themselves will supplant and displace more and more of the high-value and high-technology production inside the United States and other major democracies.

Further, the Chinese regime knows, though the U.S. does not yet perceive this, that it will use its membership in the UN and the WTO, as well as other political means, to rally a broad majority of developing countries against the U.S. and other major industrial democracies. The purpose will be to change the conditions of international trade in favor of China and regimes that defer to China and take positions against the U.S. This development would also increase the risk of resistance by the U.S.

A foreshadowing of possible events to come was the success in May 2001 of China, Russia, and their common partner Cuba in having a group of dictatorships and democracies remove the U.S. from the UN Human Rights Commission for the first time since 1947. This led Rep. Henry Hyde, chairman of the House International Relations Committee, to say, "This is a deliberate attempt to punish the United States for telling the truth when it comes to human rights violations across the globe."[16]

The pursuit of dominance by China is described here as occurring in eight phases. These phases can overlap and continue in parallel. The timing of each new phase will depend, in part, on decisions made by the Chinese regime as it resolves factional differences about strategy and tactics, as well as on China's perception of the risks it is taking as it moves toward the next phase. Also, it is quite possible, as will be discussed in the concluding chapter, for the U.S. and its allies to prevent the success of a number of these phases and, in the early stages, to do this without military conflict. This projection of events leading to a possible future is intended as a suggestive guide and not a literal prediction. The dates for each phase are unknowable, but an illustrative timeline is included to provide a sense of scale. Events could move in a negative direction much more quickly or slowly depending on decisions made by the leadership of the United States and its allies.

I. Normalization with the Industrial Democracies, 1978–Continuing

As the post-Mao Chinese regime decided on the four modernizations in 1978, it also agreed that its objectives in industry, agriculture, science, technology, and military development could best be achieved by obtaining both economic resources and advanced technology from the most advanced industrial democracies. Deng Xiaoping said then, "Peace and development are the dominant trends of the times." As already discussed, the normalization process and the mostly one-way access to the markets of the U.S. and other major countries have resulted in enormous export-led economic growth for China. Since the 1990s, this has provided China with more than a trillion dollars in economic benefits from its trade surplus, foreign direct investment, and foreign economic assistance. The scale of benefits China derived from its new relationships with the world is further illustrated by Chinese government data released in the year 2000 showing that since 1978 more than 180 countries and regions of the world had contracted for foreign direct investment in China of $632 billion in 349,500 ventures. The Chinese government said further that 400 of the world's 500 largest industrial enterprises had invested in China, with 65 percent of this investment being in the industrial sector.[17]

Taken together, these economic benefits for China have meant an enormous increase in the economic resources available to the Communist regime for its domestic and international purposes. This wealth is illustrated by the fact that by the year 2000, China's foreign exchange reserves were $168 billion (plus 500 tons of gold)—as compared to roughly $11 billion in the same year for Russia.[18] China's economic benefits continue as it evades many of its obligations as a World Trade Organization member.

II. ASIAN REGIONAL PERSUASION /COERCION, 1980S–CONTINUING

By the mid 1980s, the Chinese leadership knew that its economic modernization program would be effective, and it was also involved in normalization talks with Soviet leadership. The succession of Gorbachev as Secretary General and his movement toward a more conciliatory foreign policy toward China suggested that the worst of the Soviet threat was over. At this time, a close associate of Deng Xiaoping, Admiral Liu Huaqing, proposed a new strategic doctrine that aimed at the presumed threat from America: China should guarantee its future security by projecting its power beyond its coastline to control the seas and the "first island chain," including Taiwan, Japan, South Korea, the Philippines, and Indonesia. Adopting this geopolitical approach, and beginning to build the military capabilities to carry it out, showed that the Chinese regime was intent on retaking Taiwan and was also ready to move to end U.S. alliances in Asia, including those with South Korea, Japan, and the Philippines.

In 1987 and 1988, China used force against Communist Vietnam to evict it from islands China claimed in the South China Sea, and in 1992, China formally declared that it owned all the Spratly and Paracel islands, as well as Taiwan and the Senkaku/Daoyutai islands claimed by Japan. The rubber-stamp parliament passed a law asserting that China would "adopt all necessary measures to prevent and stop the harmful passage of vessels through its territorial waters [and for] PRC warships and military aircraft to expel the invaders."[19] These Chinese claims and other uses of military force have led to maritime territorial disputes with neighboring countries including Brunei, Malaysia, the Philippines, Taiwan, Vietnam, Indonesia, and Japan.

Throughout the 1990s, China resisted repeated requests by the other claimant countries to undertake multilateral negotiations about sovereignty over the islands in the South China Sea. By the late 1990s, extensive oil exploration efforts suggested that there were only small supplies of oil and gas under the South China Sea and the economic zones around the claimed islands.[20] Nevertheless, China continued with its claims, using force against the Philippines in 1994 and 1995, and building increasingly military-oriented structures on occupied islands, which Chinese media called "fortresses in the sea."

These actions are part of China's strategy of global political and economic positioning. By claiming that all the islands and the entire South China Sea were its "sovereign territory," China created a sense of uncertainty about whether it might try to restrict access to the sea lanes for U.S. allied countries such as Japan, South Korea, and others. The leaders in the region also saw that during the 1990s, the Philippines, despite a mutual-defense treaty with the United States, was given no help in countering China's military and coercive actions. In fact, the Clinton administration advised the Philippines not to make an issue of Chinese aggression. This appeasement may have led China to believe that the U.S. was ready to withdraw from military involvement in the region. This was followed by Chinese missile firings in 1995 and 1996 to coerce Taiwan, and the resulting deployment of two U.S. carrier battle groups in March 1996.

India

With respect to India, China expanded its military relationship with Pakistan and helped to build Pakistan's nuclear capabilities. At the same time, on India's other border, China developed a close military relationship with the dictatorship in Burma, providing it with weapons, assistance, and international support. China combined these geostrategic moves to contain and intimidate India with various episodes of diplomacy intended to establish improved relations. In 1988, China and India announced that they would begin discussing their border dispute stemming from China's claim to thousands of square miles of Indian territory and its occupation of territory seized from India in 1962. In 1989, Prime Minister Ghandi made the first visit to China by an Indian leader in thirty-four years and made an important concession by signing a statement that Tibet is an "autonomous region of China and [that] anti-China political activities by Tibetan elements are not permitted on Indian soil."[21] This was a noteworthy act of domination. China instructed India which political activities (not guerilla bases) were not to take place on India's territory and India publicly announced its agreement.

In 1991, China and India signed statements that were intended to begin a "new era of cooperation." This involved India again endorsing China's policy in Tibet and repeating that India "does not allow Tibetans to engage in anti-China political activities in India."[22] Despite these efforts by India to placate China in various negotiations, India discovered that China was continuing to deploy missiles and other weapons within range of India and that China was secretly building a military road in Indian territory that was under dispute. By July 1998, Prime Minister Atal Bihai Vajpayee, leader of the Hindu Nationalist Party, said after India's nuclear detonation, "Our problem is not Pakistan, our problem is China. We are not seeking [nuclear] parity with China; . . . what we are seeking is a minimal deterrent."[23] The Chinese ambassador replied to India that the Indian government had "sabotaged relations with China" by these comments.

During 1999, the Chinese military built a permanent network of metal roads and set up military bunkers on the Indian side of the Line of Actual Control, the truce line dividing the two countries thirty-seven years after the Chinese attack.[24] Further, the Chinese military made seventy-two incursions into Indian territory, and Indian sources claimed to have evidence that Jiang Zemin told the Pakistani head of state that China had done this to test the military readiness of the Indian forces.[25] Perhaps these Chinese actions were also intended to intimidate India into slowing its development of nuclear weapons.

By March 2000, India and China once again entered into a security dialogue, which continued throughout the year. This led to India and China signing a new bilateral trade agreement in February 2000. Despite these steps, only a few days after the security dialogue began, the Indian Ministry of Foreign Affairs said publicly:

> Two issues of great concern to India are China's attempt to pressure India to give up its nuclear weapons program and Beijing's longstanding assistance to Pakistan's nuclear and missile programs. The government is certainly not pleased about Beijing's continual references to the United Nations Security Council Resolution #1172 passed in June 1998 following the Indian and Pakistani nuclear test. Beijing calls on New Delhi and Islamabad to renounce their programs to build nuclear weapons and missiles. Although most of the powers, including the U.S., have stopped focusing on this resolution, China continues to harp on it. While the U.S. is looking for a way to reconcile India's nuclear security interests with the imperative of a global nonproliferation regime, China seems to be calling for an Indian submission.[26]

The state visit of India's President K. R. Narayanan to China in June 2000 made explicit the way in which China seeks to use the normalization process to further its objectives. Although the president of India was long known in India as a prominent pro-China leftist and was publicly praised by President Jiang as "an old friend of China," Jiang used the state visit for China's purposes and made no concessions to India. During the visit, the Chinese government publicly repeated its commitment to its "all-weather" ally, Pakistan, and harshly criticized the exiled Dalai Lama living in India, calling him an "arch criminal" and accusing his movement of rape, murder, and child cannibalism.[27]

In the same state visit, China refused to make any commitment to reduce its nuclear and missile technology assistance to Pakistan, refused to define the Line of Actual Control between its forces and those of India on territory China seized in 1962, and stated that the problems of the two major border areas where China claims Indian territory should be seen as "a leftover of history" that would be settled with patience some time in the future when "conditions are right."[28] An Australian expert on China commented, "The Chinese formulation that the border issue can be resolved when conditions are ripe really means when the balance of power has shifted in China's favor—as it did vis-à-vis Moscow."[29]

China also refused to provide any support for India's aspiration to have a permanent seat on the United Nation's Security Council. China made no concessions and, in the view of one Indian analyst, "China has been pursuing a policy toward India of engagement with containment. Intended to prevent the rise of India as a rival, the strategy has sought to contain India on three fronts—Pakistan, Tibet and Burma."[30] Representative Benjamin Gillman, then Chairman of the House Committee on International Relations, pointed out, "While Pakistan causes problems on India's Western border, China has been currying favor with the Burmese military government on India's eastern border by selling them nearly $2 billion of arms."[31] Commenting on the June 2000 state visit, a major Indian newspaper wrote, "Over the years India has gone out of its way to attend to China's security concerns, principally over Tibet. However, the Chinese have had a strange way of reciprocating: they aided Pakistan in the making of nuclear weapons and then supplied missiles that can reach Indian cities."[32] Following that state visit, which was the latest in a series of high-level Indian visits to Beijing, the U.S. government discovered that China was increasing its aid to Pakistan, for the building of "long-range missiles that could carry nuclear weapons."[33]

Chinese maps show that the Kashmir region claimed by both India and Pakistan is disputed, except for the one-fifth of Kashmir that is occupied by China, which is shown as part of China; as is the eastern Indian state of Arunachal Pradesh, which China has partly occupied. This may be why, in June 2000, the president of India said to President Jiang, "It is true that the border problems have been left to us by history, but these problems should be resolved and not left again to history. This is not something we should bequeath to future generations."[34] President Jiang, however, made no movement toward compromise or toward the genuine settlement of this issue.

When second-ranking Chinese Communist leader Li Peng visited the prime minister of India in January 2001, both pledged their countries would forge a "new dynamic relationship" and conduct a "security dialogue." Yet at the same time, General S. Padmanabhan, chief of the Indian Army General Staff, said publicly, "We have some problems" on the LAC (Line of Actual Control), and a month later the Indian military again publicly expressed serious concerns about Chinese military intrusions and road building on the Indian side of the LAC.[35]

India has attempted to counter China's growing military power. It established closer naval cooperation with Japan and planned to conduct naval exercises with Vietnam in the South China Sea and with South Korea in the East China Sea.[36] Most importantly, in October 2000, President Putin of Russia made a state visit to India, during which both countries agreed that they would create a "strategic partnership," which Prime Minister Atal Bihari Vajpayee made clear would not revive the alliance the Soviet Union and India had during the Cold War.[37] The joint Russian-Indian statement indicated that both agreed on the need to "build a multipolar global structure," and President Putin said their discussions had confirmed "the coincidence of long-term national and geopolitical interests between India and Russia."[38] The Russia-India strategic partnership includes an agreement that Russia would sell India a significant quantity of weapons—including tanks, jet fighter aircraft, and a used medium-sized aircraft carrier—as well as a significant amount of Russian technology and other assistance to be used in the development of nuclear power in India.

During his state visit, President Putin said, "Our cooperation with India is not directed against any third country . . . we see this as one of the balancing factors for the world."[39] He might have been referring to the fact that both India and Russia might wish to balance the rising power of China. Perhaps Putin's objective was not only to sell Russian weapons but also to preempt any possible India-Japan or India-United States security relationships. President Clinton made a state visit to India in March 2000, and Prime Minister Vajpayee had made a return visit to the United States in September 2000. Both countries decided on an improved political and commercial relationship. However, in the interest of nonproliferation and limiting the prospects for an India-Pakistan nuclear war, the U.S. continued to urge India to adhere to the comprehensive nuclear test ban treaty and thereby restrict its further development of nuclear weapons.[40] Russia made no such suggestions. The issue of the United States-India security relationship remained to be considered in the future.

The visit of Indian Prime Minister Atal Bihari Vajpayee to China in the summer of 2003 continued this one-sided pattern. Once again, China extracted the statements it wanted from the Indian prime minister about Taiwan and Tibetan exiles in India and obtained even more when Mr. Vajpayee changed from India's long-standing position that Tibet was an "autonomous" region within China, calling it instead, "part of the territory of China." He also acceded to China's proposal to reopen an ancient trade route into Tibet from Sikkim, "without a formal Chinese recognition that Sikkim was part of India."[41] Meanwhile, there was no discussion of the disputed border areas, merely an agreement to continue twenty-two years of indeterminate discussions about the border. Neither did India even raise the question of China's continuing weapons of mass destruction and ballistic missile assistance to Pakistan. The Indian foreign minister, Yashwant Sinha, said this was not brought up because, "If we manage to come closer together, then the proclivity for China to do something that is not in India's interests declines."[42]

As one Indian analyst summed up the situation, "India's China policy continues to live on hope," even as China steps up "its strategic containment of India as part of the strategy to deter the rise of any peer rival in Asia."[43] Another Indian analyst described China's increasing dominance over India with a rhyme: "China moves events; India moves files. China never relents; India only smiles."[44]

Geostrategic Positioning: Four Dimensions

In the new century, as China continued to maintain the flow of economic and technological benefits from the United States, the EU, Japan, and Taiwan, its strategy had four operational dimensions. First, to establish a mood of friendly relations with neighboring states while making no concessions on existing disputes; second, to intensify military cooperation with states hostile to the U.S.; third, to establish relations with a large number of developing countries in the hope of taking a leadership position among them in the United Nations, the WTO and other international forums; and, fourth, to prepare the conditions for future strategic denial by obtaining control over major sea lanes and having a near monopoly of some key high-technology inputs required by all advanced industrial countries.

Neighboring States

China has been exceptionally successful in establishing the new Russia-China alignment, and through that relationship a concurrent normalization with the other bordering post-Soviet republics of Kazakhstan, Uzbekistan, Tajikistan, and Kyrgyzstan. China has involved Russia in this process to reduce any Russian concerns about China seeking an exclusive or dominant position in the former Soviet regions of central Asia. At the same time, as these countries have moved to normalize relations and reduce disputes about their shared borders, China has also moved to purchase large quantities of oil and gas from Russia, as well as from Kazakhstan.[45] China seeks to diversify its sources of potential future oil imports from the Middle East and Central Asia. China is also worried about the stability of its Muslim-dominated Xinjiang province and hopes to have the sympathy of the neo-Communist regimes in Kazakhstan, Tajikistan, and Kyrgyzstan, all of which have an Islamic cultural-religious heritage and which also border Xinjiang.[46] By establishing friendly relations with those governments in Central Asia, which are also concerned about potential Muslim unrest and opposition to their one-party rule, China both secures its Western border and reduces the prospect of assistance coming across the border to opponents of its rule.

The relationship between China and Pakistan developed depth in 1978 after the Soviet-supported Communist coup in Afghanistan. In those years, China viewed the Soviet Union as the country seeking world dominance and worked with Pakistan to provide support for the anti-Communist armed resistance movement inside Afghanistan, also supported by the United States. In the next two decades, the relationship deepened and expanded and, for China, a major purpose was to use Pakistan to counterbalance the potential power of India.

In November 1999, General Musharraf took power through a coup in Pakistan. While the U.S. and other major democracies were concerned by the violation of constitutional principles, China simply recognized the new government and repeated that it does not interfere in the internal affairs of states. President Jiang received General Musharraf as his first visitor of the new millennium in January 2000. Both sides repeated that they observed the five principles of peaceful coexistence, and Jiang said, "China is willing to develop good neighborly relations with all neighboring countries. . . . China will never interfere in other's internal affairs and over the years the two peoples have been able to understand and support each other and to devote their efforts to consolidating and developing Sino-Pakistani friendly, cooperative relations."[47] China continued to sell Pakistan technology for nuclear weapons and missiles, to provide economic assistance, and to establish Chinese oil facilities in Pakistan. Following the June 2000 visit of the president of India to China, the foreign minister of China went to Pakistan to emphasize the continuation of the close relationship by saying, "Between China and Pakistan we enjoy this profound and traditional friendship. And our relationship is marked by an all-weather relationship."[48]

This friendship even extended to the Taliban movement, which the Pakistani intelligence service aided in gaining control of Afghanistan before the U.S. removed it following the September 11th attacks. China maintained a friendly relationship with the Taliban, despite its extremist Muslim government. Interestingly enough, there was a Taliban delegation in Beijing on September 11th 2001, and the government of China is known to have purchased materials from the U.S. cruise missile stocks ordered by President Clinton following the Al-Qeada attack on American African embassies. This is rumored to have included an intact Tomahawk missile that failed to detonate.

North Korea and South Korea

While China has normal relations with South Korea and wants to continue these, the two countries have a number of disputes over maritime boundaries for oil exploration and fishing.[49]

China and Russia both share a border with Communist North Korea, which in turn has a demilitarized zone and fortified border with democratic South Korea. Because of the economic dynamism of South Korea, the Soviet Union decided to normalize relations with it in 1990, and China did the same in 1992. China and South Korea have subsequently established a significant economic and trading relationship.

North Korea maintains a massive military force, larger than one million, and in the 1990s undertook the development of nuclear weapons in addition to its conventional chemical and biological weapons arsenals.[50] The ruler of North Korea from its founding by the Soviet Union in 1949 until his death in July 1994 was Kim Il-song. He was succeeded by his son Kim Jong-il, and the institutionalized Communist regime continued the policies of massive military investment in spite of severe economic problems and shortages, which led to enormous suffering for the people of North Korea including years of widespread starvation.

As North Korea moved closer to having the ability to produce nuclear weapons, which could strike South Korea, Japan, or other neighboring countries using its air force or ballistic missiles, the U.S. sought to end the risk of further nuclear weapons development. That led, in October 1994, to the Agreed Framework, whereby North Korea would receive significant quantities of fuel to provide electricity instead of relying on nuclear reactors and there would be assistance to build two nuclear reactors for electrical supply that would not produce material that could also be used for nuclear weapons. This involved cooperation among the United States, South Korea, and Japan to provide the resources, which included humanitarian assistance on a large scale. It also required Communist China to support this settlement. However, it has since been revealed that North Korea did not end its attempt to acquire nuclear weapons, and there are also indications that the same is true of its search for ICBMs.[51]

Russia and China cooperated to encourage North Korea to move toward the symbolic normalization of relations with South Korea. This occurred in June 2000. There were hopes this would lead to a genuine process of accommodation between North and South Korea, but the evidence suggests this was a stratagem against U.S. missile defense. While the ministers of defense of North and South Korea met on a South Korean island in December 2000, the South Korean government noted that in the many months since the June 2000 summit meeting there had been virtually no progress in reducing the size and forward deployment of the North Korean military forces that continued to face South Korea.[52] North Korea must still be considered a hostile, anti-U.S. state. Nearly a year after the June 2000 summit, it had not changed its military deployment, which positions it for rapid attack, and continued its military buildup. The CIA director testified publicly to Congress in February 2001 that North Korea was expanding its arsenal of missiles and continued its "military first" policies.[53] In April 2001, the chief of the General Staff in North Korea said that the 1.1-million-strong army was prepared for "an all out struggle against U.S. imperialists [who seek to] invade and dominate Asia."[54] In May 2001, Kim Jong-il told a delegation of European Union leaders that he would extend the moratorium on a new ICBM until 2003, but that his regime would continue selling ballistic missiles to any country with the money to pay for them.[55]

In the autumn of 2002, when confronted with evidence by the United States, the North Korean regime admitted it had been violating the 1994 agreements from their very inception. Further, it said it was determined to produce nuclear weapons, that it was giving notice of its withdrawal from the nonproliferation treaty, and that any attempt to impose sanctions or take any actions against its nuclear weapons program would mean immediate war. The North Korean news agency said that "as a stick is necessary to beat away a wolf, so too [nuclear] weapons are needed to fight the imperialists." Given the connections between North Korea and the Khan network, as well as their repeated warnings that they would seriously consider the sale of nuclear weapons to states or even individuals, the issue of North Korean proliferation is one of the highest concerns.

The United States proposed negotiations to include Japan, South Korea, China, and Russia, but North Korea insisted that it would negotiate only with the United States on a bilateral basis, and China supported this position.[56] The United States asked China to persuade North Korea not to leave the nonproliferation treaty, but the Chinese leadership responded that it had "no influence" with North Korea. This claim was made despite the fact that more than half of North Korea's fuel oil and 80 percent of its food imports come from China. China also supplies most of the expertise, training, and many of the components for its weapons of mass destruction and ballistic missile programs.

As the negotiations have continued, it appears that the Chinese, and possibly the Russians, are seeking a common goal of pulling the South Korean delegation over to the side that blames the U.S. for the stalled nature of these talks, even though it has been North Korea that has refused fair and equitable deals. This is likely part of the larger Chinese strategy to neutralize the Korean Peninsula, which would remove American forces from their Northeastern territory and free their Northern fleet.

China joined Russia in strongly opposing any U.S.-led military action to remove

Saddam Hussein in Iraq, notwithstanding Iraq's failure to comply with the unanimous Security Council Resolution 1441 of November 2002, which required it to account for all of its weapons of mass destruction. As the U.S. moved forward with political, diplomatic, and military preparations, North Korea became increasingly explicit about its military threats. Among its threats, North Korea said it would turn South Korea "into a sea of fire."[57]

There was every indication, also, that there was collusion between North Korea and China in attempting to open a "second front" of threat and danger as a possible means of deflecting the United States from its planned military action against the Saddam Hussein regime. A demonstration of this could be seen in the unsuccessful North Korean attempt to force an American reconnaissance plane to land on its territory. This would have created an immediate crisis by giving North Korea American military hostages; just as China had in April 2001 when its fighter aircraft caused damage to an American reconnaissance plane, forcing it to make an emergency landing on China's Hainan Island. The staging of the reconnaissance plane incident seemed taken directly from the Chinese experience.

In March 2003, North Korea admitted to the United States that it already had nuclear weapons and that it was going to produce additional nuclear weapons in the coming months. Some months later, it was reported that the CIA concluded, "North Korea has begun reprocessing spent nuclear fuel rods into plutonium for weapons."[58] This was all the more significant since a senior U.S. official had been quoted as concluding, "Once they start reprocessing, it's a bomb a month."[59]

After the U.S. began military action to remove Saddam Hussein from power in March 2003, there was a noticeable change in the statements and actions of China and Russia concerning North Korean nuclear weapons. Now both powers said that they favored the continuation of a nuclear-free Korea. China facilitated one round of negotiations between the U.S. and North Korea in April 2003 and persuaded North Korea to participate, in part, by temporarily cutting off its access to food and fuel from China.

The crisis with North Korea is one example of a situation that involves risks of war and of terrorists obtaining nuclear weapons. The United States seeks to assure that North Korea dismantles its existing nuclear weapons and the facilities to manufacture them, ends its threat to sell these to terrorists, and halts the transfer of ballistic missiles and technology to other state sponsors of terror, such as Iran.

China and Russia are the most important allies of North Korea and, as the August 2003 negotiations began, it was reported that both "oppose any pressure on North Korea."[60] When that diplomatic meeting in China ended with no results, except for the repetition of North Korean threats to detonate a nuclear bomb, China said the U.S. was the "main obstacle" to a peaceful settlement and Russia agreed.[61]

The outlines of China's purposes might well be to trade the verified dismantling of North Korea's nuclear weapon production capabilities for the removal of U.S. forces from South Korea and the de facto end of the U.S.-South Korean security alliance. In this, China seems to have support from Russia, all in the name of peace and stability in the Korean Peninsula. In other words, China appears not to seek just the denuclearization of the Korean Peninsula, but the neutralization of this key U.S. ally in North East Asia.

Japan

China and Japan normalized relations in 1972 and, shortly thereafter, the United States and China did the same. Following China's economic opening in 1978, Japan has been one of the largest contributors of bilateral assistance and credits to China. In 1998, President Jiang made a state visit to Japan, and in 1999, the prime minister of Japan visited China. Intending to reassure the Japanese, Li Peng said in a December 1999 visit, "China will not pose a threat to other countries even as it becomes more highly developed." Li Peng continued that the "China threat" theory is raised by people "hostile to China and is aimed at hindering China's development."[62] That statement intended to reassure Japan echoed a similar one made by President Jiang in 1998, and may well have raised questions in the mind of the Japanese leadership and public about why China seems so intent on refuting a concern that Japan had not raised.

ASEAN

The ten countries comprising the Association of South East Asian Nations are an important group of China's neighbors. These countries have a total population of roughly 450 million, including about 35 million ethnic Chinese who have a major economic role in a number of the countries. China established very close political and military relations with the military dictatorship in Burma and with Prime Minister Mahathir Mohammed of Malaysia, who has moved toward authoritarianism and has been critical of efforts by the U.S. to encourage pro-democracy movements in his country and the region. Mahathir has been very friendly to China for some years.

The military regime in Indonesia, established in 1965 after the Chinese supported Communist coup attempt, ended in 1998. The transitional process led to the election of a parliament, which then chose Abdurrahman Wahid as president. Wahid said that one of his top priorities would be closer relations with China, and his first official visit abroad was to Beijing in December 1999. That state visit involved the affirmation by Presidents Jiang and Wahid of the five principles of peaceful coexistence, a commitment to a broad range of exchanges and relationships between China and Indonesia, and an endorsement by Indonesia of a special relationship among ASEAN, China, Japan, and South Korea, which had been meeting together as "ASEAN plus three" since 1997.[63]

China has also given attention to developing normal relations with the tiny sultanate of Brunei. As a net importer of oil, China may well seek oil supplies from Indonesia, Malaysia, and Brunei in the future. China has a large and growing economic presence through commercial relations with the orderly, prosperous, mostly ethnic Chinese, tiny island state of Singapore.

China has said, as noted, that disputes with other countries about territory and islands in the South China Sea region should be "shelved" until some future time. China has also said that to the Philippines. There have been steps toward normalization with the Philippines, including the visit of China's prime minister to Manila in November 1999, which led to bilateral agreements to expand trade, as well as high-level exchanges among parliament and other groups.[64] Yet the Philippines has continued to insist on its territorial rights to some of the islands in the South China Sea. There were two incidents in July 1999 when Philippine naval ships "accidentally" rammed and sank Chinese fishing ships, which the Philippines claimed were in its waters.[65] There were joint military exercises between the Philippines and the United States in the South China Sea in November 1999, and thereafter the ambassador of China to the Philippines said that China would not "exert its will over other countries concerning the Spratly Islands ... because China will be more concerned with developing its economy over the next fifty years."[66]

Nevertheless, as occasional discussions, exchanges, and commerce between China and the Philippines continue, it is noteworthy that in February 2000, after the Philippine navy boarded Chinese fishing boats, which it said were in its territorial waters, and detained the crews, the Chinese government said that the Philippines should "stop interfering in China's internal affairs and refrain from creating new troubles."[67] This was rare candor on the part of China in this phase of its activities, telling the government of the Philippines directly that it considers the entire South China Sea and all of its islands to be "internal affairs."

A year later, in February 2001, the Philippines discovered that despite its protests, China had increased the presence of its fishing boats (which often collect intelligence) in the Scarborough Shoal, six hundred miles from China and sixty miles from the Philippines. China responded to Philippine objections by saying it was conducting "sovereignty patrols" and that the Philippines should "respect the sovereignty of China."[68]

At the end of March 2001, the security advisor to the Philippine president expressed concern over a "pattern" of Chinese incursions aimed at dominance. This led the Chinese embassy in Manila to repeat its claim that the disputed Scarborough Shoal is "an integral part of Chinese territory."[69] These official assertions of sovereignty by China are a preview of future events as it becomes stronger.

Ironically, it is the three Communist states within ASEAN, Vietnam, Cambodia, and Laos, with which China has had the worst relations during the 1990s. This was essentially because Cambodia and Laos were linked to Vietnam following Vietnam's invasion of Cambodia in 1979 to remove the Chinese-backed Pol Pot regime; they were thus allied with the Soviet Union during the years of Moscow-Beijing hostility. China invaded Communist Vietnam in 1979 and had attacked Vietnamese-disputed islands in the 1980s. In addition, China had continued its support for the dreaded Khmer Rouge Communist guerillas against the pro-Soviet Communist regime in Cambodia from 1979 through the 1990s, until the Khmer Rouge disbanded following the death of its tyrannical leader, Pol Pot.

As part of its strategy to be friendlier to neighboring countries, China normalized relations with Vietnam in 1991. When Chinese Prime Minister Li Peng visited Vietnam in December 1992, he said that both countries should "shelve territorial disputes" and develop closer economic relations.[70] Yet in 1994, China sent warships to the South China Sea to stop Vietnam from building an oil-drilling platform on a site that both countries claimed, and the Chinese Foreign Ministry said that Vietnam's drilling activities have "gravely encroached on China's sovereignty and maritime interests."[71] Not long after, both countries agreed to "disagree, but keep talking."[72] In 1996, China and Vietnam reopened a railroad line, and from 1997 to 1999, both sides removed landmines from their border. This was a sign that they were ready to develop closer economic relations.[73] That was followed by a December 1999 agreement between China and Vietnam on their land border and a visit to China by the president of Vietnam in December 2000.[74] In November 2000, President Jiang completed normalization with the Communist border powers by making state visits to both Cambodia and Laos. China promised Cambodia more than $200 million in economic aid and signed a range of economic cooperation agreements with both Laos and Cambodia.[75] Only days before President Jiang's visit to Cambodia and Laos, the foreign minister of India visited Laos and announced that India had established a new partnership with ASEAN. This was "widely seen as an attempt to counter Chinese influence."[76]

At the end of 2000, having established "normal relations" with all ASEAN member countries, the prime minister of China, Zhu Rongji, proposed that China and ASEAN establish a free-trade area by the year 2002, finally accomplished with the signing of the agreement in November 2004. He said this would "further facilitate the unfettered exchange of goods, capital and information."[77] China did not propose the inclusion of Japan and South Korea in this regional free trade area between itself and the ASEAN countries. Also, the Chinese prime minister said that this new grouping should involve greater dialogue on political and security matters, as well as on trade.

The effects of this treaty could include increased Chinese access to the information and capital-technological resources of the ASEAN countries. China would continue to limit access to its own market and information through its authoritarian controls. At the same time, it could also be the beginning of a process whereby China creates increased economic links with the ASEAN countries that leads to their becoming more economically dependant on China and perhaps, over time, subservient to China on security issues. In other words, this would mark the beginning of a sphere of Chinese political dominance that has the form of a partnership for economic cooperation.

While some intelligence and special operations cooperation with the U.S. in the war on terror might continue, this might be the prototype of the "new political and economic order" China seeks. For example, the economic links established among the ASEAN countries and China could be structured to result in significant personal financial gains for important ASEAN elites. China would then use these profitable relationships inside the ASEAN countries discreetly to encourage those governments to end most arrangements for cooperation with American military forces. Examples would include denying the U.S. and its allies landing rights, ship visits, electronic facilities, or anything else that would have a bearing on the military effectiveness of U.S., Indian, or Japanese forces in the region.

States Hostile to the United States

A significant element of China's foreign policy derives from its view that the enemy of my main enemy (the United States) might be useful in the future. China began its relations with Iran and Iraq by making large profits through the sale of weapons to both during their long and devastating war from 1980 to 1988. Since then, China has deepened its relations with what might be called an anti-U.S. Muslim axis of states, most of which are significant oil producers. These include Saddam's Iraq (2.2 million barrels per day oil production, or mbpd), Iran (3.8 mbpd), Libya (1.5 mbpd), Algeria (1.4 mbpd), Syria (.45 mbpd), and Sudan (oil production began in 1999).[78] These countries also have very large proven reserves of oil. Iraq has 112 billion barrels, Iran 90 billion, and Libya 30 billion,[79] in contrast to China's reserves of 24 billion barrels and the 21 billion of U.S. reserves. China provides many of these countries with political support, investment, the sale of weapons including missiles, and the technology and components for weapons of mass destruction. It is also a customer for their oil exports. At the same time, in the frequent high-level meetings that are held with leaders in those countries, China expresses complete support for the Palestinian cause against that of Israel. Perhaps that and the fact that these are also repressive regimes explain why these countries ignore China's repression of Muslims in Xinjiang-East Turkestan.

An example of this occurred when President Khatami of Iran visited China in July 2000, the third visit by an Iranian president to China since 1993. Initially, he asked to worship at the mosque in Urumqi, the capital of Xinjiang. The Chinese government responded that it was concerned about anti-Chinese riots by Muslims and suggested instead that President Khatami worship at a mosque in Beijing. Khatami did this and subsequently agreed with China that fundamentalist Muslim groups active in Central Asia should be condemned. Perhaps this was not only to curry favor with powerful, rich China, but also because most of these are hostile to Shiite Islam as practiced in Iran.[80]

The military regime in Sudan, established by a coup in 1986, became Islamic fundamentalist and repressed the mostly Christian population in the south. It has been opposed for years by an armed insurgency, the Sudan People's Liberation Army. After the discovery of oil, the Chinese National Petroleum Company began operations in Sudan, and China began to provide support for the National Islamic Front government there. There were reports in August 2000 that China had sent large numbers of personnel, including prisoners and soldiers, by aircraft and ship to guard the oilfields in Sudan.[81] These reports were buttressed by the fact that the guerillas opposing the Sudan government reportedly captured Chinese personnel and that the Sudanese military said that "thousands of Chinese security personnel were available for action."[82]

During the 1990s, China and Communist Cuba moved toward closer relations after decades of distance, when Cuba had taken the Soviet side in the dispute with China. Jiang visited Cuba in 1993. Castro visited China in 1995, and in 1999 the two countries established military relations. The Chinese took over control and significantly upgraded a facility in Cuba to intercept U.S. communications that was built by the Soviets and recently abandoned by the Russians. In fact, an interesting example of the coordination between seemingly disparate anti-American governments came in July 2003, when all private and government U.S. satellite transmission aimed at encouraging the people of Iran was jammed by this, now Chinese-operated, facility in Cuba.

A number of high-ranking Chinese and Cuban military delegations have visited each other and the range of weapons systems China is delivering has expanded. Given China's production, sale, and deployment of large numbers of short- and medium-range ballistic missiles (which can be nuclear armed), there is an obvious threat for China to actually deploy ballistic missiles to Cuba (for example, to deter the U.S. from providing certain weapons to or giving military support to Taiwan). In April 2001, President Jiang visited Cuba during the course of a six-country tour of Latin America and said China "supports the Cuban people's fight to safeguard state sovereignty . . . and reject foreign intervention and threats."[83] Presumably this meant ostensible "threats" from the U.S. Jiang also provided $350 million in loans for Cuba, signed nine cooperation agreements, and said, "Politically we support and understand each other."[84]

From Cuba, Jiang went to meet Castro's close friend and other political partner in the new Cuba-China-Venezuela triangle, Colonel Hugo Chavez, the radical authoritarian president of oil-rich Venezuela, with reserves of 73 billion barrels. Venezuela is currently a major supplier of oil to the United States, which China sees as a competitor for oil imports it will need in the future as its economy continues to grow. China purchased a major oil field in Venezuela in 1997.

Colonel Chavez visited Beijing in December 1998 after his election, before he was inaugurated as president in February 1999. Chavez also made a state visit to China in 2000, during which both sides expressed their interest in expanding economic cooperation. President Chavez also visited Saddam Hussein in Iraq and other anti-U.S. oil-rich states such as Iran and Libya. Chavez has repeatedly expressed his admiration for Castro and his Communist regime; he has visited Castro a number of times, donated oil at far lower prices, and joined with Cuba in support of the Communist-armed insurgents in Colombia and radicals in Ecuador and Bolivia.[85]

As the China-Russia alignment has developed since 1996, Russia has also provided more political and military support to many of the same countries as China—those hostile to the United States. Andrei Kozyrev, Russia's first foreign minister, criticized this very succinctly:

Putin's foreign policy looks like a red star cocktail to me. It is the old stuff, the anti-Americanism, spiced by the support of rogue regimes from Slobodan Milosevic to Saddam Hussein, with the addition of commercial interests.[86]

The decision by Putin to make the first visit to Latin America by a Russian leader to the Castro regime in Cuba in December 2000 demonstrates yet another parallel in Russian and Chinese foreign policy. Putin took with him to Cuba not only Russian businessmen, but also Defense Minister Igor Sergeiev. China had also sent its defense minister to reopen its relationship with Cuba in 1999.[87] Putin said he is not reestablishing the Soviet-Cuban alliance, yet his visit provided welcome support to the Castro regime and included Putin's comment that there is "full consideration of Russian and Cuban positions in crucial international issues."[88] Putin also met with Castro to visit the 1,500 Russian officers who staff the Russian electronic espionage facility in Cuba.[89]

With support from Castro and China, along with billions of dollars in oil revenues, it is likely that Chavez will seek to help radicals in a number of Latin American countries establish pro-Castro/Chavez anti-U.S regimes. It is possible that through political warfare methods and clandestine armed subversion Colombia, Ecuador, Bolivia, and Peru might align with Venezuela and Cuba in a radical bloc of states opposed to the U.S. This would serve Chinese and, perhaps, Russian interests, by distracting the United States, creating insecurities in its hemisphere, which could reduce the willingness of the U.S. to become involved in other parts of the world—the Pacific region, for example.

Key Third World States

In the 1990s, China was increasingly active in establishing political, economic, and often military relationships with Third-World states that are not yet hostile to the United States. China imports some of its Middle Eastern oil from Yemen and Oman.[90] China has sought to develop closer relations with Saudi Arabia, selling that country medium-range ballistic missiles in the late 1980s and seeking to expand economic relations since then. Saudi Arabia has the world's largest reserves of oil, 262 billion barrels, and produces 9 million barrels of oil daily with the capacity to produce 10.5 million. By itself, this could meet China's import needs in the year 2020. In November 1999, President Jiang made a state visit to Saudi Arabia, and in his address to Crown Prince Abdullah said: "The Chinese and Arab people have learned from each other and their friendly relations can trace back to ancient times. . . . China and the Arabic countries are all developing countries. . . . China has all along . . . supported the just cause of the Arab people and their just rights and interests [against Israel]. The Arabic countries have lent China their support on Taiwan and a number of other issues."[91] President Jiang also visited the United Arab Emirates (which produces 2.5 mbpd) and Nigeria (2.2 mbpd, with oil reserves of 23 billion barrels). Egypt, which controls the strategically important Suez canal, has also received a great deal of attention from China. By the year 2000, President Mubarak of Egypt had visited China seven times. President Jiang made a state visit to Egypt in April 2000 and, at the same time, visited Israel, where he also met with Palestinian leaders.[92] Jiang said that China's relations with Egypt could be summed up as "mutual understanding with deep friendship and comprehensive cooperation."[93]

In 1996, President Jiang visited six African countries. This was the beginning of markedly increased Chinese overtures to a number of African countries and was described by China's foreign minister as a decision to "pay more attention to developing its friendship and ties of cooperation with African nations [to develop] twentieth-century oriented relationships of long-term stability and full cooperation with African countries."[94] In 1999, China's foreign minister, Tang Jiaxuan, visited Egypt, Kenya, Uganda, and Zambia, while Vice President Hu Juntao visited Madagascar, Ghana, the Ivory Coast, and South Africa. In January 2000, Foreign Minister Tang visited Nigeria, Namibia, Zambia, and the Seychelles, while another senior Chinese official simultaneously visited Ghana, Benin, Togo, Botswana, and Madagascar.[95] China also has provided economic assistance and undertaken projects in Namibia and Zimbabwe, both ruled by presidents who had led Marxist-Leninist guerilla groups. In September 2000, Foreign Minister Tang outlined China's intention to lead the developing nations in a "nondominant" way, viewed as an alternative to the American approach of "hegemonism."[96] China also has established cooperative relations with South Africa, the most advanced economy in Africa, reportedly including the Chinese purchase of high-tech weapons and radar systems from South Africa.[97]

In Latin America, China has relations with many countries, but has given special attention to the largest and most populous country, Brazil, (which produces 1.1 mbpd of oil). In addition to their partnership in building and launching an "earth resource surveillance satellite," the two countries agreed in April 2001 to conduct exchanges and share high technology in biotechnology, genetics, and information sciences.[98] If radical anti-U.S. groups took power in Colombia (.8 mbpd) or Ecuador (.35 mbpd), it is quite likely that China would purchase their oil exports if the United States sought to impose any kind of economic restrictions. In the next years, it should also be assumed that China may also attempt to establish a closer relationship with Mexico, which is strategically located on the southern border of the United States, has very large oil reserves, and is a significant oil producer and exporter (3 mbpd, with 48 billion barrels in reserve). Most likely, however, in view of possible U.S. sensitivities, China might not attempt to do this until it had accomplished the objectives that define the next two phases to be discussed.

Key Sea Lanes: Strategic Denial

As part of its global strategy, China during the 1990s established organizations linked to the regime astride the major sea lanes and ports of the world. One key instrument is the China Ocean Shipping Company (COSCO). This government-owned entity has close ties to the Chinese military and was described as the "Merchant Marine arm of the PLA" by a former chairman of the Joint Chiefs of Staff.[99] This organization is the second-largest shipping company in the world and has been used by China to transport missiles and weapons of mass destruction components, and to conduct "massive smuggling operations around the world, including to the United States" of weapons, drugs, and illegal aliens.[100] Only the determined opposition of Republican members of Congress such as Duncan Hunter and Christopher Cox prevented the Clinton administration from granting this organization use of the former U.S. naval base in Long Beach, California.

The China Ocean Shipping Company has a major presence in the affluent, strategically located island state of Singapore, as well as at the main port in Malaysia (Port Klang), which is at the Straits of Malacca, through which nearly half the world's shipping trade passes and through which U.S. naval ships move on their way to and from East Asia. After going through the shipping lanes of South East Asia—Malacca, Sundra, Lombok, the Strait of Singapore—ships on their way to China, Japan, South Korea, and the Philippines must pass through the South China Sea. Here, China's claim to sovereignty over all of the islands and all of the South China Sea constitutes a potential point of future confrontation should China seek to restrict or deny access to the South China Sea to the ships of any particular country with which it might have a dispute or which it might be pressuring. The establishment of "fortresses in the sea," the building of a runway capable of basing Chinese jet fighters and bombers on one of the Paracel Islands and other Chinese actions already taken, make clear that it is building the military capability to seek to dominate or control the South China Sea at some time in the future.

Studies done for the United States government in 1996 suggested that if these Asian shipping lanes were closed, it would affect nearly half the world's shipping and the diversion to longer routes would sharply increase shipping, insurance, and freight rates; but the probability of such closing was then estimated to be low.[101] That estimate may have been correct for that time period. However, looking to the future, in the context of the new Russia and China alignment, as well as China's greater military capability and geostrategic positioning, that may change. As Manning said, closing or restricting the shipping lanes of Southeast Asia would be "the economic equivalent of a weapon of mass destruction."[102] In itself this could be a source of enormous political pressure on the states of Southeast Asia as well as on Japan and South Korea.

The Panama Canal

In 1997, the Republic of Panama decided that it would auction the rights to the management of ports at both ends of the Panama Canal to the highest bidder with a demonstrated capability to take over this activity from the United States, which, by treaty, would be leaving the canal zone at the end of 1999. A major American company entered the bidding, as did Hutchinson International Terminals, a subsidiary of a Chinese company based in Hong Kong. China was determined to win the bidding process and used corrupt means to influence the government of Panama in its favor. According to a published report, Panama preemptively closed the bidding, secretly changed the rules, and "simply awarded the contract to Hutchinson before the American or other firms could even know what was happening."[103] The U.S. ambassador to Panama, William J. Hughes, objected to the "unorthodox" bidding process, to no avail. Representatives Duncan Hunter and Dana Rohrabacher expressed grave concerns about the strategic implications of what was, in effect, China's acquisition of control over the ports on both ends of the Panama Canal, and Senate Majority Leader Trent Lott called for an investigation.[104]

The Panama Canal is a strategic transit point of great military importance to the United States because it permits the movement of naval forces between the Atlantic and the Pacific at a great saving of time as compared to alternate routes. Further, shipments through the Panama Canal account for about 13 percent of total world trade and about 15–20 percent of U.S. trade, including about 40 percent of grain exports.[105] The air and naval facilities the United States gave up as part of its withdrawal from the Panama Canal zone at the end of December 1999 were also extremely important to the United States, and the contract won by the

Chinese/Hong Kong company gives it "first option" to take over the ports of Rodman Naval Station as well as an operating area at former U.S. Albrook Air Force Base.[106] When Senate Majority Leader Trent Lott made a formal inquiry to the Clinton administration in 1999 about the strategic implications of China's gaining control of these ports, the administration minimized the importance and described this as an entirely commercial matter. Assistant Secretary of Defense Brian E. Sheridan testified to Congress that the Panama Canal had become less important for U.S. commerce, though he did admit it remains "highly important" and described the Chinese company that had taken over the ports as a "British" company long based in Hong Kong.[107]

In fact, the Hong Kong company that owned Hutchinson International Terminals is the Hutchinson Whampoa Company, bought by Hong Kong entrepreneur Li Ka-shing in 1979. U.S. government reports reveal that this individual has more than $1 billion in assets invested in Mainland China and has a long history of close relations with the Chinese government and the Chinese military.[108] One U.S. government report, as quoted by Gertz, said that "Hutchinson Whampoa group's owner, Hong Kong tycoon Li Ka-shing, has extensive business ties in Beijing and has compelling financial reasons to maintain a good relationship with the Chinese leadership."[109] Another U.S. government report said that Li Ka-shing "is willing to use his business influence to further the aims of the Chinese government."[110] The Chinese government has given Li exclusive rights of first refusal over all mainland Chinese ports south of the Yangtze River and, according to Santoli, "This involves a close working relationship with the Chinese military and businesses controlled by the People's Liberation Army."[111]

The Panama acquisition is worth understanding in some detail. It illustrates how the Chinese government uses ostensibly commercial ventures by providing them with economic rewards for meeting China's strategic purposes, while also using them to hide its geostrategic positioning. In the case of the Panama Canal, it is noteworthy that there were three levels of organization: Hutchinson Whampoa, the Hong-Kong owned company; then its subsidiary Hutchinson International Terminals, the organization acquiring ports in Panama and in other countries; then a subsidiary that would actually manage the Panama port, the Panama Ports Company. The last of these is also partly owned by a Chinese company, China Resources Enterprise, which an in-depth investigation by Senator Thompson found to be a conduit for "espionage, economic, political and military."[112] Perhaps former Secretary of Defense Casper Weinberger summarized it best when he testified in hearings on this issue in 1999 that any attempt at interference with the operations of the Panama Canal could be "catastrophic" for U.S. national security interests in a crisis, and he went on to say that the control of the ports by a Chinese-owned company poses a real threat because, "The company would not be able to survive if they don't do something the Chinese government tells them to."[113] As U.S. Representative Duncan Hunter said, "The Panama Canal continues to be a critical chokepoint for the movement of American forces and supplies. Indeed, as the U.S. Navy has shrunk from 550 ships at the start of the 1990s to about 350 ships today, the ability to ship units rapidly between oceans is vital. The strategists in Beijing are certainly aware of this."[114] The most frequent users of the Panama Canal are first, the United States; second, Japan; and third, China and Taiwan at about the same level. This could mean that control of the ports at both ends of the Panama Canal and the ever-growing Communist Chinese presence in Panama might provide opportunities for China to indirectly pressure both Taiwan and Japan in the future.

In the year 2000, among the thirty-four countries of Latin America, Mainland China had diplomatic ties with eighteen, while sixteen recognized Taiwan. This is a point of important competition for China, which wants to end the recognition of Taiwan by any state. Panama is a small, politically fragile republic with a population of about three million. Communist Cuba has long used Panama as a base for covert operations, including running weapons to Communist guerilla groups in Latin America and for financial operations to evade the U.S. embargo. The Chinese presence in Panama has grown markedly since it gained control of the ports, with more than one hundred thousand Mainland Chinese persons in Panama and $2 billion in total trade conducted between Mainland China and Panama (compared with $400 million in trade between Panama and Taiwan).[115]

During the 1990s, China increased its investments in Latin America by 400 percent, to about $8.2 billion. This involves Chinese investments and relationships with more than two hundred businesses and joint venture enterprises in Latin America.[116] A mission to Panama sent by Representative Dana Rohrabacher in 1999 found that "Panama has become the central base of operations for Communist China in Latin America ... [coordinated by] a senior intelligence officer who operates out of an office on the top floor of a bank building in Panama City with a staff of fourteen."[117] From the Chinese point of view, it now has a new strategic, political, and economic presence in Panama, an ally in Communist Cuba, close ties with the radical military dictatorship in Venezuela, and sees the prospect that the United States may become very preoccupied with the destabilization of Colombia, Bolivia, Ecuador, Peru, and perhaps several of the Central American countries again. From China's perspective, all this would certainly be another means of reducing the U.S. military presence and effectiveness in the Pacific region, where China has more immediate objectives.

China also has a major presence along the shipping lanes of the eastern Caribbean with the China Ocean Shipping Company having a large operation in Freeport, Bahamas. Not far from there, China has a military and electronic intelligence presence and operation in Cuba as a result of the 1999 agreement.

The Suez Canal

China's courtship of President Mubarak of Egypt led to an agreement giving China major facilities at Port Said, the gateway to the Suez Canal. This is one of the world's busiest ship transit zones and is a very important transit route for U.S. aircraft carriers and other naval ships. China also has its naval and intelligence facilities in the Indian Ocean in Burma and, through the building of an inland waterway between its territory and the Rangoon River, access to the Bay of Bengal and the Indian Ocean.[118]

As a result of the success of its export-led economic growth, China has become more dependent on maritime access for its continued economic development, as well as for oil and energy imports. This caused China to be concerned that the preeminent maritime power, the U.S., might be able to exert diplomatic pressures by cutting or restricting its access to imports. This concern was expressed in the conclusion to China's 1998 Report on National Defense: "The quickening of economic globalization and the intensification of the regional blocs render the economic development of a country more vulnerable to outside influences and impacts."[119]

The systematic use of political influence, money, and commercial organizations by China to establish a large and growing presence in all of the major chokepoints of the world's sea lines of communication could be seen as defensive—China wants to be sure that no power could or would restrict access for its shipping. It can also be seen as preparation for possible future actions to deny or restrict sea access to other states, perhaps in indirect ways in order to put political pressure on governments highly dependent on these maritime chokepoints, such as Taiwan, Japan, the Philippines, South Korea and others. This would become more visible in the next phases of China's movement toward dominance.

III. Asian Preponderance: Taking Control of Taiwan
(2005–2008?)

Since 1949, a major objective of the Chinese regime has been to take control of Taiwan. China has diplomatic relations with about 140 countries. To obtain economic benefits and opportunities with China, these countries must accept what the mainland calls "China's Taiwan" as an internal issue for China. This has left Taiwan with diplomatic recognition by only twenty-nine small states among the world's 192 governments.

Before leaving his positions as secretary general of the Communist Party and president of China, Jiang Zemin said in the fall of 2000 that China would take control of Taiwan during the lifetime of his generation of Party leaders.[120] There are three possible ways in which China and Taiwan could come together: first, through a process of mutual consensual cooperation and agreement without coercion. Taiwan has said that could occur when China has evolved into a political democracy. Second, Communist China could use military force to overwhelm Taiwan. As discussed, it is building and deploying the military capabilities to do exactly that. The vice chairman of the Central Military Commission, General Zhang Wannian, said, "It is inevitable that a war will break out over the Taiwan straits within the current five year plan (between 2001 and 2005),"[121] General Zhang went on to describe the means for a preemptive ballistic missile strike on Taiwan, which would include the use of electromagnetic pulse warheads that could "instantly paralyze Taiwan's [electric] power supply." That would be intended to immobilize Taiwan's air and naval forces.[122] For China, the problems with a military attack on Taiwan include the risk that the United States would provide assistance and the possibility that conflict with the United States could cause massive damage to Mainland China, especially if China were to use nuclear weapons against the United States, as it has threatened. Another problem is that even without the United States assisting Taiwan, the Chinese military and Party could not be sure about the outcome of a war with Taiwan and the political effects within Mainland China of a conflict that could involve large casualties, serious economic setbacks, deprivations for the Chinese people, and the real risk of a popular revolt against the Party.

Also, Mainland China wants to obtain control of Taiwan's highly educated scientists, engineers, and skilled workers with their high-technology production facilities intact. This would then contribute immediately to the significant expansion of China's economic, technological, and military capabilities. Another argument against a military attack on Taiwan for the Communist regime is that it could lead to large-scale economic restrictions by the United States, Japan, and other major industrial democracies, including denial of China's access to their markets, technology, capital, and investment resources. The Party may believe that this is a small risk given its view of the "greed of capitalists" and their strong influence on their governments, and given its experience with the short duration of most of the economic restrictions following the Tiananmen massacre. Many in the regime might argue that economic sanctions would last only a few months and would be a comparatively small economic price to pay compared to the national benefits of reunification. However, the Communist government could not be sure, and a prolonged period (several years) of denial of access to the U.S., Japanese, and European Union markets, especially before China would have the ability to retaliate by denying the industrial democracies high-technology exports, which it monopolized and they needed,[123] could undermine sharply its economic growth—which, in turn, could lead to significantly increased political protest and problems for the regime.

INTIMIDATE WITH FORCE, SEDUCE WITH MONEY

Therefore, the method that might work best for Communist China would be to do what then-President Jiang summarized as "Intimidate with force and seduce with money." The intimidation derives from the ever-increasing international isolation of Taiwan and the repeated threats of invasion, combined with military maneuvers and the visible buildup of Chinese military capabilities. This is intended to make the leaders and people of Taiwan believe takeover is inevitable if they cannot find the means to defend themselves.

The "seduce with money" part of the stratagem would focus on the main business leaders in Taiwan, most of whom have significant economic interests in Mainland China, since the Taiwanese have invested more than $70 billion on the mainland. In Hong Kong, China found that its best allies in helping it take control before and after July 1997 were the wealthy business tycoons who also wanted the favor of the Chinese government to help their investments on the mainland prosper. China is pursuing the same strategy in Taiwan.

Though the candidate of the Democratic Progressive Party won the presidency of Taiwan with 39 percent of the vote in March 2000, he made clear to China that he would not move toward independence, despite that having been part of his party's platform in opposition to the Nationalist Party. Nevertheless, China isolated President Chen Shui-bian and demanded that any discussions be preceded by his unequivocal acceptance of the "One China" principle. At the same time, according to an informed report, "During the months after Chen took office, China . . . has [been] courting Taiwan's influential businessmen and most other political parties in an attempt to isolate the president."[124] This courtship has included "covert support from Beijing . . . [for] Taiwanese industrial and commercial circles . . . [who are] urging the government to end any restrictions on Taiwanese investment in the People's Republic."[125]

Workers in Taiwan have been able to increase their wages significantly as Taiwan has become more prosperous, productive, and democratic. As a result, during the 1990s many Taiwanese manufacturers used the legal fiction of Hong Kong-based companies to move to the low-wage Chinese mainland, "despite Taiwanese laws banning direct cross-strait investments."[126] For some years, Taiwan produced nearly 80 percent of the world's most advanced computer chips—a product needed by all the industrial democracies. By December 2000, there were reports that almost half of Taiwan's computer-chip production had moved to Mainland China, including one factory established by Winston Wang, the son of major Taiwan industrialist Wang Yung-ching, who set up a large-scale plant in China jointly with the son of President Jiang Zemin.[127] In that same month, the chairman of the board of one of Taiwan's major computer-chip manufacturers publicly criticized his government's policy of limiting investment in Mainland China and said that his company would be investing in Mainland China to take advantage of the preferential conditions offered by China, because that is the only way his company could be competitive globally.[128]

Beginning in April 2000, China told Taiwan companies that any support for President Chen would cause difficulties for them on the mainland and conversely, that their support for unification would help their businesses on the mainland. China carried out that threat against several companies, and *Far Eastern Economic Review* reported one example:

> Taiwan petrochemical giant Chi Mei says its six factories on the Mainland have been subjected to tax, customs, environmental inspections since mid-May because of chairman Han Wen-lung's outspoken support for Chen, and in the past for Taiwanese independence.[129]

The combination of China's economic pressures on Taiwanese businessmen and the threat that they would be excluded from the Chinese market in the future has worked. This strategy brought about a growing insistence that they would invest more in the mainland and also contributed to the political and economic difficulties experienced by the newly elected government of Taiwan. All this was a preview of the pressures to come.

By 2001, it was estimated that more than $10 billion in capital had left Taiwan. A serious economic crisis deepened and the Taiwan stock market dropped about 50 percent.[130] The Nationalist Party prime minister, whom President Chen had appointed in order to establish a more broad-based government, resigned and was replaced by an individual from the Democratic Progressive Party, while the Nationalists in the parliament opposed most of President Chen's initiatives. At the same time, China invited about one-third of the 221 members in Taiwan's parliament to visit China, as well as inviting a number of Taiwanese political leaders, including the vice chairman of the Communist's old enemy, the Nationalist Party. He visited the mainland and met with senior Communist officials. President Chen said that China was "working very hard to sabotage the internal unity of Taiwan . . . [and] we are concerned that some people and some groups here are receptive to China's wooing and can't distinguish between friend and foe, lack a sense of caution, and a sense of crisis. Our most important matter in internal affairs is to establish a sense of friend and foe."[131]

By early 2003, Beijing pointed out that three hundred thousand Taiwanese lived on the mainland, that Taiwanese take three million trips between Taiwan and the mainland each year, that 60 percent of Taiwan overseas investment is on the mainland, and that trade is $90 billion annually, with a large surplus for Taiwan.[132] The Chinese government official said "stabilizing the situation in the Taiwan Strait" is very important to Beijing's goals of economic progress and good relations with America while also warning about President Chen's "creeping independence."[133]

The Chinese Communist Party has decades of successful united front political action experience in maneuvering among and manipulating groups within society to gain its objectives. It is hard to know exactly when and how this process of dividing and manipulating elements in Taiwan could bring about acceptance by Taiwan's government of China's political terms for its taking control, while continuing to promise that Taiwan would be a special administrative region able to maintain its own institutions and way of life for fifty years—"just like Hong Kong." Most likely, significant elements of Taiwan's business leadership will have a key role in this, and China undoubtedly would promise full amnesty to the Nationalists as the Communist regime did once before when it wanted to win them over. The benefit to China in pursuing its objectives through political and covert action is that the outcome would appear to be entirely the result of decisions made by the Taiwanese themselves. This would remove the prospect that any outside country could or would help to prevent "reunification," and it would also remove any possibility that China's success in taking control of Taiwan would lead to significant economic sanctions or isolation of China. Taken without political or military cost, an intact Taiwan would be an immense prize for China, with its gross national product of $289 billion (1999), its high-technology industries, skilled labor force, and $90 billion in foreign exchange holdings.

As China pursues these purposes in the next years, it will simultaneously use its political and economic influence within the new ASEAN "regional free trade area" to persuade countries in Southeast Asia to restrict or completely deny U.S. and allied military forces access to their territory. Once China has taken control of Taiwan, it is quite possible that China could discreetly persuade Malaysia, Singapore, Thailand, and perhaps Indonesia to no longer permit U.S. military forces access to their territories, even for ship visits. This might be all the more likely if China had used force to take control of Taiwan and the United States had done nothing. China would tell these countries that they—and not the "paper tiger"— should be the guarantor of their security.

As this process of discreetly expelling the U.S. military was occurring, China could seek to use the North Korea-South Korea normalization process and its political and economic relations with both Koreas as a basis for urging South Korea to end its security alliance with the United States. The largest inducement would be for China (and perhaps Russia) to guarantee that North Korea would destroy its nuclear weapons in return for the removal of all U.S. military forces from South Korea and the termination of this alliance. Further, this could involve the use of North Korea's sympathizers in South Korea to demand this in the name of peace and normalization, along with political proposals stimulated by friends of China in South Korea—for example, prominent businessmen who have significant investments in China or Russia. China might even secretly encourage North Korea to make apparently daring and dramatic promises to redeploy and reduce its military forces capable of reaching South Korea, in return for South Korea ending the security relationship with the United States.

Or, there might be secret suggestions by North Korea (encouraged by China) that it could become more threatening and increase its nuclear arsenal and its military deployment for surprise attack if South Korea failed to take advantage of all of the "progress made during the normalization" and show its resolve to "work for peace" by ending the "out-of-date" security relationship with the United States. After Communist China took control over Taiwan, South Korea could be given incentives or be subject to pressures involving the supply of oil and energy from governments friendly to China. Either South Korea acts "peacefully" by ending its participation in "Cold War military blocs" or it could face reductions in the supply of energy imports, or face possible restrictions on the flow of energy by ship to South Korea. China or its "strategic partners" might selectively prevent or "closely inspect" ships bound for South Korea from using the South China Sea, or the sea lanes near Southeast Asian states, over which China might by then have consistent indirect influence.

All of these actions could be taken in a discreet way by China, with the purpose of encouraging and inducing South Korea to end its security relationship with the United States and bring about the removal of U.S. forces and bases there without this being visible to most of the population in South Korea or to the world at large. This would open the way to the next major phase in China's movement toward dominance.

IV. Asian Dominance: The End of the U.S. Alliance with Japan (2008–2012)

After taking control of Taiwan and contributing discreetly to the neutralization of South Korea, China's next foreign-policy priority would be the end of the U.S.-Japanese security alliance. This would virtually remove United States military presence from East Asia and leave China the dominant power there. The Chinese stratagem for accomplishing this would probably have three aspects: reassuring Japan of China's peaceful intentions; providing encouragement and profit incentives for political and business groups within Japan to press for their government to adopt an "independent" or "normal" foreign policy, meaning the end of alliance with the U.S.; and, to the extent necessary, coercive diplomacy and actions aimed at the Japanese government that would be as invisible as possible.

An example of China's policy of reassurance toward Japan was the offer made by President Jiang to establish a "constructive strategic Sino-Japanese partnership for the 21st Century."[134] In President Jiang's visit to Japan in 1998 and Japanese Prime Minister Obuchi's visit to China in 1999, both sides discussed the importance of broadening their already wide-ranging economic cooperation. For many years Japan has reached out to China through extensive direct investment, trade, and also by means of a large aid program. As part of the preparations for those summits, Japan reported that it had provided 2.3 trillion Japanese Yen (about $23 billion) in loans to China for 127 projects and would offer 390 billion Yen (about $4 billion) in 1999 and the year 2000. In addition, Japan provided $2 billion in grant assistance and a fund for technological cooperation in the years 1991 to 1998.[135]

China rarely acknowledges Japanese aid, but often expresses its view of how Japan should conduct its foreign policy. For example, during a July 1999 meeting in Beijing between Prime Minister Obuchi of Japan and Prime Minister Zhu of China, the Chinese prime minister said that the high-level meetings between Japan and China had established clearly that Japan will uphold three principles which he defined as "the path of peaceful national construction, . . . its defense-only policy, and being a nuclear-free country and not becoming a military power."[136] A month later, the foreign ministry of China spelled out its view that Japan being a nuclear-free country meant that it would abide by "the three principles of non-possession, non-production and non-importation of nuclear weapons."[137]

Having taken control of Taiwan and proclaiming its peaceful intentions, China would seek to expand business and cooperative economic relationships with Japan, and might also seek to reassure Japan by its visible conduct on Taiwan. China, in its 1990s offer to Taiwan, stipulated that as a Special Administrative Region, it would maintain its own government and administration, its own military, and its "way of life." This was similar to what China had said about Tibet, Xinjiang, and most recently Hong Kong, before taking control in 1997. Just as a group of wealthy businessmen were key allies of China in establishing effective control over Hong Kong while leaving daily life and most institutions unchanged, so too China could do the same in Taiwan. Instead of appearing, initially, to build up Taiwan as a geopolitical and military strongpoint for further coercive military moves in Asia, if China followed this geostrategic route to domination it would do everything possible to make it appear that daily life continued in Taiwan as before. Of course, as in Hong Kong the government institutions would have to be "restructured" so that the mainland would assure its de facto control over its "province," and there would be some limitations on freedom of speech, assembly, and expression, and thereby limitations on representation. But this could be phased in a subtle and gradual way so that they were not easily visible for some years.

Likewise, Japan would be reassured of China's peaceful intentions if South Korea, as a result of apparent or real normalization with North Korea, had ended or was in the process of ending its alliance with the United States and did not seem to be subject to open military threats and pressures from North Korea or China.

One dimension of China's geopolitical strategy intended to end the Japan-U.S. security alliance might focus on business groups in Japan that have long been involved with China. If China's economic growth continues through the year 2008, when this phase is assumed to begin, it would be likely that China would have accumulated additional years of trade surpluses. At the rate of the 1990s, that could mean cumulative $400–600 billion in trade surplus earnings, giving China the largest foreign-exchange reserves in the world. To these would be added those of Hong Kong and Taiwan, probably on the order of $450 billion (in 1999 dollars) or greater. China would most likely have a dominant role in the ASEAN "Free Trade Region" it promoted. As a result, China could well offer selected Japanese business interests new opportunities for profit through access to China's low-cost labor and its market of 1.8 billion people, including China and the "Chinese Asia Free Trade Agreement" (CAFTA) commercial region.

After the Soviet threat receded, the security debate within Japan involved three points of view: those in favor of the U.S.-Japan security relationship; those supporting Japanese reliance on the UN Security Council and a policy of international civic responsibility but no military involvement; and, third mostly pacifists favoring an independent approach with either the complete elimination of the Japanese armed forces or a minimal army.[138] The pacifist view opposes armed forces on philosophical grounds and also holds that the U.S. and Japanese relationship should be transformed into an economic and cultural partnership, while "U.S. military forces should gradually be removed from Japanese territory. Only by transforming this relationship in this manner can Japan pursue an omnidirectional peace strategy as a truly sovereign nation."[139]

In this century, another group opposing Japan's military alliance with the U.S. has become stronger—the ultranationalists. Their resurgence, in the view of a Japanese historian, has come because "There is a feeling of emergency here and we are very worried," both about the rise of China and about the long economic decline of Japan.[140] This group wants Japan to change its constitution so that rearmament is possible "and be prepared to go it alone in a world . . . full of threats to its survival."[141] These ultranationalists are opposed to both China and the U.S., which they see as limiting, not enhancing Japan's capacity to defend itself. Will there be a "Weimar Japan," a defeated power that moves from reconstruction, to democratic prosperity, to economic crisis, and then to ultranationalism in the face of a menacing, rising nearby power? A combination of international and internal political factors could well isolate those in Japan favoring the continuation of the security alliance with the United States.

After China has taken Taiwan, and as other U.S. military security relationships in Asia were unraveling, many Japanese might conclude that the United States no longer had the ability or the will to meet any security commitments it might make to Japan.[142] Therefore, it would be an unwise course to continue the Japan-U.S. security alliance instead of accepting an offer from China for a "strategic partnership," likely to be coupled with a treaty of friendship and nonaggression. China could also promise Japan that once it had ended its alliance with America, Beijing would guarantee that North Korea would unequivocally end its nuclear weapons/ballistic missile program and cease its threats against Japan.

The Japanese-Chinese friendship association was established in 1950 and has, over the decades, been strongly supported by the Chinese government as a means to create a positive relationship with Japan.[143] The thirteenth anniversary of the normalization of diplomatic relations was marked by a reception in the Great Hall of the People for thirteen thousand Japanese guests, including Prime Minister Koizumi and many members of the Japanese business sector.[144] Since both the Soviet Union and China were greatly concerned about the possibility of Japanese rearmament, and especially since both wanted at all costs to prevent Japan from developing nuclear weapons, it is evident that both China and Russia would have extensive networks of open and clandestine supporters, agents of influence, and spies in Japan.

This would be the time when all of these Chinese and Russian internal political contacts, agents, sympathizers, and resources could be activated in combination with elements of the business sector that had developed profitable relationships with China, in order to create a strong public movement within Japan for an end to the U.S.-Japan Security Treaty. In addition to its emphasis on "peace" as the preferred choice for Japan, rather than "Cold War" alliance, such a movement might also try to identify and mobilize all those with continuing resentment against the U.S. for such things as the military defeat of Japan in World War II, the use of two atomic bombs against Japan, the military occupation, the continued presence of nearly fifty thousand U.S. military forces, the economic costs and inconvenience associated with U.S. military bases and, of course, the times when individual U.S. military personnel have committed crimes against Japanese citizens, often against young women.

If China decided to add discreet or hidden coercion to this mix, it has a number of possibilities. By this time, China's currency might well be dominant in Asia and highly significant in the world. China could threaten Japan's prosperity and exports by threatening to discreetly devalue the Chinese currency, undermining Japan's ability to export and, thereby, threatening its economy. China might threaten, in tandem with Russia, to reduce supplies of energy to Japan imported through joint Chinese-Russian pipeline facilities transporting energy from the Russian Far East.[145] Other potential means of discreet coercion might be to restrict the supplies of oil for Japan indirectly, through China's friendly relations with Middle Eastern producers or through compliant ASEAN oil producers (Malaysia, Brunei, and Indonesia).

Another coercive action might be for China to simply occupy disputed territory both claim. A Chinese perspective on the territorial disputes in the South China Sea with Japan written in the 1990s states that Japan's claims were "constraining China's territorial policy and interfering in China's sovereignty over the Nansha (Spratly) Islands and the Diaoyutai (Senkaku) Islands."[146] China might, for example, occupy the Senkaku/Diaoyutai reefs/islets, partially submerged, uninhabited reefs, that are claimed by both China and Japan. Such an action would pose a direct challenge to the Japan-U.S. security relationship. Japan would view this as requiring full U.S. support for its territorial integrity against an act of aggression by China. However, by this time, the United States would have few if any bases other than in Japan, and China would probably have acquired many more nuclear warheads on ICBMs. It is possible that China would openly or secretly threaten a nuclear strike against cities in the United States, as it did in the case of Taiwan, should America interfere in this dispute about China's "sovereign territory." But even without such a dramatic Chinese threat, the apparent irrelevance of control over the Senkaku/Diaoyutai islets would make it unlikely that the U.S. would want to risk conflict with China over the issue. Under those circumstances, it is most likely that the U.S. would advise Japan privately (as it did with the Philippines in the 1990s) to ignore this Chinese incursion on territory claimed by Japan (which the U.S. had also recognized as under Japanese control).

Thereupon, the next Chinese message to Japan would be that this demonstrates the unreliability, weakness, and decadence of the United States. Without U.S. support, Japan would most likely acquiesce to China and reconsider its security policy. This could be the final step, guaranteeing that Japan would decide to end the military alliance with the United States.

Another means of discreet coercion could involve China's restricting transit through the South China Sea or a number of other Southeast Asian straits for oil/natural gas ships bound for Japan. This could be done indirectly if various ASEAN countries under Chinese pressure and with Chinese support stopped energy tankers, perhaps by raising issues concerning cargo safety, "documentation," or "proper insurance of the ships"—all requiring lengthy inquiries for each ship. This would be a more problematic approach because, from the point of view of the United States, it would violate a broad global principle of freedom of navigation and freedom of the seas, and is more likely to lead to U.S. military support for Japan and to a greater risk of U.S.-Chinese conflict, unless China were to back down from such a hypothetical threat.

In the context of the events described in phases one, two, and three having already occurred, political action alone without Chinese coercion, discreet or otherwise, might be enough to bring about a political decision by Japan to end the alliance with the United States and become another "partner" whose security is "guaranteed" by China. Once that had occurred, it is quite likely that the Philippines would soon follow. Most likely, China would also offer the Philippines a "partner-ship" and a treaty of peace and nonaggression. China might also use some of the same incentives for businesspersons, prominent politicians, and political groups in the Philippines to establish support there for its withdrawal from the security alliance from the United States.

Australia and New Zealand might be ignored in this phase, though there might be efforts to also use political action methods in both countries to bring about an end first to New Zealand's military relations with the U.S. This could be used as a precedent for efforts to encourage "peace-loving" groups in Australia to end the Australian-U.S. security relationship and then be rewarded with an "expanding economic cooperative partnership" with China. Whether or not that occurred, by the end of this phase, with the end of the U.S.-Japan security treaty and the removal of the U.S. military presence from Japan, China would be dominant in Asia.

Although the October 2000 Russia-India partnership was viewed by India as a means of counterbalancing China, its effect might instead have been, during these years, to give India a false sense of reassurance as Russia, in fact, supported, cooper-ated with, or ignored China as it moved toward dominance in Asia.

V. The De Facto End of NATO:
The Neutralization of Western Europe (2010–2014)

From the point of view of Putin's Russia and Communist China, the end of U.S. alliances in Asia and the withdrawal of U.S. forces from all bases in Asia (except perhaps for a few U.S. territories such as Guam) would certainly constitute impor-tant progress toward a more "multipolar world." The immediate consequences would be that daily life would continue in the individual countries of Asia, although their economic and technological dependence on and cooperation with China would certainly increase.

Undoubtedly, China would now persuade Japanese companies to make their most advanced high technology available to the mainland, the technology Japan had been reluctant to provide for many years. China would have a special interest in obtaining Japanese high technology and skilled personnel for its military programs, and they would be well paid initially. Japan, South Korea, and other former U.S. allies in Asia would experience no Chinese or Russian military occupation or belli-cose words—on the surface, all country states would maintain their full sovereignty, and everything would seem to be the same. There would be a focus on "peace and commerce" in Asia. As a result, it might appear to many that international tensions were fewer with the United States only involved economically and not in security alliances.

With those apparently positive examples in Asia, it is possible that some political groups within Western Europe, especially on the left and among rightist ultranationalists, would begin to question the reason for continuing the military alliance with the United States in the North Atlantic Treaty Organization. There has always been a significant portion of political leaders and the public in Western Europe inclined to view NATO as unnecessary during and after the Cold War.[147] The Soviet Union was always very active and effective in providing encouragement and material support for groups in Western Europe that opposed NATO or sought to limit the deployment of certain types of weapons by NATO.[148] It is quite likely that Russia could launch a "peace campaign" of cordial diplomacy and a wide range of activities intended to make clear to the citizens in the European NATO countries that there is no further conceivable danger from Russia and, therefore, no need for Cold War era military blocs. Since 1992, Russia pointed to the end of the Warsaw Pact alliance, urged that the Organization for Security and Cooperation in Europe replace the Cold War "blocs," and often said there was no need for the continuation of NATO.

At the same time, China might suggest to Russia that in order to make this peace campaign even more effective, it should offer to unilaterally reduce its offensive strategic nuclear weapons and its tactical nuclear weapons to very low numbers, calling on the United States, Britain, and France to do the same. China might privately suggest that Russia reduce its total offensive strategic nuclear forces to about three hundred nuclear warheads, approximately half those assumed to be in the arsenals of the United Kingdom and France in 2000. This would be a sharp reduction from the 1,750 warheads that the U.S. and Russia had agreed in 2002 would be their totals by 2007. Such a dramatic nuclear weapons reduction initiative might be viewed as a major breakthrough opportunity and could well evolve toward an agreement between the United States, Russia, the United Kingdom, France, China, India, and Pakistan to set very low numbers of nuclear forces and an inspection system to verify such destruction. By this time (2010), China might claim to have only about one hundred strategic nuclear warheads and offer to open its facilities for inspection as part of this multilateral reduction, which would also leave the U.S. with three hundred strategic nuclear warheads.

In parallel with this Russian peace initiative and the proposal for agreed sharp reductions in offensive nuclear weapons, China might offer strong economic inducements to business interests in Europe and to European countries to persuade them to take the position that it was time for "Cold War bloc politics" to end. China might begin to transfer many of its contracts and commercial opportunities from the firms of the United States to those in Western Europe. China has often used economic means of this kind in its past diplomacy and might also transfer its by-now globally important currency dealings from the U.S. dollar to the Euro, thereby strengthening the Euro and weakening the dollar. What is envisioned here is a large-scale, comprehensive set of economic steps by China designed to benefit those in

Europe who became active in persuading their governments to end the NATO alliance.

The European Union agreed in December 2000 that it would establish an independent military force independent of NATO. At the time this was being considered, then U.S. Secretary of Defense William Cohen told a meeting of NATO foreign ministers that unless European force were directly linked to NATO, the alliance could become "a relic of the past."[149] Cohen went on to say, "If we had a competing institution that was established, that would be inconsistent with military effectiveness. If in fact there was any element of using the [EU] force structure in a way to simply set up a competing headquarters . . . NATO could become a relic."[150] It is quite conceivable, as events unfolded in Asia leading up to this future time period, that the Europeans would have expanded the size and functions of the independent force in order to be sure that they had the capabilities needed for their own defensive purposes, irrespective of decisions made by the United States. This is all the more likely in view of the strategic opposition from France and Germany to the U.S. liberation of Iraq in 2003. This would be another dimension contributing to the dissolution of the U.S.-European NATO alliance.

If the Russian and Chinese political, military, and economic offers, inducements, and accompanying political actions and measures had not yet produced the desired result, it is quite possible that a number of regimes friendly to China, which were also major suppliers of oil and energy to Europe (Russia, Iran, Libya, Sudan, Venezuela, and others), might quietly link the price of oil to the question of whether a European country were a member of NATO or not. Membership in NATO would require paying 50 to 100 percent more for energy imports from China's oil-rich friends in comparison with a European country that had ended "bloc politics." That would have very negative effects on the economy of any European country that did not leave NATO.

Taken together, a concerted "peace campaign" by Russia, in combination with substantial economic inducements by China and a widespread perception that the end of U.S. alliances in Asia had produced no negative effects, could lead to the end of NATO by the voluntary withdrawal of one European country after another. This might even be accompanied by European-Russian-Chinese friendship and nonaggression pacts that would be described as the new "Eurasian peace consensus."

VI. China Obtains the Russian Far East, China Is Dominant over Russia (2014–2020)

It would take several years for the United States to remove all of its bases and forward deployed forces from Europe. As in Asia, following the end of the security alliance with the United States daily life would seem to continue as it had before.

There would be no open military threats from Russia, much less from China. The Europeans would be pleased with the many new economic and commercial opportunities they had in China and China's (and therefore Asia's) shift from the dollar to the Euro. China would probably suggest that its currency be dominant in Asia and the Euro for most other world regions. Its purpose would be to end the era of the U.S. dollar as the global currency.

While the advanced economies of Europe and Japan provided China with an ever-growing volume of high-technology products and skills, there might be a sense of nagging concern about China's dominance in the production and export of a number of vital high-technology components needed by all industrial countries with advanced economies and information systems. The pattern would be for China to acquire the most advanced technology from Europe and Japan, copy and slightly or significantly improve on it, ignore any protests about "pirating" high tech, then export it at one-fifth the previous price. This would bankrupt competition in Japan and Europe, and China would become the sole supplier of a growing number of essential inputs for all advanced economies. China may also become skilled at using its relations with developing countries to reshape the World Trade Organization in its interests.

Yet, most would perceive this as a time of peace and stability. China and Russia would have congratulated each other on their success in using mostly political and economic means to bring about a "multipolar world" and on the diminished international role of the United States. Many in the United States would be quite content to have an end to the political, economic, and military burdens that the United States had carried in providing for the defense of former allies in Asia and in Europe.

Russia would probably have made progress economically but still be experiencing a number of problems and lagging behind China in its pace and depth of high-technology economic development. Russia would have continued selling China, for hard currency, its most advanced weapons and technology, including its most advanced military systems.

Therefore, it would come as a surprise to Russian leaders when China made its private offer: China would purchase the oil- and mineral-rich territory of the Russian Far East for $100 billion and provide Russia a continuing royalty payment for fifty years of 20 percent of the hard-currency earnings China obtained from its intensive development of these resources. In the formal written offer, China makes no mention of the fact that it had always been China's view that this vast territory was stolen from China by the unequal treaty of 1860 and that during the period of military alliance in the 1950s, China had often requested the return of this territory from the Soviet Union. However, those points were made by the Chinese in conversations with the Russian negotiators.

We recall that Russia had reduced its offensive nuclear forces, along with the United States, to a few hundred (in Phase V), as part of the incentive for the Europeans to end the NATO alliance. As the Russian government, with some shock, considers this offer and its meaning, China goes on to reveal to the Russian leadership that it had an offensive strategic nuclear force of approximately five thousand warheads (not one hundred as claimed) and also that it had developed, built, and deployed secretly a highly effective national missile defense system. This was derived from a synthesis of advanced Russian, United States, and Chinese technology and had been thoroughly tested in secret. China provides Russia with evidence that its missile defense system really exists and works against both Russian and U.S. forces. China tells the Russian government not to discuss this offer publicly and indicates that the reason China has done this was to guarantee world peace and to further the development of the new "international political and economic order" it has sought since the 1990s.

A part of the Chinese offer not revealed to all Russian officials is that China would add another $30 billion to the purchase price for the Russian Far East in order to purchase all of Russia's offensive strategic nuclear forces, as well as its biological and chemical weapons. These would be secretly transported to China by special Chinese units, which would wear Russian military uniforms while on Russian territory in order to minimize the risk of "misunderstanding" or of counteractions by elements of the Russian military or public. At the start, and again at the conclusion of the project, China would deposit $20 million in Swiss or other designated foreign bank accounts for each of the senior Russian political and military leaders who agree and who oversee the implementation of the weapon transfers, which would occur before China assumed control of the Russian Far East. Of course, this would all be done secretly.

Though no military threats have been made, it is evident to the Russian side that China is determined to take this territory from Russia and is prepared to use its offensive nuclear forces and national missile defense to defeat decisively any Russian attempt at resistance. As a result, the Russian government first secretly transfers its strategic forces, all nuclear warheads, and its chemical and biological weapons. Later it agrees to publicly "sell" the Far Eastern territories. With great fanfare, the Russian leadership describes the new arrangement as part of the deepening of the Russian-Chinese strategic partnership for the twenty-first century.

VII. The United States Is Geopolitically Isolated, China Is Preponderant in the World (2020–2023)

Once China reveals its much larger-than-claimed and assumed offensive strategic nuclear force and deployed national missile defense to Russia, it realizes that the

United States would soon have word of this new reality. Therefore, the Chinese government privately communicates the facts to the United States government and couples this with a statement prohibiting the United States from adding to its now small nuclear weapons arsenal of several hundred warheads and from taking any steps of any kind to deploy a national missile defense system or to develop its existing capabilities further. This is done secretly so that the leadership in the United States could comply with minimal political consultation or embarrassment. China adds verbally to its written command to the United States that it will take military action using whatever weapons it chooses against the territory of the United States should there should be any noncompliance by the United States. China makes it clear that its sole purpose is to safeguard world peace, stability, and the five principles of peaceful coexistence.

The United States now finds itself in a world without allies. All the Asian countries are now part of the "cooperation sphere" with China, while the European countries have adapted to their new political and economic relationship with both Russia and China. The United States remains highly dependent on oil imports (approximately 10–15 million barrels a day), and China now has dominant influence with most major oil exporters so that it could bring about a reduction or cut off oil exports to the United States through governments with which it has friendly relations.

In essence, China now controls, through governments that were in effect allied with, dependent on, or subservient to it, most exports of oil to any country in the world, as well as all the major sea lanes of the world, including the Panama and Suez Canals. As before, China prefers to exercise its dominance discreetly through secret payments or threats and through the actions of other governments. China privately informs the United States that if it wishes to continue receiving any more imported oil, if it wants its shipping to have access to the Panama Canal, the Suez Canal, or any of the world's major sea lanes, and if it wants to avoid a cut-off of key high-tech components now made only in China on which its economy depends, it must agree to give up its veto in the UN Security Council.

To avoid massive economic problems, most likely including severe depression, the United States agrees. The UN Charter was amended so that only China had a veto and countries subservient to China are guaranteed a majority on the U.N. Security Council. China then arranges that the UN Security Council would direct that the United States and all other countries in the world, except China, would be prohibited from conducting any research, development, or deploying any form of national missile defense or regional missile defense.

Further, in order "to maintain world peace and stability," the new UN Security Council passes a resolution requiring that all nuclear powers, except China, fully and completely dismantle their offensive nuclear forces and the means of delivery with full inspection to be undertaken and supervised by a UN agency led and staffed by China. Evasion by any nuclear power of this UN Security Council Resolution would be met immediately with a cut off of oil imports and the prohibition of any trade or international air/sea transport into or out of that particular country and could also lead to punitive military strikes by China, acting on behalf of the United Nations.

VIII. China Is Dominant in the World (2025–?)

Once these UN Security Council Resolutions have been implemented by the United States under Chinese-led supervision and inspection, China would be the dominant power in the world. Only China would have offensive nuclear weapons and delivery systems and only China would have a national missile defense system. Therefore, China could control the actions of major and minor states simply by issuing orders, and if these were met with evasion or noncompliance, China could threaten punishment beginning with economic deprivations and ending with the threats of ever-increasing military destruction.

To preserve "peace and stability," China would have the UN, now under its control, establish a "United Nations monitoring and inspection system"—led and mostly staffed by Mainland Chinese military and intelligence personnel. This would make certain that there would be no further production of nuclear, chemical, or biological weapons or delivery systems, or of any missile defense capability in the United States, Russia, Japan, the United Kingdom, France, Israel, India, Pakistan, or any other relevant country. This monitoring system might require many thousands of personnel and all costs would be paid by the countries under review (except, perhaps, for Pakistan).

China, under the five principles of peaceful coexistence, would of course "fully respect the sovereignty of all countries." But, in the interests of preventing war and the possibility of any future direct or indirect aggression, such as foreign intelligence services seeking to stir up discontent within China, among the Uygur Muslims or Tibetans, China could have the UN Security Council also require the following:

- the complete dismantling of all intelligence and espionage/covert action related services and capabilities in the U.S., Russia, Japan, India, Europe, Israel;
- the removal to China of all operational files of these intelligence services, along with the "temporary assignment" of knowledgeable personnel from each of the countries under review to guide a Chinese-led "Truth Commission," in a full and complete examination of all intelligence activities,

sources, and methods used in the preceding twenty years by each of the major powers.

Once these steps had been substantially completed, all the major powers—the United States, Russia, Japan, Europe, and India—would have been strategically disarmed. The next step would be for China, through the UN Security Council or directly, to require that "in the interests of world peace and development" the major powers also sharply reduce their conventional military forces—perhaps by 80 percent. It is quite likely that China would require that the most advanced aircraft, submarines—including all ballistic missile submarines—warships, aircraft carriers and the like, be transported to China, disarmed under Chinese military control, in a phased process. The various national military crews would then remain in China "temporarily" as long as required to train Chinese military personnel in the full and complete operation of these complex systems. It is quite likely that these foreign military personnel would never return to their countries.

At the same time, Chinese military personnel with secure communications to China would take up residence at all major military bases on the territories of the major powers and would supervise the 80-percent reduction in forces and the destruction of heavy weapons (such as artillery, older tanks, etc) that were not shipped back to China. All the expenses of this large undertaking would be paid by the major industrial democracies, which at this time would be required to pay annually the first "world peace tax," set at 5 percent of their GDP (Russia, India, Pakistan, and developing countries would be exempt). This would reimburse China for its contributions and costs in bringing about world disarmament and peace (Pax Sinica) through its leadership. This tax (equivalent in year 2000 U.S. dollars and GDP of $10 trillion to $500 billion, or $1,300 per capita) could be paid in products, services, or gold, and would represent the first economic effect of China's global dominance visible to the general public.

In due course—after the full disarmament process had been completed and China assured itself that it had taken all the international steps needed to assure and maintain its global dominance—there would be additional requirements that the former imperial invading powers pay reparations to China for the consequences of their exploitive or aggressive actions during China's decades of weakness (1800–1949). These reparation payments might be very substantial, perhaps 10 percent of GDP annually. Over time, this would serve to transfer enormous resources from the U.S., Europe, and Japan to China, providing the Communist regime with wealth that could further build up its military and technological capacities. These payments could also lead to major improvements in living conditions for the average citizen, which might solidify the rule of the Party. No doubt, the payment of these reparations would significantly lower real incomes and the standard of living in the subordinate countries, especially Japan, the U.S., and Western Europe, which would probably be required to pay the most.

This relatively benign view of the consequences of a globally dominant Communist China might be called the Chinese imperial approach: take tribute, assure no military threat, but let the subject countries maintain their own political, social, and cultural practices. There are far worse possibilities, as can be seen in the tragic repression and brutality used by Communist China against the people of Tibet, against any Chinese who defied the edicts of the Communist Party, as well as in the mass terror inflicted on disarmed and helpless men, women, and children by the Chinese-supported Khmer Rouge Communist regime after its victory in Cambodia (1975–79). There are also the tragic examples of Soviet terror, mass killings, and imprisonment under Stalin, or of Nazi rule and mass extermination under Hitler when ideological dictatorships committed enormous crimes against humanity. There really is no way to know how repressive and brutal a globally dominant Communist China might become. Unfortunately, the historical pattern is that of expansionist, unopposed dictatorships becoming even more vicious and repressive over time.

The tragic history of modern dictatorships of the extreme right and the extreme left teaches that it would be best that the political scenario described above never became reality—starting with China's dominance of Asia. In the concluding chapters, we will discuss how the United States and its allies can work to ensure that the grim prospects of a globally dominant Chinese Communist dictatorship never comes to pass and, instead, that both China and Russia will evolve peacefully in the years ahead.

IV. WINNING THE PEACE: A COMPREHENSIVE STRATEGY

19 Russia and China's Two-Track Policies: Destination Unknown

"There is a hope in the region [Asia] that China will become rich and benevolent. The fear is that China will become rich and aggressive."

— ADMIRAL DENNIS BLAIR, commander in chief,
U.S. Pacific Forces, 2001

"We have a stake in Russia's success. . . . [We hope] for a Russia that is truly great, a greatness measured by the strength of its democracy."

— PRESIDENT GEORGE W. BUSH, Warsaw, Poland,
June 15, 2001

In the immediate aftershock of September 11th, there were reasonable grounds to hope the relations with both China and Russia had been set on a more positive footing. President Jiang promised Chinese cooperation in the war against terror. President Putin responded with concrete actions, opening Russian skies to U.S. aircraft attacking the Taliban and Al Qaeda in Afghanistan and encouraging several Central Asian regimes to permit U.S. forces to operate from their territory.

Meanwhile, the cordial November 2001 summit in Crawford, Texas between Presidents Bush and Putin led to an agreement on major cuts in both countries' nuclear weapons. Then, in December of 2001, a new NATO-Russia council was established to bring Russia closer to NATO, Europe's bedrock security alliance.

If this were the whole story, the wishful-thinking approach of so many might be justified. As we have seen, however, this is far from the whole story. In fact, in the months following September 11, 2001, both China and Russia continued and even strengthened their cooperation with what President Bush called the "Axis of Evil"— Iran, Iraq, and North Korea. These regimes actively support international terrorism and are secretly working on developing weapons of mass destruction.

Since the end of the Cold War, China has been North Korea's primary supplier of both weapons of mass destruction and the technologies to produce them. This is primarily done through various Chinese companies, which are all government-owned and generally have links to high-level Chinese Communist Party officials.[1] It has also been done through Pakistan and the Khan network, which, as described earlier, is also a major recipient of Chinese WMD and missile assistance.[2] Similarly, Chinese companies have helped Iran build several chemical and biological weapons-related facilities. China has also provided equipment and engineering assistance, including direct-design assistance, and even sold a new generation of highly accurate, solid-fueled ballistic missiles that are much more capable than anything Iran currently deploys.[3] Chinese companies have also upgraded Iraq's air-defense capabilities.[4] The CIA reports that since the Gulf War, Iraqi WMD and missile-production capabilities have actually increased, with the probable assistance of foreign technology and expertise.[5] The unnamed foreign power could also be China, especially since the greatest improvement was the development of a solid-fueled missile capability, an area in which China is a leader.

Meanwhile, Russian Foreign Ministry officials held a major meeting in Moscow with senior Iraqis to highlight Iraq's position as "Russia's leading partner in the Arab world."[6] In December 2001 Putin publicly "cautioned the United States against attacking Iraq . . . saying he expects to be consulted before the U.S. antiterrorism campaign is expanded to other nations."[7]

As for Iran, Russia continued its weapons and nuclear sales and assistance, which the United States contends advance that country's covert program to build nuclear weapons. After September 11, 2001, despite expressed U.S. opposition, Putin continued the nuclear-assistance program begun by Russia in 1995. Russia has contended its actions have no bearing on Iran's development of nuclear weapons, but a senior State Department official said in November 2001 that "Russian cooperation is a significant accelerator for the Iranian process for acquiring nuclear weapons," a view also expressed in the biyearly CIA report to Congress on these issues.[8]

China and Russia are pursuing a two-track strategy toward the United States that seems invisible to many in the foreign-policy community. The first, more overt, and seemingly benign track seeks to maintain the aura of normal relations with the United States and other democracies so they will continue providing vitally needed economic benefits. A good example was the first Bush-Putin meeting in July 2001, during which Putin, to wide praise in the West, agreed to discuss offensive strategic forces and defensive systems together. Bush viewed this as a step toward the "new framework for peace" that went beyond rigid adherence to the 1972 Anti-Ballistic Missile Treaty.[9] The president simultaneously announced he would send Treasury Secretary Paul O'Neill and Secretary of Commerce Don Evans to Moscow to discuss increased U.S. direct economic investment in Russia.[10]

When it comes to China, Bush has, since his very first months in office, used almost the same language as Clinton in announcing his support for continuing full access for China's exports to the U.S. market. As stated earlier, China's mostly one-way trade with the U.S. allowed China to accumulate a trade surplus of about $862 billion since 1990, entirely defraying the cost of that country's massive conventional and nuclear military buildup. Current U.S. policy also supports the flow of U.S. direct investment into China, as well as billions of dollars annually in subsidized loans from the World Bank, the Asian Development Bank, and access to billions for Chinese companies in U.S. capital markets.

The second track of China and Russia's strategy toward the U.S. is to use mostly discreet or covert means to oppose or limit the United States on security issues and to divide America from its allies. This was the preferred KGB approach when Putin served there from 1975 to 1991. During much of that time, the KGB supported a major propaganda effort to "remove the image of the Soviet Union as an enemy" from the view of governments and citizens in the U.S., Europe, and Japan. This second track, including the effort not to be perceived as a threat in the U.S. or by most countries, has also been China's approach during the post-Tiananmen/Jiang years.

Obviously, as far as the U.S. is concerned, these two tracks lead in very different directions and ultimately to very different destinations; escalating tensions, a rise in global terrorism, and outright conflict leading to war is just one—and not the least likely—of those destinations. Clearly, we desperately need an eyes-wide-open U.S. strategy that combines clear objectives with flexible, pragmatic actions—the kind learned during the Cold War—to protect U.S. international interests. The ultimate aim of such a policy is much higher, however: We should seek not just to assure our major interests while preserving the peace with China and Russia, but also to create the foundations of a lasting peace with both countries through a peaceful strategy to help those in Russia and China who seek the development of truly democratic governments in their countries. These will respect the rule of law: domestic law, human rights, and international law.

How to Win Friends and Influence (Erstwhile) Enemies

Two fundamental perspectives underlie this comprehensive strategy. The foreign policy of states is shaped not only by their calculus of risks and opportunities, but also by the political character of their regimes. Genuine democracies are virtually always peaceful and do not initiate the use of force or coercion. Therefore, the fundamental U.S. concerns for human rights and political democracy abroad should constitute a major practical, not just rhetorical, aspect of U.S. policy toward Russia and China. There are peaceful, open actions the U.S. can and should take to encourage progress in this domain in both countries.

This new U.S. strategy includes two broad dimensions. First, we must act to limit and prevent any further deterioration of the U.S. security situation. This means we should:

1. speak truthfully about U.S. actions and purposes in the world and also about Russian and Chinese actions;
2. strengthen the political and military alliances of the United States;
3. build a missile defense for the U.S. and key allies; and
4. prevent or reduce the theft or unauthorized sale to China and Russia of advanced military technology.

Second, we must act to promote positive changes both inside Russia and China and, more immediately, in their international behavior. For Russia, this would include incentives for strengthening peaceful, democratic reform. At the same time, Russia must be helped to understand that while peaceful, normal relations with China are positive, the continuing sale of a variety of advanced weapons to China and its strategic cooperation with China against the U.S. is neither in the Russian national interest nor in the interest of peace. For China, active support for peaceful, democratic change within the country should be combined with a shift of U.S. policy from unconditional to realistic engagement.

It is also important that economic relations with both Russia and China promote, rather than undermine, fundamental U.S. national security interests. Since 1989, U.S. trade policy with China has been contrary to U.S. national security interests because it helped the Communist regime accumulate an enormous trade surplus that has been used, in part, to support its neoimperial world strategy and the development and purchase of advanced weapons systems. China's official international statements, military preparations, and military publications make evident that these new weapons are aimed at U.S. forces in the Pacific region and at U.S. cities. The current U.S. trade relationship with China has helped the nuclear-armed Communist dictatorship grow ever more wealthy and well armed. While political repression deepened during the 1990s, the regime has become more assertive and coercive internationally. This was illustrated by its actions and claims in the South China Sea during the April 2001 harassment and near-fatal damaging by a Chinese jet fighter of a U.S. reconnaissance plane in international airspace.

With China and Russia, economic relations should not and cannot be an end in themselves, nor can they be separated from U.S. national security concerns. It is in America's most immediate, basic, and overriding interest that these two nuclear-armed regimes be deterred from aggression, especially following their new alliance. It is time for the U.S. to use economic statecraft with China and with Russia. As will be discussed in the following pages, this means that economic benefits from the

U.S. should be provided or withheld on the basis of the actions of both regimes, rather than, as in the 1990s, continuing to flow irrespective of their challenging or potentially hostile actions. The enormous economic benefits the U.S. provides directly or facilitates can and should constitute a major instrument used to meet the new China-Russia strategic challenges in a peaceful way, without the need for the threat or use of force.

20 The Other Axis: China and Russia—America's Foremost Strategic Challenge

> "With our intercontinental missiles we have the Americans by the throat."
> —KHRUSHCHEV *speaking to Mao, July 1958*

This new China-Russia strategic axis is explicitly intended to counter the United States around the world and provide the basis for a still-undefined "new political and economic order" that China has declared to be a major global objective and which Putin endorsed at his first summit with Jiang. This raises a fundamental issue: in looking to the next years in this new century, should Russia and China be viewed as essentially cooperative international powers or do one or both pose a strategic threat to the U.S. and its allies? Several major risks of potential conflict are suggested by the analysis of the internal and international political evolution of Russia and China.

A MORE DANGEROUS WORLD

The new China-Russia strategic axis makes the world more dangerous. For the first time in forty years, the U.S. faces these nuclear-armed major powers coordinating their international actions and openly or secretly providing each other with military guarantees in the event of conflict with the U.S. or other countries. There are a number of risks deriving from this new Chinese-Russian strategic cooperation.[1]

Since 1996, Russia has increasingly accepted and repeated most of Communist China's views about international politics and about the U.S.; for example, that the U.S. seeks to dominate the world. In July 2000, Putin spoke of the "economic and power domination of the United States." Therefore, the U.S. must be balanced, contained, and opposed by a "multipolar" international system to be established with the support of the China-Russia axis. Even after the post-September 11th era of cooperation, Russia's Foreign Ministry said in 2002 that a major task of Russian foreign policy was to keep the U.S. from acting on its own in the world.

Second, the Chinese view of the treaty with Russia emphasizes that when one of the parties "experiences military aggression," the other signatory state should, when requested, "provide political, economic, and military support and launch joint attacks against the invading forces." Most believe this applies to Taiwan; however, it also applies to all of China's territorial claims, including those based on questionable historical accounts. This was illustrated by Chinese actions following the April 2001 collision between a U.S. reconnaissance aircraft and a Chinese jet interceptor. China defines virtually all of the South China Sea and its islands as its sovereign territory. If the United States should threaten or take any type of counteraction (political, economic, or military) against China to uphold the rights of U.S. or allied aircraft or ships in that international air and sea space, or to help allies or other countries defend themselves against coercion by China—which has territorial disputes with eleven neighboring countries including Japan and India—China could define this as "blackmail" and a violation of its "sovereignty." China officially stated in 2001 that a U.S. regional missile defense in Asia would be an "infringement on its sovereignty."

In any situation that China determines to be a violation of sovereignty, it would then hope to draw Russia in militarily. This could pose serious additional military risks to the U.S., as illustrated by the February 2001 Russian military exercises that included simulated nuclear attacks against U.S. military units viewed as opposing a Chinese invasion of Taiwan.[2] This was a very disturbing event. It suggested the truth of Chinese claims since the Jiang-Putin summit of July 2000 that Putin had agreed that Russia would use its military forces against the U.S. in Asia in the event of conflict, should China attempt to coerce Taiwan into "reunification." Hard-liners in China are very likely to assume that the U.S. would never dare risk conflict with both Russia and China on behalf of Taiwan. Their perception or, in a worse case, the reality of Russian military support for China could make them more willing to threaten or actually use force. They would assume that during a crisis, whatever it might have declared in advance, the U.S. would back down. This is exactly how unexpected, unintended major wars happen.

A third negative consequence has been the ever-increasing Russian military sales and other support for the buildup of Chinese advanced weapons systems specifically targeted at U.S. air, sea, and electronic military capabilities and vulnerabilities in the Pacific. For example, the Russian antiship missiles that accompany the two Russian destroyers already delivered (and the four more to come), skim the ocean at over twice the speed of sound, can carry nuclear warheads, and were designed to sink U.S. aircraft carriers. In the 1990s, Russia sold China about $9 to $20 billion in advanced weapons systems (jet fighters, submarines, destroyers, antiair/missile systems) aimed at U.S. forces, with another $20 billion in weapons and high-technology sales planned through 2004. The income from these sales also helps Russia further modernize its strategic nuclear forces, which have about four thousand warheads on about one thousand ICBMs.

A fourth negative result has been that Russia and China are working together and in parallel to oppose the U.S. decision to deploy national or Asian regional missile defenses. Their opposition failed to halt the Bush administration's wise decision to develop and deploy a limited national missile defense for the continental U.S. or the continuation of the development of regional systems in cooperation with our allies in Europe and the Asian Pacific region. However, even as they hold discussions on this issue with Washington, China and Russia are continuing to try and persuade other nations such as India, as well as U.S. allies opposed to these systems, to form a unified international front against such defensive systems. At the same time, Russia has sold China one of its most advanced weapons (S-300), originally designed to shoot down the Pershing medium-range missile, as well as aircraft and cruise missiles. Russia has also sold China a similar medium-altitude, antiair/missile system (Tor-M1) in such quantity that China is now, in effect, deploying its own missile/air defense system on its coast.[3]

Fifth, Russia and China have provided weapons of mass destruction components, technology, and expertise to a number of dictatorships such as North Korea, Iran, and Libya that are hostile to the U.S. and its allies. Russia and China have also established military supply links with Cuba and with the pro-Castro Chavez regime in Venezuela. The risk of regional conflicts increases as all these dangerous regimes become militarily stronger and believe that they are backed by both China and Russia.

But the most significant challenge to the United States, at least early on, is more likely to come from Chinese-Russian political and covert actions aimed at reducing Washington's international role. As one example, consider the defeat in 2001 of the U.S. proposal for "smart sanctions" against Iraq: First China extracted economic concessions from Washington in return for not using its veto in the UN Security Council to stop the U.S. plan, then Russia stepped in with a veto.

Examples of possible Russian-Chinese political cooperation may well include actions to intimidate and lure Taiwan into accepting China's terms; to continue the North Korean partial or pseudonormalization as a means for postponing U.S. missile defense and encouraging South Korea to shift away from its alliance with the U.S.; and to use Chinese economic opportunities for financially pressed Japanese businesses, in tandem with the possibility of Russian territorial concessions on the Kurile Islands, to persuade Japan that it should end its security alliance with the U.S.

In May 2001, Russian and Chinese officials announced they would coordinate policy toward Columbia and Cuba. Russia and China have political and military relations with Cuba, as well as electronic monitoring based there and aimed at the U.S. This joint policy might well include more help for Castro as he works with the Chavez regime to support anti-U.S. radical groups seeking to take power in Columbia and other politically fragile Latin American countries. Jiang and Putin might see this as a way of keeping the United States occupied near its borders and less involved in Eurasia. This policy has also led to the recent addition of China to the OAS as an observer. It is also one of the key factors behind the increasing number of leftist regimes throughout the Latin American region.

In addition to the challenges deriving directly from the China-Russia axis, another broad domain of risk stems from the fact that China has officially declared that no Asian country, including Japan, should have a security alliance with the United States. China intends to be dominant in Asia. President Jiang Zemin summarized its approach as " to intimidate with force and seduce with money."

Of equal concern is the possible reemergence of an authoritarian dictatorship in Russia under President Putin or a successor, whether ultranationalist or Communist. Our in-depth analysis of President Putin has included insights into his personal development, his work in the Soviet foreign intelligence service (KGB), and his actions since assuming the presidency of Russia on January 1, 2000. Putin is an intelligent, disciplined, and systematic leader, determined to assure that Russia is, in his words, a "strong state," under a "dictatorship of law" and that Russia has a major role in the world.[4] Putin declares his support for political democracy and movement toward a market-oriented economy, but the evidence to date suggests that Russia is gradually moving toward a more autocratic path. As Russia moved toward dictatorship, Putin would attempt to maintain a Potemkin democracy for the purpose of deceiving the major democracies, so that they would continue providing needed economic support for Russia.

The ever-closer relationship between Russia and China strengthens the authoritarian tendencies within Russia, thereby increasing the risk that it will become more aggressive internationally. As the Chinese government develops relations with the Putin government, the Chinese Communist Party has revived direct relations with the Communist Party in Russia and also ties between the Chinese and Russian parliaments. These multiple relationships, all coordinated from the Chinese side through its Communist Party, provide many opportunities to cultivate allies in Russia and to fan suspicion of the U.S. and of democracy. This is especially true of China's ever-expanding and mutually profitable relationships with the Russian military and its military production and research entities.

In spite of their two-track strategy, it is evident that the China-Russia axis could result in greater distance from and disputes or conflicts with the U.S. Even after September 11th, President Putin has sought to divide the European NATO powers from the U.S. on major issues and has established new alliances and relationships with regional powers such as Iran. He has also expanded or reestablished relations with virtually all of the former pro-Soviet client dictatorships, all of which also have growing military and political relationships with China and all of which are hostile to the United States and its allies.

So far the evidence along with illustrative, plausible international political scenarios illuminate China's current geopolitical strategy that blends business-economic, diplomatic, political-propaganda, and covert actions with selective, intermittent military intimidation for the purpose of moving toward dominance in

Asia, Eurasia, and perhaps the world without a major war.[5] This is in keeping with the advice of the ancient Chinese strategic thinker, General Sun Tzu, who said, "The supreme excellence is not winning battles . . . but breaking the enemy's resistance without fighting." At the same time, miscalculation or impatience by hardliners in China might lead to a military conflict over Taiwan, the South China Sea, Japan, India, or some other object of China's ambitions, which could involve the U.S. in a way that could be extremely destructive for both, whether or not it escalated to nuclear strikes by China.

21 A Prudent and Proactive U.S. Strategy

We turn now to the discussion of a prudent, coherent, and proactive U.S. national security strategy involving all dimensions of U.S. international activities toward Russia, toward China, and with respect to the China-Russia strategic alignment. Such an approach has a number of facets. We start with the importance of forthrightly informing the world about U.S. interests and actions. Truth is indeed the best policy.

TELLING THE TRUTH ABOUT U.S. INTERNATIONAL PURPOSES AND ACTIONS

From 1989 to 1991, as first the Soviet Empire and then the Soviet Union unraveled, China shifted from its position that the Soviet Union wanted to dominate the world to the view that this was the purpose of the United States. Increasingly during the 1990s, China has repeated this allegation on many occasions in virtually every international forum. Beginning in 1996, as the China-Russia "strategic partnership" was first declared, the new Russian Foreign Minister, Yevgeny Primakov, shifted the Russian position from one of seeking cooperation with the United States to a posture criticizing the alleged intention of the United States to seek a "unipolar" world, meaning one in which it would dominate. Instead, Russia agreed to use the Chinese formulation that the world should be "multipolar."[1]

Through a series of summit meetings and declarations, and ever closer cooperation that increased after the 1999 NATO bombing campaign against the Milosevic regime in Serbia—jointly opposed by Russia and China—these views coalesced into a list of accusations against the United States. Putin and Jiang individually and together expressed these in their various summit meetings beginning in July 2000. Russia also joined China in arguing that the current international system must be replaced by a "new political and economic order," still unspecified.

Quite remarkably, there is little evidence that the United States has responded to these repeated and very serious allegations made year after year by two of the

CHINA: THE GATHERING THREAT

world's most important and highly armed countries. The United States government, for the most part, seems to have decided to ignore these statements as though they had no bearing on reality. Instead, the United States continued providing very important economic benefits for Russia and for China, while seeming to pretend that their words and actions in moving toward the new China-Russia alliance were irrelevant.

It is time for the United States government to speak forthrightly about these repeated and untrue allegations. It is important that the United States make clear directly to the leaders and citizens of Russia and of China, and of all other countries, that the United States has no territorial or other claims on any country in the world. In modern history, the U.S. has never sought to conquer or annex any territory, despite having been in a position to do so as a result of its political, economic, and military preeminence at the end of World War II, for example. In 1945, while Europe, Russia, Japan, and, to a large extent, China were devastated and in ruins as a result of years of combat on their territories, the United States had armed forces of 12 million, more than 5,000 aircraft, 5,000 warships, a monopoly of nuclear weapons, an intact homeland governed democratically, and nearly half the world's economic production.

This was the time when the United States, if it had sought dominance over other countries, might well have attempted to exercise it. Instead, the United States disarmed unilaterally by reducing its 12 million combat forces to fewer than 1.5 million within fifteen months of the end of the war. This supported the establishment of the United Nations to bring about a hoped-for new era of collective security against aggressor states through mutual agreement and preventive action.

The United States established alliances in Europe and Asia only after the aggressive actions of the Soviet Union showed a need for collective self-defense. For fifty years, the defensive alliances in which the United States participated never used force. This changed with the 1999 humanitarian intervention in Kosovo, where the U.S. and NATO purpose was to help defend nearly one million Muslim men, women, and children of Albanian ethnicity who were being expelled, physically abused, and murdered by the military forces of the Milosevic dictatorship. The U.S. and NATO intervention was undoubtedly spurred, in part, by the tragic consequences that had followed international passivity in Rwanda five years earlier, when, in a matter of months, nearly 800,000 civilians were murdered in terrible interethnic rampages by brutal minorities among the Hutu and Tutsi peoples. It was the joint opposition of China and Russia in 1999 that prevented the passage of a UN Security Council resolution endorsing the rescue of one million Kosovo Muslims.

During the 1990s, the U.S. involvement in peacekeeping and peacemaking in Iraq, the former Yugoslavia, and Haiti was reluctant and done in the spirit of service to the cause of peace and human rights. It was also in accord with resolutions of the UN Security Council. The United States sought to have the European countries work together to mitigate the conflicts in the Yugoslav Federation that began in 1991 and became involved diplomatically and then militarily at the request of European democratic governments who felt that only the U.S. could provide the range of political and military resources that were needed. The UN Security Council explicitly authorized all the actions of the United States and its allies against the Serbian dictatorship and other extremists in Yugoslavia, with the important exception of the 1999 air campaign.

The obvious reason that China and Russia were brought closer together and became even more critical of the United States after the NATO bombing campaign against Milosevic in the spring of 1999 was that they feared this could be a precedent for U.S.-led intervention against their use of force on their own territories when they were in combat against armed opposition groups such as the Muslim Chechens in Russia, or Muslim Uygurs and Tibetan Buddhists in China. While their theoretical concern might be understood, it is evident that prudence would assure that the United States would never consider military countermeasures on the territories of Russia and China.

It was the aggression of Saddam Hussein against peaceful Kuwait in 1990 that led to the establishment of a military coalition authorized by the UN Security Council and led by the U.S. that defeated Iraq's armies and liberated Kuwait. Thereafter, the coalition demonstrated its defensive character and principled conduct by withdrawing its force of over 500,000, which in the hands of an aggressive power intent on dominating the world could certainly have been used to take de facto control over the Persian Gulf states that possess the world's most important source of oil supplies and reserves. The United States did not consider, much less take, any such action.

Ever since the expulsion of Saddam Hussein from Kuwait in 1991 and the severe defeat inflicted on Iraqi military forces, the military and political actions of the United States and Great Britain sought to assure the implementation of UN Security Council requirements on Saddam Hussein's government for verifying the dismantling of its weapons of mass destruction. The issue is not why the United States and United Kingdom at times threatened and used force against the regime when it refused compliance with UN Security Council requirements, but rather, why China and Russia repeatedly took the side of the Iraqi regime despite its aggression and noncompliance with the UN Security Council, which they repeatedly say should be the guiding institution in international politics.

This leads to another dimension of truth that needs to be stated clearly: An enormous threat to peace is posed by the ever-increasing transfer of components and technology for weapons of mass destruction by China and Russia to a number of hostile and dangerous terrorist-supporting regimes. After September 11, 2001, President Bush correctly spoke with increasing intensity about the threat, and he took action to remove Saddam Hussein from Iraq. However, the U.S. needs to be more vigorous in communicating the facts about China's and Russia's role in spreading WMD to the world.[2] The U.S. needs to be more effective in dramatizing how the proliferation of weapons of mass destruction might result in immense tragedy for countries near these hostile regimes, such as those in Europe, South Korea, Israel, and other friendly states in the Middle East; as well as countries more distant, such as the United States. They could also threaten even Russia and China.

It is, after all, true that Russia and China have undertaken repression against Muslim peoples and they supported Milosevic's actions against Muslim Kosovars. Also, it is China and Russia that have led the way to the Shanghai Cooperative Organization with the neo-Communist Central Asian dictatorships, aimed first at defeating not only the genuine Islamic extremist terrorists who threaten their own positions, but also any and all opposition or separatist group under the banner of fighting the three evils of terrorism, extremism, and separatism. This, as Russia and China continue to sell weapons of mass destruction components and technology to various terrorist-sponsoring states. It is quite possible that shifts in policy by the current or future regimes in those countries—Iran has expressed interest in joining the SCO, for example—might lead them to use these weapons of mass destruction to threaten Russia and China unless both cease the repression of Islamic groups.

The Truth about Communist China

It is also important to tell the truth about Communist China. Its actions demonstrate that while pursuing active commercial diplomacy to enhance its economic development and mostly avoiding visible conflict, China is also an expansionist, coercive, manipulative dictatorship. It is using the results of foreign investment and trade to become stronger in every dimension in the pursuit of its global agenda. Pretending that China is a cooperative and peaceful power, as was done by the Clinton administration, did not make it so, nor will it do so in the future. China's negative international actions include its persistent and coercive, even if at times intermittent, pursuit of territorial claims against eleven neighboring countries (India and Japan among them), its continuing and repeated violation of international weapons limitation agreements and promises, its continuing proliferation, and its assertive program of illegal acquisition of military technology. These actions mark the Communist regime of China as a strategic competitor that might well initiate conflict that could involve the United States and result in many human and material losses on all sides, including the possibility of nuclear war. It is time for the United States government to summarize the facts of Chinese actions in the world and make these known to the people of the United States and to the leaders and peoples of countries threatened by China.

At the same time, while the current regime in China is both internationally cooperative in some aspects and dangerous in others, it is important to understand that the actions of the Chinese government could be much worse. A more hard-line group of leaders might seek to pursue China's expansionist agenda more quickly and could do this through far more active indirect aggression (such as secret coercion of foreign leaders, assassinations, political destabilization, expanding its arming and funding of terrorist and guerilla groups) or through more assertive military coercion and aggression. That this is not being done may well be a tactical decision deriving from the oft-repeated phrase among Chinese hardliners that, at present, China must "bide its time and build its capabilities." This means China currently needs to avoid appearing threatening to the U.S. so that there will be no risk of losing access to the American market that provides so many of the resources that permit China to have an ever greater political, economic, and military weight in the world.

It is also important to understand that the Chinese regime could evolve toward greater moderation at home and toward genuinely peaceful cooperation abroad. We witnessed such a transformation in the early Yeltsin years as former longtime Soviet Communists responded to opportunities resulting from a greater measure of pluralism permitted by a Communist regime and decided to seek to establish democracy and have a positive, constructive relationship with the United States and the major democracies. That opportunity was partially lost with Russia, though it might be regained there, and it should be encouraged with China.

U.S. ASSISTANCE

The United States invented the idea and practice of foreign assistance when it helped peoples and governments struggling to recover from the devastation of World War I and then World War II. The United States led the way in the creation of the World Bank, the International Monetary Fund, and other institutions to promote economic growth and stability in all countries of the world. It is important to tell the governments and peoples of the world that the United States has committed since 1945 more than $500 billion of its people's funds for foreign economic assistance, at a cost to U.S. citizens of $2 trillion, since the government had to borrow the funds for these foreign aid programs. The United States is the primary contributor to the World Bank, the IMF, and the United Nations, all institutions that seek to have a positive and beneficial impact abroad.

Silence by the United States and the major democracies in the face of the relentless accusations by Communists, ultranationalists, and others in Russia, that the economic problems of Russia were caused deliberately by the West in order to weaken Russia, only serves to give credence to such totally fictitious accusations. It is time to tell the truth about the efforts of the United States and the West to provide help for Russia from the very start of its post-Soviet transition in 1992.

Though virtually never mentioned by leaders in either Russia or the United States, it is important to emphasize that from 1992 to 2002, the United States has provided the twelve post-Soviet republics with nearly $35 billion in assistance and credits, of which $18 billion went to Russia. Further, in those same years, the major democracies and international financial institutions which they support have provided Russia with more than $120 billion in international assistance, as well as tens of billions of dollars in additional savings through repeated cancellations or restructuring of Russia's external debt.

Russia's economic problems did not occur because of the West, but in spite of this very significant assistance. President Putin himself told the Russian people in April 2001 that it was Russian individuals and organizations that were removing approximately $20 billion dollars annually in funds that should have been invested inside Russia.[3] The funding of the Russian economy, both in growth and distributive terms, is a matter for the Russian people to face and correct. It is not the fault of the United States.

Another truth the United States needs to communicate is that since the unraveling of the Soviet Union, overall U.S. military forces have been reduced by nearly 50 percent, U.S. nuclear weapons deployed in Europe have been reduced by 90 percent, the U.S. has reduced its strategic nuclear warheads by 30 percent, agreed with Russia in 1993 to reduce its strategic nuclear warheads from 9,000 at the time to 3,500 by 2003. This had been delayed to 2007 because the Communists in the Russian parliament refused until 2001 to ratify the START II agreements signed by Presidents Bush and Yeltsin in 1993. Then in 2002, Presidents George W. Bush and Putin agreed to reductions to the level of about 2,000 warheads by 2012. These U.S. military reductions have been voluntary and significant, indicating a lack of any aggressive intent toward Russia or toward China, much less any intention to dominate the world.

ALLIANCES AND SECURITY RELATIONSHIPS

The extraordinary web of alliances and security relationships set up by America's far-seeing statesmen after World War II have indeed stood as they envisioned: a firewall between regional conflicts that erupt from time to time and the spread of those conflicts into another full-scale worldwide conflagration. They have protected against aggression, served as regional stabilizers, and provided the security that has allowed the great leaps in economic and democratic development we have seen erupt over great swatches of our globe: in Europe, Asia, and Latin America in particular. With the end of the Cold War, some said those alliances were no longer necessary. They couldn't be more wrong.

The new challenges posed by Islamic international terrorism, China, and the China-Russia alliance and other regional alliances working in coordination require the exact opposite: they require that the United States act to strengthen, reinvigorate, and modernize all of these alliance relationships in political, military, and economic terms. In addition, the United States should seek to establish a new defensive alliance with India, a democracy with a population of 1.1 billion that has been invaded by China in the past and that is menaced by continuing Chinese territorial claims and encirclement through China's relations with Burma and Pakistan.

With the accession of Poland, Hungary, and the Czech Republic in 1999, and Bulgaria, Estonia, Latvia, Lithuania, Romania, Slovakia, and Slovenia, the North Atlantic Treaty Organization includes twenty-six countries, with a combined population of about 645 million, a combined gross national product of over $18 trillion, and combined armed forces totaling nearly 4.2 million. This defensive alliance has served the interests of all member countries well since its establishment in 1949.

The future task of the United States and the other NATO members is to strengthen the political and military cohesion of the alliance, even though there may be differences among member governments on major issues such as missile defense and the removal of the Saddam Hussein regime in Iraq. The past history of the alliance demonstrates that democratic governments can disagree about some important issues of foreign policy while maintaining unity on core questions, such as the need to maintain military forces that can deter and defeat potential aggressors and help maintain and restore peace, as in the former Yugoslavia.

The administration of President George W. Bush demonstrated at times in its first term that it understood the importance of improving the level of political consultation and dialogue with NATO members. Secretary of State Colin Powell, Secretary of Defense Donald Rumsfeld, and other senior administration officials participated in NATO meetings and met with European NATO leaders to discuss a range of issues, most important among them, U.S. plans for missile defense. In mid-June 2001, President Bush traveled to Europe, where he met with all the NATO leaders, as well as with those of the European Union and with President Putin.

The NATO alliance held together very well during the air campaign against the Serbian dictatorship in 1999. At that time, the European members of the alliance agreed that they needed to take military action, despite the lack of UN Security Council agreement caused by the China-Russia vetoes. They also agreed on the need to strengthen their military forces in order to increase their ability to be full and equal partners with the United States. Yet, by 2001, they had failed to meet the military goals they had set, and NATO Secretary General, Lord Robertson, said the result of this is, "If a crisis comes along, the capability will not be there [among the

European members]."[4] European NATO members spend only about 60 percent as much as the United States on defense, and, since 1999, only eleven of nineteen NATO members have increased defense spending, when inflation is considered.[5] To strengthen the NATO alliance, it is important that both the European members and the United States fund the military forces that are jointly agreed upon as being necessary to preserve the peace.

At the same time the NATO alliance is strengthened, there can and should be an effort to link Russia with the democracies of Europe. Looking to the future, President Bush, speaking in Warsaw following his first meeting with all the NATO leaders, said that the United States believed "in NATO membership for all of Europe's democracies that seek and are ready to share the responsibility that NATO brings. The question of 'when' may still be up for debate . . . the question of 'whether' should not be."[6] At the same time, Bush said, "The Europe we are building must also be open to Russia . . . we look forward to the day when Russia is fully reformed, fully democratic, and closely bound to . . . Europe's great institutions— NATO and the European Union."[7]

An important step in this direction was taken in May 2002 when NATO agreed that Russia should become a participant in its discussions—though it would not have a veto over its actions. Most likely, this new Russian access to NATO facilitated Putin's efforts (with China as a silent partner) to persuade France, Germany, and Belgium to join in opposing the U.S.-led removal of Saddam Hussein in 2003. Hopefully, there will also be more constructive effects.

There is a great need to strengthen U.S. alliance and security relationships in Asia. During the Clinton years, China had the preeminent place in U.S. foreign policy toward Asia. This was vividly illustrated by the fact that Beijing decided it could publicly tell President Clinton that he should not visit Japan nor any other Asian country on his way to or from his state visit to China in 1998. When the United States agreed to this, and President Clinton flew over Japan on his way to and from China, it can only have had a negative effect on the U.S.-Japan alliance, the most important defense relationship in Asia.

The U.S. has security alliances with Japan, South Korea, the Philippines, Australia, Thailand, and naval visit/maintenance agreements with Singapore. The first need is to increase the level of political consultation, dialogue, and support from the United States. An example of the kinds of actions needed after years of neglect by the preceding administration was the invitation by President Bush to the prime minister of Japan, Junichiro Koizumi, to visit the United States for consultations in June 30, 2001. This was months before the visit of President Bush to China in October 2001. The crises in Iraq and North Korea in 2002 and 2003 would bring the U.S. and Japan into frequent, constructive action.

The military dimension of the Asian security alliances also requires strengthening. This includes the need for more frequent and more realistic defensive military exercises that reflect the ever-growing military capabilities of China, including its emphasis on electronic and information warfare weapons. In March 2000, the U.S. Commander in Chief of the Pacific, Admiral Dennis Blair, informed the U.S. Congress that his command was significantly vulnerable and underfunded in matters of Command, Control, Communications, Computers, and Intelligence (C4I) and that his central headquarters in Hawaii were located in conventional buildings within mortar distance of major public highways and vulnerable to destruction through air, missile, or terrorist attack.[8] This and other potential operational problems should be remedied.

Australia, which performs important electronic support functions for the entire Pacific region, has built a new central command, communications, and intelligence facility, which, unfortunately, is also located in a conventional structure that could be quickly destroyed by missile, air, or terrorist attack. These are only examples of a range of operational military vulnerabilities that could tempt hard-line elements in the Chinese military to conclude that their preferred tactic of "victory in one strike" using "asymmetric warfare" is indeed achievable and feasible. It is time to be serious about building the full array of defensive and offensive military forces that can deter and cope with the present and future military capabilities that China is developing and purchasing from Russia.

There is also an economic dimension to strengthening alliance relationships in Asia. All the allied and friendly countries in Asia depend significantly for their economic well-being on their exports to the United States. Since 1980, China has had the same open access to the U.S. market as have U.S. Asian allies and friends. However, China has maintained restrictions on access to its markets for U.S. exports. In addition, the dictatorship in China has kept wages there lower in comparable areas of production than in the friendly Asian countries where political pluralism and democracy have resulted in rising wages.[9] In 1994, China unilaterally devalued its currency, which made its exports to the United States far cheaper than those of friendly Asian countries. The economic result has been that China's trade surplus with the United States has increased rapidly each year, reaching an estimated $130 billion in the year 2004.

Much of this increase in China's exports derived directly from having replaced exports from friendly Asian countries. This, in turn, contributed to their serious economic crisis, which lasted from 1997 through 2000 and required more than $100 billion dollars in IMF support to permit their economies to adapt to reduced export earnings and inflows of foreign capital. In the words of one insightful analysis, "Throughout the 1990s, the unlimited market access China received [to the U.S.] not only crowded out the products of other Asian countries. It encouraged global investors to shift capital to the People's Republic where the brightest prospects for earning big returns involve exporting to the United States. The impact has been felt from South Korea to India, but particularly in Southeast Asia and Indonesia."[10] It is time to shift trade opportunities in Asia from China to American allies and security partners. By doing this, the U.S. would bring its national security and its commercial interests into balance.

As stated by the perceptive analyst William Hawkins, "Trade is best used to reinforce relationships based on shared interests and values. When it comes to commerce and diplomacy, the United States should always favor friends over rivals."[11] Hawkins also points out that such an alliance strengthening shift in trade opportunities would also be better for American exporters, since the Pacific Rim states import twelve times as many U.S.-made products as does China.[12] Further, once these allied countries obtain preferential treatment over China in trade, "Capital will flow into their economies, reversing the dangerous trends of the 1990s," permitting their people to live better, supporting political stability, and strengthening the overall alliance relationship with the U.S.[13]

The first alliance system established by the United States after World War II was the Rio Treaty, which in 1947 brought the United States together with the countries of Latin America in a collective security coalition that continues to the present. This alliance has been strengthened by the trend among the thirty-four Latin American countries toward democracy since the 1980s and by initiatives to reinforce the political relationship with closer trade relations. Examples are the North American Free Trade Area, with Canada and Mexico, which began in 1994, and the broader free trade area that was envisioned at the April 2001 Summit of the Americas, which President Bush said should be open to all countries in the hemisphere that have democratic forms of government. This was an important and new linkage of opportunities for virtually free trade with the United States among all Latin American countries, but only as long as they maintain political democracy.

The threats to this Western hemisphere alliance derive from the Communist dictatorship in Cuba, which in 1999 established political and military relationships with China and reestablished relationships with Russia following Putin's visit in December 2000. Castro and his regime are close to and linked with Communist guerillas in Columbia, the radical regime of Colonel Hugo Chavez in Venezuela, and other radical, anti-U.S. armed and unarmed groups in the hemisphere. It is important for the U.S. to participate with Latin American democracies in prudent preventive actions to avoid the serious risk of political destabilization supported by Castro and Chavez backed by Chinese military supplies and investments or other funds.

MISSILE DEFENSE

When historians look back on the partisan battles over missile defense of the last twenty years, they will no doubt shake their heads at the folly of a nation that so long delayed using its technological prowess to protect itself from the growing threat of nuclear missile attack. If we are lucky, the fallout of this delay will be only metaphorical, the folly of delay will have no lasting consequences. If we are not lucky, the fallout may be only too real, leading to an enormous loss of life.

More than twenty countries now have ballistic missile programs.[14] During and since the 1990s, China and Russia sold increasing amounts of technology, components, and technical assistance for weapons of mass destruction to anti-U.S. dictatorships. All of these regimes allocate large amounts of money to developing ballistic missiles with ever-longer ranges, which could carry nuclear, biological, or chemical warheads to attack allies of the United States and the United States itself.

In 1983, President Reagan proposed that the United States build a complete defense against ballistic missile attack, having in mind the ten thousand nuclear warheads on Soviet missiles. This led to funding for research and development and significant political opposition to the idea from the Soviet Union, even though it had been working energetically for years to develop its own missile defense.[15] Opposition also came from some European allied governments and from an important proportion of mostly Democratic members in the U.S. Congress, even though public-opinion polls indicated overwhelming bipartisan support.

During the 1990s, the discussion of missile defense shifted to protecting the U.S. and its allies in Europe, Asia, and the Middle East against the smaller numbers of missiles that the state sponsors of terrorism might have available at present or in coming years, as well as protecting the United States and its allies against missiles that might be launched by China, Russia, or third powers by accident or without authorization. There are potentially serious risks deriving from the technical deterioration of the Russian command and control system and the potential for instability there or in the anti-U.S. dictatorships.[16]

After the first Putin-Jiang summit in July 2000, China and Russia announced that they were "firmly opposed to the United States developing missile defense for its territory," and they also opposed any "nonstrategic missile defense system," which they said could "undermine the security interests of other countries."[17] This was also the time when both powers warned that establishing a missile defense would "have the most grave adverse consequences, not only for the security of Russia, China and other countries, but also for the security of the United States."[18]

The strong Chinese opposition to missile defense stemmed from its concern that if the U.S. were able to defend itself and its allies, China's nuclear weapons would be less effective in preventing the United States from taking actions that China opposed. For example, China has used threats of nuclear attack against U.S. cities to argue that the U.S. should not give any military assistance to Taiwan should Beijing decide to use coercion or military attack to establish its control.

It has been documented that Russia violated the antiballistic missile treaty during the 1980s by building large radars for "territorial defense."[19] Further, one respected expert and former U.S. Department of Defense official concluded that the Soviet Union had in place a defense "against long-range ballistic missiles specifically prohibited by the ABM accord."[20] This judgment is based on the work of William T. Lee, a career analyst of Soviet military forces with the Central Intelligence Agency and the Defense Intelligence Agency. After examining Soviet deployment of thousands of surface-to-air interceptors (SA-5 and SA-10/A-300) and large numbers of phased array radars, Lee concluded the following: by the 1980s, the Soviet Union had linked together a system of radars into a system capable of coordinating and managing the interception not only of aircraft, cruise, and medium-range ballistic missiles, but also of intercontinental ballistic missiles. He further concluded that the interceptor systems were capable of destroying incoming ballistic missiles and/or their separated warheads in the terminal phase.[21] Mr. Lee further contended that the memoirs of prominent Soviet system designers and military commanders written during the 1990s supported his conclusions.

However, this view has reportedly not been accepted as the consensus view in the U.S. government. There is agreement that the large radar discovered at Krasnoyarsk constituted a violation of the ABM treaty, but not that the Soviet Union/Russia had built a first-generation national ABM system. Reportedly, some are skeptical about Mr. Lee's conclusions because the U.S. has had difficulty developing interceptors capable of destroying missiles or warheads in the terminal phase. The Soviet systems Lee mentions have a maximum altitude of 24 kilometers (about 72,000 feet) and, therefore, are restricted to interceptions in the terminal phase. This important question—does Russia have a complete national missile defense?— should be examined in an objective way by the Bush administration, especially as the number of U.S. offensive warheads is reduced.[22]

The Soviet Union/Russia contended that its SA-10/A-300 system did not violate the ABM treaty because it was only effective against medium-range ballistic missiles but not against long-range ballistic missiles. Yet this seems dubious on its face, since a terminal intercept system that is effective against incoming warheads delivered over medium ranges could also be effective against those delivered from intercontinental ranges. The question would be whether Russia has the radar tracking capacity to target the ICBMs in time to activate the defensive interceptors. Whether Russia has a rudimentary intercontinental missile defense system remains an important, debated issue. If Mr. Lee is correct, Russia already has a first-generation antilong-range ballistic missile system.

There were credible reports that in 2001 China and Russia began cooperating to establish a joint air defense system over their territories most likely to include the Central Asian countries allied with them in the Shanghai Cooperative Organization.

It would be logical to assume that this joint system would further develop the first-generation missile defense system (SA-10/A-300) that both powers have. This would make it all the more urgent that the U.S. move from intention to actual deployment of national and regional missile defenses.

On May 1, 2001, President George W. Bush stated that the U.S. would build a missile defense system and cut "to the lowest possible number" its strategic nuclear weapons.[23] To Russia he said, "We are not and must not be strategic adversaries," but rather, the U.S. and Russia should "work together to replace this [ABM] treaty with a new framework that reflects a clear and clean break from the past."[24] Bush went on to say that the U.S. and Russia should

> leave behind the constraints of an ABM treaty that perpetuates a relationship based on distrust and mutual vulnerability . . . [there should be a] new cooperative relationship, it should look to the future, not to the past, it should be reassuring rather than threatening, it should be premised on openness, mutual confidence, and mutual opportunities for cooperation, including in the area of missile defense . . . and perhaps one day we can even cooperate in a joint defense.[25]

This echoed the Reagan offer to the USSR in 1983 to combine missile defense with sharp reductions in offensive nuclear warheads. Reagan offered to share this defensive system with the Soviet Union and said missile defense would permit mankind to move from the mutual assured destruction that was the underlying premise of the ABM treaty to mutual assured survival.[26] The bipartisan consensus among the U.S. public for moving forward with missile defense is reflected in many years of support, as seen in opinion poll data (in the year 2000, 80 percent were favorable), as well as in the passage by Congress of the National Missile Defense Act of 1999. This was signed into law by President Clinton on July 22, 1999, and established U.S. policy "to deploy as soon as is technologically possible an effective National Missile Defense system."[27]

The Bush administration moved to attempt to persuade U.S. allies in Europe and Asia that missile defense was necessary to their security. Secretary of Defense Rumsfeld said that the U.S. would begin with "rudimentary defenses" and by 2004 would deploy systems with the ability to defend against threats from North Korea, Iran, Iraq, and others.[28] He also said that the U.S. system would go beyond the approach that the Clinton administration considered of using only ground-based interceptors to attempt the destruction of ballistic-missile-delivered warheads in their final approach. Instead, Rumsfeld said that the Bush administration would seek to destroy attacking missiles in every phase of flight: the initial boost phase, when the missile is on a predictable course for some minutes and is very hot and easy for sensors to quickly find and can be destroyed by lasers or other means; the mid-flight phase, when the attacking missile could be destroyed by air-, sea-, or space-based systems; and the final approach to target, when ground-based systems would try to destroy the individual warheads before they could reach their targets.

The 1972 ABM Treaty does not prohibit the development or deployment of defenses for specific regions, for deployed military forces, or against medium-range ballistic missiles. This had been the argument used by the Soviet Union/Russia for fielding thousands of its SA-10/A-300 interceptors, which it contended were effective against aircraft, cruise missiles, and medium-range missile, but not against ICBMs.

The United States has developed a number of regional defense systems, which, if linked together, could implement the approach outlined by Secretary Rumsfeld. This includes the Navy's plan for area ballistic missile defense systems, which would be carried by AEGIS cruisers. These ships could launch interceptors at ballistic missiles during the boost phase or the mid-flight phase.[29] These ships could also be moved to focus on countries that were or became more threatening, such as North Korea. Lasers capable of destroying missiles have been successfully tested[30] and also deployed in tests on aircraft. Beginning in 1999, the U.S. Army successfully tested its Theater High Altitude Area Defense System (THAAD), intended to destroy incoming enemy missiles/warheads with ground-based interceptors.[31] The United States is also developing antimissile systems that can be mounted on aircraft.

In addition to protecting the United States and its allies, a multifaceted missile defense system could also be used to reduce the risk of war or escalation between states that are hostile to each other and that have developed ballistic missiles and highly destructive warheads: North Korea vs. South Korea and Japan, India vs. Pakistan, or China vs. India. If tensions rose between two such countries and war seemed imminent, one insightful analyst has written, "The United States could dispatch an AEGIS cruiser to the region with instructions to intercept any ballistic missile fired by either side. Such a capability in American hands would be highly stabilizing, reducing the likelihood of conflict, discouraging the use of offensive missiles, reassuring both sides."[32] In the case of hostile anti-U.S. regimes, a missile defense would make their investments in ballistic missiles useless and could, therefore, discourage the continuing efforts to build these offensive capabilities.

Opponents of missile defense among some U.S. allies in Europe and in the United States have said that moving away from the 1972 ABM treaty would lead to an expansion of offensive nuclear ballistic missile forces in a number of countries. For example, Senator Joseph Biden, Chairman of the Foreign Relations Committee of the U.S. Senate, contended in June 2001 that China would likely move immediately to increase its ICBM force from about 24 to 300 or 400 launchers within a matter of a few years. That in turn, he suggested, would lead India to expand its offensive missile force, and most likely result in Japan developing nuclear weapons and its own force of hundreds of ICBMs.[33] Senate Majority Leader Tom Daschle summarized the concerns of many Democratic members of Congress opposed to missile defense, saying that it would "undermine our nation politically, economically, and strategically."[34] This assumption that missile defense would spur increased deployment of offensive missiles to overcome it is the core of the judgment underlying opposition to this approach.

The statement made by President Putin following his first summit meeting with President Bush on June 16, 2001, reinforced that viewpoint. Putin said that if the U.S. moved toward missile defense outside the framework of the ABM treaty or an agreement with Russia, his country would not make any threats. "We cannot force anyone to do the things we would like them to," he said. "At least for the coming 25 years," he continued, American missile defenses "will not cause any substantial damage to the national security of Russia."[35] Nevertheless, he said Russia would "reinforce our capability" by "mounting [more] multiple warheads on our missiles" and that it would only cost "a meager sum."[36] As a result, Putin warned that the strategic "nuclear arsenal of Russia will be augmented multifold," most likely meaning that instead of reducing the number of strategic nuclear warheads to 3,500 (the Start II requirement by 2007) or 2,000 (as projected for Start III), Russia might keep its current 4,000 warheads or add more. Without question, Putin's initial comments could have provided the basis for further international and domestic opposition to U.S. missile defense, had he not at his second meeting with Bush in July 2001 agreed on discussions linking cuts in offensive weapons with missile defense. This was followed by Russian acquiescence in the U.S. decision to terminate its obligations under the ABM treaty and the joint Russian-U.S. agreement in May 2002 to sharply reduce offensive strategic warheads. This was a positive agreement and contradicted the pessimistic predictions of those opposing missile defense.

Concerning China, the evidence we have discussed indicates that with or without a U.S. missile defense, it has been making determined efforts to develop the new missiles that will expand its strategic nuclear missile forces as rapidly as possible since the 1990s. In the latest published U.S. Department of Defense estimates, China could have 30 ICBMs by 2005 and 60 by 2010.[37] In addition, it is quite possible that China will meet its target of placing its new ballistic missile submarine (Type 094) in service by 2005, with an additional such submarine each year until 2012. Each submarine can carry 20 JL-2 ICBMs with a range of 6,000 miles, and each may have six or more warheads (e.g., 120+ warheads per submarine). This means that by 2008, China might well have about 50 land-based ICBMs (each with about three warheads), plus two of its new ballistic missile submarines with 240 warheads, for a total of more than 400 warheads capable of reaching U.S. territory.

Although the U.S. missile defense system as it is currently being deployed is not intended to defend against such large forces, it is highly unlikely that any other countries could establish arsenals even close to the size of that in Russia or the possible Chinese force. However, it is a fact that the U.S. and its allies could "counter the effect of additional . . . missiles [or warheads] simply by adding to the capacity of our defensive system."[38] Once defensive systems have been developed and deployed, they can be expanded to counter more and more offensive missiles and warheads, thereby reducing the incentive of states to spend the resources to develop or expand their nuclear attack systems. In comparison with doing nothing or only adding to U.S. offensive nuclear attack systems to reinforce the "balance of terror," the defensive system has the great advantage that it never attacks people, poses no risk of accidental use, and is never used first. Missile defenses are only used to destroy ballistic missiles that have been launched by accident or in a purposeful effort to kill millions of persons in the U.S. and allied countries. Their success against virtually all the missiles launched by Iraq in 2003 illustrated the life-saving character of U.S. missile defenses.

A second frequent opposition argument is that there is no point having a missile defense against the small hostile dictatorships such as North Korea, because they can always smuggle a nuclear, chemical, or biological weapon of mass destruction into the United States in a suitcase. A thoughtful commentator answered:

> By that logic we should dismantle our continental antiaircraft defenses . . . the Navy should strip the fleet of antiaircraft and antimissile defenses because the enemy—as demonstrated in Yemen against the USS Cole—can always sneak in with a little harbor boat and blow you up anyway. . . . Yes, an enemy might slip in a suitcase. But that is not easy. It requires a conspiracy. It requires coordination, timing. It requires many people acting in concert for a long period of time. It risks penetration and error and disruption and defection.
>
> Compare that to a dictator sitting by a console in his capital with a button that will reliably, immediately and incontestably incinerate a half-dozen American cities. There is a huge order of magnitude difference between that threat and the smuggled suitcase."[39]

A missile defense system could assure that dictators armed with long-range missiles and weapons of mass destruction do not have the confidence that any of their missiles would ever reach their intended targets. Therefore, it is far more likely that instead of attempting to add offensive ballistic missiles in the face of a clear U.S. and allied determination to build and expand defensive systems to whatever degree were necessary, they would instead abandon this method of aggressive coercion and terror. It also would have the benefit of reducing China's incentive to expand its offensive ballistic missile systems.[40]

At the same time, with or without missile defense, the U.S. must continue its other efforts in homeland defense to prevent hostile states and groups from launching additional terrorist attacks inside the U.S. According to recent figures, the U.S. is spending $30–60 billion, depending on which programs you include in the estimate, on homeland security. Those same figures estimate that missile defense would cost an additional $4 billion annually, or about $14 per citizen per year. Even if that cost were three to ten times higher, it would be a tiny fraction of the U.S. GDP and far, far less than the costs and suffering what would result from even a limited nuclear missile attack against one or a few American cities.

SECURE MILITARY AND MILITARY-RELATED TECHNOLOGY

Is China the superpower of spying and technology theft?

In 1999, a bipartisan committee of the U.S. House of Representatives issued a report that revealed a stunning pattern of espionage by China extending over many years, through which it stole the most important secrets of America's most advanced nuclear weapons, missiles, and aircraft.[41] The Clinton administration accepted and concurred with the findings and stated that appropriate corrective measures would be taken. Yet many months later, Senators Joseph Lieberman and Fred Thompson issued a report criticizing the continuing lack of improvements.

Both Communist China and Russia are seeking to modernize their most advanced weapon systems, and both are attempting to obtain military and military-related technology in the United States through espionage, subterfuge, and purchase when possible. It is essential that the United States act with seriousness and competence to restrict the flow of these technologies to China, Russia, to all of their allies, and to the hostile anti-U.S. regimes that sponsor terrorism.

Quite clearly, so far all of the U.S. and allied expressions of concern about stopping the proliferation of weapons of mass destruction to hostile dictatorships sponsoring terrorism has failed to accomplish this goal. The two countries, which the U.S. government for years has publicly identified as most responsible for this continuing proliferation of weapons of mass destruction, are China and Russia. Therefore the United States should allocate the skilled manpower and budget resources necessary to accomplish the following actions:

1. Maintain the integrity of and control over classified information within the U.S. government and among all U.S. contractors with sensitive military technology information.
2. Significantly improve and expand U.S. counterintelligence operations in order to prevent, deter, and defeat Chinese, Russian, and other espionage operations. From 1975 to 2000, more than 127 U.S. citizens were convicted

for spying, most on behalf of the Soviet Union/Russia, and some for China.[42] The repeated spy scandals of the 1990s and the compendium of information in the Cox Report on successful Chinese military espionage led Congress to instruct President Clinton to improve U.S. security. This resulted in Clinton signing a Presidential Decision Directive on the eve of his departure from office on December 28, 2000, entitled "U.S. Counterintelligence Effectiveness—Counterintelligence for the 21st Century." Instead of the "piecemeal and parochial" approach in place up to then, it urged, in the words of Senator Richard Shelby, then Chairman of the Intelligence Committee in the U.S. Senate, a "more policy driven . . . proactive . . . approach to identifying . . . the information to be protected . . . enhanced information sharing between counterintelligence elements."[43] The administration of President Bush should make this a major priority.

3. Terminate all launches of U.S. satellites on the rockets of Russia or China or any other foreign country except for close U.S. allies. These launches in China have given that country the experience, technology, and additional financial resources to bring about important improvements in its military ballistic missile capabilities since the systems are so similar. This is fundamentally contrary to U.S. national security interests. The EU drafted a new code of conduct on missile proliferation in 2002. While still urging advanced states to "exercise the necessary vigilance" when aiding other country's space launch programs, the new language would be more lenient than the current restriction under the MTCR (Missile Technology Control Regime) rules.[44] The U.S. should resist such liberalization and should cease violating the spirit of the rules itself by indirectly aiding China's missile program through the launching of satellites on its rockets in the commercial interest of a few U.S. corporations.

4. Military exchanges with Russia, China, and other major powers that are not allies should focus on building understanding and relationships among the participants. They should help foreign military personnel understand the truth and the fruits about U.S. international purposes and activities as discussed earlier. They should not involve the transfer of military skills from the United States to these other countries. A good example of what should not happen: in the 1980s the United States showed representatives of China's Central Military Commission a training center where it simulated military operations by potential opponents using their tactics and weaponry. Sun Tzu said, "If you know your enemy and know yourself, you will not lose in 100 battles." The Chinese military by the year 2000 had copied the United States and established a military facility that specialized in simulating the military tactics of the United States and other potential

opponents. As described by General Xiao Deqiao, "Training is held strictly in accordance with the commands and orders used in foreign armies."[45]

5. The U.S. must restore the full, objective functioning of the elements of the Department of Defense, such as the Defense Technology Security Administration (DTSA) and the intelligence community responsible for the review of the potential military sensitivity of U.S. defense technology exports.[46] The "export virtually everything" approach of the Clinton administration resulted in pressures on and a weakening of these organizations. In the summer of 2003, the Department of Commerce and others in the Bush administration urged that permission be granted to one or two U.S. corporations to export highly advanced computers to China that could be used in nuclear weapon design. The commercial and bureaucratic pressures resembled those in the Clinton administration, according to informed congressional staffers. In the present and future, the reviewing organizations must be fully staffed by competent professionals who are able to provide independent analyses of the national security implications of possible military or dual-use technology exports.

6. The United States should expel all companies that function as fronts for the Chinese People's Liberation Army or for any other military or intelligence-related entities in China, Russia, or any other nonallied state. Investigative reporter Kenneth R. Timmerman wrote that a high-tech area of California could be called "China's 22nd province," because there were hundreds of such front companies for the Chinese military and military production system with offices there, many listing no telephone numbers or having any of the facilities for normal business operations.[47]

7. Restore an effective multilateral entity, such as the Coordinating Committee on Trade with Communist Countries (COCOM), which for so many years served to prevent the U.S. and its main allies from exporting military technologies to the former Soviet Union and its allied states. In 1999, the U.S. Congress urged that this step be taken in view of the relative ineffectiveness of the existing multilateral organizations such as the Nuclear Suppliers Group (NSG), the Missile Technology Control Regime (MTCR), and the Wassanar Arrangement of Conventional Arms and Dual-Use Goods and Technologies.[48] In April 2001, a bipartisan congressional study group, involving leading members of both the House and the Senate, recommended improving the U.S. export control process and also working to strengthen "multilateral export controls based on ... enhanced defense cooperation with close allies and friends."[49] This provides a good basis for making rapid progress in this little-known but very significant domain of international policy.

8. Some thousands of Chinese have been permitted to be employed as skilled staff in advanced-technology companies in the U.S. This should no longer be permitted because it simply amounts to a transfer of very important militarily relevant human skills to China.

All of these suggested actions are peaceful and within the sovereign right of the United States. If they are coordinated as an overall policy, they will begin to make positive changes in U.S. relations with China, Russia, and the world.

22 Russia: Incentives for Democracy and Cooperation with the West

$\mathbf{A}$s we have seen, Russia today straddles the fence. The opportunity is there to move toward a strong, permanent Russian democracy, but President Putin has continued playing it both ways at home and abroad.

On the eve of his first summit meeting with President Putin in June 2001, President Bush, speaking in Warsaw, Poland, made clear his hope and intention to establish a cooperative relationship with a Russia that has become "fully reformed, fully democratic and closely bound to the rest of Europe."[1]

At the conclusion of two hours of direct conversation with President Putin President Bush said that this was "an important step in building a constructive, respectful relationship. . . . When Russia and the United States work together in a constructive way, we can make the world a safer and more prosperous place."[2] President Putin responded that they had "found a good basis to start building on our cooperation, counting on a pragmatic relationship between Russia and the United States . . . we bear a special responsibility for maintaining common peace and security in the world, for building a new architecture of security in the world."[3]

Those statements reflected the possibility that a new, genuinely cooperative relationship might be established with Russia. However, during the Yeltsin years there were many similar hopeful statements, even as Russia moved ever closer to China. After two years as president, one experienced observer described Putin as "antidemocratic . . . crack[ing] down on the new freedoms without curbing the old corruption" and "duplicitous" and "untrustworthy" abroad.[4] There have been important new dimensions of Russia-U.S. cooperation after September 11, 2001. It remains true that future U.S. policy must be to provide Russia with a clear choice—not rhetorically but in fact —between continuing and perhaps increased economic benefits in the event of international cooperation and democratization or the loss of economic benefits if Russia's negative directions in international and domestic policy continue.

Yet with some important exceptions under Putin, Russia has pursued much the same international strategy that seems to have worked so well for China. This involves seeking to improve its economy by obtaining the maximum amount of economic benefits from the major industrial democracies through trade, investments, credits/loans, and assistance, accompanied by the diplomacy of normal relations. While receiving these economic benefits, Russia at the same time selectively and often discreetly opposes and seeks to reduce the geopolitical influence of the U.S. throughout the world.

Further, Putin has continued and expanded much of what might be termed the neo-Soviet foreign policy initiated by Primakov in the mid-1990s, reestablishing and increasing political-military relationships with virtually all the anti-U.S. dictatorships that were Soviet clients and allies.[5] This was especially visible in the Middle East, the center of world energy supplies and reserves, where Russia had been using "investment, development [assistance], diplomacy and military cooperation," including sales of components for weapons of mass destruction, to move a " long way toward bringing both Baghdad and Tehran into its orbit."[6]

Taken together with the dominance Russia has exerted over potential oil production from the Caspian Sea region and the bordering former Soviet republics, the result is that Russia was, until the removal of Saddam Hussein in 2003, "within reach of controlling one-third of the region's estimated 650 billions barrels of oil [reserves] and one-half or more of the area's approximately 1,800 trillion cubic feet of natural gas."[7] Putin had also agreed on May 14, 2001, with Colonel Chavez, president of Venezuela and a major supplier of foreign oil to the U.S., to coordinate efforts between Russia and the OPEC oil cartel (of which Russia is not a member) to maintain high oil prices. These help the Russian economy, which, in 1999 grew for the first time in eleven years at a rate of 5 percent and at 8 percent in 2000, the direct result of larger export earnings derived from higher oil prices (which went from $12/barrel in February 1999 to an average of about $30/barrel over the next two years).

In the Middle East, Russian actions to gain control of Caspian Sea oil supplies— and its links to Iran through weapons sales, political support, and diplomacy—add to both the geopolitical/military risks and economic pressures faced by the U.S. and its allies such as Turkey and Israel. The Russian neo-Soviet links in the Middle East paralleled and reinforced the actions of China and their weapons sales to oil-rich state sponsors of terror. Further, until the removal of the Saddam Hussein regime, there was an important oil-geopolitical aspect to the actions of Russia and China that may explain why both were so tenacious in supporting the brutal dictatorship despite its violation of UN Security Council resolutions from 1998–2003. With six of eleven OPEC members having an anti-U.S. position and political-military links with Russia and with Chavez of Venezuela as the driving force for higher oil prices since 1999, the OPEC cartel had an important role in causing the U.S. and global economic downturn of 2000–2003. As Chavez worked with Iraq and Iran to cause even higher oil prices in 1999, the U.S. Federal Reserve saw the resulting Producer Price Index increase and began raising interest rates, which then ended the stock-market boom and opened the way to the decline in U.S. economic growth. If Russia is able to coordinate prices with Chavez and OPEC, which has 39 percent of world production and 75 percent of world reserves, this might also come to include the six Shanghai Cooperative Organization members (14 percent of production, 9 percent of reserves), for a total of 53 percent of world production and 85 percent of global oil reserves. This could lead to potentially decisive pricing power, which might be used against the leading oil importers—the U.S., the EU, and Japan.[8]

Create Incentives for a Peaceful, Democratic Russia

To date, neither the U.S. nor any of the major industrial democracies have attempted seriously to use the enormous potential influence of the economic resources/benefits they provide to Russia, combined with the those of the international financial organizations which they fund and control, to affect either the external actions or the internal political evolution of Russia or China. The time has come for a new approach. The U.S. and as many of the major industrial democracies as can be persuaded to participate should give Russia a choice: It can continue receiving the current level of economic benefits and potentially receive significantly more if its actions are those of a peaceful, cooperative state which is maintaining the key institutions of political democracy. Otherwise, the more Russia acts as a geopolitical or military ally of China, or if Russia continues selling weapons of mass destruction to dangerous dictatorships that support international terrorism, or if Russia moves toward the restoration of dictatorship internally, whether nationalist or Communist, it would lose economic benefits.

The previous U.S. approach of overlooking and ignoring the many Soviet-like actions of Russia has failed. The new policy proposed here has a chance of success, in part, because it would give Putin and his associates tangible, material incentives for positive changes. It would also give the moderate, pro-Western and pro-democratic leaders and groups within Russia, who still exist and can be heard at home and abroad, practical arguments in the Russian national interest as they press for positive changes.

Putin often states that improving the Russian economy is his first priority. Problems of the Soviet command economic system and its years of heavy military spending, coupled with the difficulties of transition, has led to steady declines in the Russian economy since 1989, with a ten-year cumulative loss in economic output of 42 percent—far worse than in the U.S. during the Great Depression of the 1930s.[9] The welcome economic growth since 1999, fueled by higher world oil prices, has brought important economic improvements. But Russia still had international debts totaling an estimated $144 billion in 2001 and a very modest inflow of foreign direct investment, only $4 billion in the year 2000 out of an annual global total flow of $1 trillion (from 1991 to 2000 Russia received an actual total of only $14.5 billion).[10] Further, living conditions for a large portion of the Russian population remain very difficult, with an average monthly wage in December 2000 of $109 (3,100 rubles) and an estimated 50 million Russians, 35 percent of the total population, living below the barest subsistence level of $43 (1,185 rubles) per month.[11] At the same time, as Putin said, Russians have exported nearly $20 billion in capital annually—more than $220 billion during the post-Soviet years. This loss of resources partially explains Russia's economic troubles, not Western policy, as the Communists and ultranationalists have repeated since 1992.

In fact, the United States and the industrial democracies have made clear that they want to help Russia succeed and they provided more than $120 billion in aid and credits from 1992–1999 to the former Soviet republics, with half of U.S. bilateral aid (about $35 billion) going to Russia. In February 2000, a number of Western creditors wrote off nearly $12 billion of Russian foreign commercial debt.[12]

But Western good intentions and well-intended assistance have, for the most part, not been acknowledged or made widely known to the Russian leadership and public, nor has it been able to overcome the legacy of seventy-four years of Communist rule. A new policy of incentives and disincentives must link the U.S. and other democracies' given or withheld economic benefits with Russian actions. That, in turn, requires some specificity about which Russian actions might be met with reduced economic benefits and which would be rewarded.

Russia To End Military Aspects of Its Alliance with Communist China—or Lose Economic Benefits

China defines the July 2001 China-Russia Good-Neighborly Treaty of Friendship and Cooperation as involving a mutual obligation to provide military support if either party considers itself the subject of military attack or "blackmail." The Russian military exercises of February 2001, involving the simulated use of its conventional and nuclear forces to attack U.S. forces in the Pacific in the context of a Taiwan scenario, suggested that Russia accepts the Chinese view that any U.S. effort to help Taiwan defend itself would constitute "aggression" against China. Such a Russian military alliance with a nuclear-armed Communist state that has territorial demands and disputes with ten neighboring countries in addition to its Taiwan claims is inherently dangerous. It risks giving hard-line elements in the Chinese regime a false sense of confidence that if they threaten to strike U.S. forces in Asia to prevent U.S. actions they find unacceptable,[13] the combination of Russian nuclear forces and Chinese missile threats will surely lead the U.S. to back down. Such a military alliance risks developing a momentum of its own toward confrontation, since it could make hardliners in both countries more impatient and confident. It is profoundly counter to the security interests of the U.S. and its allies.

Unless Russia explicitly renounces the military component of its alliance with China, the U.S. should make clear that it views this as a threat. In response, behind the scenes the U.S. should outline the economic costs for Russia could include the following:

A. Termination of U.S. support for any restructuring of the $144 billion Russian international debt; this would have immediate negative effects on Russian economic prospects.

B. Termination of most U.S. bilateral assistance programs to Russia, except for democracy assistance and verified Cooperative Threat Reduction aid in dismantling Russian weapons of mass destruction; currently this would cut off about $450 million annually.[14]

C. Termination of various U.S. programs to give Russia greater access to the U.S. market, as well as to Ex-Im Bank credits; the U.S. would oppose World Bank/IMF funds for Russia.

D. The administration would urge the U.S. Congress to immediately end further consideration of normal trade relations with Russia and suspend its access to U.S. capital markets; this would reduce export earnings and impose significant economic stress on Russia.

Russia To End Sales of Weapons of Mass Destruction and Related Technology

This not only includes to the hostile dictatorships supporting terrorism, but also incentives to reduce sharply sales of advanced weapons to China, and gain equal funds in consumer grants. A large proportion of the advanced weapons systems Russia is selling to China provide military capabilities that directly threaten U.S. forces, bases, and allies in the Pacific region. Examples include *Kilo* submarines, the *Sovremeny* destroyer and its sea-skimming high-speed antiship missiles, all designed to sink U.S. aircraft carriers and their escorting ships. In fact, most of these weapons systems have no other possible target than the U.S. or Japan, since no other powers possess the military systems they are designed to destroy.

Russia is also selling technology, components, and expertise for weapons of mass destruction to Iran (missiles, nuclear aid), Syria, and North Korea. Years of discussion and Russian promises to cease, have, as in the case of China, led to little result. In fact, the Putin government clearly sees these sales, as well as those to China, providing economic benefits (employment, hard-currency earnings), supporting Russian military modernization, and restoring for Russia the Soviet-era geopolitical network of states that "counterbalance" the U.S.

There are two aspects to a new U.S. policy: disincentives and incentives. If Russia decides to continue in this pattern, the U.S. should take the same four steps as outlined above. No special U.S. economic benefits should flow to a Russia that has gone beyond the Soviet Union in weapons exports dangerous to the U.S., because these now also include advanced weapons for China. The U.S. should, in that case, also seek to persuade its allies in Europe and Asia to end or reduce their economic benefits for Russia—including bilateral and multilateral aid, investments, and international debt rescheduling.

However, this should be coupled with a very attractive incentive. If Russia would withdraw from the military aspect of the alliance with China, sharply cut its weapons sales to China (reducing them by 80 percent to include all the most advanced systems which threaten U.S. forces), and if it ends all transfers of nuclear, biological, chemical weapons (WMD) and their delivery systems to state sponsors of terrorism, the U.S. and the major democracies would establish a fund to provide Russia with annual grants, not loans, for the development of its consumer products sector. These grants would continue for seven years at an increasing amount adjusted for inflation, beginning with the average value of the declared annual value of Russia's military/WMD exports to China and state sponsors of terrorism for the years 1999–2001, provided Russia kept fully to its commitments to cease these military exports. Most likely, this would cost about $5 to $7 billion annually and would fully replace the other income Russia would forego.[15]

To assure transparency and avoid the problems of corruption and diversion that have marked much well-intentioned Western aid for Russia since 1992, this Consumer Products Fund would be administered and staffed by U.S. personnel, fluent in Russian, who would award grants on the basis of proposals submitted by Russian citizens. The government of Russia could indicate its priorities, recommend for and against particular projects, but for all proposals the final grant decisions would be made by the U.S. Fund staff, which would also establish accounting and oversight criteria and procedures.

For the U.S. and participating democracies, the resources for this endeavor should come from the defense budgets, since this would be a constructive investment in reducing future military risks.

Enhancing Russia Domestic Development
A committee of the Russian parliament found recently that years of Communist regime neglect of the water, electrical, transportation, waste disposal and other infrastructure systems meant that Russia faces a potentially catastrophic series of problems in the next years. In fact, the *Duma* report expressed the concern that the failure of electrical or other infrastructure systems could cause fires, explosions, and other sudden shocks to such an extent that the political authorities might mistakenly conclude Russia was either under military attack or under a well-coordinated terrorist assault. In the view of Evgeny Yasin, a former Minister of the Economy and

spokesperson for the Russian national electrical monopoly, Russia might need up to $300 billion in the next five to seven years to repair its physical infrastructure.[16]

Assuming that Russia has explicitly moved away from a military alliance with China, has ended WMD exports to hostile states, has sharply reduced advanced weapons sales to China, and maintains or enhances genuine political democracy, the U.S. should propose another very significant economic benefit for Russia: a Fund for Civilian Infrastructure Modernization that could allocate about $10 billion annually in grants and $20 billion annually in long-term, low-interest loans over the next seven years. To assure transparency and the effective use of the resources within Russia, this fund would operate on the same basis as the Civilian Products Fund. Disbursements would only continue provided Russia met the conditions set and provided that it remained possible to administer it with full assurances concerning the end-use of the expenditures.

The total cost of these two incentives, which would be additional to existing aid programs for Russia, would be approximately $17 billion annually in grants and $20 billion annually in long-term credits for seven years, or about $259 billion. This is a significant investment by the citizens of the democracies. Clearly, it would require resources from a number of the industrial democracies. The NATO countries have a combined GDP of $18,510 billion and adding Japan ($3,450 billion) brings the total GDP of the major democracies to about $24 trillion.[17] The annual grants would amount to a negligible portion of this combined GDP (0.07 percent) and adding in the long-term credits would increase this to about two-tenths of one percent of the GDP (0.16 percent). These funds should be seen as a positive investment for peace and national security, in place of undoubtedly significant defense budget increases that would be required by the U.S. and its allies if Russia continued or expanded its pattern of negative international actions, most especially a de facto military alliance with China.

Help Russia Understand the Threat from China

The U.S. should and did welcome a normal, peaceful relationship between Russia and China during their decade-long process of reestablishing normal relations and settling most of their border. But since the China-Russia strategic alignment began in 1996, the trajectory of the new relationship has been in an anti-U.S. direction, spurred on especially by China's intention to remove the U.S. from Asia. It is not in Russia's national interest to serve China's geopolitical purposes by remaining as its strategic ally against the U.S., and it is not in U.S. national interests that this continue. Therefore, the U.S. should seek to discreetly persuade Russia that while maintaining a peaceful relationship with China it should end the geopolitical and military cooperation making China more powerful and potentially more threatening to Russia.

China Has Immense Territorial Claims on Russia

As a first step, it is important to remind Putin, the current Russian leadership, and the Russian people that the U.S. has no territorial claims of any kind on Russia or any other country. In contrast, Communist China has on numerous occasions formally demanded that Russia "return" a large amount of territory in Russia and Central Asia, including virtually all of the Russian Far East, which contains 80 percent of Russian natural resources. China has repeatedly and formally alleged that these lands were " stolen" by "illegal" acts of the former Russian Empire.

Putin was born in 1952, and most of his key associates are the same age. Therefore, the current Russian leadership has little or no personal memory of the era of deepest Sino-Soviet hostilities; it is important to recall the bitter disputes during the Sino-Soviet alliance. This included white-hot hostile rhetoric, China's territorial demands (never formally rescinded), and the mutual preparations for nuclear and conventional war during the 1960s and into the early 1970s.

Russian leaders and citizens might also reflect on the implications of the fact that when much of the four-thousand-mile Soviet-Chinese border was agreed upon in 1990, the Soviets wanted the settlement to be in perpetuity, but China agreed only upon a thirty-year settlement, until 2020. This means that China reserved the right to reopen and review the border demarcation at that time— exactly the method China uses with many other neighboring states, "shelving disputes" until a later time when China expects to be much stronger.[18]

If present trends were to continue, it is estimated that by 2015 China might have a population of 1.4 billion, with the world's largest or second largest economy (though with a per capita income much less than that of the U.S.), thousands of nuclear warheads, and a highly advanced military and civilian technological infrastructure.[19] In contrast, the population of Russia is expected to fall from the present 146 million to about 133 million. Under the Start II accord, Russian strategic forces are to decline to 3,500 warheads by 2007, and to about 2,000 warheads by 2012 under the terms of the Bush-Putin accord of 2002.

The Stalin Mistake: Arming the Potential Aggressor

The Russian leadership and public should consider whether by selling Russia's most advanced weapons to strengthen Communist China it might be repeating the mistake Stalin made with Germany between the first and second world wars. At that time, Stalin violated the Treat of Versailles, facilitating Germany's secret rearmament by selling weapons and by providing training for German officers and military units. The Soviet purpose was to use Germany as a means of earning foreign exchange to aid Soviet industrialization and military modernization and to "balance" the power of Britain and France.

This is remarkably similar to the current Russian rationale for its weapons sales and military links to China. But these two democratic countries had reduced their military forces after the end of World War I and, like the U.S. today, had no aggressive designs on the Soviet Union. The result was that Soviet weapons, training, and support helped to create the Hitler war machine that invaded and devastated Russia from 1941 to 1945.

As Russians leaders would well understand, it is hard to know when a Communist politburo might decide to coerce or become aggressive against a neighboring country. Examples include the Soviet intervention in neutral Afghanistan from 1978 to 1989, or China's sudden invasion of India in 1962 and Vietnam in 1979 and 1988. What is clear from the history of the Communist regime in China is that it is capable of sudden reversals of policy and of sudden military attack or coercive demands against even large neighbors such as India. Russian leaders who choose to reflect on the issue thoughtfully would understand that, quite often, Communist regimes become more coercive as they become stronger in military and economic terms—as is projected for China.

Gradual Annexation: The Rising Tide of Illegal Chinese Immigration

Aside from China's formal demands for the "return" of territory from Russia, the long Russia-China border in the Far East has about 8 million Russians on one side and about 300 million Chinese on the other. There is a great deal of illegal Chinese emigration into Russia, with estimates ranging from 1 to 3 million by 2001. President Putin, in visiting the region, said unless Russia became more effective in the economic development of the Russian Far East, within a few years the population there would be speaking Chinese, Japanese, and Korean.[20] Russian *Duma* member Viktor Ilyukhin, a leader of the Movement in Support of the Army, said in January 2001 that 1.5 million Chinese would soon gradually move into the Russian Far East as a result of China's "secret doctrine to counteract overpopulation in it own country . . . by means of active migration of Chinese to the regions of Russia east of the Urals."[21] This process is being aided, he said, by Chinese business persons in Russia who themselves had moved into Russia illegally over the last eight years, but now were settled and able to help other Chinese slip into Russia.

Controlling illegal immigration over long borders is always difficult, as can be seen in the porous U.S. border with Mexico. There, despite increased U.S. enforcement efforts, fences, patrols, and mostly honest U.S. officials, an estimated two million Mexicans enter illegally each year. Russia faces limited resources, problems of corruption, criminal gangs in China and Russia involved in illegal immigration, and the real possibility that both corruption and policy in China may facilitate ever more illegal immigration into Russia.[22]

Russian and Central Asian officials who have firsthand experience feel this risk most acutely; therefore, they are the least willing to compromise with China on border demarcation issues. For example, where China proposed "joint economic development" (which usually means a de facto Chinese takeover as Chinese businessmen and immigrants far outnumber Russians) of disputed islands in the Amur river, the governor of the Khabarovsk region ruled this out. He said the territory had been Russian "since time immemorial . . . we will develop the island's economy no matter how much the Chinese side dislikes this."[23] Further, he said that the Russian foreign minister, the head of the Security Council, and the patriarch of Moscow all shared his viewpoint. A similar concern over Chinese encroachment was shown in Central Asia, even the Shanghai Pact, as a majority in the largely acquiescent parliament of Kyrgyzstan voted to suspend further demarcation of the border with China because of concerns that China was gaining too many concessions.[24] If present economic and demographic trends continue, the officials facing China in the border regions clearly fear a gradual, silent process of annexation through Chinese illegal immigration and business expansion.

China's Geostrategic Moves against Russia

Russia and China have very important differences concerning Pakistan and India. China seeks not only to keep the territory it took from India by force in 1962, but it has further claims and intends to dominate India so that China will be the leading power in Asia. In contrast, the former Soviet Union forged an alliance with India to balance and "contain" China. Putin has reestablished a close political and military supply relationship with India, which both Russia and India say is not an alliance but which seems quite close to it. This dynamic may have a great deal of importance within the Shanghai Cooperative Organization, as both Pakistan and India have expressed an interest in joining the SCO.

China's close relations with Pakistan have been part of its strategy to encircle and intimidate India. Pakistan created the Taliban movement in 1996, which ruled most of Afghanistan until removed by a U.S.-led coalition in the fall of 2001. The Taliban, in turn, has been an important source of military support and funds for Islamic guerrilla and militant political organizations such as al-Qaeda and the armed Chechens, which Russia has tried to suppress in two bloody conflicts. Theoretically, the Shanghai Pact brings Russia and China together against all the armed Islamic groups in Eurasia. In fact, since China believes its repression has been effective against the Muslim Uygurs on its territory, it gave priority to maintaining good relations with Pakistan even during the years when Pakistan supplied weapons and support to the Taliban, which then helped the anti-Russian Chechens. One informed observer said that, even after the 2001 Shanghai Pact, weapons from China continued to be sent through Pakistan to the Taliban and then to the armed Chechen fighters, contrary to Chinese promises to Russia of cooperation in halting these supplies.[25]

This is an issue where Russia and the U.S. have been on the same side, since both are the targets of armed groups formerly aided by the Taliban or by the terrorist coordinator Osama bin Laden, who operates from Afghanistan.[26] In December 2000, the U.S. and Russia sought UN Security Council approval for an arms embargo and economic sanctions against the Taliban regime. But China, described in a news report as "an ally of Pakistan and widely suspected of sending arms, soldiers and military advisers to the Taliban regime,"[27] abstained. In April 2001, Russia sought UN Security Council sanctions against Pakistan for its support of the Taliban regime, which continued arming the Chechen guerrillas.[28] Russia views the issue of Islamic insurgency as its greatest proximate national security threat. Therefore, the fact that China chooses to pursue its geopolitical agenda against India rather to genuinely cooperate in seeking to end the supply of weapons from the Taliban should also raise questions in Moscow about China's present and future reliability, whether or not it has signed two treaties with Russia.

During the decades of Soviet-Chinese hostility, one of China's strategies against Moscow was to cultivate close relations with other anti-Soviet Communist regimes, such as those in Albania and Yugoslavia. In this way, China sought to create more political opposition to Soviet leadership in the "Communist camp" and also to cause Moscow to be concerned that if it used force against China to its east, China's Communist friends might attack the Soviet Union or its allies from the west or offer China bases and facilities for open or covert anti-Soviet military operations.

This rather obscure but important history of inter-Communist hostilities and war preparations becomes relevant to the future of Russian relations with China because the evidence suggests that China is currently establishing close relations on Russia's Western border with Ukraine and with Belarus, which is ruled by a restored Communist regime. In April 2001, President Jiang Zemin and Belarus President Alexander Lukashenka held a summit meeting in Beijing, where they signed a number of economic, cultural, and "military-technical" cooperation agreements, a major part of China-Belarus trade.[29] The Chinese and Belarus defense ministers also met and said they would expand military cooperation "in all fields."[30] This relationship with China, strongly supported by the Communist parties of Belarus, Russia, and China, gives Beijing access to advanced military technology; and, more importantly, provides a potential source of influence on Russian policy and politics since Belarus is a nominally equal partner in the Russia-Belarus confederation.

China has also been courting the regime in Ukraine with offers of expanded trade, aid, and agreements on "military-technical" cooperation. Ukraine contains production facilities for some of the most advanced ballistic missiles, aircraft, and other military systems of the former Soviet Union. In April 2001, Ukrainian President Leonid Kuchma met with the director of weapons development of the Chinese Peoples Liberation Army, General Cao Gangchuan, and agreed that

Ukraine would provide China with advanced technology, especially in aircraft building.[31] Kuchma also accepted an invitation to visit Jiang in China.

Two examples of Chinese-Ukrainian cooperation should be of concern to Russia. First, China has used Ukraine to obtain military technology that Russia did not want to provide to China. It is reported that China paid $20 million to obtain the technology to "maintain engines on its Russian designed fighter aircraft, a capability that Moscow has refused to transfer."[32] Ukraine also sold China the technology to permit it to manufacture gas turbines, which would enable China to build larger, more powerful naval vessels.[33] Undoubtedly, there are many more such efforts by Beijing to obtain the military technology it wants—whether or not Russia wants to share this with China.

Another revelation that should trouble Moscow is the report that Ukraine has agreed to provide language and other relevant training for Chinese spies who will be working to obtain all types of military-industrial secrets from Russia. Since this unusual Ukraine-China "education/technical assistance" contract became public, it is likely that Putin will attempt to persuade Ukraine to cancel the arrangement. Additionally, there have been a number of cases of Chinese espionage against Russia that have become public, usually focused on Beijing's effort to steal Russian military technology. In early 1999, Chinese spies were caught, and in May 1999 they were convicted of sending China spare parts and components for the Su-27 Russian jet fighter aircraft.[34]

China's ambassador to Russia said at the time that there was no need for Chinese spying because "technological cooperation between Russia and China has been developing successfully through open channels which are based on mutual benefit and mutual confidence."[35] Yet China continued its spying, seen in the fact that in April 2001, border guards in Kazakhstan found two suspicious containers on a train bound for China that were lead-lined and emitting strong radiation. This suggested an effort to smuggle nuclear weapons or components to Beijing.[36] In May 2001, a Russian court convicted a Chinese citizen of using the cover of a commercial company in the Russian Far East to steal military secrets over a period of some years.[37] These known events suggest many more incidents that are as yet undiscovered or unreported. This pattern of surrounding and spying on Russia should raise questions in Moscow about how long China intends to be its "trustworthy strategic partner."

The United States has every reason to help Russia perceive the risks posed by China, an ever richer, more heavily armed Communist regime just across a long land border. Now we shall turn to new proposals for U.S. policy toward China.

23 China: Realistic Engagement, Not Unconditional Engagement

"With our intercontinental missiles we have the Americans by the throat."
—KHRUSHCHEV, speaking to Mao, July 1958

China policy from both sides of the political aisle has been mired in fantasy, as if the country were a giant Rorschach on which American public officials project their own ideas and political predilections. For a long time, including during the horrors of Mao's mass murder of his own people, Communist China was the darling of many on the left. Today, many among the economic determinists of the right—along with many big-business allies—see nothing in China but an emerging market that can yield bubbling profits. It is time to make a realistic reappraisal of our interests in China, including the threats and opportunities China presents, and then establish a prudent policy based on reality.

There have been two very different international contexts for China-U.S. relations since the normalization, which began in 1971. The first was the era of the Cold War between the Soviet Union and the Warsaw Pact countries on one side and the U.S. and its NATO and Asian allies on the other. The second was the post-Cold War era, after 1991, when the Soviet Union unraveled, the Warsaw Pact ended, and its former members in Eastern Europe became fully independent—with many making transitions to democracy. Ironically, during most of the three decades spanning these two different international situations, the main elements of U.S. policy toward Communist China remained much the same. Essentially, this policy permitted China access to the U.S. market on the same basis as U.S. allies, ignored or downplayed China's international aggression and coercion, and was mostly unchanged by Communist internal repression—though at all times voicing ineffectual rhetorical concern about the human rights of the Chinese people.

The rationale for the continuity in U.S. policy, however, changed. During the Cold War years, the emphasis was on China's utility in balancing Soviet power; in the post-Soviet era, the policy rested on a hope, often repeated by U.S. presidents from Carter through the second President Bush, that economic modernization in China would lead to political pluralism, then to political democracy and a peaceful China.[1] This policy of unconditional engagement failed, as can be seen in the facts of Chinese international and domestic actions, especially since the Tiananmen repression in 1989 and the new China-Russia strategic axis.

The time has come for a new policy toward the nuclear-armed Communist dictatorship in China. Such a change is essential to safeguard the national security interests of the United States and its Asian allies and to reduce the risk of conflict with China. A prudent and feasible new policy will use the immense economic benefits that the U.S. provides China as an incentive for it to end its international coercive, aggressive actions; to end its transfer of weapons of mass destruction components and expertise to state sponsors of terrorism; and to comply with its obligations under the UN Declaration of Human Rights and the two UN covenants on economic, social, and political rights, which it voluntarily signed in the 1990s. This is a sensible approach for the U.S., because it is China that gains massive trade surpluses annually by selling more than 40 percent of its exports to the U.S., and it is China that urgently needs the economic benefits provided by its access to the U.S. market, U.S. direct investment, and U.S.-funded international financial organizations. China's exports to the U.S. are also a major part of its overall economy, accounting for about 9 percent of its GDP and 15 percent of its manufacturing output. In contrast, the U.S. sells less than 1.4 percent of its exports to China, and these constitute a miniscule fraction of U.S. economic activity (.001 percent).[2]

It is time for the U.S. to view China realistically. China's successful strategy since 1971 has meant that even though it was China that needed the U.S. for its purposes, it was the U.S. that made tangible concessions while China made virtually none and failed to carry out the few promises it made. For example, after the 1960 break with Moscow, the Communist regime in China strongly opposed both the Soviet "revisionists" and the American "imperialists." It was the Soviet Union, with its ever-growing arsenal of nuclear-tipped ballistic missiles and its large, well-equipped conventional military forces across their long border that was the immediate threat to China. The Soviet ruler, Nikita Khrushchev, had experienced years of meetings with Mao Zedong, during which China insisted a nuclear war with "American imperialism" was inevitable, demanded the return of large amounts of Soviet territory allegedly "stolen" from China, and asked Moscow to provide China with both nuclear weapons and ballistic missiles so that it could build its own more quickly.

After Khrushchev had a heated, intense confrontation with Mao in 1959, Moscow cancelled all of its extensive military assistance programs and nearly all its economic aid for China, beginning the rift between the two major Communist powers. In 1960, at a world meeting of Communist parties, which unsuccessfully attempted to reconcile the two major Communist powers, Khrushchev described Mao as a "megalomanic war-monger," and Mao accused Khrushchev of trying to sell China out to the U.S. and abandoning true Communism.[3] Reportedly, in 1964, Khrushchev was removed from power partly because he was determined to launch preemptive nuclear attacks on Chinese nuclear and missile-production facilities to prevent China from developing its own nuclear weapons (which were first tested on the day Khrushchev was removed).[4]

In the next years, there were additional Soviet nuclear and conventional attack preparations and threats, leading China to seek normalization with the U.S. as a way of counterbalancing the Soviet Union. The U.S. provided immense help to China by opposing any Soviet nuclear attack on China and by giving the Chinese regime valuable intelligence information on Soviet military activities. The U.S. expected that the normalization of relations would be helpful against the Soviet Union. But, it was Communist China, although torn apart internally by the self-inflicted cruelties of Mao's Cultural Revolution and under direct threat of Soviet attack and intervention, that gained the most in the first years of normalization (1971–79), while the U.S. obtained none of its immediate objectives with China during the Mao years.[5]

By 1979, post-Mao China had shifted to its current strategy of economic and military modernization based on exports to the industrial democracies and the use of foreign direct investment, purchase, and clandestine operations to obtain advanced Western technology. This was accompanied by the establishment of formal diplomatic relations with the U.S. During these remaining Cold War years (1979–89), U.S. policy was to facilitate China's economic modernization through virtually open access for its exports to the U.S. market—Most Favored Nation trade status was granted by the U.S. in 1980 and renewed each year thereafter, bringing with it foreign direct investment and billions of dollars in international economic aid.

After the Soviet Union succeeded in helping pro-Soviet movements take power in eleven countries in the 1970s, China and the U.S. cooperated in helping the armed resistance in Afghanistan, which opposed the new pro-Moscow Afghan Communist regime backed by 120,000 Soviet troops. By 1989, the Afghan armed resistance had forced the Soviet Union to withdraw its forces, though the Afghan Communist regime continued in power until 1992, when the Soviet Union dissolved. During the 1980s, China permitted the U.S. to have facilities on its territory to monitor Soviet military developments.

In this context of limited but important strategic cooperation against what China called the Soviet drive for world hegemony or dominance, President Carter and his successors said nothing about the internal political situation in China. When Wei Jingsheng and other courageous Chinese citizens contended publicly in 1979 that China needed a "fifth modernization," political democracy, the result was a nineteen-year prison sentence and the persecution of those who agreed with him. The small, struggling pro-democracy movements in China found that, in contrast with the attention being given to the human rights dissidents in the Soviet Union, they were virtually ignored by U.S. leaders and administrations until the 1989 repression in Tiananmen Square.

Nevertheless, during the 1980s, as first the agricultural and then industrial economic changes succeeded in raising living standards for some of the population, and as the Chinese regime permitted thousands of Chinese students and officials to travel to the United States and other democracies, there was some modest movement toward cultural and political liberalization. This derived in part from the decisions of the Chinese Communist Party to reduce the regimentation of personal life, end the fanatical persecution campaigns of the Mao years, and to permit some "lifestyle" variety, such as the choice of daily clothing.

Yet, at the same time, hard-line elements of the Chinese Communist Party opposed the new openness to Western cultural influences as "spiritual pollution" and denounced the willingness of a few senior Communist leaders to consider various institutional means to limit the arbitrary power of the Communist Party as "bourgeois liberalization." Elections for urban councils, even though only Communist or government-approved candidates could compete, were cancelled after one round in 1980 (though they were continued in about 20 to 30 percent of villages). Student demonstrations seeking political liberalization were suppressed in 1983 and again in 1986. Communist hardliners then persuaded the paramount leader, Deng Xiaoping, to remove the reform-oriented secretary general of the Communist Party, Hu Yaobang. It was his death in April 1989 that sparked the peaceful pro-democracy Tiananmen demonstrations by one million students, later joined by workers, which then spread to twenty-three cities in China.

This was when the Chinese Communist Party leadership went into hiding, prepared to wage a civil war against the pro-democratic groups if any elements of the military supported them, and even prepared for flight into exile. The regime then assembled its military forces and, on June 4, 1989, attacked the peaceful students and workers in Tiananmen Square, killing and wounding thousands throughout Beijing. The regime then undertook a national pogrom of political repression involving executions and the imprisonment of about forty thousand persons. The Chinese Communist elite's experience of brief but intense fear of being removed from power and its ferocious repression strengthened their determination never again to risk the loss of political control. That was further reinforced by the fact that just as the Tiananmen massacre was happening, the Solidarity movement in Poland overwhelmingly won the June 4, 1989, elections, the first free vote permitted in Communist Europe. This opened the way for the unraveling of the Central European Communist regimes, followed by the December 1991 dissolution of the Soviet Union.

The former president of China, Jiang Zemin, the former head of the National People's Congress, Li Peng, and virtually the entire current military leadership of China were leaders in the Tiananmen repression and the subsequent dual policy of economic-military modernization combined with more stringent political repression and religious-ethnic persecution. For the Chinese Communist hardliners, the end of Communism in Central Europe proved the point they had made throughout the 1980s—the institutionalization of any degree of genuine political pluralism and of the rights of citizens to free political speech, assembly, and association pose unacceptable risks to Communist rule. Further, the Communist leadership concluded that the U.S., through its ostensible strategy of "peaceful evolution," had caused the unraveling of Communism in Eastern Europe and intended the same for China. Therefore, the Chinese Communist Party once again declared the U.S. the "main enemy."

The brutal actions in Tiananman Square and throughout China led President George H. W. Bush to respond with the withdrawal of some U.S. economic benefits and to end most U.S. cooperation in improving China's military systems. But, China kept access to the U.S. market for its exports on a Most Favored Nation basis and received $26 billion in World Bank subsidized loans during the four years 1989–93. This policy toward China, called "constructive engagement," was criticized in detail in 1992 by the candidate who would become the democratic nominee for the presidency. Governor Clinton said the Bush policy toward China was a "dismal failure," and that the Bush administration was "coddling ... dictators," even though the Chinese Communist leadership refused "to allow the Chinese people to exercise their basic rights" and despite "Chinese sales of sophisticated weapons to regimes such as Syria and Iraq ... Iran, Libya."[6]

In May 1993, President Clinton issued an Executive Order specifying the conditions China would have to meet within a year in order to be eligible for the renewal of its Most Favored Nation access to U.S. markets in 1994. These conditions included "that China adhere to the UN Universal Declaration of Human Rights," which would mean that China would permit genuine freedom of speech, assembly, association, and religion, and end "arbitrary arrest, detention or exile."[7]

The response from China was to ignore the Clinton conditions, to brief the leadership of the Chinese Communist Party throughout the nation that the U.S. was again the "main enemy" and to quietly urge the many U.S. corporations profiting from the manufacture of products with low-cost labor in China or hoping for present or future profits from business with China to urge the unconditional renewal of MFN. This is what occurred. In May 1994, President Clinton removed all conditions on the renewal of Most Favored Nation trading status for China, declaring "there are far more likely to be human rights advances when it [China] is not under the cloud of annual renewal of MFN."[8]

During the annual congressional and public discussions about whether to renew the U.S. grant to China of unconditional access to the U.S. market, political leaders in both major parties used economic determinist arguments. Clinton repeatedly said giving China full access to the U.S. market would improve its economy and that this would result in political liberalization and ultimately political democracy. Clinton also said this would promote U.S. national security because the U.S. President George W. Bush echoed this in 2001, when he said, "Trade freely with China and time is on our side."[9]

FAILURES OF U.S. UNCONDITIONAL ENGAGEMENT: NATIONAL SECURITY INTERESTS

In fact, since 1994 the current U.S. policy has failed in terms of U.S. national security interests. China has behaved more aggressively internationally. It has occupied disputed islands by force, claimed sovereignty over the international South China Sea, and fired medium-range ballistic missiles near the Republic of China on Taiwan in 1995 and again in 1996 in an effort to prevent the completion of Taiwan's transition to democracy. As pointed out by Herbert London, the "peace through commerce" theory is most dramatically refuted again (as it was by the two world wars of the twentieth century) by China's actions toward Taiwan. Despite the ever-increasing number of Taiwanese businessmen living in China and the very important $70 billion in Taiwanese direct investment in China, along with growing levels of trade, China has increased its military buildup and threats since the mid-1990s.

During these years, Communist China has used a significant part of the more than $1.1 trillion in trade surplus it gained from 1990 to the present to modernize its military forces, with special emphasis on developing capabilities against U.S. forces in the Pacific. Currently, China is estimated to have about three hundred deployed nuclear warheads, with twenty-four capable of reaching the U.S. China's land-based ICBMs have large nuclear warheads (five megatons) designed to totally destroy large cities. As revealed in the Cox Report, the PRC has supplemented its own technological capacities through an intense program of espionage and the successful theft of nuclear secrets from the U.S., as it further expands its strategic and regional nuclear arsenal.[10]

Contrary to repeated promises and assurances, Communist China—identified by the CIA as the major proliferator of weapons of mass destruction in the world—has continued to provide these dangerous capabilities to North Korea, Iran, and Iraq, among other states; as well as directly or indirectly aiding non-state actors such as the Khan network. It could well be said that China is directly responsible for the fact that the long-running conflict between Pakistan and India now has the additional risk of escalating to a nuclear war—China provided Pakistan with the missile and nuclear technology and components. China also uses billions of trade surplus dollars to buy Russian advanced weapons. This, in turn, contributes to Russia's ability to unilaterally upgrade its nuclear missile forces, which currently have four thousand warheads capable of reaching the U.S.

Besides providing China with the money and technology to increase its military power, current U.S. policy has two additional negative consequences for national security. As pointed out by the insightful political-economist William Hawkins, although trade presumes a benefit to both participants:

> in the case of trade between American corporations and the Beijing regime, the gain to the corporations takes the form of private profit while the gain to the regime is an increase in its military-industrial capabilities. This increase in China's strength poses a threat to American national interests. The cost of meeting that threat-not to mention the cost of not meeting it—swamps the private commercial gains in scale and importance to our country.[11]

Second, the companies from the U.S. and other democratic countries, instead of influencing the Chinese regime to make positive changes "seek to protect their own interests. They lobby Washington to "appease" China.[12] In effect, very influential and wealthy sectors of American society become "the allies of adversary regimes."[13] This is because contemporary businesses in the democracies view their sole purpose as maximizing profits and persuading their governments to adopt policies conducive to this result. It is up to their governments to establish policies to safeguard national security.

The Chinese dictatorship has become adept over the decades at providing incentives for foreign companies and businesspersons to be supportive of China's purposes in their home countries by granting or withholding business contracts and opportunities. It also is ready to threaten commercial retaliation if any companies act in ways that displease the regime. Beijing's threat to ban the importation of any future Disney films because it objected to the content of a U.S.-made film concerning its actions in Tibet is a routine example of attempted censorship abroad by the dictatorship. On a larger scale, the official *China News* reported during the reconnaissance aircraft incident in April 2001 that the prospects for the European Airbus consortium have "grown bigger in the wake of the recent tensions in Sino-U.S. relations, which industry analysts believe will take their toll on Boeing, Airbus's major rival in the burgeoning Chinese market." Chinese officials were quoted to the effect that politics and business could hardly be handled separately.[14] This practice of the Chinese regime to punish or reward foreign businesses may explain why private U.S. corporations would violate U.S. law to provide China with information that markedly improved the reliability of its intercontinental ballistic missiles aimed at U.S. cities.

FAILURES OF UNCONDITIONAL ENGAGEMENT: HUMAN RIGHTS/POLITICAL PLURALISM

Current U.S. policy has also failed in terms of concerns about human rights and hope for movement toward political pluralism in China. Since 1950, China has accepted the obligations of the UN Universal Declaration of Human Rights, which guarantees the freedoms of thought, religion, expression, peaceful assembly, and association. During the 1990s, the regime signed two further UN conventions on human rights. But, as the Department of State has documented in its annual reports on human rights, during and since the 1990s political, religious, and ethnic repression continued and worsened.

One of these in-depth assessments concluded that the Chinese regime's "human rights record deteriorated sharply" in 1998, that political repression and religious persecution deepened. "The Government's . . . extremely limited tolerance of public dissent, fear of unrest, and the limited scope or inadequate implementation of laws protecting basic freedoms" has led to violations of internationally accepted human-rights norms throughout 2002.[15]

A reported 230,000 persons are confined in forced labor camps without the opportunity for judicial review.[16] All in detention are vulnerable to torture and degrading conditions. Among many, many examples of suffering in Chinese forced-labor camps documented in the writings of Harry Wu and Wei Jingsheng, both former prisoners, is the report that since 1999 thousands of members of the meditation and exercise group Falun Gong have been put in forced-labor camps, prison, or psychiatric facilities. Several hundred of those in detention have died from torture, neglect, and abuse.[17] The Falun Gong has also stated that Chinese police and prison officials subject female members under arrest to group rape by police and guards.[18] The Chinese dictatorship also publicly announces the execution of more human beings annually than all the remaining countries of the world combined. China announced that over four thousand executions were carried out in 2002, although it is estimated that the true number ranges from ten to twenty thousand annually.[19] The regime has also established a gruesome, lucrative, and corrupt international and domestic trade in organs taken from those executed.[20]

Contrary to the repeated hopeful assertions of U.S. presidents and political leaders from both parties that more free trade will necessarily bring about institutional changes resulting in more freedom in China, that has not occurred in the domain of political life. Despite all the economic changes and the 400 percent growth in the economy since 1979, the Communist regime has not moved toward political pluralism or greater respect for human, civic, and religious rights in China.

Despite this, various U.S. business coalitions promoting free trade make contrary assertions. One of these wrote that U.S. trade with and investment in China "leads to greater personal and political freedom."[21] In fact, the Chinese regime and the business sector in China, both domestic- and foreign-owned, have an economic incentive for the continuation of the dictatorship because that prevents free, independent labor unions or other forms of worker association, thereby making it easier to keep wages at the lowest levels. Since most foreign investors and many Chinese and state-owned businesses earn their highest profits from export sales to the U.S. and other industrial democracies, the lower the wages in China, the greater the profits for the Chinese regime. This is exactly the reverse of the expected liberalizing effects often described as leading inevitably to political pluralism and then political democracy.

Other arguments for the liberalizing effect of open trade with China include that it would "weaken the coercive power of the state, create a democratically minded middle class . . . expose the populace to ideas from abroad."[22] But Lawrence Kaplan notes this is not happening in China: there is "no effective system of property rights," which means that the Communist state can exercise control over any business, and all need good relations with state and Party officials. In fact, most major Chinese businessmen are either current or former state and/or Party elites. The small middle-class remains dependent on state and political connections and is susceptible to the regime's nationalist and other propaganda delivered through the controlled media. The Internet is under state surveillance with the "portal, bankrolled by Intel and Goldman Sachs" reminding users "to avoid 'topics which damage the reputation of the state' and warns that it will be 'obliged to report you to the Public Security Bureau' if you don't."[23]

It is also a historical fact that while economic modernization does sometimes lead to political pluralism and democracy, "not every capitalist economy has produced a democratic government. One hundred years ago in Germany and Japan, 30 years ago in countries such as Argentina and Brazil, and today in places like Singapore and Malaysia, capitalist development has buttressed rather than undermined authoritarian regimes. And these models are beginning to look a lot more like contemporary China."[24] Kaplan also points out that the economic modernization process in China was designed to hinder the emergence of political freedom, as can be seen in the means of coercion maintained and used by the regime and by its actions to keep the state in direct control of the "commanding heights of China's economy," meaning all critical industries.[25]

FAILURES OF UNCONDITIONAL ENGAGEMENT:
U.S. WORKER AND ECONOMIC INTERESTS

The current U.S. policy toward China has also failed in economic terms. While obtaining full access to the U.S. market and major access to the markets of the EU and Japan for its exports, China itself has used a policy of managed trade. It keeps its markets mostly closed, except for imports it considers useful. As a result of China's 1994 devaluation and of its access to free markets for its products made by unfree, very low-cost but often highly skilled labor, China has obtained a cumulative trade surplus from 1990 to 2004[26] with the U.S., EU, and Japan of $1.5 trillion ($862 billion with the United States alone).[27] During 1990 to 2000, China also received upwards of $320 billion in foreign direct investment and more than $60 billion in subsidized loans from the World Bank and other Western-financed development institutions.

We have already seen that this more than $1 trillion in economic benefits from the U.S. and other industrial democracies since 1990 have not led to a more peaceful or a less politically repressive China—quite the contrary. Little known is the size of the trade surplus China has obtained from the U.S. and also that few U.S. companies are able to make any profit whatsoever from their business activities in China. It is also little-known that China seeks to extract advanced proprietary technology from U.S. and other foreign companies as a condition of their being permitted to invest. A U.S. government study found that a "majority of industry representatives . . . clearly stated that technology transfers are required to do business in China" and that "U.S. high-tech firms seem willing to pay the price—technology transfers—in exchange for limited market access."[28]

Proponents of international trade such as the U.S. Department of Commerce contend that each $1 billion in exports creates 11,000– 20,000 jobs.[29] At the same time, the Economic Policy Institute concludes that each $1 billion in imports cost 11,000–20,000 jobs.[30] Free trade is not intended to mean mostly one-way trade with a dictatorship such as China. As we look at China's trade surplus of $862 billion since 1990, we can estimate that this cost 7–12 million jobs, representing 5–8 percent of the civilian labor force in May 2003.[31] Richard L. Trumka, Secretary-Treasurer of the AFL-CIO, said, "When consumer demand is met with imports instead of domestic production, existing jobs can be lost . . . we now have fewer manufacturing jobs in the U.S. than we did in 1965."[32]

China intends to use U.S., Western, Russian, and its own commercial and military technology to produce high-value and high-technology products with its low-cost labor that will more and more undersell and supplant products made in the democracies, causing even more world production to shift to its territory. This would mean that the working people living in the democracies would have to compete with low-cost Chinese labor, which is under a dictatorship. The result could well be falling living standards for workers in the U.S. and other industrial democracies, along with future large-scale financial losses for many of the major Western companies that might find themselves undersold around the world by Chinese production skills they helped to create.[33]

It was often stated that some of the unilateral economic advantages that have been so useful to China would end once it joined the World Trade Organization (WTO). In theory, WTO membership would require China to open its economy, although the decision of the Bush administration to give in to China's demand that it have the preferences of a "developing country" will reduce requirements on China to open its market.[34] However, even this lesser opening assumes that the WTO rules would actually be obeyed by China or enforced by the majority of WTO members needed for any effective action.

Given China's poor record of compliance with innumerable international commitments it has made in virtually every domain, including in its economic relations; and given China's willingness to use all means, including bribery, covert action, and coercion to influence or intimidate foreign leaders and governments, it is an open question whether China will actually obey the rules of the WTO. It is more likely that China will ignore or feign compliance with rules that it views as inconvenient. At the same time, WTO membership gives exporters from China access to the markets of the 144 member countries, permitting China to use its low-cost, unfree labor force to undersell national producers in many, many countries.[35] This would both further enrich the regime in China and could cause potentially severe economic and perhaps political problems in any countries China targeted for massive exports; for example, U.S. regional allies such as Japan, South Korea, the Philippines, and U.S. neighbors such as Mexico.

China received Permanent Normal Trade Relations from the U.S. in 2000 and was admitted to the World Trade Organization in late 2001. During the first months of WTO membership, "there have been a number of areas where China has failed to meet its commitments."[36] For example, China failed to open its markets to U.S. agricultural exports, while simultaneously using its new WTO access to undersell U.S. agricultural producers in their traditional markets. More of this duplicity is likely.

Given China's declared goal of establishing and leading a global "new political and economic order," it is also possible that China will conduct an intense but subtle open and secret campaign to change the WTO rules to favor itself and create additional economic costs for the U.S. As of 2003, there were 144 member states of WTO[37] and while decisions on admitting new members or amending key provisions of agreements both require a two-thirds majority of all members, interpretations of trade agreements and the waiving of obligations on a particular member can be approved by if only 38 percent of members vote in favor.[38] This provides an opening for China, which would most probably use the theme of "fairness for developing countries" as it attempted to rally 38 percent of the WTO members (most of which are developing countries) in its favor. Undoubtedly, this is part of the reason for China's global strategic activism.[39]

A preview of how China might work against the U.S. in the WTO could be seen at the Seattle ministerial meeting in 1999, which was supposed to launch a new "round" of trade negotiations. The top priority of the U.S. is to open world agricultural markets to American farm exports. China, participating at the meeting with observer status, sided with those defending their home markets under the banner of "food security." When the Seattle talks failed to launch a new WTO round, EU Trade Commissioner Pascal Lamy claimed victory when the talks collapsed, saying that Europe had formed important new alliances, including one with China against the U.S. proposal.

Another example of how China has used multilateral organizations against the U.S., in concert with elements of European political opinion, was the May 2001 removal of the U.S. from the UN Human Rights Commission, the first time since its founding in 1947. This was done by a secret, majority vote of 53 voting members that included many of the world's dictatorships such as China, Cuba, Libya, Vietnam, and also secret coordination between China, other anti-U.S. dictatorships, the pro-Castro regime of Chavez in Venezuela, and apparently several European democracies.[40] Further, Sudan, a Chinese partner in oil development, which U.S. Secretary of State Colin Powell called "the biggest single abuser of human rights on the face of the earth," was voted a member of the commission, leading Powell to comment that the two events "send one very, very scary, shocking message."[41] China said this expulsion resulted from the U.S. use of human rights as a weapon, Cuba said the U.S. was rejected because of its "arrogance . . . and coercive methods . . . in international bodies," while Sen. Jesse Helms, Chairman of the U.S. Senate Foreign Relations Committee, concluded, "Countries like China, Cuba and Sudan will no longer be subject to the careful scrutiny that the United States has always demanded."[42]

U.S.-China trade is frequently described in the U.S. media "as a $116 billion relationship." This made it seem to have a large economic importance for the U.S. (e.g., for business and for jobs in the export sector). In fact the "$116 billion relationship" meant that China exported $100 billion in products to the U.S. and the U.S. exported $16 billion to China.[43] U.S. exports to China have very little effect on the U.S. economy, but China's trade with the U.S. is essential to that regime meeting its declared highest priority goal of continuing its economic growth and military modernization. From the Chinese regime's perspective, its dollar trade-surplus earnings from its exports to the U.S. are the key to maintaining the rate of economic growth considered essential to assuring what it calls "social stability" and avoiding large-scale public expressions of disaffection that could threaten its control.

To reach its economic, military, and power-oriented goals, China needs continued favorable access for its exports to the U.S. market. These facts in the early years of the twenty-first century make clear that it is China that needs the U.S. economically, while the U.S. has little if any need for China, though the U.S. seeks peaceful and normal relations with China as with all countries. Given the failures of the U.S. policy of unconditional engagement with China, and given the new challenges of the China-Russia strategic axis, the time has come for a new U.S. policy.

REALISTIC ENGAGEMENT WITH CHINA

The alternative to the current U.S. policy toward Communist China, which we have termed unconditional engagement, is not isolation, but rather a policy of realistic engagement. An essential element is using the enormous economic benefits accruing to China from trade with and investments from the U.S. as an incentive for acting peacefully and cooperatively internationally and for its compliance domestically with the human-rights commitments China has freely assumed.

In the domain of trade, U.S. policy would first make clear that there are two parts to China's exports to the U.S.: the reciprocal portion, which matches the amount of U.S. exports to China permitted by that regime in the previous year; and the very large amount that China gains each year in trade-surplus dollars from the U.S., which we will define as the one-way market access opportunity portion. The new policy proposed here would permit China to continue exporting to the U.S. on the basis of strict reciprocity but would transfer half of the one-way market access opportunity portion from China to U.S. allies in the Pacific Rim and permit China to have the rest only if it had met three explicit conditions.

This new policy would replace China's current access under the U.S. legislated Permanent Normal Trade Relations and under the WTO, once China has actually entered, with the following:

1. China may export to the U.S. in the current year the same value of goods the U.S. was permitted to export to China in the preceding year; for the year 2000 this would have meant China could have exported about $13 billion, the value of U.S. exports to China in 1999.

2. The U.S. would grant half of China's one-way market access opportunities to U.S. allies among the Asian countries. Using the year 2001 as an example, this would mean that half of China's $84-billion trade surplus with the U.S. in the year 2000 gained from its one-way market access opportunity would be shifted to U.S. Asian allies to strengthen them politically and economically.

3. The U.S. would grant China the other half of its year 2000 one-way market access opportunity (or about $42 billion), provided China met three conditions:

   a. ended its aggressive/coercive actions in its territorial disputes with eleven neighboring states and participated in genuine good-faith multilateral as well as bilateral negotiations to resolve these;

   b. ended completely its proliferation of weapons of mass destruction, including components, technology, expertise to the seven hostile terrorist sponsoring states;[44] and

   c. had begun good-faith, serious, and verifiable implementation of the human-rights commitments to which China has freely obligated itself by signing the UN Declaration of Human Rights, the UN Covenant on Economic and Social Rights, and the UN Covenant on Political Rights.

The legislation establishing this new approach to trade with China should also specify that the U.S. president would appoint a bipartisan commission with full access to all relevant U.S. government information that would make a determination, annually, whether or not China had met the three conditions. If these three conditions had not been met, China's permitted exports to the U.S. for the next year would be limited to the amount of U.S. exports to China in the previous year, the reciprocal trade portion. Further, if China had not met the three conditions, no U.S. persons or organizations would be permitted to make any further direct investments in China, except for investments in environmental cleanup; nor would any Chinese-based persons or organizations, state or private, be permitted to raise money in U.S. capital markets. If the conditions had been met, Chinese entities would be permitted to raise funds in the U.S. only if they were not linked to the military, intelligence, or secret police, and if they did not use persons confined in prison or forced labor to manufacture their products.[45]

This new approach to trade, investment, and financing opportunities for China would be strongly opposed by the Chinese regime, by many U.S. corporations, and by many U.S. China experts who have tended to believe and hope, against years of contrary evidence, that economic modernization would lead to political pluralism and liberalization. However, many groups and individuals concerned about national security, human rights, religious persecution, and environmental protection would support a trade policy that is fair to U.S. workers and to the overwhelming majority of U.S. businesses that do not export to or from China and which are vulnerable to the unfair competition from its unfree and coerced labor force. There could be a very broad political coalition in support of this realistic engagement approach.

Such a new policy would also mean that for the first time since 1979, the U.S. would be using its sovereign right to grant or withhold access to its market and financial resources as an incentive for China to make positive international and domestic changes. This is a peaceful and prudent means of action in the cause of national security and the maintenance of peace. So far, China has had it both ways—it has obtained major economic benefits from the U.S. while simultaneously working to intimidate the U.S. and its allies by arming and practicing to attack U.S. Pacific forces and threatening to destroy major U.S. cities.

This policy of realistic engagement would bring about a debate within the Chinese Communist regime. Those more concerned with continuing economic modernization might contend that China had to become less aggressive internationally, for now, and that it needed to move in the direction of implementing or appearing to implement its UN human-rights agreements. The more hard-line Communists would most likely oppose any changes, they would argue that the "greedy capitalists" making profits from using low-cost Chinese labor to make products for export to the U.S. would soon bring their political influence to bear and change the new policy. They would recall President Clinton's backing away from his somewhat similar 1993 statement of conditions China would have to meet by 1994 in order to have a renewal of its full access to the U.S. market, and they would contend that the same retreat would happen again. But if the U.S. held to these trade and financial aspects of the new policy of realistic engagement for two or more years, it might well encourage the beginning of positive changes within the regime and within China.

The strategy of realistic engagement with China also includes the other aspects of this comprehensive new U.S. strategy toward the China-Russia axis already discussed: telling the truth about the U.S. and about China; strengthening defensive alliance relationships with friendly countries in Asia; and developing and deploying missile defense, including Asian regional missile defense, as rapidly as feasible, especially as a result of North Korea's admission that it has nuclear warheads and its repeated threats of war since the fall of 2002.

There should also be a continuation and increase in sensible people-to-people programs of all types with China. Military-to-military exchanges can be continued, provided the U.S. makes efforts to assure that the focus is on the role, strength, and determination of the U.S. military; and its role in a democracy, including issues of transparency of military budgets and activities. The U.S. should assure that no transfer of war-fighting skills or techniques occurs.[46]

Educational exchanges and opportunities for Chinese to study in the U.S. are a good idea and should be expanded, but they need to be balanced. To date, the overwhelming proportion of the tens of thousands of Chinese students enrolled at U.S. colleges and universities have studied the sciences, mathematics, and engineering. These fields emphasize skills directly relevant to advancing China's military and high-technology sectors. In contrast, virtually all U.S. exchange students in China study languages, literature, and other subjects in the humanities. Reciprocity would suggest that China's guest students and faculty in the sciences, engineering, and high technology should be limited to about 20 percent of the total, with U.S. guest students and faculty having reciprocal opportunities in China. The other 80 percent should be distributed among the humanities and social sciences on both sides. This would make educational exchange less a one-way extraction by China of U.S. high-technology skills and more of a process for mutual learning about each other's societies.

A more realistic U.S. policy should also include a focused and coherent effort to enlarge relations with pro-democracy groups and to encourage and assist those who are working on behalf of human rights and a peaceful evolution toward political democracy in China and Russia.

24 Encouraging Democracy and Human Rights in Russia and China

"A single spark can start a prairie fire."

—Mao

"The linkage between development and rights is too loose. . . . the time frame too long and the results too uncertain to make economic engagement a substitute for direct policy."

—Professor Andrew Nathan, Columbia University

"Drastic changes could come suddenly, the tide could turn in a single day. . . . we must preserve stability above all else. . . . We must raise our guard against unexpected events and shocks."

—Jiang Zemin

Peace made with dictatorships will never be secure. Underlying every other aspect of U.S. policy toward Russia and China, therefore, must be the ultimate goal of their political liberalization leading to true democratic institutions in those countries. This should never be far from our thoughts, because that is what humanity demands. However, the foremost reason is because history demonstrates that a free people, who are free to choose, do not wage aggressive war. The only ultimately reliable deterrence is democracy.

Despite political liberalization since the Soviet era, the observance of human rights and the continuation of progress toward political democracy in Russia are fragile. Signs of regression in the Putin era include increased monitoring and assertiveness by the internal security, federal police, and prosecuting authorities, as well as a number of government actions that have reduced the independence of the national television and other major media. In China, the Communist regime has been and remains adamant that it will not permit any movement toward political pluralism or democracy. As the Chinese economy, foreign direct investment, and hard-currency trade surpluses grew during the 1990s, the Communist regime increased its political and religious repression. A major aspect of a comprehensive U.S. strategy toward both countries should be to encourage peaceful progress in the observance of human rights, the preservation and deepening of political democracy in Russia, and the emergence of political pluralism leading to political democracy in China.

The hallmarks of a political democracy include the observance of basic human rights such as the rights to life and liberty, as well as the freedoms of political speech, assembly, association, and religion; together with a reasonably open, competitive process for selecting government leaders. The U.S. national interest in the encouragement of democracy can be seen in the fact that the post-World War II era demonstrates that political democracies virtually never initiate the use of force in international politics, though they have been willing to use force in self-defense against both direct and indirect aggression. Therefore, the U.S. has never been under military threat from any state that is democratically governed. Virtually all of the world's democracies are allies of the U.S. or cooperate with the U.S. in a range of constructive international tasks.[1]

The democratic transformation of Germany, Japan, Italy, and Austria after World War II, and of Central Europe and the Baltics after 1989, demonstrates that the citizens of many countries can establish democracy even after long periods of dictatorship. We have also seen that the foreign policy of states is determined by the character of their political regime. Those countries became peaceful once their citizens were able to replace fascist or Communist regimes with democracy. These historical transformations also have shown that timely, effective, external assistance can help those within a country who seek to establish and nurture the institutions of political democracy.[2]

Therefore, it is in the national interest of the U.S. that existing democracies or emerging democracies, such as in Russia, are preserved; and that more states, especially powerful ones such as China, make a successful transition to genuine democracy. Further, from the viewpoint of fundamental U.S. values, we see that the history of the post-World War II era also demonstrates that at all levels of economic development, political democracies are more successful than dictatorships in safeguarding human rights and in providing improved living conditions for their citizens.

In 1982, President Reagan, having seen positive results from his policy of supporting citizens' efforts to have democracy replace rightist dictatorships in Latin America,[3] began a new effort by the U.S. to encourage democracy abroad. Speaking to the British parliament, Reagan announced his proposal for the establishment of a National Endowment for Democracy saying:

> We are approaching the end of a bloody century plagued by a terrible political invention-totalitarianism. . . . Yet, optimism is in order, because day by day democracy is proving itself to be a not-at-all fragile flower. . . . Still, it needs cultivating. If the rest of this century is to witness the gradual growth of freedom and democratic ideals, we must take actions to assist the campaign for democracy.

We must be staunch in our conviction that freedom is not the sole preroga-
tive of a lucky few, but the inalienable and universal right of all human beings.
So states the United Nations Universal Declarations of Human Rights, which
among other things guarantees free elections.

The objective I propose is quite simple to state: to foster the infrastructure
of democracy, the system of a free press, unions, political parties, universities
which allow a people to choose their own way to develop their own culture to
reconcile their own differences through peaceful means.

This is not cultural imperialism, it is providing the means for genuine self-
determination and protection for diversity. Democracy already flourishes in
countries with very different cultures and historical experiences. It would be
cultural condescension, or worse, to say that any people prefer dictatorship to
democracy.[4]

President Reagan went on to observe that as the Western Europeans had for
several decades provided "open assistance to fraternal, political and social institutions
to bring about peaceful and democratic progress [especially] Germany's political
foundations," he would propose to Congress that the U.S. establish a bipartisan institution to promote democracy abroad.[5] This became the National Endowment for
Democracy, a government funded but privately managed institution that provides
open assistance for emerging pro-democratic leaders and movements in countries
throughout the world.[6] This new organization was formally proposed by President
Reagan in 1983, funded by the U.S. Congress in 1984, and has continued to function
since that time on a modest annual budget of approximately $35 million dollars.

The National Endowment for Democracy (NED) has four component institutions: the National Democratic Institute (NDI), which is linked to the Democratic
party of the U.S. and works mainly with democratic parties of the center-left; the
International Republican Institute (IRI), which is associated with the Republican
party in the U.S. and works mostly with democratic parties of the center-right; the
Free Trade Union Institute (FTUI), which has the mission of encouraging and
supporting the development of independent pro-democratic organized-labor
movements in countries where these do not yet exist and there is an opportunity to
create such institutions; and the Center for International Private Enterprise (CEIP),
which has the task of helping individuals in the business community abroad build
independent business associations that can help articulate the interests of the
private sector in society and help it play a legitimate political role in a pluralist
democratic political process.

Illustrating bipartisan agreement about these goals as they would apply to
China, President Clinton in 1993 proposed making China's observance of the UN
Universal Declaration of Human Rights a condition for its receiving full normal

trade access to the U.S. market. Clinton backed away from that in 1994. Nevertheless, in 1995, President Clinton stated that one of three "central goals" of his foreign policy was "to promote democracy abroad."[7]

From the national interest perspective, encouraging democracy in Russia and China as well as elsewhere in the world can be seen as part of an overall approach to increasing U.S. national security through positive and peaceful actions that prevent the emergence of future threats or reduce current ones. Funding for these activities should be considered part of the U.S. national security budget rather than under the rubric of foreign assistance.

We can distinguish between two types of democratization activities. There are those that can be seen as part of an ongoing, open effort involving a range of U.S.-funded democracy assistance and voluntary associations that seek to encourage pro-democracy leaders and groups emerging in a broad variety of countries. Usually, there is a sense that this democratization assistance may involve many years of effort and that there is not a specific time frame or defined sequence of events during which such assistance can be decisive.

I call the second broad type of democratization activities strategic democratization. This involves countries where the U.S. has a compelling or immediate national security interest in the ultimate success of pro-democratic movements. Among the most important examples are nuclear-armed Russia, which is in the midst of a complex process of political transition where a return to an authoritarian regime is possible; and nuclear-armed Communist China, where the regime intends to suppress all pro-democratic and human-rights movements in order to ensure the continuity of its dictatorship.

It is evident that the Reagan and, to some extent, the first Bush administration carried out strategic democratization.[8] However, it was the Clinton administration that defined the national security aspects most explicitly, stating in its 1995 National Security Strategy that its policy of promoting democracy was "not a democratic crusade [but] a pragmatic commitment to see freedom take hold where that will help us most."[9] This Clinton White House document stated further: "We must target our effort to assist states that affect our strategic interests, such as those with large economies, critical locations, nuclear weapons, or the potential to generate refugee flows into our own nation or into key friends or allies."[10] Russia and China meet those criteria. Turning to Russia and China we can summarize some of the actions that the United States should take.

RUSSIA

As of 2004, among the fifteen post-Soviet states, only the three Baltic states were in a defined process of transition to democracy; Russia, Ukraine, and Georgia are in a situation of de facto cogovernance, where both pro-democratic and authoritarian tendencies compete within the governing institutions and society. Seven Central Asian republics are governed by the former republic-level Communist leadership who emulate Communist China—support for aspects of the market economy, while permitting virtually no real political opposition. They continue in power through Soviet-style managed national elections. In Belarus and Tajikistan, there has been a virtually complete Communist restoration. This is a bleak picture. The future political evolution of Russia is of greatest importance to the U.S. because of its strategic nuclear weapons, its foreign policy, and also because it could well provide an example that could positively affect the other republics.

For Russia, the results of the post-Soviet years (1992–2004) have been mixed. Positive aspects include: the maintenance of substantial levels of personal freedom and human rights for the Russian peoples, including the return of religious freedom (the exceptions are linked to internal war situations such as those in Chechnya); the holding of five reasonably free and competitive national elections;[11] the existence of many associational groups free of government control; and the avoidance of open military conflict with any post-Soviet republics (such as Ukraine) or any other country. Negative aspects include: continuing economic problems and poor living conditions for a large part of the population; large-scale corruption derived in part from the Communist era and from special privileges granted to or taken by financial barons linked to the Yeltsin "party of power"; the expansion of organized crime beyond its Soviet-era role; the fact that one of the largest, best-organized, political parties continues to be the authoritarian Russian Communist Party, with an estimated twenty thousand local branches and more than six hundred thousand members; and the absence of broadly supported, strong pro-democratic political parties and pro-democratic labor unions.

This current situation results from the decisions and actions of the Russian leaders and people since 1992. Yet it also derives in part from the failure of the large U.S. and Western assistance programs to provide far greater resources and support early in 1992 and 1993, and on a continuing basis, to help Russians build genuinely pro-democratic political parties and independent labor unions that could have provided an alternative to the parties representing the views of the party of power, the Communists, or the ultranationalists.

The much-too-small level of help for the emerging democratic parties and labor unions can be seen in the fact that from 1992 to 2000, while total U.S. bilateral expenditures to help Russia were $18 billion ($9 billion in grants), only about $26 million was provided to help build democratic parties and labor unions.[12] The U.S. was fortunate to have organizations with experience in helping emerging democratic parties and labor unions, the IRI, the NDI and the Free Trade Union Institute. All have done good work in Russia with very limited resources. Both NDI and IRI believe they could reach many more pro-democratic groups with more funds, and they also have empirical data documenting the effectiveness of their work.[13]

An example of effective and very timely pro-democracy assistance was the work of the late Dr. Robert Krieble, an American entrepreneur who decided in 1988 to establish an organization "to assist emerging countries in the former Soviet empire to make the transition from Communism to democratic capitalism and provide assistance in the form of direct political and economic training programs."[14] In November 1989, on the day the Berlin Wall was opened, Dr. Krieble and associates, including experienced American political strategist Paul Weyrich, were in Moscow, planning the beginning of their pro-democracy seminars in Russia and other post-Soviet republics. In Dr. Krieble's words, they "provided training in the ideas, institutions, and practical methods of democracy in action."[15] From 1989 to 1995, the Krieble organization held two hundred conferences in eighty-one cities of the former Soviet Union and Eastern Europe, involving sixteen thousand grass-roots leaders.

Many of the leading pro-democratic and proreform leaders in the post-Communist states of Europe and the former Soviet Union were inspired and helped to become more effective through their participation in these programs. Among the most well-known of these emerging pro-democracy leaders who were helped by Dr. Krieble's efforts was Boris Yeltsin and his proreform team, who competed against the Communist Party and the ultranationalists to win the presidency of the Russian Federation in June 1991. The Krieble organization provided important information and practical advice on the methods of democratic electoral competition to Yeltsin, his team, and to many other Russian reformers in 1990 and 1991—long before any U.S. government-sponsored efforts had begun.[16]

This had a history-changing impact, because it was Yeltsin's June 1991 election as president of the Russian Federation, combined with his courage, that provided the basis for rallying public resistance to the hard-line Communist coup attempt in August 1991. Since the Soviet Communist Party was still in power and was determined that its Communist candidate should win the June 1991 Russian Federation presidential election, Yeltsin might not have won that election without the help provided by Dr. Krieble. Without Yeltsin as the president of the Russian Republic, the hard-line Communist coup plotters would probably have succeeded in extinguishing the opportunity for the transition to democracy.

It is essential that the U.S. and other democracies make a clear distinction between pro-democratic leaders and organizations and those that are antidemocratic, helping only those judged to be genuinely dedicated to democracy. In some cases, there has been a misguided view that any political assistance must be given to all competing political parties and organizations, whether pro- or antidemocratic. This was done by the Organization for Security and Cooperation in Europe

(OSCE) in the 1996 elections, held under the terms of the Dayton Accord in the former Yugoslavia (Bosnia-Herzegovina). This is a totally self-defeating approach; it belies common sense and a prudent concern for the objective, the establishment of democratic institutions.

In March 1992, two members of the U.S. Congress, Senator John McCain, a Republican, and Representative Dave McCurdy, a Democrat, expressed what have turned out to be very wise and prescient concerns about the direction of U.S. and Western assistance. They wrote that the plans for assistance to Russia and the other post-Soviet republics were "unimaginative and partial" and:

> economic and technical assistance for private business and financial enterprises . . . [while] necessary and commendable . . . does not address the need for new institutions..is only a partial solution . . . [and] will fail utterly . . . [if not] linked to the prospect for democracy. . . . There can be no effective civil laws and property rights—and therefore, no free market system—without a firm new political and social contract.[17]

They correctly predicted that the "macroeconomic assistance strategies proposed by debt-laden bankers at the International Monetary Fund and the European Bank for Reconstruction and Development . . . could amount to pouring water into a sieve."[18] To increase the prospects for the development and consolidation of political democracy in Russia, McCain and McCurdy proposed, just as the U.S. had done with great success in the process of encouraging democracy in post-Nazi Germany, so too in post-Communist Russia and in the other former Soviet republics, about fifty "Democracy Houses" should be established. These would be staffed by "Teams of experienced Americans (joined by representatives of other democracies) [with] language . . . skills . . . practical expertise in fields such as law, education, business, labor, politics, public administration, human rights . . . [and] Team members should be prepared to stay in residence for at least two years."[19]

The purpose behind this important proposal was that the American staff in the Democracy Houses, with their linguistic skills and knowledge of the national and local political realities, could "assess obstacles to the development of free institutions . . . coordinate public and private assistance efforts from abroad" and encourage the development of "a culture of freedom."[20] All of these purposes remain relevant to the current situation in Russia. Therefore, this idea should be implemented as soon as possible with a staff of experienced, competent, dedicated, and well-compensated Americans who have the relevant language and practical institutional development/inspirational skills, together with an in-depth knowledge of the past and current political and economic conditions in Russia and the former Soviet Union. This knowledge can be acquired by short, intense competently designed courses, but it is essential so that the American experts have enough understanding of the political context for their work. This reduces the chances that they will be misled by Russian individuals and groups claiming to have democratic, free-market, and reformist intentions; but that are either only interested in obtaining the external funding or intend to undermine and preempt support for the genuine democrats nationally or in a particular locality.

Each Democracy House would most likely have at least one representative from each of the four components of the National Endowment for Democracy: the two political party institutes (NDI, IRI), one or more from the free-labor organization (FTUI), and one from the free-market/business association development group (CIPE). These organizations have years of experience in Russia and, therefore, are in a position to work even more effectively in the future as the level of funding increases. In addition, there should be one or more persons working to encourage independent media. The earlier free media assistance program ended because it was believed that its work had been successfully completed. It should be reestablished. The cost for establishing such Democracy Houses would likely be about $40 to $50 million annually, assuming that thirty would be immediately established in Russia.[21]

A few might also be established in Latvia, Lithuania, Estonia, and Ukraine, but the authoritarian regimes in the remaining post-Soviet republics would be unlikely to allow such organizations. There might also be opposition in Russia from the Communists, the ultranationalists, and, most likely, from elements of Putin's broad-based political party, especially those associated with Primakov. China would also likely urge Putin not to permit this. If the term "Democracy House" served as the catalyst for such opposition, the concept could still be implemented, using a designation such as Centers for Technical Assistance Coordination. Effective U.S. pro-democracy assistance in Russia, just like aid in the event of humanitarian emergencies such as earthquakes, should continue whether or not Russia met the conditions discussed earlier for the establishment of the American-staffed economic growth organizations.

The three highest priorities for this work in Russia should be: to encourage the growth and development of the genuinely pro-democratic national political parties such as Yabloko and the Union of Right Forces; to foster the growth and development of the independent, pro-democratic labor-union movement (the Communist unions still enroll about 90 percent of the unionized workers in Russia); and to assist those seeking to maintain or develop politically independent but pro-democratic print and electronic media. There should be an immediate increase in funding for democratic parties and labor-union development from the average levels in the 1990s of less than $2 million per year to no less than $20 to $30 million annually. The free media assistance program should be funded in the range of $5–$10 million per year. These are very small amounts in relation to the hundreds of millions spent annually by the U.S. aid program for Russia since 1992, and if additional funds cannot be obtained, these democracy assistance programs should have priority.

Efforts should also be made to restructure other aspects of U.S. and Western economic assistance to assure greater accountability and to develop ways to link some of the economic assistance funds to the development of democratic political parties and labor unions. Finally, the entire democratic assistance effort for both Russia and China should, in fact, become a top priority of the president. A single coordinator for the assistance program for Russia, the post-Soviet republics, and China should report directly to the president on at least a monthly basis. This would increase the prospects that the highest levels of the entire executive branch would give sustained interest and attention to the encouragement of democracy in Russia and China as a matter of the highest national interest.[22]

THE PEOPLE'S REPUBLIC OF CHINA

In 1997, the Republican leadership of the U.S. House of Representatives declared that the goal of U.S. policy toward China should be to help the Chinese people establish a free, democratic government.[23] During his June 1998 state visit to China, President Clinton said in words echoing President Reagan's 1982 speech urging U.S. aid to encourage democracy abroad:

> We are convinced that certain rights are universal—not American rights or European rights or rights for developed nations, but the birthright of people everywhere, now enshrined in the United Nations Universal Declaration of Human Rights—the right to be treated with dignity; the right to express one's opinions, to choose one's own leaders, to associate freely with others, and to worship, or not, freely, however one chooses.[24]

As he was leaving China, Clinton said further, "I believe that there can be, and I believe that there will be" democracy in China, "but there are powerful forces resisting change, as evidenced by continuing governmental restrictions on free speech, assembly and freedom of worship."[25]

These words express a bipartisan consensus that the goal of U.S. policy in China should be to maintain normal relations with this large, important country, while encouraging its peaceful evolution into a political democracy that will respect the human rights of its citizens and be peaceful internationally. However, there has also been a bipartisan assumption that continuing the pattern of unconditional economic and commercial relations, which since 1980 has been highly advantageous to China, will in itself lead to political democracy.

We have already discussed the evidence proving this assumption false, as seen in the history of the last two centuries, where economic modernization has at times increased the power of authoritarian states and fueled their expansionist impulses (imperial Germany and imperial Japan), rather than leading to political pluralism and democracy. The economic-determinist assumption about the development of political democracy has been disproved in China by the history of the post-Mao era, where the regime has kept its dictatorship intact while the economy and society have changed dramatically. A noted expert on China, Professor Andrew Nathan of Columbia University, wrote: "The linkage between development and rights is too loose, . . . the time frame too long and the results too uncertain to make economic engagement a substitute for direct policy" on behalf of human rights and democracy.[26]

In fact, nowhere has political democracy simply emerged from the process of economic modernization and growth. It has to be sought, struggled for, and established by individuals who have reached a firm decision that this form of government would be better for their country than the current dictatorship and who have decided to take action to bring about a new system of governance. This is a decision of the mind and of the heart, and it is a decision that in any dictatorship carries immense risk and requires courage to translate into action. The role of the U.S. and other democracies in such a process of movement toward political democracy is to provide a positive example as a prosperous, peaceful democracy, and also to move from the repetition of rhetorical hopes for human rights and democracy in China to giving encouragement and practical assistance that helps the individuals who seek to liberalize the political system.

It is a great irony that, since the 1950s, the Chinese Communist Party has imagined that the U.S. has pursued a secret strategy to bring about the "peaceful evolution" of countries from Communism to democracy, when in the case of China, the U.S. government has done almost nothing but talk about the inevitability of this transformation through economic change and international trade. Now is the time for an open but discreet strategy to assist those inside China and abroad who seek a peaceful evolution to genuine political democracy in China.

Those, especially in the U.S. and in other democratic governments, who believe this is impossible or unlikely, might reflect on recent history. In 1988, it seemed that the Communist regimes of Europe might last decades longer, but in 1989, the courage shown for many years in Eastern Europe by a very few democratic dissidents set the stage for the mass protests leading first to the unraveling of Communism in Eastern Europe, then to the dissolution of the Soviet Union. While the end of Communism seemed to come suddenly in Eastern Europe, in fact it occurred in Poland after more than a decade of continuous struggle by the few who founded and the hundreds of thousands and then millions who subsequently became members of the Solidarity movement.

While the citizens of Poland liberated themselves, they needed and received help from abroad. An important example for post-Tiananmen China is President Reagan's decision to facilitate assistance for the Solidarity movement in Poland after the December 1981 repression and mass arrest of its leaders. This assistance from the U.S. and other democracies, provided through a variety of institutions including the U.S. labor movement, helped to sustain the morale and underground organization of Solidarity and provided the tangible resources the Solidarity leaders needed to continue acting as a peaceful, pro-democratic opposition to the Polish Communist regime. It was this continuous effort and the loyalty of millions to the repressed Solidarity movement year after year, along with Gorbachev's decision to seek the reform of Soviet Communism, that finally led the Polish Communist regime to permit its reemergence and agree to its participation in partially free elections in June 1989, in the hope this would bring an end to labor protests and strikes. Something similar could occur in China.

A second important example is the success of the democratic opposition in Serbia, where the Communist dictator, Slobodan Milosevic, was removed by popular protests in October 2000. That regime had caused immense suffering since 1991 by inciting intergroup wars. Milosevic fell quickly, after fifty-five years of Communist dictatorship. During thirty of these years, significant market-oriented changes and extensive trade took place, while personal travel within democratic Europe and other countries was permitted. None of these measures succeeded in ending the Communist dictatorship. But once the people of Serbia were given help in removing Milosevic and a number of his top officials, Serbia began a transition to political democracy.

This visible event followed what had been a long, seemingly hopeless struggle by brave pro-democratic leaders and groups that lasted nearly a decade and received ever-increasing support from democracies abroad.[27] In the final six months of the citizens' effort to remove the dictator, Thomas Carothers from the Carnegie Endowment estimates that U.S. public and private groups spent about $40 million and the European democracies spent about the same amount to help the Serbian people organize and implement their quest for democracy.[28]

As in all cases where aggressive dictators are replaced by democratizing regimes, the results have been good for the people of Serbia and immensely important in reducing further threats of aggression and war in the former Yugoslavia and in the entire region. China supported Milosevic with political, financial, and covert means, and the Beijing regime has undoubtedly studied those events with the purpose of trying to assure that nothing similar ever occurs in China. The arrest and subsequent transfer of Milosevic to stand trial for war crimes before the International Tribunal in Holland will reinforce the determination of the Chinese

Communist Party never to be overthrown or risk its hold on power through elections. But the intention of dictators to keep power does not guarantee that outcome, as has been evident in many countries since the 1980s.

A Strategy for Democratization in China

There are four major groups that will be most important in the process of political liberalization in China:

1. The hundreds of millions of Chinese citizens who want fair, legal and effective government. They want their system to work properly and they are becoming increasingly dissatisfied because of the serious problems of daily life they see as caused by the Party;
2. political reform elements within the Chinese Communist Party;
3. pro-democracy citizens of China;
4. pro-democracy Chinese living in exile in the U.S. and other democratic countries.

Each of these groups is important; all can and must be reached by a comprehensive pro-democracy strategy. A peaceful process of evolution toward democracy—one involving the gradual or apparently sudden political transformation of the regime (after years of nearly invisible struggle)—can lead to the Communist Party losing its monopoly of power without fear of violent or painful retribution. The example of post-Communist transitions in Europe with amnesty, personal safety, and equal rights for virtually all former members of the ruling Communist parties and regimes provides a basis for tacit or open cooperation between the pro-democratic groups and the reform elements of the Party. We shall briefly discuss each of these four groups and then consider how they can be reached by a realistic, peaceful, pro-democracy strategy.

Citizens Seeking Fair, Legal, Effective Governance: Vulnerabilities of the Regime
Among China's estimated 1.3 billion population, there are hundreds of millions of citizens who want the government to follow its own constitution and laws and who object to arbitrary, illegal taxes, bribes, demands, and threats from a wide variety of local, provincial, and national officials of the regime and the Party. Despite impressive economic growth, China has a series of very significant problems that are causing ever-rising levels of discontent, especially among many of the nine hundred million persons living in the countryside.

This is compounded by enormous and ever-increasing inequalities in income and in living conditions, and by widespread regime and Party corruption, which then-President Jiang Zemin frequently denounced publicly. Corruption continues to become more widespread. Jiang told a senior Party meeting that corruption is "blackening the hearts" of Party officials, that "several leading cadres are exchanging power for money and power for sex," and that members of the Party "must control their spouses and children" so that they cease their corrupt business activities.[29]

It is widely known in China that the children of senior Party leaders have become very wealthy by using their political connections to assure their success in business deals, most of which require approval by the state. These wealthy adult children of the Party's Politburo and Central Committee members are popularly known as "princelings," and one of the most wealthy is former President Jiang's son, Jiang Mianheng. He is a U.S.-educated electrical engineer, undoubtedly intelligent, who has become one of China's major business owners, including "an airline, a telecommunications company and a newly completed state of the art computer chip manufacturing plant" (in partnership with one of Taiwan's wealthiest computer chip makers), which his father tried to hide with "a veil of secrecy . . . to avoid the taint of corruption."[30]

Mao warned that "a single spark can start a prairie fire." The Party in China is concerned that the ever-increasing levels of corruption, visible to the population in both the towns and the country side (where many farmers live poorly while Party officials have elegant houses and drive imported SUVs) will provoke widespread rebellion against a regime no longer viewed as legitimate. For that reason, since 1999, the Party has prosecuted corrupt officials more vigorously. In the first eight months of a recent year, more than twenty-three thousand criminal corruption cases were pursued. The number of officials under investigation increased by about 12 percent annually during the later 1990s.[31]

A member of the Chinese Academy of Sciences, Hu Angang, estimates that corruption costs China the equivalent of 8 percent of GDP annually (about $90 billion per one trillion of GDP) in lost taxes and tariffs.[32] In addition, the National Audit Bureau of China found that in 1999 more than $15 billion in government funds had been "skimmed off unauthorized projects" with most "ending up in private hands."[33]

One example was the use by the Ministry of Water Resources of $72 million to build a twenty-eight-story "office building" in Beijing, where the ministry only needed one or two floors. For the rest of the building " the ministry's mandarins envisioned restaurants, a hotel and conference center. . . . Rent was . . . supposed to spill into a secret coffer."[34] This corrupt project took money directly away from the maintenance of a "national network of canals, reservoirs, dams and dikes," vitally necessary to provide water for farmers and to avoid floods. The diversion in this ministry was revealed as totaling $360 million in 1999 alone. The report included the words of a poor farmer from central China who was directly affected: "We won't get anything from the land this year because there is no water now."[35]

On November 8, 2000, the official Chinese media broke its silence about the biggest corruption scandal up to then, the diversion over several years of more than $6 billion from the government by large-scale smuggling operations in the east coast port city of Xiamen. This led to months of press coverage involving "tales of money, sex, power, illicit videotaping, tapped phones" among the smugglers.[36] The trial revealed that "the entire system was for sale," and among the first eighty-four defendants, fourteen were sentenced to death, twelve to life in prison, and fifty-eight to other prison terms.[37]

In a remarkably candid 2001 report prepared for the Party Central Committee and published as a book in China, two major causes of growing public unrest were identified: widespread corruption within the Party and government; and the increasing inequalities of income, which it said were at "an alarm level," not only between the few wealthy and the vast majority of still-poor Chinese, but also between the cities and the countryside and between the rapidly developing coastal east and the stagnant interior and Western regions of China.[38] A highly respected Chinese economist, He Qinglian, blacklisted by the regime because of her objectivity, estimates that China's upper class accounts for about 1 percent of the population (13 million of 1.3 billion persons). The middle class is about 16 percent of the population (208 million), and the remaining 83 percent is poor— divided between the working poor, about 50 percent (650 million) who eke out a living and the 30 percent (390 million) who live in extreme poverty. These included the estimated 100–200 million "floating" persons, a homeless population in the towns and cities without legal residences, regular employment, or access to any public services.[39]

The combination of corruption, sharp income inequalities, and the authoritarian power of the Communist Party have led to growing resentment among the nine hundred million living in the countryside; and this has led to a cycle of increasingly frequent, larger, and more violent demonstrations. As described in the Party's own May 2001 report, "In recent years [there have been] rising numbers of group incidents and their scale has been expanding, frequently involving over a thousand or even ten thousand people."[40] Also, the growing numbers of demonstrations have become more assertive, with the report prepared for the Party saying: "Protesters frequently seal off bridges and block roads, storm Party and government offices, coercing Party committees and government and there are even criminal acts such as attacking, trashing, looting and arson."[41]

Many in the countryside are angry because they remain poor while the local Party members become rich by taxing them and charging them fees, legal and illegal. They are angry because after some improvement in the early 1980s when the communes were replaced by the leasing of land to individual farmers, the state still owns all the land. The farmers have long-term leases and they must pay the taxes on the land even when they decide not to farm because they can no longer earn enough to make it worthwhile. As a result, "Many continue farming simply to defray the taxes due, even though their crops fail to cover expenses."[42] A major reason for the ever-higher taxes and fees is that the number of Party officials the farmers must support keeps increasing. Before it was censored by the regime, a candid Party-owned newspaper, *Southern Weekend*, published the appeal of a farmer who wrote that in the last ten years, the number of Party officials in his town had increased three-fold (300 percent). In another rural region, the fees collected from four thousand farmers were used to support one thousand Party.[43]

When ten thousand angry farmers demonstrate, as in Yuandu in 2000, the regime sends truckloads of the paramilitary Peoples Armed Police to end the protest, using whatever degree of force may be required. Usually, some hundreds of farmers are injured or arrested, and some will be sent to detention or forced-labor camps.[44] At the current stage of public mobilization, the regime retains the armed might to prevail, but just as a prairie wildfire can spread quickly, this could change very rapidly in the future if protests spread and coercive organizations begin to doubt their mission or lose confidence in the ultimate outcome.

This is especially true since in China there are severe problems in both the countryside and cities. As noted, the current population of those with no employment and legal residence in towns is estimated at 100–200 million out of an urban population of about 400 million. In addition, the government plans to reduce employment in the state-owned and affiliated enterprises, which account for about 65 percent of China's GDP, and about the same proportion of its enterprise employment (about 275 million). This is likely to result in additional millions of unemployed persons in the towns and cities.[45] China has not yet established a social insurance/unemployment insurance system to assist these workers as they seek to make a transition to new jobs, ostensibly in the expanding private sector. This urban unemployment could increase even more, since China has joined the WTO. If China actually implements some or most of its WTO obligations, there will be further unemployment as certain types of imports reduce the demand in China for some Chinese-made products.

These urban unemployment problems may well be compounded by the fact that China is facing serious macroeconomic difficulties, which so far have been little noticed and little discussed publicly in China or abroad. China has enormous unfunded pension liabilities from the state-owned and affiliated enterprises. These are estimated by the World Bank at between $500 and $800 billion (or from 50 to 80 percent of GDP).[46] This means many retiring or laid-off workers will not receive the pensions they were expecting. Also, Chinese banks and other financial institutions, having made loans on the basis of Party directions and personal connections, have nonperforming loans estimated at $200–$300 billion (20 to 30 percent of GDP). Officially, China reports a debt of just 20 percent of GDP, a very sustainable amount, but the former chief of the World Bank mission there estimates that the total debt-to-GDP ratio may be 150 percent, or about $1.5 trillion in state debts—an amount that suggests systemic fragility and potentially very serious economic problems ahead.[47]

The Chinese stock market has become very important to the estimated 58 million Chinese who have stock accounts. It performed very well during the 1990s, as China's export-led economic growth continued, and was hardly affected by the decline in the U.S. stock market that followed the year 2000 reductions in the valuation of U.S. high-technology firms and lowered values in the world's other stock markets. But, an analysis by Business Week finds that China's stocks and other financial instruments are highly risky due to a lack of transparency, systematic fraud, market manipulation, and because many of the listed Chinese companies are in dubious financial condition due to their large, hidden, bad debts. This assessment concludes that the price increases in Chinese stocks have been driven by artificial scarcity of stocks, swindles, and insider trading; further, it warns that China is using false data to sell stock in troubled Chinese companies to U.S. investors and pension funds.[48]

Taken together, these facts suggest that China is extremely vulnerable to a major financial/stock market crisis, which could cause further disaffection from the regime in urban areas—both among average workers and among the most well-off, including the Party elite and many Party members who have a large portion of their savings in stocks. These financial problems would be seen as the fault of the Party and will be blamed on a combination of its denial, manipulation, incompetence, corruption, and the inability in a dictatorship to discuss these matters openly and therefore take preventive actions.

While the problems affecting hundreds of millions of poor farmers and poor city and town residents are building resentment, a large-scale financial or stock crisis or crash would cause direct personal financial losses to the Communist and business elite and to the urban middle and upper class. It is estimated that for the well-off, 80 percent of personal savings are now in financial instruments. China's internal financial vulnerabilities have immense political implications, including the prospect that a financial crisis and losses could alienate many of the elite and well-off from the present regime. As noted in the May 2001 report for the Party, those participating in protests "are expanding from farmers and retired workers [lack of pensions] to include workers still on the job, individual business owners, decommissioned soldiers and even officials, teachers and students."[49] Urban unrest is on the rise.

China also has very severe environmental problems. As with the former Soviet Union and other Communist states, the regime gave no priority to preventing these severe threats to health nor did the views of citizens have any influence. China has major problems of urban air pollution, with five of the world's ten most polluted cities.[50] China has more toxic water pollution than the whole of the Western world combined. Eighty percent of its lakes and rivers are polluted, acid rain occurs in 25 percent of its territory, and China produces 14 percent of world carbon emissions—its per capita emissions are 75 percent higher than those of Brazil, which has an economy of comparable size. In Beijing and other cities, particulate emissions are four times the World Health Organization maximum safe level, and sulfur dioxide levels are twice the safe maximum.[51] All these and other environmental problems increase discontent in both the countryside and in the towns and cities, and they are also perceived as the direct responsibility of the Party.

In spite of the high overall growth rates of the Chinese economy, these facts of everyday life trouble hundreds of millions of its citizens in both rural and urban areas. This is setting the stage for an expansion of protest against the Communist regime and brings to mind the words an American president used to describe another major Communist state, which subsequently experienced a major transformation:

> We are witnessing . . . a crisis where the demands of the economic order are conflicting directly with those of the political order. . . . The crisis is happening . . . in the home of Marxism-Leninism. . . . It is the Soviet Union [China] that runs against the tide of history by denying human freedom and human dignity to its citizens. . . . What we see here is a political structure that no longer corresponds to its economic base, a society where productive forces are hampered by political ones.[52]

Such insights may be occurring to some within the Chinese Communist Party who may believe that reform and change is the best way to keep the Party in power and may also be best for China.

Reform Elements within the Chinese Communist Party

The Chinese Communist Party has an estimated 70 million members and large national, provincial, and local organizations, all led by Secretary General Hu, the nine-member Standing Committee of the Politburo, the Politburo, and the Central Committee.[53] As with all organizations, there are factions throughout the CCP based on patron-client relationships among higher- and lower-ranking persons, personal factors, and as a result of differences in views about what the Party should do now and in the future.

At present, there are generally perceived to be three main coalitions: the dominant Jiang Zemin group, which gives highest priority to economic and military modernization while using whatever repression seems necessary to retain power. The hardliners, led by Li Peng, see a need for more internal repression and are more willing to threaten or use force to take control of Taiwan. Li Peng was a catalyst for the Tiananman massacre and subsequent political persecution campaign. The smallest group, personified by Li Ruihuan, head of the consultative branch of the legislature, is perceived to be the most popular with the general public and consistently speaks openly about the need for the Party to broaden its appeal, tolerate diversity in views, and find ways to increase the participation of citizens in politics.[54]

During the 1980s, there were those at the highest levels of the Chinese Communist Party who made the case for movement toward some political reform. They mostly used functional arguments: the need for more predictable rules in order to foster economic growth, therefore the need to increase the authority of the government institutions and reduce the daily role of the Party; the need for greater professionalism in administration of a new, more complex economy and, therefore, the need for more objective criteria for selecting and promoting government officials rather than simply using their Party history and connections; the need for more objective, factual data about economic, social, and attitudinal trends in the society, therefore, the need for somewhat greater openness in social science research, inquiry, and even in journalism.[55] The hardliners in the Party precipitated the 1989 Tiananmen repression to complete the removal from leadership of the 1980s Party reformers and provide the pretext for reasserting hard-line control of the Party.[56]

However, in 2002, a new era began opening, one in which there are four catalysts that could lead either to reforms or to greater repression. These include: the continuing changes in the Chinese economy and society and the shift toward high-technology production and employment outside state production organizations, about 35 percent of the work force; the serious, growing internal problems of China widely perceived as the responsibility of the Party (corruption, severe inequalities of income, unemployment, mounting unrest, increasing organized crime, severe environmental pollution, water shortages); ideological shifts and uncertainties within the Party; and the likely intense struggle for succession within the Party, always a weak point of dictatorships.

The announced succession process is that Jiang Zemin, his senior-level appointees (and therefore his group), along with about half of all senior Party officials who comprise the "third generation" of CCP rulers (first Mao, second Deng, third Jiang) would resign from most of their Party and government positions over the next several years as a result of decisions ratified at the Sixteenth Party Congress in October 2002.[57] Since the third generation witnessed and experienced the life-and-death, secret inter-Party conspiracies, maneuverings, and preparations for an inter-Communist civil war that followed the death of Mao in 1976, Jiang wants an orderly succession.

Jiang is following what Deng did in the early 1980s, when he resigned from most

Party and government positions in the months following the Sixteenth Party Congress but kept control of the military until late 2004 as chairman of the Party's Central Military Commission. This is the point of senior authority over the military that is under the direct control of the Party rather than the government. Together with the promotion to Secretary General and then president of Jiang's intended successor and protégé, Vice President Hu Jintao, this could permit Jiang to follow in Deng's path as the "paramount leader," guiding China's key strategic decisions behind the scenes for some years.[58]

The "fourth generation," whether linked to Hu Jintao or followers of Li Peng, are Party officials who were directly responsible for implementing the repression of political, religious, and ethnic movements following the 1989 Tiananmen massacre. Therefore, it is likely that the Chinese regime would expect to continue using repression by the secret police and the recently enlarged Peoples Armed Police, forced-labor camps, tightened censorship, and the threat the return of persecution campaigns, such as that Jiang launched against the Falun Gong movement in 1999. The aim would be to contain dissatisfaction until China had used additional years of economic benefits from the U.S. and other democracies to build a more broadly based economy and expand its strategic nuclear and other advanced military forces. The current Party assumption is that domestic unrest can and will be contained and that China's economic growth would provide the political, economic, and military instruments needed to have an international role that includes the domination of Asia, and which assures access to needed supplies of oil, natural gas, high technology, fresh water, and other resources on China's terms.

Despite these purposes, there might, nevertheless, be some opening for change toward reform in the Party, due to the combination of China's growing internal problems, public dissatisfaction, and the coming shift in leadership to the fourth generation. This will be followed by the arrival of the post-Cultural Revolution fifth generation, now in their late 30s and 40s, in key implementing/management positions such as vice ministers and heads of departments in the Party and regime. Nearly all of the fourth and fifth generations are far better educated than the Jiang generation. Some even studied in the U.S. or other democracies. There are reports that Hu Jintao was identified in the 1980s with some of the reform thinking of then-Secretary General Hu Yaobang, who was removed by the hardliners, and that he has some reform ideas in mind.[59]

Also, there may be an opening for political reform within the Party because of the unsettling effects and rethinking brought on by the ideological redefinition launched by Jiang Zemin. His purpose has been to keep the loyalty of the Party members and help maintain the cohesion and relevance of Chinese Communism by adapting the ideology to the visible realities of contemporary China. Since the Party's establishment in 1921, it has kept essentially the same Leninist precepts, with a few additions by Mao and then by Deng. Despite Deng's proclamation of "socialism with Chinese characteristics," permitting internal and international economic opening, the Party continued to define itself as the "vanguard of the proletariat," consisting of workers and peasants, people "without property." The major purpose of the Party was to assure "the dictatorship of the proletariat," meaning that workers and peasants would rule the other classes, such as owners of land or businesses, people "with property." It was this purpose that justified the fact that the military would be directly under the primary control of the Party, rather than of the government.[60]

To update the ideology, Jiang Zemin declared the "Theory of the Three Representatives," that the Party should represent and lead the most advanced economic, technological, and cultural elements of the society. Therefore, people from all groups and classes, even those "with property," must be welcomed into the Party.[61] A senior Party official commenting on this said, "Obviously, well-educated people—and to a considerable extent, entrepreneurs and professionals with property and wealth—are best positioned to make advances in economic and technological fields."[62] This led, in 2001, to the Party inviting business people to join and to proposed amendments of the basic charter and principles changing the goal of the Party from the "dictatorship of the proletariat" to "economic development for all," opening the Party to all social groups. A senior Party official said that Jiang and other members of the Politburo "are keen that China excels in the knowledge economy. The goal of the Party should then be the spreading of knowledge as well as knowledge-based wealth, not class struggle."[63]

This reformulation of core principles and positions may be self-evident to many of the Party elite in Beijing and Shanghai, but it is probably a source of ideological confusion and uncertainty among millions of the Party rank and file throughout the vast land. One astute observer, Al Santoli, notes that Jiang's new ideology is "creating an identity crisis" for millions of Party members. The *Far Eastern Economic Review* called it an implicit betrayal of blue-collar workers who are not part of the knowledge economy. This, at the time when those workers are facing rising unemployment, no unemployment insurance, and unfunded pensions, as the Party-regime restructures domestic production away from the state-linked factories and has entered the WTO.[64] Discontent among workers has also increased because enterprise managers now have salaries up to three hundred times more than those of workers, not counting corrupt income, compared with three or four times higher in the 1970s.[65] Also, while the National People's Congress consisted of about 27 percent workers in 1978, that declined steadily to fewer than 11 percent by 1997.[66] This ideological redefinition could play a larger-than-anticipated role in deciding whether the Party remains functionally united or begins to separate into distinct national factions that might, over time, begin to approximate competing political coalitions, possibly evolving into competing political parties.

POSSIBLE STAGES OF PARTY EVOLUTION TOWARD POLITICAL REFORM

Most organizations, including ruling Communist parties, only move toward reformist changes when their existing methods of action seem not to be working. It is for this reason that a major catalyst for Party reform could be the proposed U.S. policy we have called realistic engagement. This would remove China's lucrative one-way market access opportunities to the U.S. unless the regime changed internationally and began implementing the UN Declaration of Human Rights and the other UN political-social covenants it has signed. That action would require Party leadership to choose between moving toward political reform and confronting far more internal unrest due to economic dislocations caused by the loss of what have been, in effect, massive subsidies from the U.S.

When the first Bush administration imposed economic sanctions after Tiananmen, the Party initially responded by some lessening of repression. More than eight hundred political prisoners were released. But then the U.S. reassured the Chinese leadership that it would renew MFN and trade relations could continue. That ended the internal impetus toward some reform at that time. Ironically, the massive economic benefits from the U.S., the EU, and Japan, instead of encouraging political reform have subsidized the maintenance of the political dictatorship in an unchanged form, with documented increased political repression during the 1990s—the years of China's greatest macroeconomic growth and ever larger trade surpluses. Whether the pressure for reform of the Party's method of rule comes from the Chinese people, from inside the Party, from the U.S. and perhaps other major democracies, or from all of these, the following briefly discusses possible stages of reformist evolution.

After the fanaticism of Mao, the Deng era was marked by the end of the mass persecution campaigns, the economic opening, and a significant decline in the regimentation of daily life. Jiang moved the Party away from class struggle and the dictatorship of the proletariat to the goals of inclusion for all groups, especially those linked to the most advanced sectors of the economy and high technology on behalf of economic development. But the Party still rules China, and within the Party, the Politburo rules—all the election processes within the Party are, in reality, selection processes from the top down. Based on what is known of discussions within the Party, the experience of the Gorbachev-era Soviet Union, and other Communist change processes, we might define four stages of political evolution in China as: reform Communism; "socialist democracy"; limited social democracy; and genuine political democracy.

Reform Communism

In reform Communism, there would be an openness to genuine debate within the Party on the major issues; an effort as in the 1980s to shift more of the daily functions of the state to government institutions; and the beginning of genuine, competitive elections within the Party, perhaps starting at the local level, then moving up to the provincial and national levels. For example, the Seventeenth Party Congress to meet in 2007 might consist of genuinely elected Party members. This intra-Party openness would, of course, mean that Party and other media would need to be more open in debating and discussing alternative approaches and solutions for pressing national problems. The shift of the Party from day-to-day management to the role of overall national strategy and policy direction might also be accompanied by the legislature, the National Peoples Congress, becoming more involved in some degree of genuine consultation and oversight. There was a hint of this in the February 2001 session, when the leading government institution, the State Council (cabinet), ordered all ministers and vice ministers to remain in Beijing during the two-week session of the legislature so they could attend some of the sessions and would be available to answer questions if requested.[67]

"Socialist Democracy"

The next phase, what some Party members refer to as "socialist democracy," would continue to keep the Party in ultimate control but see a devolution of day-to-day authority to the government institutions, possibly broadening the electoral process for the government. "Elections" have been held at the village level in some hundreds of thousand of villages since 1980.These have been mostly pseudoelections, since the Party and the local government select the competing candidates (when there is competition), and, as one well-informed observer noted, "When the Communist candidate does not win the votes are recounted until he does."[68] Reformers within the Party spoke in 2000 of expanding elections in China from the village level to include the county level by 2003, to the towns and cities by 2008, to the provincial level by 2013, and, in some form, to the national level by 2018.[69] Yet, as the Soviet Union demonstrated over many decades of national elections, the form of elections does not necessarily indicate or lead to any genuine liberalization. Stalin summed up his view: "I do not care how the votes go, I only care about who counts the votes." A sign that expanding meaningless elections might accomplish little is that some in the Party reportedly are considering the "socialist democracy" approach more as a means of reducing the threat or pressure for democratization from the West.[70]

Nevertheless, there is the possibility of a broadening of public debate about alternative policies for China as a result of such elections, provided there is also some degree of opening in the media. This might also be the stage during which the control over the military shifts from the Party to the government, a change which could have important effects. As one Party reformer told the insightful, experienced observer, Willy Wo-lam Lap, "If there is no more necessity for class struggle . . . the PLA's role should be mostly for national defense and it should become a state, not a Party, army."[71]

"Limited Social Democracy"

The limited "social democracy" stage being considered by some Party reformers would involve national elections, in which the existing eight "opposition parties" that the Communist regime has maintained and financed since 1949 would become visible again and be allowed to "compete" with the Communist Party. They might win some seats in the legislature, their leaders might hold some cabinet posts, they might even have some media of their own, but their role and visibility inside China would be limited to assure that the Party kept the reins of power. This would have the double purpose of containing and coopting opposition groups within China and of attempting to demonstrate to the democratic world, especially European social democratic parties, that China was in fact "really changing" and, presumably, should be rewarded with additional financial benefits, investments, and technology. In a sense, this would be a return to Mao's " New Democracy," the initial years of Communist rule when the Party used its United Front methods to control and guide the opposition parties and persuade potential opponents of the Party that coexistence would be possible for them. This facilitated the Party's systematic actions to destroy its perceived enemies one at a time.

However, in Poland, what was intended in 1989 as a controlled opening toward and limited political role for Solidarity went far beyond what had been expected or intended by that Communist regime. This type of opening, especially in the context of a serious international effort to encourage and help pro-democratic Chinese exiles, who could work with proreform elements within the Party and pro-democratic elements in the society, might have a larger-than-intended effect. No doubt, Party hardliners will make this point as they resist strongly even this limited "social democracy." Quite possibly, that dispute could either divide the Party, lead to the expulsion of the hardliners, or lead to their success (as in the 1980s) and a regression to more harsh forms of the dictatorship.

There are no currently known plans within the Party for a transition to genuine political democracy. However, in the context of changing events within China, it might occur if the Party leadership faced a situation where they risked defeat or where they could negotiate a transition that would provide for their continuing participation as one of several other genuinely competing political parties in China. Here the experience of the Communist parties in Eastern Europe is instructive. Many changed their professed ideology by accepting the rules of democratic politics, and many leaders of renamed and professedly reformed Communist parties won election to the presidency (Poland, Hungary, Bulgaria, the Baltics) and continued to play an important national role. These examples might persuade many Party leaders that this could be the future of a reformed Communist Party of China, if pro-democratic groups in China and abroad succeed.

Genuine Political Democracy

Prodemocratic Citizens of China

There are perhaps hundreds of thousands or millions of citizens of China who have reached a firm but still-private decision that the history of their country and the various alternative political systems in the modern era make clear that democracy would be best for the people of their country. There has been a tradition of support among some intellectuals for constitutional democracy since the beginning of the twentieth century.[72] The number of those quietly hoping for a transition to political democracy in China has undoubtedly increased as a result of the visible success of Taiwan in establishing a prosperous modern economy and democracy, while avoiding the terror and corruption of mainland Communism.

At present, leaders with this view are most often found among the university-educated, although many workers and farmers have undoubtedly also come to this conclusion as a result of their experience of past suffering and current exploitation under the dictatorship. An example of how quickly the support for democracy might become visible, even in the current political context, was the rapid expansion in 1998 of the newly established China Democratic Party to twenty thousand registered members in ten provinces within a few months. This group of brave organizers inside China received encouragement and financial support from pro-democracy Chinese exiles. Those involved in China and abroad hoped the China Democracy Party would not be repressed because it acted openly, complying with the legal requirements for the registration of civic associations, and because of the state visit of President Clinton. Unfortunately, the regime immediately set out to crush the China Democracy Party by arresting all the organizers and intimidating all those who had joined. This, along with the persecution of the Falun Gong, was a major part of the reason that political repression increased markedly after 1998.[73]

The ranks of pro-democracy Chinese could be rapidly increased by many religious believers, as well as ethnic minorities such as Muslim Uygurs and Tibetans. Many among these would also favor genuine political democracy because they would expect that they would then have the liberty to live according to their beliefs without persecution. Members of the Falun Gong movement, estimated to number in the tens of millions and having experienced harsh persecution since late 1999, would also be likely to favor political democracy. This is also likely to be true of all the workers who would like to establish genuinely independent labor unions to mitigate the harsh conditions and low pay experienced by most urban laborers.[74] This suggests that although the core group of Chinese citizens actively committed to political democracy may be comparatively small, it could quickly expand once there seemed to be real opportunities to pursue this alternative without the risk of immediate arrest and punishment. One American of Chinese descent wrote after twenty years of work in China that in the next years "The central government will not be able to fight all those who challenge it . . . the consequence will be the end of Chinese institutions as they now exist."[75]

We should recall that a small group of courageous activists in Communist Eastern Europe kept the flame of human rights and democracy alive year after year during the 1970s and 1980s, until a change in circumstances opened the way to freedom. That was the combination of citizen activism and the Soviet decision in the autumn of 1989, having just withdrawn its forces after ten years of bloody, unsuccessful combat in Afghanistan, not to suppress profreedom demonstrations in Eastern Europe with military force as it had in 1953, 1956, and 1968. If the Chinese regime refrained from using force against domestic demonstrations, there might well be a "prairie fire" of citizens seeking more freedom.

Prodemocracy Chinese Exiles

In addition to those looking toward democracy inside China, there are tens of thousands of Chinese exiles living in the U.S. and in other democratic countries. Some support the current regime, many want no involvement in anything having to do with politics in China, and some have a strong commitment to helping to bring about a transition to democracy in their homeland. Many of these genuinely prodemocracy exiles are of the Tiananman generation. They have hope for the future because they saw what could be accomplished through spontaneous action. They know the vulnerabilities of the regime and understand the discontent in the society. The pro-democracy exiles include individuals of all ages and together they account for many thousands in the U.S. alone.

They are an especially important group because their experience of life in the U.S. and other democracies has taught them that political democracy does not solve the problems of a society, rather it provides a means for citizens to debate and make public policy decisions without coercion and force as they seek to improve their lives. Therefore, having lived in a democracy and having adopted the goal of political democracy for China, they are likely to be realistic about the opportunities and limitations. They also have a depth of intuitive and analytical understanding of their country, and of its various regions, that can make them exceptionally effective in identifying, inspiring, encouraging, and providing practical assistance. In the initial years of a pro-democracy effort, these pro-democratic Chinese exiles are likely to be an indispensable bridge to their pro-democracy compatriots within China.

The success of the Serbian pro-democratic organizations in removing the Communist dictator and regime in October 2000 led the Chinese Party to conclude that this was "an antisocialist conspiracy spearheaded by the United States."[77] Sources revealed that this was discussed at length at a meeting of the Politburo Standing Committee and that Jiang Zemin said the Party had to draw lessons from this event: "Drastic changes could come suddenly, the tide could turn in a single day . . . we must preserve stability above all else. . . . We must raise our guard against unexpected events and shocks." This, in turn, produced increased restrictions on the Internet, the media, the arrest of a number of frequent visitors to China, some U.S. residents or citizens, and additional efforts to make certain that no independent civic groups could be formed or function.[78]

The officially sanctioned nongovernment organizations that Kaplan notes "impress so many Western observers" are described by Andrew Nathan of Columbia University as a Potemkin façade, where "Almost every ostensibly independent organization—institutes, foundations, consultancies is linked to the Party-state network," even sports and business associations.[79] This illustrates the effort at control of political life by the Chinese regime and makes clear that only pro-democratic Chinese exiles are likely to have the knowledge, understanding and informal relationships to facilitate the flow of outside assistance to genuinely pro-democratic individuals and groups on the mainland.

For that very reason, the Chinese regime, like most other dictatorships, makes a wide range of efforts to undermine and demoralize pro-democracy Chinese exiles and their organizations. This is done by attempting to penetrate them and then cause ideological and personal disputes within the organizations. It is done through defamation and sabotage, such as accusing genuine pro-democracy activists of being Communist "plants." All exile groups have factions and factional disputes (just like democratic and Communist parties), and all have members who are under great stress because they must work full-time to provide for themselves and their families, because they are concerned about possible reprisals against relatives in China, and because they are discouraged by the lack of support they receive in the U.S. from private or public sources. Most of all, they are perplexed and disappointed by the repetition year after year of the false theory that free trade will in itself bring progress on human rights and democracy. This seems to many of the pro-democracy exiles to represent the political influence of private business, which seems to have convinced the U.S. government to focus only on business today while giving occasional rhetorical attention to human rights and leaving the issue of democracy for a distant tomorrow.

THE PROGRAM FOR DEMOCRACY IN CHINA

A strategy to encourage a peaceful transition to political democracy in China should be understood as requiring ten to twenty years of competent and increasing effort, although, as Jiang Zemin said, unanticipated events could bring this about much more quickly. We might also recall the insight about regime change spoken by a leader of a successful attempt to end a major one: "Revolution is impossible, until it is inevitable."[80]

The essence of a peaceful pro-democracy strategy involves giving the people and the natural leaders in each of the four groups in China (which we have discussed) the information and encouragement that will lead them to take practical steps to bring the Party first toward greater observance of its own laws, constitution, and existing international human rights commitments; then to make changes in the direction of political liberalization. This requires the establishment of an organization to plan, coordinate, and implement these activities, which might be named the Program for Democracy in China (PDC). Genuinely pro-democratic Chinese exiles and citizens of the U.S. and other participating democracies who share a commitment to the purposes and have relevant skills would staff it. It should follow the example of the National Endowment for Democracy and be a private nongovernmental organization that receives funds appropriated by the U.S. Congress and which may also seek contributions from individuals and foundations based in the U.S. and other democracies. The European Union should be invited to contribute additional funds and participate, as should all other major democracies, provided this does not cause any dilution of the fundamental purposes or strategy as will be outlined. Mr. Christopher Patten, the last British Governor General of Hong Kong who significantly expanded democratic participation there (which led Beijing to call him "a sinner of a thousand years"), said the EU should support the observance of human rights and a transition to an open society in China.[81] To reduce the chances that the Beijing regime will penetrate the organization and disrupt it from within, all individuals to be employed directly should be screened using the full information resources of the U.S. government, as has been done for many years with similar entities such as Radio Free Europe and Radio Free Asia.

What might be an appropriate budget for this endeavor? In May 2001, Senators Joseph Lieberman and Jesse Helms made a bipartisan proposal that the U.S. allocate $100 million annually to provide direct assistance to individuals in Communist Cuba (with a population of 12 million) who are working for human rights, democracy, a more open media, and for the families of political prisoners and other victims of repression.[82] During the decades when the 100 million persons in Eastern Europe were under Communist rule, the latest annual budgets of Radio Free Europe (RFE) were about $170 million.[83] We have learned from the positive results and from the testimony of all the pro-democracy activists who were encouraged to keep up their struggle by this organization what a wise and valuable investment that was. If we were to extrapolate from the RFE experience, taking into account that China's population is thirteen time larger than that of Eastern Europe, this would suggest an ultimate budget of about $3.6 billion annually. Since encouraging democracy in China is a means of reducing the risk of war, including nuclear war, these funds should be considered part of the budget for national security and defense. Nevertheless, it is highly unlikely that this effort could obtain public funds of this magnitude and, in any case, it would need to develop and grow over time.

A reasonable initial publicly funded budget might be about $500 million, to be evenly divided between expenditures for a competent and dedicated staff of mature individuals and for programmatic activities. This would permit an initial staff of about nine hundred persons to be based in Washington DC and in other cities of the U.S. with large Chinese-American communities; in Singapore, Thailand, Taiwan, Indonesia, countries with large ethnic Chinese populations; and in Hong Kong, if possible and prudent. This budget might increase at about 25 percent annually over a ten-year period, if the organization proved itself effective. The PDC could also seek additional funding from private sources in the democracies as long as these were not granted with restrictions on use that conflicted with its essential activities.

The Program for Democracy in China (PDC) would undertake four main types of activities: analysis; communication; assistance for pro-democratic individuals in China and for pro-democratic Chinese abroad; and, monitoring/reporting on China's actions and relationships with the major democracies, Russia, the major international financial institutions, the United Nations, the World Trade Organization, developing countries, other Communist states, and the state sponsors of terrorism.

Analysis
The analysis function would include an effort to obtain factual information on the most significant political, economic, and social events and trends within China, beginning at the national level. Then, as experience and resources permitted, this would also include the provincial, city/town, and rural district levels. This information would then be used to produce an objective weekly overview of events in Chinese (using the major dialects, including Mandarin and Cantonese) and in English for subsequent communication in China; to Chinese pro-democratic exiles in the U.S. and throughout the world; to the largest overseas Chinese communities; and to political leaders, civic groups, experts, and interested citizens in the U.S. and the major democracies.

There would also be in-depth analysis of the words and actions of key political participants in China at the national, provincial, and local levels to identify those who are the most repressive as well as those who are potentially reform-oriented or pro-democratic. This would include persons in the Party or government who might consider or be attempting reforms. Virtually, all this analytic work would be based on all available open sources, including the daily monitoring of the Chinese media and official statements as currently done by the U.S.-government-funded Foreign Broadcast Information Service (FBIS). An effort would also be made to obtain facts and judgments from the pro-democratic Chinese exiles working in or with the organization (which would include individuals from all the main provinces, cities, and towns of China), as well as from reliable sources in the various communities of Chinese abroad who often have family and business ties to Mainland China. In addition, innovative ways could be developed to permit persons in China with valuable information to provide it anonymously, and this could be assessed for reliability.

In essence, the Program for Democracy in China would serve as China's free media reporting about events in China to the citizens of China and those abroad who are deeply concerned about China. In this, it would follow the example of Radio Free Europe (for Eastern Europe) and Radio Liberty (for the former Soviet Union). These important institutions were described by one of the architects of their approach as helping the peoples in Communist countries understand that "their road to freedom lay not in waiting for the day when a 'war of liberation' would rescue them but in achieving by themselves a series of day to day advances . . . specific short term reforms in their regimes . . . that would gradually lead to the whittling away of Communist authority."[84]

Gregory Fossedal, in his valuable discussion points out that in the 1960s, then director of the freedom radios Edward R. Murrow, "continually stressed news about liberalization within the [Soviet] bloc." Thus small or large positive steps in one Communist country would immediately become known in the others, and this often would result in movements within the Communist parties or pressure from social groups for similar steps. For example, the Communist regime in Hungary could take a specific liberalizing step without Soviet objection. So why not also in Czechoslovakia or Poland?[85] As Fossedal summed up this dimension, the reformist members of ruling Communist parties need "do-it-yourself kits in Marxist repair and road maps to a more democratic socialism."[86] The same idea could be applied in China by providing the people and Communist Party members there with factual information about any examples of reforms or liberalization within any of the cities, towns, or provinces within China, as well as in other Communist countries (Vietnam, Cambodia, Laos, Cuba) or other dictatorships that might have relevance for China.

Communications
To illustrate the communications activities we shall list possible themes for the four

audiences in China, perhaps with different emphases and methods. These would also apply to the overseas Chinese communities and to pro-democratic Chinese exiles in the U.S. and elsewhere. The means to be used would include news items provided to the full range of the world media: broadcasts, articles in print, the Internet, Chinese-language television, Internet, and newspapers intended for Chinese living outside of China, especially in democratic countries. Much of this might seep into China through informal contacts, but we can expect that many commercial media organizations will not give much space or attention to this inside China reporting.

Therefore, Radio Free Asia, a U.S.-funded organization that broadcasts directly to China and other countries in Asia, should have its budget increased from the current $22 million to about $80 million, so that it can transmit the increased information likely to emerge from this new initiative. In addition, the Program for Democracy in China would use the Internet to transmit information into China. It would use the latest technology to evade the extensive Internet controls that have been established by the regime, and it would provide a daily Internet report for further transmission by pro-democracy Chinese exiles who would use their own systems, developed in recent years, to evade regime censorship.[87] Also, the information might be packaged in innovative ways, such as on computer discs, through burst transmissions from satellites, and on microfilm or microdots, so that visitors to China might pass it along to individuals there who could then reproduce it for further discreet distribution.

Illustrative examples of communications themes, using the information deriving from the analysis work, include the following:

1. Performance of the Chinese government—major issues: national, provincial, local
   a. rural living conditions, incomes, education, health and social services
   b. urban living conditions, incomes, education, health and social services
   c. living conditions of the poorest 30 percent and what the government is/is not doing to help
   d. corruption, trends, new cases involving Party members
   e. water for drinking and for farming, trends, actions/inaction by the government
   f. China's expenditures and investment of human and technological resources in advanced weapons systems, trends, facts, possible alternative uses for those resources to solve the problems of China's people, with examples such as how the July 2001 expenditure of $2 billion for Russian jet fighter aircraft could instead have provided the following for the Chinese people . . .
   g. environmental pollution/problems

2. Human rights /persecution by the regime: national, provincial, local
    a. Overall numbers in forced-labor camps, detention, executions
    b. By specific forced-labor camp or detention facility: total persons held, proportion of deaths and severe illnesses, proportions and cases of torture, abuse; names of current commanders/Party officials supervising, including the most brutal guards, the most humane guards/commanders (if any)
    c. Over time: by names of individual commanders/guards/police officials and where they work; lists of cases of abuse, torture, names of victims, dates, consequences (death, severe illness, incapacity/mutilation)
    d. Over time: names of victims of persecution/political prisoners by category: pro-democracy/human rights activists; religious believers by faith; Falun Gong; ethnic minorities; Muslim Uygurs; Tibetans . . .
    e. Transmittal of this data on a regular basis to the free world media in summary form, to democratic governments and parliaments, to the UN Human Rights Commission and to the International Court of Justice at the Hague (examples of China's violation of international agreements)
    f. Dissemination to the citizens at large and to the police/forced-labor camp authorities of a synthesis of China's international obligations under the UN Declaration of Human Rights, the UN Covenant on Political Rights, UN Covenant on Economic and Social Rights; [Encourage the establishment throughout China of citizens committees to monitor and report on China's violations of these international commitments]
3. Repression and reform: debates and trends within the Chinese Communist Party and government
    a. Debates and different views on the approach to specific major problems, e.g., corruption, unemployment, income inequalities, the extremely poor 30 percent, fraud in the stock market, the hidden financial crisis
    b. Debates and differing views on the overall Party/state strategy for China with an emphasis on the groups competing for the succession to rule
4. Examples and specific cases of successful Communist reform and of successful peaceful transitions from Communism to democracy, including the facts and specific examples of Communist Party members having a normal life and political opportunities in the new post-Communist democracies (e.g., Poland, Hungary, Czech Republic, Lithuania, Estonia, Latvia)

5. Proposals from pro-democratic Chinese groups and exiles (abroad, and also from inside, if possible) for new approaches to improving life in China and dealing with some of the major problems affecting the people
6. A synthesis of the ideas and institutions of political democracy as presented in different countries and how these might improve life in China
7. Specific proposals for political liberalization within the Communist Party
8. Specific proposals for a peaceful transition from rule by the Communist Party to political democracy

Assistance for Prodemocratic Chinese in China and Abroad

The very existence of the Program for Democracy in China, as well as its analytic and communications activities, will have an immediate and positive effect on pro-democracy Chinese in exile and in Mainland China. Many of the individuals working for the committee will be pro-democratic Chinese exiles. They would have a program budget for assistance activities that might be about $250 million per year, out of the total initial budget of $500 million. Some of those funds could be used to help organize pro-democracy groups of Chinese exiles in the United States, in major democracies, and in countries with large Chinese communities. These pro-democracy organizations, in turn, can use a variety of creative means to distribute the information and communications products that we have discussed. They can try to turn the tide of opinion within the Chinese community abroad toward the idea that, like Taiwan, the people of China can govern themselves as free individuals without the coercion of the Communist Party. At the same time, they can attempt to persuade the governments and citizens of major democracies that China can and should be a democracy in the not too distant future.

These assistance activities can, over time, contribute to a change in the policy of the United States and other democracies toward China. The new policy would be one of conditioning China's access to the economic benefits from any democratic country to tangible movement within China, toward compliance with the UN Declaration of Human Rights and the other UN covenants signed by China. At the same time, efforts could be made to persuade the international development banks, private investors, pension funds, and corporations, not to provide additional money for production in China until it had met those conditions, allowing Chinese workers to organize for better wages and working conditions.

The people who can best identify and get help to pro-democratic Chinese living in Mainland China are the pro-democratic Chinese individuals living abroad. They visit their families and friends. They have business and professional connections in China, as well as years of relationships with individuals there. As a result, they can make reasonable judgments about which individuals might have the commitment, the courage, and the ability to take peaceful action for human rights and political liberalization. That judgment is the most difficult task in providing political assistance and it is the most essential, because it is people who bring about political liberalization.

The program could create and provide short courses to train pro-democratic Chinese exiles in the skills needed for effective, peaceful political activism. These skills include establishing organizations, developing political campaigns, initially using symbols and functional arguments that can lead to liberalization within the context of the Communist system. It would also be useful to provide the practical means needed for political activism such as computers, faxes, modems, Internet access, printing facilities; and, not least, funds to support a core group of activists and their families so they can devote full time to their task. It would also be important to help the families of victims of political repression with tangible assistance and support, as well as to take up the cause of their loved ones.

There are many examples of successful grassroots organizations within Communist countries that grew from small beginnings to include hundreds of thousands, then millions of people. The Chinese Communist regime understands that and will be determined to crush every effort at independent political activity and activism for reform, human rights, and political democracy. Therefore, an initial focus of assistance for organizational efforts inside China could be on improving living conditions of specific groups of disadvantaged persons. This would include the millions working in terrible conditions in urban factories; the tens of millions of homeless and unemployed; and the hundreds of millions of extremely poor peasants who are in deepening poverty because of the regime's shortcomings in providing economic opportunities and water.

It would also be good for activists to take up the cause of Chinese who have been unfairly treated by the regime in a very visible way. A good example are the more than 1.3 million people forced to leave their homes so that the Three Gorges damns could be built. They have not received the promised new homes, farmland, or compensation; one of these farmers said, "The government treats us like vagrants."[88] There are an additional one million people who are to be moved, and they have heard about the difficult fate awaiting them. The result has been that thousands have joined local protests and, according to Santoli, "Observers fear . . . force being used to silence protest and exert Communist Party control over a massive project rife with corruption . . . credible accounts have emerged of violence and intimidation by authorities."[89] This is exactly the kind of situation that activists could use to demonstrate the cruelty, arbitrariness, corruption, and economic shortcomings of the Communist regime. Unfortunately, there will be many other such circumstances in the future.

These are first and only illustrative thoughts about political assistance. The details of a strategy and approach would emerge once the program has been established and begun its analytic and information work. Political assistance and pro-democratic political activism in China will always be an existential process—pursuing a constant goal with a variety of approaches, depending on events in the country and opportunities created by the decisions and action or inaction of the Communist rulers.

MONITORING OF RELATIONS AMONG CHINA, THE U.S., AND THE WORLD

The United States has laws prohibiting the importation of products made by slave labor. In spite of this, China consistently exports such products anyway. The Program for Democracy in China should compile an overview of existing laws and regulations in the United States and in all the democracies that reflect efforts to prevent trade with China from directly or indirectly supporting forced-labor camps, the secret police, and the military production complex. Then there is a need for in-depth research on whether the U.S. and major democracies are actually enforcing their own laws and regulations. The findings should be made public every six months and should be communicated to the leadership of the executive branch, the legislature, the media, and concerned citizens groups, along with recommendations for action that could result in better enforcement of such laws.

The committee should also monitor the World Bank, the Asian Development Bank, and other multilateral financial organizations that are supported by funds from the U.S. and other major democracies. The focus would be on whether the billions of dollars in low-interest loans granted by these organizations to Communist China were providing support for any elements of its apparatus of coercion, including forced-labor camps. In the case of the World Bank, Harry Wu has documented that over a period of years, hundreds of millions of dollars in World Bank loans provided support for China's use of prison-camp labor and for China's forced resettlement of Han Chinese in predominantly Muslim Uygur areas in Xinjiang province.[90]

The Program for Democracy in China should also seek to monitor and report on the actual working conditions in factories within China that are owned or co-owned by companies or investors from the United States, the European Union, Japan, Taiwan, and other major democracies. Although it has been repeatedly stated by foreign investors in China that they are bringing the methods of work and human relationships from the democracies to China through their investments, there is a large amount of anecdotal evidence to the contrary. In fact, the National Labor Committee investigation of U.S. companies in China was surprised to find, "American companies are taking advantage and prolonging human and labor rights abuses by paying substandard wages and punishing workers who seek to state or raise grievances."[91] Two former political prisoners, Harry Wu and Wei Jingsheng, have worked with the U.S. National Labor Committee for Human Rights to provide photographic evidence of inhumane working conditions in Chinese factories exporting to the United States. One report documented wages "as low as 3 cents an hour, 98-hour work weeks, compulsory unpaid overtime, a ban on talking during work hours, 24-hour prison-like surveillance and unsanitary conditions."[92] The committee could publicize the result of its inquiries, briefly describing the working conditions and then name the U.S. and other foreign investors directly benefiting from that production facility. These reports might be distilled into a rating system and perhaps even published as newspaper advertisements in the democracies with the intention of exerting political and consumer pressure on corporations to improve working conditions in their Chinese factories.

"Parliament in Exile"

As the Communist dictatorship in China begins to unravel, it will also be important to begin building political parties and civic associations that will serve to represent the interests of the people in a democratic political system that might emerge. One way to prepare for that would be for the pro-democratic Chinese exiles to meet for several days once a year, to debate and consider practical proposals for solving a wide range of China's current problems. The analytic work of the Program for Democracy in China, along with the work of scholars, experts, and international organizations, would provide a large amount of data that skilled individuals could use to formulate practical policy proposals.

For the first few years, such an annual meeting should include debate about different suggestions in different domains of public policy. Each year the two or three most salient views in each policy area could be synthesized and a summary of the proposals published as a brief book, which also could be made available on the Internet. At some point, the pro-democratic Chinese exile participants might find themselves clustering in two or three groups having different views across the range of policy issues. They might be on the customary spectrum of democratic left, center, and democratic right. This process might establish a substantive basis for the formation of coalitions that could become political parties.

A next step might be for the annual convention to become a "parliament in exile," in which two or three political coalitions or political parties would make their differing proposals to solve China's current problems. They would then engage in spirited and free debate with each other. At the end of this process, votes might be taken. A synthesis of the proposals, the proceedings, and the final "legislation" might then be published annually and distributed through all available means within China and abroad. The purpose would not be to create a government in exile, but rather to give individuals who might be among those returning to a China in transition from Communism to democracy experience in formulating practical policy proposals and engaging in civil debate with those of different views. This could also provide examples of how informed individuals, not bound by the Party dictatorship and censorship, might approach and discuss practical solutions to China's problems.

History offers no guarantees about the future. China may become democratic in the next years or not for decades. We know that a nuclear-armed Communist China, where the regime controls an economy with an advanced technology sector and is far better armed, would be a state that could become ever more dangerous. We know that economic and commercial relations do not in themselves produce political liberalization or political democracy. We know that Communist regimes can reform and evolve from reform Communism to political democracy. We know that this is better for their people and for peace—these are the lessons of the transitions in Eastern Europe since 1989 and in Western Europe and Japan since 1945.

The possibility that the people of China could follow the path of peaceful self-liberation from Communism as shown by the peoples of Eastern Europe would be much greater if the United States were to establish an institution such as the Program for Democracy in China. It could then work to encourage a peaceful transition in that vast land where Communist rule imposed such tragic suffering for decades. We do know that a democratic China is likely to be a peaceful China. These are goals we should seek.

Relations among the United States, Russia and China in the coming years will have immense consequences both globally and regionally in the fields of democratic development, economic well-being, security, and human rights. The policy of the United States toward China and Russia has the possibility of having either a profoundly positive or extremely dangerous negative impact on their political evolution and foreign policies. With realistic leadership, skill, foresight, and effective action, it is possible to turn back the momentum by hardliners in both China and Russia that would lead to aggression and confrontation.

The realistic U.S. policies that we have discussed could increase the prospects for peaceful relations with both Russia and China by maintaining the U.S. and allied military capabilities needed for effective deterrence, while also encouraging the positive internal political evolution of both countries. On the other hand, failure to engage in a realistic, principled, and comprehensive policy on the part of the West in general and the United States in particular will lead us to the most disastrous of situations in terms of our economy, our own way of life, and our geostrategic position in the world. Most importantly, though, is the very real threat as outlined in this book of a war of mutual miscalculation that could quickly spiral out of control from a local conventional conflict over Taiwan or the South China Sea to a nuclear exchange between the U.S. and China, in which the whole world would end up losing. So let us go forward learning from history and not repeating the same mistakes that Churchill spoke about when he said, "There never was a war in all history easier to prevent by timely action . . . but no one would listen. . . . We surely must not let that happen again."

Acknowledgments

Unfortunately, prior to Dr. Menges' death he did not have the opportunity to acknowledge and thank those who contributed to the production and publication of this book. Those that knew him best knew that he was gracious beyond measure and in that spirit, we who are trying to carry on his work have endeavored to provide a proper accounting of those involved in this great work.

Dr. Menges held his literary agent Mr. Michael Bourret, of Dystel and Goderich Literary Management, in the highest regard and appreciated the long hours and efforts that Michael devoted to the publication of this book. Michael's hard work following the authors death highlights a professionalism rarely seen in today's world.

Mr. Joel Miller of Nelson Current has demonstrated levels of honor that are often lacking in the world of publishing. His efforts on moving this book forward and ensuring as wide an audience as possible were appreciated by Dr. Menges and by those of us who assisted in this labor. The author was extremely grateful for the assistance of good friends Mr. William Chatfield and Mrs. Jayna Davis in bringing him into contact with Joel Miller and Nelson Current.

Dr. Menges was always grateful for the insights and encouragement as well as the nearly life long friendship he had with Dr. Herbert London, president of the Hudson Institute. Dr. London was always a source of great wisdom and direction for Dr. Menges throughout their decade's long relationship.

Dr. Ken Weinstein, vice president of the Hudson Institute was also helpful and a source of great support during the writing of this book as well as the efforts to ensure that it went forward following the death of Dr. Menges. The author would also have wanted to acknowledge the support and assistance provided by the staff of the Hudson Institute in Washington D.C. whom he regularly relied upon in the closing years of his professional work.

In Dr. Menges' long career, he had the privilege and pleasure of knowing many great individuals. Two of these who played a particularly significant role in this project by their support and friendship are Mr. Max Singer and Ambassador Curt

Winsor. Dr. Menges held both of these men in the highest possible regard and viewed them each as champions in the cause of freedom. Dr. Ira Strauss, who possesses a vast knowledge about Russia discussed his insights with Dr. Menges and was also helpful and supportive.

Those who provided key support during the research and writing of this book should also be recognized. They include: Mr. R. Daniel McMicheal and Mr. Michael W. Gleba of the Sarah Scaife Foundation, Tim and Leesa Donner, Anita Winsor Edwards, and Ambassador Curt Winsor of The William H. Donner Foundation, Ms. Abby S. Moffat and Mrs. Dianna Spencer of The Shelby Cullom Davis Foundation, Mr. Owen and Bernadette Smith of the Sophia and William Casey Foundation.

Dr. Menges would also want to recognize the contributions and express his deep appreciation for the contributions of his research assistants, Mr. Christopher Brown and Mr. Marcus Sgro. Marcus had the opportunity of working on the book for several years throughout its initial production whereas Christopher had the honor to assist in several series of updates and the final publication.

Dr. Menges was also deeply grateful for the excellent assistance of the interns who aided his research for this book including: Ms. Rachel Birthisel of The George Washington University, Ms. Kelani Chan of John Hopkins University, Ms. Emilie Cougenioux of Wellesley College, Mr. Kevin DeCorla-Souza of the College of William and Mary, Mr. Rick Liu of Georgetown University, Ms. Golnar Oveyssi of the University of Virginia, Mr. Austin Turner of Georgetown University.

Finally, there are three that need to be singled out for special recognition. First, the immeasurable support and love of Dr. Menges' caring wife Mrs. Nancy Menges which can not be overstated. She has worked tirelessly to see that her husband's work continues and her love was one of the main drivers in Dr. Menges' life. Second the love and support of his son, Christopher Menges. Dr. Menges wanted to ensure that he would inherit a safer and more secure world. Finally, this book was made possible by the author's love of humanity and his belief in the inherent God given right of all people everywhere to live in freedom and peace. To that end Dr. Menges' life and this work represent his offering at the 'altar of freedom'. To those throughout the world who still seek to throw off the shackles of tyranny, this book was inspired by your cause and is a testament to his hope that you too will one day be free.

Notes

Introduction

1. Hourly pay in manufacturing in 2001 was $16.14 in the U.S. and $0.61 in China according to the U.S. Bureau of Labor Statistics and the *China Statistical Yearbook.* 2. Elizabeth Becker and Edmund L. Andrews, "The Currency of China Is Emerging as a Tough Business Issue in the U.S.," *New York Times,* August 26, 2003. 3. National Intelligence Council, *Foreign Missile Developments and the Ballistic Missile Threat to the United States Through 2015* (December 2001). 4. Central Intelligence Agency, *Unclassified Report to Congress on the Acquisition of Technology Relating to Weapons of Mass Destruction and Advanced Conventional Munitions, 1 January Through 30 June 2003* (Washington, DC, 10 November 2003). 5. U.S. Department of Defense, *Selected Military Capabilities of the PRC* (Washington, DC, April 1997), as cited in Mark A. Stokes, *China's Strategic Modernization: Implications for the United States* (Carlisle Barracks, Pa.: U.S. Army War College, 1999), 97. 6. Numbers of weapons and warheads compiled from the U.S. House of Representatives Select Committee; Rep. Christopher Cox, Chairman; *United States National Security and Military Commercial Concerns with the People's Republic of China* (1999), 75, hereafter cited as the Cox Report; and International Institute for Strategic Studies, *The Military Balance 2003–2005.* The information on the amounts of nuclear material comes from the Center for Nonproliferation Studies *China's Fissile Material Production and Stockpile.* 7. Immanuel C. Y. Hsu, Chapters 35–37, in *The Rise of Modern China* (New York and Oxford: Oxford University Press, 1995).

Chapter 1

1. Edward Timperlake and William C. Triplett II, Chapter 2 of *Red Dragon Rising* (Washington, DC: Regnery, 1999). 2. Quoted in *The Weekly Standard,* February 2002, 8. 3. China's trade with the U.S. resulted in a Chinese trade surplus with the U.S. from 1990 to 2000 of $442 billion, and a surplus of $80 billion in 2001. 4. Statement made at World Economic Forum Meeting, Davos (Switzerland), January 2000. 5. Quoted in Matt Pottinger, "China's President Assails Corruption as Threat to Party," *Washington Times,* April 2, 2000, C13. 6. *The Economist,* March 2–8, 2002. Hard currency reserves for China were $211.8 billion and for Hong Kong $111.3 billion, for a total of $323.1 billion. 7. Steven W. Mosher, *Hegemon* (San Francisco: Encounter, 2000), 7. 8. Deng's statement is quoted and expounded upon in Yu Yunyao, "Epoch-Making Significance of Hiding our Capabilities to Bide our Time," [in Chinese], *Liaowang,* March 17, 2003. Yu is the exec-

utive vice president of the Central Party School of the Communist Party of China, and *Liaowang* is a Communist Party weekly news and analysis magazine. **9.** *Far Eastern Economic Review,* October 3, 1996. **10.** *Cheng Ming (Hong Kong),* [in Chinese], January 4, 2000, broadcast on "Part 3 Asia-Pacific," *Summary of World,* BBC, January 6, 2000, FE/D3730/F2. **11.** Statement made at a forum chaired by the author at George Washington University, February 19, 1998. **12.** For example, see the Joint Russia-China communiqué following the summit meeting between Presidents Yeltsin and Jiang, FBIS (CHI), 11 August 1996. See Chapter 19 for an in-depth discussion. **13.** Joint Russia-China communiqué, FBIS (CHI), 10 December 1999. **14.** Russia-China communiqué, December 10, 1999. **15.** George Tenet, Director of the CIA, speaking to the U.S. Congress, February 7, 2001 and February 6, 2002. **16.** *Treaty of Good-Neighborliness and Friendly Cooperation Between the People's Republic of China and the Russian Federation,* 24 July 2001, http://www.fmprc.gov.cn/eng/wjdt/2649/t15771.htm. **17.** For an overview of this secret indirect warfare as waged by both sides in the Cold War, see Constantine C. Menges, *The Twilight Struggle* (Washington, DC: AEI Press, 1990). **18.** Mosher, *Hegemon,* Chapter 2. **19.** Mosher, *Hegemon,* Chapter 2. **20.** Mosher, *Hegemon,* Chapter 2. **21.** Ross H. Monroe, "Eavesdropping on the Chinese Military: Where It Expects War—Where It Doesn't," *Orbis,* Summer 1994, 1#17. **22.** Monroe, "Eavesdropping."

Chapter 2

1. Mosher, *Hegemon,* 19; this draws on Mosher's excellent discussion. **2.** Mosher, *Hegemon,* 19#20. **3.** Mosher, *Hegemon,* 21#26. **4.** Mosher, *Hegemon,* 21#26. **5.** Jean-Louis Margolin, "China: A Long March into Night," in *The Black Book of Communism: Crimes, Terror, Repression,* ed. Courtois et al., 468 (Cambridge, Mass.: Harvard University Press, 1999). **6.** Mosher, *Hegemon,* 38. **7.** Margolin, "China," 468. **8.** This historical overview draws on Hsu, parts V and VI, Rise of Modern China; and Mosher, Chapter 3, *Hegemon.* **9.** Margolin, "China," 471. **10.** Margolin, "China," 471. **11.** Margolin, "China," 473. **12.** Margolin, "China," 479. **13.** Timperlake and Triplett, *Red Dragon Rising,* 58. **14.** Mosher, *Hegemon,* 37. **15.** Immanuel Chung-Yueh Hsu, *Rise of Modern China* (Cambridge: Oxford University Press, 1999), 649. **16.** Hsu, *Rise of Modern China,* 646. **17.** Quoted in Margolin, "China," 474. **18.** Bruce Gilley, *Tiger on the Brink: Jiang Zemin and China's New Elite* (Berkeley, CA: University of California Press, 1998), 33#35. **19.** Hsu, *Rise of Modern China,* 650. **20.** Hsu, *Rise of Modern China,* 646. **21.** Hsu, *Rise of Modern China,* 649. **22.** Hsu, *Rise of Modern China,* 650. **23.** Richard C. Thornton, *The Bear and the Dragon: Sino-Soviet Relations and the Political Evolution of the Chinese People's Republic, 1949–1971* (New York: American-Asian Educational Exchange, 1972), 8. **24.** Hsu, *Rise of Modern China,* 652. **25.** Dimitry Volkogonov, *Autopsy of an Empire* (New York: The Free Press, 1998), 136. The author was a Soviet military officer and historian, and was given access to secret Soviet-era Party and government archives; these are verbatim quotations from the transcripts of the meetings (made by the translators). **26.** Volkogonov, *Autopsy of an Empire,* 136. **27.** Hsu, *Rise of Modern China,* 661. **28.** Hsu, *Rise of Modern China,* 661. **29.** John Kenneth Knaus, *Orphans of the Cold War: America and the Tibetan Struggle* (New York: Public Affairs Press, 1999), 47. **30.** Knaus, *Orphans,* 47. **31.** Volkogonov, *Autopsy of an Empire,* 155. **32.** Volkogonov, *Autopsy of an Empire,* 155. **33.** Volkogonov, *Autopsy of an Empire,* 155. **34.** Volkogonov, *Autopsy of an Empire,* 159. **35.** Volkogonov, *Autopsy of an Empire,* 162. **36.**

Timperlake and Triplett, *Red Dragon Rising*, 60. **37.** Text of a letter from the Dalai Lama to Mr. William Triplett, as cited in Timperlake and Triplett, *Red Dragon Rising*, 54. **38.** Margolin "China," 464, estimates 10 to 20 percent of the 2.2 million people of Tibet have died as a result of the Chinese occupation. **39.** Geoffrey Smith, "China Missiles on Plateau Threaten India, Gilman Warns," *Washington Times*, April 9, 2000, C9; see also Eric S. Margolis, *War at the Top of the World: The Struggle for Afghanistan, Kashmir and Tibet* (New York: Routledge, 2000). **40.** Julia Taft, U.S. Special Coordinator for Tibetan Issues, speaking to the U.S. Congress, April 2000, as cited in Smith, "China Missiles." **41. Margolin,** "China," 472. **42.** Margolin, "China," 479. **43.** Margolin, "China," 479. **44.** Margolin, "China," 479. **45.** Hsu, *Rise of Modern China*, 653. **46.** Margolin, "China," 480. **47.** There was precedent for these from the Imperial era. **48.** Andrew J. Nathan, *China's Transition* (New York: Columbia University Press, 1997), 52. **49.** Nathan, *China's Transition*, 52. **50.** Hsu, *Rise of Modern China*, 654. **51.** Hsu, *Rise of Modern China*, 653. **52.** Margolin, "China," 480. **53.** Margolin, "China," 481. **54.** Margolin, "China," 482 **55.** Margolin, "China," 482. **56.** Margolin, "China," 483. **57.** Margolin, "China," 483. **58.** Margolin, "China," 489. **59.** Jung Chang, *Wild Swans* (New York: Anchor Doubleday, 1991), 192. **60.** Chang, *Wild Swans*, 181. **61.** Chang, *Wild Swans*, 195-200. **62.** Hsu, *Rise of Modern China*, 957. **63.** Hsu, *Rise of Modern China*, 957. **64.** Nathan, *China's Transition*, 24. **65.** Hsu, *Rise of Modern China*, 690. **66.** Hsu, *Rise of Modern China*, 690. **67.** John K. Fairbank, *China: A New History* (Cambridge, Mass.: Belknap Press of Harvard University Press, 1992), 364. **68.** Hsu, *Rise of Modern China*, 663. **69.** Hsu, *Rise of Modern China*, 836. **70.** Hsu, *Rise of Modern China*, 836. **71.** Cited in Hsu, *Rise of Modern China*, 677. **72.** Harold C. Hinton, *China's Turbulent Quest* (New York: MacMillan, 1970), 67, as cited in Mosher, *Hegemon*, 16. This discussion draws heavily on Mosher's excellent summary of the 1954–1958 confrontation. **73.** Dwight David Eisenhower, *Mandate for Change, 1953–1956* (New York: Doubleday, 1963), 442–463. **74.** Hsu, *Rise of Modern China*, 677. **75.** Mosher, *Hegemon*, 55. **76.** Mosher, *Hegemon*, 55–56. **77.** Mosher, *Hegemon*, 18. **78.** Mosher, *Hegemon*, 18. **79.** Mosher, *Hegemon*, 18. **80.** Thornton, *Bear and the Dragon*, 14. **81.** Thornton, *Bear and the Dragon*, 15–16. **82.** Chang, *Wild Swans*, 221. **83.** Hsu, *Rise of Modern China*, 664. **84.** Hsu, *Rise of Modern China*, 656. **85.** This account derives from records on the Soviet side, as cited in Volkogonov, *Autopsy of an Empire*, 231–233. **86.** Volkogonov, *Autopsy of an Empire*, 232. **87.** Mosher, *Hegemon*, 25. **88.** Volkogonov, *Autopsy of an Empire*, 232. **89.** Volkogonov, *Autopsy of an Empire*, 232. **90.** Mosher, *Hegemon*, 57. **91.** Mosher, *Hegemon*, 57. **92.** Mosher, *Hegemon*, 57. **93.** Mosher, *Hegemon*, 24. **94.** Hsu, *Rise of Modern China*, 657. **95.** Margolin, "China," 425; R. J. Rummel, *Death by Government* (New Brunswick, N.J.: Transaction Publishers, 1994), 97, estimates 28 million deaths. **96.** Margolin, "China," 425. **97.** Wei Jingsheng, *The Courage to Stand Alone* (New York: Penguin Books, 1997), 246–247. **98.** Thornton, *Bear and the Dragon*, 18. Only a few of these troops, however, were given any serious military training; the vast majority of militia personnel were simply names in books and received only drill and firearms training in school. **99.** Estimate by Deng Xiaoping, as cited in Nathan, *China's Transition*, 16. **100.** Volkogonov, *Autopsy of an Empire*, 232. Volkogonov quoted directly from the Soviet archives. **101.** Volkogonov, *Autopsy of an Empire*, 233. **102.** Volkogonov, *Autopsy of an Empire*, 233. **103.** Volkogonov, *Autopsy of an Empire*, 234. **104.** Hsu, *Rise of Modern China*, 694. **105.** Mao proclaimed this position in 1958 as the "Three Red Banners"—the Party Line, the

Great Leap Forward, and the rural communes. **106.** Hsu, *Rise of Modern China*, 694–695. **107.** Hsu, *Rise of Modern China*, 694–695. **108.** Thornton, *Bear and the Dragon*, 23–24. **109.** Timperlake and Triplett, *Red Dragon Rising*, 61–62. China subsequently declared a unilateral cease-fire and withdrew from some of the territory it had occupied but continued to pressure India on the border issue. **110.** Hsu, *Rise of Modern China*, 681. **111.** Chong Pin Lin, *China's Nuclear Weapons Strategy* (Lexington, Mass: D. C. Heath, 1988), 44–45. **112.** Chong, *China's Nuclear Weapons Strategy*, 46.

Chapter 3

1. Chang, *Wild Swans*, 239. See also Hsu, Chapter 8 of *Rise of Modern China*, for a discussion of the Cultural Revolution. **2.** Chang, *Wild Swans*, 239. **3.** Chang, *Wild Swans*, 274. **4.** Chang, *Wild Swans*, 275. **5.** Chang, *Wild Swans*, 275. **6.** Thornton, *Bear and the Dragon*, 27. **7.** Hsu, *Rise of Modern China*, 697. **8.** Thornton, *Bear and the Dragon*, 31. **9.** Hsu, *Rise of Modern China*, 697. **10.** Hsu, *Rise of Modern China*, 701. **11.** John W. Lewis and Xue Litai, *China's Strategic Seapower* (Stanford, Calif.: Stanford University Press, 1994). **12.** Hsu, *Rise of Modern China*, 700. **13.** Hsu, *Rise of Modern China*, 700. **14.** Margolin, "China," 519. **15.** Hsu, *Rise of Modern China*, 700. **16.** Hsu, *Rise of Modern China*, 702. **17.** Hsu, *Rise of Modern China*, 701. **18.** Hsu, *Rise of Modern China*, 702. **19.** Ken Ling, *Red Guard: From Schoolboy to "Little General" in Mao's China*, trans. Miriam London and Ta-ling Lee (London: Macdonald and Company, 1972) 18–21. **20.** Chang, *Wild Swans*, 284–285. **21.** Chang, *Wild Swans*, 286. **22.** Margolin, "China," 528. **23.** Margolin, "China," 528. **24.** Margolin, "China," 534. **25.** Margolin, "China," 534. **26.** Jean-Luc Domenach, *Chine: L'archipel oublie* (Paris: Fagard, 1992), 211, as cited in Margolin, "China," 513. **27.** Rummel, *Death by Government*, 100–101. **28.** Margolin, "China," 534. **29.** Margolin, "China," 519; Deng Xiaopeng estimated that three million party members were punished, as cited in Nathan, *China's Transition*, 16. **30.** Nathan, *China's Transition*, 16. **31.** Margolin, "China," 524. **32.** Margolin, "China," 524. **33.** Juan Linz, "Totalitarian and Authoritarian Regimes," in *Handbook of Political Science*, ed. Fred I. Greenstein and Nelson W. Polesby, 3:175–411 (Reading, Mass.: Addison-Wesley, 1975). **34.** Please see the table for the detailed citation of the various sources. **35.** Margolin, "China," 464; and Hongda Harry Wu, *Laogai, the Chinese Gulag*, trans. Ted Slingerland (Boulder, Colo.: Westview Press, 1992). **36.** Fairbank, *China: A New History*, 690–691 estimates 20–30 million deaths while Margolin, "China," estimates 20–43 million deaths. **37.** Nathan, *China's Transition*, 16. **38.** Rummel, *Democide* (New Brunswick, N.J.: Transaction Publishers, 1992). See also http://www.hawaii.edu/rummel/chinatabletab8.1. **39.** Nathan, *China's Transition*, 22.

Chapter 4

1. Thornton, *Bear and the Dragon*, 58. **2.** As cited in Thornton, *Bear and the Dragon*, 53. **3.** Thornton, *Bear and the Dragon*, 53. **4.** Thornton, *Bear and the Dragon*, 53. **5.** Thornton, *Bear and the Dragon*, 53. **6.** Edgar Snow, *Red Star over China* (New York: Grove Press, 1961), 96, cited in Hsu, *Rise of Modern China*, 682. **7.** Snow, *Red Star over China*, 96, cited in Hsu, *Rise of Modern China*, 682. **8.** Hsu, *Rise of Modern China*, 683. **9.** Hsu, *Rise of Modern China*, 683. **10.** Hsu, *Rise of Modern China*, 684. **11.** Joseph Allsop, "Thoughts Out of China—I Go vs. No Go," *New York Times Magazine*, 11 March 1973, 11. **12.** Thornton, *Bear and the Dragon*, 56. **13.** Hsu, *Rise of Modern China*, 702.

14. Fairbank, *China: A New History,* 397–398. 15. Hsu, *Rise of Modern China,* 684. 16. Thornton, *Bear and the Dragon,* 61. 17. Thornton, *Bear and the Dragon,* 61. 18. Hsu, *Rise of Modern China,* 684. 19. Hsu, *Rise of Modern China,* 685–686. Hsu informs us that by mid-1973, the Chinese were reported to have fifteen missiles with a range of 1,200 miles and fifteen to twenty missiles with a range of 2,300 miles. 20. Hsu, *Rise of Modern China,* 709–710. 21. Hsu, *Rise of Modern China,* 711. 22. Cited in Hsu, *Rise of Modern China,* 711. 23. Cited in Hsu, *Rise of Modern China,* 713. 24. Hsu, *Rise of Modern China,* 713. 25. Hsu, *Rise of Modern China,* 714. 26. Hsu, *Rise of Modern China,* 714. 27. Hsu, *Rise of Modern China,* 713, note 19. 28. Hsu, *Rise of Modern China,* 715. 29. Richard M. Nixon, "Asia after Vietnam," *Foreign Affairs,* vol. 46, October 1967, 121. 30. Vernon A. Walters, *Silent Missions* (New York: Doubleday and Co., 1978), 525. 31. James Mann, *About Face* (New York: Knopf, 1998), 121. 32. Mann, *About Face,* 28. 33. Hsu, *Rise of Modern China,* 726. 34. John Holdridge, *War and Peace with China* (Washington, DC: Dacor-Bacon House, 1994), 124. 35. Mann, *About Face,* 33. 36. Mann, *About Face,* 33. 37. Robert C. McFarlane, *Special Trust* (Cadell & Davies, 1994), 150. 38. Mann, *About Face,* 34. 39. President Nixon's daily diary, 18 February 1972, as cited in James Mann, *About Face,* 13–14. 40. *Examiner* (San Francisco), February 21, 1972, as cited in Hsu, *Rise of Modern China,* 727. 41. Hsu, *Rise of Modern China,* 728. 42. Mann, *About Face,* chapter 2. 43. Shanghai Communiqué, as cited in Hsu, *Rise of Modern China,* 729. 44. Nixon's notes as cited in Mann, *About Face,* 42. 45. Mann, *About Face,* 44. 46. Mann, *About Face,* 15. 47. Mann, *About Face,* 45. 48. Mann, *About Face,* 50. 49. Richard H. Solomon, *Chinese Political Negotiating Behavior* (Santa Monica, Calif.: Rand Corporation, 1995), 47. 50. Mann, *About Face,* 52. 51. Hsu, *Rise of Modern China,* 763–774. 52. Roxanne Witke, *Comrade Chiang Ch'ing* (Boston, Mass.: 1977), 37–38, as cited in Hsu, *Rise of Modern China,* 771. 53. Hsu, *Rise of Modern China,* 764. 54. Hsu, *Rise of Modern China,* 765. 55. Hsu, *Rise of Modern China,* 766. 56. Hsu, *Rise of Modern China,* 768.

Chapter 5
1. Hsu, *Rise of Modern China,* 836. 2.Hsu, *Rise of Modern China,* 776. 3.Hsu, *Rise of Modern China,* 776. 4. Hsu, *Rise of Modern China,* 776. 5. Hsu, *Rise of Modern China,* 803. 6. Hsu, *Rise of Modern China,* 776. 7. Hsu, *Rise of Modern China,* 832. 8. Hsu, *Rise of Modern China,* 779. 9. *People's Daily,* 1 July 1978, 3, as cited in Hsu, *Rise of Modern China,* 779. 10. Hsu, *Rise of Modern China,* 781. 11. Hsu, *Rise of Modern China,* 841, referring to the Third Plenum of the Eleventh Party Congress. 12. Merle Goldman and Roderick McFarquhar, "Dynamic Economy, Declining Party-State" in ed. Goldman and Macfarquar, *The Paradox of China's Post-Mao Reforms* (Cambridge, Mass.: Harvard University Press, 1999), 5. 13. Deng Xiaoping, *Building Socialism with Chinese Characteristics* (Peking: Foreign Languages Press, 1985), 35–40, 49—*52, 58—*59, 70—*73. 14. Hsu, *Rise of Modern China,* 785. 15. For perspective on this pattern of successful Soviet indirect aggression see Menges, *Twilight Struggle.* 16. Hsu, *Rise of Modern China,* 787. 17. *New York Times,* 21 May 1978, as cited in Hsu, *Rise of Modern China,* 787. The "marauders" were the Cuban forces, and the Soviet threats of "military force" referred to Hungary (1956), Czechoslovakia (1968), and perhaps Poland as the Solidarity movement was emerging. 18. Mann, *About Face,* 87. 19. Mann, *About Face,* 87. 20. Mann, *About Face,* 86. 21. Mann, *About Face,* 91. 22. Mann, *About Face,* 91. 23. Hsu, *Rise of Modern China,* 795. 24. Hsu, *Rise of Modern China,* 796. 25. Hsu, *Rise of Modern China,*798. 26. Hsu, *Rise*

of Modern China, 789. **27.** Mann, *About Face,* 95. **28.** Mann, *About Face,* 95. **29.** Hsu, *Rise of Modern China,* 793. **30.** Hsu, *Rise of Modern China,* 793. **31.** Hsu, *Rise of Modern China,* 793. **32.** Hsu, *Rise of Modern China,* 794. **33.** Hsu, *Rise of Modern China,* 794. **34.** Mann, *About Face,* 97. **35.** Mann, *About Face,* 98. **36.** Mann, *About Face,* 98. **37.** Mann, *About Face,* 99. **38.** Mann, *About Face,* 99. **39.** Hsu, *Rise of Modern China,* 794. **40.** Timperlake and Triplett, *Red Dragon Rising,* 63. **41.** Timperlake and Triplett, *Red Dragon Rising,* 63. **42.** Hsu, *Rise of Modern China,* 798. **43.** Hsu, *Rise of Modern China,* 975. **44.** Hsu, *Rise of Modern China,* 843. **45.** Hsu, *Rise of Modern China,* 844. **46.** Hsu, *Rise of Modern China,* 897. **47.** Hsu, *Rise of Modern China,* 845. **48.** Hsu, *Rise of Modern China,* 845. **49.** Hsu, *Rise of Modern China,* 849. **50.** Hsu, *Rise of Modern China,* 849–851. **51.** Hsu, *Rise of Modern China,* 851. **52.** Hsu, *Rise of Modern China,* 853. **53.** As cited in footnote to the resolution on the reform of the economic system, Third Plenum, Twelfth Central Committee, Chinese Communist Party, October 1984, 20; as cited in Hsu, *Rise of Modern China,* 854–5. **54.** Hsu, *Rise of Modern China,* 855. **55.** Hsu, *Rise of Modern China,* 856. **56.** Hsu, *Rise of Modern China,* 856. **57.** Shenzhen, Xiamen, Zhuhai, Fuzhou. **58.** Goldman op cit, 9. **59.** Hsu, *Rise of Modern China,* 897. **60.** Hsu, *Rise of Modern China,* 897. **61.** Hsu, *Rise of Modern China,* 860–861. **62.** Hsu, *Rise of Modern China,* 817–824. **63.** As cited in Goldman, op cit, 11. **64.** Hsu, *Rise of Modern China,*826. **65.** Hsu, *Rise of Modern China,* 826. **66.** Hsu, *Rise of Modern China,* 827. **67.** Goldman op cit, 11. **68.** Goldman op cit, 11. **69.** Goldman and MacFarquhar, "Dynamic Economy," 12. **70.** Goldman and MacFarquhar, "Dynamic Economy," 12. **71.** Goldman and MacFarquhar, "Dynamic Economy," 13. **72.** Goldman and MacFarquhar, "Dynamic Economy," 13. **73.** Mann, *About Face,* 101. **74.** Mann, *About Face,* 247. **75.** Mann, *About Face,* 248. **76.** Mann, *About Face,* 101. **77.** Mann, *About Face,* 101. **78.** Mann, *About Face,* 101, 102. **79.** As cited in Mann, *About Face,* 103. **80.** Mann, *About Face,* 102. **81.** Mann, *About Face,* 103. **82.** Sophia Woodman, "Wei Jingsheng's Life-long Battle for Democracy" as cited in Wei, *Courage to Stand Alone,* 259. **83.** This discussion derives from the insightful book by Merle Goldman, *Sowing the Seeds of Democracy in China* (Cambridge, Mass.: Harvard University Press, 1994), especially Chapters 1 and 2. **84.** Goldman, *Sowing the Seeds,* 3. **85.** Goldman, *Sowing the Seeds,* 3. **86.** Merle Goldman, "The Emergence of Politically Independent Intellectuals," in ed. Goldman and McFarquar, *Paradox,* 295. **87.** Goldman, "Politically Independent Intellectuals," 299. **88.** Goldman, "Politically Independent Intellectuals," 300. **89.** Goldman, "Politically Independent Intellectuals," 301. **90.** Mann, *About Face,* 106. **91.** Mann, *About Face,* 135–136. **92.** Mann, *About Face,* 111. **93.** Mann, *About Face,* 114. **94.** Mann, *About Face,* 129. **95.** George Schultz, *Turmoil and Triumph* (New York: Scribner's, 1993), 382. **96.** Mann, *About Face,* 127. **97.** Mann, *About Face,* 130. **98.** Mann, *About Face,* 131. **99.** Mann, *About Face,* 132. **100.** Mann, *About Face,* 134. **101.** Mann, *About Face,* 140. **102.** As cited in Mann, *About Face,* 146. **103.** Schultz, *Turmoil and Triumph* 388–389. **104.** Hsu, *Rise of Modern China,* 856–857. **105.** Hsu, *Rise of Modern China,* 856. **106.** Elizabeth J Perry, "Crime, Corruption, and Contention," in ed. Goldman and MacFarquhar, *Paradox,* 815. **107.** Goldman and MacFarquhar, 323–324. **108.** As cited in Richard Baum and Alexi Shevshenko, "The 'State of the State,'" in Goldman and MacFarquhar, *Paradox,* 349. **109.** *Newsweek,* Hong Kong edition, June 6, 1988, 25–6.

Chapter 6

1. Hsu, *Rise of Modern China,* 882. **2.** Hsu, *Rise of Modern China,* 882. **3.** Hsu, *Rise of Modern China,* 38. **4.** Hsu, *Rise of Modern China,* 857–858. **5.** Hsu, *Rise of Modern China,*

857. 6. Hsu, *Rise of Modern China*, 883. 7. Hsu, *Rise of Modern China*, 884. 8. These decisions still exist but only apply to whomever Jiang Zemin does not like. 9. Hsu, *Rise of Modern China*, 873-874. 10. Mann, *About Face*, 157–158. 11. Mann, *About Face*, 157–158. 12. Mann, *About Face*, 157–158. 13. Hsu, *Rise of Modern China*, 875. 14. Hsu, *Rise of Modern China*, 884–885. 15. Hsu, *Rise of Modern China*, 886. 16. Hsu, *Rise of Modern China*, 886–887. 17. Hsu, *Rise of Modern China*, 886. 18. Hsu, *Rise of Modern China*, 887. 19. As cited in Mann, *About Face*, 158. 20. Hsu, *Rise of Modern China*, 887–888. 21. Hsu, *Rise of Modern China*, 889. 22. Hsu, *Rise of Modern China*, 890–891. 23. Hsu, *Rise of Modern China*, 892–893. 24. Hsu, *Rise of Modern China*, 895. 25. Hsu, *Rise of Modern China*, 897. 26. Hsu, *Rise of Modern China*, 897. 27. Hsu, *Rise of Modern China*, 901, footnote 49. 28. As cited in Mann, *About Face*, 177. 29. Mann, *About Face*, 178–180. 30. Mann, *About Face*, 180. 31. Mann, *About Face*, 179. 32. Cited in Hsu, *Rise of Modern China*, 928. 33. Hsu, *Rise of Modern China*, 928. 34. Hsu, *Rise of Modern China*, 929. 35. Hsu, *Rise of Modern China*, 929. See also Andrew S. Nathan and Percy Link, ed., *The Tiananmen Papers* (New York: Public Affairs, 2001). 36. Hsu, *Rise of Modern China*, 931–932. 37. Hsu, *Rise of Modern China*, 933. 38. Paul H. B. Godwin, "Party-Military Relations," in ed. Goldman and MacFarquhar, *Paradox*, 76–99. 39. Hsu, *Rise of Modern China*, 935, indicates that the Twelfth, Twentieth, Twenty-fourth, Twenty-seventh, Twenty-eighth, Thirty-eighth, Fifty-fourth, Sixty-third, Sixty-fourth, and Sixty-fifth armies would be involved in the repression at Tiananmen Square. 40. Richard Baum, *Burying Mao* (Princeton, N.J.: Princeton University Press), 162. 41. Orville Schell, *Mandate of Heaven* (New York: Simon and Schuster, 1994), 103. 42. Timperlake and Triplett, *Red Dragon Rising*, 30. 43. Timperlake and Triplett, *Red Dragon Rising*, 31. 44. Timperlake and Triplett, *Red Dragon Rising*, 31. 45. Yi Mu and Mark Thompson, *Crisis at Tiananmen:Reform and Reality in Modern China* (San Francisco: China Books and Periodicals, 1989), 55. 46. Timperlake and Triplett, *Red Dragon Rising*, 32#33. 47. Timperlake and Triplett, *Red Dragon Rising*, 32. 48. Hsu, *Rise of Modern China*, 935. 49. Hsu, *Rise of Modern China*, 935. 50. Hsu, *Rise of Modern China*, 936. 51. Timperlake and Triplett, *Red Dragon Rising*, 24. 52. Timperlake and Triplett, *Red Dragon Rising*, 24. 53. Timperlake and Triplett, *Red Dragon Rising*, 24. 54. Hsu, *Rise of Modern China*, 936. 55. David Aikman, speaking to the Subcommittee on International Operations and Human Rights, U.S. House of Representatives, December 18, 1996, as cited in Timperlake and Triplett, *Red Dragon Rising*, 27. 56. Jan Wong, *Red China Blues* (New York: Doubleday, 1996), 259–260. 57. Wong, *Red China Blues*, 265. 58. Wong, *Red China Blues*, 268. 59. Former estimates from Hsu, *Rise of Modern China*, 37, The larger estimates are from communist-owned Hong Kong newspaper *Wenwei Pao*, as cited in Timperlake and Triplett, *Red Dragon Rising*, 26. 60. As cited in Hsu, *Rise of Modern China*, 937. 61. Timperlake and Triplett, *Red Dragon Rising*, 42. 62. Liu Binyan, "Deng's Phyrric Victory," *The New Republic*, October 22, 1989. 63. Margolin, "China," 542. 64. Margolin, "China," 542. 65. Wong, *Red China Blues*, 271–272. 66. Mann, *About Face*, 192. 67. Hsu, *Rise of Modern China*, 939.

Chapter 7

1. Hsu, *Rise of Modern China*, 945. 2. Hsu, *Rise of Modern China*, 945. 3. Li, op. cit., 205. 4. Mann, *About Face*, 195. 5. Mann, *About Face*, 196. 6. Mann, *About Face*, 197. 7. Mann, *About Face*, 205. 8. Mann, *About Face*, 201. 9. Mann, *About Face*, 208. 10. Mann, *About Face*, 208. 11. Mann, *About Face*, 208–209. 12. Hsu, *Rise of Modern China*, 960. 13. Jonathan Sanford, *China and the Multilateral Development Banks*, Congressional

Research Service, May 6, 1997, 6. **14.** Sanford, *China*, 6. **15.** Sanford, *China*, derived from information on page 7. **16.** Hsu, *Rise of Modern China*, 960. **17.** The Wisconsin Project on Nuclear Arms Control, *U.S. Exports to China, 1988–1998: Fueling Proliferation*, April 1999, 113. **18.** Mann, *About Face*, 202. **19.** Mann, *About Face*, 221. **20.** Mann, *About Face*, 222. **21.** Mann, *About Face*, 223. **22.** Mann, *About Face*, 224. **23.** The United States–led coalition inflicted tens of thousand of casualties on the Iraqi forces while sustaining 613 of its own. See Michael R. Gordon and Bernard E. Trainor, *The Generals' War: The Inside Story of the Conflict in the Gulf* (New York: Little, Brown, 1995). **24.** Richard Bernstein and Ross H. Munro, *The Coming Conflict with China* (New York: Alfred A. Knopf, 1997), 44. This discussion derives significantly from the material in Chapter 1 of this insightful and important book. **25.** U.S. House of Representatives, *Russia's Road to Corruption*, September 2000, 128; hereafter referred to as House Report. **26.** Mann, *About Face*, and Wisconsin Project, *U.S. Exports*. **27.** U.S. Department of Defense, *Report to Congress Pursuant to Section 12-26 of the FY98 National Defense Authorization Act* (Washington, DC, October 1998), 9. **28.** See table on China's ballistic missiles, long-, medium-, and short-range for further details and sources. **29.** Quotation as cited in Mann, *About Face*, 45. **30.** Cited in Mann, *About Face*, 23. **31.** As cited in Mann, *About Face*, 23. **32.** Cited in Mann, *About Face*, 27. **33.** U.S. Newswire, "Clinton Criticizes Bush Decision to Renew China's Most Favored Nation Status," June 3, 1992.

Chapter 8

1. Mann, *About Face*, Chapters 15–16 has an excellent discussion of these issues. **2.** http://www.un.org/Overview/rights.html. **3.** Dianne E. Rennack, *China: U.S. Economic Sanctions* (Washington, DC, Congressional Research Service, May 30, 1997), 27. **4.** John Mintz, "NSC Papers Trace Concern on Export Waivers for China," *Washington Post*, June 11, 1998, A10. **5.** Mintz, "NSC Papers," A10. **6.** As quoted in Aron L. Friedberg, "Arming China Against Ourselves" *Commentary*, July–August 1999, 29. The following discussion draws upon facts listed in this excellent article. **7.** Rennack, *China: U.S.*, 27–29. **8.** Friedberg, "Arming China," 29. **9.** Friedberg, "Arming China," 29. **10.** Friedberg, "Arming China," 46. **11.** Bernstein and Munro, *Coming Conflict with China*, 46–47. **12.** Bernstein and Munro, *Coming Conflict with China*, 47. **13.** Wisconsin Project, *U.S. Exports*, Introduction. **14.** *Trading With The Enemy: How the Clinton Administration Armed China*, Video (American Investigator, 2000). **15.** Friedberg, "Arming China," 30. **16.** Greg Gerardi and Richard Fisher, "China's Missile Tests Show More Muscle," *Jane's Intelligence Review*, March 1, 1997. The C-SS-X-7/DF-15, a solid-fueled, mobile missile with a range of 370 miles and the capacity to have either a neutron bomb or a conventional explosive payload of about 1,100 pounds. **17.** The content of this U.S. government report is published in Bill Gertz, *Betrayal:How the Clinton Administration Undermined American Security* (Washington, DC: Regenery Publishers, 1999), 268. **18.** U.S. Newswire, *Transcript of Remarks by President Clinton at Press Conference on China Trade Status*, May 26, 1994. **19.** Cox Report, 75. **20.** Cox Report, 84. **21.** Barton Gelman, "U.S. and China Nearly Came to Blows in 1996," *New York Times*, June 21, 1998, A1. **22.** James Mann, "Between China and the U.S.," *The Washington Post*, January 10, 1999. **23.** Mann, "China and the U.S." **24.** Lewis and Xue, *China's Strategic Seapower*, 325. **25.** Richard

Fisher, "China's Missiles Over the Taiwan Strait: A Political and Military Assessment" (paper, Conference on the People's Liberation Army, September 1996), 5. **26.** Friedburg, "Arming China," 30. **27.** Friedburg, "Arming China," 30. **28.** Friedburg, "Arming China," 30. **29.** Friedburg, "Arming China," 30. **30.** Friedburg, "Arming China," 30. **31.** Dumbaugh, *China–U.S. Relations,* 24; RNC Chronology, *Washington Times,* May 28 1998. **32.** RNC Chronology, *Washington Times,* June 25, 1998. **33.** Dumbaugh, *China–U.S. Relations,* 24; RNC Chronology, *Washington Times,* May 28 1998; 1998, and Kerry Dumbaugh, *China–U.S. Relations: Chronology of Developments During the Clinton Administration,* Congressional Research Service, July 25, 2000, 12. **34.** For detailed analysis of the virtually identical similarities between the Chinese ICBM, the C-SS-4, and the Long March missile used for satellite launches, see the Cox Report. **35.** Mann, "China and the U.S.," C2. **36.** Dumbaugh, *China–U.S. Relations,* 24; RNC Chronology, *Washington Times,* May 28, 1998. **37.** *Trading With the Enemy.* **38.** Gelman, "U.S. and China," A1. **39.** Patrick Tyler, *A Great Wall* (New York: Twentieth Century Foundation, 1999), 32. **40.** Mann, "China and the U.S." **41.** Mann, "China and the U.S." **42.** Mann, "China and the U.S." See also the important account by Notra Trulock in "Kindred Spirit." **43.** RNC Chronology, *Washington Times,* May 25, 1998. **44.** Jeff Gerth, "President's Top Security Adviser Questioned by Senate Committee," *New York Times,* July 1, 1999. **45.** Cox Report, 75–84. **46.** Gerth, "President's Top Security Adviser Questioned by Senate Committee." **47.** Cox Report, xix. **48.** Cox Report, xvii. **49.** Dumbaugh, *China–U.S. Relations,* 24; RNC Chronology, *Washington Times,* May 28 1998; **50.** Senate Government Affairs Committee, *Investigation of Alleged Improper Activities in Connection with the 1996 Federal Election Campaign,* Report 105–167. Three insightful discussions of this issue are Edward Timperlake and William C. Triplett II, *The Year of the Rat: How Bill Clinton Compromised U.S. Security for Chinese Cash* (Washington, DC: Regnery Publishers, 1998); Gertz, *Betrayal;* and Kenneth R. Timmerman, *Selling Out America* (Philadelphia: Xlibris Corp., 2000). **51.** *Washington Post,* July 20, 1999, A1. **52.** Wisconsin Project *Risk Report.* **53.** A U.S. Government report detailed these efforts in September 1996, as cited in Bill Gertz, *Betrayal* (Washington, DC: Regnery, 1999), 266. **54.** Dumbaugh, *China–U.S. Relations,* 12. **55.** Dumbaugh, *China–U.S. Relations,* 14. **56.** Dumbaugh, *China–U.S. Relations,* 15. **57.** Dumbaugh, *China–U.S. Relations,* 15. **58.** Dumbaugh, *China–U.S. Relations,* 15. **59.** Dumbaugh, *China–U.S. Relations,* 18. **60.** William J. Clinton, "China and the National Interest," *U.S. Department of State Dispatch,* vol. 8, no. 9, 1. **61.** Office of the White House Press Secretary, transcript of press conference by President Clinton and President Jiang Zemin, October 29, 1997. **62.** Dumbaugh, *China–U.S. Relations,* CRS-23. **63.** Dumbaugh, *China–U.S. Relations,* CRS-19. **64.** *Trading With the Enemy.* **65.** Gertz, "China Summit Missile Pact Unlikely," *Washington Times,* June 21, 1998, A6. **66.** John M. Broder, "Clinton on Chinese TV endorses Freedom," *New York Times,* July 2, 1998. **67.** Terrence Hunt, "Clinton Ends 9 Day China Trip, Sees Democracy for Chinese," Associated Press, July 4, 1998. **68.** John M. Broder, "Clinton Optimistic on China's Future as He Heads Home," *New York Times,* July 4, 1998. **69.** Jim Hoagland, "Spinning Off to China," *The Washington Post,* June 21, 1998, C7. **70.** Dumbaugh, *China–U.S. Relations,* 31. **71.** "Watching Closely for Changes in Relationships with Taiwan and Enhancing Military Leadership Awareness of the Current Situation" (manuscript, Central Military Commission of the Communist

Party of China, August 10, 1999), 7; hereafter cited as CMC. **72.** CMC, 3. **73.** CMC, 5. **74.** CMC, 7. **75.** CMC, 12. **76.** CMC, 12. **77.** CMC, 12. **78.** CMC, 7. **79.** CMC, 9. **80.** CMC, 11. **81.** CMC, 11. **82.** CMC, 13. **83.** Dumbaugh, *China–U.S. Relations,* 31. **84.** *CRM,* no. 281, February 28, 2000. **85.** *CRM,* no. 281, as quoted in the *Ching Chi Jih Pao* (Hong Kong), February 2000. **86.** *CRM,* Februry 24, 2000, citing *Sing Tao Jih Pao* (Hong Kong). **87.** John Pomfret, "Chinese Military Backs Beijing's Latest Warning to Taiwan," *Washington Post,* February 24, 2000, A17. **88.** Bill Gertz, "China Warns U.S. of Missile Strike," *Washington Times,* February 29, 2000, A1. Pomfret, "Chinese Military," also discusses the military threat but in less direct terms. **89.** Pomfret, "Chinese Military." **90.** John J. Tkacik, Jr.China-Taiwan Dialogue Could Begin at the APEC Summit by Executive Memorandum #767 Heritage foundation August 21, 2001. **91.** *CRM,* March 1, 2000. **92.** As cited in Pomfret, "Chinese Military." **93.** Pomfret, "Chinese Military." **94.** *CRM,* no. 285, March 8, 2000. **95.** *CRM,* as quoted in *Ping Kuo Jih Pao (Apple Daily)* (Hong Kong), March 23, 2000. **96.** *CRM,* April 22, 2000. **97.** *CRM,* May 23, 2000, as reported in *Taiyang Pao* (Hong Kong). **98.** *CRM,* reporting from the *South China Morning Post,* May 16, 2000. **99.** *CRM,* May 23, 2000, from *Taiyang Pao* (Hong Kong), May 18, 2000. **100.** Eric Eckholm, "China and Japan Affirm, Ties Despite Tensions," *New York Times,* August 30, 2000, A12. **101.** Dumbaugh, *China–U.S. Relations,* 32. **102.** Dumbaugh, *China–U.S. Relations,* 32. **103.** *The International Report Early Warning,* August 2000. **104.** John Pomfret, "China Expands Crackdown on Religions Not Recognized by State," *Washington Post,* September 5, 2000, A19. **105.** Pomfret, "China Expands Crackdown." **106.** "Need to Move Forward With Prudence," excerpts from remarks by President Bill Clinton, as published in the *Washington Post,* September 2, 2000, A14. **107.** Paisley Dodds, "Putin, NATO Allies Praise Missile Defense Decision," *Washington Post,* September 2, 2000, A15. **108.** Bill Gertz, "Clinton Delays Missile Defense," *Washington Times,* September 2, 2000, A1. **109.** Charles Babbington, "Clinton's Decision Poses Challenges to Gore/Bush," *Washington Post,* September 2, 2000, 14. **110.** David Sanger, "Clinton Planning Diplomatic Whirl on Upcoming Trip, *New York Times,* September 5, 2000, A1. **111.** Sanger, "Clinton Planning Diplomatic Whirl." **112.** Charles Hutzler, "Jiang to Keep Heat on Missile Defense," *Washington Times,* September 5, 2000, A9. **113.** Bill Gertz, "China Aids Pakistani 'Rogue' Missile Program, CIA Says," *Washington Times,* February 27, 2001, A10. On loosening computer controls, see *Information Weekly,* January 10, 2001. **114.** Dumbaugh, *China–U.S. Relations,* 3.

Chapter 9
1. House Policy Committee, *U.S.–China Relations: A Policy for Freedom,* Washington, DC, October 1997. **2.** House Policy Committee, *U.S.–China Relations.* **3.** House Policy Committee, *U.S.–China Relations,* 2. **4.** House Policy Committee, *U.S.–China Relations,* 3. **5.** House Policy Committee, *U.S.–China Relations,* 4. **6.** House Policy Committee, *U.S.–China Relations,* 4. **7.** Dumbaugh, *China–U.S. Relations,* 21. **8.** Dumbaugh, *China–U.S. Relations,* 24. **9.** Timperlake and Tripplet, *Red Dragon Rising,* 190 and the biannual public reports to Congress from the Director of Central Intelligence, 1997–Present. **10.** Dumbaugh, *China–U.S. Relations,* 24; RNC Chronology, *Washington Times,* May 28 1998. **11.** Dumbaugh, *China–U.S. Relations,* 25. **12.** Dumbaugh, *China–U.S. Relations,* 25. **13.** Dumbaugh, *China–U.S. Relations,*

26. **14.** Bill Gertz, "China Adds Six ICBMs to Arsenal," *Washington Times*, July 21, 1998, A1. **15.** Dumbaugh, *China–U.S. Relations*, 25. **16.** Gertz, "China Summit," A6. **17.** Gertz, "China Summit," A6. **18.** Eric Schmitt, "Helms Said Clinton Tried to Protect China by Waiving Curbs on Satellite Exports," *New York Times*, June 12, 1998, A8. **19.** See Executive Summary, *Report of the Commission to Assess the Ballistic Missile Threat to the United States* (Washington, DC, July 15, 1998), hereafter cited as the Rumsfeld Report. **20.** Rumsfeld Report, 10. **21.** Rumsfeld Report, 10. **22.** Rumsfeld Report, 11. **23.** Rumsfeld Report, 11. **24.** Rumsfeld Report, 11. **25.** Rumsfeld Report, 12. **26.** Rumsfeld Report, 12. **27.** Rumsfeld Report, 12. **28.** Cox Report. **29.** Dumbaugh, *China–U.S. Relations*, 30. **30.** Dumbaugh, *China–U.S. Relations*, 29. Also, Bill Gertz, "China Makes Move on Spratlies," *Washington Times*, January 4, 1999, A1. **31.** For the best analysis of these issues see Timperlake and Triplett, *Year of the Rat* and Timmerman, *Selling Out America.* **32.** Andrew Cain, "China's Zhu Denies Spying, Nuke Theft," *Washington Times*, April 9, 1999, A1. **33.** Cain, "China's Zhu Denise Spying," A1. **34.** Dumbaugh, *China–U.S. Relations*, 30. **35.** Dumbaugh, *China–U.S. Relations*, 31. **36.** Tom Carter, "U.S. Sees Human Rights Eroding in China," *Washington Times*, February 27, 1999, A9. **37.** Tony Marshall, "Albright Uses Diplomacy with Chinese," *Washington Times*, January 13, 1999, A12. **38.** Dumbaugh, *China–U.S. Relations*, 30. **39.** Cox Report, vol. 1, ii. **40.** Cox Report, vol. 1, ii. **41.** Cox Report, vol. 1, iii. **42.** Cox Report, vol. 1, vi. **43.** Bill Gertz, "Chinese Believed Preparing for a Nuclear Weapons Test," *Washington Times*, May 11, 2001, A5. **44.** Cox Report, vol. 1, xii. **45.** Cox Report, vol. 1, xiv. This refers to the currently deployed 7,500-mile ICBM [CSS-4] that was based in large part on both United States and Russian technologies brought to Communist China by Dr. Qian, whom we discussed earlier. **46.** Cox Report, vol. 1, xiii. **47.** Cox Report, vol. 1, x. **48.** Cox Report, vol. 1, xi. Here, White House response to sworn interrogatories was that the President had been briefed early in 1998. On other occasions, President Clinton said that he had been briefed in July 1997. **49.** Cox Report, vol. 1, ix. **50.** Cox Report, vol. 1, xx. **51.** Cox Report, vol. 1, xxi. **52.** Dumbaugh, *China–U.S. Relations*, 24; RNC Chronology, *Washington Times*, May 28 1998. **53.** Brian Bergstein, "Satellite Maker Loral files for Chapter 11," Associated Press, July 15, 2003. **54.** People's Republic of China, "Facts Speak Louder Than Words and Lies Will Collapse by Themselves: Further Refutation of the Cox Report" (Information Office of the State Council, July 15, 1999), as cited in Shirly Kan, CRS Report, op. cit. August 8, 2000, 41. **55.** "White House Response Shares Concerns of Cox Panel on Nuclear Security Lapses," *Washington Times*, May 26, 1999, A11; Donald Lambrough, "GOP Candidates Denounce Clinton for Security Lapses," *Washington Times*, May 26, 1999, A11. **56.** Lambrough, "GOP Candidates Denounce Clinton." **57.** Lambrough, "GOP Candidates Denounce Clinton." **58.** Bill Sammon, "Clinton Distances Himself From Scandal, Agrees to Implement Security Measure," *Washington Times*, May 26, 1999, A1. **59.** David E. Sanger, "U.S. Eases Restrictions on Selling Fast PCs to Russia, China," *New York Times*, July 2, 1999, A1.

Chapter 10

1. Richard Pipes, *The Russian Revolution* (New York: Vintage Press, 1991), 159. **2.** Volkogonov, *Autopsy of an Empire*, 23. **3.** Volkogonov, *Autopsy of an Empire*, 24. **4.** Volkogonov, *Autopsy of an Empire*, 94–95. **5.** For additional information on the political terror during this period, see Robert Conquest, *The Great Terror: A Reassessment* (New York: Oxford University Press, 1990). 6. Volkogonov, *Autopsy of an Empire*, 81.7. Volkogonov, *Autopsy of an Empire*, 73. 8. Volkogonov, *Autopsy of an Empire*, 73. 9. For an interesting discussion of the period, see Stephen F. Cohen, *Bukharin and the Bolshevik Revolution: A Political Biography* (New York: Oxford University Press, 1982). 10. Volkogonov, *Autopsy of an Empire*, 76. 11. Volkogonov, *Autopsy of an Empire*, 72. 12. Paul Johnson, *Modern Times* (New York: Harper Colophon Books, 1983), 66–71. 13. For discussion, see Moshe Lewin, *Lenin's Last Struggl* (New York: Pantheon, 1968). To be sure, at least part of Lenin's vitriolic comments about Stalin reflected the latter's recent ill-mannered behavior toward Lenin's wife, Nadezhda Krupskaya. 14. Volkogonov, *Autopsy of an Empire*, 104. 15. The noted British historian, Alan Bullock suggests that Hitler borrowed many of his ideas from Stalin's totalitarian state, rather than vice versa, as has been alleged by Soviet historians. See Bullock's *Hitler and Stalin: Parallel Lives* (New York: Random House, 1992). 16. Stalin's rule is in many ways the most crucial issue in Soviet history. Especially worthy of note are the two volumes by Robert Tucker, *Stalin as Revolutionary: 1879–1929: A Study in History and Personality* (New York: Norton, 1974), and *Stalin in Power: The Revolution from Above* (New York: Norton, 1990). Differing interpretations may be found in Leon Trotsky, *The Revolution Betrayed* (Garden City, N.Y.: Doubleday, Doran, and Co., Inc., 1937) and Adam Ulam, *Stalin: The Man and his Era* (New York: Viking Press, 1973). For a broad discussion of the Great Terror, see Robert Conquest's classic study, *The Great Terror: A Reassessment.* Figures on the Soviet terror, however, are subject to change. In 1992, for the first time, the KGB officially stated that between 1933 and 1945 the Soviet state executed 7 million people. (See RFE/FL *Research Report,* May 1, 1992, 3.) Western observers, including Conquest, have placed the figure for those years as high as 33 million dead. 17. Volkogonov, *Autopsy of an Empire*, 139. 18. Volkogonov, *Autopsy of an Empire*, 108. 19. Volkogonov, *Autopsy of an Empire*, 108. 20. Volkogonov, *Autopsy of an Empire*, 109. 21. Among other things, the Hitler-Stalin pact gave the Soviet leadership the means to forcibly annex the Baltic republics of Lithuania, Latvia, and Estonia, independent since their escape from Russia's empire in 1917. 22. This point is made by, among others, Harrison Salisbury in *The 900 Days: The Siege of Leningrad* (New York: Harper and Row, 1969). 23. For an excellent discussion of the Stalin phenomenon, particularly its relationship to both Czarist autocracy and the Leninist state, see Mitchell Cohen's article "Theories of Stalinism: Revisiting a Historical Problem," *Dissent*, Spring 1992, 190. 24. For an overview of the methods of Soviet indirect aggression, see Menges, *Twilight Struggle.* 25. Volkogonov, *Autopsy of an Empire*, 156. 26. See Volkogonov, *Autopsy of an Empire*, 151–166 for a discussion of the Korean War. 27. Volkogonov, *Autopsy of an Empire*, 169. 28. Volkogonov, *Autopsy of an Empire*, 169. 29. Volkogonov, *Autopsy of an Empire*, 110. 30. See Volkogonov, *Autopsy of an Empire*, 151 for Gulag numbers and page 72 for information on informers. 31. Volkogonov, *Autopsy of an Empire*, 186–188. 32. Volkogonov, *Autopsy of an Empire*, 107. 33. Volkogonov, *Autopsy of an Empire*, 207. 34. Volkogonov, *Autopsy of an Empire*, 151. 35. Volkogonov, *Autopsy of an Empire*, 232. 36. Volkogonov, *Autopsy of an Empire*, 237–240. 37. Volkogonov, *Autopsy of an Empire*, 264. 38. Volkogonov, *Autopsy of an Empire*, 274. 39. Volkogonov, *Autopsy of an Empire*, 180. 40. Volkogonov, *Autopsy of an Empire*, 180. 41. From 1975 to 1979, pro-Soviet movements took power with help from the Soviet Union and its allies in the following countries: Afghanistan, Angola, Ethiopia, Mozambique, South Yemen, Cambodia, Laos, South Vietnam, Grenada, and Nicaragua. For an in-depth analysis see Menges, *Twilight Struggle*. **42.** Volkogonov, *Autopsy of an Empire*, 283. **43.** For a discussion of environmental problems in the Soviet Union, see Murray Feshbach and Alfred Friendly, Jr., *Ecocide in the USSR* (New York: Basic Books, 1992). **44.** Volkogonov, *Autopsy of an Empire*, 281. **45.** Peter Reddaway, *Uncensored Russia: Protest and Dissent in the Soviet Union* (New York: American Heritage Press, 1972). **46.** Volkogonov, *Autopsy of an Empire*, 340–346. **47.** Volkogonov, *Autopsy of an Empire*, 178. **48.** Volkogonov, *Autopsy of an Empire*, 330. **49.** Volkogonov, *Autopsy of an Empire*, 347. **50.** Volkogonov, *Autopsy of an Empire*, 359. **51.** Peter Pry, *War Scare: Nuclear Countdown after the Soviet Fall* (Atlanta, Ga.: Turner Publications, 1997). **52.** Volkogonov, *Autopsy of an Empire*, 384.

Chapter 11

1. Volkogonov, *Autopsy of an Empire*, 438. **2.** Volkogonov, *Autopsy of an Empire*, 467–469. **3.** Volkogonov, *Autopsy of an Empire*, 492. **4.** Volkogonov, *Autopsy of an Empire*, 494–495. **5.** Volkogonov, *Autopsy of an Empire*, 263. **6.** Menges, *Twilight Struggle*. **7.** Volkogonov, *Autopsy of an Empire*, 483. **8.** Volkogonov, *Autopsy of an Empire*, 492. **9.** Volkogonov, *Autopsy of an Empire*, 455. **10.** Volkogonov, *Autopsy of an Empire*, 473–474. **11.** See Lewin, *Lenin's Last Struggle*. Lenin's perception of the Party's direct role in governing is exemplified by his choice of General Secretary, a position he considered largely ceremonial. By selecting Stalin for this office, a man generally thought to be a minor figure in the Bolshevik Party and for whom Lenin held little regard, Lenin indicated his desire to work through established governmental organs. **12.** Carl Linden, "Gorbachev and the Fall of the Marxian Prince in Europe and Russia" in Carl Linden and Jan Prybyla, *Russia and China on the Eve of A New Millenium* (New Brunswick: Transaction Publishers, 1997), 72–77. **13.** Linden, "Gorbachev," 74. **14.** James Millar, "The Importance of Initial Conditions in Economic Transitions," *Journal of Socio-Economics*, vol. 26, no. 4, 383–384, Table 2. **15.** Linden, "Gorbachev," 76. **16.** Linden, "Gorbachev," 76. **17.** Linden, "Gorbachev," 75. **18.** Dmitry Mikheyev, *Russia Transformed* (Indianapolis, Ind.: Hudson Institute, 1996), 76. **19.** Mikheyev, *Russia Transformed*, 97. **20.** Mikheyev, *Russia Transformed*, 76. **21.** Mikheyev, *Russia Transformed*, 76. (Emphasis Mikheyev's.) **22.** Millar, "Economic Transitions," 383-384, Table 2. **23.** Volkogonov, *Autopsy of an Empire*, 473–474. **24.** Volkogonov, *Autopsy of an Empire*, 474. **25.** *Izvestiya TsKPSS*, no. 9, 1990, 19-25. **26.** For an in-depth analysis, see Constantine C. Menges, *The Future of Germany and the Atlantic Alliance* (Washington, DC: American Enterprise Institute, 1990). **27.** Alfred Evans, "Gorbachev's Unfinished Revolution," *Problems of Post-Communism*, January–April 1991, 135. **28.** Robert Kaiser, *Why Gorbachev Happened* (New York: Simon and Schuster, 1991), 436–437. **29.** Mikheyev, *Russia Transformed*, 77. **30.** Mikheyev, *Russia Transformed*, 77; Kaiser, *Why Gorbachev Happened*, 442. **31.** Mikheyev, *Russia Transformed*, 78. **32.** Mikheyev, *Russia Transformed*, 78. **33.** Kaiser, *Why Gorbachev Happened*, 444. **34.** Kaiser, *Why Gorbachev Happened*, 444. **35.** Kaiser, *Why Gorbachev Happened*, 445. **36.** Kaiser, *Why Gorbachev Happened*, 445. **37.** Kaiser, *Why Gorbachev Happened*, 446. **38.** Linden, "Gorbachev," 83. **39.** Volkogonov, *Autopsy of an Empire*, 513. **40.** Mikheyev, *Russia Transformed*, 78. **41.** Mikhail Gorbachev, *The August Coup*

(New York: HarperCollins, 1991), 31–32. **42.** Gorbachev, *August Coup,* 43. **43.** Gorbachev, *August Coup,* 46. **44.** *Novoe vremya,* no. 45, 1991; *Rossiyskaya gazeta,* November 6, 1992. **45.** For an excellent discussion of the coup and its aftermath, see the symposium in *Problems of Communism,* November/December 1991. This journal dissolved in 1992 but was reestablished with the author as the founding editor at George Washington University in 1994 as *Problems of Post-Communism.*

Chapter 12

1. Boris Yeltsin, *Midnight Diaries* (New York: Public Affairs Press, 2000), 72. **2.** Yeltsin, *Midnight Diaries,* 24. **3.** Yegor Gaidar, *Days of Defeat and Victory* (Seattle:University of Washington Press, 1999), provides an overview of the views held by Yeltsin's economic group led by Gaidar. See especially chapters 4 and 5. **4.** Gaidar, *Defeat and Victory.* **5.** Yegor Gaidar, "Russia Needs to Three Kinds of Economic Aid—and Quickly," *Financial Times,* January 22, 1992), 15. **6.** John P. Hart and Philip J. Kaiser, *Russia's Economic Program* (Washington DC: CRS Issue Brief, Library of Congress, March 26, 1992), 1. **7.** Hart and Kaiser, *Russia's Economic Program,* 1. **8.** *Financial Times,* April 3, 1992. **9.** Alexander Lukin, "Forcing the Pace of Democratization," *Journal of Democracy,* April 1999, 39. **10.** Gaidar, *Defeat and Victory,* 129. **11.** James R. Millar, ed., *Politics, Work and Daily Life in the USSR* (Cambridge, Mass.: Cambridge University Press, 1988), 43–45. **12.** Konstantin Simis, *USSR: The Corrupt Society* (New York: Simon and Schuster, 1982), 86–87. **13.** As paraphrased by David Remnick, "Dons of the Don," *New York Review,* July 16, 1992), 47. **14.** Nikolai Shmelyov and Vladimir Popov, *The Turning Point: Revitalizing the Soviet Economy* (New York: Doubleday, 1989), 199. **15.** Shmelyov and Popov, *The Turning Point,* 199. **16.** This is the estimate of the late physicist and democratic dissident Andrei Sakharov, cited by Hedrick Smith, *The New Russians* (New York: Random House, 1990), 266–267. **17.** Smith, *The New Russians,* 265. **18.** Smith, *The New Russians,* 91. **19.** Gaidar, *Defeat and Victory,* 142. **20.** John Lyold, "Burdened but Unbowed," *Financial Times,* April 3, 1992. **21.** Gaidar, *Defeat and Victory,* 145. **22.** Yeltsin, *Midnight Diaries,* 103. **23.** Yeltsin, *Midnight Diaries,* 162–166. **24.** Victor Sheinis, *The Politics of Russian Reform* (Washington, DC: Program on Transition to Democracy, George Washington University, 1992). **25.** Petro, *Rebirth of Russian Democracy,* 174. **25.** Yeltsin, *Midnight Diaries,* 106. **27.** Yeltsin, *Midnight Diaries,* 106. **28.** Zolten Baranay, "Controlling the Military: A Partial Success," *Journal of Democracy,* April 1999, 57. **29.** Baranay, "Controlling the Military," 59. **30.** For a contrasting analysis that raises the prospect of gains for the antireform groups, see Constantine C. Menges, "The U.S. Can Help Russia's Democrats," *Christian Science Monitor,* November 1, 1993; and Constantine C. Menges, *The Russian Crisis and the Clinton Administration* (Washington DC: Program on Transitions to Democracy, George Washington University, October 1993). **31.** Vladimir Schlapentokh (lecture, University of Michigan at the American Association for the Advancement of Slavic Studies, November 20, 1994). **32.** Michael McFaul, *Russia's 1996 Presidential Election* (Stanford, Calif.: Hoover Institution Press, 1997), 83. **33.** Remarkably, the head of the Central Bank during the hyperinflation years, Gerashenko, was returned to that position by the government of Prime Minister Primakov, which was established after the economic crisis of 1998. **34.** Yeltsin, *Midnight Diaries,* 103. **35.** Gaidar, *Defeat and Victory,* 172. **36.** Yeltsin,

Midnight Diaries. 37. Baranay, "Controlling the Military," 54–55. 38. Baranay, "Controlling the Military," 56. 39. Baranay, "Controlling the Military," 56. 40. Baranay, "Controlling the Military," 58–59. 41. Baranay, "Controlling the Military," 59. 42. General Rokhlin died a mysterious death in July 1998, ostensibly at the hands of his wife, but questions remain as to whether he was involved with an effort to organize some of the military against Yeltsin at the time. 43. Baranay, "Controlling the Military," 60. 44. Yeltsin, *Midnight Diaries,* 139. 45. Gaidar, *Defeat and Victory.* 46. Andrei Illarinov, "The Roots of the Economic Crisis," *Journal of Democracy,* vol. 10, no. 2, 1999, 68–82. 47. David Hoffman, "Tycoons Take the Reigns in Russia," *The Washington Post,* August 28, 1999, A1. 48. Hoffman, "Tycoons Take the Reigns." 49. Hoffman, "Tycoons Take the Reigns." 50. Hoffman, "Tycoons Take the Reigns." 51. See David Sutter, *Darkness at Dawn* (New Haven, Conn.: Yale University Press, 2003). 52. Keith Bush, *The Economy of Russia* (Washington, DC: Center for Strategic and International Strategy, 1999), 25. 53. Bush, *The Economy of Russia,* 25. 54. A discussion of the 1996 campaign can be found in McFaul, *Russia's 1996 Presidential Election.* 55. Yeltsin, *Midnight Diaries,* 24–25. 56. Yeltsin, *Midnight Diaries,* 23. 57. McFaul, *Russia's 1996 Presidential Election,* 81. Yeltsin, *Midnight Diaries,* 25–29 describes some of the important help he received. 58. The author saw these programs on Russian television while there in the spring of 1996. 59. McFaul, *Russia's 1996 Presidential Election,* 82. 60. McFaul, *Russia's 1996 Presidential Election,* 8, Table 1. 61. Yeltsin, *Midnight Diaries,* 64. 62. Yeltsin, *Midnight Diaries,* 66. 63. *Washington Post,* February 22, 1997. 64. Otto Latsis, "Russia: Man on His Own," *Freedom in the World, 1997-1998* (Washington, DC: Freedom House, 1998), 23. 65. Latsis, "Russia," 24. 66. Yeltsin, *Midnight Diaries,* 240. 67. Yeltsin, *Midnight Diaries,* 94. 68. Yeltsin, *Midnight Diaries,* 100. 69. See the economic results chart. 70. Yeltsin, *Midnight Diaries,* 106–7. 71. Yeltsin, *Midnight Diaries,* 108–9. 72. Michael Gordon, "In Russia, Reformers Fall, Wealthy Insider Triumphs," *New York Times,* August 27, 1998, A10. 73. Yeltsin, *Midnight Diaries,* 100. 74. Yeltsin, *Midnight Diaries,* 94.78. Among the specific aspects cited by Illarionov in his analysis is the fact that while the Russian banking system had maintained a level foreign exchange balance in 1993 and 1994, beginning in 1995, the balance became increasingly negative. By 1998, the negative balance had grown from a debt of $11 billion in 1996 and $21 billion to $32 billion in 1997—nearly one third of all bank assets. op. cit., 79. 75. Yeltsin, *Midnight Diaries,* 78. 76. This is described in detail in David Satter, "The Rise of the Russian Criminal State," *Monitor,* 1998. 77. Yeltsin, *Midnight Diaries,* 78. 78. Yeltsin, *Midnight Diaries,* 91 and 94. 79. Gordon, "In Russia, Reformers Fall." 80. Michael Wines, "Drive to Impeach Russian President Crumbles in Duma," *New York Times,* May 16, 1999, A1. 81. Wines, "Drive to Impeach." 82. Wines, "Drive to Impeach." 83. Wines, "Drive to Impeach." 84. Celestine Bohlen, "Yeltsin's Opposition Delays Impeachment Votes," *New York Times,* April 13, 1999, A5. 85. Bohlen, "Yeltsin's Opposition." 86. Sergi Shargorodsky, "Stepashin Able to Climb Ladder After Some Missteps Along Way," *Washington Times,* May 20, 1999, A10. 87. Celistine Bohlen, "Stepashin is Easily Confirmed as Russian Prime Minister," *New York Times,* May 20, 1999, A3. 88. David R. Sands, "Yeltsin Triumphs in Battle with Parliament," *Washington Times,* May 20, 1999, A1. 89. Cited in Michael Waller, ed., *RRM,* no. 619, April 6, 1999. 90. *Moscow Times,* April 21, 1999, as cited in *RRM,* no. 629, May 4, 1999. 91. *Moscow Times,* April 21, 1999. 92. Celestine Bohlen,

"Kremlinology 101: The More Things Change . . .," *New York Times,* May 24, 1999, A1. **93.** "Chubais on Stepashin and the Irreversibility of Russian Reform," (issue brief, Carnegie Endowment for International Peace, Washington DC, May 19, 1999), 1. **94.** David Satter, "The Rise of the Russian Criminal State," *Prism,* 1999, 10. **95.** "Russian Organized Crime," *The Economist,* August 28–September 3, 1999, 18. **96.** *Freedom in the World: 1997–1998* (Washington, DC, 1998), 432–433. **97.** *Freedom in the World: 1997–1998,* 432–433. **98.** *Freedom in the World: 1997–1998,* 432–433. **99.** *Freedom in the World: 1997–1998,* 431. **100.** *Freedom in the World: 1997–1998,* 431. **101.** See poll data previously cited.

Chapter 13
1. Vladimir Putin, *First Person* (New York: Public Affairs Press, 2000). This revealing book is taken from a series of interviews with Putin as well as with friends of the family, former teachers, and coaches. It was composed by Natalia Gvorykn, Natalia Dimakova, and Andre Kolesnikov, published in Russia just before the March 2000 presidential election and then translated into English and published in this edition in June 2000. **2.** Putin, *First Person,* 9. **3.** Putin, *First Person,* 9. **4.** Putin, *First Person,* 18. **5.** Putin, *First Person,* 19. **6.** Putin, *First Person,* 22. **7.** Putin, *First Person,* 36. **8.** Putin, *First Person,* 42. **9.** Putin, *First Person,* 42. **10.** Putin, *First Person,* 50. **20.** Putin, *First Person,* 50. **21.** Center for Security Policy, "Who is Vladimir Putin" (Washington, DC, January 5, 2000); summary of an analysis by Stratfor.com. **22.** Putin, *First Person,* 70. **23.** Putin, *First Person,* 80–81. In fact, it was not until 1995 that all Soviet forces had left East Germany and other East European countries. **24.** Putin, *First Person,* 85. **25.** Putin, *First Person,* 86–87. **26.** Putin, *First Person,* 89. **27.** Putin, *First Person,* 93. **28.** Putin, *First Person,* 94. **29.** Putin, *First Person,* 96. **30.** Putin, *First Person,* 128. **31.** These allegations were part of the media attack on Yeltsin in 1999 that he saw as a prelude to defeat in the 2000 presidential election. The charges have never been proven or disproved. In January 2001, Pavel Borodin was arrested as he attempted to enter the United States to attend the presidential inauguration. The arrest occurred pursuant to an international warrant issued by the Swiss government. Borodin was subsequently extradited to Switzerland. **32.** Center for Security Policy, "Who Is Vladimir Putin." **33.** Putin, *First Person,* 131. **34.** As quoted in Putin, *First Person,* 139. **35.** Putin, *First Person,* 139–140. **36.** Putin, *First Person,* 138. **37.** The factual information in the discussion of Chechnya, unless otherwise indicated, has been drawn from the report, Jim Nichol, *Chechnya Conflict: Recent Developments,* Congressional Research Service, May 3, 2000. **38.** Nichol, *Chechnya Conflict,* 2. **39.** Putin, *First Person,* 141. **40.** Nichol, *Chechnya Conflict,* 3. **41.** Nichol, *Chechnya Conflict,* 3. **42.** Nichol, *Chechnya Conflict,* 7. **43.** Nichol, *Chechnya Conflict,* 15. **44.** Nichol, *Chechnya Conflict,* 14. **45.** International Republican Institute, *Russian Election Review,* December 24, 1999. Totals as reported in *Segodnya* December 21, 1999; the proportion of votes and proportion of seats differ because half the seats are decided through a direct vote and half through a party list. Only parties receiving 5 percent are eligible to be represented in the Duma, and therefore, there is a redistribution of half of the seats based upon the proportion of the total vote received leading to the apparently odd fact that the communists would win 24% of the vote and have 111 seats and Unity would win 23 percent and have only 76 seats. **46.** Putin, *First Person.* **47.** Putin, *First Person.* **48.** Ariel Cohen, "From Yeltsin to Putin: Milestones on

an unfinished journey," *Policy Review,* April/May 2000, 41. **49.** *RRM,* January 20, 2000. **50.** Nichol, *Chechnya Conflict,* 11. **51.** *RRM,* June 2, 2000. **52.** *RRM,* January 25, 2000. **53.** *RRM,* February 8, 2000. **54.** Stuart D. Goldman, *Russia,* Congressional Research Service, August 10, 2000, 5–6. **55.** Stuart D. Goldman, *Russian Presidential Election: 2000* (Washington, DC, Congressional Research Service, March 24, 2000), 3. **56.** Goldman, *Russian Presidential Election: 2000,* 3. **57.** As published in *Kommersant* (Moscow), May 3–4, 2000, cited in Waller ed., *RRM,* May 13, 2000. **58.** *Kommersant,* May 3–4, 2000. **59.** *Kommersant,* May 3–4, 2000. **60.** *Kommersant,* May 3–4, 2000. **61.** Vladimir Putin, State of the Nation address, Reuters, July 7, 2000. **62.** Reuters, July 8, 2000. **63.**Reuters, July 8, 2000. **64.** This was issued by *TASS,* the Russian news agency, on May 13, 2000 and cited in Waller ed., *RRM,* May 25, 2000. **65.** Yeltsin, *Midnight Diaries.* **66.** Putin, State of the Nation. **67.** Putin, State of the Nation. **68.** See also Michael Wines, "Putin Describes an Ill Russia and Prescribes Strong Democracy," *New York Times,* July 9, 2000, 3. **69.** U.S. Department of State, *Country Reports on Human Rights Practices – 2000: Russia* (Washington, DC, February 26, 2000), as published on the internet. **70.** Patrick E. Tyler, "Talkative Putin Demonstrates Value of Cyberspace," *New York Times,* March 7, 2001, A6. **71.** Vladimir Putin, Annual Presidential Address to the Federal Assembly, May 16, 2003. **72.** As cited in Fred Hiatt, "A Bipolar Bear," *Washington Post,* February 12, 2001, A21. **73.** U.S. Department of State, *Human Rights Practices—2000: Russia.* **74.** U.S. Department of State, *Human Rights Practices—2000: Russia.* **75.** U.S. Department of State, *Human Rights Practices—2000: Russia,* 9. **76.** U.S. Department of State, *Human Rights Practices—2000: Russia,* 9. **77.** U.S. Department of State, *Human Rights Practices—2000: Russia,* 8. **78.** U.S. Department of State, *Human Rights Practices—2000: Russia,* 7. **79.** U.S. Department of State, *Human Rights Practices—2000: Russia,* 9. **80.** Putin, State of the Nation. **81.** U.S. Department of State, *Human Rights Practices—2000: Russia.* **82.** U.S. Department of State, *Human Rights Practices—2000: Russia.* **83.** Yeltsin, *Midnight Diaries,* 96. **84.** The facts cited in this discussion of the media are summarized in U.S. Department of State, *Human Rights—2000, Russia,* 10–11. **85.** U.S. Department of State, *Human Rights—2000, Russia,* 10–11. **86.** RFE/RL, *(Un)Civil Societies,* February 16, 2001. **87.** David Sands, "Gusinsky: Kremlin Controls Media," *Washington Times,* May 4, 2001, A11. **88.** Sands, "Gusinsky," A11. **89.** RFE/RL, *(Un)Civil Societies,* September 24, 2000. **90.** Berezovsky, "Our Reverse Revolution," A27. **91.** Putin, State of the Nation, July 7, 2000. **92.** Yeltsin, *Midnight Diaries,* 231. **93.** Cited in Yeltsin, *Midnight Diaries,* an article from the *Los Angeles Times,* February 16, 2001. **94.** Yeltsin, *Midnight Diaries.* **95.** U.S. Department of State, *Reports on Human Rights—2000: Russia,* 11. **96.** U.S. Department of State, *Reports on Human Rights—2000: Russia,* 11. **97.** RFE/RL, *Newsline,* July 11–15, 2000. **98.** RFE/RL, *Newsline,* July 26, 28, 31, 2000. **99.** RFE/RL, *Newsline,* July 26, 28, 31, 2000. **100.** Boris Berezovsky, "Our Reverse Revolution," *Washington Post,* October 16, 2000, A27. **101.** Putin, State of the Nation, 7. **102.** U.S. Department of State, *Reports on Human Rights—2000: Russia,* 16. **103.** U.S. Department of State, *Reports on Human Rights—2000: Russia,* 16. **104.** Putin, State of the Nation, 8. **105.** U.S. Department of State, *Reports on Human Rights—2000: Russia.* **106.** U.S. Department of State, *Reports on Human Rights—2000: Russia.* **107.** Vladimir Putin, Annual Address to the Federal Assembly, April 3, 2001, from BBC Monitoring Service (of Russian television in Moscow), internet version, 7. **108.** U.S. Department of State, *Reports on Human*

Rights—2000: Russia, 16. **109.** RFE/RL *(UnCivil) Societies,* February 28, 2001. **110.** Michael Wines, "Reviving a Tactic, KGB Heir Acts on Anonymous Accusations," *New York Times,* February 15, 2001, A7; subsequent quotations also from this article. **111.** Waller, *RRM,* February 17, 2001. **112.** Wines, "Reviving a Tactic," A7. **113.** Peter Baker and Susan Glasser, "Putin Consolidates Power But Wields It Unsteadily," *Washington Post,* March 26, 2001, A1. **114.** "Russia's Spy Trials," *Washington Post,* March 14, 2001, A24. **115.** "Russia's Spy Trials," A24, and the subsequent cases mentioned. **116.** "Russia's Spy Trials," A24. **117.** "Russia's Spy Trials," A24. **118.** Waller, *RRM,* May 24, 2000. **119.** "Yeltsin Slams Putin over Anthem," *Washington Times,* December 8, 2000, A17. **120.** Peter Baker, "Russians to Feel a Patriotic Push," *Washington Post,* March 14, 2001, A18. **121.** Reported by the liberal opposition daily *Segodnya,* February 5, 2001, cited in Waller, *RRM,* February 7, 2001. **122.** Baker, "Russians to Feel a Patriotic Push," A18. **123.** Baker, "Russians to Feel a Patriotic Push," A18.

Chapter 14

1. Andrei Kozyrev, *Russia: A Chance for Survival,* Foreign Affairs, spring 1992. **2.** David Hoffman, "U.S. Opens World Conference Today on Assistance to Soviet Nations," *Washington Post,* January 22, 1992, A26. **3.** Thomas Friedman, "Bush to Press Congress for $645 million to ex-Soviet Lands," *New York Times,* January 23, 1992, A1. **4.** John Lyold, "Burdened but Unbowed," *Financial Times,* April 3, 1992. **5.** Robert McFadden, "Leaders Gather in New York to Chart a 'New World Order,'" *New York Times,* January 31, 1992, A1. **6.** Thomas Friedman, "Baker and Yeltsin Agree on U.S. Aid in Scrapping Arms," *New York Times,* February 18, 1992. **7.** Michael Weins, "Accord at Summit," *New York Times,* June 17, 1992, A1. **8.** Weins, "Accord at Summit." **9.** Serge Schmemann, "Bush and Yeltsin Sign Pact Making Deep Missile Cuts," *New York Times,* January 4, 1993, A1. **10.** Michael Gordon, "Russians Fault U.S. on Shifting Ukraine's Arms," *New York Times,* June 7, 1993, A1. **11.** For example, Ira Straus, *Problems of Post-Communism,* Fall 1994. **12.** Serge Schemann, "Yeltsin Tiptoeing on Sensitive Issues," *New York Times,* April 4, 1993. **13.** The U.S., the UK, Germany, France, Italy, and Japan. **14.** Daniel Williams, "Rich Nations Approve Aid to Russia," *Washington Post,* April 16, 1993, A1. **15.** Douglas Jehl, "Clinton is 'Four Square' Behind Yeltsin, but Expects Russian Election Soon," *New York Times,* October 5, 1993, A19. **16.** Robert H. Donaldson and Jospeh L. Nogee, *The Foreign Policy of Russia* (Armonk, NY: M. E. Sharpe, 1998), 125–126. **17.** As cited in Terry McNeal, *The Russian Security Agenda* (London: Atlantic Council of the United Kingdom, 1996), 8. **18.** As told to the author by a senior Yeltsin administration official in the Kremlin, June 1992. **19.** See McNeal, *Russian Security Agenda,* 9–17. **20.** McNeal, *Russian Security Agenda,* 12. **21.** Cited in McNeal, *Russian Security Agenda,* 13. **22.** McNeal, *Russian Security Agenda,* 13. **23.** Vladimir Putin, Address to the Federal Assembly, May 16, 2003. **24.** Putin address. **25.** Stephen Blank, *Proliferation and Counter Proliferation in Russian Strategy,* MSS, February 1999, 27. **26.** Blank, *Proliferation,* 25. **27.** McNeal, *Russian Security Agenda,* 17. **28.** Blank, *Proliferation,* 9. **29.** Blank, *Proliferation,* 9. **30.** Blank, *Proliferation,* 21. **31.** See Constantine Menges, ed., *Partnerships for Peace, Democracy and Prosperity* (Maryland: University Press of America, 1997). **32.** Stephen Blank and Alvin Z. Rubinstein, "Is Russia Still a Power in Asia," *Problems of Post-Communism,* March/April 1997, 42. **33.** Blank and Rubinstein, "Is Russia Still a Power," 43. **34.** Cited in James P. Scanlin, "The Russian Idea from Dostoevskii to Zyuganov," *Problems of Communism,* July–August 1996, 39. **35.** Blank and Rubenstein, "Is Russia Still a Power," 41. **36.** Blank and Rubenstein, "Is Russia Still a Power," 41. **37.** Blank and Rubenstein, "Is Russia Still a Power," 41. **38.** Memorandum from the meeting of President Clinton and President Yeltsin, March 1996 in Moscow, as published in Gertz, *Betrayal,* 275. **39.** Executive Order no. 12938, November 14, 1994, as cited in Gertz, *Betrayal,* 71. **40.** Senate Committee on Government Operations, Subcommittee on International Security, *The Proliferation Primer,* January 1998, 17. **41.** Central Intelligence Agency, *The Acquisition of Technology Relating to Weapons of Mass Destruction and Advanced Conventional Munitions,* July–December 1996, as published in *Proliferation Primer,* 85–91. Other reports of the director of Central Intelligence are quoted in Gertz, *Betrayal,* 179–190. **42.** Gertz, *Betrayal,* 166–191. **43.** Gertz, *Betrayal,* 177. **44.** Gertz, *Betrayal,* 179. **45.** Gertz, *Betrayal,* 179. **46.** Scott Parish, "Primakov in Terran," *OMRI Daily Digest,* December 30, 1996, as cited in Cohen, 1. **47.** Bill Gertz, "Russian Spies Active in Balkans, CIA Says," *Washington Times,* March 23, 1999, A1. **48.** Gertz, "Russian Spies." **49.** Craig R. Whitney, "Russia and NATO Sign Cooperation Pact," *New York Times,* March 28, 1997, A1. **50.** FBIS (NES), December 21, 1998. **51.** FBIS (SOV), December 22, 1998. **52.** Constantine Menges and Mihajlo Mihajlov, "Expansion Visions in Russia," *Washington Times,* February 1999. **53.** *Bilt,* November 13, 1998, also cited in Menges and Mihajlov. **54.** Associated Press, "Excerpts from Clinton and Yeltsin's Remarks: 'Peace and Stability,'" *New York Times,* September 3, 1998, A10. **55.** From the text of President Clinton's address to the nation on March 24, 1999, as published in the *Washington Times,* March 25, 1999, A14. **56.** Betsey Pisik, "Yeltsin in 'Shock,' Recalls Diplomat," *Washington Times,* March 25, 1999, A14. **57.** Pisik, "Yeltsin in 'Shock.'" **58.** Teimurkhanov Elchin, "Six MiGs Found on Russian Airplane," *Washington Times,* March 24, 1999, A11. **59.** Elchin, "Six MiGs." **60.** Andrei Kozyrev, as quoted by RFE/RL and cited in *RRM,* no. 624 (April 14, 1999). **61.** Andrei Kozyrev, *Moscow News,* March 30–April 5, 1999, as cited in *RRM,* no. 622 (April 12, 1999). **62.** Bill Salmon, "Accord Keeps Russia in Kosovo, Sharing Sectors," *Washington Times,* June 19, 1999, A1. **63.** William Drozdiak and Charles Babington, "Western Powers to Help Russia Cut Debt," *Washington Post,* June 20, 1999, A24. **64.** Drozdiak and Babington, "Western Powers." **65.** *RRM,* no. 654 (June 29, 1999). **66.** *RRM,* no. 654. **67.** David Stout, "Russian Bombers Face Off Against American Fighters," *New York Times,* July 1, 1999, A3. **68.** Stout, "Russian Bombers." **69.** Stout, "Russian Bombers." **70.** Michael Gordon, "Maneuvers Show Russian Reliance on Nuclear Arms," *New York Times,* July 10, 1999, A1. **71.** William Drozdiak "NATO, Russia Resume Relations," *Washington Post,* July 24, 1999, A14. **72.** David Sands, "Premier Arrives to Meet Clinton About Yugoslavia," *Washington Times,* July 26, 1999, A13. **73.** Sands, "Premier Arrives." **74.** Bill Gertz, "Russians Told to Cut Number of Spies in the U.S.," *Washington Times,* July 26, 1999, A1. **75.** Gertz, "Russians Told to Cut." **76.** "Who'll Lead Ukraine?" *The Economist,* October 23, 1999, 56. **77.** Reported by NTV in Moscow on February 12, 2001, as cited in *RRM,* February 14, 2001. **78.** Peter Baker, "For Georgia, Russia Remains an Intimidating Neighbor," *Washington Post,* May 6, 2001, A23. **79.** Interview of Russian First Deputy Foreign Minister Vyacheslav Trubnikov, published in "There Is a Limit to Moscow's Concessions" [in Russian], *Nezavisimaya Gazeta,* May 12, 2004. Retrieved from the Russian Embassy to

Canada's website, July 22, 2004. **80.** Bill Gertz and Rowan Scarborough, "Inside the Rings: Kilos to Taiwan," *Washington Times,* June 25, 2004. **81.** David Hoffman, "Russia Sets Guidelines Governing Diplomacy," *Washington Post,* July 11, 2000, A17. **82.** Hoffman, "Russia Sets Guidelines." **83.** Vladimir Putin, speaking to the Ministry of Foreign Affairs in Moscow, RFE/RL *Security Watch,* vol.2, no. 5, cited in *RRM,* January 29, 2001. **84.** William Drozdiak, "Putin, EU Leaders to Cooperate on Energy, Balkans," *Washington Post,* March 24, 2001, A15. **85.** Michael Gordon, "Putin Seeks Allies in Quest to Fight U.S. Missile Plan," *New York Times,* June 11, 2000, A8. **86.** Arnaud De Borchgrave, "Reassessing Russia's Security Interests," *Washington Times,* March 14, 2001, A18. **87.** De Borchgrave, "Reassessing Russia's Security." **88.** Helle Bering, "A Russian Game of Chess, Putin Is a Better Player than Yeltsin," *Washington Times,* March 14, 2001, A19. **89.** Mike Allen, "Bush Calls for Missile Shield," *Washington Post,* May 2, 2001, A1. **90.** Reuters, February 4 2001, as cited in *RRM,* February 7, 2001. **91.** Patrick E. Tyler, "Global reaction to Missile Plan is Cautious," *New York Times,* May 3, 2001, A10. **92.** *Times of London,* August 12, 2000. **93.** Patrick E. Tyler, "High Level Shake-Up, Putin Replaces Russia's Defense, Interior, and Nuclear Energy Chiefs," *New York Times,* March 29, 2001, A8. **94.** Peter Baker and Susan B. Glasser, "In Kremlin Shuffle, Putin Puts Loyalists in Key Security Jobs," *Washington Post,* March 29, 2001, A18. **95.** Tyler, "High Level Shake-Up." **96.** Bill Gertz, "Russian Forces Conduct Massive War-Games Exercise," *Washington Times,* February 15, 2001, A1. **97.** Gertz, "Russian Forces." **98.** Bill Gertz, "U.S. Spy Satellites Pinpoint Russian Nuclear Arms in Baltics," *Washington Times,* February 15, 2001, A1. **99.** Gertz, "U.S. Spy Satellites." **100.** *Rossiya* (Moscow), cited in *RRM,* February 21, 2001. **101.** Susan Glasser, "Russia, Iran Renew Alliance Meant to Boost Arms Trade," *Washington Post,* March 13, 2001, A14. **102.** Glasser, "Russia, Iran Renew Alliance." **103.** Michael Wines, "Putin to Sell Arms and Nuclear Help to Iran," *New York Times,* March 13, 2001, A7. **104.** Patrick Tyler, "Russians Question Wisdom of their Coziness with Iran," *New York Times,* March 16, 2001, A8. **105.** Jon Boyle, "New Energy Chief Key to Arms Control," *Washington Times,* March 20, 2001, A13. **106.** Remarks by President Bush and Russian President Putin, www.whitehouse.gov, September 27, 2003. **107.** Gordon, "Maneuvers." **108.** Gertz, *Betrayal,* 43. **109.** Gertz, *Betrayal,* 43. **110.** Gertz, *Betrayal,* 44. **111.** Gertz, *Betrayal,* 46–47. **112.** Gertz, *Betrayal,* 47. **113.** Gertz, *Betrayal,* 45. **114.** Gertz, *Betrayal,* 45. **115.** Gertz, *Betrayal,* 48. **116.** Gertz, *Betrayal,* 48. **117.** Cited in Gertz, *Betrayal,* 38. **118.** Cited in Gertz, *Betrayal,* 38–39. **119.** Cited in Gertz, *Betrayal,* 36. **120.** Cited in Gertz, *Betrayal,* 36.

Chapter 15
1. People's Republic of China, "National Defense" (White Paper, Information Office of the State Council, October 2000). **2.** *CRM,* no. 109 (August 20, 1998). **3.** See Bill Gertz, "Chinese Exercise Targets Taiwan, *Washington Times,* January 26, 1999. **4.** People's Republic of China, "China's National Defense" (White Paper, Information Office of the State Council, July 27, 1998), 3; and John Pomfret, "China Said to Show New Candor in Defense Paper," *Washington Post,* July 29, 1998, A16. **5.** Pomfret, "China Said to Show New Candor." **6.** PRC, "National Defense." **7.** Maria rost Rublee, "Foreign Policy Responses to Aggressive Territorial Moves: The Case of the Spratly Islands," *International Affairs Review,* Summer 1996, 55. **8.** David G. Winncek, "The

South China Sea Dispute: Background Briefing," (manuscript, February 11, 1999), 2. Other useful sources on this issue include: John H. Nore with David Gregory, *Chokepoints: Maritime Economic Concerns in Southeast Asia* (Washington, DC, National Defense University Press, 1996); Scott Snyder, *The South China Sea Dispute: Prospects for Preventive Diplomacy* (Washington, DC: U.S. Institute of Peace, August 1996); and Rublee, "Foreign Policy." **9.** Winncek, "South China Sea," 4. **10.** Rublee, "Foreign Policy." **11.** Winncek, "South China Sea," 4. **12.** Department of State, *United States Policy on the South China Sea,* May 1995. **13.** Department of State, *United States Policy.* **14.** Richard Fisher, *PLA Modernization Gains Momentum,* Heritage Foundation March 1997, 2; and Rublee, "Foreign Policy," 26.**15.** Winncek, "South China Sea," 5. **16.** Winncek, "South China Sea," 6. **17.** Al Santoli (briefing, The Heritage Foundation, February 11, 1999); also Peter Schaefe, "Between China and the Deep Blue Sea," *Washington Times,* February 11, 1999, A21. This article also mentions an August 1998 Congressional Research Service Study showing "an official Chinese map of Chinese territorial waters that run down the coast of Vietnam and run down the coast of Malaysia and Brunei, and back up the coast of the Philippine islands of Palau and Luzon." **18.** Bill Gertz, "China Makes Upgrades to Island Base," *Washington Times,* February 11, 1999, A12. **19.** As cited in Gertz, "China Makes Upgrades." **20.** Gertz, "China Makes Upgrades." **21.** Winncek, "South China Sea," 4. **22.** James Webb, "Warily Watching China," *New York Times,* February 23, 1999. **23.** Gertz, "China Makes Upgrades." **24.** Webb, "Warily Watching China." **25.** *CRM,* no. 157 (January 20, 1999). **26.** House International Relations Committee, Subcommittee on Asia and the Pacific, *U.S. Security Concerns in Asia,* testimony of Admiral Dennis C. Blair, March 8, 2000, 19–20. **27.** John Lewis and Xue Litai, *China's Strategic Seapower* (Palo Alto, Calif: Stanford University Press, 1994), 226–230. **28.** June Dreyer, "China's Military Relations with and Strategy Towards Japan" in ed. James R. Lilley and David Shambaugh, *China's Military Faces the Future* (Washington, DC: M. E. Sharpe and AEI, 2000). **29.** Robert S. Ross, *Managing a Changing Relationship: China's Japan Policy in the 1990s* (Carlisle Barracks, Penn.: U.S. Army War College, 1996), 9; see also John Pomfret, "Rocky Road for China-Japan Talks," *Washington Post,* August 29, 2000, A14. **30.** Ross, *Managing a Changing Relationship,* 7. **31.** Ross, *Managing a Changing Relationship,* 12. **32.** Ross, *Managing a Changing Relationship,* 11. **33.** People's Republic of China, "History Proves Diaoyutai Islands are Chinese Territory," www.china-embassy.org, February 2000, 2. **34.** PRC, "History Proves," 2. **35.** Masayoshi Kanabayashi, "Japan, China's Competing Claim on Pacific Isles Centers on Oil," *Wall Street Journal,* June 29 and July 21, 1999. **36.** Eric Eckholm, "China and Japan Affirm Ties Despite Tension and Rivalry," *New York Times,* August 30, 2000, A12. **37.** Eckholm, "China and Japan." **38.** Pomfret, "Rocky Road." **39.** Pomfret, "Rocky Road." **40.** Kanabayash, "Japan, China's Competing Claim." **41.** Eckholm, "China and Japan." **42.** Agence France-Presse, "India Claims Beijing Placed Nukes in Tibet," *Washington Times,* May 4, 1998. **43.** Agence France-Presse, "India Claims." **44.** Agence France-Presse, "India Claims." **45.** Statement distributed by the Office of Congresswoman Nancy Pelosi, June 1998. **46.** Senate Select Committee on Intelligence, *Worldwide Threat 2001: National Security in Changing World,* statement of Director of Central Intelligence George J. Tenet, February 7, 2001; and Senate Select Committee on Intelligence, *Global Threats and Challenges through 2015,* statement of the director of the Defense Intelligence Agency, Vice Admiral Thomas R. Wilson, February 7, 2001. **47.** Due in significant part to the reports of Bill Gertz in the *Washington Times* and Jeff Gerth in the *New York Times* and the public reports mandated by the U.S. Congress, as discussed earlier. **48.** This information is drawn from the following three government sources: Central Intelligence Agency, *Unclassified Report to Congress on the Acquisition of Technology Relating to Weapons of Mass Destruction and Conventional Munitions, 1 July–31 December 1999,* August 9, 2000, 9; Central Intelligence Agency, *Unclassified Report to Congress on the Acquisition of Technology Relating to Weapons of Mass Destruction and Conventional Munitions, January 1–June 30, 1998,* August 9, 1999, 9; and the Cox Report. **49.** CIA report, August 9, 2000. **50.** CIA report, August 9, 2000. **51.** Senate Select Committee, *The Worldwide Threat in 2000,* 2. **52.** Senate Select Committee, *Global Threats and Challenges,* 14. **53.** CIA report, August 9, 2000. **54.** Bill Gertz, "China-Iraq military axis is 'troubling,' Bush says; Beijing denies violating U.N.-imposed sanctions" *Washington Times,* February 23, 2001. **55.** Wisconsin Project on Nuclear Arms Control, Chart: "China's Dangerous Exports," *U.S. Exports to China, 1988–98: Fueling Proliferation* (April 1999). **56.** Defense Intelligence Agency, February 2001, 14. **57.** Wisconsin Project, "China's Dangerous Exports." **58.** CIA Report, August 9 2000, 7. **59.** Cox Report, vol. 1, xxvii. **60.** Cox Report, vol. 1, xxvii. **61.** Senate Select Committee, *Worldwide Threat in 2000,* 2. **62.** Senate Select Committee on Intelligence, *Global Threats and Challenges,* 14. **63.** Senate Select Committee on Intelligence, *Worldwide Threat in 2000,* 3. **64.** Shirley A. Kan, *Chinese Proliferation of Weapons of Mass Destruction: Current Policy Issues,* Congressional Research Service, July 18, 2000, 1. The various promises are summarized in this excellent review of China and proliferation; the specific voluntary guidelines of the MCTR are that those agreeing would not transfer missiles that can deliver a warhead larger than 500 kg or about 1,100 lbs. at a distance of greater than 100 km (60 mi.). **65.** Kan, *Chinese Proliferation.* **66.** U.S. Department of State, *United States Relations with the People's Republic of China,* 1997, 3. **67.** Department of State, *United States Relations,* 3. **68.** Text of statement by Senator John Ashcroft at the U.S.-China Summit, May 14, 1998, 1. **69.** Ashcroft, U.S.-China Summit. **70.** Ashcroft, U.S.-China Summit. **71.** Document cited in Gertz, *Betrayal,* 286. **72.** Bill Gertz, "Pakistan Gets More Chinese Weapons," *Washington Times,* August 9, 2000, A1. **73.** Bill Gertz, "China Breaks Vow, Sends North Korea Missile Materials," *Washington Times,* January 6, 2000. **74.** Gertz, "China Breaks Bow." **75.** Mark Magnier, "China Tests Seen as Impetus for North Korea Missile Launch," *Los Angeles Times,* August 4, 1999, 1. **76.** *South China Morning Post,* June 1998, as cited in *CRM,* no. 90 (June 30, 1998). **77.** There are many examples of this threat, which has been repeated since 1995 on a number of occasions by senior Chinese officials. Examples are to be found in Jane Perlez, "Hopes for Improved Ties with China Fade," *New York Times,* February 12, 1999, A6; and "China Warns U.S. on Taiwan Missile Shield," *New York Times,* February 12, 1999, A6. **78.** "North Korea Admits Selling Missiles," *Washington Times,* June 17, 1998, A1 and A17. **79.** Pomfret, "China Said to Show New Candor." **80.** Kan, *Chinese Proliferation.* **81.** Bill Gertz, "Chinese Ship Arms Parts to Pakistan," *Washington Times,* June 4, 1998, A1. **82.** Bill Gertz, "Clinton to Discuss Missiles and China," *Washington Times,* June 7, 1998, A1. **83.** See *The International Reports: Early Warning,* vol. 18, no. 15 (September 1, 2000): 5. **84.** Bill Gertz, "Iran Set for Another

Flight Test of Missile," *Washington Times,* September 8, 2000, A1. **85.** David Sanger, "Clinton and China Leader Meet, but with Little Gain," *New York Times,* September 9, 2000, A5. **86.** Timperlake and Tripplet, *Red Dragon Rising,* 114. This discussion derives significantly from their excellent discussion on pages 114–117. **87.** U.S. Arms Control and Disarmament Agency, *Threat Control Through Arms Control: Annual Report to Congress, 1996,* August 13 1997, 87. **88.** United States Department of Defense, Office of the Secretary, *Proliferation, Threats, and Response,* April 1996, 9. **89.** Timperlake and Triplett, *Red Dragon Rising,* 115. **90.** Timperlake and Triplett, *Red Dragon Rising,* 225. **91.** Timperlake and Triplett, *Red Dragon Rising,* 225. **92.** Timperlake and Triplett, *Red Dragon Rising,* 116. **93.** Timperlake and Triplett, *Red Dragon Rising,* 116. **94.** Timperlake and Triplett, *Red Dragon Rising,* 116. **95.** Zalmay Khalizad, Abram N. Shulsky, Daniel L. Byman, Roger Cliff, David T. Orleski, David Schlapak, Ashley Talas: *The United States and a Rising China: Strategic and Military Implications,* Santa Monica, Calif.: RAND Corporation, 1999), 41; hereafter cited as RAND 1999. **96.** Khalizad et al., RAND 1999, 41. **97.** Tripplet and Timperlake, *Red Dragon Rising,* 116.

Chapter 16

1. See Zalmy M. Kalizad, et al., *The United States and a Rising China: Strategic and Military Implications* (Washington, DC and Santa Monica, Calif.: RAND Corporation, 1999), 43, for an overview of the time sequence of the development and deployment of China's missiles. See also the chart on missiles in this book. **2.** See U.S. Department of Defense, *Annual Report on the Military Power of the People's Republic of China,* report to Congress, June 2000, 7; hereafter cited as Defense Report, June 2000. **3.** Defense Report, June 2000. **4.** U.S. Department of Defense, *Annual Report on the Military Power of the People's Republic of China,* report to Congress, June 1, 2004; hereafter cited as Defense Report, June 2004. **5.** Defense Report, June 2004. **6.** Defense Report, June 2000, 7. **7.** Stokes, *China's Strategic Modernization,* 15. **8.** The Maldon Institute, *China's Espionage: Impact on U.S. Policy* (Washington, DC: 1999), 2; hereafter cited as Maldon. **9.** Hsu, *Rise of Modern China.* **10.** Maldon, 2. **11.** An excellent overview is Nicholas Etifmiadies, *Chinese Intelligence Operations* (Arlington, Va.: Newcomb Publishers, 1998). **12.** Etifmiadies, *Chinese Intelligence Operations.* **13.** Cox Report, 178–9. **14.** Entifmiades reports that Mr. Chin was recruited by the Communists in the 1940s. **15.** Maldon, 4. **16.** Walter Pincus, "U.S. Cracking Down on China's Nuclear Data," *Washington Post,* February 16, 1999, A7. **17.** Shirley A. Kan, *China: Suspected Acquisition of U.S. Nuclear Weapons Data,* Congressional Research Service, August 2000, 41. **18.** Pincus, "U.S. Cracking Down." **19.** For a thorough and well researched discussion of the Wen-ho Lee case, including information from principles involved in the investigation, see Bill Gertz, *The China Threat* (Washington, DC: Regnery, 2000), 142–170. Much of this discussion is based on the material provided in this important book. **20.** Gertz, *China Threat,* 156. **21.** "Excerpts from Testimony at Congressional Hearing in the Wen-ho Lee Case," *New York Times,* September 27, 2000, A14. **22.** "Wen-ho Lee Case." **23.** "Wen-ho Lee Case." **24.** U.S. Government, *Foreign Collection Against the Department of Energy: The Threat to U.S. Weapons and Technology,* 1998, cited in the Appendix of Gertz, *China Threat,* 222. **25.** A report published by Robert Woodward, February 19, 1997, as discussed in Gertz, *China Threat,* 15–18. **26.** As cited in Gertz, *China Threat,* 27. **27.** For a more in-depth discussion, see Timperlake and Tripplet; also Timmerman, *Selling Out America,* Chapters 2 and 5. **28.**

For example, see Timperlake and Tripplet, *Year of the Rat;* Gertz, *Betrayal;* and Timmerman, *Selling Out America.* **29**. Timperlake and Tripplet, *Year of the Rat,* xxv–xxvi. **30**. "China's Chief of Intelligence Reassigned," *Washington Post,* July 3, 1999, A6. **31**. As cited in Gertz, *China Threat,* 24. **32**. As cited in Gertz, *China Threat,* 25. **33**. Gertz, *China Threat,* 25–26. Both Mr. Labella and FBI Director Lewis Freeh called for independent counsels to investigate the campaign situation in 1996, but the attorney general did not accept that recommendation. **34**. Gertz, *China Threat,* 31. **35**. Cited in Gertz, *China Threat,* 28. **36**. Cox Report, xxxiii. **37**. Cox Report, xxxiv. **38**. As cited in Gertz, *China Threat,* 73. **39**. This material is drawn from the interesting account in Timmerman, Chapter 8, "The PLA and the USA," *Selling Out America,* 176–189. **40**. Jeff Fielder of the AFL-CIO, cited in Timmerman, 181. **41**. Timmerman, *Selling Out America,* 338. **42**. U.S. Department of Commerce, Bureau of Technology Administration, *U.S. Technology Transfers to the People's Republic of China,* 1999, 5. **43**. Department of Commerce, *U.S. Technology.* **44**. Shirley A. Kan, *China: Possible Missile Technology Transfers from Possible U.S. Transfer of Technology: Background and Chronology,* Congressional Research Service, July 20, 2000, 2. **45**. Kan, *China: Possible Missile Technology,* 4. **46**. Kan, *China: Possible Missile Technology,* 13, cites a CIA comparison of the Chinese space launch vehicle and the long range intercontinental ballistic missile (DF-5/CSS-4). **47**. Kan, *China: Possible Missile Technology,* 11. **48**. As cited in Kan, *China: Possible Missile Technology,* 12. **49**. Henry Solkolski, "U.S. Satellites to China: Unseen Proliferation Concerns," *International Defense Review,* 1994. **50**. Defense Report, June 2000, 7. **51**. Defense Report, June 2000, 7. **52**. Defense Report, June 2000, 7. **53**. Defense Report, June 2000, 7. **54**. Defense Report, June 2000, 7. **55**. Defense Report, June 2000, 6. **56**. Stokes, *China's Strategic Modernization,* 93–4. **57**. Stokes, *China's Strategic Modernization,* 94. **58**. Stokes, *China's Strategic Modernization,* 96. **59**. Stokes, *China's Strategic Modernization,* 94. **60**. National Intelligence Council, *Foreign Missile Developments and the Ballistic Missile Threat to the United States Through 2015,* December 2001. **61**. See David Smith, "Sun Txu and the Modern Art of Countering Missile Defense," *Jane's Intelligence Review,* January 2000, 36. **62**. Smith, "Sun Txu." **63**. Defense Report, June 2004. **64**. "Peoples Liberation Navy Overview," The Federation of American Scientists, http://www.fas.org/man/dod-101/sys/ship/row/plan/index.html. **65**. Department of Defense, *Selected Military Capabilities of the PRC,* April 1997, as cited in Stokes, *China's Strategic Modernization,* 97. **66**. Stokes, *China's Strategic Modernization,* 97. **67**. Yang Shang Zheng, *China's Nuclear Arsenal* (internet article, National University of Singapore, March 16, 1996). **68**. See, for example, the Cox Report and Kenneth Timmerman, "Chinese Missiles in the New World Order," *The Washington Times,* May 24, 2000, A20. The author describes how information from a Chinese defector revealed that many of the breakthroughs in the Chinese nuclear weapons program in the 1990s were directly attributable to information provided by U.S. companies. **69**. Khalizad, et al, 43. **70**. Defense Report, June 2004, 22. **71**. Defense Report, June 2004, 22. **72**. For estimated future deployments, see Gertz, *China Threat.* **73**. Defense Report, 1999, 17. **74**. Defense Report, 2000, 17, and Michael Pillsbury, *The U.S.-China Military Balance in 2020,* July 1999, 15. **75**. Defense Report, 2000, 17, and Pillsbury, 15. **76**. U.S.-China Economic and Security Review Commission, *Hearing on Military Modernization and Cross-Straits Balance,* statement of Richard Fisher, February 6, 2004. **77**. Pillsbury, *U.S.-China Military Balance,* 15. **78**. Pillsbury, *U.S.-China Military Balance,* 18. **79**. Pillsbury, *U.S.-China Military Balance,* 16. **80**. Lyle J. Goldstein, Undersea

Dragons—China's Maturing Submarine Force Hearing on Military Modernization and Cross-Straits Balance U.S.-China Economic and Security Review Commission, February 6, 2004. 81. Defense Report, 2003. 82. Defense Report, 2003. 83. Defense Report, 2003. 84. Defense Report, June 2004. 85. Defense Report, June 2004, 26. 86. Defense Report, June 2004, 26. 87. Goldstein, Undersea Dragons. 88. Defense Report, 2000, 19; Defense Report, June 2004. 89. Defense Report, 2000, 20. 90. Stokes, *China's Strategic Modernization*, 25. 91. Stokes, *China's Strategic Modernization*, 26. 92. As cited in Stokes, *China's Strategic Modernization*, 28. 93. Stokes, *China's Strategic Modernization*, 29. 94. Stokes, *China's Strategic Modernization*, 30. 95. Stokes, *China's Strategic Modernization*, 43. 96. Stokes, *China's Strategic Modernization*, 43. 97. Stokes, *China's Strategic Modernization*, 44. 98. Defense Report, 2000, 9. 99. Defense Report, 2000, 11. 100. House International Relations Committee, Subcommittee on Asia and the Pacific, *Security Concerns in Asia*, statement of Admiral Dennis C. Blair, USN, Commander in Chief, U.S. Pacific Command, March 8, 2001, 21–22. 101. House International Relations Committee, March 8, 2001, 21–22. 102. Elizabeth Becker, "FBI Warns That Chinese May Disrupt U.S. Web Sites," *New York Times*, Saturday, April 28, 2001. 103. Defense Report, 2000, 11. 104. Defense Report, 2000, 11. 105. Stokes, *China's Strategic Modernization*, 44, provides the $200 billion investment figure. 106. Stokes, *China's Strategic Modernization*, 12. 107. Pillsbury, *U.S.-China Military Balance*, 18. 108. Defense Report, 2000, 15. 109. This was reported to the U.S. government and is described in Gertz, *China Threat*, 73. 110. Stokes, *China's Strategic Modernization*, 139. 111. Michael Pillsbury, *Chinese Views of Future Warfare* (Washington, DC: National Defense University Press, 1997); and *China Debates the Future Strategic Environment* (Washington, DC: National Defense University Press, 1999). 112. Pillsbury, *China Debates the Future*, 66–67. 113. Pillsbury, *China Debates the Future*. 14. Pillsbury, *China Debates the Future*. 115. Defense Report, 2000, 7. 116. Qiao Liang and Wang Xiangshui, *Unrestricted Warfare* (Beijing: PLA Literature and Arts Publishing House, 1999). 117. Liang and Xiangshui, 121. 118. Report of the Defense Science Board Task Force on Information Warfare, Washington, DC 1995, 28, as cited in Tripplet and Timperlake, 137. 119. Tripplet and Timperlake, 122–126. 120. Defense 2000 Report, 9–10. 121. Defense 2002 Report, 2002. 122. For further reading, see Stokes; Tripplet & Timperlake; Pillsbury. 123. Pillsbury, 1999, 14. 124. Central Military Commission.

Chapter 17

1. For a discussion of these conflicts and political negotiations, see Menges, *Twilight Struggle*. 2. U.S. House of Representatives, *Russia's Road to Corruption*, September 2000, 151; hereafter referred to as House Report. 3. House Report, 151. 4. House Report, 151. 5. See chart on Russian Military Sales to China 1992–2000. 6. See Alexander V. Nemets and John L. Scherer, "Sino Russian Military Relations: The Fate of Taiwan and the New Geopolitics," (manuscript, 1999), 72. This is an important analysis that uses Chinese and Russian sources to document both the Chinese military buildup and Russian military sales to China. The table on Russian military sales derives in significant part from the work done by these two authors. 7. House Report, 152. 8. House Report, 152. 9. House Report, 153. 10. House Report, 153. 11. House Report, 154. 12. Sino-Russian joint statement [in Chinese], *Xinhua* (Beijing), trans. FBIS (CHI) 97–079, April 23, 1997. 13. Nemets and Scherer, *Sino-Russian Military Relations*, 72. 14. House Report, 154. 15. People's Republic of China, "China and Russia: Review

of Bilateral Relations" (Ministry of Foreign Affairs, February 2000), 5. **16.** Sino-Russian joint statement [in Chinese], *Xinhua* (Beijing), trans. FBIS (CHI) 97–315, November 11, 1997. **17.** For background on Soviet activities in support of regimes hostile to the United States in the Middle East see Menges, *Twilight Struggle,* 338–349. **18.** Sino-Russian joint statement [in Chinese], *Xinhua* (Beijing), trans. FBIS (CHI)-98-327, November 23, 1998. **19.** Cited in Speaker's Report, Ch 10. **20.** PRC, "China and Russia," 8. **21.** Speaker's Report, 154. **22.** Speaker's Report, 155. **23.** Joint statement at the summit of 1999 [in Chinese], *Xinhua,* Beijing, trans. FBIS (CHI), August 26, 1999. **24.** FBIS, August 26, 1999. **25.** FBIS, August 26, 1999. **26.** Cited in House Report, 155. **27.** Nemets and Scherer, *Sino-Russian Military Relations,* 73, 299. **28.** Nemets and Scherer, *Sino-Russian Military Relations,* 69. **29.** Nemets and Scherer, *Sino-Russian Military Relations,* 69. **30.** Nemets and Scherer, *Sino-Russian Military Relations,* 99. **31.** Nemets and Scherer, *Sino-Russian Military Relations,* 98, 99, 100, 101. **32.** Nemets and Scherer, *Sino-Russian Military Relations,* 101. **33.** Nemets and Scherer, *Sino-Russian Military Relations,* 146. **34.** Eric Eckholm, "A Bristling Yeltsin Reminds Clinton of Russia's A Arms," *New York Times,* December 10, 1999, A14. **35.** Eckholm, "Bristling Yeltsin." **36.** Eckholm, "Bristling Yeltsin." **37.** Nemets and Scherer, 149, footnote 8; they also refer to an article published in *Segodnia,* December 10, 1999, 1. **38.** Eckholm, "Bristling Yeltsin." **39.** PRC-Russia Leaders Joint Communiqué [in Chinese], *Xinhua* (Beijing), trans. FBIS (CHI), December 10, 1999. **40.** David Hoffman, "Russia Sets Guidelines Governing Diplomacy," *Washington Post,* July 11, 2000, 17. **41.** Hoffman, "Russia Sets Guidelines." **42.** "North Koreans Watch Reforms at Work," *Washington Times,* June 6, 1999, C12. **43.** *Straits Times* (Singapore), February 9, 2000. **44.** *RRM,* no. 747, February 21, 2000. **45.** Eric Eckholm "North Korean in China for Three Secret Days," *New York Times,* May 16, 2000, A6. **46.** Associated Press, "Putin: We've Established Now . . . Personal Relations," *Washington Post,* June 5, 2000, A11. **47.** Alessandra Stanley, "Putin Travels to Rome to Promote Russian Arms Control Alternative," *New York Times,* June 6, 2000, A1. **48.** Roger Cohen, "Warm Welcome for 'Putin the German,'" *New York Times,* June 15, 2000, A12. **49.** Cohen, "Warm Welcome." **50.** Howard W. French, "Koreas Reach Accord, Seeking Reconciliation After 50 Years," *New York Times,* June 15, 2000, A1. **51.** Jane Perlez, "North Korea's Missile Pledge Paves the Way for New Talks," *New York Times,* June 22, 2000, A8. **52.** "North Korea Vows to Continue 'Self Defense' Missile Program," *New York Times,* July 13, 2000, A14. **53.** "North Korea Vows." **54.** *New York Times,* September 25, 2000. **55.** Howard W. French, "Japanese Press North Korea on Old Kidnappings," *New York Times,* October 15, 2000, 16. **56.** French, "Japanese Press North Korea." **57.** FBIS (CHI), July 7, 2000. **58.** *People's Daily* (Beijing), July 17, 2000, trans. FBIS (CHI), July 18, 2000. **59.** Craig S. Smith, "Russia and China Unite in Criticism of U.S. Antimissile Plan," *New York Times,* July 19, 2000, A6. **60.** Putin-Jiang joint statement on ABM [in Chinese], July 18, 2000, *Xinhua* (Beijing), trans. FBIS (CHI), July 18, 2000; and Ted Plafker, "U.S. anti-missile plan draws more fire," *Washington Post,* July 18, 2000, A1. **61.** Beijing *Xinhua* English (Beijing), July 18, 2000, trans. FBIS (CHI), July 19, 2000. **62.** FBIS, July 19, 2000. **63.** *Tai Yang Pao* (Hong Kong), July 24, 2000. **64.** "Putin Praises North Korea's Kim," *Washington Post,* July 21, 2000, A24. **65.** Calvin Sims, "Group of 8 Pledges to Help Poor Countries," *New York Times,* July 24, 2000, A6. **66.** Marc Lacey, "Putin Bends Clinton's Ear Hoping to Halt Missile Shield," *New York Times,* July 22, 2000, A6. **67.** Lacey, "Putin Bends Clinton's Ear." **68.**

National Intelligence Council *Foreign Missile*, 9. **69.** House Report, 155. **70.** As cited in House Report, 156. **71.** *New York Times,* October 26, 1999, as cited in Nemets and Scherer, 98. **72.** Nemets and Scherer, *Sino-Russian Military Relations,* 130. **73.** Nemets and Scherer, *Sino-Russian Military Relations,* 100–101. **74.** "Sergeiev Warns of Danger to Strategic Stability from U.S. NMD," *Nezavisimaya Gazazeta,* June 22, 2000, 1; as cited in House Report, 143. **75.** Peter Pry, *War Scare.* **76.** Daniel Williams, "Russian to Cut Armed Forces," *Washington Post,* September 9, 2000, A1. **77.** Patrick E. Tyler, "Russia Poised to Cut Military by One Third," *New York Times,* September 10, 2000, A16. **78.** Bill Gertz, "Letter Showed Gore Made Russian Deal," *Washington Times,* October 17, 2000, A1. **79.** John M. Broder, "Despite Secret '95 Pact by Gore, Russian Arms Sales to Iran Go On," *New York Times,* October 13, 2000, A1. **80.** As cited by Gertz, "Letter Showed Gore." **81.** Nemets and Scherer, 8–9. **82.** Aleksandr V. Nemets, "China-Russia Military Report," *World Security Network,* vol. 1, no. 1 (February 1, 2000), 4, ww.globalsecuritynews.com. **83.** Nemets, "China-Russia Military Report." **84.** John Pomfret, "Russians Help China Modernize its Arsenal; New Military Ties Raise U.S. Concerns," *Washington Post,* February 10, 2000, A17. **85.** Floyd Spence, "China in the Ascendancy: A Growing Threat to National Security," *National Security Report,* vol. IV, no. 2, May 2000, 3. **86.** House Report, 160. **87.** Nemets and Scherer, *Sino-Russian Military Relations,* cite the DIA report, 63. **88.** Nemets and Scherer, *Sino-Russian Military Relations,* 73. **89.** House Report, 160. **90.** House Report, 158. **91.** House Report, 158. **92.** Bill Gertz, "Russia Readies Warship for China," *Washington Times,* July 12, 2000, 1. This story also mentions the fact that Russian crews will participate in manning the *Sovremenny* destroyers delivered to China—presumably during the training of the Chinese crews. **93.** As cited in House Report, 159. **94.** Cited in House Report. **95.** Nemets & Scherer, *Sino-Russian Military Relations,* 152. **96.** As cited in House Report, 159. **97.** House Report, 159. **98.** Robert L. Maginnis, "Trade Dollars Might Finance Military Power," *Los Angeles Times,* May 22, 2000; also, FBIS (CHI)–2000–0112. **99.** J. Michael Waller, *RRM,* no. 694, October 11, 1999. **100.** *Tai Yang Pao* (Hong Kong), February 2, 2000, as cited in Santoli, *CRM,* no. 277, February 15, 2000. **101.** *Tai Yang Pao.* **102.** Nemets and Scherer, *Sino-Russian Military Relations,* 37. **103.** *Sino-Russian Military Relations,* 223. **104.** Reuters, February 29, 2000. **105.** House Report, 161. **106.** Agence France-Presse, "Pact with Russia Will Buy Fighters, Tanks, and Carrier," *Washington Times,* October 5, 2000, A11. **107.** Celia W. Dugger, "Putin Joins India Discussion On How to Use Atomic Plans," *New York Times,* October 6, 2000, A7. **108.** These reports were published in the Associated Press and Reuters, and cited in Nemets and Scherer, *Sino-Russian Military Relations,* 191. **109.** *Moscow Commersant* [in Russian], September 14, 2000, 10, trans. FBIS (SOV), September 14, 2000. **110.** See Nemets, *China-Russia Military Report,* 2. **111.** *ITAR-TASS* (Moscow) [in English], March 30, 2001. **112.** "China and Russia Re-enter Military Cooperative Alliance," *Tai Yang Pao* (Hong Kong), January 8, 2001. **113.** "China and Russia." **114.** Nemets, *China-Russia Military Report,* 3. **115.** House Report, 61.

Chapter 18

1. Hsu, *Rise of Modern China,* 662. **2.** Hsu, *Rise of Modern China,* 662. **3.** People's Republic of China, "Report on National Defense" (State Council, October 2000), 2. See www.chinaguide.org/e-white/2000/20. **4.** This includes disputes with three of fourteen bordering states and eight of eleven neighboring states; see chart "China: Geostrategic Positioning" for details. **5.** PRC, "Report on National Defense," 2. **6.** Agence France-Presse, July 18, 2000. **7.** Defense Report, 2000, 2. **8.** David Sanger, "U.S. Would Defend Taiwan, Bush says," *New York Times*, April 26, 2001, A1. **9.** Michael Pillsbury, *China Debates the Future Security Environment* (Washington DC: National Defense University Press, 2000). See the views of Chinese strategists in Chapter 3, "China and India, Dangerous Democracies." **10.** Pillsbury, *China Debates*, Chapter 5, "Geopolitical Power Calculations." **11.** Robert A. Manning, *The Asian Energy Factor* (New York: Polygrave, 2000), 104. **12.** ExxonMobil, one of the world's largest oil companies, projects global demand for oil at 150 mbpd in 2010 and global supply at about 75 mbpd unless substantial new production begins quickly; see *New York Times*, February 15, 2001, A31. **13.** Public Statements of Soviet General Secretary Nikita Khrushchev in 1957 and 1958, as cited in N. H. Mager and Jacques Katel, *Conquest Without War* (New York: Simon and Schuster, 1961), 55–58. **14.** Gen Xu Hezhen, "Focus on Psychological War Under the Background of Larger Military Strategy," *Zhongguo Junshi* Kexue (Beijing), October 2000. **15.** General Zhang Wannian, at the end of the year 2000 as discussed earlier in this chapter. **16.** Juliet Ellperin, "House Votes to Block Payment of UN Dues," *Washington Post*, May 11, 2001. **17.** "China Said World's Second Largest Foreign Funds Recipient," *Xinhua* (Beijing), December 8, 2000, trans. FBIS (CHI), 001200. **18.** Department of Energy, *Energy Information Administration, China*, April 2000, 10. **19.** This law was published by *Xinhua* (Beijing), February 25, 1992, trans. FBIS (CHI), February 28, 1992, 2–3. **20.** Manning, *Asian Energy Factor*. **21.** Barbara Croset, "Indian-China Statement Angers Tibetan Exiles," *New York Times*, January 3, 1989, 11. **22.** Mark Fineman, "China and India launch new era of cooperation," *Los Angeles Time*, December 17, 1991, A6. **23.** John F. Burns, "India, Eye on China, Insist It Will Develop Nuclear Deterrent," *New York Times*, July 7, 1998, A7. **24.** *Calcutta Telegraph*, February 1, 2000, as cited in *CRM*, March 7, 2000. **25.** *CRM*, March 7, 2000. **26.** FBIS (CHI) March 9, 2000. **27.** Brahma Chellaney, "India Goes to China with Hat in Hand," *Washington Times*, June 9, 2000, A16. **28.** Chellaney, "India Goes to China." **29.** Chellaney, "India Goes to China." **30.** Chellaney, "India Goes to China." **31.** Chellaney, "India Goes to China." **32.** Chellaney, "India Goes to China." **33.** David E. Sanger and Eric Schmitt, "Reports say China is Siding Pakistan on Missile Project," *New York Times*, July 2, 2000, A1. **34.** Chellaney, "India Goes to China." **35.** *Hindustan Times* (New Delhi), January 15, 2001 and *The Pioneer* (New Delhi), February 12, 2001. **36.** Chellaney, "India Goes to China." **37.** Pamela Constable, "India and Russia Agree to Create Strategic Alliance," *Washington Post*, October 4, 2000, A15. **38.** Constable, "India and Russia Agree." **39.** Constable, "India and Russia Agree." **40.** Constable, "India and Russia Agree." **41.** Brahma Chellany, "India Kowtows to China," *Washington Times*, July 5, 2003, A6. **42.** Chellaney, "India Kowtows." **43.** Chellany, "India Kowtows." **44.** Mr. Puri, cited in "Two Systems, One Grand Rivalry," *The Economist*, June 21, 2003, 22. **45.** Manning, *Asian Energy Factor*, Chapter 5. The author mentions China's commitment of $4.3 billion to buy 60 percent of Kazakhstan's main oil company and a 60-percent share of its oil fields, as well as $4.5 million to build a pipeline from Kazakhstan to Xin Jiang province along with a shorter pipeline from Kazakhstan to Iran. **46.** Manning, *Asian Energy Factor*, 108. **47.** FBIS (CHI), January 18, 2000. **48.** "Beijing Separates Ties with India,

Pakistan," *Washington Times,* July 24, 2000. **49.** Robert Dujarric, ed., *Korea: Security Pivot Northeast Asia* (Indianapolis: The Hudson Institute, 1998), 67. **50.** U.S. Defense Intelligence Agency, *North Korea: The Foundations for Military Strength, Update 1995,* 1995. **51.** See the insightful discussion in Donald Kagan and Fredrick W. Kagan, Chapter 16, *While America Sleeps* (New York: St. Martin's Press, 2000). **52.** Deutsche Press Agentur, September 25, 2000. It may be worth noting that the Chinese defense minister, Chi Haotian, visited North Korea in October 2000, to celebrate the fiftieth anniversary of China entering the war against the U.S. and UN, an event in which he personally took part as a political commissar with Chinese troops. **53.** Bill Gertz, "North Korea Continues Military Buildup," *Washington Times,* February 12, 2001, A1. **54.** "North Korea Vows Anti-U.S. struggle," *Washington Times,* April 25, 2001, A15. **55.** Doug Struck, "North Korean Leader to Continue Sale of Missiles," *Washington Post,* May 5, 2001, A13. **56.** Associated Press, "China Rejects U.S. Appeal on North Korea," February 24, 2003. **57.** Li Yongyan, "Risky Business: A History Lesson for Kim Jong-il," *South China Morning Post,* March 11, 2003. **58.** Bill Gertz, "CIA Shifts on North Korean Nukes," *Washington Times,* July 4, 2003. **59.** David Sanger, "U.S. Sees Quick Start of North Korea Nuclear Site," *New York Times,* February 28, 2003. **60.** *New York Times,* August 18, 2003, 1. **61.** Joseph Kahn, "U.S. Stand Could Stall Korean Talks, China Says," *New York Times,* September 3, 2003. **62.** Round up on Li visit to Japan, FBIS (CHI), 1999-1612. **63.** "Joint Communiqué Marks Whaid's Visit," FBIS (CHI), December 3, 1999. **64.** FBIS (CHI), November 27, 1999. **65.** FBIS (CHI), July 20, 1999; FBIS (CHI), July 25, 1999. **66.** FBIS (EAS), December 7, 1999. **67.** "PRC spokesman on dispute with Philippines," trans. FBIS (CHI), February 2, 2000. **68.** AFP February 8, 2001, in *CRM,* February 14, 2001. **69.** *Philippine Star* (Manila), March 30, 2001. **70.** "China, Vietnam Should Shelve Territorial Issue, Lipeng Says," *Washington Post,* December 3, 1992, A40. **71.** Phillip Shannon, "China Sends Warships to Vietnam Oil Site," *New York Times,* July 21, 1994, A17. **72.** "China, Vietnam Hold Formal Talks on Longtime Land and Sea Disputes," *Los Angeles Times,* August 20, 1994, A21. **73.** "China Clears Mines in Vietnam Border Zone," *New York Times,* November 30, 1997, 1–12, and FBIS (CHI), August 11, 1999, reporting on Chinese soldiers removing the last landmines on the Vietnamese border. **74.** *Washington Times,* December 8, 2000, A16. **75.** Joshua Kurlantzick, "China's Influence Waxes as Washington's Wanes," *Washington Times,* December 4, 2000, A1. **76.** Kurlantzick, "China's Influence Waxes." **77.** "China Outlines Need for Free Trade Zone," *New York Times,* November 22, 2000, A9. **78.** Oil production figures cited here come from the U.S. Department of Energy, Energy Information Administration OPEC fact sheet, October 6, 2000 and Chapter 16. **79.** OPEC Fact Sheet. **80.** *Taheri,* June 22, 2000, vol. 14, no. 118. **81.** Christina Lam, "Chinese Forces Sent to Sudan," *Washington Times,* August 27, 2000, A1. **82.** Lam, "Chinese Forces." **83.** *Xinhua* (Beijing) [in Chinese], April 13, 2001, cited in *CRM,* April 17, 2001. **84.** *Granma* (Havana) [in Spanish], April 14, 2001, as cited in *CRM,* April 17, 2001. **85.** Andres Oppenheimer, "Neighbors Say Chavez Aids Violence," *Miami Herald,* December 5, 2000, A1. **86.** Patrick E. Tyler, "Putin Nurturing Friendships of Soviet Era, Casting a Wide Net," *New York Times,* December 13, 2000, A8. **87.** Andrew Cawthorne, "Russian President Will Visit Havana," *Washington Times,* December 13, 2000, A16. **88.** *RRM,* December 20, 2000. **89.** *RRM,* December 20, 2000. **90.** Manning, *Asian Energy Factor,* Chapter 5; in 1999 Yemen produced .4 mbpd. **91.**

Jiang Zemin's Riyadh speech, trans. FBIS (CHI), November 3, 1999. **92.** Jiang Zemin discusses cooperation with Egypt's Mubarak, FBIS (CHI), April 17, 2000. **93.** FBIS (CHI), April 17, 2000. **94.** "Beijing's Charm Offensive," *International Report/Early Warning,* February 18, 2000, 3. **95.** "Beijing's Charm Offensive." **96.** "Beijing's Charm Offensive." **97.** Reuters, "South Africa Set to Sell High Tech to China," *Washington Times,* February 3, 1997, A9. **98.** *Jornal Brasil* (Rio De Janeiro), April 19, 2001. **99.** Admiral Thomas Moorher, cited in Robert L. Macginnis, "Trade Dollars Might Finance Military Power," *Los Angeles Times,* May 22, 2000. **100.** Al Santoli, *The Panama Canal in Transition* (Washington DC: American Foreign Policy Council, June 23, 1999), 4. **101.** John H. Nor, *Chokepoints: Maritime Concerns in Southeast Asia* (Washington, DC: National Defense University Press, 1996), as cited in Manning, *Asian Energy Factor,* 202. The author was with the Center for Naval Analysis. **102.** Manning, *Asian Energy Factor,* 205. **103.** *Charleston Daily Mail* (South Carolina), March 29, 1997. **104.** For a very insightful discussion see Gertz, *China Threat,* Chapter 5. **105.** Santoli, *Panama Canal,* 1. **106.** Santoli, *Panama Canal,* 7. **107.** Gertz, *China Threat,* 86. **108.** Gertz, *China Threat,* Chapter 5; and Santoli, *Panama Canal,* 5–6. **109.** Gertz, *China Threat,* 89. **110.** Gertz, *China Threat,* 88. **111.** Santoli, *Panama Canal,* 6. **112.** As cited by Santoli, *Panama Canal,* 5. **113.** As cited in Gertz, *China Threat,* 86. **114.** As cited in Gertz, *China Threat,* 92. **115.** Santoli, *Panama Canal,* 4. **116.** Gertz, *China Threat,* 84. **117.** Santoli, *Panama Canal,* 4. **118.** Andrew Selth "Burma and Superpower Rivalries in the Asia Pacfic" US Naval War College Review Spring 2002 Vol L.V. No. 2119. PRC, "National Defense Report," 1998. **120.** Willy Wo-lop Lam (presentation, American Enterprise Institute, November 17, 2000). Mr. Lam was recently removed from the *South China Morning Post* of Hong Kong for political reasons. **121.** *Defense and Foreign Affairs Digest,* November 20, 2000, as cited in *CRM,* November 28, 2000. **122.** *CRM,* November 28, 2000. The description of the scenario given by General Zhang is almost exactly that offered in the very interesting novel by Chuck Devore and Steven W. Mosher, *China Attacks* (buybooksontheweb.com, 2000). **123.** Such as key computer chips, 80 percent of which are currently produced in Taiwan. **124.** John Pomfret, "Taiwanese Leader Voices Confidence in the Face of Turmoil," *Washington Post,* October 5, 2000, A22. **125.** "Economic Warfare," *International Report/Early Warning,* December 1, 2000, 8. **126.** "Economic Warfare." **127.** "Taiwan Semiconductor Group to Invest in Mainland China," Taipei Central News Agency, December 8, 2000. **128.** "Taiwan Semiconductor Group." **129.** Bruce Gilley and Julian Baum, "Crude Tactics," *Far Eastern Economic Review,* June 28, 2000, 25. This article also gives total Taiwan investment in the mainland as $40 billion as of June 2000. **130.** Pomfret, "China Said to Show New Candor." **131.** Pomfret, "China Said to Show New Candor." **132.** Eric Eckholm, "Chinese are Tempting Taiwan by Dangling Economic Fruit," *New York Times,* June 28, 2003, A4. **133.** Eckholm, "Chinese are Tempting Taiwan." **134.** Willy Wo-Lop Lam, "Containment Under Fire," *South China Morning Post,* April 26, 2000. **135.** *Xinhua* (Beijing) [in Chinese], trans. FBIS (CHI), October 18, 1999. **136.** "Zhu Rongji-Obuchi Hold Talks in Beijing," FBIS (CHI), July 19, 1999. **137.** FBIS (CHI), October 21, 1999. **138.** Michael M. Machizuki, "American and Japanese Strategic Debates" in Mochizuki, ed., *Toward a True Alliance* (Washington, DC: Brookings Institution Press, 1997). **139.** Machisuzki, "American and Japanese Strategic Debates," 68. **140.** Howard W. French, "Japan's Resurgent Far

Right Tinkers with History," *New York Times,* March 25, 2001, 3. **141.** French, "Japan's Resurgent Far Right." **142.** I have called this the "Munich Effect," where the leading democracy loses credibility against an expansionist authoritarian power. See "The Chinese Puzzle," *Washington Post,* March, 2000. **143.** "Japanese-Chinese Friendship Association Holds New Year Meeting," FBIS (CHI), January 30, 2000. This meeting, held in Beijing, included three hundred friends of China from all walks of life in Japan and the Japanese vice minister of foreign affairs. The meeting discussed their activities over the past fifty years and the fact that two thousand Japanese members of the association would plant trees at the Great Wall in Beijing and hold a large Chinese National Treasures exhibit in Japan. **144.** *Xinhua* (Beijing), October 28, 2002; FBIS (CHI) October 28, 2002. **145.** Manning, *Asian Energy Factor,* 204, discusses a joint Chinese-Russian-Japanese energy relationship moving energy from Sakhalin to Japan, which, by the end of 1991, had received investments of $143 million from American and Japanese companies. Other, larger energy pipelines were also possible, although Manning did not believe these would be commercially feasible by 2010. **146.** As quoted in Michael Pillsbury, *China Debates the Future Security Environment* (Washington, DC: National Defense University, 2000), 129. **147.** See Constantine Menges, *The Future of Germany and the Atlantic Alliance* (Washington DC: AEI Press, 1991), Chapter 4. Poll data from 1970 to 1988 shows public support for NATO in France at 40–50 percent during the peak Cold War years. This was true in other European NATO members as well, but contrasted with much higher support in Germany and the United Kingdom. **148.** Menges, *Future of Germany.* **149.** Douglas Hamilton and Charles Aldinger, "EU Force Could Spell NATO's End, Cohen Says," *Washington Post,* December 6, 2000, A28. **150.** Hamilton and Aldinger, "EU Force."

Chapter 19

1. This has been documented by Bill Gertz in his book *The China Threat* and in articles for the *Washington Times.* "Axis of Evil" WMD and missile programs and Russian and Chinese assistance to them is discussed from a holistic viewpoint in Constantine Menges and M. Sgro, *Deadly Weapons: North Korea, Iran, Iraq's Weapons of Mass Destruction and Ballistic Missiles* (Hudson Institute, January 2003). **2.** David Sanger and James Dao, "U.S. Says Pakistan Gave Technology to North Korea," *New York Times,* October 17, 2002, A1. See also Menges and Sgro, *Deadly Weapons.* **3.** Central Intelligence Agency, *Unclassified Report to Congress on the Acquisition of Technology Relating to Weapons of Mass Destruction and Advanced Conventional Munitions, 1 July Through 31 December 2003,* November 2004. **4.** Bill Gertz, "China Fortifying Iraq's air-defense system," *The Washington Times,* February 20, 2002, A3. **5.** Central Intelligence Agency, *Iraq's Weapons of Mass Destruction Programs,* October 2002. **6.** "Russia-Iraq Bond as Oil Slides," *Moscow Times,* November 27, 2001. **7.** Sharon LaFraniere, "Putin Warns Against Expanding War to Iraq," *Washington Post,* December 18, 2001, A24. **8.** Eli J. Lake, "From Russia (to Iran) With Love," *Weekly Standard,* December 10, 2001, 17; the CIA report referenced was dated December 2000. **9.** The major Western media ignored the fact that senior Russian officials immediately "changed" the optimistic interpretation by Marshall Igor Sergeev, advisor to the president for strategic security, stating that any movement away from the ABM Treaty would have "irreversible" consequences, including loss of control over "the entire system of deterrence and counterbalances." RFE/RL Newsline, July 30, 2001. **10.** Don Evans, "Time to Get Down to Business with Russia," *Washington Post,* July 27, 2001, A31. The Secretary of Commerce wrote from Moscow to report that he was seeking to "create an American and Russian business dialogue" to "present a business perspective to both governments" and that in the fall of 2001 he would "lead a business mission of American business owners to Russia . . . with particular emphasis on small and medium business."

Chapter 20
1. See Chapter 19. **2.** Bill Gertz, "Russian Forces Help China in Mock Conflict," *Washington Times,* April 30, 2001, A1. **3.** Based on the work of Nemetz and Sherer. **4.** See Chapter 8. **5.** See Chapter 18.

Chapter 21
1. See Chapter 14, "U.S.-Russia Relations, 1992–2000." **2.** See Chapters 8 and 9. **3.** President Putin, Annual Address to the Russian Legislature, April 2001. **4.** Michael R. Gordon, "Armies of Europe Failing to Meet Goals, Sapping NATO," *New York Times,* June 7, 2001, A6. See also Christopher Donnelly "Reshaping European Armed Forces for the 21st Century" (Analytic Paper, NATO, September 29, 2000). **5.** Gordon, "Armies of Europe." **6.** "Bush's Vision: We Will Not Trade Away the Fate of Free Europe's Peoples," *New York Times,* June 16, 2001, A8. **7.** "Bush's Vision." **8.** See Chapter 8-9. **9.** "With labor costs less than 10 percent of those of Korea and Taiwan, China continues to gain market share from its neighbors and now runs a larger trade surplus with the U.S. than Japan does." Gene Koretz, "A Golden Age for China?" *Business Week,* July 9, 2001; 28. **10.** William Hawkins and Alan Tonnelson, "Bush Strategy: An Odd Way of Treating Our Allies," *Los Angeles Times,* May 27, 2001. **11.** William Hawkins, "Production Center of the World: Should We Be Trading with Asian Friends and Foes Alike?" *Washington Times,* June 6, 2001, A19. **12.** Hawkins, "Production Center of the World." **13.** Hawkins, "Production Center of the World." **14.** Including, in addition to the five long established nuclear powers: North Korea, Pakistan, India, Iran, Iraq, Syria, Libya. **15.** The extensive Soviet programs were documented in unclassified reports published by the Reagan administration during the 1980s. **16.** See Pry, *War Games* and Gertz, *Betrayal;* also Chapter 14. **17.** Ted Plafker, "China Joins Russia in Warning U.S. on Shield," *Washington Post,* July, 19, 2001, A1. **18.** Plafker, "China Joins Russia." **19.** Frank Gaffney, "With Friends Like These . . . ," *Washington Times,* June 5, 2001, A17, drawing on the book by William T. Lee, *The ABM Treaty Charade: A Study in Elite Illusion and Delusion* (Washington, DC: Council for Social and Economic Studies, 1997). **20.** Gaffney, "With Friends Like These." **21.** Lee, *ABM Treaty Charade.* **22.** Such an assessment was suggested by Frank Gaffney and discussed in Melanie Kirkpatrick, "Does Russia Already Have a National Missile Defense," *Wall Street Journal,* March 6, 2001. **23.** David Lee Sanger and Steven Lee Myers, "Bush's Missile Plan: . . . Bush Seeks a Missile Shield Along with Nuclear Cuts . . . ," *New York Times,* May 2, 2001, A1. **24.** Sanger and Myers, "Bush's Missile Plan," A1. **25.** Sanger and Myers, "Bush's Missile Plan," A8. **26.** In 1979, the author published one of the first articles urging missile defense and wrote "it might accomplish what 11 years of SALT negotiations have failed to do—it would provide Moscow

with a reason to agree on significant and verified reductions in strategic forces since we could counter the effect of additional Soviet missiles simply by adding to the capacity of our defense system." See Constantine Menges, "SALT II—A Real Shell Game: U.S. Must Push Anti-Missile System," *Los Angeles Times*, July 10, 1979. **27.** Public Law 106-38, as cited in Baker Spring and James H. Anderson, *Missile Defense* (Washington, DC: The Heritage Foundation, 2000), 1. This act passed the House with 317 votes in support, including 214 Republicans and 103 Democrats. It passed the Senate by a vote of 97 to 3. **28.** "Rumsfeld Gives Allies Look at Missile Defense," *Washington Times*, June 8, 2001 A13. **29.** Roberto Suro, "Sea Based Missile Defense Supported," *Washington Post*, May 27, 2000, A1 and Bill Gertz, "Navy Developing Plan for Sea Based Missile Defense," *Washington Times*, May 30, 2000, A3. **30.** James Glanz, "U.S. Says Missile Defense Laser Passes a Test," *New York Times*, May 4, 2000, A14. **31.** "Defense Missile Blasts Test Target," *Washington Times*, June 11, 1999. **32.** Richard Perle, "A Better Way to Build a Missile Defense," *New York Times*, July 13, 2000. **33.** Joseph Biden, speaking on *Meet the Press*, NBC, June 17, 2001. **34.** "Mr. Bush, Meet Mr. Putin," *Washington Times*, June 16, 2001, A11. **35.** Patrick E. Tyler, "Putin Says Russia Would Add Arms to Counter Shield, *New York Times*, June 19, 2001, A1. **36.** Tyler, "Putin Says Russia Would Add Arms." **37.** U.S. Department of Defense, *FY-04 Report to Congress on PRC Military Power Pursuant to the FY2000 National Defense Authorization Act*, June 1, 2004. **38.** Menges, "SALT II." **39.** Charles Krauthammer, "Dense on Missile Defense," *Washington Post*, May 11, 2001, A45. **40.** The CIA reported in 2002 that China would triple its ICBM force by 2007. See National Intelligence Council, *Foreign Missile Developments.* **41.** Cox Report; see also Chapters 8 and 9. **42.** Richard Shelby, *Intelligence and Espionage in the 21st Century* (Washington DC: The Heritage Foundation, May 18, 2001), 1. **43.** Shelby, *Intelligence and Espionage,* 6. **44.** Brooks Tigner, "EU Hopes Code of Conduct Will Cool Missile Proliferation," *Defense News*, July 9–15, 2001, 1, 4. **45.** "China's Blue Army," *Junshi Wenzhai* (Beijing), [in Chinese], November 1, 2000, trans. and cited in *CRM*, December 12, 2000. **46.** Reps. Dan Burton, Curt Weldon, and Dana Rohrabacher wrote to the secretary of defense in May 2001 to express their support for an effective DTSA. See Bill Gertz and Roman Scarborough, "Inside the Ring," *Washington Times*, June 15, 2001, A12. **47.** Timmerman, *Selling Out America,* Chapter 8. **48.** CSIS *Study Group on Enhancing Multilateral Export Controls for U.S. National Security,* April 2001, 1. **49.** CSIS, *Multilateral Export Controls.*

Chapter 22

1. As reported in the *New York Times*, June 16, 2001, A8. **2.** "Two Leaders Talk about a 'Productive' Exchange," *New York Times*, June 17, 2001, A8. **3.** "Two Leaders Talk." **4.** William Safire, "Putin's China Card," *New York Times*, June 18, 2001, A29. **5.** Syria, Libya, Iran, Iraq, North Korea, and Cuba, among others. **6.** Ilan Berman, *Russia and the Mideast Vacuum* (Washington DC: Institute for Advanced Strategic and Policy Studies, June 2001), 13. **7.** Berman, *Russia and the Mideast,* citing *Oil and Gas Journal* and *World Oil.* U.S. government estimates available at http://www.eia.doe.gov. **8.** See the author's table "The New Geopolitics of Oil" 1999 production/reserve data, Appendix. **9.** Keith Bush, *The Russian Economy in May 2001* (Washington DC: Center for Strategic and International Studies, May 2001), 5. **10.** Bush, *Russian Economy,* 3–4.

11. Bush, *Russian Economy,* 3–4. 12. Bush, *Russian Economy,* 4. 13. Such actions range from helping Taiwan defend itself to building and regional missile defense to maintaining alliances with Japan and other powers. 14. "Russia Happy with Bush's Move to Release Nunn-Lugar Money," *Interfax,* January 16, 2003. 15. This is an estimate based upon the previous discussion of Russian exports to China (Chapter 15) and the annual public testimony of the U.S. intelligence organizations, which offer examples of types of weapons transferred but do not try to estimate costs or resulting earnings for Russia. 16. Cited by Ariel Cohen, *An Agenda for the Bush-Putin Summit* (Washington, DC: Heritage Foundation, June 11, 2001), 2. 17. *The CIA World Factbook,* 2002; http://www.cia.gov/factbook. 18. See Chapter 18. 19. See China, Russia, U.S. Forecast, 2000-25 chart and sources [AG chart for appendix or text to be dec] 20. RIA, "Oreanda," *Blagoveschensk,* July 21, 2000. 21. *Segodnya* (Moscow), January 11, 2001. 22. For example, "Thirty Chinese Nationals Detained for Violations of Border Rules" [in Russian], *Itar-Tass* (Moscow), January 19, 2001. 23. *Interfax* (Moscow), January 23, 2001. 24. *Kyrgyz* Radio One (Bishkek), [in Russian], June 19, 2001, trans. FBIS (SOV), June 19, 2001. 25. Comment made by Josef Bogdansky, a well-informed staff member in the U.S. Congress, at a public luncheon with visiting Russian officials in Washington DC, June 19, 2001. 26. Among other attacks, the U.S. government held bin Laden responsible for the terrorist bombing of two U.S. embassies in East Africa in 1998. 27. Evelyn Leopold, "Russia, U.S. Call for Arms Embargo and Sanctions," *Washington Times,* December 8, 2000, A16. 28. Barbara Crossette, "Russia Seeks Sanctions Against Pakistan for Aid to Taliban," *New York Times,* April 9, 2001, 4. According to Crossette, UN sources say that Russia, India, and Iran have been providing military support for the armed opponents of the Taliban inside Afghanistan. 29. *Itar-Tass* (Moscow), April 24, 2001 in *CRM,* May 8, 2001. 30. *Xinhua* (Beijing), April 24, 2001, in *CRM,* May 8, 2001. 31. *UT1* (Ukranian government channel), April 19, 2001, trans. FBIS (SOV), April 19, 2001. 32. Robert Sae-Liu, "Beijing Beats Ban on Aircraft Technology," *Jane's Defense Weekly,* January 10, 2001. 33. Ong Hwee-Hwee, "Ukraine Deal a Big Boost for China's Naval Capability, *Straits Times* (Singapore), May 14, 2001.
34. Robert Karnoi, "Smuggling Plot is Foiled by Russia," *Jane's Defense Weekly,* May 19, 1999. 35. Vladimir Isachenkov, "China Ambassador Mum on Spy Arrest," Associated Press (Moscow), May 20, 1999. 36. *Itar-Tass* (Moscow), April 6, 2001. 37. *Itar-Tass* (Moscow), May 21, 2001.

Chapter 23

1. This has been eloquently documented and discussed by James Mann and Patrick Tyler, op. cit. 2. See chart comparing forecasts for the U.S., China, and Russia in the Appendix. 3. Harry Schwartz, "Khrushchev-Mao Clashes on Party Issues Revealed," *New York Times,* February 12, 1961. 4. See the discussion in Chapter 9. 5. See Chapter 9. 6. U.S. Newswire, "Clinton Criticizes Bush Decision to Renew China's Most Favored Nation Status," *Los Angeles Times,* June 3, 1992. 7. See Chapter 8 for a more detailed discussion. 8. Chapter 8, note 14. 9. Cited in Lawrence Kaplan, "Why Trade Won't Bring Democracy to China," *New Republic,* July 9–16, 2001. 10. See Chapters 8–9. 11. William Hawkins, "Our Strategic Trade Partner?" *Weekly Standard,* June 21, 1999. 12. William Hawkins, "Big Business vs. National Security," *Weekly Standard,* January 18,

1999). 13. Hawkins, "Big Business." 14. "A Bright Signal to Airbus," *China Daily* (Hong Kong), May 7, 2001. 15. U.S. Department of State, *China: Country Reports on Human Rights Practices—2002*, 2003. 16. Department of State, *China: Country Reports* 17. Department of State, *China: Country Reports.* 18. "China Sect Says Police Rape Women," Associated Press (Beijing), July 16, 2001. 19. "China Sect." 20. This is denied by the regime, e.g. Philip P. Pan, "China Attacks Doctor For U.S. Testimony," *Washington Post*, July 5, 2001, A10. There is overwhelming evidence, including objec- tions by Chinese families to the sale of organs of their executed family members, which has been published by a small weekly on a web-site in China; see, John Pomfret, "Rare Chinese Newspaper Exposé Details Prisoner Organ Harvests," *Washington Post*, July 31, 2001, A14. 21. Cited in Hawkins, "Big Business." 22. Kaplan, "Why Trade Won't Bring Democracy." 23. Kaplan, "Why Trade Won't Bring Democracy." 24. Kaplan, "Why Trade Won't Bring Democracy." This point is also made in Constantine Menges, "China: Economic Modernization, Liberalization, Democracy," *Washington Times*, May 24, 2000, A20. 25. Kaplan, "Why Trade Won't Bring Democracy." 26. 2004 total is based on best estimates as of November 2004; see China Trade With U.S. EU and Japan Chat. 27. See table on trade in Chapter 13. 28. U.S. Bureau of Export Administration, *U.S. Commercial Technology Transfers to the People's Republic of China*, 1999; as cited in Hawkins, "Our Strategic Trade Partner?" 29. U.S.-China Security Review Commission, *Report to Congress*, July 2002, 53. 30. U.S.-China Security Review Commission, *Report to Congress*, 53. 31. http://www.bls.gov/news.release/empsit.t01.htm. 32. U.S.-China Security Review Commission, *Report to Congress*, 52. 33. The severe economic risks and negative consequences of the current one-way trade system with China, as well as other impor- tant global trends, are discussed in Alan Tonelson, *The Race to the Bottom* (Boulder, Colo.: Westview, 2000). 34. Hawkins, "China Trade Prospects Grow Dimmer," *American Economic Alert*, Friday, February 09, 2001, http://www.tradealert.us/ view_art.asp?Prod_ID=181. 35. "Breakthrough Moves China to the Verge of Joining WTO," *Washington Times*, July 5, 2001, A15 36. U.S.-China Security Review Commission, *Report to Congress*, 77. 37. http://www.wto.org/english/ thewto_e/whatis_e/tif_e/org6_e.htm. 38. Jeffrey J. Schott, *WTO: Organization and Procedure* (Washington, DC: Institute for International Economics, 2000), 4. The technical provision is that a "majority of three quarters of WTO members" may make these decisions, i.e. half of 75 percent equals 37.5 percent. 39. This was discussed in Chapter 16. 40. Warren P. Strobel, "Removal from UN Human Rights Panel Surprises U.S.," Knight Rider/Tribune News Service, May 5, 2001. 41. Strobel, "Removal from UN." 42. Strobel, "Removal from UN." 43. Hawkins, "Big Business." The data cited here is for 1998, but the proportions have remained about the same. See chart on trade in Chapter 13. 44. The Department of State Counterterrorism Office lists the following as state sponsors of international terrorism: Iran, Iraq, Syria, Libya, Cuba, North Korea, and Sudan. See *Patterns of Global Terrorism*, Annual Report 2000, http://www.state.gov/s/ct/rls/pgtrpt/2000/index.cfm?docid=2441. 45. Initiatives of this type have been suggested by Roger W. Robinson of the Center for Security Policy and were proposed as U.S. legislation by Sen. Fred Thompson in the year 2000. 46. For example, the changes in this domain proposed by Bush administration Secretary of Defense Rumsfeld in the spring of 2001 were a very positive step.

Chapter 24

1. Among 192 sovereign states, the most authoritative survey of political regimes finds that: 86 states, with 41 percent of the world's population, are democracies; 58. states, with 24 percent of the world's population, including Russia, are "partly free," meaning their governments observe some elements of respect for human rights and personal freedom; and 48 states with 35 percent of the world's population, including China, are dictatorships. See *Freedom in the World: The Annual Survey of Political Rights and Civil Liberties, 2002–2003* (Washington DC: Freedom House, 2003). 2. The literature on democratic political development includes: William A. Douglas: *Developing Democracy* (Washington, DC: Heldref Publications, 1972); Gregory A. Fossedal, *The Democratic Imperative: Exporting the American Revolution* (New York: Basic Books, Inc., 1989); Joshua Muravchik, *Exporting Democracy: Fulfilling America's Destiny,* 1991); Larry Diamond: *Promoting Democracy in the 1990s: Actors and Instruments, Issues and Imperatives* (New York: Carnegie Corporation, 1995); Constantine C. Menges, "The U.S. and the Encouragement of Democracy Abroad," in W. Bruce Weinrod and Paula J. Dobriansky, ed., *U.S. International Leadership in the 21st Century* (McLean, Va.: The Potomac Foundation, 2000). 3. The author was directly involved in proposing a national fund for the encouragement of democracy abroad in the late 1970s and 1980s in the design of President Reagan's pro-democratic policy for Latin America, which Reagan summarized in January 1981 as opposition to the extreme right and the extreme left, while providing support for all genuinely democratic political groups. See Menges, *Twilight Struggle.* 4. Ronald Reagan, Address to members of the British parliament, June 8, 1982; cited in Ronald Reagan, *Speaking My Mind: Selected Speeches* (New York: Simon and Schuster, 1989), 110–117. 5. Reagan, *Speaking My Mind.* 6. The author, along with several Democrats and Republicans, proposed such an idea in the 1970s, and the author had a direct role in urging Cabinet-level leaders of the Reagan administration and President Reagan to establish this new organization as a means of making the encouragement of democracy part of U.S. policy, but doing it openly. 7. White House, *National Security Strategy of Engagement and Enlargement,* 1995, 1. 8. Examples would include Central America, the Philippines, Panama, Eastern Europe after 1989, and the assistance proposals for the post-Soviet republics in 1992. 9. White House, *National Security Strategy,* 23. 10. White House, *National Security Strategy,* 23. 11. In the years 1993, 1995, 1996, 1999, and 2000. 12. White House, *National Security Strategy,* 23. 13. Personal communication from NDI and IRI with the author, November 1998. The positive results of their work are documented by a pattern of proportionally more votes for the pro-democratic parties in the cities and regions where IRI and NDI have had programs prior to the various elections. 14. Robert Krieble in Constantine Menges, ed., *Partnerships for Peace, Democracy and Prosperity* (Lanham, Md.: University Press of America, 1997), 113. 15. Krieble, *Partnerships for Peace,* 114. 16. For an interesting analysis of the work of Dr. Krieble and his associates, see Arthur H. Matthews, *Agents of Influence* (Washington DC: Krieble Institute of the Free Congress Foundation, 1995), particularly Chapters VI and XI. 17. Dave McCurdy and John McCain, "Democracy Corps for a Soviet Recovery," *Washington Post,* March 15, 1992, C7. 18. McCurdy and McCain, "Democracy Corps," C7. Western grants and loans totaling about $120 billion from 1992 to 2000 were matched by the movement of about $160 billion in

funds out of Russia through legal and illegal means. **19.** McCurdy and McCain, "Democracy Corps," C7. The individual who sparked this good initiative and worked with members of Congress to further the idea was Penn Kemble, who subsequently served in the Clinton administration as deputy director and acting director of the U.S. Information Agency. **20.** McCurdy and McCain, "Democracy Corps," C7. **21.** In 1992, Penn Kemble, the originator of the concept, estimated the cost for fifty Democracy Houses at about $32 million; accounting for inflation and a smaller number, $40 to $50 million is a reasonable current estimate. **22.** For a critical assessment of a more comprehensive set of proposals to improve the U.S. aid program to Russia, see Constantine Menges, "An Initial Assessment of U.S. Aid to Russia 1992–1996," [in Russian], *Demokratizatsiya,* vol. 4, no. 4, Fall 1996, 538–560. **23.** U.S. House Republican Conference, *The China Policy Bills: The People's Republic of China—A Policy for Freedom,* October 30, 1997. **24.** William J. Clinton, "Promoting Human Rights in China" (speech given in China, June 29, 1998); see http://www.white-house.gov/WH/Work/062998.html. **25.** John M. Broder, "Clinton Optimistic on China's Future as He Heads Home," *New York Times,* July 4, 1998. **26.** As cited in Kaplan, "Why Trade Won't Bring Democracy." **27.** R. Jeffrey Smith, "Yugoslav Masses Seize Belgrade," *Washington Post,* October 6, 2000, A1. See also the interesting discussion of the important role played by international democracy assistance in Thomas Carothers, "Ousting Foreign Strongmen: Lessons from Serbia," *Policy Brief* (Washington, DC: Carnegie Endowment for International Peace, May 2001). **28.** Smith, "Yugoslav Masses Seize Belgrade." **29.** Matt Pottinger: "China's President Assails Corruption as Threat to Party," *Washington Times,* April 2, 2000, C13. **30.** Damien McElroy, "Chinese President Concerned as the Son Also Rises," *The Scotsman,* December 11, 2000, 8. **31.** "Can China Tame the Corruption Beast?" *Business Week,* December 18, 2000, 197; estimates based on the work of Pei Minxin with the Carnegie Endowment for International Peace, Washington, DC. **32.** "Can China Tame." **33.** Craig S. Smith, "Graft in China Flows Freely, Draining the Treasury," *New York Times,* October 1, 2000, A4. **34.** Smith, "Graft in China," A4. **35.** Smith, "Graft in China," A4. **36.** "A City Ruled by Crime," *Far Eastern Economic Review,* November 30, 2000, 15. **37.** "A City Ruled by Crime," 15. **38.** Eric Eckholm, "China's Inner Circle Reveals Big Unrest and Lists Causes," *New York Times,* June 3, 2001. This is an excellent summary of the candid Party report by the Organization Department of the CCP Central Committee, "China Investigation Report 2000-2001: Studies of Contradictions Among the People Under New Conditions" [in Chinese], Beijing, 2001. **39.** Calum Macleod, "China's Poverty Time Bomb," *South China Morning Post,* April 20, 2001. This article also points out that "Premier Zhu Rongi warned that a 1999 survey put China's Gini Coefficient, an international index of income inequality at .39 'close to the international danger level' of .4. . . . Most experts agree that a more accurate estimate . . . is .458 . . . some claim the figure is . . . .59." **40.** Eckholm, "China's Inner Circle." **41.** Eckholm, "China's Inner Circle." **42.** Craig S. Smith, "China's Farmers Rebel Against Bureaucracy," *New York Times,* September 17, 2000, A1. **43.** Smith, "China's Farmers Rebel," A1. **44.** Smith, "China's Farmers Rebel," A1. **45.** Wayne Morrison, *The Growth of the Private Sector in China and Implications for China's Accession to the WTO,* Congressional Research Service, April 3, 2000, 7. **46.** Pieter Bottelier, former Chief of Mission, World Bank, Beijing (lecture, SAIS, Johns Hopkins

University, Baltimore, Md., March 2001). **47.** Bottelier (lecture, March 2001). **48.** *Business Week,* March 12, 2001, as cited in *CRM,* March 27, 2001. **49.** Eckholm, "China's Inner Circle." **50.** House Policy Committee, *China's Environmental Destruction,* July 6, 1998. **51.** House Committee, *China's Environmental Destruction.* **52.** Reagan, *Speaking My Mind,* 110–117. **53.** The 'Communist Party of China, http://www.chinatoday.com/org/cpc/ (updated February 18, 2001). **54.** This summary of Li Ruihuan's views comes from the *Far Eastern Economic Review,* May 3, 2001 as cited in *CRM,* June 21, 2001. **55.** This alludes to the issues discussed by Merle Goldman in her excellent analysis of the emergence of liberalizing influences within the Party; see Chapter 5. **56.** See the revelations of the manipulation by the hardliners in their own words through documents smuggled out of China compiled by Zhang Liang, a pseudonym for a CCP member seeking reform. Published in Andrew J. Nathan and Perry Link, *The Tiananmen Papers* (New York: Public Affairs Press, 2001). **57.** Willy Wo-Lap Lam, "Appealing to the Modern Comrade," *South China Morning Post,* January 11, 2000, 20. **58.** The estimate that 50 percent of senior Party and government officials will retire comes from the *Far Eastern Economic Review,* October 26, 2000, cited in *CRM,* November 21, 2000. **59.** Willy Wo-Lap Lam (lecture, American Enterprise Institute, Washington, DC, November 29, 2000). **60.** Lam, "Appealing to the Modern Comrade," 20. **61.** Lam, "Appealing to the Modern Comrade," 20, provides an excellent overview of this change and the quotes from a senior Party official are from this article. **62.** Lam, "Appealing to the Modern Comrade," 20. **63.** Lam, "Appealing to the Modern Comrade," 20. **64.** *CRM,* November 21, 2000 offers this view and cites the *Far Eastern Economic Review,* October 26, 2000. **65.** Anita Chan and Robert A. Senser, "China's Troubled Workers: Sweatshop Socialism," *Foreign Affairs,* March/April 1997. **66.** Chan and Senser, "China's Troubled Workers." **67.** Pamela Pun, "NPC Ready to Quiz Ministers," *Hong Kong Mail,* February 27, 2001. **68.** Lam (lecture, November 29, 2000). **69.** Lam (lecture, November 29, 2000). **70.** Lam (lecture, November 29, 2000). **71.** Lam, "Appealing to the Modern Comrade," 20. **72.** This is discussed in Hsu, *Rise of Modern China.* **73.** A coalition of pro-democracy Chinese exile organizations in the U.S., the the Free China Movement, was established in June 1998 at a founding conference at George Washington University. It had a major role in encouraging the formation of the China Democracy Party. The author has been an advisor to the Free China Movement since its inception. The increased repression is documented Department of State, *China: Country Reports.* **74.** Chan and Senser, "China's Troubled Workers." **75.** Gordon G. Chang, *The Coming Collapse of China* (New York: Random House, 2001), xix–xx. **76.** Lam, "Leadership Itchy over Yugoslavia's People Power," *South China Morning Post,* November 10, 2000, 18. **77.** Lam, "Leadership Itchy." **78.** Reuters (July 21, 2001), reports that China closed two thousand Internet cafes and ordered six thousand others to suspend operations; cited in *CRM,* July 30, 2001. **79.** Cited in Kaplan, "Why Trade Won't Bring Democracy to China." **80.** Spoken by Leon Trotsky and cited in Chang, *Coming Collapse of China.* **81.** Jasper Becker, "EU Must Push for Transition to an Open Society, Says Patten," *South China Morning Post,* May 22, 2001. **82.** Christoher Marquis, "Helms and Lieberman Seek to Aid Dissidents in Cuba," *New York Times,* May 16, 2001, A8. A proportionate expenditure for China would be about $10 billion annually ($100 million times 100, the multiple of the Chinese population as compared to that of Cuba). **83.** According to the *BBG and BIB Annual Reports,* the annual budget of RFE/RL in 1988 was $169,664,500 and in 1989, $170,564,836. The amount of the 1988 budget equals about $249,158,038 in current dollars, assuming 3 percent inflation annually; the adjusted number for the 1989 budget would be about $243,184,672. Further, Gregory A. Fossedal indicates that in 1985 the total budget for RFE, RL, VoA, and other USIA operations, as well as the National Endowment for Democracy, was less than $500 million. See Gregory A. Fossedal, *The Democratic Imperative: Exporting the American Revolution* (New York: Basic Books, Inc., 1989). **84.** Alan A. Michie, *Voices Through the Iron Curtain* (New York: Dodd, Mead, 1963), 143–154. **85.** Michie, *Voices Through the Iron Curtain,* 103. **86.** Michie, *Voices Through the Iron Curtain,* 109. **87.** Richard Long, of the Free China Movement, has managed with only minimal financial support to establish a daily internet report that reaches an estimated 240,000 persons in China, and which has continued since 1998 despite the increased political repression. **88.** *Washington Times,* July 1, 2001 as cited in *CRM,* July 3, 2001. **89.** *Washington Times,* July 1, 2001. **90.** See Wu, *Laogai* and http://www.laogai.org. **91.** U.S. China Security Review Commission, p. 95; citing *"Made in China": The Role of U.S. Companies in Denying Human and Workers' Rights,* New York, National Labor Committee, 2000. **92.** Al Santoli, ed., "China's 'Strike Hard' Campaign vs Dissidents during U.S. Trade Vote; Harry Wu, Wei Jingsheng Describe Chinese Factory Conditions," *CRM,* no. 305, May 15, 2000. The article summarizes the findings of the U.S.-based National Labor Committee for Human Rights.

Index